# RESEARCH METHODS FOR BUSINESS

## Fifth Edition

# RESEARCH METHODS FOR BUSINESS

## A Skill-Building Approach

Fifth Edition

Uma Sekaran and Roger Bougie

A John Wiley and Sons, Ltd, Publication

This edition first published 2009

Copyright © 2009 John Wiley & Sons Ltd

*Registered office*

John Wiley & Sons Ltd, The Atrium, Southern Gate, Chichester, West Sussex, PO19 8SQ, United Kingdom

For details of our global editorial offices, for customer services and for information about how to apply for permission to reuse the copyright material in this book please see our website at www.wiley.com.

The right of the author to be identified as the author of this work has been asserted in accordance with the Copyright, Designs and Patents Act 1988.

Reprinted August 2010, October 2010

*Library of Congress Cataloging-in-Publication Data*

Sekaran, Uma.

  Research methods for business : a skill building approach/Uma Sekaran and Roger Bougie. – 5th ed.

    p. cm.

  Includes bibliographical references and index.

    ISBN 978-0-470-74479-6 (pbk.)

1. Business–Research–Methodology.   I. Bougie, Roger.   II. Title.

  HD30.4.S435 2010

  650.072–dc22

2009021660

A catalogue record for this book is available from the British Library.

Set in 10/12.5pt Palatino-Roman by Thomson Digital, India

Printed in Great Britain by TJ International Ltd, Padstow, Cornwall

*To my husband, ARC Sekaran.*

# CONTENTS

About the authors                                                                    xvii

Preface                                                                               xix

Chapter 1   Introduction to research                                                    1
What is research?                                                                       2
Business research                                                                       2
   Definition of business research                                       3
   Research and the manager                                              3
Types of business research: applied and basic                                           5
   Applied research                                                      6
   Basic or fundamental research                                         7
Managers and research                                                                   9
The manager and the consultant–researcher                                              10
   The manager–researcher relationship                                   11
Internal versus external consultants/researchers                                       12
   Internal consultants/researchers                                      12
   External consultants/researchers                                      13
Knowledge about research and managerial effectiveness                                  14
Ethics and business research                                                           15
Summary                                                                                15
Discussion questions                                                                   16

Chapter 2   Scientific investigation                                                   17
The hallmarks of scientific research                                                   19
   Purposiveness                                                         19
   Rigor                                                                 19
   Testability                                                           20
   Replicability                                                         20

Precision and confidence                                                      21

Objectivity                                                                   22

Generalizability                                                              22

Parsimony                                                                     23

Some obstacles to conducting scientific research in the
management area                                                               23

The hypothetico-deductive method                                             24

The seven-step process in the hypothetico-deductive method                   24

Review of the hypothetico-deductive method                                   28

Other types of research                                                      30

Case studies                                                                 30

Action research                                                              31

Summary                                                                      31

Discussion questions                                                         32


Chapter 3    The research process: the broad problem area
             and defining the problem statement                              35

Broad problem area                                                           36

Preliminary information gathering                                            37

Nature of information to be gathered                                         37

Literature review                                                            38

Conducting the literature review                                             39

Defining the problem statement                                               45

What makes a good problem statement?                                         45

The research proposal                                                        47

Managerial implications                                                      50

Ethical issues in the preliminary stages of investigation                    50

Summary                                                                      51

Discussion questions                                                         52

Practice projects                                                            53

Appendix                                                                     55

Some online resources useful for business research                           55

Bibliographical databases                                                    60

APA format for referencing relevant articles                                 61

Referencing and quotation in the literature review section                   64

Chapter 4    The research process: theoretical framework
                   and hypothesis development                                    67
The need for a theoretical framework                                            69
Variables                                                                       69
    Types of variables                                                          70
Theoretical framework                                                           80
    The components of the theoretical framework                                 80
    Theoretical framework for the example of air safety violations              82
Hypothesis development                                                          86
    Definition of a hypothesis                                                  87
    Statement of hypotheses: formats                                            87
    Directional and nondirectional hypotheses                                   88
    Null and alternate hypotheses                                               88
Hypothesis testing with qualitative research: negative case analysis           92
Managerial implications                                                         95
Summary                                                                         96
Discussion questions                                                            96
Practice project                                                                99

Chapter 5    The research process: elements of
                   research design                                             101
The research design                                                            102
Purpose of the study: exploratory, descriptive, hypothesis testing
(analytical and predictive), case study analysis                               103
    Exploratory study                                                          103
    Descriptive study                                                          105
    Hypothesis testing                                                         108
    Case study analysis                                                        109
    Review of the purpose of the study                                         109
Type of investigation: causal versus correlational                             110
Extent of researcher interference with the study                               111
Study setting: contrived and noncontrived                                      114
Unit of analysis: individuals, dyads, groups, organizations, cultures          116
Time horizon: cross-sectional versus longitudinal studies                      119
    Cross-sectional studies                                                    119
    Longitudinal studies                                                       119

Review of elements of research design                                      120
Managerial implications                                                    122
Summary                                                                    123
Discussion questions                                                       123


Chapter 6   Measurement of variables:
                operational definition                                     125
How variables are measured                                                 126
Operationalization of variables                                            127
   Operationalization: dimensions and elements                            129
   Operationalizing the (multidimensional) concept of
     achievement motivation                                                129
   What operationalization is not                                         135
   Review of operationalization                                            136
International dimensions of operationalization                             137
Summary                                                                    137
Discussion questions                                                       137


Chapter 7   Measurement: scaling, reliability, validity                    139
Scales                                                                     141
   Nominal scale                                                           141
   Ordinal scale                                                           142
   Interval scale                                                          143
   Ratio scale                                                             145
   Review of scales                                                        148
Rating scales                                                              149
   Dichotomous scale                                                       149
   Category scale                                                          149
   Semantic differential scale                                            150
   Numerical scale                                                         150
   Itemized rating scale                                                   151
   Likert scale                                                            152
   Fixed or constant sum scale                                            152
   Stapel scale                                                            153
   Graphic rating scale                                                    153

Consensus scale                                                      154
Other scales                                                         154
Ranking scales                                                       155
   Paired comparison                                                 155
   Forced choice                                                     155
   Comparative scale                                                 156
International dimensions of scaling                                  156
Goodness of measures                                                 157
   Item analysis                                                     157
   Validity                                                          158
   Reliability                                                       161
Reflective versus formative measurement scales                      163
   What is a reflective scale?                                       163
   What is a formative scale and why do the items of a formative
      scale not necessarily hang together?                          163
Summary                                                             165
Discussion questions                                                165
Appendix                                                            167
   Examples of some measures                                        167

Chapter 8   Data collection methods                                 179
Sources of data                                                     180
   Primary sources of data                                          181
   Secondary sources of data                                        184
Data collection methods                                             184
   Interviewing                                                     186
   Questionnaires                                                   197
   Other methods of data collection                                 211
   Multimethods of data collection                                  216
   Review of the advantages and disadvantages of different data
      collection methods and when to use each                       217
   Setting from which data are gathered                             218
International dimensions of surveys                                  218
   Special issues in instrumentation for cross-cultural research     219
   Issues in data collection                                        219

Managerial implications 220
Ethics in data collection 220
  Ethics and the researcher 221
  Ethical behavior of respondents 221
Summary 222
Discussion questions 222

Chapter 9    Experimental designs 225
The lab experiment 228
  Control 229
  Manipulation of the independent variable 229
  Controlling the contaminating exogenous or "nuisance" variables 231
  Internal validity of lab experiments 233
  External validity or generalizability of lab experiments 233
The field experiment 234
  External validity 234
Trade-off between internal and external validity 235
Factors affecting the validity of experiments 235
  History effects 235
  Maturation effects 236
  Testing effects 237
  Selection bias effects 238
  Mortality effects 238
  Statistical regression effects 239
  Instrumentation effects 239
Identifying threats to validity 240
Internal validity in case studies 241
Review of factors affecting internal and external validity 242
Types of experimental design and validity 242
  Quasi-experimental designs 243
  True experimental designs 245
Simulation 249
Ethical issues in experimental design research 251
Managerial implications 252
Summary 253

| | |
|---|---|
| Discussion questions | 253 |
| Appendix | 255 |
| Further experimental designs | 255 |
| | |
| Chapter 10 Sampling | 261 |
| Population, element, sample, sampling unit, and subject | 262 |
| Population | 262 |
| Element | 263 |
| Sample | 263 |
| Sampling unit | 263 |
| Subject | 263 |
| Parameters | 264 |
| Reasons for sampling | 264 |
| Representativeness of samples | 265 |
| Normality of distributions | 265 |
| The sampling process | 266 |
| Defining the population | 267 |
| Determining the sample frame | 267 |
| Determining the sampling design | 267 |
| Determining the sample size | 268 |
| Executing the sampling process | 268 |
| Probability sampling | 270 |
| Unrestricted or simple random sampling | 270 |
| Restricted or complex probability sampling | 270 |
| Review of probability sampling designs | 275 |
| Nonprobability sampling | 276 |
| Convenience sampling | 276 |
| Purposive sampling | 276 |
| Review of nonprobability sampling designs | 278 |
| Examples of when certain sampling designs would be appropriate | 278 |
| Simple random sampling | 278 |
| Stratified random sampling | 282 |
| Systematic sampling | 283 |
| Cluster sampling | 284 |
| Area sampling | 284 |

Double sampling 284
Convenience sampling 285
Judgment sampling: one type of purposive sampling 285
Quota sampling: a second type of purposive sampling 286
Sampling in cross-cultural research 287
Issues of precision and confidence in determining
  sample size 287
  Precision 287
  Confidence 288
Sample data, precision, and confidence in estimation 289
Trade-off between confidence and precision 290
Sample data and hypothesis testing 291
Determining the sample size 293
Importance of sampling design and sample size 296
Efficiency in sampling 297
Sampling as related to qualitative studies 297
Managerial implications 298
Summary 298
Discussion questions 299

Chapter 11   Quantitative data analysis 303
Getting the data ready for analysis 306
  Coding and data entry 306
  Editing data 308
  Data transformation 310
Getting a feel for the data 311
  Frequencies 313
  Measures of central tendency and dispersion 316
  Relationships between variables 319
Excelsior Enterprises – descriptive statistics part 1 322
Testing goodness of data 324
  Reliability 324
  Validity 327
Excelsior Enterprises – descriptive statistics part 2 327
Summary 331
Discussion questions 331

Chapter 12    Quantitative data analysis:
                     hypothesis testing                                         335
Introduction                                                                    336
Type I errors, type II errors, and statistical power                            336
Choosing the appropriate statistical technique                                  337
Testing a hypothesis about a single mean                                        339
Testing hypotheses about two related means                                      340
Testing hypotheses about two unrelated means                                    345
Testing hypotheses about several means                                          346
Regression analysis                                                             348
    Standardized regression coefficients                                        351
    Regression with dummy variables                                             351
    Multicollinearity                                                           352
    Testing moderation using regression analysis: interaction effects           354
Other multivariate tests and analyses                                           355
    Discriminant analysis                                                       356
    Logistic regression                                                         356
    Conjoint analysis                                                           357
    Two-way ANOVA                                                               358
    MANOVA                                                                      358
    Canonical correlation                                                       359
Excelsior Enterprises – hypothesis testing                                      359
    Overall interpretation and recommendations to the president                 361
Data warehousing, data mining, and operations research                          363
Some software packages useful for data analysis                                 364
Summary                                                                         365
Discussion questions                                                            365


Chapter 13    Qualitative data analysis                                         369
Introduction                                                                    369
Data reduction                                                                  372
Data display                                                                    382
Drawing conclusions                                                             382
Reliability and validity in qualitative research                                384
Some other methods of gathering and analyzing qualitative data                  385

Content analysis                                                            385
Narrative analysis                                                          386
Summary                                                                     386
Discussion questions                                                        387

Chapter 14    The research report                                           389
The report                                                                  390
The written report                                                          390
The purpose of the written report                                           391
The audience for the written report                                         394
Characteristics of a well-written report                                    395
Contents of the research report                                             396
Integral parts of the report                                                397
Oral presentation                                                           402
Deciding on the content                                                     403
Visual aids                                                                  403
The presenter                                                               404
The presentation                                                            404
Handling questions                                                          404
Summary                                                                     405
Discussion questions                                                        405
Appendix                                                                    407
Report 1: Sample of a report involving a descriptive study                  407
Report 2: Sample of a report where an idea has to be "sold"                 412
Report 3: Sample of a report offering alternative solutions and
    explaining the pros and cons of each alternative                        415
Report 4: Example of an abridged basic research report                      418

A final note to students                                                    423

Statistical tables                                                          425

Glossary                                                                    435

Bibliography                                                                449

Index                                                                       457

# ABOUT THE AUTHORS

**Uma Sekaran** was Professor Emerita of Management, Southern Illinois University at Carbondale (SIUC), Illinois. She obtained her MBA degree from the University of Connecticut at Storrs, and her PhD from UCLA. She was the Chair of the Department of Management and also the Director of University Women's Professional Advancement at SIUC when she retired from the University and moved to California to be closer to her family.

Professor Sekaran authored or co-authored eight books, 12 book chapters, and more than 55 refereed journal articles in the management area, and presented more than 70 papers at national, international, and regional management conferences. She also won recognition for significant research contributions to cross-cultural research from US and international professional organizations. She received Meritorious Research Awards both from the Academy of Management and SIUC, and was conferred the Best Teacher Award by the University.

**Roger Bougie** is a Lecturer in the Department of Marketing at Tilburg University (The Netherlands), where he teaches courses in Marketing and Business Research Methods. He has received a number of teaching awards, including the Best Course Award for his course on Business Research Methods.

Dr Bougie's main research interest is in emotions and their impact on consumer behavior. He obtained his PhD from Tilburg University in 2005. His dissertation was nominated for the Dutch Marketing Science Award 2005 and his publications have appeared in, amongst others, the *Journal of the Academy of Marketing Science*. Dr Bougie is ad hoc reviewer for the *Journal of the Academy of Marketing Science*, the *Journal of Business Research*, and *Marketing Letters*.

# PREFACE

I have used this book in my research methods course with great success for more than ten years. Over these years the book has helped thousands of my own students, as well as many more around the world, to carry out their research projects. The great strength of *Research Methods for Business* is that students find it clear, informal, and nonintimidating. I have tried to maintain these strengths and Uma's style in the fifth edition.

## Changes in the fifth edition

The chapters on scientific investigation, the broad problem area and defining the problem statement, measurement of variables, experimental designs, sampling, and quantitative data analysis have all been substantially revised. A second chapter on quantitative data analysis and a chapter on qualitative data analysis have been added to the book. Additional real-life cases and examples are presented to introduce students to the world of business research.

As in previous editions, the simple and informal style of presenting information has been maintained and the focus on practical skill building preserved. The book provides numerous examples to illustrate the concepts and points presented. Users will also note the variety of examples from different areas of the world – Europe, Asia, and America – as well as different areas of business – human resources management, production, operations management, business policy and strategy, organizational behavior, marketing, information systems, accounting, and finance. It is hoped that students will find research interesting, nonintimidating, and of practical use.

Data analysis is illustrated through the current SPSS Version 16.0 in the data analysis chapter.

Most chapters in the book include *managerial implications* of the contents discussed, emphasizing the need for managers to understand research. The *ethical considerations* involved in conducting research are also clearly brought out. The dynamics of *cross-cultural research* in terms of instrument development, surveys, and sampling are discussed, which, in the context of today's global economy, will be useful to students.

I expect that students and instructors alike will enjoy this edition. Students should become effective researchers, helped by the requisite knowledge and skills acquired by the study of this book.

## Companion websites

Lecturers and students have a dedicated companion website available from www.wileyeurope.com/college/sekaran

Lecturers will find an extensive Test Bank, PowerPoint slides, and an Instructor's Manual, which offers a valuable additional teaching aid. Students will find an online glossary, quizzes, and walkthrough videos explaining how to use SPSS.

## Acknowledgments

The Marketing Department of Tilburg University has been a very pleasant and inspiring working environment. I would like to thank all my colleagues for their feedback on earlier versions of this book. Thank you Rik Pieters and Marcel Zeelenberg for teaching me most of what I know about research.

Several people have been extremely helpful in writing this book. I want to thank Deborah Egleton for giving me the opportunity to revise the book and for being very supportive and patient throughout the process of writing this revised edition. Finally, I would like to thank the reviewers for their insightful comments on earlier drafts of the chapters.

Roger Bougie

The first edition of this book *Research Methods for Business* was published in 1984. I am pleased that it has served the needs of students during the last 25 years in three continents—North America, Europe and Asia. Roger Bougie has been instrumental in changes in the Fifth Edition, and with his contributions, we hope that the book will serve the needs of students during the next 25 years.

Uma Sekaran

# CHAPTER 1

## Introduction to research

## Topics discussed

- What is research?
- Business research
- Types of business research: applied and basic
- Managers and research
- The manager and the consultant–researcher
- Internal versus external consultants/researchers
- Knowledge about research and managerial effectiveness
- Ethics and business research

## CHAPTER OBJECTIVES

After completing Chapter 1 you should be able to:

1. Describe what research is and how it is defined.
2. Distinguish between applied and basic research, giving examples, and discussing why they fall into one or the other of the two categories.
3. Explain why managers should know about research.
4. Discuss what managers should and should not do in order to interact most effectively with researchers.
5. Identify and fully discuss specific situations in which a manager would be better off using an internal research team, and when an external research team would be more advisable, giving reasons for the decisions.

6. Discuss what research means to you and describe how you, as a manager, might apply the knowledge gained about research.
7. Be aware of the role of ethics in business research.

## What is research?

Just close your eyes for a minute and utter the word *research* to yourself. What kinds of images does this word conjure up for you? Do you visualize a lab with scientists at work with Bunsen burners and test tubes, or an Einstein-like character writing dissertations on some complex subject, or someone collecting data to study the impact of an advertising campaign on sales? Most certainly, all these images do represent different aspects of research. **Research**, a somewhat intimidating term for some, is simply the process of finding solutions to a problem after a thorough study and analysis of the situational factors. Managers in organizations constantly engage themselves in studying and analyzing issues and hence are involved in some form of research activity as they make decisions at the workplace. As is well known, sometimes managers make good decisions and the problem gets solved, sometimes they make poor decisions and the problem persists, and on occasions they make such colossal blunders that the organization gets stuck in the mire. The difference between making good decisions and committing blunders lies in how managers go about the decision-making process. In other words, good decision making fetches a "yes" answer to the following questions: Do managers identify where exactly the problem lies, do they correctly recognize the relevant factors in the situation needing investigation, do they know what types of information are to be gathered and how, do they know how to make use of the information so collected and draw appropriate conclusions to make the right decisions, and, finally, do they know how to implement the results of this process to solve the problem? This is the essence of research and to be a successful manager it is important to know how to go about making the right decisions by being knowledgeable about the various steps involved in finding solutions to problematic issues. This is what this book is all about.

## Business research

Business research can be described as a systematic and organized effort to investigate a specific problem encountered in the work setting, which needs a solution. It comprises a series of steps that are designed and executed with the goal of finding answers to the issues that are of concern to the manager in the work environment. This means that the first step in research is to know where the problem areas exist in the organization, and to identify as clearly and specifically as possible the problems that need to be studied and resolved. Once a problem that needs attention is clearly defined, steps can be taken to gather information, analyze the data, and determine the factors that are associated with the problem and then solve it by taking the necessary corrective measures.

This entire process by which we attempt to solve problems is called research. Thus, research involves a series of well-thought-out and carefully executed activities that enable the manager to know how organizational problems can be solved, or at least considerably minimized. Research thus encompasses the processes of inquiry, investigation, examination, and experimentation. These processes have to be carried out systematically, diligently, critically, objectively, and logically. The expected end result would be a discovery that helps the manager to deal with the problem situation.

Identifying the critical issues, gathering relevant information, analyzing the data in ways that help decision making, and implementing the right course of action, are all facilitated by understanding business research. After all, decision making is simply a process of choosing from among alternative solutions to resolve a problem and research helps to generate viable alternatives for effective decision making. Knowledge of research thus enables you to undertake research yourself in order to solve the smaller and bigger problems that you will encounter in your job as a treasurer, controller, brand manager, product manager, marketing and sales officer, project manager, business analyst, or consultant. What's more, it will help you to discriminate between good and bad studies published in (professional) journals, to discriminate between good and bad studies conducted by research agencies, to discriminate between good and bad research proposals of research agencies, and to interact more effectively with researchers and consultants.

The difference between the manager who uses common sense alone to analyze and make a decision in a given situation, and the investigator who uses a scientific method (discussed in the next chapter) is that the latter does a systematic inquiry into the matter and proceeds to describe, explain, or predict phenomena based on data carefully collected for the purpose.

## Definition of business research

We can now define business research as an *organized, systematic, data-based, critical, objective, scientific inquiry or investigation into a specific problem,* undertaken with the purpose of finding answers or solutions to it. In essence, research provides the necessary information that guides managers to make *informed* decisions to successfully deal with problems. The information provided could be the result of a careful analysis of data gathered first-hand or of data that are already available (in the company, industry, archives, etc.). Data can be *quantitative* (as generally gathered through structured questions) or *qualitative* (as generated from the broad answers to specific questions in interviews, or from responses to open-ended questions in a questionnaire, or through observation, or from already available information gathered from various sources).

## Research and the manager

An experience common to all organizations is that the managers thereof encounter problems, big and small, on a daily basis, which they have to solve by making the right decisions. In business, research is usually primarily conducted to resolve problematic issues in, or inter-related among, the areas of accounting, finance, management, and marketing. In *Accounting*, budget control systems, practices, and procedures are frequently examined. Inventory costing methods, accelerated depreciation, time-series behavior of quarterly earnings, transfer pricing, cash recovery rates, and taxation methods are some of the other areas that are researched. In *Finance*, the operations of financial institutions, optimum financial ratios, mergers and acquisitions, leveraged buyouts, intercorporate financing, yields on mortgages, the behavior of the stock exchange, and the like, become the focus of investigation. *Management* research could encompass the study of employee attitudes and behaviors, human resources management, the impact of changing demographics on management practices, production operations management, strategy formulation, information systems, and the like. *Marketing* research could address issues pertaining to consumer decision making, customer satisfaction and loyalty, creating a competitive advantage, product image, advertising, sales promotion, marketing channel management, pricing, new product development, and other marketing aspects.

Exhibit 1 gives an idea of some commonly researched topical areas in business.

---

**EXHIBIT 1    Some commonly researched areas in business**

1. Employee behaviors such as performance, absenteeism, and turnover.
2. Employee attitudes such as job satisfaction, loyalty, and organizational commitment.
3. Supervisory performance, managerial leadership style, and performance appraisal systems.
4. Employee selection, recruitment, training, and retention.
5. Validation of performance appraisal systems.
6. Human resource management choices and organizational strategy.
7. Evaluation of assessment centers.
8. The dynamics of rating and rating errors in the judgment of human performance.
9. Strategy formulation and implementation.
10. Just-in-time systems, continuous-improvement strategies, and production efficiencies.
11. Updating policies and procedures in keeping with latest government regulations and organizational changes.
12. Organizational outcomes such as increased sales, market share, profits, growth, and effectiveness.
13. Consumer decision making.
14. Customer relationship management.
15. Consumer satisfaction, complaints, customer loyalty, and word-of-mouth communication.
16. Complaint handling.
17. Delivering and performing service.

18. Product life cycle, and product innovation.
19. Impression management, logos, and image building.
20. Product positioning, product modification, and new product development.
21. Cost of capital, valuation of firms, dividend policies, and investment decisions.
22. Risk assessment, exchange rate fluctuations, and foreign investment.
23. Tax implications of reorganization of firms or acquisition of companies.
24. Collection of accounts receivable.
25. Development of effective cost accounting procedures.
26. Qualified pension plans and cafeteria-type benefits for employees.
27. Deferred compensation plans.
28. Installation of effective management information systems.
29. Advanced manufacturing technologies and information systems.
30. Design of career paths for spouses in dual-career families.
31. Creative management of a diverse workforce.
32. Cultural differences and the dynamics of managing a multinational firm.
33. Alternative work patterns: job sharing, flexitime, flexiplace, and part-time work.
34. Downsizing.
35. Participative management and performance effectiveness.
36. Differences in leadership positions, salaries, and leadership styles.
37. Instrument development for assessing "true" gender differences.
38. Installation, adaptation, and updating of computer networks and software suitable for creating effective information systems for organizations.
39. Installation of an effective data warehouse and data mining system for the organization.
40. Keeping ahead of the competition.

Not only are the issues within any subarea related to many factors within that particular system, but they must also be investigated in the context of the external environment facing the business. For example, economic, political, demographic, technological, competitive, and other relevant global factors could impinge on some of the dynamics related to the firm. These have to be scrutinized as well to assess their impact, if any, on the problem being researched.

# Types of business research: applied and basic

Research can be undertaken for two different purposes. One is to solve a current problem faced by the manager in the work setting, demanding a timely solution. For example, a particular product may not be selling well and the manager might want to find the reasons for this in order to take corrective action. Such research is called **applied research**. The other is to generate a body of knowledge by trying to comprehend how certain problems that occur in organizations can be solved. This is called **basic research**.

It is quite possible that some organizations may, at a later stage, apply the knowledge gained by the findings of basic research to solve their own problems. For instance, a university professor may be interested in investigating the factors that contribute to absenteeism as a matter of mere academic interest. After gathering information on this topic from several institutions and analyzing the data, the professor may identify factors such as inflexible work hours, inadequate training of employees, and low morale as primarily influencing absentee-ism. Later on, a manager who encounters absenteeism of employees in his organization may use this information to determine if these factors are relevant to that particular work setting.

In sum, research done with the intention of applying the results of the findings to solve specific problems currently being experienced in an organization is called **applied research**. Research done chiefly to make a contribution to existing knowledge is called **basic, funda-mental, or pure research**. The findings of such research contribute to the building of knowledge in the various functional areas of business; they teach us something we did not know before. Such knowledge, once generated, is usually later applied in organizational settings for problem solving.

## Applied research

The following examples, following two situations cited in *Business Week*, should provide some idea of the scope of business research activities.

### EXAMPLE

1. Apple's iPod fueled the company's success in recent years, helping to increase sales from $5 billion in 2001 to $32 billion in the fiscal year 2008 (which ended on September 30). Growth for the music player averaged more than 200% in 2006 and 2007, before falling to 6% in 2008. One reason for this decrease in sales is that iPod owners see little or no reason to upgrade, especially with the crumbling economy. As a result, some analysts believe that the fourth quarter of 2008 will be the first quarter since the iPod was introduced in 2001 that sales will decline from the year-earlier quarter. What's more, they believe that the number of iPods sold will drop 12% in 2009, to about 48 million units. "The reality is there's a limited group of people who want an iPod or any other portable media player," one analyst says. "So the question becomes, what will Apple do about it?"

2. As Chinese consumers grow wealthier, they are increasingly willing to spend extra money on more expensive, but healthier, drinks. A Chinese company, China Huiyuan Juice Group, has leveraged its early-mover advantage and strong brand name to become the leading 100% juice and nectar beverage company in China. China Huiyuan Juice Group wants to grow bigger but it is lacking the distribution network, financial resources, and management to do so.

In an effort to diversify its presence in one of the world's fastest-growing beverage markets, Coca-Cola has announced that it wants to buy China Huiyuan Juice Group. Three major shareholders of Huiyuan, with a collective shareholding of 66% in the Chinese company, have already accepted Coca-Cola's offer. Whether both companies will benefit from this merger is uncertain: mergers can succeed or fail for many reasons. Recent research has shown that cultural differences might be a major cause of post-merger difficulties.

The two preceding examples illustrate the need for applied research, whereby existing problems can be solved through investigation and good managerial decision making.

## Basic or fundamental research

### EXAMPLE

Right from her days as a clerical employee in a bank, Sarah had observed that her colleagues, though extremely knowledgeable about the nuances and intricacies of banking, were exerting very little effort to improve the efficiency and effectiveness of the bank in the area of customer relations and service. They took on the minimum amount of work load, availed themselves of long tea and lunch breaks, and seemed unmotivated in their dealings with the customers and the management. That they were highly knowledgeable about banking policies and practices was clearly evident from their mutual discussions about these as they processed applications from customers. Sarah herself was very hardworking and enjoyed her work with the customers. She always used to think what a huge waste it was for talented employees to goof off rather than to work hard and enjoy their work. When she left the bank and did her dissertation for her PhD, her topic of investigation was Job Involvement, or the ego investment of people in their jobs. The conclusion of her investigation was that the single most important contributory factor to job involvement is the fit or match between the nature of the job and the personality predispositions of the people engaged in performing it. For example, challenging jobs allowed employees with high capabilities to get job-involved, and people-oriented employees got job-involved with service activities. Sarah then understood why the highly intelligent bank employees could not get job-involved or find job satisfaction in the routine jobs that rarely called for the use of their abilities.

Subsequently, when Sarah joined the Internal Research Team of a Fortune 500 company, she applied this knowledge to solve problems of motivation, job satisfaction, job involvement, and the like, in the organization.

The above is an instance of basic research, where knowledge was generated to understand a phenomenon of interest to the researcher. Most research and development departments in various industries, as well as many professors in colleges and universities, do basic or fundamental research, so that more knowledge is generated in particular areas of interest to industries, organizations, and researchers. Though the objective of engaging in basic research is primarily to equip oneself with additional knowledge of certain phenomena and problems that occur in several organizations and industries with a view to finding solutions, the knowledge generated from such research is often applied later for solving organizational problems.

As stated, the primary purpose of conducting basic research is to generate more knowledge and understanding of the phenomena of interest and to build theories based on the research results. Such theories subsequently form the foundation of further studies on many aspects of the phenomena. This process of building on existing knowledge is the genesis for theory building, particularly in the management area.

Several examples of basic research can be provided. For instance, research into the causes and consequences of global warming will offer many solutions to minimize the phenomenon, and lead to further research to determine if and how global warming can be averted. Although research on global warming might primarily be for the purpose of understanding the nuances of the phenomenon, the findings will ultimately be applied and useful to, among others, the agricultural and building industries.

Many large companies also engage in basic research. For instance, General Electric Company generates knowledge concerning the different applications of electrical energy, their motto being "We bring good things to life." Computer companies in the Silicon Valley are constantly engaged in generating the know-how to increase the usefulness of micro-computers in industry, which benefits managers and technicians in all organizations. This, ultimately, results in increased sales of computers for them.

University professors engage in basic research in an effort to understand and generate more knowledge about various aspects of businesses, such as how to improve the effectiveness of information systems, integrate technology into the overall strategic objectives of an organization, assess the impact of logos, increase the productivity of employees in service industries, monitor sexual harassment incidents at the workplace, increase the effectiveness of small businesses, evaluate alternative inventory valuation methods, change the institutional structure of the financial and capital markets, and the like. These findings later become useful for application in business situations.

As illustrated, the main distinction between applied and basic business research is that the former is specifically aimed at solving a currently experienced problem, whereas the latter has the broader objective of generating knowledge and understanding of phenomena and problems that occur in various organizational settings. Despite this distinction, both types of research follow the same steps of systematic inquiry to arrive at solutions to problems. As current or prospective practicing managers in organizations, you will be directly or indirectly engaged in applied research. You will also be keeping abreast of new basic knowledge generated by being in regular touch with published research in the business journals related to your sphere of work, some of which may very well be relevant and applicable to your own business organization.

In sum, both applied and basic business research are scientific in nature, the main difference being that the former is undertaken specifically to solve a current business problem whereas the latter is primarily resorted to because of the importance of the subject to the researcher. A deeper understanding of the phenomenon is useful for its own sake as well as for application later, as needed. Both basic and applied research have to be carried out in a scientific manner (discussed in the next chapter) so that the findings or results generated by them can be relied upon to effectively solve the problem investigated. It is, however, possible that some applied research may have a shorter time frame than some basic research.

# Managers and research

Managers with knowledge of research have an advantage over those without. Though you yourself may not be doing any major research as a manager, you will have to understand, predict, and control events that are dysfunctional within the organization. For example, a newly developed product may not be "taking off," or a financial investment may not be "paying off" as anticipated. Such disturbing phenomena have to be *understood* and explained. Unless this is done, it will not be possible to *predict* the future of that product or the prospects of that investment, and how future catastrophic outcomes can be *controlled*. A grasp of research methods enables managers to understand, predict, and control their environment.

A thought that may cross your mind is that, because you will probably be bringing in researchers to solve problems instead of doing the research yourself, there is no need to bother to study research. The reasons for its importance become clear when one considers the consequences of failing to do so. With the ever-increasing complexity of modern organizations, and the uncertainty of the environment they face, the management of organizational systems now involves constant troubleshooting in the workplace. It would help if managers could sense, spot, and deal with problems *before* they got out of hand. Knowledge of research and problem-solving processes helps managers to identify problem situations before they get out of control. Although minor problems can be fixed by the manager, major problems warrant the hiring of outside researchers or consultants. The manager who is knowledgeable about research can interact effectively with them. Knowledge about research processes, design, and interpretation of data also helps managers to become discriminating recipients of the research findings presented, and to determine whether or not the recommended solutions are appropriate for implementation.

Another reason why professional managers today need to know about research methods is that they will become more discriminating while sifting through the information disseminated in business journals. Some journal articles are more scientific and objective than others. Even among the scientific articles, some are more appropriate for application or adaptation to particular organizations and situations than others. This is a function of the sampling design, the types of organizations studied, and other factors reported in the journal articles. Unless the manager is able to grasp fully what the published empirical research really conveys, she or he is likely to err in incorporating some of the suggestions such publications offer. By the same token, managers can handle with success their own problems at considerable cost savings by studying the results of "good" (discussed in the next chapter) published research that has addressed similar issues.

There are several other reasons why professional managers should be knowledgeable about research and research methods in business. First, such knowledge sharpens the sensitivity of managers to the myriad variables operating in a situation and reminds them frequently of the multicausality and multifinality of phenomena, thus avoiding inappropriate, simplistic notions of one variable "causing" another. Second, when managers understand the research reports about their organizations handed to them by professionals, they are equipped to take intelligent, educated, calculated risks with known probabilities attached to the success or failure of their decisions. Research then becomes a useful decision-making tool rather than a mass of incomprehensible statistical information. Third, if managers become knowledgeable about scientific investigations, vested interests inside or outside the organization will not prevail. For instance, an internal research group within the organization will not be able to distort information or manipulate the findings to their advantage if managers are aware of the biases that can creep into research and know how data are analyzed and interpreted. As an example, an internal research team might state that a particular unit to which it is partial (for whatever reason) has shown increased profits and hence should be allocated more resources to buy sophisticated equipment to further enhance its effectiveness. However, the increased profit could have been a one-time windfall phenomenon due to external environmental factors such as market conditions, bearing no relation whatever to the unit's operating efficiency. Thus, awareness of the different ways in which data may be camouflaged will help the manager to make the right decision. Fourth, knowledge about research helps the manager to relate to and share pertinent information with the researcher or consultant hired for problem solving.

In sum, being knowledgeable about research and research methods helps professional managers to:

1. Identify and effectively solve minor problems in the work setting.
2. Know how to discriminate good from bad research.
3. Appreciate and be constantly aware of the multiple influences and multiple effects of factors impinging on a situation.
4. Take calculated risks in decision making, knowing full well the probabilities associated with the different possible outcomes.
5. Prevent possible vested interests from exercising their influence in a situation.
6. Relate to hired researchers and consultants more effectively.
7. Combine experience with scientific knowledge while making decisions.

## The manager and the consultant–researcher

Managers often need to engage a consultant to study some of the more complex, time-consuming problems that they encounter, as in the case of Apple discussed earlier. It is thus important to be knowledgeable about how to effectively interact with the consultant (the terms researcher and consultant are used interchangeably), what the manager–researcher relationship should be, and the advantages and disadvantages of internal versus external consultants.

## The manager–researcher relationship

During their careers, it often becomes necessary for managers to deal with consultants. In such cases, the manager must not only interact effectively with the research team, but must also explicitly delineate the roles for the researchers and the management. The manager has to inform the researchers what types of information may be provided to them and, more importantly, which of their records will *not* be made available to them. Such records might include the personnel files of the employees, or certain trade secrets. Making these facts explicit at the very beginning can save a lot of frustration for both parties. Managers who are very knowledgeable about research can more easily foresee what information the researchers might require, and if certain documents containing such information cannot be made available, they can inform the research team about this at the outset. It is vexing for researchers to discover, at a late stage, that the company will not let them have certain information. If they know the constraints right from the beginning, the researchers might be able to identify alternate ways of tackling the problems and to design the research in such a way as to provide the needed answers.

Beyond specifying the roles and constraints, the manager should also make sure that there is congruence in the value systems of management and the consultants. For example, the research team might very strongly believe and recommend that reduction of the workforce and streamlining would be the ideal way to significantly cut down operating costs. Management's consistent philosophy, however, might be *not* to fire employees who are experienced, loyal, and senior. Thus, there might be a clash of ideologies between management and the research team. Research knowledge will help managers to identify and explicitly state, even at the outset, the values that the organization holds dear, so that there are no surprises down the road. Clarification of the issue offers the research team the opportunity to either accept the assignment and find alternative ways of dealing with the problem, or regret its inability to undertake the project. In either case, both the organization and the research team will be better off having discussed their value orientations, thus avoiding potential frustration on both sides.

Exchange of information in a straightforward and forthright manner also helps to increase the rapport and trust levels between the two parties, which in turn motivates the two sides to interact effectively. Under this setup, researchers feel free to approach the management to seek assistance in making the research more purposeful. For instance, the research team is likely to request that management inform the employees of the ensuing research and its broad purpose to allay any fears they might entertain.

To summarize, while hiring researchers or consultants the manager should make sure that:

1. The roles and expectations of both parties are made explicit.
2. Relevant philosophies and value systems of the organization are clearly stated and constraints, if any, are communicated.
3. A good rapport is established with the researchers, and between the researchers and the employees in the organization, enabling the full cooperation of the latter.

# Internal versus external consultants/researchers

## Internal consultants/researchers

Some organizations have their own consulting or research department, which might be called the Management Services Department, the Organization and Methods Department, R & D (research and development department), or some other name. This department serves as the internal consultant to subunits of the organization that face certain problems and seek help. Such a unit within the organization, if it exists, is useful in several ways, and enlisting its help might be advantageous under some circumstances, but not others. The manager often has to decide whether to use internal or external researchers. To reach a decision, the manager should be aware of the strengths and weaknesses of both, and weigh the advantages and disadvantages of using either, based on the needs of the situation. Some of the advantages and disadvantages of both internal and external teams are now discussed.

### Advantages of internal consultants/researchers

There are at least four advantages in engaging an internal team to do the research project:

1. The internal team stands a better chance of being readily accepted by the employees in the subunit of the organization where research needs to be done.
2. The team requires much less time to understand the structure, the philosophy and climate, and the functioning and work systems of the organization.
3. They are available to implement their recommendations after the research findings have been accepted. This is very important because any ''bugs'' in the implementation of the recommendations may be removed with their help. They are also available to evaluate the effectiveness of the changes, and to consider further changes if and when necessary.
4. The internal team might cost considerably less than an external team for the department enlisting help in problem solving, because they will need less time to understand the system due to their continuous involvement with various units of the organization. For problems of low complexity, the internal team would be ideal.

### Disadvantages of internal consultants/researchers

There are also certain disadvantages to engaging internal research teams for the purposes of problem solving. The four most critical ones are:

1. In view of their long tenure as internal consultants, the internal team may quite possibly fall into a stereotyped way of looking at the organization and its problems. This inhibits any fresh ideas and perspectives that might be needed to correct the problem. This is definitely a handicap for situations in which weighty issues and complex problems are to be investigated.

2. There is scope for certain powerful coalitions in the organization to influence the internal team to conceal, distort, or misrepresent certain facts. In other words, certain vested interests could dominate, especially in securing a sizable portion of the available scant resources.
3. There is also a possibility that even the most highly qualified internal research teams are not perceived as "experts" by the staff and management, and hence their recommendations may not get the consideration and attention they deserve.
4. Certain organizational biases of the internal research team might, in some instances, make the findings less objective and consequently less scientific.

## External consultants/researchers

The disadvantages of the internal research teams turn out to be the advantages of the external teams, and the former's advantages work out to be the disadvantages of the latter. However, the specific advantages and disadvantages of the external teams may be highlighted.

### Advantages of external consultants/researchers

The advantages of the external team are:

1. The external team can draw on a wealth of experience from having worked with different types of organizations that have had the same or similar types of problems. This wide range of experience enables them to think both divergently and convergently rather than hurry to an instant solution on the basis of the apparent facts in the situation. They are able to ponder over several alternative ways of looking at the problem because of their extensive problem-solving experience in various other organizational setups. Having viewed the situation from several possible angles and perspectives (divergently), they can critically assess each of these, discard the less viable options and alternatives, and focus on specific feasible solutions (think convergently).
2. The external teams, especially those from established research and consulting firms, might have more knowledge of current sophisticated problem-solving models through their periodic training programs, which the teams within the organization may not have access to. Because knowledge obsolescence is a real threat in the consulting area, external research institutions ensure that their members are current on the latest innovations through periodic organized training programs. The extent to which internal team members are kept abreast of the latest problem-solving techniques may vary considerably from one organization to another.

### Disadvantages of external consultants/researchers

The major disadvantages in hiring an external research team are as follows:

1. The cost of hiring an external research team is usually high and is the main deterrent, unless the problems are critical.

2. In addition to the considerable time the external team takes to understand the organization being researched, they seldom get a warm welcome, nor are readily accepted by employees. Departments and individuals likely to be affected by the research study may perceive the study team as a threat and resist them. Therefore, soliciting employees' help and enlisting their cooperation in the study is a little more difficult and time-consuming for external researchers than for internal teams.

3. The external team also charges additional fees for their assistance in the implementation and evaluation phases.

Keeping in mind these advantages and disadvantages of internal and external research teams, the manager who desires research services has to weigh the pros and cons of engaging either before making a decision. If the problem is a complex one, or if there are likely to be vested interests, or if the very existence of the organization is at stake because of one or more serious problems, it would be advisable to engage external researchers despite the increased costs involved. However, if the problems that arise are fairly simple, if time is of the essence in solving moderately complex problems, or if there is a system-wide need to establish procedures and policies of a fairly routine nature, the internal team would probably be the better option.

Knowledge of research methods and appreciation of the comparative advantages and disadvantages of external and internal teams help managers to make decisions on how to approach problems and determine whether internal or external researchers are the appropriate choice to investigate and solve the problem.

# Knowledge about research and managerial effectiveness

As mentioned, managers are responsible for the final outcome by making the right decisions at work. This is greatly facilitated by research knowledge. Knowledge of research heightens the sensitivity of managers to the innumerable internal and external factors of a varied nature operating in their work and organizational environment. It also helps to facilitate effective interactions with consultants and comprehension of the nuances of the research process.

Sophisticated technology such as simulation and model building is now available and may lend itself to profitable application in certain business areas. The recommendations of the external consultant who is proficient in this technology and urges its application in a particular situation may make no sense to, and might create some misgivings in, the manager not acquainted with research. Even superficial knowledge of these techniques helps the manager to deal with the researcher in a mature and confident manner, so that dealing with "experts" does not result in discomfort. As the manager, *you* will be the one to make the final decision on the implementation of the recommendations made by the research team. Remaining objective, focusing on problem solutions, fully understanding the recommendations made, and why and how they have been arrived at, make for good managerial decision making. Although company traditions are to be respected, there may be occasions where today's rapidly changing turbulent environment demands the substitution or re-adaptation of some of these traditions, based on research findings. Thus, knowledge of research greatly enhances the decision-making skills of the manager.

# Ethics and business research

**Ethics** in business research refers to a code of conduct or expected societal norm of behavior while conducting research. Ethical conduct applies to the organization and the members that sponsor the research, the researchers who undertake the research, and the respondents who provide them with the necessary data. The observance of ethics begins with the person instituting the research, who should do so in good faith, pay attention to what the results indicate, and, surrendering the ego, pursue organizational rather than self-interests. Ethical conduct should also be reflected in the behavior of the researchers who conduct the investigation, the participants who provide the data, the analysts who provide the results, and the entire research team that presents the interpretation of the results and suggests alternative solutions.

Thus, ethical behavior pervades each step of the research process – data collection, data analysis, reporting, and dissemination of information on the Internet, if such an activity is undertaken. How the subjects are treated and how confidential information is safeguarded are all guided by business ethics. We will highlight these as they relate to different aspects of research in the relevant chapters of this book.

There are business journals such as the *Journal of Business Ethics* and the *Business Ethics Quarterly* that are mainly devoted to the issue of ethics in business. The American Psychological Association has established certain guidelines for conducting research, to ensure that organizational research is conducted in an ethical manner and the interests of all concerned are safeguarded. As stated, we will discuss the role of ethics in the chapters that follow, insofar as it is relevant to the various steps in the research process.

## SUMMARY

In this chapter we examined what research is, the two types of research (applied and basic), some commonly researched topical areas in business, why managers should know about research for good decision making, effective relationships between the manager and the consultant–researcher, and the advantages and disadvantages of external and internal consultants. We also saw how managerial effectiveness is enhanced by knowledge of research and highlighted some of the areas where ethical issues deserve attention in the conduct of business research. In the next chapter we will examine what "scientific" investigation is.

## DISCUSSION QUESTIONS

1.  Why should a manager know about research when the job entails *managing* people, products, events, environments, and the like?
2.  For what specific purposes is basic research important?
3.  When is applied research, as distinct from basic research, useful?
4.  Why is it important to be adept in handling the manager–researcher relationship?
5.  Explain, giving reasons, which is more important, applied or basic research.
6.  Give two specific instances where an external research team would be useful and two other scenarios when an internal research team would be deployed, with adequate explanations as to why each scenario is justified for an external or internal team.
7.  Describe a situation where research will help you as a manager to make a good decision.
8.  Given the situations below:
    a.  discuss, with reasons, whether they fall into the category of applied or basic research
    b.  for Scenario 1, explain, with reasons, who will conduct the research.

### Scenario 1
### To acquire or not to acquire: that is the question

Companies are very interested in acquiring other firms, even when the latter operate in totally unrelated realms of business. For example, Coca-Cola has announced that it wants to buy China Huiyuan Juice Group in an effort to expand its activities in one of the world's fastest-growing beverage markets. Such acquisitions are claimed to "work miracles." However, given the volatility of the stock market and the slowing down of business, many companies are not sure whether such acquisitions involve too much risk. At the same time, they also wonder if they are missing out on a great business opportunity if they fail to take such risk. Some research is needed here!

### Scenario 2
### Reasons for absenteeism

A university professor wanted to analyze in depth the reasons for absenteeism of employees in organizations. Fortunately, a company within 20 miles of the campus employed her as a consultant to study that very issue.

### Scenario 3
### Effects of service recovery on customer satisfaction

A research scientist wants to investigate the question: What is the most effective way for an organization to recover from a service failure? Her objective is to provide guidelines for establishing the proper "fit" between service failure and service recovery that will generalize across a variety of service industries.

# CHAPTER 2

## Scientific investigation

## Topics discussed

- The hallmarks of science
  - Purposiveness
  - Rigor
  - Testability
  - Replicability
  - Precision and confidence
  - Objectivity
  - Generalizability
  - Parsimony
- Limitations to scientific research in management
- The building blocks of science and the hypothetico-deductive method of research
- The seven steps of the hypothetico-deductive method
  - Identify the broad problem area
  - Define the problem statement
  - Develop hypotheses
  - Determine measures
  - Data collection
  - Data analysis
  - Interpretation of data
- Other types of research
  - Case studies
  - Action research

## CHAPTER OBJECTIVES

After completing Chapter 2 you should be able to:

1. Explain what is meant by scientific investigation, giving examples of both scientific and nonscientific investigations.
2. Explain the eight hallmarks of science.
3. Briefly explain why research in the organizational behavior and management areas cannot be completely scientific.
4. Describe the building blocks of science.
5. Discuss the seven steps of the hypothetico-deductive method, using an example of your own.
6. Describe the processes of induction and deduction.
7. Appreciate the advantages of knowledge about scientific investigation.

Managers frequently face issues that call for critical decision making. Managerial decisions based on the results of scientific research tend to be effective. In Chapter 1, we defined research as an organized, systematic, data-based, critical, objective, scientific inquiry into a specific problem that needs a solution. Decisions based on the results of a well-done scientific study tend to yield the desired results. It is necessary to understand what the term *scientific* means. Scientific research focuses on solving problems and pursues a step-by-step logical, organized, and rigorous method to identify the problems, gather data, analyze them, and draw valid conclusions from them. Thus, scientific research is not based on hunches, experience, and intuition (though these may play a part in final decision making), but is purposive and rigorous. Because of the rigorous way in which it is done, scientific research enables all those who are interested in researching and knowing about the same or similar issues to come up with comparable findings when the data are analyzed. Scientific research also helps researchers to state their findings with accuracy and confidence. This helps various other organizations to apply those solutions when they encounter similar problems. Furthermore, **scientific investigation** tends to be more objective than subjective, and helps managers to highlight the most critical factors at the workplace that need specific attention so as to avoid, minimize, or solve problems. Scientific investigation and managerial decision making are integral aspects of effective problem solving.

The term *scientific research* applies to both basic and applied research. Applied research may or may not be generalizable to other organizations, depending on the extent to which differences exist in such factors as size, nature of work, characteristics of the employees, and structure of the organization. Nevertheless, applied research also has to be an organized and systematic process where problems are carefully identified, data scientifically gathered and analyzed, and conclusions drawn in an objective manner for effective problem solving.

Do organizations always follow the rigorous step-by-step process? No. Sometimes the problem may be so simple that it does not call for elaborate research, and past experience might offer the necessary solution. At other times, exigencies of time (where quick decisions are called for), unwillingness to expend the resources needed for doing good research, lack of knowledge, and other factors might prompt businesses to try to solve problems based on hunches. However, the probability of making wrong decisions in such cases is high. Even such business ''gurus'' as Lee Iacocca confess to making big mistakes due to errors of judgment. *Business Week*, *Fortune*, and the *Wall Street Journal*, among other business periodicals and newspapers, feature articles from time to time about organizations that face difficulties because of wrong decisions made on the basis of hunches and/or insufficient information. Many implemented plans fail because not enough research has preceded their formulation.

# The hallmarks of scientific research

The hallmarks or main distinguishing characteristics of scientific research may be listed as follows:

1. Purposiveness
2. Rigor
3. Testability
4. Replicability
5. Precision and confidence
6. Objectivity
7. Generalizability
8. Parsimony

Each of these characteristics can be explained in the context of a concrete example. Let us consider the case of a manager who is interested in investigating how employees' commitment to the organization can be increased. We shall examine how the eight hallmarks of science apply to this investigation so that it may be considered ''scientific.''

## Purposiveness

The manager has started the research with a definite aim or purpose. The focus is on increasing the commitment of employees to the organization, as this will be beneficial in many ways. An increase in employee commitment will translate into less turnover, less absenteeism, and probably increased performance levels, all of which will definitely benefit the organization. The research thus has a **purposive** focus.

## Rigor

A good theoretical base and a sound methodological design add **rigor** to a purposive study. Rigor connotes carefulness, scrupulousness, and the degree of exactitude in research investigations. In the case of our example, let us say the manager of an organization asks 10 to 12 of its employees to indicate what would increase their level of commitment to it. If, solely on the basis of their responses, the manager reaches several conclusions on how employee commitment can be increased, the whole approach to the investigation is unscientific. It lacks rigor for the following reasons:

1. The conclusions are incorrectly drawn because they are based on the responses of just a few employees whose opinions may not be representative of those of the entire workforce.
2. The manner of framing and addressing the questions could have introduced bias or incorrectness in the responses.
3. There might be many other important influences on organizational commitment that this small sample of respondents did not or could not verbalize during the interviews, and the researcher has therefore failed to include them.

Therefore, conclusions drawn from an investigation that lacks a good theoretical foundation, as evidenced by reason 3, and methodological sophistication, as evident from 1 and 2 above, are unscientific. Rigorous research involves a good theoretical base and a carefully thought-out methodology. These factors enable the researcher to collect the right kind of information from an appropriate sample with the minimum degree of bias, and facilitate suitable analysis of the data gathered. The following chapters of this book address these theoretical and methodological issues. Rigor in research design also makes possible the achievement of the other six hallmarks of science that we shall now discuss.

## Testability

If, after talking to a random selection of employees of the organization and study of the previous research done in the area of organizational commitment, the manager or researcher develops certain hypotheses on how employee commitment can be enhanced, then these can be tested by applying certain statistical tests to the data collected for the purpose. For instance, the researcher might hypothesize that those employees who perceive greater opportunities for participation in decision making will have a higher level of commitment. This is a hypothesis that can be tested when the data are collected. A correlation analysis will indicate whether the hypothesis is substantiated or not. The use of several other tests, such as the chi-square test and the *t*-test, is discussed in Chapters 11 and 12.

Scientific research thus lends itself to testing logically developed hypotheses to see whether or not the data support the educated conjectures or hypotheses that are developed after a careful study of the problem situation. Testability thus becomes another hallmark of scientific research.

## Replicability

Let us suppose that the manager/researcher, based on the results of the study, concludes that participation in decision making is one of the most important factors that influences the commitment of employees to the organization. We will place more faith and credence in these findings and conclusion if similar findings emerge on the basis of data collected by other organizations employing the same methods. To put it differently, the results of the tests of hypotheses should be supported again and yet again when the same type of research is repeated in other similar circumstances. To the extent that this does happen (i.e., the results are *replicated* or repeated), we will gain confidence in the scientific nature of our research. In other words, our hypotheses have not been supported merely by chance, but are reflective of the true state of affairs in the population. **Replicability** is thus another hallmark of scientific research.

## Precision and confidence

In management research, we seldom have the luxury of being able to draw "definitive" conclusions on the basis of the results of data analysis. This is because we are unable to study the universe of items, events, or population we are interested in, and have to base our findings on a sample that we draw from the universe. In all probability, the sample in question may not reflect the exact characteristics of the phenomenon we are trying to study (these difficulties are discussed in greater detail in Chapter 10). Measurement errors and other problems are also bound to introduce an element of bias or error in our findings. However, we would like to design the research in a manner that ensures that our findings are as close to reality (i.e., the true state of affairs in the universe) as possible, so that we can place reliance or confidence in the results.

**Precision** refers to the closeness of the findings to "reality" based on a sample. In other words, precision reflects the degree of accuracy or exactitude of the results on the basis of the sample, to what really exists in the universe. For example, if I estimated the number of production days lost during the year due to absenteeism at between 30 and 40, as against the actual figure of 35, the precision of my estimation compares more favorably than if I had indicated that the loss of production days was somewhere between 20 and 50. You may recall the term *confidence interval* in statistics, which is what is referred to here as precision.

**Confidence** refers to the probability that our estimations are correct. That is, it is not merely enough to be precise, but it is also important that we can confidently claim that 95% of the time our results will be true and there is only a 5% chance of our being wrong. This is also known as the *confidence level*.

The narrower the limits within which we can estimate the range of our predictions (i.e., the more precise our findings) and the greater the confidence we have in our research results, the more useful and scientific the findings become. In social science research, a 95% confidence level – which implies that there is only a 5% probability that the findings may *not* be correct – is accepted as conventional, and is usually referred to as a significance level of 0.05 ($p = 0.05$). Thus, precision and confidence are important aspects of research, which are attained through appropriate scientific sampling design. The greater the precision and confidence we aim at in our research, the more scientific is the investigation and the more useful are the results. Both precision and confidence are discussed in detail in Chapter 10 on Sampling.

## Objectivity

The conclusions drawn through the interpretation of the results of data analysis should be objective; that is, they should be based on the facts of the findings derived from actual data, and not on our own subjective or emotional values. For instance, if we had a hypothesis that stated that greater participation in decision making would increase organizational commitment, and this was not supported by the results, it would make no sense if the researcher continued to argue that increased opportunities for employee participation would still help! Such an argument would be based, not on the factual, data-based research findings, but on the subjective opinion of the researcher. If this was the researcher's conviction all along, then there was no need to do the research in the first place!

Much damage can be sustained by organizations that implement non-data-based or misleading conclusions drawn from research. For example, if the hypothesis relating to organizational commitment in our previous example was not supported, considerable time and effort would be wasted in finding ways to create opportunities for employee participation in decision making. We would only find out later that employees still kept quitting, remained absent, and did not develop any sense of commitment to the organization. Likewise, if research shows that increased pay is not going to increase the job satisfaction of employees, then implementing a revised, increased pay system will only drag down the company financially without attaining the desired objective. Such a futile exercise, then, is based on nonscientific interpretation and implementation of the research results.

The more objective the interpretation of the data, the more scientific the research investigation becomes. Though managers or researchers might start with some initial subjective values and beliefs, their interpretation of the data should be stripped of personal values and bias. If managers attempt to do their own research, they should be particularly sensitive to this aspect. **Objectivity** is thus another hallmark of scientific investigation.

## Generalizability

**Generalizability** refers to the scope of applicability of the research findings in one organizational setting to other settings. Obviously, the wider the range of applicability of the solutions generated by research, the more useful the research is to the users. For instance, if a researcher's findings that participation in decision making enhances organizational commitment are found to be true in a variety of manufacturing, industrial, and service organizations, and not merely in the particular organization studied by the researcher, then the generalizability of the findings to other organizational settings is enhanced. The more generalizable the research, the greater its usefulness and value. However, not many research findings can be generalized to all other settings, situations, or organizations.

For wider generalizability, the research sampling design has to be logically developed and a number of other details in the data-collection methods need to be meticulously followed. However, a more elaborate sampling design, which would doubtless increase the generalizability of the results, would also increase the costs of research. Most applied research is generally confined to research within the particular organization where the problem arises, and the results, at best, are generalizable only to other identical situations and settings. Though such limited applicability does not necessarily decrease its scientific value (subject to proper research), its generalizability is restricted.

## Parsimony

Simplicity in explaining the phenomena or problems that occur, and in generating solutions for the problems, is always preferred to complex research frameworks that consider an unmanageable number of factors. For instance, if two or three specific variables in the work situation are identified, which when changed would raise the organizational commitment of the employees by 45%, that would be more useful and valuable to the manager than if it were recommended that he should change ten different variables to increase organizational commitment by 48%. Such an unmanageable number of variables might well be totally beyond the manager's control to change. Therefore, the achievement of a meaningful and parsimonious, rather than an elaborate and cumbersome, model for problem solution becomes a critical issue in research.

Economy in research models is achieved when we can build into our research framework a lesser number of variables that explain the variance far more efficiently than a complex set of variables that only marginally add to the variance explained. **Parsimony** can be introduced with a good understanding of the problem and the important factors that influence it. Such a good conceptual theoretical model can be realized through unstructured and structured interviews with the concerned people, and a thorough literature review of the previous research work in the particular problem area.

In sum, scientific research encompasses the eight criteria just discussed. These are discussed in more detail later in this book. At this point, a question that might be asked is why a scientific approach is necessary for investigations when systematic research by simply collecting and analyzing data would produce results that could be applied to solve the problem. The reason for following a scientific method is that the results will be less prone to error and more confidence can be placed in the findings because of the greater rigor in application of the design details. This also increases the replicability and generalizability of the findings.

# Some obstacles to conducting scientific research in the management area

In the management and behavioral areas, it is not always possible to conduct investigations that are 100% scientific, in the sense that, unlike in the physical sciences, the results obtained will not be exact and error-free. This is primarily because of difficulties likely to be encountered in the measurement and collection of data in the subjective areas of feelings, emotions, attitudes, and perceptions.

These problems occur whenever we attempt to quantify human behavior. Difficulties might also be encountered in obtaining a representative sample, restricting the generalizability of the findings. Thus, it is not always possible to meet all the hallmarks of science in full. Comparability, consistency, and wide generalizability are often difficult to obtain in research. Still, to the extent that the research is designed to ensure purposiveness, rigor, and the maximum possible testability, replicability, generalizability, objectivity, parsimony, and precision and confidence, we would have endeavored to engage in scientific investigation. Several other possible limitations in research studies are discussed in subsequent chapters.

# The hypothetico-deductive method

Scientific research pursues a step-by-step, logical, organized, and rigorous method (a *scientific* method) to find a solution to a problem. The hypothetico-deductive method, popularized by the Austrian philosopher Karl Popper, is a typical version of the scientific method. The hypothetico-deductive method provides a useful, systematic approach to solving basic and managerial problems. This systematic approach is discussed next.

## The seven-step process in the hypothetico-deductive method

The **hypothetico-deductive method** involves the seven steps listed and discussed next.

1. Identify a broad problem area
2. Define the problem statement
3. Develop hypotheses
4. Determine measures
5. Data collection
6. Data analysis
7. Interpretation of data

### Identify a broad problem area

A drop in sales, frequent production interruptions, incorrect accounting results, low-yielding investments, disinterestedness of employees in their work, customer switching, and the like, could attract the attention of the manager and catalyze the research project.

## Define the problem statement

Scientific research starts with a definite aim or purpose. To find solutions for identified problems, a problem statement that states the general objective of the research should be developed. Gathering initial information about the factors that are possibly related to the problem will help us to narrow the broad problem area and to define the problem statement. Preliminary information gathering, discussed in greater detail in Chapter 3, involves the seeking of information in depth, of what is observed (for instance the observation that our company is losing customers). This could be done by a literature review (literature on customer switching) or by talking to several people in the work setting, to clients (why do they switch?), or to other relevant sources, thereby gathering information on what is happening and why. Through any of these methods, we get an idea or a "feel" for what is transpiring in the situation. This allows us to develop a specific problem statement.

## Develop hypotheses

In this step variables are examined as to their contribution or influence in explaining why the problem occurs and how it can be solved. The network of associations identified among the variables is then theoretically woven, together with justification as to why they might influence the problem. From a theorized network of associations among the variables, certain hypotheses or educated conjectures can be generated. For instance, at this point, we might hypothesize that specific factors such as overpricing, competition, inconvenience, and un-responsive employees affect customer switching.

A scientific hypothesis must meet two requirements. The first criterion is that the hypothesis must be *testable*. A famous example of a hypothesis that is not testable is the hypothesis that God created the earth. The second criterion, and one of the central tenets of the hypothetico-deductive method, is that a hypothesis must also be *falsifiable*. That is, it must be possible to disprove the hypothesis. According to Karl Popper, this is important because a hypothesis cannot be confirmed; there is always a possibility that future research will show that it is false. Hence, failing to falsify (!) a hypothesis does not prove that hypothesis: it remains provisional until it is disproved. Hence, the requirement of falsifiability emphasizes the tentative nature of research findings: we can only "prove" our hypotheses until they are disproved.

The development of hypotheses and the process of theory formulation are discussed in greater detail in Chapter 4.

## Determine measures

Unless the variables in the theoretical framework are measured in some way, we will not be able to test our hypotheses. To test the hypothesis that unresponsive employees affect customer switching, we need to *operationalize* unresponsiveness and customer switching. Measurement of variables is discussed in Chapters 6 and 7.

## Data collection

After we have determined how to measure our variables, data with respect to each variable in the hypothesis need to be obtained. These data then form the basis for data analysis. Data collection is extensively discussed in Chapters 5, 8, 9, and 10.

## Data analysis

In the data analysis step, the data gathered are statistically analyzed to see if the hypotheses that were generated have been supported. For instance, to see if unresponsiveness of employees affects customer switching, we might want to do a correlational analysis to determine the relationship between these variables.

Hypotheses are tested through appropriate statistical analysis, discussed in Chapter 12. Analyses of both quantitative and qualitative data can be done to determine if certain conjectures are substantiated. Qualitative data refer to information gathered in a narrative form through interviews and observations. For example, to test the theory that budgetary constraints adversely impact on managers' responses to their work, several interviews might be conducted with managers after budget restrictions are imposed. The responses from the managers, who verbalize their reactions in different ways, might then be organized to see the different categories under which they fall and the extent to which the same kinds of responses are articulated by the managers.

## Interpretation of data

Now we must decide whether our hypotheses are supported or not by interpreting the meaning of the results of the data analysis. For instance, if it was found from the data analysis that increased responsiveness of employees was negatively related to customer switching (say, 0.3), then we can deduce that if customer retention is to be increased, our employees have to be trained to be more responsive. Another inference from this data analysis is that responsiveness of our employees accounts for (or explains) 9% of the variance in customer switching ($0.3^2$). Based on these deductions, we are able to make recommendations on how the "customer switching" problem may be solved (at least to some extent); we have to train our employees to be more flexible and communicative.

Note that even if the hypothesis on the effect of unresponsiveness on customer switching is not supported, our research effort has still been worthwhile. Hypotheses that are not supported allow us to refine our theory by thinking about why it is that they were not supported. We can then test our refined theory in future research.

In summary, there are seven steps involved in identifying and resolving a problematic issue. To make sure that the seven steps of the hypothetico-deductive method are properly understood, let us briefly review an example in an organizational setting and the course of action taken in the seven steps.

## Example of the application of the hypothetico-deductive method in organizations

### The CIO Dilemma

#### Identifying the broad problem area

The Chief Information Officer (CIO) of a firm observes that the newly installed Management Information System (MIS) is not being used by middle managers as much as was originally expected. The managers often approach the CIO or some other "computer expert" for help or, worse still, make decisions without facts. "There is surely a problem here," the CIO exclaims. The CIO develops the following broad problem statement: "What should be done to increase the use of the newly installed MIS by our middle managers?"

#### Defining the problem statement

Talking to some of the middle-level managers, the CIO finds that many of them have very little idea as to what MIS is all about, what kinds of information it can provide, and how to access it and utilize the information. The CIO uses the Internet to explore further information on the lack of use of MIS in organizations. The search indicates that many middle-level managers – especially the old-timers – are not familiar with operating personal computers and experience "computer anxiety." Lack of knowledge about what MIS offers is also found to be another main reason why some managers do not use it. This information helps the CIO to narrow the broad problem area and to define the problem statement: "To what extent do knowledge-related factors affect the use of MIS by middle managers?"

#### Hypothesizing

The CIO develops a theory incorporating all the relevant factors contributing to the lack of access to the MIS by managers in the organization. From such a theory, the CIO generates various hypotheses for testing, one among them being: *Knowledge of the usefulness of MIS would help managers to put it to greater use.*

#### Development of measures and data collection

The CIO then develops a short questionnaire measuring the various factors theorized to influence the use of the MIS by managers, such as the extent of knowledge of what MIS is, what kinds of information MIS provides, how to gain access to the information, and the level of comfort felt by managers in using computers in general, and finally, how often managers have used the MIS in the preceding three months.

**Data analysis**

The CIO then analyzes the data obtained through the questionnaire to see what factors prevent the managers from using the system.

**Interpretation**

Based on the results, the manager deduces or concludes that managers do not use MIS owing to certain factors. These deductions help the CIO to take necessary action to rectify the situation, which might include, among other things, organizing seminars for training managers on the use of computers, and MIS and its usefulness.

## Review of the hypothetico-deductive method

The hypothetico-deductive method involves the seven steps of identifying a broad problem area, defining the problem statement, hypothesizing, determining measures, data collection, data analysis, and the interpretation of the results. Deductive reasoning is a key element in the hypothetico-deductive method. In **deductive reasoning**, we start with a general theory and then apply this theory to a specific case.

Hypothesis testing is deductive in nature because we test if a general theory (for instance the theory that "customer satisfaction is based on the service quality dimensions of responsiveness, reliability, assurance, tangibles, and empathy") is capable of explaining a particular problem; the problem that catalyzed our research project (for instance, complaints about the service quality our company provides). Hence, service quality theory is used to make predictions about relationships between certain variables in our specific situation; for instance, that there is a positive relationship between perceived employee responsiveness and satisfaction of our customers. In a similar vein, marketing researchers often deduce the consequences of changes in the marketing mix based on existing (marketing) models.

**Inductive reasoning** works in the opposite direction: it is a process where we observe specific phenomena and on this basis arrive at general conclusions. Along these lines, the observation of a first, second, and third white swan may lead to the proposition that "all swans are white". In this example, the repeated observation of a white swan has led to the conclusion that all swans are white. According to Karl Popper it is not possible to "prove" a hypothesis by means of *induction*, because no amount of evidence assures us that contrary evidence will not be found. Observing 3, 10, 100, or even 10 000 white swans, does not justify the conclusion that "all swans are white" because there is always a possibility that the next swan we will observe will be black. Instead, Popper proposed that science is accomplished by *deduction*.

However, despite Popper's criticism on induction, both inductive and deductive processes are often used in research. Indeed, many researchers have argued that both theory generation (induction) and theory testing (deduction) are essential parts of the research process. The following example illustrates this point.

Sometimes, hypotheses that were not originally formulated do get generated through the process of induction. That is, after the data are obtained, some creative insights occur and, based on these, new hypotheses are generated to be tested later. The Hawthorne experiments are a good example of this. In the relay assembly line, many experiments were conducted that increased lighting and the like, based on the original hypothesis that these would account for increases in productivity. But later, when these hypotheses were not substantiated, a new hypothesis was generated based on observed data. The mere fact that people were chosen for the study gave them a feeling of importance that increased their productivity whether or not lighting, heating, or other effects were improved, thus the coining of the term the *Hawthorne effect!* This example shows that both deductive and inductive processes are applied in scientific investigations. Although both deductive and inductive processes can be used in quantitative and qualitative research, deductive processes are more often used in causal and quantitative studies, whereas inductive research processes are regularly used in exploratory and qualitative studies.

In sum, theories based on deduction and induction help us to understand, explain, and/or predict business phenomena. When research is designed to test some specific hypothesized outcomes, for instance to see if controlling aversive noise in the environment increases the performance of individuals in solving mental puzzles, the following steps ensue. The investigator begins with the theory that noise adversely affects mental problem solving. The hypothesis is then generated that if the noise is controlled, mental puzzles can be solved more quickly and correctly. Based on this, a research project is designed to test the hypothesis. The results of the study help the researcher to deduce or conclude that controlling the aversive noise does indeed help the participants to improve their performance on mental puzzles. This method of starting with a theoretical framework, formulating hypotheses, and logically deducing from the results of the study is known as (you probably recognized it already) the hypothetico-deductive method. Here is another example of the hypothetico-deductive research process.

## EXAMPLE

A sales manager might observe that customers are perhaps not as pleased as they used to be. The manager may not be certain that this is really the case but may experience anxiety and some uneasiness that customer satisfaction is on the decline. This process of observation or sensing of the phenomena around us is what gets most research – whether applied or basic – started. The next step for the manager is to determine whether there is a real problem and, if so, how serious it is. This problem identification calls for some preliminary data gathering. The manager might talk casually to a few customers to find out how they feel about the products and customer service. During the course of these conversations the manager might find that the customers like the products but are upset because many of the items they need are frequently out of stock, and they perceive the salespersons as not being helpful. From discussions with some of the salespersons, the manager might discover that the factory does not supply the goods on time and promises new delivery dates that it fails, on occasion, to keep.

Salespersons might also indicate that they try to please and retain the customers by communicating the delivery dates given to them by the factory.

Integration of the information obtained through the informal and formal interviewing process helps the manager to determine that a problem does exist and to define the *problem statement* as follows: "How do delays affect customer satisfaction?" It also helps the manager to formulate a theoretical framework of all the factors contributing to the problem. In this case, there is a network of connections among the following factors: delays by the factory in delivering goods, the notification of later delivery dates that are not kept, the promises of the salespersons to the customers (in hopes of retaining them) that cannot be fulfilled, all of which contribute to customer dissatisfaction. From the theoretical framework, which is a meaningful integration of all the information gathered, several *hypotheses* can be generated and tested to determine if the data support them. Concepts are then *operationally defined* so that they can be measured. A research design is set up to decide on, among other issues, how to *collect* further data, *analyze* and *interpret* them, and finally, to provide an answer to the problem. The process of drawing from logical analysis an inference that purports to be conclusive is called deduction. Thus, the building blocks of science provide the genesis for the hypothetico-deductive method of scientific research.

# Other types of research

Case studies and action research are sometimes used to study certain types of issues. These will be briefly discussed now.

## Case studies

**Case studies** involve in-depth, contextual analyses of similar situations in other organizations, where the nature and definition of the problem happen to be the same as experienced in the current situation. As in the hypothetico-deductive studies, hypotheses can be developed in case studies as well. However, if a particular hypothesis has *not* been substantiated in even a single other case study, no support can be established for the alternate hypothesis developed.

Case study, as a problem-solving technique, is not often undertaken in organizations because such studies dealing with problems similar to the one experienced by a particular organization of a particular size and in a particular type of setting are difficult to come by. Moreover, authentic case studies are difficult to find because many companies prefer to guard them as proprietary data. However, by carefully scrutinizing documented case studies, the manager is in a position to obtain several clues as to what factors might be operating in the current situation and how the problem might be solved. Picking the right cases for study, and understanding and correctly translating the dynamics to one's own situation, are critical for successful problem solving. It should be noted that case studies usually provide qualitative rather than quantitative data for analysis and interpretation. However, the application of case study analysis to certain organizational issues is relatively easy. For example, a study of what contributes to the successful installation of a good management information system in organizations similar to the one that is planning to install it, and the practical application of that knowledge would be very functional.

## Action research

**Action research** is sometimes undertaken by consultants who want to initiate change processes in organizations. In other words, action research methodology is most appropriate while effecting planned changes. Here, the researcher begins with a problem that is already identified, and gathers relevant data to provide a tentative problem solution. This solution is then implemented, with the knowledge that there may be unintended consequences following such implementation. The effects are then evaluated, defined, and diagnosed, and the research continues on an ongoing basis until the problem is fully resolved.

Thus, action research is a constantly evolving project with interplay among problem, solution, effects or consequences, and new solution. A sensible and realistic problem definition and creative ways of collecting data are critical to action research. An example of a situation where action research would be useful is given below.

### EXAMPLE

The vice president of CDS Co. wants to introduce a new system of bookkeeping that is likely to meet with some resistance from the Accounting Department. Based on the past experience in the organization, the VP would like to seek a solution to the problem of employee resistance.

There are several other methods of obtaining data for research purposes, such as through focus groups, panels, observational studies, projective techniques, and interactive media, as we shall see in Chapter 8.

### SUMMARY

In this chapter we obtained a general understanding of what constitutes scientific research and examined the hallmarks of scientific investigations. We also discussed, with examples, the steps involved in the hypothetico-deductive method of studying a problem in order to solve it. When managers realize the value of scientific investigation, they are able to understand and readily accept the need for "good" research. This offers the opportunity to effectively solve complex problems encountered in the workplace. The manager also realizes that although organizational research cannot offer 100% accuracy in results, choices and trade-offs among the various criteria of scientific investigation can be made to obtain valid results for good decision making.

This chapter also briefly touched on case studies and action research. Several methods of collecting data and analyzing them for these types of research are discussed at length in Chapter 8.

## DISCUSSION QUESTIONS

1. Describe the hallmarks of scientific research.
2. What are the steps in hypothetico-deductive research? Explain them, using an example not in the book.
3. One hears the word *research* being mentioned by several groups such as research organizations, college and university professors, doctoral students, graduate assistants working for faculty, graduate and undergraduate students doing their term papers, research departments in industries, newspaper reporters, journalists, lawyers, doctors, and many other professionals and nonprofessionals. In the light of what you have learned in this chapter, which among the aforementioned groups of people do you think may be doing "scientific" investigations in the areas of basic or applied research? Why?
4. Explain the processes of deduction and induction, giving an example of each.
5. If research in the management area cannot be 100% scientific, why bother to do it at all? Comment on this statement.
6. Critique the following research done in a service industry as to the extent to which it meets the hallmarks of scientific investigation discussed in this chapter.

## EXAMPLE

### The Friendly Telephone Company

Customer complaints were mounting, and letters of complaint detailing the problems they experienced with the residential telephone lines were constantly pouring in at the Friendly Telephone Company. The company wanted to pinpoint the specific problems and take corrective action.

Researchers were called in, and they spoke to a number of customers, noting the nature of the specific problems they faced. Because the problem had to be attended to very quickly, they developed a theoretical base, collected relevant detailed information from a sample of 100 customers, and analyzed the data. The results promise to be fairly accurate with at least an 85% chance of success in problem solving. The researchers will make recommendations to the company based on the results of data analysis.

7. Strictly speaking, would the use of case studies be considered scientific research? Why or why not?
8. What is action research? Describe a specific situation where action research would be warranted.
9. Comment on the following situation.

## EXAMPLE

### The dilemmas of Dorothy Dunning

Dorothy Dunning, Chief Production Manager, was on top of the world just two years ago. In her nontraditional job, she was cited to be the real backbone of the company, and her performance was in no small measure responsible for the mergers the institution was contemplating with other well-known global corporations.

Of late though, the products of the company had to be recalled several times owing to safety concerns. Quality glitches and production delays also plagued the company.

To project a good image to consumers, Dunning developed a very reassuring website and made sweeping changes in the manufacturing processes to enhance the quality of the product, minimize defects, and enhance the efficiency of the workers. A year after all these changes, the company continues to recall defective products!

Inductive.
Observation → Pattern → Tentative Theory → Theory.

Deductive research.
Theory → Hypothesis → Observation → Confirm

# CHAPTER 3

## The research process: the broad problem area and defining the problem statement

## Topics discussed

- The broad problem area
- Preliminary data gathering
- Some information vital for research
  - Background information on the organization: contextual factors
  - Prevailing knowledge on the topic
- Literature review
  - Reasons for the literature review
  - Conducting the literature review
    - Identifying relevant sources
    - Extracting the relevant information
    - Writing up the literature review
- Problem definition
- The research proposal
- Managerial implications
- Ethical issues
- Appendix:
  - Online databases
  - Bibliographical indexes
  - Referencing in the APA format
  - Referencing and quotation in the literature review section

## CHAPTER OBJECTIVES

After completing Chapter 3 you should be able to:

1. Identify problem areas that are likely to be studied in organizations.
2. Discuss how problem areas can be identified in work settings.
3. State research problems clearly and precisely.
4. Explain how primary and secondary data help the researcher to develop a problem statement.
5. Develop relevant and comprehensive bibliographies for any organizational research topic.
6. Write a literature review on any given topic, documenting the references in the prescribed manner.
7. Develop a research proposal.
8. Apply all you have learned to a group project that might be assigned.

# Broad problem area

Identification of the broad problem area through the process of observing and focusing on the situation was discussed briefly in Chapter 2. A "problem" does not necessarily mean that something is seriously wrong with a current situation that needs to be rectified immediately. A problem could also indicate an interest in an issue where finding the right answers might help to improve an existing situation. Thus, it is fruitful to define a problem as any situation where a gap exists between the actual and the desired ideal states.

Examples of broad problem areas that a manager could observe at the workplace are as follows:

1. Training programs are perhaps not as effective as anticipated.
2. The sales volume of a product is not picking up.
3. Minority group members in organizations are not advancing in their careers.
4. The newly installed information system is not being used by the managers for whom it was primarily designed.
5. The introduction of flexible work hours has created more problems than it has solved in many companies.

Once we have identified the broad problem area, it needs to be narrowed down to a specific problem statement after some preliminary information is gathered by the researcher. This may be through interviews and literature research.

# Preliminary information gathering

## Nature of information to be gathered

Unstructured interviews, structured interviews, and a review through existing sources of information will help us to narrow the broad problem area and to define a specific problem statement. Although the exact nature of the information needed for this purpose depends on the type of problem we are addressing, it may be broadly classified under two headings:

1. Background information on the organization – that is, the contextual factors.
2. Prevailing knowledge on the topic – that is, relevant findings from previous research.

Certain types of information, such as the background details of the company, can be obtained from available published records, the website of the company, its archives, and other sources. Other types of written information, such as company policies, procedures, and rules, can be obtained from the organization's records and documents. Data gathered through such existing sources are called **secondary data**. That is, they are data that already exist and do not have to be collected by the researcher. Some secondary sources of data are statistical bulletins, government publications, published or unpublished information available from either within or outside the organization, data available from previous research, case studies and library records, online data, company websites, and the Internet in general. In contrast, certain other types of information are best obtained by observing events, people, and objects, or by administering questionnaires to individuals. Such data gathered for research from the actual site of occurrence of events are called **primary data**. It is often beneficial to simultaneously gather primary and secondary data. On the one hand, secondary data can help you to focus further interviews more meaningfully on relevant aspects found to be important in the literature. On the other hand, the interviews may help you to search for relevant topics in secondary sources.

## Background information on the organization

It is important for the researcher or the research team – especially if an outside agency conducts the research – to be well acquainted with the background of the company or organization studied. Such background information might include, among other things, the contextual factors listed below, which may be obtained from various published sources.

1. The origin and history of the company – when it came into being, business it is in, rate of growth, ownership and control, and so on.
2. Size in terms of employees, assets, or both.
3. Charter – purpose and ideology.
4. Location – regional, national, or other.

5. Resources – human and others.
6. Interdependent relationships with other institutions and the external environment.
7. Financial position during the previous five to ten years, and relevant financial data.
8. Information on structural factors (for instance roles and positions in the organization and number of employees at each job level, communication channels, control systems, work-flow systems).
9. Information on the management philosophy.

Information gathered on the foregoing aspects will be useful in talking knowledgeably with managers and other employees in the company and raising the appropriate issues related to the problem. Along these lines, an understanding of these factors might be helpful in arriving at a precise problem formulation. Depending on the situation, the type of problem investigated, and the nature of some initial responses received, certain aspects may have to be explored in greater depth than others.

### Prevailing knowledge on the topic

A literature review should help the researcher to identify and highlight the important variables that are related to the problem. This is important because it ensures that the research is structured on work already done and that it builds on the foundation of prevailing knowledge. A review of the literature thus ensures that no important variable that has in the past been found repeatedly to have had an impact on the problem is ignored in the process of defining the problem statement. Indeed, it is possible that some of the critical variables are never brought out in the interviews you administer, either because the employees cannot articulate them or are unaware of their impact, or because the variables seem so obvious to the interviewees that they are not specifically stated. If there are variables that are not identified during the interviews but influence the problem critically, then research done without considering them is an exercise in futility. In such a case, the true reason for the problem will remain unidentified even at the end of the research. To avoid such possibilities the researcher needs to delve into all the important research relating to the particular problem area.

# Literature review

A **literature review** is a step-by-step process that involves the identification of published and unpublished work from secondary data sources on the topic of interest, the evaluation of this work in relation to the problem, and the documentation of this work. We have just explained how a literature review helps the researcher to develop a good problem statement: it ensures that no important variable is overlooked in the process of defining the problem. A review of the literature also serves some other functions. For instance, sometimes the investigator might spend considerable time and effort in "discovering" something that has already been thoroughly researched. A literature review would prevent such a waste of resources in reinventing the wheel. A survey of the literature also facilitates the creative integration of the information gathered from the structured and unstructured interviews with what has been found in previous studies. In other words, it gives a good basic framework to proceed further with the investigation. A good literature review thus provides the foundation for developing a comprehensive theoretical framework from which hypotheses can be developed for testing.

In sum, a good literature review ensures that:

1. Important variables that are likely to influence the problem situation are not left out of the study.
2. A clearer idea emerges as to what variables will be most important to consider (parsimony), why they are considered important, and how they should be investigated to solve the problem. Thus, the literature survey helps the development of the theoretical framework and hypotheses for testing.
3. The problem statement can be made with precision and clarity.
4. Testability and replicability of the findings of the current research are enhanced.
5. One does not run the risk of "reinventing the wheel"; that is, wasting effort on trying to rediscover something that is already known.
6. The problem investigated is perceived by the scientific community as relevant and significant.

## Conducting the literature review

The first step of the literature review involves the identification of the various published and unpublished materials that are available on the topic of interest, and gaining access to these.

### Data sources

The quality of a literature review depends on a cautious selection and reading of books, academic and professional journals, reports, theses, conference proceedings, unpublished manuscripts, and the like. Academic books and journals are, in general, the most useful sources of information. However, other sources such as professional journals, reports, and even newspapers may also be valuable because they can provide you with specific, real world information about markets, industries, or companies. Therefore, as a rule, you will need to use a combination of information resources. The precise combination of resources depends on the nature and the objectives of your research project.

### Textbooks

Textbooks are a useful source of theory in a specific area. An advantage of textbooks is that they can cover a broad range of topics. What's more, textbooks can cover a topic much more thoroughly than articles can. Hence, textbooks offer a good starting point from which to find more detailed sources such as journal articles, theses, and unpublished manuscripts. A downside of textbooks is that they tend to be less up to date than journals.

### Journals

Both academic and professional journals are important sources of up-to-date information. Articles in academic journals have generally been peer-reviewed: this means that the articles have been subject to the scrutiny of experts in the same field before being accepted for publication. *Review articles* (that may or may not contain a meta-analysis: a type of data analysis in which the results of several studies are combined and analyzed as if they were the results of one large study) summarize previous research findings to inform the reader of the state of existing research. Review articles are very useful because they provide an overview of all the important research in a specific area. *Research articles* are reports of empirical research, describing one or a few related studies. The conceptual background section of a research article provides a compact overview of relevant literature. Research articles also provide a detailed description of the purpose of the study, the method(s) used, and the results of the study.

Articles in professional journals are a valuable source of recent developments in the field and of facts and figures. What's more, they may provide you with a feel for the practical relevance of a problem.

### Theses

PhD theses often contain an exhaustive review of the literature in a specific area. Most PhD theses include several empirical chapters. These chapters often have the same structure and characteristics as academic journal articles. Note that not every empirical chapter of a thesis is eventually published in an academic journal.

### Conference proceedings

Conference proceedings can be useful in providing the latest research, or research that has not (yet) been published. Conference proceedings are very up to date, and for this reason this information source is quite valuable if you are working in a relatively new area or domain. Not every manuscript presented at a conference is eventually published in an academic journal; hence you must critically assess the quality of this information source.

### Unpublished manuscripts

The APA defines an unpublished manuscript as any information source that is not "officially" released by an individual, publishing house, or other company. Examples of unpublished manuscripts may include papers accepted for publication but still "in press," data from an unpublished study, letters, manuscripts in preparation, and personal communications (including e-mails). Unpublished manuscripts are often very up to date.

### Reports

Government departments and corporations commission or carry out a large amount of research. Their published findings provide a useful source of specific market, industry, or company information.

### Newspapers

Newspapers provide up-to-date business information. They are a useful source of specific market, industry, or company information. Note that opinions in newspapers are not always unbiased.

### The Internet

The amount of information that can be found on the World Wide Web is enormous. You can search for (the details of) books, journals and journal articles, and conference proceedings, as well as for specialized data such as company publications and reports. The number of newspapers, magazines, and journals that is available electronically is growing rapidly.

Note that the Internet is unregulated and unmonitored. Moreover, developing an Internet page is easy and cheap. For this reason, the Internet provides exceptional challenges in determining the usefulness and reliability of information. A helpful source that may help you to assess the quality of online information is Cooke (2001). You can also find useful information on the Internet itself; several universities have developed useful guidelines to assess the quality of information found on the Internet (check, for instance, http://www.lib. berkeley.edu/TeachingLib/Guides/Evaluation.html).

Search engines such as Google and Yahoo! can help you to find relevant information. For instance, Google Scholar, which can be accessed from the Google homepage, can help you to identify academic literature, such as peer-reviewed papers, theses, books, abstracts, and articles from academic publishers, universities, and other scholarly organizations.

## Searching for literature

Previously, one had to manually go through several bibliographical indexes that are compiled periodically, listing the journals, books, and other sources in which published work in the area of interest could be found. With modern technology, locating sources where the topics of interest have been published has become much easier. Almost every library today has computer online systems to locate published information. Computerized databases provide a number of advantages. First, they save enormous amounts of time. Second, they are comprehensive in their listing and review of references. Third, gaining access to them is relatively inexpensive. For these reasons the researcher can focus on material most central to the research effort.

You will benefit from spending some time on becoming familiar with the online resources that your library provides. Most libraries have the following electronic resources at their disposal:

- Electronic journals. Your library is probably subscribed to journals that are published or made available online. You may want to find out which journals are provided online by your library.
- Full-text databases. Full-text databases provide the full text of the article. Find out which full-text databases are provided by your library.
- Bibliographic databases. Bibliographic databases display only the bibliographic citations; that is, the name of the author, the title of the article (or book), source of publication, year,

volume, and page numbers. These contain the same information as can be found in the Bibliographic Index books in libraries, which are periodically updated, and include articles published in periodicals, newspapers, books, and so on. Some useful indexes are provided in the appendix to this chapter.
- Abstract databases. Abstract databases also provide an abstract or summary of articles. They do not provide the full text of an article or manuscript.

Some of these databases are listed in the appendix at the end of this chapter. Some important research databases available on the World Wide Web are also provided in the appendix. Databases include, among others, listings of journal articles, books in print, census data, dissertation abstracts, conference papers, and newspaper abstracts that are useful for business research.

## Evaluating the literature

Accessing the online system and searching for literature in the area of interest will provide a comprehensive bibliography on the subject. Because the search for literature can sometimes provide as many as one hundred or more results, you will have to carefully select relevant books and articles.

A glance at the *titles* of the articles or books will indicate which of them may be pertinent and which others are likely to be peripheral to the contemplated study. The *abstract* of an article usually provides an overview of the study purpose, general research strategy, findings, and conclusions. A good abstract thus provides you with enough information to help you to decide whether an article is relevant for your study. An article's *introduction* also provides an overview of the problem addressed by the research and specific research objectives. The introduction often ends with a summary of the research questions that guide the study. The problem statement, research questions, and/or the research objectives give you a feel for what the researcher is studying and thus for the relevance of the article to your study. In a similar fashion, the *table of contents* and the *first chapter of a book* may help you to assess the relevance of the book.

A good literature review needs to include references to the key studies in the field. For this reason, articles and books that are often cited by others must be included in your literature review, even if these articles and books were written thirty or even forty years ago. Of course, more recent work should also be incorporated in your literature survey, since recent work will build on a broader and more up-to-date stream of literature than older work.

To assess the quality of *recent* research (indeed, in this case you cannot use the number of citations as an indicator of the quality of an article) you could ask the following questions:

- Is the main research question or problem statement presented in a clear and analytical way?
- Is the relevance of the research question made transparent?
- Does this study build directly upon previous research?
- Will the study make a contribution to the field?
- Is there a theory that guides the research?

- Is the theory described relevant and is it explained in an understandable, structured, and convincing manner?
- Are the methods used in the study explained in a clear manner (description of methods)?
- Is the choice of certain methods motivated in a convincing way (justification of methods)?
- Is the sample appropriate?
- Are the research design and/or the questionnaire appropriate for this study?
- Are the measures of the variables valid and reliable?
- Has the author used the appropriate quantitative and/or qualitative techniques?
- Do the conclusions result from the findings of the study?
- Do the conclusions give a clear answer to the main research question?
- Has the author considered the limitations of the study?
- Has the author presented the limitations in the article?

The quality of the journal that published an article can also be used as an indicator of the quality of an article. Important questions in this respect are: "Is the journal peer-reviewed; that is, do all articles have to undergo a review process before they are published?" and "What is the impact factor of the journal?" The impact factor of a journal can be viewed as the average number of citations in a year given to those papers in the journal that were published during a given period (usually the two preceding years). Because important articles are cited more often than articles that are not important, the impact factor of a journal is frequently used as a proxy for the importance of that journal to its field.

In sum, some criteria for assessing the value of articles or books are: the relevance of the issues that are addressed in the article or book, the importance of a book or article in terms of citations, the year of publication of the article or book, and the overall quality of the article or book.

All the articles considered relevant to your study can be listed as references, using the appropriate referencing format, which is discussed in the appendix to this chapter.

## Documenting the literature review

As stated earlier, the purpose of the literature review is to help the researcher to develop a good problem statement. A review of the literature identifies and highlights the important variables, and documents the significant findings from earlier research that will serve as the foundation on which the theoretical framework for the current investigation can be built. Documenting the literature review is important to convince the reader that (1) the researcher is knowledgeable about the problem area and has done the preliminary homework that is necessary to conduct the research, and (2) the theoretical framework will be structured on work already done and will add to the solid foundation of existing knowledge.

A point to note is that the literature survey should bring together all relevant information in a cogent and logical manner instead of presenting all the studies in chronological order with bits and pieces of uncoordinated information. A good literature review also leads one logically to a good problem statement.

There are several accepted methods of citing references in the literature survey section and using quotations. The *Publication Manual of the American Psychological Association* (2001) offers detailed information regarding citations, quotations, references, and so on, and is one of the accepted styles of referencing in the management area. Other formats include *The Chicago Manual of Style* (2003), and Turabian's *Manual for Writers* (2007). As stated earlier, details of the referencing style and quotations based on the APA Manual (2001) are offered in the appendix at the end of this chapter.

Let us take *a portion* of a completed literature review and examine how the activity has helped to (1) introduce the subject of study, (2) identify the problem statement, and (3) build on previous research to offer the basis from which to get to the next steps of the theoretical framework and hypothesis development.

## EXAMPLE

### Organizational effectiveness

Organization theorists have defined organizational effectiveness (OE) in various ways. OE has been described in terms of objectives (Georgopolous and Tannenbaum, 1957), goals (Etzioni, 1960), efficiency (Katz and Kahn, 1966), resources acquisition (Yuchtman and Seashore, 1967), employee satisfaction (Cummings, 1977), interdependence (Pfeffer, 1977), and organizational vitality (Colt, 1995). As Coulter (2002) remarked, there is little consensus on how to conceptualize, measure, or explain OE. This should, however, not come as a surprise to us since OE models are essentially value-based classifications of the construct (the values being those of the researchers) and the potential number of models that can be generated by researchers is virtually limitless. Researchers are now moving away from a single model and are taking contingency approaches to conceptualizing OE (Cameron, 1996; Wernerfelt, 1998; Yetley, 2001). However, they are still limiting themselves to examining the impact of the dominant constituencies served and the organization's life cycle on OE instead of taking a broader, more dynamic approach (Dahl, 2001, p. 25).

From the above extract, several insights can be gained. The literature review (1) introduces the subject of study (organizational effectiveness), (2) highlights the problem (that we do not have a good conceptual framework for understanding what OE is), and (3) summarizes the work done so far on the topic in a manner that convinces the reader that the researcher has indeed surveyed the work done in the area of OE and wants to contribute to the understanding of the concept, taking off on the earlier contingency approaches in a more creative way. The scholar has carefully paved the way for the next step, which is to develop a more viable and robust model of organizational effectiveness. This model will be logically developed, integrating several streams of research done in other areas (such as cross-cultural management, sociology, etc.), which will be woven further into the literature review. Once the scholar has explicated the framework as to what constitutes OE and what the factors that influence it are, the next step is to develop testable hypotheses to see if the new model is indeed viable.

After gathering preliminary information the researcher should be able to delineate a logical, well-defined, and sharply focused problem for research investigation. This delineation or definition of the problem, which is the next step in the research process, is now discussed.

# Defining the problem statement

After the interviews and the literature review, the researcher is in a position to narrow down the problem from its original broad base and define the issues of concern more clearly. It is critical that the focus of further research, or in other words, the problem, be unambiguously identified and defined. No amount of good research can find solutions to the situation if the critical issue or the problem to be studied is not clearly pinpointed.

## What makes a good problem statement?

The problem statement introduces the key problem that is addressed in the research project. A **problem statement** is a clear, precise, and succinct statement of the specific issue that a researcher wishes to investigate. There are three key criteria to assess the quality of the problem statement: it should be relevant, feasible, and interesting.

A problem statement is relevant if it is meaningful from a managerial perspective, an academic perspective, or both. From a *managerial* perspective, research is *relevant* if it relates to (1) a problem that currently exists in an organizational setting or (2) an area that a manager believes needs to be improved in the organization. As an example of a problem that currently exists, a situation might present itself where a manager receives written complaints from women in some departments that they are not being "treated right" by the bosses. From the generalized nature of these complaints, the manager might become aware that he is facing a gender-related problem situation, but may not be able to pinpoint what exactly it is. That is, the matter calls for further investigation before the exact problem can be identified and attempts made to resolve it. On the other hand, the following is an example of a situation requiring improvement. If the company has already formulated policies on discrimination and sexual harassment, and legitimate complaints of discrimination continue to come in, then it is obvious that the policies are ambiguous and need to be redefined in terms of how they have been framed, how they are understood, or how they are enforced.

## EXAMPLE

It is very important that symptoms of problems are not defined as the real problem. For instance, a manager might have tried to increase productivity by increasing the piece rate, but with little success. Here the real problem may be the low morale and motivation of employees who feel they are not being recognized as valuable contributors to the system and get no "praise" for the good work that they do. The low productivity may merely be a symptom of the deep-rooted morale and motivation problem. Under these conditions, a higher piece rate will not improve productivity! Thus, finding the "right" answers to the "wrong" problem definitions will not help. Hence, it should be recognized that correct problem identification is extremely critical for finding solutions to vexing issues. Frequently, managers tend to describe the problem in terms of symptoms. Rather than accepting it as such, the researcher needs to identify the problem more accurately. One way of determining that the problem, rather than the symptom, is being addressed is to ask the question (after gathering sufficient information through interviews and literature searches), "Is this factor I have identified an antecedent, the real problem, or the consequence?" These terms can be discussed in the context of the earlier example of low productivity. The real issue or problem here is low morale and motivation. The consequence of the problem is low productivity. Note that the consequence (or effect) of low motivation can also manifest itself in absenteeism, sabotage, or any number of other adverse effects for the firm. The real problem that needs to be addressed in this case, hence, is not productivity, but motivation. The antecedent of the problem (i.e., the contributing factor) in the given situation seems to be nonrecognition of the employees' contributions. Until such time as the employees are recognized for their work, their motivation and morale will not improve, nor will their productivity, as a consequence. Without addressing the central issue, if more money is given, or better equipment installed to increase productivity, the desired results will not ensue because the right problem has not been addressed.

From an *academic* perspective, research is *relevant* if: (1) nothing is known about a topic, (2) much is known about the topic, but the knowledge is scattered and not integrated, (3) much research on the topic is available, but the results are (partly) contradictory, or (4) established relationships do not hold in certain situations. If you base your research report on the "nothing is known" argument, you will have to prove that your claim is right. The observation that much is known about a topic, but that the knowledge is scattered and not integrated also provides a good basis for a research report. Your task is, however, a difficult one, since it is expected that you will present an integrated overview of the topic. A research project that aims to reconcile contradictory findings or to establish boundary conditions is also a real challenge.

A good problem statement is relevant but also *feasible*. A problem statement is feasible if you are able to answer the problem statement within the restrictions of the research project. These restrictions are possibly related to time and money, but also to the availability of respondents, the expertise of the researcher (a problem statement may be too difficult to answer), and the like. A frequent problem in terms of feasibility is that the problem statement is too broad in scope. Indeed, it is important that you develop a narrowly defined question that can be investigated within a reasonable amount of time, and with a reasonable amount of money and effort. For instance, the problem statement "How do consumers behave?" is far too general to investigate.

A third characteristic of a good problem statement is that it is *interesting* to you. Research is a time-consuming process and you will go through many ups and downs before you present the final version of your research report. It is therefore vital that you are genuinely interested in the problem statement you are trying to answer, so that you can stay motivated throughout the entire research process.

## EXAMPLE

### Examples of well-defined problem statements

1. To what extent do the structure of the organization and type of information systems installed account for the variance in the perceived effectiveness of managerial decision making?
2. To what extent has the new advertising campaign been successful in creating the high-quality, customer-centered corporate image that it was intended to produce?
3. How has the new packaging affected the sales of the product?
4. Has the new advertising message resulted in enhanced recall?
5. How do price and quality rate on consumers' evaluation of products?
6. Is the effect of participative budgeting on performance moderated by control systems?
7. Does better automation lead to greater asset investment per dollar of output?
8. Does expansion of international operations result in an enhancement of the firm's image and value?
9. What are the effects of downsizing on the long-range growth patterns of companies?
10. What are the specific factors to be considered in creating a data warehouse for a manufacturing company?

When you have defined the problem statement you are ready to start your research. First, however, you need to communicate the problem statement and a number of other important aspects of the study – such as the scope of the study, the procedures to be followed, the time frame, and the budget – to all the parties involved.

# The research proposal

Before any research study is undertaken, there should be an agreement between the person who authorizes the study and the researcher as to the problem to be investigated, the methodology to be used, the duration of the study, and its cost. This ensures that there are no misunderstandings or frustrations later for either party. This is usually accomplished through a research proposal, which the researcher submits and gets approved by the sponsor, who issues a letter of authorization to proceed with the study.

The **research proposal** drawn up by the investigator is the result of a planned, organized, and careful effort, and basically contains the following:

1. The purpose of the study.
2. The specific problem to be investigated.
3. The scope of the study.
4. The relevance of the study.
5. The research design offering details on:
   a. The sampling design.
   b. Data collection methods.
   c. Data analysis.
6. Time frame of the study, including information on when the written report will be handed over to the sponsors.
7. The budget, detailing the costs with reference to specific items of expenditure.
8. Selected bibliography.

Such a proposal containing the above features is presented to the manager, who might seek clarification on some points, want the proposal to be modified in certain respects, or accept it in toto. A model of a simple research proposal to study the frequent turnover of newly recruited employees is presented below.

## EXAMPLE

### Model 3.1 Research proposal to study retention of new employees

**Purpose of the study**

To find a solution to the recurring problem of 40% employee turnover within the first three years of their recruitment, and more specifically to:

a. Draw up a profile of the employees who quit;
b. Assess if there are any special needs of the new recruits that require to be met; and
c. Determine the reasons for employees leaving the organization in the first three years.

**Problem statement**

How can small to medium-sized firms increase the organizational commitment of their employees?

**Scope of the study**

This research analyzes the problem of high turnover of employees within *small to medium-sized firms*.

### Relevance of the study

The cost of employee turnover to firms has been estimated to be up to 150% of the employees' remuneration package (Schlesinger and Heskett, 1991). There are both direct and indirect costs involved. Direct costs relate to leaving costs, replacement costs, and transition costs, while indirect costs relate to the loss of production, reduced performance levels, unnecessary overtime, and low morale. The results of this study provide managers with the means to decrease the costs of employee turnover.

### The research design (i.e., details of the study)

*Survey instruments.* First, we will interview a small number of employees who have joined the company in the last three years. Based on these exploratory findings, we will administer a questionnaire to the employees who have joined the company in the last three years.

*Data collection.* The interviews will be conducted during office hours in the Conference Hall of the organization at a prearranged time convenient to the interviewees. The questionnaire will be given to the employees to be completed by them in their homes and returned anonymously to the box set up for the purpose by the specified date. They will all be reminded two days before the due date to return their questionnaires, if not already done.

### Time frame

The time frame necessary for completion of this research project is approximately five months. During these five months, periodic reports will be provided on the progress being made.

### Budget

The budget for this project is in Appendix A.

### Selected bibliography

Bateman, T.S. and Strasser, S. (1984). A Longitudinal Analysis of the Antecedents of Organizational Commitment. *The Academy of Management Journal*, 27, (1), 95–112.

Lachman, L. and Aranya, N. (1986). Evaluation of alternative models of commitments and job attitudes of professionals, *Journal of Occupational Behavior*, 7, 227–243.

Meyer, J. and Allen, N. (1997). *Commitment in the Workplace: Theory, research and application*. Thousand Oaks: Sage.

Meyer, J., Stanley, D., Herscovitch, L. and Topolnytsky, L. (2002). Affective, continuance and normative commitment: a meta-analysis of antecedents, correlates and consequences. *Journal of Vocational Behavior*, 63, 20–52.

Schlesinger, L., & Heskett, J. (1991). The Service-Driven Service Company. *Harvard Business Review*, 69, 71–81.

Vandenberghe, C., Bentein, K. and Stinglhamber, F. (2002). Affective commitment to the organization, supervisor and work group: antecedents and outcomes. *Journal of Vocational Behavior*, 64, 47–71.

Once the proposal is accepted, the researcher conducts the research, going through the appropriate steps discussed in the research design process.

# Managerial implications

Managers sometimes look at the symptoms in problematic situations and treat them as if they are the real problems, getting frustrated when their remedies do not work. Understanding the *antecedents–problem–consequences* sequence and gathering the relevant information to get a real grasp of the problem go a long way towards pinpointing it.

Managers' inputs help researchers to define the broad problem area and confirm their own theories about the situational factors impacting the central problem. Managers who realize that correct problem definition is critical to ultimate problem solution do not begrudge the time spent in working closely with researchers, particularly at this stage.

A well-developed research proposal allows managers to judge the relevance of the proposed study. However, to make sure that the objectives of the study are actually being achieved, managers must stay involved throughout the *entire* research process. Information exchange between the manager and the researcher during all the important stages of the research process will definitely enhance the managerial relevance and the quality of the research effort.

# Ethical issues in the preliminary stages of investigation

Preliminary information is gathered by the researcher to narrow the broad problem area and to define a specific problem statement. In many cases, the researcher interviews decision makers, managers, and other employees to gain knowledge of the situation so as to better understand the problem. Once a problem is specified and a problem statement is defined, the researcher needs to assess his or her research capabilities; if the researcher does not have the skills or resources to carry out the project, he or she should decline the project. If the researcher decides to carry out the project, it is necessary to inform all the employees – particularly those who will be interviewed for preliminary data gathering through structured and unstructured interviews – of the proposed study (though it is not necessary to acquaint them with the actual reasons for the study, because this might bias responses). The element of unpleasant surprise will thus be eliminated for the employees. It is also necessary to assure employees that their responses will be kept confidential by the interviewer/s and that individual responses will not be divulged to anyone in the organization. These two steps make the employees comfortable with the research undertaken and ensure their cooperation. Employees should not be forced to participate in the study. When employees are willing to participate in the study, they have the right to be protected from physical or psychological harm. They also have a right to privacy and confidentiality. Attempts to obtain information through deceptive means should be avoided at all costs.

## Checklist for dealing with ethical considerations and dilemmas during the first stages of the research process

- Why is this research project worth doing?
- How does the organization benefit from this project?
- What impact, if any, does your research have on the organization?
- Do you have the skills and resources to carry out this research project?
- Have you informed all the employees of the research project? Why not?
- Do you explain the purpose of your research to the participants? Why not?
- Are participants given the opportunity to decline participation?
- Are participants able to withdraw their consent at any point? How?
- Does the research cause you to have access to sensitive information? How will you ensure the confidentiality of this information?
- How will you ensure individual respondents cannot be identified from any research reports or papers that are produced?
- Are there any possible negative effects (long or short term) on your participants (including any physical or psychological harm)?
- How will you report back from the research to your participants?
- Where ethical dilemmas have arisen, what steps have you taken to resolve these?

## SUMMARY

In this chapter we learned about the first steps in the research process: identifying the broad problem area and defining the problem statement. Preliminary data gathering through interviews and a literature review was also discussed since this is key to defining the problem statement. We ended this chapter by describing the functions and format of the research proposal. In particular, we discussed how managers can identify the broad problem area through observation, how preliminary data can be collected through unstructured and structured interviews and literature reviews, and how the problem can be honed. The appendix to this chapter offers information on (1) online databases, (2) bibliographical indexes, (3) the APA format for references, and (4) notes on referencing previous studies and quoting original sources in the literature review section.

In Chapter 4 we will examine the next step in the research process: the development of hypotheses.

## DISCUSSION QUESTIONS

1. Explain the preliminary data collection methods.
2. Why is it important to gather information on the background of the organization?
3. Should a researcher *always* obtain information on the structural aspects and job characteristics from those interviewed? Give reasons for your answer with examples.
4. How would you go about doing a literature review in the area of customer satisfaction?
5. What is the purpose of a literature review?
6. Why is appropriate citation important? What are the consequences of not giving credit to the source from which materials are extracted?
7. "The problem definition stage is perhaps more critical in the research process than the problem solution stage." Discuss this statement.
8. Why should one get hung up on problem definition if one already knows the broad problem area to be studied?
9. Offer a clearly focused problem statement in the broad area of corporate culture.
10. After studying and extracting information from all the relevant work done previously, how does the researcher know which particular references, articles, and information should be given prominence in the literature review?
11. Below is the gist of an article from *Business Week*. After reading it:
    a. identify the broad problem area
    b. define the problem
    c. explain how you would proceed further.

### EXAMPLE

While Chrysler's minivans, pickups, and sport utility vehicles take a big share of the truck market, its cars trail behind those of GM, Ford, Honda, and Toyota. Quality problems include, among other things, water leaks and defective parts.

12. What is the problem statement in the following situation?

### EXAMPLE

## Employee loyalty

Companies benefit through employee loyalty. Crude downsizing in organizations during the recession crushed the loyalty of millions. The economic benefits of loyalty embrace lower recruitment and training costs, higher productivity of workers, customer satisfaction, and the boost to morale of fresh recruits. In order that these benefits are not lost, some companies, while downsizing, try various gimmicks. Flex leave, for instance, is one. This helps employees receive 20% of their salary, plus employer-provided benefits, while they take a 6- to 12-month sabbatical, with a call option on their services. Others try alternatives like more communication, hand holding, and the like.

**13.** How would you define the problem in the following case?

### EXAMPLE

## Accounting gets radical

The GAAP (Generally Accepted Accounting Principles) do an unacceptable job of accounting for the principal activities of information age companies. Today, investors are in the dark because the accounting is irrelevant. The basic purpose of accounting is to provide useful information to help investors make rational investment, credit, and similar decisions, but today's most important assets and activities – intellectual capital and work knowledge – are totally ignored.

Professor Robert A. Howell wants to reform the accounting system with the goal of making clear the measurement of how companies produce cash and create value.

### PRACTICE PROJECTS

**I.** Do the project assigned below, following the step-by-step process outlined:

   **i.** Compile a bibliography on any one of the following topics, or any other topic of interest to you, from a business perspective: (a) service quality; (b) product development; (c) open-market operations; (d) information systems; (e) manufacturing technology; (f) assessment centers; (g) transfer pricing.

  **ii.** From this bibliography, select 15 references that include books, periodicals, and newspaper items.

 **iii.** Based on these 15 articles, write a literature review using different forms of citation, as described in the appendix.

  **iv.** Formulate a problem statement.

II. Visit the following websites and answer the questions below.

    **i.** Visit    IBM     http://www.ibm.com and
                 Ford     http://www.ford.com

What similarities and differences do you notice?

    **ii.** Visit    Intel         http://www.intel.com
                 Microsoft   http://www.microsoft.com and
                 Apple     http://www.apple.com

Write a paragraph on each of these companies.

III. Gain access to the online system in your library and (a) generate a list of the references that relate to the performance of General Motors, and (b) obtain the abstracts of these studies.

IV. Access the online system and obtain a list of references that deal with product image.

# APPENDIX

## Some online resources useful for business research

### Online databases

Databases contain raw data stored on disks or CD-ROM. Computerized databases can be purchased that deal with statistical data, financial data, texts, and the like. Computer network links allow the sharing of these databases, which are updated on a regular basis. Most university libraries have computerized databases pertaining to business information that can be readily accessed. Some of the databases useful for business research are listed below:

1. **ABI/INFORM Global** and **ABI/INFORM** provide the capability to search most major business, management, trade and industry, and scholarly journals from 1971 onward. The information search can be made by keying in the name of the author, periodical title, article title, or company name. Full texts from the journals and business periodicals are also available on CD-ROM and electronic services.
2. **The Business Periodicals Index (BPI)** provides an index of business and management periodicals, and is available online and on CD-ROM.
3. **Dow Jones Factiva** products and services provide business news and information. The collection of more than 14 000 sources includes *The Wall Street Journal, the Financial Times*, Dow Jones and Reuters newswires and the Associated Press, as well as Reuters Fundamentals, and D&B company profiles.
4. **EconLit** is a comprehensive index of journal articles, books, book reviews, collective volume articles, working papers, and dissertations.
5. **The International Bibliography of the Social Sciences (IBSS)** is an online resource for social science and interdisciplinary research. IBSS includes over 2.5 million bibliographic records relating to the four core social science subjects of anthropology, economics, politics, and sociology.
6. **PsycINFO** is an abstract database of psychological literature from the 1800s to the present. PsycINFO contains bibliographic citations, abstracts, cited references, and descriptive information of scholarly publications in the behavioral and social sciences.
7. **RePEc (Research Papers in Economics)** is a collaborative effort of volunteers in 63 countries to enhance the dissemination of research in economics. The heart of the project is a decentralized database of working papers, journal articles, and software components.

The following databases can also be accessed through the Internet: Business and Industry Database,[1] Guide to Dissertation Abstracts, Guide to Newspaper Abstracts, Periodicals Abstract, Social Science Citation Index, STAT-USA, Conference Board Cumulative Index (covers publications in business, finance, personnel, marketing, and international operations).

*Note:* A cumulated annotated index to articles on accounting and in business periodicals arranged by subject and by author is also available. The Lexis-Nexis Universe provides specific company and industry information including company reports, stock information, industry trends, and the like.

## On the Web

Some of the many websites useful for business research that can be accessed through a browser such as Internet Explorer are provided below.

### General

Bureau of Census: www.census.gov

Business Researcher's Interests: www.brint.com/interest.html

Business Week Online: http://www.businessweek.com/. The journal *Business Week* online from 1995 until now.

China & World Economy: http://www.iwep.org.cn/wec/

Company Annual Reports: www.annualreports.com

Economic Journals on the web: http://www.oswego.edu/~economic/journals.htm

Euromoney Publications: http://www.euromoney.com/contents/publications/euromoney/. The journal *Euromoney* online from 1995 until now. Registration required.
Eurostat: http://epp.eurostat.ec.europa.eu/portal/page?_pageid=1090,30070682,1090_33076-576&_dad=portal&_schema=PORTAL. Eurostat is the site of the Statistical Office of the European Community. It provides direct access to the latest and most complete statistical information available on the European Union, the EU members, the euro-zone, and other countries.

Forbes Magazine: http://www.forbes.com/forbes/. The journal *Forbes Magazine* online from August 1997 until now.

FT.com TotalSearch: http://news.ft.com/home/europe. FT.com's TotalSearch gives you access to more than ten million free newspaper and magazine articles alongside results gathered from leading online news sources. TotalSearch also incorporates a definitive web

---

[1] Includes information on whether the company is private or public, description of business, company organization and management, product lines and brand names, financial information, stock and bond prices and dividends, foreign operations, marketing and advertising, sales, R & D, and articles available on the company in newspapers and periodicals.

guide in association with Business.com, a leader in business website classification. You can search in the *Financial Times*, the *Guardian*, and *Wall Street Journal* from 1996 until now, or you can refine your search for the *Finanical Times* only.

Harvard Business School Publishing: www.hbsp.harvard.edu

I.O.M.A.: www.ioma.com/ioma/direct.html. This site links to business resources that include financial management, legal resources, small business, human resources, and Internet marketing.

List of Economics Journals: http://netec.mcc.ac.uk/WebEc/journals.html

STAT-USA: www.stat-usa.gov

Wall Street Executive Library: http://www.executivelibrary.com/. Business sites on newspapers, magazines, government, financial markets, company and industry, law, marketing and advertising, statistics, etc.

Wall Street Journal: http://online.wsj.com/public/us

## Accounting

ARN: http://www.ssrn.com/arn/index.html. The Accounting Research Network (ARN) was founded to increase communication among scholars and practitioners of accounting worldwide. ARN encourages the early distribution of research results by publishing abstracts of top quality research papers in three journals: *Auditing, Litigation and Tax Abstracts*, *Financial Accounting Abstracts*, and *Managerial Accounting Abstracts*. The journals publish abstracts of articles dealing with empirical, experimental, and theoretical research in financial and managerial accounting, auditing, and tax strategy. ARN is a division of the Social Science Research Network (SSRN).

BUBL link to accounting: http://bubl.ac.uk/link/a/accountinglinks.htm Links to accounting resources, companies, departments, societies, and journals.

Internal Auditing World Wide Web (IAWWW): http://www.bitwise.net/iawww/ A warehouse of information and knowledge pertaining to the internal auditing profession and functions across all associations, industries, and countries.

## Business and management

Academy of Management: www.aomonline.org

ASTD home page: www.astd.org. The ASTD (American Society for Training and Development) has information on shifting paradigms from training to performance.

Bnet: http://www.bnet.co.uk/. Bnet is a richly interconnected knowledge bank containing information and learning materials about business and management. It is organized to deliver a wide range of information on essential skills and recommended good practice in business and management.

Business information on the Internet: http://www.rba.co.uk/sources/. A selection of key business information sites on the Internet, compiled by Karen Blakeman.

Business information on the Internet: http://www.crosscut.net/research/business.html. Using the Internet for college research, maintained by Terry Dugas.

Corporate Information: http://www.corporateinformation.com/. Starting point to find corporate information from around the world.

European Business Directory: http://www.europages.com/home-en.html

Fortune: http://www.fortune.com/. Also contains the Fortune 500 List (500 American companies and 500 global companies with financial data and their home pages).

GlobalEDGE: http://globaledge.msu.edu/ibrd/ibrd.asp. A directory of international business resources categorized by specific orientation and content. Each resource has been selected and reviewed by the globalEDGE TM Team.

Kompass: http://www.kompass.com/. Addresses and business information of 1.5 million companies worldwide.

Latest management research and practice: http://www.mcb.co.uk/lmrp/jourhome.htm. Internet journal (site also includes Internet links) produced by MCB University Press which is composed of articles on management previously published in other MCB University Press journals. All articles are available in full text in the AdobeAcrobat PDF format. 1996 onwards (approx. ten issues a year).

Moreover: http://www.moreover.com/. Moreover Technologies provides companies with real-time news and information from every online source that impacts their business.

Society for Human Resource Management: www.shrm.org

Wall Street Central: http://www.wscentral.com/. An access point for all kinds of information on companies and financial markets.

Wall Street Executive Library: http://www.executivelibrary.com/. Business sites on newspapers, magazines, government, financial markets, company and industry, law, marketing and advertising, statistics, etc.

### Financial economics

CNN financial network: http://money.cnn.com

FEN: http://www.ssrn.com/fen/index.html. The Financial Economic Network (FEN) is a division of the Social Science Research Network (SSRN).

FINWeb: http://finweb.com/. FINWeb is a financial economics website managed by James R. Garven. The primary objective of FINWeb is to list Internet resources providing substantive information concerning economics and finance-related topics.

MFFAIS: http://www.mffais.com/. Mutual Fund Facts About Individual Stocks. A reference site that shows you (among other things) which and how many mutual funds sold shares in a specific company. And the only one that lists more than just the top ten fundholders of a company.

Standard & Poor's Micropal: http://www.micropal.com/. A detailed and free service analyzing funds from all major markets.

## Marketing

Academic marketing journals: http://www.tilburguniversity.nl/faculties/feb/marketing/links/journal1.html

Current research in marketing: http://www.bauer.uh.edu/parks/crim/crim0000.htm.

KnowThis: http://www.knowthis.com/. Marketing virtual library, offering an objective and unbiased resource for marketing basics, market research, Internet marketing, marketing plans, advertising, and much more.

Marketing links: http://www.tilburguniversity.nl/faculties/feb/organisation/dept/mar/links/. Collected by Tilburg University, Department of Marketing & Marketing Research.

# Bibliographical databases

The following indexes help in compiling a comprehensive bibliography on business topics.

1. Bibliographic Index. A cumulative bibliography of bibliographies – an index that lists, by subject, sources of bibliographies.
2. Business Books in Print. This indexes, by author, title, and business subject, the books in print in the areas of finance, business, and economics.
3. Business Periodicals Index. This is a cumulative subject index covering 270 business periodicals.
4. Management Information Guide. This offers bibliographic references in many business areas.
5. Human Resource Management Abstracts. This is an index of articles that deal with the management of people and the subject area of organizational behavior.
6. Psychological Abstracts. This summarizes the literature in psychology, covering several hundred journals, reports, monographs, and other scientific documents.
7. Public Affairs Information Service Bulletin. This has a selective subject index of books, yearbooks, directories, government documents, pamphlets, and over a thousand periodicals relating to national and international economic and public affairs.
8. Work Related Abstracts. This contains abstracts of articles, dissertations, and books relating to labor, personnel, and organizational behavior.

# APA format for referencing relevant articles

A distinction has to be made between a bibliography and references. A **bibliography** is a listing of work that is relevant to the main topic of research interest arranged in alphabetical order of the last names of the authors. A **reference list** is a subset of the bibliography, which includes details of all the citations used in the literature review and elsewhere in the paper, arranged, again, in alphabetical order of the last names of the authors. These citations have the goals of crediting the authors and enabling the reader to find the works cited.

At least three modes of referencing are followed in business research. These are based on the format provided in the *Publication Manual of the American Psychological Association* (APA) (2001), the *Chicago Manual of Style* (2003), and the Turabian style (2007). Each of these manuals specifies, with examples, how books, journals, newspapers, dissertations, and other materials are to be referenced in manuscripts. Since the APA format is followed for referencing by many journals in the management area, we will use this below to highlight the distinctions in how books, journals, newspaper articles, dissertations, and so on, are referenced. In the following section we will discuss how these references should be cited in the literature review section. All the citations mentioned in the research report will find a place in the References section at the end of the report.

## Specimen format for citing different types of references

### Specimen format for referencing

*Book by a single author*

Leshin, C. B. (1997). *Management on the World Wide Web*. Englewood Cliffs, NJ: Prentice Hall.

*Book by more than one author*

Cornett, M., Wiley, B.J., & Sankar, S. (1998). *The pleasures of nurturing*. London: McMunster Publishing.

*More than one book by the same author in the same year*

Roy, A. (1998a) *Chaos theory*. New York: Macmillan Publishing Enterprises.

Roy, A. (1998b). *Classic chaos*. San Francisco, CA: Jossey Bamar.

*Edited book*

Pennathur, A., Leong, F.T., & Schuster, K. (Eds). (1998). *Style and substance of thinking*. New York: Publishers Paradise.

*Chapter in an edited book*

Riley, T., & Brecht, M.L. (1998). The success of the mentoring process. In R. Williams (Ed.) *Mentoring and career success*, pp. 129–150. New York: Wilson Press.

*Book review*

Nichols, P. (1998). A new look at Home Services [Review of the book Providing Home Services to the Elderly by Girch, S.] *Family Review Bulletin, 45,* 12–13.

*Journal article*

Jeanquart, S., & Peluchette, J. (1997). Diversity in the workforce and management models. *Journal of Social Work Studies, 43* (3), 72–85.

Deffenbacher, J. L., Oetting, E. R., Lynch, R. S. & Morris, C. D. (1996). The Expression of Anger and its Consequences. *Behaviour Research and Therapy, 34,* 575–590.

*Journal article in press*

Van Herpen, E., Pieters, R. & Zeelenberg, M. (2009), When Demand Accelerates Demand: Trailing the Bandwagon, *Journal of Consumer Psychology,* in press.

*Conference proceedings publication*

Yeshwant, M. (1998). Revised thinking on Indian philosophy and religion. In S. Pennathur (Ed.), *Proceedings of the Ninth International Conference on Religion,* (pp. 100–107). Bihar, India: Bihar University.

*Doctoral dissertation*

Kiren, R.S. (1997). *Medical advances and quality of life.* Unpublished doctoral dissertation, Omaha State University.

*Paper presentation at conference*

Bajaj, L.S. (1996, March 13). *Practical tips for efficient work management.* Paper presented at the annual meeting of Entrepreneurs, San Jose, CA.

*Unpublished manuscript*

Pringle, P.S. (1991). *Training and development in the '90s.* Unpublished manuscript, Southern Illinois University, Diamondale, IL.

*Newspaper article, no author*

The new GM pact. (1998, July 28). *Concord Tribune,* p.1.

## Referencing nonprint media

*Film*

Maas, J.B. (Producer), & Gluck, D.H. (Director). (1979). *Deeper into hypnosis* (film). Englewood Cliffs, NJ: Prentice Hall.

*Cassette recording*

Clark, K.B. (Speaker). (1976). *Problems of freedom and behavior modification* (Cassette Recording No. 7612). Washington, DC: American Psychological Association.

*Electronic source*

Author, I. (1998). Technology and immediacy of information [Online] Available at http://www.bnet.act.com

*Online document, no author identified, no date*

GVU's 18th WWW customer survey. (n.d.). Retrieved March 24th, 2009, from http://www.bb.gotech.edu/gvu/user-surveys/survey-2008-10/

*Report from private organization, available on organization's website*

Philips UK. (2009, March 23). *U.S. Department of Energy honors Philips for significant advancement in LED lighting.* Retrieved March 24th, 2009, from http://www.philips.co.uk/index.page

*Message posted to online forum or discussion group*

Davitz, J. R. (2009, February, 21). How medieval and renaissance nobles were different from each other [Msg 131]. Message posted to http://groups.yahoo.com/group/Medieval_Saints/message/131

# Referencing and quotation in the literature review section

Cite all references in the body of the paper using the author–year method of citation; that is, the surname of the author(s) and the year of publication are given in the appropriate places. Examples of this are as follows:

**a.** Todd (1998) has shown . . .
**b.** In recent studies of dual-career families (Hunt, 1999; Osborn, 1998) it has been . . .
**c.** In 1997, Kyle compared dual-career and dual-earner families and found that . . .

As can be seen from the above, if the name of the author appears as part of the narrative as in the case of (a), the year of publication alone has to be cited in parentheses. Note that in case (b), both the author and the year are cited in parentheses, separated by a comma. If the year and the author are a part of the textual discussion as in (c) above, the use of parentheses is not warranted.

Note also the following:

1. Within the same paragraph, you need not include the year after the first citation so long as the study cannot be confused with other studies cited in the article. An example of this is:

   Gutek (1985) published her findings in the book entitled *Sex and the Work place*. Gutek indicated . . .

2. When a work is authored by *two* individuals, always cite both names every time the reference occurs in the text.
3. When a work has *more than two* authors but fewer than six authors, cite all authors the first time the reference occurs, and subsequently include only the surname of the first author followed by ''*et al.*'' as per the example below:

   Sekaran, U., Martin, T., Trafton, N. and Osborn R. N. (1980) found  . . .  (first citation)
   Sekaran *et al.* (1980) found  . . .  (subsequent citations)
4. When a work is authored by *six or more* individuals, cite only the surname of the first author followed by *et al.* and the year for the first and subsequent citations. Join the names in a multiple-author citation in running text by the word *and*. In parenthetical material, in tables, and in the reference list, join the names by an ampersand (&). Examples are given below.
   **a.** As Tucker and Snell (1989) pointed out . . .
   **b.** As has been pointed out (Tucker & Snell, 1989), . . .
5. When a work has no author, cite in text the first two or three words of the article title. Use double quotation marks around the title of the article. For example, while referring to the newspaper article cited earlier, the text might read as follows:

   While examining unions (''With GM pact,'' 1990).

6. When a work's author is designated as "Anonymous," cite in text the word *Anonymous* followed by a comma and the date: (Anonymous, 1979). In the reference list, an anonymous work is alphabetized by the word *Anonymous*.

7. When the same author has several works published in the same year, cite them in the same order as they occur in the reference list, with the in press citations coming last. For example:

   Research on the mental health of dual-career family members (Sekaran, 1985a, 1985b, 1985c, 1999, in press) indicates . . .

8. When more than one author has to be cited in the text, these should be in the alphabetical order of the first author's surname, and the citations should be separated by semicolons as per the illustration below:

   In the job design literature (Aldag & Brief, 1976; Alderfer, 1972; Beatty, 1982; Jeanquart, 1998), . . .

Personal communication through letters, memos, telephone conversations, and the like, should be cited in the text only and not included in the reference list since these are not retrievable data. In the text, provide the initials as well as the surname of the communicator together with the date, as in the following example:

L. Peters (personal communication, June 15, 1998) feels . . .

In this section we have seen different modes of citation. We will next see how to include quotations from others in the text.

## Quotations in text

Quotations should be given exactly as they appear in the source. The original wording, punctuation, spelling, and italics must be preserved even if they are erroneous. The citation of the source of a direct quotation should always include the page number(s) as well as the reference.

Use double quotation marks for quotations in text. Use single quotation marks to identify the material that was enclosed in double quotation marks in the original source. If you want to emphasize certain words in a quotation, underline them and immediately after the underlined words, insert within brackets the words: *italics added*. Use three ellipsis points ( . . . ) to indicate that you have omitted material from the original source. See example that follows later.

If the quotation is of more than 40 words, set it in a free-standing style starting on a new line and indenting the left margin a further five spaces. Type the entire quotation double spaced on the new margin, indenting the first line of paragraphs five spaces from the new margin, as shown below.

In trying to differentiate dual-earner and dual-career families, Sekaran (1986) states:

Various terms are used to refer to dual-earner families: dual-worker families, two-paycheck families, dual-income families, two-job families, and so on. Spouses in dual-earner families may both hold jobs, or one of the partners may hold a job while the other pursues a career . . .

The distinction between dual-career and dual-earner families also gets blurred when spouses currently holding jobs are preparing themselves both educationally and technically to move up in their organization. (p. 4)

If you intend publishing an article in which you have quoted extensively from a copyrighted work, it is important that you seek written permission from the owner of the copyright. Make sure that you also footnote the permission obtained with respect to the quoted material. Failure to do so may result in unpleasant consequences, including legal action taken through copyright protection laws.

# CHAPTER 4

## The research process: theoretical framework and hypothesis development

## Topics discussed

- The need for a theoretical framework
- Variables
  - Dependent variable
  - Independent variable
  - Moderating variable
  - Mediating variable
- The theoretical framework and its three basic features
- Hypothesis development
  - Definition
  - If–then statements
  - Directional and nondirectional hypotheses
  - Null and alternate hypotheses
- Managerial implications

## CHAPTER OBJECTIVES

After completing Chapter 4, you should be able to:

1. Identify and label variables associated with any given situation.
2. Trace and establish the links among the variables and evolve a theoretical framework.

**3.** Develop a set of hypotheses to be tested and state them in the null and the alternate.
**4.** Apply what has been learned to a research project.

In the previous chapter the focus was on learning how to narrow down and clearly define the research problem. But mere definition of the problem does not solve it. How, then, does one proceed further? The answer is by going through the entire process as shown in the research process model in Figure 4.1. The next two steps are designated steps 4 and 5 and are indicated by the shaded portions in the figure. Step 4 relates to evolving a theoretical framework and step 5 deals with deriving testable hypotheses. In this chapter we shall discuss both topics in some depth.

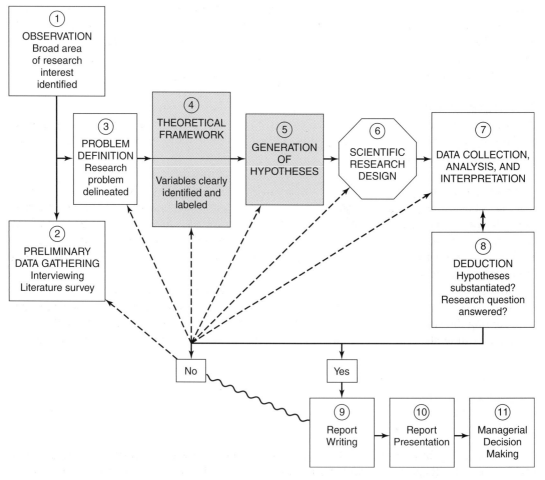

Figure 4.1: The research process and where this chapter fits in.

As you proceed through this chapter, in various places you are instructed to work through certain exercises. Doing them at that time, before reading further, will help you in becoming adept at formulating theoretical frameworks in a logical manner without getting confused.

# The need for a theoretical framework

After conducting the interviews, completing a literature review, and defining the problem, you are ready to develop a theoretical framework. A theoretical framework is the foundation of hypothetico-deductive research as it is the basis of the hypotheses that you will develop. A theoretical framework represents your beliefs on *how* certain phenomena (or variables or concepts) are related to each other (a model) and an explanation of *why* you believe that these variables are associated with each other (a theory). Both the model and the theory flow logically from the documentation of previous research in the problem area. Integrating your logical beliefs with published research, taking into consideration the boundaries and constraints governing the situation, is pivotal in developing a scientific basis for investigating the research problem.

The process of building a theoretical framework includes:

1. Introducing definitions of the concepts or variables in your model.
2. Developing a conceptual model that provides a descriptive representation of your theory.
3. Coming up with a theory that provides an explanation for relationships between the variables in your model.

From the theoretical framework, then, testable hypotheses can be developed to examine whether your theory is valid or not. The hypothesized relationships can thereafter be tested through appropriate statistical analyses. Hence, the entire research rests on the basis of the theoretical framework. Even if testable hypotheses are not necessarily generated (as in some applied research projects), developing a good theoretical framework is central to examining the problem under investigation.

Since the theoretical framework offers the conceptual foundation to proceed with the research, and since a theoretical framework involves nothing more than identifying the network of relationships among the variables considered important to the study of any given problem situation, it is essential to understand what a variable means and what the different types of variables are.

# Variables

A **variable** is anything that can take on differing or varying values. The values can differ at various times for the same object or person, or at the same time for different objects or persons. Examples of variables are production units, absenteeism, and motivation.

### EXAMPLE

*Production units:* One worker in the manufacturing department may produce one widget per minute, a second might produce two per minute, a third might produce five per minute. It is also possible that the same member might produce one widget the first minute and five the next minute. In both cases, the number of widgets produced has taken on different values, and is therefore a variable.

*Absenteeism:* Today, three members in the sales department may be absent; tomorrow, six members may not show up for work; the day after, there may be no one absent. The value can thus theoretically range from "zero" to "all" being absent, on the absenteeism variable.

*Motivation:* The levels of motivation of members to learn in the class or in a work team might take on varying values ranging from "very low" to "very high." An individual's motivation to learn from different classes or in different work teams might also take on differing values. Now, how one *measures* the level of motivation is an entirely different matter. The factor called motivation has to be reduced from its level of abstraction and operationalized in such a way that it becomes measurable. We will discuss this in Chapter 6.

## Types of variables

Four main types of variables are discussed in this chapter:

1. The dependent variable (also known as the criterion variable).
2. The independent variable (also known as the predictor variable).
3. The moderating variable.
4. The mediating variable.

Variables can be discrete (e.g., male/female) or continuous (e.g., the age of an individual). Scale levels of variables are discussed in Chapter 7. Extraneous variables that confound cause-and-effect relationships are discussed in Chapter 9 on Experimental Designs. In this chapter we will primarily concern ourselves with the four types of variables listed above.

### Dependent variable

The **dependent variable** is the variable of primary interest to the researcher. The researcher's goal is to understand and describe the dependent variable, or to explain its variability, or predict it. In other words, it is the main variable that lends itself for investigation as a viable factor. Through the analysis of the dependent variable (i.e., finding what variables influence it), it is possible to find answers or solutions to the problem. For this purpose, the researcher will be interested in quantifying and measuring the dependent variable, as well as the other variables that influence this variable.

## EXAMPLE

A manager is concerned that the sales of a new product, introduced after test marketing it, do not meet with his expectations. The dependent variable here is "sales". Since the sales of the product can vary – they can be low, medium, or high – it is a variable; since sales is the main focus of interest to the manager, it is the dependent variable.

A basic researcher is interested in investigating the debt-to-equity ratio of manufacturing companies in southern Germany. Here, the dependent variable is the ratio of debt to equity.

A vice president is concerned that the employees are not loyal to the organization and, in fact, seem to switch their loyalty to other institutions. The dependent variable in this case is "organizational loyalty". Here again, there is variance found in the levels of organizational loyalty of employees. The V.P. might want to know what accounts for the variance in the loyalty of organizational members with a view to controlling it. If he finds that increased pay levels would ensure their loyalty and retention, he can then offer inducement to employees by way of pay rises, which will help control the variability in organizational loyalty and keep them in the organization.

It is possible to have more than one dependent variable in a study. For example, there is always a tussle between quality and volume of output, low-cost production and customer satisfaction, and so on. In such cases, the manager is interested to know the factors that influence all the dependent variables of interest and how some of them might differ in regard to different dependent variables. These investigations may call for multivariate statistical analyses.

Now do Exercises 4.1 and 4.2

## EXERCISE 4.1

An applied researcher wants to increase the performance of bank employees in a particular branch.

What is the dependent variable in this case?

## EXERCISE 4.2

A marketing manager believes that limiting the availability of a product increases product desirability.

What is the dependent variable here?

### Independent variable

It is generally conjectured that an **independent variable** is one that influences the dependent variable in either a positive or negative way. That is, when the independent variable is present, the dependent variable is also present, and with each unit of increase in the independent variable, there is an increase or decrease in the dependent variable. In other words, the variance in the dependent variable is accounted for by the independent variable. To establish that a change in the independent variable *causes* a change in the dependent variable, *all four* of the following conditions should be met:

1. The independent and the dependent variable should covary: in other words, a change in the dependent variable should be associated with a change in the independent variable.
2. The independent variable (the presumed causal factor) should precede the dependent variable. In other words, there must be a time sequence in which the two occur: the cause must occur before the effect.
3. No other factor should be a possible cause of the change in the dependent variable. Hence, the researcher should *control for* the effects of other variables.
4. A logical explanation (a theory) is needed about why the independent variable affects the dependent variable.

Because of the time sequence condition, experimental designs, described in Chapter 9, are often used to establish causal relationships.

## EXAMPLE

Research studies indicate that successful new product development has an influence on the stock market price of the company. That is, the more successful the new product turns out to be, the higher will be the stock market price of that firm. Therefore, the success of the new product is the *independent variable*, and stock market price the *dependent variable*. The degree of perceived success of the new product developed will explain the variance in the stock market price of the company. This relationship and the labeling of the variables are illustrated in Figure 4.2.

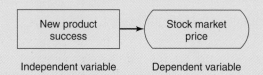

Figure 4.2: Diagram of the relationship between the independent variable (new product success) and the dependent variable (stock market price).

Cross-cultural research indicates that managerial values govern the power distance between superiors and subordinates. Here, power distance (i.e., egalitarian interactions between the boss and the employee, versus the high-power superior in limited interaction with the low-power subordinate) is the subject of interest and hence the dependent variable. Managerial values that explain the variance in power distance comprise the independent variable. This relationship is illustrated in Figure 4.3.

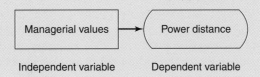

Independent variable          Dependent variable

**Figure 4.3:** Diagram of the relationship between the independent variable (managerial values) and the dependent variable (power distance).

Now do Exercises 4.3 and 4.4.

List the variables in these two exercises individually, and label them as dependent or independent, explaining why they are so labeled. Create diagrams to illustrate the relationships.

## EXERCISE 4.3

A manager believes that good supervision and training will increase the production level of the workers.

## EXERCISE 4.4

A marketing manager believes that selecting physically attractive spokespersons and models to endorse their products increases the persuasiveness of a message.

### Moderating variable

The **moderating variable** is one that has a strong *contingent* effect on the independent variable–dependent variable relationship. That is, the presence of a third variable (the moderating variable) modifies the original relationship between the independent and the dependent variables. This becomes clear through the following examples.

## EXAMPLE

It has been found that there is a relationship between the availability of reference manuals that manufacturing employees have access to, and the product rejects. That is, when workers follow the procedures laid down in the manual, they are able to manufacture products that are flawless. This relationship is illustrated in Figure 4.4(a).

Although this relationship can be said to hold true generally for all workers, it is nevertheless contingent on the inclination or urge of the employees to look in the manual every time a new procedure is to be adopted. In other words, only those who have the interest and urge to refer to the manual every time a new process is adopted will produce flawless products. Others who do not consult the manual will not benefit and will continue to produce defective products. This influence of the attributes of the worker on the relationship between the independent and the dependent variables can be illustrated as shown in Figure 4.4(b).

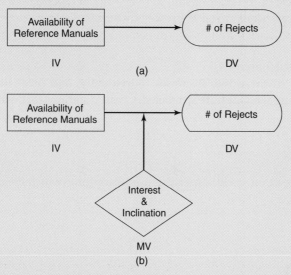

**Figure 4.4: (a)** Diagram of the relationship between the independent variable (availability of reference manuals) and the dependent variable (rejects); **(b)** diagram of the relationship between the independent variable (availability of reference materials) and the dependent variable (rejects) as moderated by the moderating variable (interest and inclination).

As in the above case, whenever the relationship between the independent variable and the dependent variable becomes contingent or dependent on another variable, we say that the third variable has a moderating effect on the independent variable–dependent variable relationship. The variable that moderates the relationship is known as the moderating variable.

## EXAMPLE

Let us take another example of a moderating variable. A prevalent theory is that the diversity of the workforce (comprising people of different ethnic origins, races, and nationalities) contributes more to organizational effectiveness because each group brings its own special expertise and skills to the workplace. This synergy can be exploited, however, only if managers know how to harness the special talents of the diverse work group; otherwise they will remain untapped. In the above scenario, organizational effectiveness is the dependent variable, which is positively influenced by workforce diversity – the independent variable. However, to harness the potential, managers must know how to encourage and coordinate the talents of the various groups to make things work. If not, the synergy will not be tapped. In other words, the effective utilization of different talents, perspectives, and eclectic problem-solving capabilities for enhanced organizational effectiveness is contingent on the skill of the managers in acting as catalysts. This managerial expertise then becomes the moderating variable. These relationships can be depicted as in Figure 4.5.

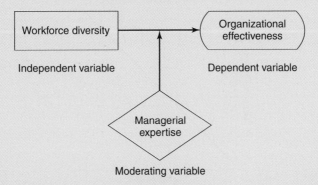

**Figure 4.5:** Diagram of the relationship among the three variables: workforce diversity, organizational effectiveness, and managerial expertise.

## The distinction between an independent variable and a moderating variable

At times, confusion is likely to arise as to when a variable is to be treated as an independent variable and when it becomes a moderating variable. For instance, there may be two situations as follows:

1. A research study indicates that the better the quality of the training programs in an organization and the greater the growth needs of the employees (i.e., where the need to develop and grow on the job is strong), the greater is their willingness to learn new ways of doing things.
2. Another research study indicates that the willingness of the employees to learn new ways of doing things is *not* influenced by the quality of the training programs offered by the organizations to *all* people without any distinction. Only those with high growth needs seem to have the yearning to learn to do new things through specialized training.

In the above two situations, we have the same three variables. In the first case, the training programs and growth need strength are the independent variables that influence employees' willingness to learn, this latter being the dependent variable. In the second case, however, the quality of the training program is the independent variable, and while the dependent variable remains the same, growth need strength becomes a moderating variable. In other words, only those with high growth needs show a greater willingness and adaptability to learn to do new things when the quality of the training program is improved. Thus, the relationship between the independent and dependent variables has now become contingent on the existence of a moderator.

The above illustration makes it clear that even though the variables used are the same, the decision as to whether to label them dependent, independent, or moderating depends on how they affect one another. The differences between the effects of the independent and the moderating variables may be visually depicted as in Figures 4.6(a) and 4.6(b). Note the steep incline of the top line and the relative flatness of the bottom line in Figure 4.6(b).

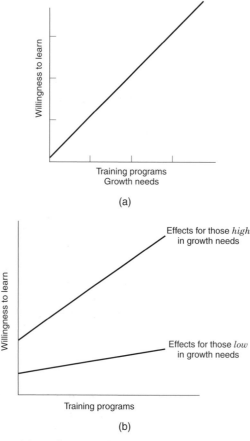

**Figure 4.6: (a)** Illustration of the influence of independent variables on the dependent variable when no moderating variable operates in the situation; **(b)** illustration of the influence of independent variables on the dependent variable when a moderating variable is operating in the situation.

Now do Exercises 4.5 and 4.6

List and label the variables in these two exercises and explain and illustrate by means of diagrams the relationships among the variables.

## EXERCISE 4.5

A manager finds that off-the-job classroom training has a great impact on the productivity of the employees in her department. However, she also observes that employees over 60 years of age do not seem to derive much benefit and do not improve with such training.

## EXERCISE 4.6

A manager finds that the intensity of e-Business adoption is positively associated with sales performance. What's more, when market uncertainty (the rate of change in the composition of customers and their preferences) is high, this positive effect is strengthened.

### Mediating variable

A **mediating variable** (or intervening variable) is one that surfaces between the time the independent variables start operating to influence the dependent variable and the time their impact is felt on it. There is thus a temporal quality or time dimension to the mediating variable. In other words, bringing a mediating variable into play helps you to model a *process*. The mediating variable surfaces as a function of the independent variable(s) operating in any situation, and helps to conceptualize and explain the influence of the independent variable(s) on the dependent variable. The following example illustrates this point.

## EXAMPLE

In the previous example where the independent variable (workforce diversity) influences the dependent variable (organizational effectiveness), the mediating variable that surfaces as a function of the diversity in the workforce is "creative synergy". This creative synergy results from a multiethnic, multiracial, and multinational (i.e., diverse) workforce interacting and bringing together their multifaceted expertise in problem solving. This helps us to understand how organizational effectiveness can result from having diversity in the workforce. Note that creative synergy, the mediating variable, surfaces at time $t_2$, as a function of workforce diversity, which was in place at time $t_1$, to bring about organizational effectiveness in time $t_3$. The mediating variable of creative synergy helps us to conceptualize and understand how workforce diversity brings about organizational effectiveness. The dynamics of these relationships are illustrated in Figure 4.7.

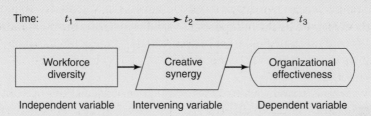

**Figure 4.7:** Diagram of the relationship among the independent, mediating, and dependent variables.

It would be interesting to see how the inclusion of the moderating variable "managerial expertise" in the foregoing example would change the model or affect the relationships. The new set of relationships that would emerge in the presence of the moderator are depicted in Figure 4.8. As can be seen, managerial expertise moderates the relationship between workforce diversity and creative synergy. In other words, creative synergy will not result from the multifaceted problem-solving skills of the diverse workforce unless the manager is capable of harnessing that synergy by creatively coordinating the different skills. If the manager lacks the expertise to perform this role, then no matter how many different problem-solving skills the

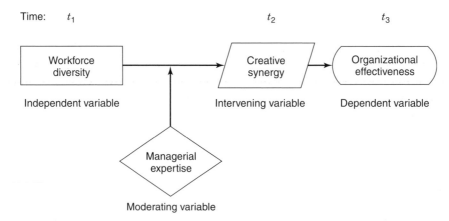

**Figure 4.8:** Diagram of the relationship among the independent, mediating, moderating, and dependent variables.

diverse workforce might have, synergy will just not surface. Instead of functioning effectively, the organization might just remain static, or even deteriorate.

It is now easy to see what the differences are among an independent variable, a mediating variable, and a moderating variable. The **independent variable** helps to *explain* the variance in the dependent variable; the **mediating variable** *surfaces at time* $t_2$ as a function of the independent variable, which also helps us to conceptualize the relationship between the independent and dependent variables; and the **moderating variable** has a *contingent effect* on the relationship between two variables. To put it differently, while the independent variable explains the variance in the dependent variable, the mediating variable does not add to the variance already explained by the independent variable, whereas the moderating variable has an interaction effect with the independent variable in explaining the variance. That is, unless the moderating variable is present, the theorized relationship between the other two variables considered will not hold.

Whether a variable is an independent variable, a dependent variable, a mediating variable, or a moderating variable should be determined by a careful reading of the dynamics operating in any given situation. For instance, a variable such as motivation to work could be a dependent variable, an independent variable, a mediating variable, or a moderating variable, depending on the theoretical model that is being advanced.

Now do Exercises 4.7, 4.8, and 4.9

## EXERCISE 4.7

Make up three different situations in which motivation to work would be an independent variable, a mediating variable, and a moderating variable.

## EXERCISE 4.8

Failure to follow accounting principles causes immense confusion, which in turn creates a number of problems for the organization. Those with vast experience in bookkeeping, however, are able to avert the problems by taking timely corrective action. List and label the variables in this situation, explain the relationships among the variables, and illustrate these by means of diagrams.

## EXERCISE 4.9

The manager of Haines Company observes that the morale of employees in her company is low. She thinks that if their working conditions are improved, pay scales raised, and the vacation benefits made attractive, the morale will be boosted. She doubts, however, if an increase in pay scales would raise the morale of all employees. Her conjecture is that those that have supplemental incomes will just not be "turned on" by higher pay, and only those without side incomes will be happy with increased pay with a resultant boost in morale. List and label the variables in this situation. Explain the relationships among the variables and illustrate them by means of diagrams. What might be the problem statement or problem definition for the situation?

# Theoretical framework

Having examined the different kinds of variables that can operate in a situation and how the relationships among these can be established, it is now possible to see how we can develop the theoretical framework for our research.

The theoretical framework is the foundation on which the entire research project is based. It is a logically developed, described, and elaborated network of associations among the variables deemed relevant to the problem situation and identified through such processes as interviews, observations, and literature review. Experience and intuition also guide the development of the theoretical framework.

It becomes evident at this stage that, to arrive at good solutions to the problem, one should first correctly identify the problem, and then the variables that contribute to it. The importance of conducting purposeful interviews and doing a thorough literature review now becomes clear. After identifying the appropriate variables, the next step is to elaborate the network of associations among the variables, so that relevant hypotheses can be developed and subsequently tested. Based on the results of hypothesis testing (which indicate whether or not the hypotheses have been supported), the extent to which the problem can be solved becomes evident. The theoretical framework is thus an important step in the research process.

The relationship between the literature review and the theoretical framework is that the former provides a solid foundation for developing the latter. That is, the literature review identifies the variables that might be important, as determined by previous research findings. This, in addition to other logical connections that can be conceptualized, forms the basis for the theoretical model. The theoretical framework represents and elaborates the relationships among the variables, explains the theory underlying these relations, and describes the nature and direction of the relationships. Just as the literature review sets the stage for a good theoretical framework, this in turn provides the logical base for developing testable hypotheses.

## The components of the theoretical framework

A good theoretical framework identifies and defines the important variables in the situation that are relevant to the problem and subsequently describes and explains the interconnections among these variables. The relationships among the independent variables, the dependent variable(s), and, if applicable, the moderating and mediating variables are elaborated. Should there be any moderating variable(s), it is important to explain how and what specific relationships they moderate. An explanation of why they operate as moderators should also be offered. If there are any mediating variables, a discussion on how or why they are treated as mediating variables is necessary. Any interrelationships among the independent variables themselves, or among the dependent variables themselves (in case there are two or more dependent variables), should also be clearly spelled out and adequately explained. Note that a good theoretical framework is not necessarily a complex framework.

There are three basic features that should be incorporated in any theoretical framework:

1. The variables considered relevant to the study should be clearly defined.
2. A conceptual model that describes the relationships between the variables in the model should be given.
3. There should be a clear explanation of why we expect these relationships to exist.

It is not always easy to come up with generally agreed-upon *definitions* of the relevant variables. More often than not, there are many definitions available in the literature (for instance, there are literally dozens of definitions of "brand image", "customer satisfaction", and "service quality" available in the marketing literature). Still, well-chosen guiding definitions of concepts are needed, because they will help you to provide an explanation for the relationships between the variables in your model. What's more, they will also serve as a basis for the operationalization or measurement of your concepts in the data collection stage of the research process. Hence, you will have to choose a useful definition from the literature (do not use dictionary definitions, they are usually too general). It is also important that you explain why you have chosen a particular definition as your guiding definition.

A *conceptual model* helps you to structure your discussion of the literature. A conceptual model describes how the concepts in your model are related to each other. A schematic diagram of the conceptual model helps the reader to visualize the theorized relationships. Hence, conceptual models are often expressed in this form. However, relationships between variables can also be adequately expressed in words. Both a schematic diagram of the conceptual model and a description of the relationships between the variables in words should be given, so that the reader can see and easily comprehend the theorized relationships.

A good model is based on a sound theory. A theory or a clear explanation for the relationships in your model is the last component of the theoretical framework. A theory attempts to explain relationships between the variables in your model: an explanation should be provided for all the important relationships that are theorized to exist among the variables. If the nature and direction of the relationships can be theorized on the basis of the findings of previous research and/or your own ideas on the subject, then there should also be an indication as to whether the relationships should be positive or negative and linear or nonlinear. From the theoretical framework, then, testable hypotheses can be developed to examine whether the theory formulated is valid or not.

Note that you do not necessarily have to "invent" a new theory every time you are undertaking a research project. In an applied research context you apply existing theories to a specific context. This means that arguments can be drawn from previous research. However, in a basic research context you will make some contribution to existing theories and models. In such a case, it is not (always) possible to use existing theories or explanations for relationships between variables. As a result, you will have to rely on your own insights and ideas.

Let us illustrate how these features are incorporated in the following example.

## EXAMPLE

### Air safety violations

In April 2008, the Federal Aviation Administration announced its second effort in three years to stop its managers in Texas from covering up air safety violations after a new investigation found the misconduct had continued. The FAA announced that the top managers of an air traffic control facility in Dallas-Fort Worth had been removed from their jobs. According to the FAA, the Transportation Department's inspector general found that in addition to letting airlines ignore their safety directives, FAA managers in Dallas-Fort Worth routinely and intentionally misclassified instances where airplanes were flying closer together than they were supposed to.

Air safety violations put the safety of airplane passengers at risk. At worst, air safety violations have the potential to cause mid-air collisions, and at the very least, air safety violations lead to increased workload for air traffic controllers and pilots. Four important factors that seem to have influenced air safety violations are poor communication among the cockpit crew members themselves, poor coordination between ground staff and cockpit crew, minimal training given to the cockpit crew, and a management philosophy that has encouraged a decentralized structure. It would be nice to know if these factors did indeed contribute to the safety violations and, if so, to what extent.

## Theoretical framework for the example of air safety violations

The dependent variable is safety violation, which is the variable of primary interest. We attempt to explain the variance in this dependent variable by the four independent variables of (1) communication among crew members, (2) communication between ground control and the cockpit crew, (3) training received by the cockpit crew, and (4) decentralization. Communication is the process of conveying information from a sender to a receiver by the use of a medium in which the communicated information is understood the same way by both sender and receiver. Training refers to the acquisition of knowledge, skills, and competencies as a result of the teaching of vocational or practical skills and knowledge that relate to specific useful competencies of the cockpit crew. Decentralization is the dispersion of decision-making governance closer to the employees.

The less the communication among the crew members themselves, the greater is the probability of air safety violations since very little information is shared among them. For example, whenever safety is threatened, timely communication between the navigator and pilot is most unlikely. Each member will be preoccupied with his or her work and lose sight of the larger picture. When ground crew fails to give the right information at the right time, mishaps are bound to occur with aborted flights and collisions. Coordination between ground and cockpit crew is at the very heart of air safety. Thus, the less coordination between ground control and cockpit crew there is, the greater the possibility of air safety violations taking place. Both of the above factors are exacerbated by the management philosophy of airlines, which often emphasize decentralization. This philosophy might have worked before the deregulation of the airlines when the number of flights was manageable. But with deregulation and increased flights overall in mid-air, and with all airlines operating many more flights, centralized coordination and control assume great importance. Thus, the greater the degree of decentralization, the greater is the scope for lower levels of communication both among in-flight staff and between ground staff and cockpit crew, and the greater the scope for air safety violations. Also, when cockpit crew members are not adequately trained, they may not have the requisite knowledge of safety standards or may suffer from an inability to handle emergency situations and avoid collisions. Thus, poor training also adds to the probability of increased safety violations. These relationships are outlined in Figure 4.9.

Note how the basic features of the theoretical framework have been incorporated in the example.

1. Identification and labeling of the dependent and independent variables have been done in the theoretical framework. Definitions have been provided.

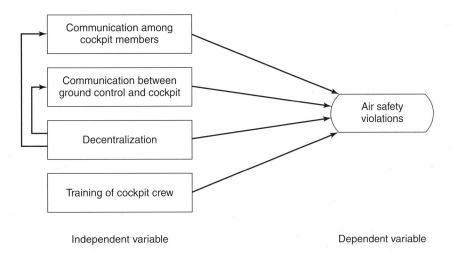

Figure 4.9: Schematic diagram for the theoretical framework in the example of air safety violations.

2.  The relationships among these variables have been schematically illustrated (see Figure 4.9).

3.  The relationships among the variables were discussed, establishing that the four independent variables are related to the dependent variable, and that the independent variable, decentralization, is related to two other independent variables, namely communication among the cockpit members and between ground control and the cockpit crew. The nature and direction of the relationship of each independent variable with the dependent variable and the relationship of decentralization to two of the other independent variables were clearly stated. For example, it was indicated that the lower the training level of the cockpit crew, the greater the chances of air safety violations. Thus, as the training is lowered, the hazard is increased, or conversely, the higher the training, the less likely are air safety violations, indicating a negative relationship between the two variables. Such a negative relationship exists between each of the independent variables, with the exception of decentralization, and the dependent variable. There is also a negative relationship between decentralization and communication among cockpit members (the more decentralization, the less communication) and between decentralization and coordination (the more decentralization, the less coordination). Why these relationships are to be expected was explained through several logical statements, such as describing why decentralization, which worked before deregulation, would not now work. More specifically, it was argued that:

    a.  lower levels of communication among cockpit crew would fail to alert the pilot to impending hazards;

    b.  poor coordination between ground control and cockpit crew would be detrimental because such coordination is the very essence of safety;

    c.  encouragement of decentralization would only reinforce poorer communication and coordination efforts;

    d.  inadequate training of cockpit crew would fail to build survival skills.

Now, out of interest, let's see if we can interject a mediating variable in the model. For example, we may say that lack of adequate training makes the pilots nervous and diffident, and this in turn explains why they are not able to confidently handle situations in mid-air when many aircraft share the skies. Nervousness and diffidence are functions of lack of training, and help to explain why inadequate training would result in air safety hazard. This scenario is depicted in Figure 4.10.

We may also substantially change the model by using (poor) training as a moderating variable, as shown in Figure 4.11. Here, we are theorizing that poor communication, poor coordination, and decentralization are likely to result in air safety violations only in such cases where the pilot in charge has had inadequate training. In other words, those who have had adequate training in deftly handling hazardous situations through simulated training sessions and so forth would not be handicapped by poor communication and coordination, and in cases where the aircraft is operated by well-trained pilots, poor communication and coordination will not result in hazards to safety.

These examples again illustrate that the same variable may be independent, mediating, or moderating, depending on how we conceptualize our theoretical model.

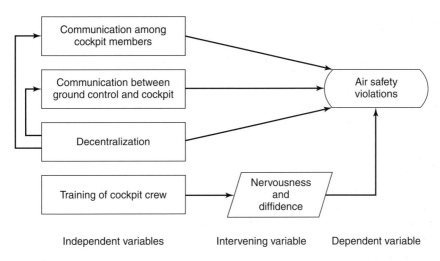

Independent variables         Intervening variable         Dependent variable

**Figure 4.10:** Schematic diagram for the theoretical framework including the mediating variable.

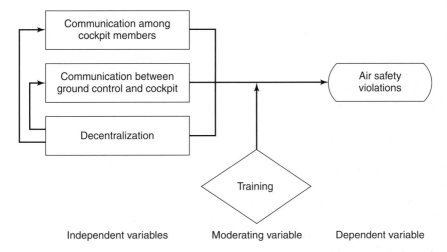

Independent variables         Moderating variable         Dependent variable

**Figure 4.11:** Schematic diagram for the theoretical framework including a moderating variable.

Now do Exercises 4.10 and 4.11

## EXERCISE 4.10

Avatars are virtual characters that can be used as representatives of a company that is using the Internet as a distribution channel. For instance, avatars can be used as shopping assistants, website guides, or as identification figures. A manager of an online company believes that avatar-mediated communication will have a positive effect on satisfaction with her company and on purchase intentions of consumers, because avatars enhance the value of information provided on the website and increase the pleasure of the shopping experience. She also believes that the positive effect of the perceived information value on satisfaction with the company and purchase intentions is stronger when customers are highly involved. Develop a theoretical framework for this situation after stating what the problem definition of the researcher would be in this case.

## EXERCISE 4.11

The probability of cancer victims successfully recovering under treatment was studied by a medical researcher in a hospital. She found three variables to be important for recovery:

• Early and correct diagnosis by the doctor.
• The nurse's careful follow-up of the doctor's instructions.
• Peace and quiet in the vicinity.

In a quiet atmosphere, the patient rested well and recovered sooner. Patients who were admitted in advanced stages of cancer did not respond to treatment even though the doctor's diagnosis was performed immediately on arrival, the nurses did their best, and there was plenty of peace and quiet in the area. Define the problem and develop the theoretical framework for this situation.

# Hypothesis development

Once we have identified the important variables in a situation and established the relationships among them through logical reasoning in the theoretical framework, we are in a position to test whether the relationships that have been theorized do, in fact, hold true. By testing these relationships scientifically through appropriate statistical analyses, or through negative case analysis in qualitative research (described later in the chapter), we are able to obtain reliable information on what kinds of relationships exist among the variables operating in the problem situation. The results of these tests offer us some clues as to what could be changed in the situation to solve the problem. Formulating such testable statements is called *hypothesis development*.

## Definition of a hypothesis

A **hypothesis** can be defined as a tentative, yet testable, statement, which predicts what you expect to find in your empirical data. Hypotheses are derived from the theory on which your conceptual model is based and are often relational in nature. Along these lines, hypotheses can be defined as logically conjectured relationships between two or more variables expressed in the form of testable statements. By testing the hypotheses and confirming the conjectured relationships, it is expected that solutions can be found to correct the problem encountered.

### EXAMPLE

Several testable statements or hypotheses can be drawn from the theoretical framework formulated in the previous example. One of them might be:

*If the pilots are given adequate training to handle mid-air crowded situations, air safety violations will be reduced.*

The above is a testable statement. By measuring the extent of training given to the various pilots and the number of safety violations committed by them over a period of time, we can statistically examine the relationship between these two variables to see if there is a significant negative correlation between the two. If we do find this to be the case, then the hypothesis is substantiated. That is, giving more training to pilots in handling crowded space in mid-air will reduce safety violations. If a significant negative correlation is not found, then the hypothesis has not been substantiated. By convention in the social sciences, to call a relationship "statistically significant," we should be confident that 95 times out of 100 the observed relationship will hold true. There should be only a 5% chance that the relationship will not be detected.

## Statement of hypotheses: formats

### If–then statements

As already stated, a hypothesis can be defined as a testable statement of the relationship among variables. A hypothesis can also test whether there are differences between two groups (or among several groups) with respect to any variable or variables. To examine whether or not the conjectured relationships or differences exist, these hypotheses can be set either as propositions or in the form of *if–then statements*. The two formats can be seen in the following two examples.

*Employees who are more healthy will take sick leave less frequently.*

*If employees are more healthy, **then** they will take sick leave less frequently.*

## Directional and nondirectional hypotheses

If, in stating the relationship between two variables or comparing two groups, terms such as *positive, negative, more than, less than*, and the like are used, then these are **directional hypotheses** because the direction of the relationship between the variables (positive/negative) is indicated, as in the first example below, or the nature of the difference between two groups on a variable (more than/less than) is postulated, as in the second example.

*The greater the stress experienced in the job, the lower the job satisfaction of employees.*

*Women are more motivated than men.*

On the other hand, **nondirectional hypotheses** are those that do postulate a relationship or difference, but offer no indication of the direction of these relationships or differences. In other words, though it may be conjectured that there is a significant relationship between two variables, we may not be able to say whether the relationship is positive or negative, as in the first example below. Likewise, even if we can conjecture that there will be differences between two groups on a particular variable, we may not be able to say which group will be more and which less on that variable, as in the second example.

*There is a relationship between age and job satisfaction.*

*There is a difference between the work ethic values of American and Asian employees.*

Nondirectional hypotheses are formulated either because the relationships or differences have never been explored and hence there is no basis for indicating the direction, or because there have been conflicting findings in previous research studies on the variables. In some studies a positive relationship might have been found, while in others a negative relationship might have been traced. Hence, the current researcher might only be able to hypothesize that there is a significant relationship, but the direction may not be clear. In such cases, the hypotheses can be stated nondirectionally. Note that in the first example there is no clue as to whether age and job satisfaction are positively or negatively correlated, and in the second example we do not know whether the work ethic values are stronger in Americans or in Asians. However, it would have been possible to state that age and job satisfaction are positively correlated, since previous research has indicated such a relationship. Whenever the direction of the relationship is known, it is better to develop directional hypotheses for reasons that will become clear in our discussions in a later chapter.

## Null and alternate hypotheses

The hypothetico-deductive method requires that hypotheses are falsifiable: they must be written in such a way that other researchers can show them to be false. For this reason, hypotheses are sometimes accompanied by null hypotheses. A **null hypothesis** ($H_0$) is a hypothesis set up to be rejected in order to support an alternate hypothesis, labeled $H_A$. When used, the null hypothesis is presumed true until statistical evidence, in the form of a hypothesis test, indicates otherwise. For instance, the null hypothesis may state that advertising does not affect sales, or that women and men buy equal amounts of shoes. In more general terms, the null hypothesis may state that the correlation between two variables is equal to zero or that the difference in the means of two groups in the population is equal to zero (or some other *definite* number). Typically, the null statement is expressed in terms of there being no (*significant*) relationship between two variables or no (*significant*) difference between two groups. The **alternate hypothesis**, which is the opposite of the null, is a statement expressing a relationship between two variables or indicating differences between groups.

To explain further, in setting up the null hypothesis, we are stating that there is no difference between what we might find in the population characteristics (i.e., the total group we are interested in knowing something about) and the sample we are studying (i.e., a limited number representative of the total population or group that we have chosen to study). Since we do not know the true state of affairs in the population, all we can do is to draw inferences based on what we find in our sample. What we imply through the null hypothesis is that any differences found between two sample groups or any relationships found between two variables based on our sample are simply due to random sampling fluctuations and not due to any "true" differences between the two population groups (say, men and women), or relationships between two variables (say, sales and profits). The null hypothesis is thus formulated so that it can be tested for possible rejection. If we reject the null hypothesis, then all permissible alternate hypotheses relating to the particular relationship tested could be supported. It is the theory that allows us to have faith in the alternate hypothesis that is generated in the particular research investigation. This is one more reason why the theoretical framework should be grounded on sound, defendable logic to start with. Otherwise, other researchers are likely to refute and postulate other defensible explanations through different alternate hypotheses.

The *null* hypothesis in respect of group differences stated in the example *Women are more motivated than men* would be:

$$H_0 : \mu_M = \mu_W$$

or

$$H_0 : \mu_M - \mu_W = 0$$

where $H_0$ represents the null hypothesis, $\mu_M$ is the mean motivational level of the men, and $\mu_W$ is the mean motivational level of the women.

The *alternate* for the above example would statistically be set as follows:

$$H_A : \mu_M < \mu_W$$

which is the same as

$$H_A : \mu_W > \mu_M$$

where $H_A$ represents the alternate hypothesis and $\mu_M$ and $\mu_W$ are the mean motivation levels of men and women, respectively.

For the nondirectional hypothesis of mean group differences in work ethic values in the example *There is a difference between the work ethic values of American and Asian employees*, the null hypothesis would be:

$$H_0 : \mu_{AM} = \mu_{AS}$$

or

$$H_0 : \mu_{AM} - \mu_{AS} = 0$$

where $H_0$ represents the null hypothesis, $\mu_{AM}$ is the mean work ethic value of Americans and $\mu_{AS}$ is the mean work ethic value of Asians.

The alternate hypothesis for the above example would statistically be set as:

$$H_A : \mu_{AM} \neq \mu_{AS}$$

where $H_A$ represents the alternate hypothesis and $\mu_{AM}$ and $\mu_{AS}$ are the mean work ethic values of Americans and Asians, respectively.

The null hypothesis for the relationship between the two variables in the example *The greater the stress experienced in the job, the lower the job satisfaction of employees*, would be $H_0$: There is no relationship between stress experienced on the job and the job satisfaction of employees. This would be statistically expressed by:

$$H_0 : \rho = 0$$

where $\rho$ represents the correlation between stress and job satisfaction, which in this case is equal to 0 (i.e., no correlation).

The alternate hypothesis for the above null, which has been expressed directionally, can be statistically expressed as:

$$H_A : \rho < 0 \text{ (The correlation is negative.)}$$

For the example *There is a relationship between age and job satisfaction*, which has been stated nondirectionally, while the null hypothesis would be statistically expressed as:

$$H_0 : \rho = 0$$

the alternate hypothesis would be expressed as:

$$H_A : \rho \neq 0$$

Having formulated the null and alternate hypotheses, the appropriate statistical tests (*t*-tests, *F*-tests) can then be applied, which indicate whether or not support has been found for the alternate hypothesis – that is, that there is a significant difference between groups or that there is a significant relationship between variables, as hypothesized.

The steps to be followed in hypothesis testing are:

1. State the null and the alternate hypotheses.
2. Choose the appropriate statistical test depending on whether the data collected are parametric or nonparametric.
3. Determine the level of significance desired ($p = 0.05$, or more, or less).
4. See if the output results from computer analysis indicate that the significance level is met. If, as in the case of Pearson correlation analysis in Excel software, the significance level is not indicated in the printout, look up the critical values that define the regions of acceptance on the appropriate table [$(t, F, \chi^2)$ – see the statistical tables at the end of this book]. This critical value demarcates the region of rejection from that of acceptance of the null hypothesis. When the resultant value is larger than the critical value, the null hypothesis is rejected, and the alternate accepted. If the calculated value is less than the critical value, the null is accepted and the alternate rejected.

Note that null hypotheses are rarely presented in research reports or journal articles. Now do Exercises 4.12, 4.13, and 4.14

## EXERCISE 4.12

For the theoretical framework developed for the Haines Company in Exercise 4.9, develop five different hypotheses.

## EXERCISE 4.13

A production manager is concerned about the low output levels of his employees. The articles that he has read on job performance frequently mention four variables as being important to job performance: skill required for the job, rewards, motivation, and satisfaction. In several of the articles it was also indicated that only if the rewards were valent (attractive) to the recipients did motivation, satisfaction, and job performance increase, not otherwise. Given this situation:

1. Define the problem.
2. Evolve a theoretical framework.
3. Develop at least six hypotheses.

EXERCISE 4.14

Retention of minority women at the workplace is becoming more and more difficult. Not finding an influential mentor in the system who is willing to help them, lack of an informal network with influential colleagues, lack of role models, and the dearth of high-visibility projects result in dissatisfaction experienced at work and the minority women ultimately decide to leave the organization. Of course, not all minority women quit the system. Only those who have the wherewithal (for example, resources and self-confidence) to start their own business leave the organization. For this situation, define the problem, develop a theoretical framework, and formulate six hypotheses.

Before concluding the discussion on hypotheses, it has to be reiterated that hypothesis generation and testing can be done both through deduction and induction. In deduction, the theoretical model is first developed, testable hypotheses are then formulated, data collected, and then the hypotheses are tested. In the inductive process, new hypotheses are formulated based on what is known from the data already collected, which are then tested. Recall from our discussions in Chapter 2 the example of the Hawthorne experiments, where new hypotheses were developed after the data already collected did not substantiate any of the original hypotheses.

In sum, new hypotheses not originally thought of, or which have been previously untested, might be developed after data are collected. Creative insights might compel researchers to test a new hypothesis from existing data, which, if substantiated, would add new knowledge and help theory building. Through the broadening of our understanding of the dynamics operating in different situations using deductive and inductive processes, we add to the total body of knowledge in the area.

# Hypothesis testing with qualitative research: negative case analysis

Hypotheses can also be tested with qualitative data. For example, let us say that, after extensive interviews, a researcher has developed the theoretical framework that unethical practices by employees are a function of their inability to discriminate between right and wrong, or due to a dire need for more money, or the organization's indifference to such practices. To test the hypothesis that these three factors are the primary ones that influence unethical practices, the researcher should look for data to refute the hypothesis. When even a single case does not support the hypothesis, the theory needs revision. Let us say that the researcher finds one case where an individual is deliberately engaged in the unethical practice of accepting kickbacks (despite the fact that he is knowledgeable enough to discriminate right from wrong, is not in need of money, and knows that the organization will not be indifferent to his behavior), simply because he wants to "get back" at the system, which "will not listen to his advice." This new discovery, through disconfirmation of the original hypothesis, known as *the negative case method*, enables the researcher to revise the theory and the hypothesis until such time as the theory becomes robust.

We have thus far seen how a literature review is done, theoretical frameworks are formulated, and hypotheses developed. Let us now illustrate this logical sequence through a mini example where a researcher wants to examine the organizational factors influencing women's progress to top management positions. The literature review and the number of variables are deliberately kept small, since the purpose is merely to illustrate how a theoretical framework is developed from the literature review, and how hypotheses are developed based on the theoretical framework.

## EXAMPLE

## Example of literature review, theoretical framework, and hypothesis development

### Introduction

Despite the dramatic increase in the number of managerial women during the current decade, the number of women in top management positions continues to be very small and static, suggesting a glass ceiling effect that women currently face (Morrison, White and Vura, 1999; O'Neil, Hopkins and Bilimoria, 2008; Van Velsor, 2000). Given the projected demographics of the workplace, which forecasts that for every six or seven women entering the workforce in the future, there will only be about three white males joining the labor market, it becomes important to examine the organizational factors that might facilitate the *early* advancement of women to top executive positions. This study is an effort to identify the factors that currently impede women's advancement to the top in organizations.

### A brief literature review

It is often declared that since women have only recently embarked on careers and entered the managerial ranks, it will take more time for them to rise to top executive positions. However, many women in higher middle management positions feel that there are at least two major stumbling blocks to their advancement: gender role stereotypes and inadequate access to critical information (Crosby, 1985; Daniel, 1998; Schein, 2007; Welch, 2001).

Gender stereotypes, or sex-role stereotypes as they are also known, are societal beliefs that men are better suited for taking on leadership roles and positions of authority and power, whereas women are more suited for taking on nurturing and helping roles (DeArmond *et al.*, 2006; Eagly, 1989; Kahn and Crosby, 1998; Smith, 1999). These beliefs influence the positions that are assigned to organizational members. Whereas capable men are given line positions and developed to take on higher responsibilities and executive roles in the course of time, capable women are assigned to staff positions and dead-end jobs. With little exposure to management of budgets and opportunities for significant decision making, women are seldom groomed for top-level positions.

Women are also excluded from the "old boys" network because of their gender. Information exchange, development of career strategies, clues regarding access to resources, and such important information vital to upward mobility are thus lost to women (*The Chronicle*, 2000). While many other factors impinge on women's upward mobility, the two variables of gender-role stereotypes and exclusion from critical information are particularly detrimental to women's advancement to senior level positions.

## Theoretical framework

The dependent variable of advancement of women to top management positions is influenced by the two independent variables – gender-role stereotyping and access to critical information. The two independent variables are also interrelated as explained below.

Gender-role stereotypes adversely impact on women's career progress. Since women are perceived as ineffective leaders but good nurturers, they are not assigned line positions in their early careers but offered staff responsibilities. It is only in line positions that managers make significant decisions, control budgets, and interact with top-level executives who have an impact on their future careers. These opportunities to learn, grow and develop on the job, and gain visibility in the system help managers to advance to top-level positions. However, since women in staff positions do not gain these experiences or have the visibility to be identified as key people in the organization with the potential to be successful top managers, their advancement to top-level positions is never considered by the system and they are always overlooked. Thus, gender-role stereotypes hinder the progress of women to the top.

Exclusion from the networks where men informally interact with one another (golf course, pubs, and so on) also precludes women from gaining access to crucial information and resources vital for their advancement. For example, many of the significant organizational changes and current events are discussed informally among men outside the work setting. Women are generally unaware of the most recent developments since they are not a part of the informal group that interacts and exchanges information away from the workplace. This definitely is a handicap. For example, knowledge of an impending vacancy for an executive position enables one to strategize to occupy that position. One can become a key contender by procuring critical information relevant to the position, get prepared to present the appropriate credentials to the right people at the right time, and thus pave the way for success. Thus, access to critical information is important for the progress of all, including women. When women do not have the critical information that is shared in informal networks, their chances of advancement to top positions also get severely restricted.

Gender-role stereotypes also hinder access to information. If women are not considered to be decision makers and leaders, but are perceived merely as support personnel, they will not be apprised of critical information essential for organizational advancement, since this is not seen as relevant for them. When both stereotyping and exclusion from critical information are in operation, there is no way that women can reach the top. These relationships are shown schematically in Figure 4.12.

In sum, both gender-role stereotypes and access to critical information significantly influence women's advancement to top-level positions in organizations and explain the variance in it.

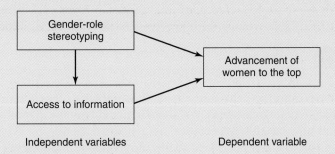

Figure 4.12: Schematic diagram of the example relating to women in managerial positions.

**Hypotheses**

1. *The greater the extent of gender stereotyping in organizations, the fewer will be the number of women at the top.*
2. *Male managers have more access to critical information than women managers in the same ranks.*
3. *There will be a significant positive correlation between access to information and chances for promotion to top-level positions.*
4. *The greater the extent of gender-role stereotyping, the less access there will be to critical information for women.*
5. *Gender-role stereotyping and access to critical information will both significantly explain the variance in promotional opportunities for women to top-level positions.*

# Managerial implications

At this juncture, it becomes easy to follow the progression of research from the first stage, when managers sense the broad problem area, to preliminary data gathering (including literature review), to developing the theoretical framework based on the literature review and guided by experience and intuition, to formulating hypotheses for testing.

It is also clear that once the problem is defined, a good grasp of the four different types of variables broadens the understanding of managers as to how multiple factors impinge on the organizational setting. Knowledge of how and for what purpose the theoretical framework is developed and the hypotheses are generated enables the manager to be an intelligent judge of the research report submitted by the consultant. Likewise, knowledge of what significance means, and why a given hypothesis is either accepted or rejected, helps the manager to persist in or desist from following hunches, which, while making good sense, do not work. If such knowledge is absent, many of the findings through research will not make much sense to the manager and decision making will bristle with confusion.

## SUMMARY

In this chapter we examined the four types of variables – dependent, independent, moderating, and mediating variables. We also discussed how the theoretical framework is developed and how testable hypotheses are generated therefrom. We saw examples where the same variable can be a dependent, independent, moderating, or mediating variable, depending on the situation. We also explained when a null hypothesis should be accepted or rejected, based on whether or not the results of hypothesis testing meet the significance test. Furthermore, we also briefly discussed the test for hypothesis validation in qualitative research. In the next chapter we will examine the basic research design issues.

## DISCUSSION QUESTIONS

1. "Because literature review is a time-consuming exercise, a good, in-depth interview should suffice to develop a theoretical framework." Discuss this statement.
2. "Good models are complex. What's more, a good model should include both moderating and mediating variables." Discuss this statement.
3. "Academic researchers usually develop more complex and elaborate models than applied researchers." Discuss this statement.
4. "In an applied research context you do not need to explain the relationships between the variables in your conceptual model." Discuss this statement.
5. There is an advantage in stating the hypothesis both in the null and in the alternate; it adds clarity to our thinking of what we are testing. Explain.
6. It is advantageous to develop a directional hypothesis whenever we are sure of the predicted direction. How will you justify this statement?

7. In recent decades, many service markets have been liberalized. For this reason, incumbent service firms are facing new competitors and must address customer switching. You are discussing the determinants of customer switching with a service firm manager. She believes that product quality, relationship quality, and switching costs are important determinants of customer switching. You agree with the contention that product quality and relationship quality are important determinants of switching. However, you believe that switching costs *moderate* the relationships between product quality, relationship quality, and customer switching. Provide arguments for this contention.

8. For the following case entitled "Sleepless nights at Holiday Inn" (published in *Business Week* and adapted here):
   a. Identify the problem
   b. Develop a conceptual model
   c. Develop at least four hypotheses

## EXAMPLE

### Sleepless nights at Holiday Inn

Just a few years ago, Tom Oliver, the Chief Executive of Holiday Hospitality Corp., was struggling to differentiate among the variety of facilities offered to clients under the Holiday flag – the *Holiday Inn Select* designed for business travelers, the *Holiday Inn Express* used by penny pinchers, and the *Crowne Plaza Hotels*, the luxurious hotels meant for the big spenders. Oliver felt that revenues could be quadrupled if only clients could differentiate among these.

Keen on developing a viable strategy for Holiday Hospitality, which suffered from brand confusion, Tom Oliver conducted a customer survey of those who had used each type of facility, and found the following. The consumers didn't have a clue as to the differences among the three different types. Many complained that the buildings were old and not properly maintained, and the quality ratings of service and other factors were also poor. Furthermore, when word spread that one of the contemplated strategies of Oliver was a name change to differentiate the three facilities, irate franchises balked. Their mixed messages did not help consumers to understand the differences, either.

Oliver thought that he first needed to understand how the different classifications would be important to the several classes of client, and then he could market the heck out of them and greatly enhance the revenues. Simultaneously, he recognized that unless the franchise owners fully cooperated with him in all his plans, mere face lifting and improvement of customer service would not bring added revenues.

9. Develop a conceptual model for the scenario below.

## EXAMPLE

Incidence of smoking in movies has started to increase again, after having declined for several decades. According to the National Cancer Institute, smoking is seen in at least three out of four contemporary box-office hits. What's more, identifiable cigarette brands appeared in about one-third of all movies in 2008. Exposure to smoking in movies is an important predictor of adolescent smoking initiation: smoking in movies has been shown to affect adolescents' intentions to start smoking. In turn, the intentions to start smoking are determined by a more positive attitude toward smoking after seeing a film character smoke. Recent research has revealed that the relationship between seeing a film character smoke and the attitude toward smoking is stronger when a person's identification with a film character increases. These findings are consistent with social learning theory, which predicts that attitudes and behaviors are modeled by observing the behaviors of others.

10. Develop a conceptual model for the following case.

## EXAMPLE

Once given, perks are extraordinarily hard to take away without sapping employee morale. The adverse effects of these cuts far outweigh the anticipated savings in dollars. Research has shown that when the reason behind the cuts is explained to employees, morale does not drop.

11. Product placement is a form of advertising in which a company's products and name are intentionally positioned in motion pictures, television programs, radio broadcasts, and the like. Product placement can take many forms: verbal mentions in dialogue, actual use by a character, or visual displays (for instance a company logo on a vehicle or billboard). Develop a theoretical framework on this issue, based on a review of the current literature. This framework should include:

- a specification and definition of an appropriate dependent variable;
- a conceptual model that describes the relationships between the dependent variable, at least one independent variable, and either a moderating or a mediating variable;
- a theory on why you would expect these relationships to exist;
- an appropriate number of testable hypotheses.

## PRACTICE PROJECT

For the topic you chose to work on for the project in Chapter 3, do the following:

i. Go through the computer-generated bibliography again.
ii. Define a problem statement that, in your opinion, would be most useful for researchers to investigate.
iii. Write up a literature review that would seem to offer the greatest potential for developing a good theoretical framework, using about 20 references.
iv. Develop the theoretical framework incorporating its five basic features, as discussed in the chapter.
v. Generate a set of testable hypotheses based on the theoretical framework.

# CHAPTER **5**

## The research process: elements of research design

## Topics discussed

- The research design
- Purpose of the study: exploratory, descriptive, hypothesis testing, case study analysis
- Type of investigation: causal versus correlational
- Extent of researcher interference with the study
- Study setting: contrived versus noncontrived
- Unit of analysis: individuals, dyads, groups, organizations, cultures
- Time horizon of study: cross-sectional versus longitudinal
- Managerial implications

## CHAPTER OBJECTIVES

After completing Chapter 5 you should be able to:

1. Understand the different aspects relevant to designing a research study.
2. Identify the scope of any given study and the end use of the results.
3. Decide, for any given situation, the type of investigation needed, the study setting, the extent of researcher interference, the unit of analysis, and the time horizon of the study.
4. Identify which of the two, a causal or a correlational study, would be more appropriate in a given situation.

# The research design

Having identified the variables in a problem situation and developed the theoretical framework, the next step is to design the research in such a way that the requisite data can be gathered and analyzed to arrive at a solution.

The various issues involved in the research design and discussed in this chapter are shown comprehensively in Figure 5.1. As may be seen, issues relating to decisions regarding the purpose of the study (exploratory, descriptive, hypothesis testing), its location (i.e., the study setting), the type it should conform to (type of investigation), the extent to which it is manipulated and controlled by the researcher (extent of researcher interference), its temporal aspects (time horizon), and the level at which the data will be analyzed (unit of analysis), are integral to research design. These are discussed in this chapter. In addition, decisions have to be made as to the type of sample to be used (sampling design), how the data will be collected (data collection methods), how variables will be measured (measurement), and how they will be analyzed to test the hypotheses (data analysis). These are discussed in subsequent chapters.

As shown in Figure 5.1, each component of the research design offers several critical choice points. The extent of scientific rigor in a research study depends on how carefully the manager/researcher chooses the appropriate design alternatives, taking into consideration its specific purpose. For instance, if a critical financial decision to invest millions of dollars in a

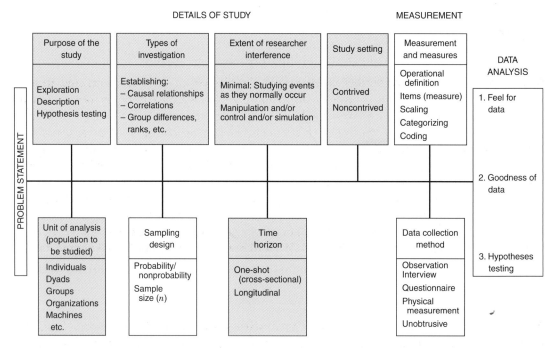

Figure 5.1: The research design.

project is to be based on the results of a research investigation, then careful attention to detail is necessary to ensure that the study has precision and has the acceptable level of confidence. This implies, as we will see later in the book, that close attention will be paid to sampling, measurement, data collection, and so on. Contrast this with the research goal of generating a profile of managers in an organization to publish a newsletter. This will not call for elaborate research design decisions.

It is important to note that the more sophisticated and rigorous the research design is, the greater the time, costs, and other resources expended on it will be. It is therefore relevant to ask oneself at every choice point whether the benefits that result from a more sophisticated design to ensure accuracy, confidence, generalizability, and so on, are commensurate with the larger investment of resources.

In this chapter we will examine the six basic aspects of research design. Specifically, we will discuss the purpose of the study, the types of investigation, the extent of researcher interference, the study setting, the unit of analysis, and the time horizon of the study (the shaded parts in Figure 5.1). The other aspects of measurement, data collection methods, sampling design, and data analysis will be elaborated in later chapters.

# Purpose of the study: exploratory, descriptive, hypothesis testing (analytical and predictive), case study analysis

Studies may be either exploratory in nature or descriptive, or may be conducted to test hypotheses. The **case study**, which is an examination of studies done in other similar organizational situations, is also a method of solving problems, or for understanding phenomena of interest and generating further knowledge in that area. The nature of the study – whether it is exploratory, descriptive, or hypothesis testing – depends on the stage to which knowledge about the research topic has advanced. The design decisions become more rigorous as we proceed from the exploratory stage, where we attempt to explore new areas of organizational research, to the descriptive stage, where we try to describe certain characteristics of the phenomena on which interest centers, to the hypothesis testing stage, where we examine whether or not the conjectured relationships have been substantiated and an answer to the research question has been obtained. We will now look at each of these in some detail.

## Exploratory study

An **exploratory study** is undertaken when not much is known about the situation at hand, or no information is available on how similar problems or research issues have been solved in the past. In such cases, extensive preliminary work needs to be done to gain familiarity with the phenomena in the situation, and understand what is occurring, before we develop a model and set up a rigorous design for comprehensive investigation.

In essence, exploratory studies are undertaken to better comprehend the nature of the problem since very few studies might have been conducted in that area. Extensive interviews with many people might have to be undertaken to get a handle on the situation and understand the phenomenon. More rigorous research could then proceed.

Some qualitative studies (as opposed to quantitative data gathered through questionnaires, etc.) where data are collected through observation or interviews, are exploratory in nature. When the data reveal some pattern regarding the phenomenon of interest, theories are developed and hypotheses formulated for subsequent testing. For example, Henry Mintzberg interviewed managers to explore the nature of managerial work. Based on the analysis of his interview data, he formulated theories of managerial roles, the nature and types of managerial activities, and so on. These have been tested in different settings through both interviews and questionnaire surveys.

Exploratory studies are also necessary when some facts are known, but more information is needed for developing a viable theoretical framework. For instance, when we want to get at the important factors that influence the advancement of women in organizations, previous studies might indicate that women are increasingly taking on qualities such as assertiveness, competitiveness, and independence. There is also a perception that a judicious blend of masculine and feminine traits – such as being strong but not tough, kind but not soft – is conducive to women's organizational advancement. These notions apart, there is a need for interviewing women managers who have made it to the top to explore all the relevant variables. This will help to build a robust theory.

In sum, exploratory studies are important for obtaining a good grasp of the phenomenon of interest and advancing knowledge through subsequent theory building and hypothesis testing.

The following is an example where exploratory research would be necessary.

## EXAMPLE

The manager of a multinational corporation is curious to know if the work ethic values of employees working in its subsidiary in Pennathur City are different from those of Americans. There is very little information about Pennathur (except that it is a small city in southern India), and since there is considerable controversy about what work ethic values mean to people in other cultures, the manager's curiosity can be satisfied only by an exploratory study, interviewing the employees in organizations in Pennathur. Religion, political, economic, and social conditions, upbringing, cultural values, and so on play a major role in how people view their work in different parts of the world. Here, since very little is known about work ethic values in India (or even whether it is a viable concept for study in that country, as per discussions in a later chapter), an exploratory study will have to be undertaken.

Many topics of interest and concern to management in the management and organizational behavior areas have been studied, and information is available in the library on these subject areas. Although few exploratory studies are currently undertaken in the management area, researchers do explore new grounds from time to time with the changing dynamics that occur in the workplace. Not long ago, for instance, exploratory research on the topics of women in management and dual-career families was conducted. Because of subsequent studies, research on these topics has now progressed beyond the exploratory stage to the hypothesis testing stage.

The same is also true of research on quality of life. At one time, exploratory studies were undertaken to understand what the concept "quality of work life" means. After extensive interviews with various groups of people, it was considered to encompass such factors as enriched jobs, healthy work environment, stress-free work relationships, job satisfaction, work role involvement, and other work-related factors. Current thinking is that the concept "quality of work life" is too narrow and limited to be useful for research and that the concept "quality of life" is more encompassing, since work and nonwork cannot be viewed as two tightly compartmentalized aspects of an individual's life. Current research now takes both the work and nonwork factors (family, community, etc.) into consideration while examining quality of life. This advancement of knowledge would not have been possible without the initial exploratory studies.

Currently, exploratory studies about organizationally relevant differences in race, ethnic, and country origins are being undertaken so that sound theories about managing a diverse work group can be evolved for the future. Such exploratory studies are necessary since we do not now know if there are differences in communication styles, interpretation schemas, superior–subordinate relationship expectations, and the like, among the groups. If conflict and stress in the system are to be reduced and productivity is to be maintained and increased in the years to come, such understanding will be essential. The demographics of the workplace are constantly changing, and learning to value differences and adopting new styles of management are important to organizational success.

Exploratory studies can be undertaken by interviewing individuals and through focus groups. For instance, if a company manufacturing cosmetics wants to obtain a thorough understanding of what it is that arouses emotive appeal for the product and induces people to buy cosmetics, several focus groups can be convened to discuss the related issues. This exploratory study will offer the necessary preliminary information for a full-fledged study on the matter, later. With the advancement of technology, the Internet and videoconferencing facilities offer the advantage of contacting focus groups online at minimal cost. An analysis of their views would be very useful for a further in-depth study. Focus groups are discussed further in Chapter 8.

It is important to note that doing a study for the first time in a particular organization does not make the research exploratory in nature; only when knowledge is scant, and a deeper understanding is sought, does the study become exploratory.

## Descriptive study

A **descriptive study** is undertaken in order to ascertain and be able to describe the characteristics of the variables of interest in a situation. For instance, a study of a class in terms of the percentage of members who are in their senior and junior years, sex composition, age groupings, number of semesters left until graduation, and number of business courses taken, can be considered descriptive in nature. Quite frequently, descriptive studies are undertaken in organizations to learn about and describe the characteristics of a group of employees, for example, the age, educational level, job status, and length of service of Hispanics or Asians working in the system. Descriptive studies are also undertaken to understand the characteristics of organizations that follow certain common practices. For example, one might want to know and be able to describe the characteristics of the organizations that implement flexible manufacturing systems (FMS), or that have a certain debt-to-equity ratio.

The goal of a descriptive study, therefore, is to offer to the researcher a profile or to describe relevant aspects of the phenomenon of interest from an individual, organizational, industry-oriented, or other perspective. In many cases, such information may be vital before even considering certain corrective steps; for example, should the organization consider changing its practices? If a study of the firms in the industry indicates that most of them resort to just-in-time systems to cut inventory costs, maybe organization Z should also seriously consider the feasibility of this practice. Or if a descriptive study stresses the need to introduce flexible work hours for parents of children under three years of age, this may have to be seriously considered, and a much more focused study initiated to decide on the matter.

A brief description of the study of advances in the textile industry might look something like this:

US Textiles has used high-tech to make huge advances in productivity and innovation. An army of reels surrounds a complex circular knitting machine at Malden Hills, feeding yarn to thousands of needles producing polyester fabric. The 3-dimensional loom has added value utility in the competitive market.

Jacquard looms, which are computer controlled at Burlington, weave miles of intricately patterned materials. Even faster looms use jets of compressed air to move the weft. The industry is being revolutionized with a 3-dimensional loom that weaves the fibers in the shape of the end product, skipping the laborious process of lamination.

Denims, which are difficult to make, are now made by computer controls and electric sensors to a so-called dye range, which ensures a shade perfectly matching customers' samples.

The fastest looms, automated spinning processes, and Sanfmi machines programmed from a desktop computer and capable of producing any type of garment are other innovations in the textile industry.

Such a description of the advances helps textile companies to gauge their progress in keeping up with the technological advances.

Descriptive studies that present data in a meaningful form thus help to:

1. Understand the characteristics of a group in a given situation.
2. Think systematically about aspects in a given situation.

3. Offer ideas for further probe and research.
4. Help make certain simple decisions (such as how many and what kinds of individuals should be transferred from one department to another).

Below are examples of situations warranting a descriptive study.

## EXAMPLE

A bank manager wants to have a profile of the individuals who have loan payments outstanding for six months and more. The profile will include details of their average age, earnings, nature of occupation, full-time/part-time employment status, and the like. This might help him to elicit further information or decide right away on the types of individuals who should be made ineligible for loans in the future.

A CEO may be interested in having a description of organizations in her industry that follow the LIFO system. In this case, the report might include the age of the organizations, their locations, their production levels, assets, sales, inventory levels, suppliers, and profits. Such information might allow comparison later of the performance levels of specific types of companies.

A marketing manager might want to develop a pricing, sales, distribution, and advertising strategy for her product. With this in mind, she might ask for information regarding the competitors, with respect to the following:

1. The percentage of companies that have prices higher and lower than the industry norm; a profile of the terms of sale; and the percentage where prices are controlled regionally instead of from central headquarters.
2. The percentage of competitors hiring in-house staff to handle sales and those that use independent agents.
3. The percentage of sales groups organized by product line, by accounts, and by region.
4. The types of distribution channels used and the percentage of customers using each.
5. The percentage of competitors spending more dollars on advertising/promotion than the firm and those spending less; a categorization of their target audience, and the types of media most frequently used.
6. The percentage of those using the web ("dot coms") to sell the product.

Descriptive studies thus become essential in many situations. Whereas qualitative data obtained by interviewing individuals may help the understanding of phenomena at the exploratory stages of a study, quantitative data in terms of frequencies, or mean and standard deviations, become necessary for descriptive studies. A report on a descriptive study of the reaction of organizational members to a proposal to introduce an on-site child care facility, for instance, might look somewhat like this:

Whereas 30% of the employees were in favor of the idea, at least 40% felt that an on-site child care facility was unnecessary. Twenty percent indicated that it would benefit only those with preschool children and hence would be unfair to the others who could not use the facility. The remaining 10% suggested the introduction of a cafeteria style of benefits, so that employees could opt for what they preferred.

More women than men were favorably inclined toward the proposal (almost 2:1). Parents with two or more preschool children overwhelmingly desired this; employees who did not belong to this category were opposed to the idea.

Employees over 50 years of age and those below 25 did not seem to favor this scheme. However, women between 25 and 45 (a total of 45 women) seemed to desire it the most.

The mean on the preference scale indicated for the child care facility by all employees is rather low (1.5 on a five-point scale), but the dispersion is rather high, the standard deviation being 1.98. This indicates that there are some who indicate a strong liking for the proposed project, while some are totally against it.

The average preference indicated by women between the ages of 30 and 45 with children is the highest (4.75 on a five-point scale) with very little dispersion (the standard deviation for this group of 42 women is 0.38). This is the group that desires the on-site facility the most.

Introductory descriptive narratives in some research reports, as you might have noticed, are drawn from government statistical publications such as the Bureau of Labor Statistics, census, and the like, from which data are culled for presentation, as and when appropriate.

## Hypothesis testing

Studies that engage in hypothesis testing usually explain the nature of certain relationships, or establish the differences among groups, or the independence of two or more factors in a situation. Examples of such studies are given below. Hypothesis testing is undertaken to explain the variance in the dependent variable or to predict organizational outcomes.

### EXAMPLE

A marketing manager wants to know if the sales of the company will increase if he doubles the advertising dollars. Here, the manager would like to know the nature of the relationship that may be established between advertising and sales by testing the hypothesis: *If advertising is increased, then sales will also go up.*

Given people's tensions on the subject of purchase of guns in these days of crime in cities big and small, a marketing researcher might be interested in predicting the factors that significantly account for the variance in people's decision to purchase guns. Here, the researcher might theorize the factors that influence people's decision to possess guns (through literature search and interviews) and then test the hypothesis that four specific variables significantly account for the variance in people's intention to buy a gun. Here again, the researcher is interested in understanding and accounting for the variance in the dependent variable – gun purchase – through hypothesis testing.

The testing of a hypothesis such as *More men than women are whistleblowers* establishes the difference between two groups – men and women – in regard to their whistle-blowing behavior.

The independence between two variables that are qualitative in nature can also be established through hypothesis testing. Consider the hypothesis: *Working the night shift (as opposed to the day shift) is related to whether or not one is married*. A $\chi^2$ test of independence will easily provide the answer to this question. As may be seen, in hypothesis testing the researcher goes beyond mere description of the variables in a situation to an understanding of the relationships among factors of interest.

## Case study analysis

As discussed in Chapter 2, case studies involve in-depth, contextual analyses of matters relating to similar situations in other organizations. We noted earlier that case studies, as a problem-solving technique, are not frequently resorted to in organizations because finding the same type of problem in another comparable setting is difficult due to the reluctance of companies to reveal their problems. Case studies that are qualitative in nature are, however, useful in applying solutions to current problems based on past problem-solving experiences. They are also useful in understanding certain phenomena, and generating further theories for empirical testing.

## Review of the purpose of the study

It is not difficult to see that in exploratory studies, the researcher is basically interested in exploring the situational factors so as to get a grip on the characteristics of the phenomena of interest. Also, pilot studies on a small scale, by interviewing individuals or gathering information from a limited number of occurrences, are not uncommon in exploratory research.

Descriptive studies are undertaken when the characteristics or the phenomena to be tapped in a situation are known to exist, and one wants to be able to describe them better by offering a profile of the factors. Hypothesis testing offers an enhanced understanding of the relationship that exists among variables. It may also establish cause-and-effect relationships. Hypothesis testing can be done with both qualitative and quantitative data. Case studies are generally qualitative in nature and are sometimes used as a tool in managerial decision making.

Methodological rigor increases as we move progressively from an exploratory study to a hypothesis-testing study, and with this, the costs of research also increase. As we will see in later chapters in this book, increases in sample size, multiple methods of data collection, development of sophisticated measuring instruments, and the like, add to research costs, though they contribute more to testability, accuracy, precision, and generalizability.

# Type of investigation: causal versus correlational

A manager should determine whether a causal or a correlational study is needed to find an answer to the issue at hand. The former is done when it is necessary to establish a definitive cause-and-effect relationship. However, if all that the manager wants is a mere identification of the important factors "associated with" the problem, then a correlational study is called for. In the former case, the researcher is keen on delineating one or more factors that are undoubtedly causing the problem. In other words, the intention of the researcher conducting a causal study is to be able to state that variable X causes variable Y. So, when variable X is removed or altered in some way, problem Y is solved. Quite often, however, it is not just one or more variables that cause a problem in organizations. Given the fact that most of the time there are multiple factors influencing one another and the problem in a chainlike fashion, the researcher might be asked to identify the crucial factors associated with the problem, rather than establish a cause-and-effect relationship.

A study in which the researcher wants to delineate the cause of one or more problems is called a causal study. When the researcher is interested in delineating the important variables associated with the problem, the study is called a correlational study. It may be of interest to know that attempts are sometimes made to establish cause-and-effect relationships through certain types of correlational or regression analyses, such as cross-lagged correlations and path analysis (Billings and Wroten, 1978; Namboodiri, Carter and Blalock, 1975). Whether a study is causal or correlational thus depends on the type of research questions asked and how the problem is defined. The following example illustrates the difference.

## EXAMPLE

A causal study question: Does smoking cause cancer?
A correlational study question: Are smoking and cancer related?

OR

Are smoking, drinking, and chewing tobacco associated with cancer? If so, which of these contributes most to the variance in the dependent variable?

The answer to the first question will help to establish whether people who do not smoke will avoid developing cancer. The answer to the second question will determine if smoking and cancer are correlated. The third situation recognizes that there are perhaps several other factors that influence cancer apart from the three identified, but do these three help to explain a significant amount of the variance in cancer? If they do, then which among the three variables examined is the one that has the greatest association with it, which is the next, and which the third? The answer to the correlational study will help determine the extent of risk of cancer that people expose themselves to by smoking, drinking, and chewing tobacco. The intention here is not to establish a causal connection between one factor and another, but merely to see if a relationship does exist among the variables investigated.

The distinction between causal and correlational studies may be made clearer by the following two examples:

## EXAMPLE

Fears of an earthquake predicted recently in the New Madrid fault zone were instrumental (i.e., causal) in an unprecedented number of house owners in the Midwest region taking out an earthquake insurance policy.

Increases in interest rates and property taxes, the recession, and the predicted earthquake considerably slowed down the business of real estate agents in the Midwest.

Note that the first example indicates a causal relationship between the earthquake prediction and earthquake insurance, whereas the second example indicates that several factors, including the predicted earthquake, influenced (not caused) the slowdown of real estate agents' business. This is a correlational study, which was not intended to establish a cause-and-effect relationship.

# Extent of researcher interference with the study

The extent of interference by the researcher with the normal flow of work in the workplace has a direct bearing on whether the study undertaken is causal or correlational. A correlational study is conducted in the natural environment of the organization with minimal interference by the researcher with the normal flow of work. For example, if a researcher wants to study the factors influencing training effectiveness (a correlational study), all that the individual has to do is develop a theoretical framework, collect the relevant data, and analyze them to come up with the findings. Though there is some disruption to the normal flow of work in the system as the researcher interviews employees and administers questionnaires in the workplace, the researcher's interference in the routine functioning of the system is minimal as compared to that caused during causal studies.

In studies conducted to establish cause-and-effect relationships, the researcher tries to manipulate certain variables so as to study the effects of such manipulation on the dependent variable of interest. In other words, the researcher deliberately changes certain variables in the setting and interferes with the events as they normally occur in the organization. As an example, a researcher might want to study the influence of lighting on worker performance; hence he manipulates the lighting in the work situation to varying intensities. Here, there is considerable researcher interference with the natural and normal setting. In other cases the researcher might even want to create an altogether new artificial setting where the cause-and-effect relationships can be studied by manipulating certain variables and tightly controlling certain others, as in a laboratory. Thus, there could be varying degrees of interference by the researcher in the manipulation and control of variables in the research study, either in the natural setting or in an artificial lab setting.

Let us give examples of research with varying degrees of interference – minimal, moderate, and excessive.

## EXAMPLE

### Minimal interference

A hospital administrator wants to examine the relationship between the perceived emotional support in the system and the stresses experienced by the nursing staff. In other words, she wants to do a correlational study. Here, the administrator/researcher will collect data from the nurses (perhaps through a questionnaire) to indicate how much emotional support they get in the hospital and to what extent they experience stress. (We will learn in a later chapter how to measure these variables.) By correlating the two variables, the answer that is being sought can be found. In this case, beyond administering a questionnaire to the nurses, the researcher has not interfered with the normal activities in the hospital. In other words, researcher interference has been minimal.

### Moderate interference

The same researcher is now no longer content with finding a correlation, but wants to firmly establish a causal connection. That is, the researcher wants to demonstrate that if the nurses had emotional support, this indeed would cause them to experience less stress. If this can be established, then the nurses' stress can definitely be reduced by offering them emotional support. To test the cause-and-effect relationship, the researcher will measure the stress currently experienced by the nurses in three wards in the hospital, and then deliberately manipulate the extent of emotional support given to the three groups of nurses in the three wards for perhaps a week, and measure the amount of stress at the end of that period. For one group, the researcher will ensure that a number of lab technicians and doctors help and comfort the nurses when they face stressful events – for example, when they care for patients suffering excruciating pain and distress in the ward. Under a similar setup, for a second group of nurses in another ward, the researcher might arrange only a moderate amount of emotional support, employing only the lab technicians and excluding doctors. The third ward might operate without any emotional support. If the experimenter's theory is correct, then the reduction in the stress levels before and after the one-week period should be greatest for the nurses in the first ward, moderate for those in the second ward, and nil for the nurses in the third ward. Here we find that not only does the researcher collect data from nurses on their experienced stress at two different points in time, but she also "plays with" or manipulates the normal course of events by deliberately changing the amount of emotional support received by the nurses in two wards, while leaving things in the third ward unchanged. Here, the researcher has interfered more than minimally.

## Excessive interference

The above researcher, after conducting the previous experiments, feels that the results may or may not be valid since other external factors might have influenced the stress levels experienced by the nurses. For example, during that particular experimental week, the nurses in one or more wards may not have experienced high levels of stress because there were no serious illnesses or deaths in the ward. Hence, the emotional support received might not be related to the level of stress experienced. The researcher might now want to make sure that such extraneous factors as might affect the cause-and-effect relationship are controlled. So she might take three groups of medical students, put them in different rooms, and confront all of them with the same stressful task. For example, she might ask them to describe in the minutest detail, the procedures in performing surgery on a patient who has not responded to chemotherapy and keep bombarding them with more and more questions even as they respond. Although all are exposed to the same intensive questioning, one group might get help from a doctor who voluntarily offers clarification and help when students stumble. In the second group, a doctor might be nearby, but might offer clarification and help only if the group seeks it. In the third group, there is no doctor present and no help is available. In this case, not only is the support manipulated, but even the setting in which this experiment is conducted is artificial inasmuch as the researcher has taken the subjects away from their normal environment and put them in a totally different setting. Here, the researcher has intervened maximally with the normal setting, the participants, and their duties. In Chapter 9 we will see why such manipulations are necessary to establish cause-and-effect relationships beyond any doubt.

As we have seen, the extent of researcher interference depends on whether the study is correlational or causal and also the importance of establishing a causal relationship beyond any doubt whatever. Most organizational problems seldom call for a causal study. In any case, researcher interference through a change in the setting in which the causal study is conducted is rarely done, except in some market research areas.

# Study setting: contrived and noncontrived

As we have just seen, organizational research can be done in the natural environment where work proceeds normally (that is, in **noncontrived settings**) or in artificial, **contrived settings**. Correlational studies are invariably conducted in noncontrived settings, whereas most rigorous causal studies are done in contrived lab settings.

Correlational studies done in organizations are called **field studies**. Studies conducted to establish cause-and-effect relationships using the same natural environment in which employees normally function are called **field experiments**. Here, as we have seen earlier, the researcher does interfere with the natural occurrence of events inasmuch as the independent variable is manipulated. For example, a manager wanting to know the effects of pay on performance should raise the salary of employees in one unit, decrease the pay of employees in another unit, and leave the pay of the employees in a third unit untouched. Here there is a tampering with, or manipulating of, the pay system to establish a cause-and-effect relationship between pay and performance, but the study is still conducted in the natural setting and hence is called a field experiment.

Experiments done to establish a cause-and-effect relationship beyond the possibility of the least doubt require the creation of an artificial, contrived environment in which all the extraneous factors are strictly controlled. Similar subjects are chosen carefully to respond to certain manipulated stimuli. These studies are referred to as **lab experiments**. Let us give some further examples to understand the differences among a field study (a noncontrived setting with minimal researcher interference), a field experiment (noncontrived setting but with researcher interference to a moderate extent), and a lab experiment (a contrived setting with researcher interference to an excessive degree).

## EXAMPLE

### Field study

A bank manager wants to analyze the relationship between interest rates and bank deposit patterns of clients. She tries to correlate the two by looking at deposits into different kinds of accounts (such as savings, certificates of deposit, golden passbooks, and interest-bearing checking accounts) as interest rates change. This is a field study where the bank manager has merely taken the balances in various types of account and correlated them to the changes in interest rates. Research here is done in a noncontrived setting with no interference with the normal work routine.

### Field experiment

The bank manager now wants to determine the cause-and-effect relationship between the interest rate and the inducement it offers to clients to save and deposit money in the bank. She selects four branches within a 60-mile radius for the experiment. For one week only, she advertises the annual rate for new certificates of deposit received during that week in the following manner: the interest rate will be 9% in one branch, 8% in another, and 10% in the third. In the fourth branch, the interest rate remains unchanged at 5%. Within the week, she will be able to determine the effects, if any, of interest rates on deposit mobilization.

The above is a field experiment since nothing but the interest rate is manipulated, with all activities occurring in the normal and natural work environment. Hopefully, all four branches chosen will be more or less compatible in size, number of depositors, deposit patterns, and the like, so that the interest–savings relationships are not influenced by some third factor. But it is possible that some other factors might affect the findings. For example, one of the areas may have more retirees who may not have additional disposable income to deposit, despite the attraction of a good interest rate. The banker may not have been aware of this fact while setting up the experiment.

## Lab experiment

The banker in the previous example may now want to establish the causal connection between interest rates and savings, beyond a doubt. Because of this, she wants to create an artificial environment and trace the true cause-and-effect relationship. She recruits 40 students who are all business majors in their final year of study and are more or less of the same age. She splits them into four groups and gives each one of them chips that count for $1000, which they are told they might utilize to buy their needs, or save for the future, or both. She offers them, by way of incentive, interest on what they save but manipulates the interest rates by offering a 6% interest rate on savings for group 1, 8% for group 2, 9% for group 3, and keeps the interest at the low rate of 1% for group 4.

Here, the manager has created an artificial laboratory environment and has manipulated the interest rates for savings. She has also chosen subjects with similar backgrounds and exposure to financial matters (business students). If the banker finds that the savings by the four groups increase progressively, keeping in step with the increasing rates of interest, she will be able to establish a cause-and-effect relationship between interest rates and the disposition to save.

In this lab experiment with the contrived setting, the researcher interference has been maximal, inasmuch as the setting is different, the independent variable has been manipulated, and most external nuisance factors such as age and experience have been controlled.

Experimental designs are discussed more fully in Chapter 9. However, the above examples show us that it is important to decide the various design details before conducting the research study, since one decision criterion might have an impact on others. For example, if one wants to conduct an exploratory, descriptive, or a correlational hypothesis-testing study, then the necessity for the researcher to interfere with the normal course of events in the organization will be minimal. However, if causal connections are to be established, experimental designs need to be set up either within the organization where the events normally occur (a field experiment) or in an artificially created laboratory setting (a lab experiment).

In summary, we have thus far made a distinction among (1) field studies, where various factors are examined in the natural setting in which daily activities go on as normal with minimal researcher interference, (2) field experiments, where cause-and-effect relationships are studied with some amount of researcher interference, but still in the natural setting where work continues in the normal fashion, and (3) lab experiments, where the researcher explores cause-and-effect relationships, not only exercising a high degree of control but also in an artificial and deliberately created setting.

In Chapter 9 we will see the advantages and disadvantages of using contrived and noncontrived settings for establishing cause-and-effect relationships. Depending on the degree to which establishment of the cause-and-effect relationship unequivocally is important to a research project, a contrived or a noncontrived setting will be relevant for causal studies. Thus, the choice of the setting becomes an important issue in research design. As stated earlier, an artificial setting is rarely called for in business research.

# Unit of analysis: individuals, dyads, groups, organizations, cultures

The **unit of analysis** refers to the level of aggregation of the data collected during the subsequent data analysis stage. If, for instance, the problem statement focuses on how to raise the motivational levels of employees in general, then we are interested in individual employees in the organization and have to find out what we can do to raise their motivation. Here the unit of analysis is the individual. We will be looking at the data gathered from each individual and treating each employee's response as an individual data source. If the researcher is interested in studying two-person interactions, then several two-person groups, also known as *dyads*, will become the unit of analysis. Analysis of husband–wife interactions in families and supervisor–subordinate relationships in the workplace are good examples of dyads as the unit of analysis. However, if the problem statement is related to group effectiveness, then the unit of analysis will be at the group level. In other words, even though we may gather relevant data from all individuals comprising, say, six groups, we aggregate the individual data into group data so as to see the differences among the six groups. If we are comparing different departments in the organization, then the data analysis will be done at the departmental level – that is, the individuals in the department will be treated as one unit – and comparisons made by treating the department as the unit of analysis.

Our research question determines the unit of analysis. For example, if we wish to study group decision-making patterns, we will probably be examining such aspects as group size, group structure, cohesiveness, and the like, in trying to explain the variance in group decision making. Here, our main interest is not in studying individual decision making but *group* decision making, and we will be studying the dynamics that operate in several different groups and the factors that influence group decision making. In such a case, the unit of analysis will be groups.

As our research question addresses issues that move away from the individual to dyads, and to groups, organizations, and even nations, so also does the unit of analysis shift from individuals to dyads, groups, organizations, and nations. The characteristic of these "levels of analysis" is that the lower levels are subsumed within the higher levels. Thus, if we study buying behavior, we have to collect data from, say, 60 individuals, and analyze the data. If we want to study group dynamics, we may need to study, say, six or more groups, and then analyze the data gathered by examining the patterns in each of the groups. If we want to study cultural differences among nations, we will have to collect data from different countries and study the underlying patterns of culture in each country. Some critical issues in cross-cultural research are discussed in later chapters.

Individuals do not have the same characteristics as groups (e.g., structure, cohesiveness), and groups do not have the same characteristics as individuals (e.g., IQ, stamina). There are variations in the perceptions, attitudes, and behaviors of people in different cultures. Hence, the nature of the information gathered, as well as the level at which data are aggregated for analysis, are integral to decisions made on the choice of the unit of analysis.

It is necessary to decide on the unit of analysis even as we formulate the research question, since the data collection methods, sample size, and even the variables included in the framework may sometimes be determined or guided by the level at which data are aggregated for analysis.

Let us examine some research scenarios that would call for different units of analysis.

## EXAMPLE

### Individuals as the unit of analysis

The Chief Financial Officer of a manufacturing company wants to know how many of the staff would be interested in attending a three-day seminar on making appropriate investment decisions. For this purpose, data will have to be collected from each individual staff member and the unit of analysis is the individual.

### Dyads as the unit of analysis

Having read about the benefits of mentoring, a human resources manager wants to first identify the number of employees in three departments of the organization who are in mentoring relationships, and then find out what the jointly perceived benefits (i.e., by both the mentor and the one mentored) of such a relationship are. Here, once the mentor and the mentored pairs are identified, their joint perceptions can be obtained by treating each pair as one unit. Hence, if the manager wants data from a sample of 10 pairs, he will have to deal with 20 individuals, a pair at a time. The information obtained from each pair will be a data point for subsequent analysis. Thus, the unit of analysis here is the dyad.

## Groups as the unit of analysis

A manager wants to see the patterns of usage of the newly installed Information System (IS) by the production, sales, and operations personnel. Here, three groups of personnel are involved and information on the number of times the IS is used by each member in each of the three groups, as well as other relevant issues, will be collected and analyzed. The final results will indicate the mean usage of the system per day or month for each group. Here, the unit of analysis is the group.

## Divisions as the unit of analysis

Procter & Gamble wants to see which of its various divisions (soap, paper, oil, etc.) have made profits of over 12% during the current year. Here, the profits of each of the divisions will be examined and the information aggregated across the various geographical units of the division. Hence, the unit of analysis will be the division, at which level the data will be aggregated.

## Industry as the unit of analysis

An employment survey specialist wants to see the proportion of the workforce employed by the health care, utilities, transportation, and manufacturing industries. In this case, the researcher has to aggregate the data relating to each of the subunits comprised in each of the industries and report the proportions of the workforce employed at the industry level. The health care industry, for instance, includes hospitals, nursing homes, mobile units, small and large clinics, and other health care providing facilities. The data from these subunits will have to be aggregated to see how many employees are employed by the health care industry. This will need to be done for each of the other industries.

## Countries as the unit of analysis

The Chief Financial Officer (CFO) of a multinational corporation wants to know the profits made during the past five years by each of the subsidiaries in England, Germany, France, and Spain. It is possible that there are many regional offices of these subsidiaries in each of these countries. The profits of the various regional centers for each country have to be aggregated and the profits for each country for the past five years provided to the CFO. In other words, the data will now have to be aggregated at the country level. As can be easily seen, the data collection and sampling processes become more cumbersome at higher levels of units of analysis (industry, country) than at the lower levels (individuals and dyads). It is obvious that the unit of analysis has to be clearly identified as dictated by the research question. Sampling plan decisions will also be governed by the unit of analysis. For example, if I compare two cultures, for instance those of India and the United States –where my unit of analysis is the country – my sample size will be only two, despite the fact that I shall have to gather data from several hundred individuals from a variety of organizations in the different regions of each country, incurring huge costs. However, if my unit of analysis is individuals (as when studying the buying patterns of customers in the southern part of the United States), I may perhaps limit the collection of data to a representative sample of a hundred individuals in that region and conduct my study at a low cost!

It is now even easier to see why the unit of analysis should be given serious consideration even as the research question is being formulated and the research design planned.

# Time horizon: cross-sectional versus longitudinal studies

## Cross-sectional studies

A study can be undertaken in which data are gathered just once, perhaps over a period of days or weeks or months, in order to answer a research question. Such studies are called **one-shot** or **cross-sectional studies**. For example:

### EXAMPLE

Data were collected from stock brokers between April and June of last year to study their concerns in a turbulent stock market. Data with respect to this particular research had not been collected before, nor will they be collected again for this research.

A drug company desirous of investing in research for a new obesity (reduction) pill conducted a survey among obese people to see how many of them would be interested in trying the new pill. This is a one-shot or cross-sectional study to assess the likely demand for the new product.

The purpose of the studies in the two foregoing examples was to collect data that would be pertinent to finding the answer to a research question. Data collection at one point in time was sufficient. Both were cross-sectional designs.

## Longitudinal studies

In some cases, however, the researcher might want to study people or phenomena at more than one point in time in order to answer the research question. For instance, the researcher might want to study employees' behavior before and after a change in the top management, so as to know what effects the change accomplished. Here, because data are gathered at two different points in time, the study is not cross-sectional or of the one-shot kind, but is carried longitudinally across a period of time. Such studies, as when data on the dependent variable are gathered at two or more points in time to answer the research question, are called **longitudinal studies**.

## EXAMPLE

UPS experienced a shutdown for 15 days during the Teamsters' walkout and its clients shifted their business to other carriers such as FedEx and the US Postal Service. After the termination of the strike, UPS tried to woo its customers back through several strategies and collected data month after month to see what progress was being made in this regard. Here, data were collected every month to assess whether UPS had regained the business volume. Since data were collected at various points in time to answer the same research question (have we regained lost ground?), the study was a longitudinal one.

A marketing manager is interested in tracing the pattern of sales of a particular product in four different regions of the country on a quarterly basis for the next two years. Since data will be collected several times to answer the same issue (tracing pattern of sales), the study falls into the longitudinal category.

Longitudinal studies take more time and effort and cost more than cross-sectional studies. However, well-planned longitudinal studies can, among other things, help to identify cause-and-effect relationships. For example, one could study the sales volume of a product before and after an advertisement, and provided other environmental changes have not impacted on the results, one could attribute the increase in the sales volume, if any, to the advertisement. If there is no increase in sales, one could conclude that either the advertisement is ineffective or it will take a longer time to take effect.

Experimental designs invariably are longitudinal studies, since data are collected both before and after a manipulation. Field studies may also be longitudinal. For example, a study of the comparison data pertaining to the reactions of managers in a company toward working women now and ten years later will be a longitudinal field study. Most field studies conducted, however, are cross-sectional in nature because of the time, effort, and costs involved in collecting data over several time periods. Longitudinal studies will certainly be necessary if a manager wants to keep track of certain factors (e.g., sales, advertising effectiveness, etc.) over a period of time to assess improvements, or to detect possible causal connections (sales promotions and actual sales data; frequency of drug testing and reduction in drug usage, etc.). Though more expensive, longitudinal studies offer some good insights.

# Review of elements of research design

This concludes the discussions on the basic design issues regarding the purpose of the study, type of investigation, extent of researcher interference, study setting, unit of analysis, and the time horizon. The researcher determines the appropriate decisions to be made in the study design based on the problem definition, the research objectives, the extent of rigor desired, and cost considerations. Sometimes, because of the time and costs involved, a researcher might be constrained to settle for less than the "ideal" research design. For instance, the researcher might have to conduct a cross-sectional instead of a longitudinal study, do a field study rather than an experimental design, choose a smaller rather than a larger sample size, and so on, thus suboptimizing the research design decisions and settling for a lower level of scientific rigor because of resource constraints. This trade-off between rigor and resources will be a deliberate and conscious decision made by the manager/researcher based on the scope of, and reasons for, the study, and will have to be explicitly stated in any written research proposal. Compromises so made also account for why management studies are not entirely scientific, as discussed in Chapter 2.

A rigorous research design that might involve higher costs is essential if the results of the study are critical for making important decisions affecting the organization's survival and/or the well-being of the vast majority of the public using the system. It is best to think about research design decision issues even as the theoretical framework is being developed. The researcher has to be very clear about each aspect discussed in this chapter before embarking on data collection.

Now do Exercises 5.1, 5.2, 5.3, 5.4, and 5.5

## EXERCISE 5.1

A foreman thinks that the low efficiency of the machine tool operators is directly linked to the high level of fumes emitted in the workshop. He would like to prove this to his supervisor through a research study.

1. Would this be a causal or a correlational study? Why?
2. Is this an exploratory, descriptive, or hypothesis-testing (analytical or predictive) study? Why?
3. What kind of a study would this be: field study, lab experiment, or field experiment? Why?
4. What would be the unit of analysis? Why?
5. Would this be a cross-sectional or a longitudinal study? Why?

## EXERCISE 5.2

Many were concerned about the operations of the infamous BCCI, the international banking institution. If the government had wished to probe into the details, would this investigation have called for:

1.  A causal or correlational study? Why?
2.  An exploratory, descriptive, or hypothesis-testing study or case analysis? Why?
3.  A field study, lab experiment, or field experiment? Why?
4.  A cross-sectional or longitudinal study? Why?

## EXERCISE 5.3

You want to examine how exposure to thin or heavy models in advertisements influences a person's self-esteem. You believe that the effect of exposure to models in advertisements depends on the extremity of the model's thinness or heaviness. Discuss the design decisions that you as a researcher will make to investigate this issue, giving reasons for your choices.

## EXERCISE 5.4

You want to investigate the specific effects of specific emotions on customers' behavioral responses to failed service encounters across industries. Discuss the design decisions that you as a researcher will make to investigate this issue, giving reasons for your choices.

## EXERCISE 5.5

Dr Larry Norton of Memorial Sloan-Kettering Cancer Center predicts that cancer treatment will undergo major changes. Several drugs are being developed to battle cancer without harming healthy tissue. It is a question of discovering which of these drugs does the job best. Design a study that would help find which drug would do the trick.

# Managerial implications

Knowledge about research design issues helps the manager to understand what the researcher is attempting to do. The manager also understands why the reports sometimes indicate data analytic results based on small sample sizes, when a lot of time has been spent in collecting data from several scores of individuals, as in the case of studies involving groups, departments, or branch offices.

One of the important decisions a manager has to make before starting a study pertains to how rigorous the study ought to be. Knowing that more rigorous research designs consume more resources, the manager is in a position to weigh the gravity of the problem experienced and decide what kind of design will yield acceptable results in an efficient manner. For example, the manager might decide that knowledge of which variables are associated with employee performance is good enough to enhance performance results and there is no need to ferret out the cause. Such a decision would result not only in economy in resources, but also cause the least disruption to the smooth flow of work for employees and preclude the need for collecting data longitudinally. Knowledge of interconnections among various aspects of the research design helps managers to call for the most effective study, after weighing the nature and magnitude of the problem encountered, and the type of solution desired.

One of the main advantages in fully understanding the difference between causal and correlational studies is that managers do not fall into the trap of making implicit causal assumptions when two variables are only associated with each other. They realize that A could cause B, or B could cause A, or both A and B could covary because of some third variable.

Knowledge of research design details also helps managers to study and intelligently comment on research proposals.

## SUMMARY

In this chapter we examined the basic research design issues and the choice points available to the manager/researcher. We discussed the situations in which exploratory, descriptive, hypothesis-testing, and case studies are called for. We examined causal versus correlational studies, and the implications of either for determining the study setting, the extent of researcher interference, and the time horizon of the study. We noted that the unit of analysis refers to the level at which data are aggregated for analysis, and that the time horizon of studies may be one-shot or longitudinal. Finally, we examined the circumstances in which each design decision would be appropriate.

## DISCUSSION QUESTIONS

1. What are the basic research design issues? Describe them in some detail.
2. Why is it important to consider basic design issues before conducting the study and even as early as at the time of formulating the research question?
3. Is a field study totally out of the question if one is trying to establish cause-and-effect relationships?
4. "An exploratory study is just as useful as a predictive study." Discuss this statement.
5. Why is the unit of analysis an integral part of the research design?
6. Discuss the interrelationships among noncontrived setting, the purpose of the study, type of investigation, researcher interference, and time horizon of study.

7. Below are three scenarios. Indicate how the researcher should proceed in each case; that is, determine the following, giving reasons:
   a. The purpose of the study
   b. The type of investigation
   c. The extent of researcher interference
   d. The study setting
   e. The time horizon for the study
   f. The unit of analysis

## Scenario 1

Ms Joyce Lynn, the owner of a small business (a women's dress boutique), has invited a consultant to tell her how her business is different from similar small businesses within a 60-mile radius with respect to use of the most modern computer technology, sales volume, profit margin, and staff training.

## Scenario 2

Mr Paul Hodge, the owner of several restaurants on the East Coast, is concerned about the wide differences in their profit margins. He would like to try some incentive plans for increasing the efficiency levels of those restaurants that lag behind. But before he actually does this, he would like to be assured that the idea will work. He asks a researcher to help him on this issue.

## Scenario 3

A manager is intrigued as to why some people seem to derive joy from work and get energized by it, while others find it troublesome and frustrating.

# CHAPTER 6

## Measurement of variables: operational definition

## Topics discussed

- Measurement of variables
- Operational definition (operationalization)
  - Dimensions and elements of concepts
  - What an operational definition is not
- International dimensions of operational definition

### CHAPTER OBJECTIVES

After completing Chapter 6, you should be able to:

1. Explain when operationalization of variables is necessary.
2. Operationally define (or operationalize) variables.
3. Describe the advantages of using existing measurement scales to operationalize variables.

Measurement of the variables in the theoretical framework is an integral part of research and an important aspect of research design (see shaded portion in Figure 6.1). Unless the variables are measured in some way, we will not be able to test our hypotheses and find answers to our research questions. In this chapter we will discuss how variables lend themselves to measurement.

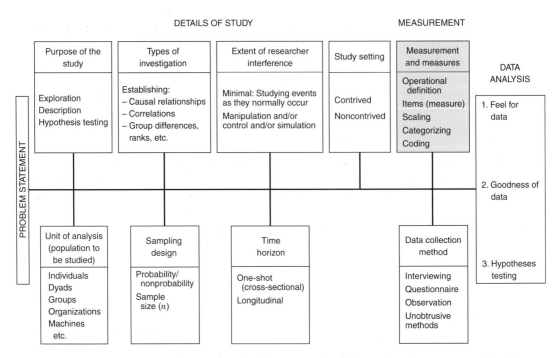

**Figure 6.1:** Research design and where this chapter fits in.

# How variables are measured

To test the hypothesis that workforce diversity affects organizational effectiveness we have to measure workforce diversity and organizational effectiveness. Measurement is the assignment of numbers or other symbols to *characteristics* (or *attributes*) of *objects* according to a pre-specified set of rules. Objects include persons, strategic business units, companies, countries, bicycles, elephants, kitchen appliances, restaurants, shampoo, yogurt, and so on. Examples of characteristics of objects are arousal-seeking tendency, achievement motivation, organizational effectiveness, shopping enjoyment, length, weight, ethnic diversity, service quality, conditioning effects, and taste. It is important that you realize that you cannot measure objects (for instance, a company); you measure characteristics or attributes of objects (for instance, the organizational effectiveness of a company). In a similar fashion, you can measure the length (the attribute) of a person (the object), the weight of an elephant, the arousal-seeking tendency of stockbrokers, the shopping enjoyment of women, the service quality of a restaurant, the conditioning effects of a shampoo, and the taste of a certain brand of yogurt.

Attributes of objects that can be physically measured by some calibrated instruments pose no measurement problems. For example, the length and width of a rectangular office table can be easily measured with a measuring tape or a ruler. The same is true for measuring the office floor area and for measuring the weight of an elephant (at least to some extent). Data representing several demographic characteristics of office personnel are also easily obtained by asking employees simple, straightforward questions, such as: "How long have you been working in this organization?" or "What is your marital status?"

The measurement of more abstract and subjective attributes is more difficult however. For instance, it is relatively difficult to measure the level of *achievement motivation* of office clerks, the *shopping enjoyment* of women, or the *need for cognition* of students. Likewise, it is not straightforward to test hypotheses on the relationship between workforce diversity, managerial expertise, and organizational effectiveness. The problem is that we cannot simply ask questions like "How diverse is your company's workforce?" or "How effective is your organization?" because of the abstract nature of the variables "workforce diversity" and "organizational effectiveness". Of course, there are solutions to this problem. One of these solutions is discussed next. But let us, before we discuss the solution, summarize the problem.

Certain variables lend themselves to easy measurement through the use of appropriate measuring instruments; for example, physiological phenomena pertaining to human beings such as blood pressure, pulse rates, and body temperature, as well as certain physical attributes such as length and weight. But when we get into the realm of people's subjective feelings, attitudes, and perceptions, the measurement of these factors or variables becomes more difficult. Accordingly, there are at least two types of variables: one lends itself to objective and precise measurement; the other is more nebulous and does not lend itself to accurate measurement because of its abstract and subjective nature.

# Operationalization of variables

Despite the lack of physical measuring devices to measure the more nebulous variables, there are ways of tapping these types of variable. One technique is to reduce these abstract notions or concepts to observable behavior and/or characteristics. In other words, the abstract notions are broken down into observable behavior or characteristics. For instance, the concept of *thirst* is abstract; we cannot see it. However, we would expect a thirsty person to drink plenty of fluids. In other words, the expected reaction of people to thirst is to drink fluids. If several people say they are thirsty, then we may determine the thirst levels of each of these individuals by the measure of the quantity of fluids that they drink to quench their thirst. We will thus be able to measure their levels of thirst, even though the concept of thirst itself is abstract and nebulous. Reduction of abstract concepts to render them measurable in a tangible way is called *operationalizing* the concepts.

Operationalizing is done by looking at the behavioral dimensions, facets, or properties denoted by the concept. These are then translated into observable and measurable elements so as to develop an index of measurement of the concept. Operationalizing a concept involves a series of steps. The first step is to come up with a definition of the construct that you want to measure. Then, it is necessary to think about the content of the measure; that is, an instrument (one or more items or questions) that actually measures the concept that one wants to measure has to be developed. Subsequently, a response format (for instance a seven-point rating scale with end-points anchored by "strongly disagree" and "strongly agree") is needed, and finally, the validity and reliability of the measurement scale has to be assessed. The next chapter discusses steps 3 and 4. In this chapter we will discuss step 2: the development of an adequate and representative set of items or questions.

## EXAMPLE

### Operationalizing the concept of need for cognition

We have just reduced the abstract concept *thirst* into observable behavior by measuring the amount of drinks people use to quench their thirst. Other abstract concepts such as need for cognition (the tendency to engage in and enjoy thinking [Cacioppo and Petty, 1982]) can be reduced to observable behavior and/or characteristics in a similar way. For instance, we would expect individuals with a high need for cognition to prefer complex to simple problems, to find satisfaction in deliberating hard and for long hours, and to enjoy tasks that involve coming up with new solutions to problems (examples taken from Cacioppo and Petty, 1982). We may thus identify differences between individuals in need of cognition by measuring to what extent people prefer complex to simple problems, find satisfaction in deliberating hard and for long hours, and enjoy tasks that involve coming up with new solutions to problems.

In 1982, Cacioppo and Petty reported four studies to develop and validate a measurement scale to assess need for cognition. In a first study, a pool of 45 items that appeared relevant to need for cognition was generated (based on prior research) and administered to groups "known to differ in need for cognition". The results of this study revealed that the 45 items exhibited a high degree of interrelatedness and thus suggested that need for cognition is a *unidimensional* construct (that is, it does not have more than one main component or dimension; we will come back to this issue further on in this chapter). This finding was replicated in a second study. Two further studies (studies 3 and 4) were carried out to validate the findings of the first two studies. The outcome of this validation process was a valid and reliable need for cognition measure containing 34 items, such as "I would prefer complex to simple problems", "I find satisfaction in deliberating hard and for long hours", and "I really enjoy tasks that involve coming up with new solutions to problems".

Now do Exercise 6.1

## EXERCISE 6.1

a. Read the paper of Cacioppo and Petty (1982) and describe how the authors generated the pool of 45 scale items that appeared relevant to need for cognition.

**b.** Why do we need 34 items to measure "need for cognition"? Why do three or four items not suffice?

## Operationalization: dimensions and elements

The examples of thirst and need for cognition illustrate how abstract concepts are operationalized by using observable and measurable elements, such as the amount of drinks people use to quench their thirst, and the extent to which people prefer complex to simple problems. You may have noticed that whereas only one item is needed to measure thirst ("how many drinks did you use to quench your thirst?"), 34 items are needed to measure need for cognition. These 34 items are needed because if we used fewer than these 34 items, our measurement scale would probably not represent the entire domain or universe of need for cognition; in other words, our measure would probably not include an adequate and representative set of items. As a consequence, our measure would not be valid.

A valid measure of need for cognition thus contains 34 items even though need for cognition is a unidimensional construct. An example of a construct with more than one dimension is aggression. Aggression has at least two dimensions: verbal aggression and physical aggression. That is, aggression might include behavior such as shouting and swearing at a person (verbal aggression), but also throwing objects, hitting a wall, and physically hurting others (physical aggresson). A valid measurement scale of aggression would have to include items that measure verbal aggression and items that measure physical aggression. A measurement scale that only included items that measure physical aggression or that only included verbal aggression items would not be valid if our aim was to measure aggression. Thus, a valid measurement scale includes quantitatively measurable questions or items that adequately represent the domain or universe of the construct; if the construct has more than one domain or dimension, we have to make sure that questions or items that adequately represent these domains or dimensions are included in our measure.

Now do Exercise 6.2

## EXERCISE 6.2

Try to come up with two unidimensional and two multidimensional abstract concepts. Explain why these concepts have either one or more than one dimension.

## Operationalizing the (multidimensional) concept of achievement motivation

Suppose that we are interested in establishing a relationship between gender and achievement motivation. To test this relationship we will have to measure both gender and achievement motivation. At this point, you will probably understand that whereas measuring gender will not cause any problems, measuring achievement motivation probably will, because the latter construct is abstract and subjective in nature. For this reason we must infer achievement motivation by measuring behavioral dimensions, facets, or characteristics we would expect to find in people with high achievement motivation. Indeed, without measuring these dimensions, facets, or characteristics we will not be able to arrive at bottom-line statements about the relationship between gender and achievement motivation.

After we have defined the construct, the next step in the process of measuring abstract constructs such as achievement motivation is to go through the literature to find out whether there are any existing measures of the concept. Both scientific journals and "scale handbooks" are important sources of existing measures. As a rule, empirical articles published in academic journals provide a detailed description of how specific constructs were measured; information is often provided on what measures were used, when and how these measures were developed, by whom, and for how long they have been in use. Scale handbooks are also a useful source of existing measurement scales. Scale handbooks, such as the *Marketing Scales Handbook* by Bruner, Hensel, and James (2005) or the *Handbook of Organizational Measurement* by Price and Mueller (1986), provide an exhaustive overview of measurement scales that have appeared in the academic literature. These handbooks help you to determine whether a measurement scale exists and, if more than one measurement scale exists, to make a logical selection between available measures. The use of existing measurement scales has several advantages. First, it saves you a lot of time and energy. Second, it allows you to verify the findings of others and to build on the work of others (this is very important in scientific research but impossible if you use measures that differ from those that our predecessors have used!). Hence, if you want to measure something, see if it has been measured before and then use this measure (adapt it to your specific needs whenever this is needed). Make sure that you document the use of existing measurement scales properly.

## EXAMPLE

### Documenting the use of existing measurement scales

Service encounter dissatisfaction and anger were measured with seven-point, multi-item rating scales adapted from previous studies (Crosby and Stephens, 1987; Izard, 1977). These scales were introduced with the following question: "How did you feel about your service experience on this particular occasion?" A seven-point, multi-item measurement scale adapted from prior research (Nasr-Bechwati and Morrin, 2003) was used to measure the desire to get even with the service provider. Scales measuring customers' behavioral intentions closely followed existing scales measuring reactions to service failure. Intentions to engage in negative word of mouth, complaint intentions (Zeithaml, Berry, and Parasuraman, 1996), and switching intentions (Oliver, 1996) were assessed by having participants indicate the degree to which they were inclined to such behavior on a seven-point rating scale, anchored by "not at all" and "very much."

There are several measures of achievement motivation available from the literature (Amabile, Hill, Hennessey, and Tighe, 1994; Gordon, 1973; Heggestad and Kanfer, 1999; Super, 1970). But what if there were no existing measure available? In such a case, we would have to develop a measure ourselves; this means that we would have to break down the concept "achievement motivation" into observable behavior or characteristics, as detailed next.

## Dimensions and elements of achievement motivation

Let us try to operationalize "achievement motivation", a concept of interest to educators, managers, and students alike. What behavioral dimensions, facets, or characteristics would we expect to find in people with high achievement motivation? They would probably have the following five typical broad characteristics, which we will call dimensions:

1. They would be driven by work; that is, they would be working almost round the clock in order to derive the satisfaction of having "achieved and accomplished."
2. Many of them would generally be in no mood to relax and direct their attention to anything other than work-related activity.
3. Because they want always to be achieving and accomplishing, they would prefer to work on their own rather than with others.
4. With mind and heart set on accomplishment and achievement, they would rather engage in challenging jobs than easy, hum-drum ones. However, they would not want to take on excessively challenging jobs because the expectation and probability of accomplishment and achievement in such jobs would not be very high.
5. They would be yearning to know how they are progressing in their jobs as they go along. That is, they would like to get frequent feedback in direct and subtle ways from their superiors, colleagues, and on occasion even their subordinates, to know how they are progressing.

Thus, we would expect those with high achievement motivation to drive themselves hard at work, find it difficult to relax, prefer to work alone, engage in challenging, but not too challenging jobs, and seek feedback. Although breaking the concept into these five dimensions has somewhat reduced its level of abstraction, we have still not operationalized the concept into measurable elements of behavior. This could be done by examining each of the five dimensions and breaking each further into its elements, thus delineating the actual patterns of behavior that would be exhibited. These should somehow be quantitatively measurable so that we can distinguish those who have high motivation from those with less. Let us see how this can be done.

### Elements of dimension 1

It is possible to describe the behavior of a person who is driven by work. Such a person will (1) be at work all the time, (2) be reluctant to take time off from work, and (3) persevere even in the face of some setbacks. These types of behavior lend themselves to measurement. For instance, we can count the number of hours employees engage themselves in work-related activities during work hours, beyond working hours at the workplace, and at home, where they are likely to pursue their unfinished assignments. Thus, the number of hours put in by them on their work is an index of the extent to which work "drives" them.

Next, keeping track of how frequently people persevere with their job despite failures is a reflection of how persevering they are in achieving their goals. A student who drops out of school due to failure to pass the first exam can by no means be deemed to be a highly persevering, achievement-oriented individual. However, a student who, despite getting D grades on three quizzes, toils day and night unceasingly in order to understand and master a course he considers difficult, is exhibiting persevering and achievement-oriented behavior. Achievement-motivated individuals do not usually want to give up on their tasks even when confronted by initial failures. Perseverance urges them to continue. Hence, a measure of perseverance could be obtained by the number of setbacks people experience on the task and yet continue to work, undaunted by failures. For example, an accountant might find that she is unable to balance the books. She spends an hour trying to detect the error, fails to do so, gives up, and leaves the workplace. Another employee in the same position stays patiently on the job, discovers the error, and balances the books, spending the entire evening in the process. In this case it is easy to tell which of the two is the more persevering by merely observing them.

Finally, in order to measure reluctance to take time off, we need only know how frequently people take time off from their jobs, and for what reasons. If an employee is found to have taken seven days off during the previous six months to watch football games, attend an out-of-town circus, and visit friends, we can conclude that the individual probably would not hesitate in taking time away from the job. However, if an individual has not been absent even a single day during the past 15 months, and has not missed work even when slightly indisposed, it is evident that he is too dedicated to work to take time off from the job.

Thus, if we can measure how many hours per week individuals spend on work-related activities, how persevering they are in completing their daily tasks, and how frequently and for what reasons they take time off from their jobs, we will have a measure of the extent to which employees are driven by work. This variable, when thus measured, would place individuals on a continuum ranging from those who are least driven by work, to those whose very life is work. This, then, would give some indication of the extent of their achievement motivation.

Figure 6.2 schematically outlines the dimensions (the several facets or main characteristics) and the elements (representative behaviors) for the concept of achievement motivation. Frequent reference to this figure will help you follow the ensuing discussions.

### Elements of dimension 2

The degree of unwillingness to relax can be measured by asking persons such questions as:

1. How often do you think about work while you are away from the workplace?
2. What are your hobbies?
3. How do you spend your time when you are away from the workplace?

Those who are able to relax would indicate that they do not generally think about work or the workplace while at home, that they spend time on hobbies, engage in leisure-time activities, and spend their waking hours with the family or in other social or cultural activities.

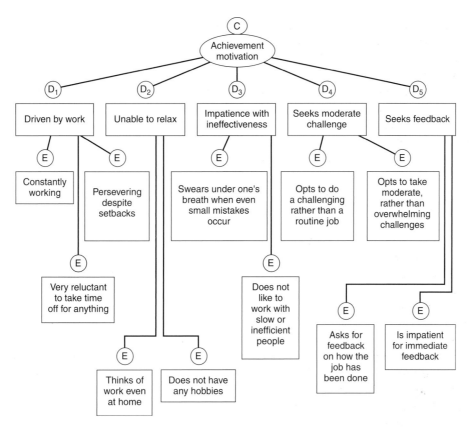

**Figure 6.2:** Dimensions (D) and elements (E) of the concept (C) "achievement motivation".

Thus, we can place employees on a continuum ranging from those who relax very well to those who relax very little. This dimension also then becomes measurable.

### Elements of dimension 3

Individuals with high achievement motivation have no patience with ineffective people and are reluctant to work with others. Whereas achievement-motivated persons in the organization may rank very high on these behavioral predispositions, there may be others who are not highly achievement motivated. The latter may not at all mind ineffectiveness in either themselves or others, and may be quite willing to work with almost anybody. Thus, impatience with ineffectiveness can also be measured by observing behavior.

### Elements of dimension 4

A measure of how excited people are at seeking challenging jobs can be had by asking employees what kinds of jobs they prefer. A number of different job descriptions could be presented – some jobs entailing stereotyped work of a routine nature, and others with gradations of challenge built into them. Employee preferences for different types of jobs could then be placed on a continuum ranging from those who prefer fairly routine jobs to those who prefer jobs with a progressive increase in challenge. Those opting for medium degrees of challenge are likely to be more achievement motivated than those who opt for either lower or higher degrees of challenge. Achievement-oriented individuals tend to be realistic and choose jobs that are reasonably challenging and within reach of accomplishment. Heedless and overconfident persons would perhaps choose the highly challenging jobs where the success is slow in coming, oblivious to whether or not the end results will be achieved. Those who are low in achievement motivation would perhaps choose the more routine jobs. Thus, those seeking moderate challenges can also be identified.

### Elements of dimension 5

Those who desire feedback seek it from their superiors, co-workers, and sometimes even from their subordinates. They want to know others' opinions on how well they are performing. Feedback, both positive and negative, indicates to them how much they are achieving and accomplishing. If they receive messages suggesting a need for improvement, they will act on them. Hence, they constantly seek feedback from several sources. By keeping track of how often individuals seek feedback from others during a certain period of time – say, over several months – employees can again be placed on a continuum ranging from those who seek extensive feedback from all sources to those who never seek any feedback from anyone at any time.

Having thus operationalized the concept of achievement motivation by reducing its level of abstraction to observable behaviors, it is possible to develop a good measure to tap the concept of achievement motivation. Its usefulness is that others could use the same measure, thus ensuring replicability. It should, however, be recognized, that any operationalization is likely to (1) exclude some of the important dimensions and elements arising from failure to recognize or conceptualize them, and (2) include certain irrelevant features, mistakenly thought to be relevant. You will recall that we earlier pointed out that management research cannot be 100% scientific because we do not have the "perfect" measuring instruments.

Operationalizing the concept, nevertheless, is the best way to measure it. However, actually observing and counting the number of times individuals behave in particular ways, even if practical, would be too laborious and time consuming. So, instead of actually observing the behavior of individuals, we could ask them to report their own behavior patterns by asking them appropriate questions, which they could respond to on some (rating) scale that we provide. In the following example we will look at the type of questions that may be asked to tap achievement motivation.

### EXAMPLE

Answers to the following questions from respondents would be one way of tapping the level of achievement motivation.

1. To what extent would you say you push yourself to get the job done on time?
2. How difficult do you find it to continue to do your work in the face of initial failure or discouraging results?
3. How often do you neglect personal matters because you are preoccupied with your job?
4. How frequently do you think of your work when you are at home?
5. To what extent do you engage yourself in hobbies?
6. How disappointed would you feel if you did not reach the goals you had set for yourself?
7. How much do you concentrate on achieving your goals?
8. How annoyed do you get when you make mistakes?
9. To what extent would you prefer to work with a friendly but incompetent colleague, rather than a difficult but competent one?
10. To what extent would you prefer to work by yourself rather than with others?
11. To what extent would you prefer a job that is difficult but challenging, to one that is easy and routine?
12. To what extent would you prefer to take on extremely difficult assignments rather than moderately challenging ones?
13. During the past three months, how often have you sought feedback from your superiors on how well you are performing your job?
14. How often have you tried to obtain feedback on your performance from your co-workers during the past three months?
15. How often during the past three months have you checked with your subordinates that what you are doing is not getting in the way of their efficient performance?
16. To what extent would it frustrate you if people did not give you feedback on how you are progressing?

The foregoing illustrates a possible way to measure variables relating to the subjective domain of people's attitudes, feelings, and perceptions by first operationalizing the concept. Operationalization consists of the reduction of the concept from its level of abstraction, by breaking it into its dimensions and elements, as discussed. By tapping the behaviors associated with a concept, we can measure the variable. Of course, the questions will ask for responses on some scale attached to them (such as "very little" to "very much"), which we will discuss in the next chapter.

## What operationalization is not

Just as it is important to understand what operationalization is, it is equally important to remember what it is not. An operationalization does not describe the correlates of the concept. For example, success in performance cannot be a dimension of achievement motivation, even though a motivated person is likely to meet with it in large measure. Thus, achievement motivation and performance and/or success may be highly correlated, but we cannot measure an individual's level of motivation through success and perform-ance. Performance and success may have been made possible as a consequence of achieve-ment motivation, but in and of themselves, the two are not measures of it. To elaborate, a person with high achievement motivation might have failed for some reason, perhaps beyond her control, to perform the job successfully. Thus, if we judge the achievement motivation of this person with performance as the yardstick, we will have measured the wrong concept. Instead of measuring achievement motivation – our variable of interest – we will have measured performance, another variable we did not intend to measure nor were interested in.

Thus, it is clear that operationalizing a concept does not consist of delineating the reasons, antecedents, consequences, or correlates of the concept. Rather, it describes its observable characteristics in order to be able to measure the concept. It is important to remember this because if we either operationalize the concepts incorrectly or confuse them with other concepts, then we will not have valid measures. This means that we will not have "good" data, and our research will not be scientific.

## Review of operationalization

We have thus far examined how to operationally define concepts and to frame and ask questions that are likely to measure the concepts. Operationalizations are necessary to measure abstract concepts such as those that usually fall into the subjective areas of feelings and attitudes. More objective variables such as age or educational level are easily measured through simple, straightforward questions and do not have to be operationalized. Luckily, measures for many concepts that are relevant in the organizational context have already been developed by researchers. While you review the literature in a given area, you might want to particularly note the reference that discusses the instrument used to tap the concept in the study, and read it. The article will tell you when the measure was developed, by whom, and for how long it has been in use. Only a well-developed instrument, which has been operationalized with care, will be accepted and frequently used by other researchers.

Now do Exercises 6.3 and 6.4

## EXERCISE 6.3

Provide an operational definition of the concept of "service quality" and develop questions that would measure service quality.

## EXERCISE 6.4

Compare your service quality measure to the measure of Zeithaml, Berry and Para-suraman (1996) presented in the *Journal of Retailing*.

**a.** How does your measure differ from this measure in terms of dimensions and elements?

**b.** Would you prefer using your own measure or the measure of Zeithaml, Berry and Parasuraman? Why?

# International dimensions of operationalization

In conducting transnational research, it is important to remember that certain variables have different meanings and connotations in different cultures. For instance, the term "love" is subject to several interpretations in different cultures and has at least 20 different interpretations in some countries. Likewise, the concept "knowledge" is equated with "jnana" in some Eastern cultures and construed as "realization of the Almighty." Thus, it is wise for researchers who hail from a country speaking a different language to recruit the help of local scholars to operationalize certain concepts while engaging in cross-cultural research.

## SUMMARY

In this chapter, we saw that any concept can be broken down into dimensions and elements for measurement through a set of items. We also discussed briefly the nuances in operational definition in cross-cultural research and were alerted to the dangers of operationalizing certain concepts in other cultures that might have different connotations.

## DISCUSSION QUESTIONS

1. Define measurement.
2. Explain why it is impossible to measure an object.
3. Provide (relevant) measurable attributes for the following objects:
   **a.** a restaurant
   **b.** a businessperson
   **c.** a consumer
   **d.** a car
   **e.** a tennis racket
   **f.** a strategic business unit
4. Why is it wrong to use correlates of a concept to measure that concept?

5. What is meant by operational definition, when is it necessary, and why is it necessary?
6. Operationalize the following:
   a. Customer loyalty
   b. Price consciousness
   c. Career success
7. Is it useful to draw on existing measures to measure abstract and subjective constructs such as customer loyalty? Why (not)?

# CHAPTER 7

## Measurement: scaling, reliability, validity

## Topics discussed

- The four types of scales
  - Nominal
  - Ordinal
  - Interval
  - Ratio
- Scaling techniques frequently used
  - Rating scales
    - Dichotomous scale
    - Category scale
    - Likert scale
    - Semantic differential scale
    - Numerical scales
    - Itemized rating scale
    - Fixed or constant sum rating scale
    - Stapel scale
    - Graphic rating scale
    - Consensus scale
  - Ranking scales
    - Paired comparisons
    - Forced choice
    - Comparative scale
- International dimensions of scaling

- Goodness of measures
  - Stability
    - Test–retest reliability
    - Parallel-form reliability
  - Internal consistency
    - Split-half reliability
    - Interitem consistency reliability
  - Validity
  - Content validity
    - Face validity
  - Criterion-related validity
    - Concurrent validity
    - Predictive validity
  - Construct validity

## CHAPTER OBJECTIVES

After completing Chapter 7, you should:

1. Know the characteristics and power of the four types of scales – nominal, ordinal, interval, and ratio.
2. Know how and when to use the different forms of rating scales and ranking scales.
3. Be able to explain stability and consistency and how they are established.
4. Be able to explain the difference between reflective and formative scales.
5. Be conversant with the different forms of validity.
6. Be able to discuss what "goodness" of measures means, and why it is necessary to establish it in research.

Now that we have learned how to operationally define (or operationalize) dimensions and elements of a variable, we need to measure them in some manner. We will examine in this chapter the types of scales that can be applied to measure different variables and subsequently see how we actually apply them. There are two main categories of attitudinal scales (not to be confused with the four different types of scales, discussed first in this chapter) – the rating scale and the ranking scale. **Rating scales** have several response categories and are used to elicit responses with regard to the object, event, or person studied. **Ranking scales**, on the other hand, make comparisons between or among objects, events, or persons and elicit the preferred choices and ranking among them. Both scales are discussed below.

# Scales

A **scale** is a tool or mechanism by which individuals are distinguished as to how they differ from one another on the variables of interest to our study. The scale or tool may be a gross one in the sense that it only broadly categorizes individuals on certain variables, or it may be a fine-tuned tool that differentiates individuals on the variables with varying degrees of sophistication.

There are four basic types of scales: nominal, ordinal, interval, and ratio. The degree of sophistication to which the scales are fine-tuned increases progressively as we move from the nominal to the ratio scale. That is, information on the variables can be obtained in greater detail when we employ an interval or a ratio scale than the other two scales. As the calibration or fine-tuning of the scale increases in sophistication, so does the power of the scale. With more powerful scales, increasingly sophisticated data analyses can be performed, which, in turn, means that more meaningful answers can be found to our research questions. However, certain variables lend themselves with greater ease to more powerful scaling than others. Let us now examine each of these four scales.

## Nominal scale

A **nominal scale** is one that allows the researcher to assign subjects to certain categories or groups. For example, with respect to the variable of gender, respondents can be grouped into two categories – male and female. These two groups can be assigned code numbers 1 and 2. These numbers serve as simple and convenient category labels with no intrinsic value, other than to assign respondents to one of two nonoverlapping, or mutually exclusive, categories. Note that the categories are also collectively exhaustive. In other words, there is no third category into which respondents would normally fall. Thus, nominal scales categorize individuals or objects into mutually exclusive and collectively exhaustive groups. The information that can be generated from nominal scaling is the calculation of the percentage (or frequency) of males and females in our sample of respondents. For example, if we had interviewed 200 people, and assigned code number 1 to all male respondents and number 2 to all female respondents, then computer analysis of the data at the end of the survey may show that 98 of the respondents are men and 102 are women. This frequency distribution tells us that 49% of the survey's respondents are men and 51% women. Other than this marginal information, such scaling tells us nothing more about the two groups. Thus, the nominal scale gives some basic, categorical, gross information.

## EXAMPLE

Let us take a look at another variable that lends itself to nominal scaling – the nationality of individuals. We could nominally scale this variable in the following mutually exclusive and collectively exhaustive categories.

| | |
|---|---|
| American | Japanese |
| Australian | Polish |
| Chinese | Russian |
| German | Swiss |
| Indian | Zambian |
| Other | |

Note that every respondent has to fit into one of the above eleven categories and that the scale allows computation of the numbers and percentages of respondents that fit into them.

Now do Exercise 7.1

### EXERCISE 7.1

Suggest two variables that would be natural candidates for nominal scales, and set up mutually exclusive and collectively exhaustive categories for each.

## Ordinal scale

An **ordinal scale** not only categorizes the variables in such a way as to denote differences among the various categories, it also rank-orders the categories in some meaningful way. With any variable for which the categories are to be ordered according to some preference, the ordinal scale would be used. The preference would be ranked (e.g., from best to worst; first to last) and numbered 1, 2, and so on. For example, respondents might be asked to indicate their preferences by ranking the importance they attach to five distinct characteristics in a job that the researcher might be interested in studying. Such a question might take the form shown in the following example.

The ordinal scale helps the researcher to determine the percentage of respondents who consider interaction with others as most important, those who consider using a number of different skills as most important, and so on. Such knowledge might help in designing jobs that are seen as most enriched by the majority of the employees.

We can now see that the ordinal scale provides more information than the nominal scale. The ordinal scale goes beyond differentiating the categories to providing information on how respondents distinguish them by rank-ordering them. Note, however, that the ordinal scale does not give any indication of the magnitude of the differences among the ranks. For instance, in the job characteristics example, the first-ranked job characteristic might be only marginally preferred over the second-ranked characteristic, whereas the characteristic that is ranked third might be preferred in a much larger degree than the one ranked fourth. Thus, in ordinal

## EXAMPLE

Rank the following five characteristics in a job in terms of how important they are for you. You should rank the most important item as 1, the next in importance as 2, and so on, until you have ranked each of them 1, 2, 3, 4, or 5.

| Job characteristic | Ranking of importance |
|---|---|
| The opportunity provided by the job to: | |
| Interact with others | — |
| Use a number of different skills. | — |
| Complete a whole task from beginning to end. | — |
| Serve others. | — |
| Work independently. | — |

scaling, even though differences in the ranking of objects, persons, or events investigated are clearly known, we do not know their magnitude. This deficiency is overcome by interval scaling, which is discussed next.

Now do Exercise 7.2

## EXERCISE 7.2

Develop an ordinal scale for consumer preferences for different brands of beer.

## Interval scale

An interval scale allows us to perform certain arithmetical operations on the data collected from the respondents. Whereas the nominal scale allows us only to qualitatively distinguish groups by categorizing them into mutually exclusive and collectively exhaustive sets, and the ordinal scale to rank-order the preferences, the interval scale lets us measure the distance between any two points on the scale. This helps us to compute the means and the standard deviations of the responses on the variables. In other words, the interval scale not only groups individuals according to certain categories and taps the order of these groups, it also measures the magnitude of the differences in the preferences among the individuals. If, for instance, employees think that (1) it is more important for them to have a variety of skills in their jobs than to complete a task from beginning to end, and (2) it is more important for them to serve people than to work independently on the job, then the interval scale would indicate whether the first preference is to the same extent, a lesser extent, or a greater extent than the second. This can be done by changing the scale from the ranking type to make it appear as if there are several points on a scale that represent the extent or magnitude of the importance of each of the five job characteristics. Such a scale could be indicated for the job design case as shown in the following example.

## EXAMPLE

Indicate the extent to which you agree with the following statements as they relate to your job, by circling the appropriate number against each, using the scale given below.

| Strongly Disagree | Disagree | Neither Agree Nor Disagree | Agree | Strongly Agree |
|---|---|---|---|---|
| 1 | 2 | 3 | 4 | 5 |

The following opportunities offered by the job are very important to me:

| | | | | |
|---|---|---|---|---|
| a. Interacting with others | 1 | 2 | 3 | 4 | 5 |
| b. Using a number of different skills | 1 | 2 | 3 | 4 | 5 |
| c. Completing a task from beginning to end | 1 | 2 | 3 | 4 | 5 |
| d. Serving others | 1 | 2 | 3 | 4 | 5 |
| e. Working independently | 1 | 2 | 3 | 4 | 5 |

Let us illustrate how the interval scale establishes the equality of the magnitude of differences in the scale points. Let us suppose that employees circle the numbers 3, 1, 2, 4, and 5 for the five items in the above example. They then indicate to us that the extent of their preference for skill utilization over doing the task from beginning to end is the same as the extent of their preference for serving customers over working independently. That is, the magnitude of difference represented by the space between points 1 and 2 on the scale is the same as the magnitude of difference represented by the space between points 4 and 5, or between any other two points. Any number can be added to or subtracted from the numbers on the scale, still retaining the magnitude of the difference. For instance, if we add 6 to all five points on the scale, the interval scale will have the numbers 7 to 11 (instead of 1 to 5). The magnitude of the difference between 7 and 8 is still the same as the magnitude of the difference between 9 and 10. Thus, the origin, or the starting point, may be any arbitrary number. The clinical thermometer is a good example of an interval-scaled instrument; it has an arbitrary origin and the magnitude of the difference between 98.6 degrees (supposed to be the normal body temperature) and 99.6 degrees is the same as the magnitude of the difference between 104 and 105 degrees. Note, however, that one may not be seriously concerned if one's temperature rises from 98.6 to 99.6, but one is likely to be so when the temperature goes up from 104 to 105 degrees!

The interval scale, then, taps the differences, the order, and the equality of the magnitude of the differences in the variable. As such, it is a more powerful scale than the nominal and ordinal scales, and has for its measure of central tendency the arithmetic mean. Its measures of dispersion are the range, the standard deviation, and the variance.

Now do Exercises 7.3 and 7.4

## EXERCISE 7.3

Measure any three variables on an interval scale.

## EXERCISE 7.4

Mention one variable for each of the four scales in the context of a market survey, and explain how or why it would fit into the scale.

## Ratio scale

The ratio scale overcomes the disadvantage of the arbitrary origin point of the interval scale, in that it has an absolute (in contrast to an arbitrary) zero point, which is a meaningful measurement point. Thus, the **ratio scale** not only measures the magnitude of the differences between points on the scale but also taps the proportions in the differences. It is the most powerful of the four scales because it has a unique zero origin (not an arbitrary origin) and subsumes all the properties of the other three scales. The weighing balance is a good example of a ratio scale. It has an absolute (and not arbitrary) zero origin calibrated on it, which allows us to calculate the ratio of the weights of two individuals. For instance, a person weighing 250 pounds is twice as heavy as one who weighs 125 pounds. Note that multiplying or dividing both of these numbers (250 and 125) by any given number will preserve the ratio of 2:1. The measure of central tendency of the ratio scale may be either the arithmetic or the geometric mean and the measure of dispersion may be either the standard deviation, or variance, or the coefficient of variation. Some examples of ratio scales are those pertaining to actual age, income, and the number of organizations individuals have worked for.

The properties of the scales, as fine-tuning is increasingly achieved, are summarized in Table 7.1. We may also see from the table how the power of the statistic increases as we move away from the nominal scale (where we group subjects or items under some categories), to the ordinal scale (where we rank-order the categories), to the interval scale (where we tap the magnitude of the differences), to the ratio scale (which allows us to measure the proportion of the differences).

You must have surmised by now that some variables, such as gender, can be measured only on the nominal scale, while others, such as temperature, can be measured on a nominal

TABLE 7.1　Properties of the four scales.

| Scale | Highlights | | | | Measures of central tendency | Measures of dispersion | Some tests of significance |
|---|---|---|---|---|---|---|---|
| | Difference | Order | Distance | Unique origin | | | |
| Nominal | Yes | No | No | No | Mode | — | $\chi^2$ |
| Ordinal | Yes | Yes | No | No | Median | Semi-interquartile range | Rank-order correlations |
| Interval | Yes | Yes | Yes | No | Arithmetic mean | Standard deviation, variance, coefficient of variation | $t, F$ |
| Ratio | Yes | Yes | Yes | Yes | Arithmetic or geometric mean | Standard deviation or variance or coefficient of variation | $t, F$ |

*Note:* The interval scale has 1 as an arbitrary starting point. The ratio scale has the natural origin 0, which is meaningful.

scale (high/low), or ordinal scale (hot/medium/low), or the interval scale through the thermometer. Whenever it is possible to use a more powerful scale, it is wise to do so.

Now that we have looked at the four types of scales, let us see, through the following examples, when and how they should be used.

## EXAMPLE

### Use of the nominal scale

The nominal scale is always used for obtaining personal data such as gender or department in which one works, where grouping of individuals or objects is useful, as shown below.

| 1. Your gender | 2. Your department |
|---|---|
| ___ Male | ___ Production |

___ Female

___ Sales
___ Accounting
___ Finance
___ Personnel
___ R & D
___ Other (specify)

## Use of the ordinal scale

The ordinal scale is used to rank the preferences or usage of various brands of a product by individuals and to rank-order individuals, objects, or events, as per the examples below.

1.  Rank the following personal computers with respect to their usage in your office, assigning the number 1 to the most used system, 2 to the next most used, and so on. If a particular system is not used at all in your office, put a 0 next to it.

    ___ Apple          ___ Hewlett-Packard
    ___ Compaq         ___ IBM
    ___ Comp USA       ___ Packard Bell
    ___ Dell Computer  ___ Sony
    ___ Gateway        ___ Toshiba
                       ___ Other (Specify)

2.  Rank the cities listed below in the order that you consider suitable for opening a new plant. The city considered the most suitable should be ranked 1, the next 2, and so on.

    ___ Cincinnati   ___ Milwaukee
    ___ Detroit      ___ Pittsburgh
    ___ Des Moines   ___ St Louis
    ___ Houston

## Use of the interval scale

The interval scale is used when responses to various items that measure a variable can be tapped on a five-point (or seven-point or any other number of points) scale, which can thereafter be summed across the items. See the example below of a Likert scale.

Using the scale below, please indicate your response to each of the items that follow, by circling the number that best describes your feeling.

|  | Strongly Disagree | Disagree | Neither Agree Nor Disagree | Agree | Strongly Agree |
|---|:---:|:---:|:---:|:---:|:---:|
|  | 1 | 2 | 3 | 4 | 5 |
| 1. My job offers me a chance to test myself and my abilities. | 1 | 2 | 3 | 4 | 5 |
| 2. Mastering this job meant a lot to me. | 1 | 2 | 3 | 4 | 5 |
| 3. Doing this job well is a reward in itself. | 1 | 2 | 3 | 4 | 5 |
| 4. Considering the time spent on the job, I feel thoroughly familiar with my tasks and responsibilities. | 1 | 2 | 3 | 4 | 5 |

## Use of the ratio scale

Ratio scales are usually used in organizational research when exact numbers on objective (as opposed to subjective) factors are called for, as in the following questions:

1. How many other organizations did you work for before joining this system? ___
2. Please indicate the number of children you have in each of the following categories:

> ___ below 3 years of age
> ___ between 3 and 6
> ___ over 6 years but under 12
> ___ 12 years and over

3. How many retail outlets do you operate? ___

The responses to the questions could range from 0 to any reasonable figure.

## Review of scales

The four scales that can be applied to the measurement of variables are the nominal, ordinal, interval, and ratio scales. The nominal scale highlights the differences by classifying objects or persons into groups, and provides the least amount of information on the variable. The ordinal scale provides some additional information by rank-ordering the categories of the nominal scale. The interval scale not only ranks, but also provides us with information on the magnitude of the differences in the variable. The ratio scale indicates not only the magnitude of the differences but also their proportion. Multiplication or division would preserve these ratios. As we move from the nominal to the ratio scale, we obtain progressively increasing precision in quantifying the data, and greater flexibility in using more powerful statistical tests. Hence, whenever possible and appropriate, a more powerful rather than a less powerful scale should be used to measure the variables of interest.

# Rating scales

The following rating scales are often used in organizational research:

- Dichotomous scale
- Category scale
- Semantic differential scale ✓
- Numerical scale
- Itemized rating scale
- Likert scale ✓
- Fixed or constant sum rating scale
- Stapel scale ✓
- Graphic rating scale
- Consensus scale

Other scales, such as the Thurstone Equal Appearing Interval Scale, and the multi-dimensional scale, are less frequently used. We will briefly describe each of the above attitudinal scales.

### Dichotomous scale

The **dichotomous scale** is used to elicit a Yes or No answer, as in the example below. Note that a nominal scale is used to elicit the response.

Do you own a car?           Yes           No

### Category scale

The **category scale** uses multiple items to elicit a single response as per the following example. This also uses the nominal scale.

Where in London do you reside?

___ East London
___ South London
___ West London
___ North London
___ Outskirts

## Semantic differential scale

Several bipolar attributes are identified at the extremes of the scale, and respondents are asked to indicate their attitudes, on what may be called a semantic space, toward a particular individual, object, or event on each of the attributes. The bipolar adjectives used might employ such terms as Good–Bad; Strong–Weak; Hot–Cold. The **semantic differential scale** is used to assess respondents' attitudes toward a particular brand, advertisement, object, or individual. The responses can be plotted to obtain a good idea of their perceptions. This is treated as an interval scale. An example of the semantic differential scale follows.

| Responsive | — — — — — — | Unresponsive |
| Beautiful | — — — — — — | Ugly |
| Courageous | — — — — — — | Timid |

## Numerical scale

The **numerical scale** is similar to the semantic differential scale, with the difference that numbers on a five-point or seven-point scale are provided, with bipolar adjectives at both ends, as illustrated below. This is also an interval scale.

How pleased are you with your new estate agent?

Extremely Pleased        7 6 5 4 3 2 1        Extremely Displeased

## Itemized rating scale

A five-point or seven-point scale with anchors, as needed, is provided for each item and the respondent states the appropriate number on the side of each item, or circles the relevant number against each item, as per the examples that follow. The responses to the items are then summed. This uses an interval scale.

### EXAMPLE

Respond to each item using the scale below, and indicate your response number on the line by each item.

| 1 | 2 | 3<br>Neither Unlikely | 4 | 5 |
|---|---|---|---|---|
| Very Unlikely | Unlikely | Nor Likely | Likely | Very Likely |

| 1 | I will be changing my job within the next 12 months. | — |
|---|---|---|
| 2 | I will take on new assignments in the near future. | — |
| 3 | It is possible that I will be out of this organization within the next 12 months. | — |

Note that the above is a balanced rating scale with a neutral point.

| | Not at All<br>Interested<br>1 | Somewhat<br>Interested<br>2 | Moderately<br>Interested<br>3 | Very<br>Much<br>Interested<br>4 |
|---|---|---|---|---|
| How would you rate your interest in changing current organizational policies? | 1 | 2 | 3 | 4 |

This is an unbalanced rating scale which does not have a neutral point.

The itemized rating scale provides the flexibility to use as many points in the scale as considered necessary (4, 5, 7, 9, or whatever), and it is also possible to use different anchors (e.g., Very Unimportant to Very Important; Extremely Low to Extremely High). When a neutral point is provided, it is a balanced rating scale, and when it is not, it is an **unbalanced rating scale**.

Research indicates that a five-point scale is just as good as any, and that an increase from five to seven or nine points on a rating scale does not improve the reliability of the ratings (Elmore and Beggs, 1975).

The itemized rating scale is frequently used in business research, since it adapts itself to the number of points the researcher wishes to use, as well as the nomenclature of the anchors, as is considered necessary to accommodate the needs of the researcher for tapping the variable.

## Likert scale

The Likert scale is designed to examine how strongly subjects agree or disagree with statements on a five-point scale with the following anchors:

| Strongly Disagree | Disagree | Neither Agree Nor Disagree | Agree | Strongly Agree |
|:-:|:-:|:-:|:-:|:-:|
| 1 | 2 | 3 | 4 | 5 |

The responses over a number of items tapping a particular concept or variable can be analyzed item by item, but it is also possible to calculate a total or summated score for each respondent by summing across items. The summated approach is widely used, and therefore the Likert scale is also referred to as a summated scale.

In the following example, the scores on the second item have to be reversed before calculating the summated score, because a high score on this item reflects an unfavorable attitude to work, whereas a high score on items 1 and 3 reflects a favorable attitude to work. This will lead to high total scores for respondents who have a favorable attitude toward work and to low total scores for respondents who have an unfavorable attitude towards work.

### EXAMPLE

Using the preceding Likert scale, state the extent to which you agree with each of the following statements:

| | | | | | |
|---|:-:|:-:|:-:|:-:|:-:|
| My work is very interesting | 1 | 2 | 3 | 4 | 5 |
| I am not engrossed in my work all day | 1 | 2 | 3 | 4 | 5 |
| Life without my work would be dull | 1 | 2 | 3 | 4 | 5 |

Whether a Likert scale is an ordinal or an interval scale is a subject of much debate. People who treat a Likert scale as an ordinal scale argue that one cannot assume that all pairs of adjacent levels are equidistant. Nonetheless, Likert scales are generally treated as interval scales.

## Fixed or constant sum scale

The respondents are here asked to distribute a given number of points across various items as per the example below. This is more in the nature of an ordinal scale.

## EXAMPLE

In choosing a toilet soap, indicate the importance you attach to each of the following five aspects by allotting points for each to total 100 in all.

| | |
|---|---|
| Fragrance | — |
| Color | — |
| Shape | — |
| Size | — |
| Texture of lather | — |
| Total points | 100 |

## Stapel scale

This scale simultaneously measures both the direction and intensity of the attitude toward the items under study. The characteristic of interest to the study is placed at the center with a numerical scale ranging, say, from $+3$ to $-3$, on either side of the item, as illustrated in the example below. This gives an idea of how close or distant the individual response to the stimulus is. Since this does not have an absolute zero point, this is an interval scale.

## EXAMPLE

State how you would rate your supervisor's abilities with respect to each of the characteristics mentioned below, by circling the appropriate number.

| | | |
|---|---|---|
| +3 | +3 | +3 |
| +2 | +2 | +2 |
| +1 | +1 | +1 |
| Adopting modern technology | Product innovation | Interpersonal skills |
| −1 | −1 | −1 |
| −2 | −2 | −2 |
| −3 | −3 | −3 |

## Graphic rating scale

A graphical representation helps the respondents to indicate on this scale their answers to a particular question by placing a mark at the appropriate point on the line, as in the following example. This is an ordinal scale, though the following example might make it look like an interval scale.

**EXAMPLE**

| On a scale of 1 to 10, how would you rate your supervisor? | | 10 Excellent<br>5 Adequate<br>1 Very bad |
|---|---|---|
| | On a scale of 1 to 10, how would you rate your supervisor      10 Excellent<br><br>5 Adequate<br><br>1 Very bad | |

This scale is easy to respond to. The brief descriptions on the scale points are meant to serve as a guide in locating the rating rather than representing discrete categories. The faces scale, which depicts faces ranging from smiling to sad (illustrated in Chapter 8), is also a graphic rating scale used to obtain responses regarding people's feelings with respect to some aspect – say, how they feel about their jobs.

## Consensus scale

Scales can also be developed by consensus, where a panel of judges selects certain items, which in its view measure the relevant concept. The items are chosen particularly based on their pertinence or relevance to the concept. Such a consensus scale is developed after the selected items have been examined and tested for their validity and reliability. One such consensus scale is the Thurstone Equal Appearing Interval Scale, where a concept is measured by a complex process followed by a panel of judges. Using a pile of cards containing several descriptions of the concept, a panel of judges offers inputs to indicate how close or not the statements are to the concept under study. The scale is then developed based on the consensus reached. However, this scale is rarely used for measuring organizational concepts because of the time necessary to develop it.

## Other scales

There are also some advanced scaling methods such as multidimensional scaling, where objects, people, or both, are visually scaled, and a conjoint analysis is performed. This provides a visual image of the relationships in space among the dimensions of a construct.

It should be noted that the Likert or some form of numerical scale is the one most frequently used to measure attitudes and behaviors in organizational research.

# Ranking scales

As already mentioned, **ranking scales** are used to tap preferences between two or among more objects or items (ordinal in nature). However, such ranking may not give definitive clues to some of the answers sought. For instance, let us say there are four product lines and the manager seeks information that would help decide which product line should get the most attention. Let us also assume that 35% of the respondents choose the first product, 25% the second, and 20% choose each of products three and four as being of importance to them. The manager cannot then conclude that the first product is the most preferred, since 65% of the respondents did not choose that product! Alternative methods used are paired comparisons, forced choice, and the comparative scale, which are discussed below.

## Paired comparison

The **paired comparison** scale is used when, among a small number of objects, respondents are asked to choose between two objects at a time. This helps to assess preferences. If, for instance, in the previous example, during the paired comparisons, respondents consistently show a preference for product one over products two, three, and four, the manager can reliably understand which product line demands his utmost attention. However, as the number of objects to be compared increases, so does the number of paired comparisons. The number of paired choices for $n$ objects will be $[(n)(n–1)/2]$. The greater the number of objects or stimuli, the greater the number of paired comparisons presented to the respondents, and the greater the respondent fatigue. Hence, paired comparison is a good method if the number of stimuli presented is small.

## Forced choice

The **forced choice** enables respondents to rank objects relative to one another, among the alternatives provided. This is easier for the respondents, particularly if the number of choices to be ranked is limited in number.

### EXAMPLE

Rank the following magazines that you would like to subscribe to in the order of preference, assigning 1 to the most preferred choice and 5 to the least preferred.

| | |
|---|---|
| *Fortune* | — |
| *Playboy* | — |
| *Time* | — |
| *People* | — |
| *Prevention* | — |

## Comparative scale

The **comparative scale** provides a benchmark or a point of reference to assess attitudes toward the current object, event, or situation under study. An example of the use of the comparative scale follows.

### EXAMPLE

In a volatile financial environment, compared to stocks, how wise or useful is it to invest in Treasury bonds? Please circle the appropriate response.

| More useful | | About the same | | Less useful |
|---|---|---|---|---|
| 1 | 2 | 3 | 4 | 5 |

In sum, nominal data lend themselves to dichotomous or category scales; ordinal data to any one of the ranking scales – paired comparison, forced choice, or comparative scales; and interval or interval-like data to the other rating scales, as seen from the various examples above. The semantic differential and the numerical scales are, strictly speaking, not interval scales, though they are often treated as such in data analysis.

Rating scales are used to measure most behavioral concepts. Ranking scales are used to make comparisons or rank the variables that have been tapped on a nominal scale.

# International dimensions of scaling

Apart from sensitivity to operational definition of concepts in other cultures, the issue of scaling also needs to be addressed in cross-cultural research. Different cultures react differently to issues of scaling. For instance, a five-point or a seven-point scale may make no difference in the United States, but could in the responses of subjects in other countries (see Sekaran and Martin, 1982; Sekaran and Trafton, 1978). Barry (1969), for instance, found that in some countries, a seven-point scale is more sensitive than a four-point scale in eliciting unbiased responses.

Recent research has shown that people from different countries differ in both their tendency to use the extremes of the rating scale (for instance 1 and 5 or 1 and 7) and to respond in a socially desirable way (De Jong, 2006). These findings illustrate that analyzing and interpreting data that are collected in multiple countries is an extremely challenging undertaking.

# Goodness of measures

Now that we have seen how to operationally define variables and apply different scaling techniques, it is important to make sure that the instrument that we develop to measure a particular concept is indeed accurately measuring the variable, and that, in fact, we are actually measuring the concept that we set out to measure. This ensures that in operationally defining perceptual and attitudinal variables, we have not overlooked some important dimensions and elements or included some irrelevant ones. The scales developed can often be imperfect, and errors are prone to occur in the measurement of attitudinal variables. The use of better instruments will ensure more accuracy in results, which in turn will enhance the scientific quality of the research. Hence, in some way, we need to assess the "goodness" of the measures developed. That is, we need to be reasonably sure that the instruments we use in our research do indeed measure the variables they are supposed to, and that they measure them accurately.

Let us now examine how we can ensure that the measures developed are reasonably good. First, an item analysis of the responses to the questions tapping the variable is carried out, and then the reliability and validity of the measures are established, as described below.

## Item analysis

Item analysis is carried out to see if the items in the instrument belong there or not. Each item is examined for its ability to discriminate between those subjects whose total scores are high, and those with low scores. In item analysis, the means between the high-score group and the low-score group are tested to detect significant differences through the $t$-values. The items with a high $t$-value (test which is able to identify the highly discriminating items in the instrument) are then included in the instrument. Thereafter, tests for the reliability of the instrument are carried out and the validity of the measure is established.

Very briefly, **reliability** is a test of how consistently a measuring instrument measures whatever concept it is measuring. **Validity** is a test of how well an instrument that is developed measures the particular concept it is intended to measure. In other words, validity is concerned with whether we measure the right concept, and reliability with stability and consistency of measurement. Validity and reliability of the measure attest to the scientific rigor that has gone into the research study. These two criteria will now be discussed. The various forms of reliability and validity are depicted in Figure 7.1.

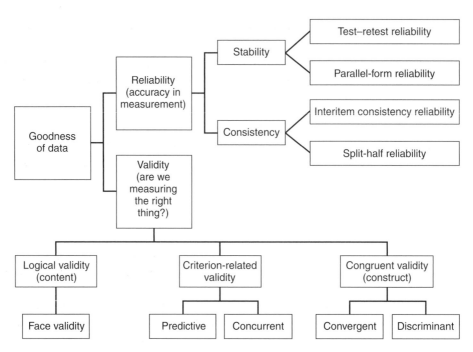

**Figure 7.1:** Testing goodness of measures: forms of reliability and validity.

## Validity

In Chapter 9 we will examine the terms *internal validity* and *external validity* in the context of experimental designs. That is, we will be concerned about the issue of the authenticity of the cause-and-effect relationships (internal validity), and their generalizability to the external environment (external validity). For now, we are going to examine the validity of the measuring instrument itself. That is, when we ask a set of questions (i.e., develop a measuring instrument) with the hope that we are tapping the concept, how can we be reasonably certain that we are indeed measuring the concept we set out to measure and not something else? This can be determined by applying certain validity tests.

Several types of validity test are used to test the goodness of measures and writers use different terms to denote them. For the sake of clarity, we may group validity tests under three broad headings: content validity, criterion-related validity, and construct validity.

### Content validity

**Content validity** ensures that the measure includes an adequate and representative set of items that tap the concept. The more the scale items represent the domain or universe of the concept being measured, the greater the content validity. To put it differently, content validity is a function of how well the dimensions and elements of a concept have been delineated.

A panel of judges can attest to the content validity of the instrument. Kidder and Judd (1986) cite the example where a test designed to measure degrees of speech impairment can be considered as having validity if it is so evaluated by a group of expert judges (i.e., professional speech therapists).

Face validity is considered by some a basic and minimum index of content validity. **Face validity** indicates that the items that are intended to measure a concept, do, on the face of it, look like they measure the concept. Some researchers do not see fit to treat face validity as a valid component of content validity.

## Criterion-related validity

**Criterion-related validity** is established when the measure differentiates individuals on a criterion it is expected to predict. This can be done by establishing concurrent validity or predictive validity, as explained below.

**Concurrent validity** is established when the scale discriminates individuals who are known to be different; that is, they should score differently on the instrument, as in the example that follows.

### EXAMPLE

If a measure of work ethic is developed and administered to a group of welfare recipients, the scale should differentiate those who are enthusiastic about accepting a job and glad of an opportunity to be off welfare, from those who do not want to work even when offered a job. Obviously, those with high work ethic values do not want to be on welfare and yearn for employment to be on their own. Those who are low on work ethic values, on the other hand, might exploit the opportunity to survive on welfare for as long as possible, deeming work to be drudgery. If both types of individual have the same score on the work ethic scale, then the test is not a measure of work ethic, but of something else.

**Predictive validity** indicates the ability of the measuring instrument to differentiate among individuals with reference to a future criterion.

### EXAMPLE

If an aptitude or ability test administered to employees at the time of recruitment is to differentiate individuals on the basis of their future job performance, then those who score low on the test should be poor performers and those with high scores good performers.

### Construct validity

Construct validity testifies to how well the results obtained from the use of the measure fit the theories around which the test is designed. This is assessed through convergent and discriminant validity, which are explained below.

Convergent validity is established when the scores obtained with two different instruments measuring the same concept are highly correlated.

Discriminant validity is established when, based on theory, two variables are predicted to be uncorrelated, and the scores obtained by measuring them are indeed empirically found to be so. Validity can thus be established in different ways. Published measures for various concepts usually report the kinds of validity that have been established for the instrument, so that the user or reader can judge the "goodness" of the measure. Table 7.2 summarizes the kinds of validity discussed here.

Some of the ways in which the above forms of validity can be established are through:

1. Correlational analysis (as in the case of establishing concurrent and predictive validity or convergent and discriminant validity).

**TABLE 7.2    Types of validity.**

| Validity | Description |
| --- | --- |
| Content validity | Does the measure adequately measure the concept? |
| Face validity | Do "experts" validate that the instrument measures what its name suggests it measures? |
| Criterion-related validity | Does the measure differentiate in a manner that helps to predict a criterion variable? |
| Concurrent validity | Does the measure differentiate in a manner that helps to predict a criterion variable currently? |
| Predictive validity | Does the measure differentiate individuals in a manner that helps predict a future criterion? |
| Construct validity | Does the instrument tap the concept as theorized? |
| Convergent validity | Do two instruments measuring the concept correlate highly? |
| Discriminant validity | Does the measure have a low correlation with a variable that is supposed to be unrelated to this variable? |

2. Factor analysis, a multivariate technique that confirms the dimensions of the concept that have been operationally defined, as well as indicating which of the items are most appropriate for each dimension (establishing construct validity).
3. The multitrait, multimethod matrix of correlations derived from measuring concepts by different forms and different methods, additionally establishing the robustness of the measure.

In sum, the goodness of measures is established through the different kinds of validity and reliability depicted in Figure 7.1. The results of any research can only be as good as the measures that tap the concepts in the theoretical framework. We need to use well-validated and reliable measures to ensure that our research is scientific. Fortunately, measures have been developed for many important concepts in organizational research and their psychometric properties (i.e., the reliability and validity) established by the developers. Thus, researchers can use the instruments already reputed to be "good," rather than laboriously developing their own measures. When using these measures, however, researchers should cite the source (i.e., the author and reference) so that the reader can seek more information if necessary.

It is not unusual for two or more equally good measures to be developed for the same concept. For example, there are several different instruments for measuring the concept of "job satisfaction". One of the most frequently used scales for the purpose, however, is the Job Descriptive Index (JDI) developed by Smith, Kendall, and Hulin (1969). When more than one scale exists for any variable, it is preferable to use the measure that has better reliability and validity and is also more frequently used.

At times, we may also have to adapt an established measure to suit the setting. For example, a scale that is used to measure job performance, job characteristics, or job satisfaction in the manufacturing industry may have to be modified slightly to suit a utility company or a health care organization. The work environment in each case is different and the wordings in the instrument may have to be suitably adapted. However, in doing this, we are tampering with an established scale, and it is advisable to test it for the adequacy of the validity and reliability afresh.

A sample of a few measures used to tap some frequently researched concepts in the management and marketing areas is provided in the appendix to this chapter.

Finally, it is important to note that validity is a necessary but not sufficient condition of the test of goodness of a measure. A measure should not only be valid but also reliable. A measure is reliable if it provides consistent results. We will now discuss the concept of reliability.

## Reliability

The **reliability** of a measure indicates the extent to which it is without bias (error free) and hence ensures consistent measurement across time and across the various items in the instrument. In other words, the reliability of a measure is an indication of the stability and consistency with which the instrument measures the concept and helps to assess the "goodness" of a measure.

## Stability of measures

The ability of a measure to remain the same over time – despite uncontrollable testing conditions or the state of the respondents themselves – is indicative of its stability and low vulnerability to changes in the situation. This attests to its "goodness" because the concept is stably measured, no matter when it is done. Two tests of stability are test–retest reliability and parallel-form reliability.

### Test–retest reliability

The reliability coefficient obtained by repetition of the same measure on a second occasion is called the **test–retest reliability**. That is, when a questionnaire containing some items that are supposed to measure a concept is administered to a set of respondents now, and again to the same respondents, say several weeks to six months later, then the correlation between the scores obtained at the two different times from one and the same set of respondents is called the test–retest coefficient. The higher it is, the better the test–retest reliability and, consequently, the stability of the measure across time.

### Parallel-form reliability

When responses on two comparable sets of measures tapping the same construct are highly correlated, we have **parallel-form reliability**. Both forms have similar items and the same response format, the only changes being the wording and the order or sequence of the questions. What we try to establish here is the error variability resulting from wording and ordering of the questions. If two such comparable forms are highly correlated (say 8 and above), we may be fairly certain that the measures are reasonably reliable, with minimal error variance caused by wording, ordering, or other factors.

## Internal consistency of measures

The **internal consistency** of measures is indicative of the homogeneity of the items in the measure that tap the construct. In other words, the items should "hang together as a set," and be capable of independently measuring the same concept so that the respondents attach the same overall meaning to each of the items. This can be seen by examining whether the items and the subsets of items in the measuring instrument are correlated highly. Consistency can be examined through the interitem consistency reliability and split-half reliability tests.

### Interitem consistency reliability

The **interitem consistency reliability** is a test of the consistency of respondents' answers to all the items in a measure. To the degree that items are independent measures of the same concept, they will be correlated with one another. The most popular test of interitem consistency reliability is Cronbach's coefficient alpha (Cronbach's alpha; Cronbach, 1946), which is used for multipoint-scaled items, and the Kuder–Richardson formulas (Kuder and Richardson, 1937), used for dichotomous items. The higher the coefficients, the better the measuring instrument.

### Split-half reliability

**Split-half reliability** reflects the correlations between two halves of an instrument. The estimates will vary depending on how the items in the measure are split into two halves. Split-half reliabilities may be higher than Cronbach's alpha only in the circumstance of there being more than one underlying response dimension tapped by the measure and when certain other conditions are met as well (for complete details, refer to Campbell, 1976). Hence, in almost all cases, Cronbach's alpha can be considered a perfectly adequate index of the interitem consistency reliability.

# Reflective versus formative measurement scales

At this moment, it is important to come back to the contention that the items of a multi-item measure should hang together as a set and be capable of independently measuring the same concept (it may give you a headache right now, but it most certainly will save you an even bigger headache in your future career as a researcher, so bear with us). The fact is that the items that measure a concept should not always hang together: this is only true for reflective, but not for formative, scales.

## What is a reflective scale?

In a **reflective scale**, the items (all of them!) are expected to correlate. Unlike the items used in a formative scale, discussed next, each item in a reflective scale is assumed to share a common basis (the underlying construct of interest). Hence, an increase in the value of the construct will translate into an increase in the value for all the items representing the construct. An example of a reflective scale is the Attitude Toward the Offer scale developed by Burton and Lichtenstein (1988). This is a six-item, nine-point summated ratings scale measuring a person's attitude about a certain product offered at a certain price. The scale is composed of five bipolar adjectives (unfavorable–favorable; bad–good; harmful–beneficial; unattractive–attractive; poor–excellent) and one disagree–agree item, introduced by the stem: "I like this deal", measured on a nine-point graphic scale. Indeed, we would expect that a more favorable attitude towards the offer would translate into an increase in the value of all the six items representing attitude towards the offer. Hence, we would expect all the six items to correlate. Note that the direction of "causality" is from the construct to the items.

## What is a formative scale and why do the items of a formative scale not necessarily hang together?

A **formative scale** is used when a construct is viewed as an explanatory combination of its indicators (Fornell and Bookstein, 1982; Fornell, 1987). Take the Job Description Index

(Smith, Kendall, and Hulin, 1969), a composite measure purporting to evaluate job satisfaction. This measure includes five dimensions: type of work (18 items), opportunities for promotion (9 items), satisfaction with supervision (18 items), co-workers (18 items), and pay (9 items). The five dimensions are seen as the five defining characteristics of job satisfaction.

The five dimensions are translated into 72 observable and measureable elements such as "Good opportunity for advancement", "Regular promotions", "Fairly good chance for promotion", "Income adequate for normal expenses", "Highly paid", and "Gives sense of accomplishment". The idea is that we would expect the first three items ("Good opportunity for advancement", "Regular promotions", and "Fairly good chance for promotion") to be correlated (after all, they all aim to measure one particular dimension of job satisfaction, that is, "opportunities for promotion"). However, these items do not necessarily correlate with the items that measure "Pay" (a second dimension), such as "Income adequate for normal expenses" and "Highly paid", because the dimension "Good opportunities for advancement" is not necessarily related to the dimension "Pay". Indeed, a first worker may have a very good salary but no opportunities for promotion, a second worker may have very good opportunities for promotion but a very poor salary, and a third worker may have a very good salary and very good opportunities for promotion.

Likewise, we would expect the items "Income adequate for normal expenses" and "Highly paid" to be correlated to each other (since both items measure pay), but we would not necessarily expect these items to correlate with the item "Gives sense of accomplishment" (because this last item does not measure pay but another dimension of the Job Description Index).

In summary, the Job Description Index includes five dimensions and 72 items. These 72 items are not necessarily related to each other, because the five dimensions they represent do not necessarily hang together.

A scale that contains items that are not necessarily related is called a formative scale. We have already explained that formative scales are used when a construct (such as job satisfaction) is viewed as an explanatory combination of its indicators (promotions, pay, satisfaction with supervision, co-workers, and work); that is, when a change in any one of the indicators (dimensions) is expected to change the score of the overall construct, regardless of the value of the other indicators (dimensions). The Job Description Index is formative in nature, since an increase in the value of one of its indicators, such as "opportunities for promotion", is expected to translate into a higher score for job satisfaction, regardless of the value of the other indicators. Thus, the Job Description Index conceptualizes job satisfaction as the total weighted score across the 72 job satisfaction items, where each item corresponds to a specific independent dimension of job satisfaction.

A good (that is, a valid) formative scale is one that represents the entire domain of the construct. This means that a valid scale should represent all the relevant aspects of the construct of interest, even if these aspects do not necessarily correlate.

While it makes sense to test the interitem consistency of reflective scales, it does not make sense to test the interitem consistency of formative scales. The reason is that we do not expect the items in a formative scale to be homogeneous; in other words we do not expect all the items to correlate. For this reason, tests of the consistency of respondents' answers to the items of a formative measure do not tell us anything about the quality of our measuring instrument.

Note that there are other methods to assess the goodness of formative scales (see, for instance, Jarvis, MacKenzie, and Podsakoff, 2003).

## SUMMARY

In this chapter, we examined the four types of scales – nominal, ordinal, interval, and ratio. We also saw what kinds of attitude rating scales and ranking scales can be used in developing instruments after a concept has been operationally defined (or operationalized). We also discussed how the goodness of measures is established by means of item analysis, and reliability and validity tests. We noted that the Likert scale and other interval-type scales, such as the numerical scale, are extensively used in organizational research since they lend themselves to more sophisticated data analysis. Finally, we discussed the goodness of measures in terms of reliability and validity and the various ways in which these can be established.

Knowledge of the different scales and scaling techniques helps managers to administer short surveys by designing questions that use ranking or rating scales, as appropriate. Awareness of the fact that measures are already available for many organizational concepts further facilitates mini-exploratory surveys by managers.

In the next chapter, we will see the different sources and methods of data collection.

## DISCUSSION QUESTIONS

1. Describe the four types of scales.
2. How is the interval scale more sophisticated than the nominal and ordinal scales?
3. Why is the ratio scale considered to be the most powerful of the four scales?
4. Briefly describe the difference between attitude rating scales and ranking scales and indicate when the two are used.
5. Why is it important to establish the "goodness" of measures and how is this done?
6. Describe the difference between formative and reflective scales.
7. Explain why it does not make sense to assess the internal consistency of a formative scale.
8. "The job involvement measure described in the appendix is reflective in nature." Comment on this statement.
9. Construct a semantic differential scale to assess the properties of a particular brand of coffee or tea.
10. Whenever possible, it is advisable to use instruments that have already been developed and repeatedly used in published studies, rather than developing our own instruments for our studies. Do you agree? Discuss the reasons for your answer.
11. "A valid instrument is always reliable, but a reliable instrument may not always be valid." Comment on this statement.

Now do Exercises 7.5 and 7.6

## EXERCISE 7.5

Develop and name the type of measuring instrument you would use to tap the following:

a. Which brands of beer are consumed by how many individuals?

b. Among the three types of exams – multiple choice, essay type, and a mix of both – which is the one preferred most by students?

c. To what extent do individuals agree with your definition of accounting principles?

d. How much people like an existing organizational policy.

e. The age of employees in an organization.

f. The number of employees in each of the 20 departments of a company.

## EXERCISE 7.6

"The Index of Consumer Sentiment Toward Marketing described in the appendix is formative in nature." Comment on this statement. Explain why it does not make sense to assess the interitem consistency of this scale.

# APPENDIX

## Examples of some measures

Some of the measures used in behavioral research can be found in the *Handbook of Organizational Measurement* by Price (1997) and in the *Michigan Organizational Assessment Package* published by the Institute of Survey Research in Ann Arbor, Michigan. Several measures can also be seen in Psychological Measurement Yearbooks and in other published books. A sample of measures from the management and marketing areas is provided in this appendix.

### Measures from management research

Below is a sample of five scales used to measure five variables related to management research.

### Job involvement

| | Strongly Disagree | Disagree | Neither Agree nor Disagree | Agree | Strongly Agree |
|---|---|---|---|---|---|
| 1. My job means a lot more to me than just money. | 1 | 2 | 3 | 4 | 5 |
| 2. The major satisfaction in my life comes from my job. | 1 | 2 | 3 | 4 | 5 |
| 3. I am really interested in my work. | 1 | 2 | 3 | 4 | 5 |
| 4. I would probably keep working even if I didn't need the money. | 1 | 2 | 3 | 4 | 5 |
| 5. The most important things that happen to me involve my work. | 1 | 2 | 3 | 4 | 5 |

*(continued)*

| | Strongly Disagree | Disagree | Neither Agree nor Disagree | Agree | Strongly Agree |
|---|---|---|---|---|---|
| 6. I will stay overtime to finish a job, even if I am not paid for it. | 1 | 2 | 3 | 4 | 5 |
| 7. For me, the first few hours at work really fly by. | 1 | 2 | 3 | 4 | 5 |
| 8. I actually enjoy performing the daily activities that make up my job. | 1 | 2 | 3 | 4 | 5 |
| 9. I look forward to coming to work each day. | 1 | 2 | 3 | 4 | 5 |

*Source:* J. K. White and R. A. Ruh (White and Ruh, 1973). Effects of personal values on the relationship between participation and job attitudes. *Administrative Science Quarterly*, **18**(4), p. 509. Reproduced with permission.

## Participation in decision making

| | Not at all | Very little | Somewhat | To a moderate extent | To a large extent |
|---|---|---|---|---|---|
| 1. In general, how much say or influence do you have on how you perform your job? | 1 | 2 | 3 | 4 | 5 |
| 2. To what extent are you able to decide how to do your job? | 1 | 2 | 3 | 4 | 5 |
| 3. In general, how much say or influence do you have on what goes on in your work group? | 1 | 2 | 3 | 4 | 5 |
| 4. In general, how much say or influence do you have on decisions that affect your job? | 1 | 2 | 3 | 4 | 5 |
| 5. My superiors are receptive and listen to my ideas and suggestions. | 1 | 2 | 3 | 4 | 5 |

*Source:* J. K. White and R. A. Ruh (White and Ruh, 1973). Effects of personal values on the relationship between participation and job attitudes. *Administrative Science Quarterly*, **18**(4), p. 509. Reproduced with permission.

## Role conflict

|  | Very False |  |  |  |  |  | Very True |
|---|---|---|---|---|---|---|---|
| 1. I have to do things that should be done differently. | 1 | 2 | 3 | 4 | 5 | 6 | 7 |
| 2. I work under incompatible policies and guidelines. | 1 | 2 | 3 | 4 | 5 | 6 | 7 |
| 3. I receive an assignment without the manpower to complete it. | 1 | 2 | 3 | 4 | 5 | 6 | 7 |
| 4. I have to buck a rule or policy in order to carry out an assignment. | 1 | 2 | 3 | 4 | 5 | 6 | 7 |
| 5. I work with two or more groups who operate quite differently. | 1 | 2 | 3 | 4 | 5 | 6 | 7 |
| 6. I receive incompatible requests from two or more people. | 1 | 2 | 3 | 4 | 5 | 6 | 7 |
| 7. I do things that are apt to be accepted by one person and not accepted by others. | 1 | 2 | 3 | 4 | 5 | 6 | 7 |
| 8. I receive an assignment without adequate resources and materials to execute it. | 1 | 2 | 3 | 4 | 5 | 6 | 7 |
| 9. I work on unnecessary things. | 1 | 2 | 3 | 4 | 5 | 6 | 7 |

*Source*: J. R. Rizzo, R. J. House and S. I. Lirtzman (1970). Role conflict and role ambiguity in complex organizations. *Administrative Science Quarterly*, **15**, p. 156. Reproduced with permission.

## Career salience

| Strongly Disagree 1 | Disagree 2 | Slightly Disagree 3 | Neutral 4 | Slightly Agree 5 | Agree 6 | Strongly Agree 7 |
|---|---|---|---|---|---|---|
| 1 | My career choice is a good occupational decision for me. | | | | | ____ |
| 2 | My career enables me to make significant contributions to society. | | | | | ____ |
| 3 | The career I am in fits me and reflects my personality. | | | | | ____ |
| 4 | My education and training are not tailored for this career. | | | | | ____ |
| 5 | I don't intend changing careers. | | | | | ____ |
| 6 | All the planning and thought I gave to pursuing this career are a waste. | | | | | ____ |
| 7 | My career is an integral part of my life. | | | | | ____ |

*Source*: U. Sekaran. (1986) *Dual-Career Families: Contemporary Organizational and Counseling Issues*. San Francisco: Jossey-Bass. Reproduced with permission.

**Least preferred co-worker scale (to assess whether employees are primarily people-oriented or task-oriented)**

Look at the words at both ends of the line before you put in your "X." Please remember that there are no right or wrong answers. Work rapidly; your first answer is likely to be the best. Please do not omit any items, and mark each item only once.

   LPC: think of the person with whom you can work least well. He may be someone you work with now, or he may be someone you knew in the past. He does not have to be the person you like least well, but should be the person with whom you had the most difficulty in getting a job done. Describe this person as he appears to you.

| Pleasant | : ___ 8 | : ___ 7 | : ___ 6 | : ___ 5 | : ___ 4 | : ___ 3 | : ___ 2 | : ___ 1 | Unpleasant |
|---|---|---|---|---|---|---|---|---|---|
| Friendly | : ___ 8 | : ___ 7 | : ___ 6 | : ___ 5 | : ___ 4 | : ___ 3 | : ___ 2 | : ___ 1 | Unfriendly |
| Rejecting | : ___ 8 | : ___ 7 | : ___ 6 | : ___ 5 | : ___ 4 | : ___ 3 | : ___ 2 | : ___ 1 | Accepting |
| Helpful | : ___ 8 | : ___ 7 | : ___ 6 | : ___ 5 | : ___ 4 | : ___ 3 | : ___ 2 | : ___ 1 | Frustrating |
| Unenthusiastic | : ___ 8 | : ___ 7 | : ___ 6 | : ___ 5 | : ___ 4 | : ___ 3 | : ___ 2 | : ___ 1 | Enthusiastic |
| Tense | : ___ 1 | : ___ 2 | : ___ 3 | : ___ 4 | : ___ 5 | : ___ 6 | : ___ 7 | : ___ 8 | Relaxed |
| Distant | : ___ 1 | : ___ 2 | : ___ 3 | : ___ 4 | : ___ 5 | : ___ 6 | : ___ 7 | : ___ 8 | Close |
| Cold | : ___ 1 | : ___ 2 | : ___ 3 | : ___ 4 | : ___ 5 | : ___ 6 | : ___ 7 | : ___ 8 | Warm |
| Cooperative | : ___ 8 | : ___ 7 | : ___ 6 | : ___ 5 | : ___ 4 | : ___ 3 | : ___ 2 | : ___ 1 | Uncooperative |
| Supportive | : ___ 8 | : ___ 7 | : ___ 6 | : ___ 5 | : ___ 4 | : ___ 3 | : ___ 2 | : ___ 1 | Hostile |
| Boring | : ___ 8 | : ___ 7 | : ___ 6 | : ___ 5 | : ___ 4 | : ___ 3 | : ___ 2 | : ___ 1 | Interesting |
| Quarrelsome | : ___ 8 | : ___ 7 | : ___ 6 | : ___ 5 | : ___ 4 | : ___ 3 | : ___ 2 | : ___ 1 | Harmonious |
| Self-assured | : ___ 8 | : ___ 7 | : ___ 6 | : ___ 5 | : ___ 4 | : ___ 3 | : ___ 2 | : ___ 1 | Hesitant |
| Efficient | : ___ 8 | : ___ 7 | : ___ 6 | : ___ 5 | : ___ 4 | : ___ 3 | : ___ 2 | : ___ 1 | Inefficient |

| Gloomy | : ___ | : ___ | : ___ | : ___ | : ___ | : ___ | : ___ | : ___ | Cheerful |
|--------|-------|-------|-------|-------|-------|-------|-------|-------|----------|
|        | 8     | 7     | 6     | 5     | 4     | 3     | 2     | 1     |          |
| Open   | : ___ | : ___ | : ___ | : ___ | : ___ | : ___ | : ___ | : ___ | Guarded  |
|        | 8     | 7     | 6     | 5     | 4     | 3     | 2     | 1     |          |

*Source*: Fred E. Fiedler. (1967). *A Theory of Leadership Effectiveness*. New York: McGraw-Hill. Reproduced with permission.

## Measures from marketing research

Below is a sample of some scales used to measure commonly researched concepts in marketing. Bruner and Hensel have done extensive work since 1992 in documenting and detailing several scores of scales in marketing research. For each scale examined, they have provided the following information:

1. Scale description
2. Scale origin
3. Samples in which the scale was used
4. Reliability of the scale
5. Validity of the scale
6. How the scale was administered
7. Major findings of the studies using the scale.

The interested student should refer to the four volumes of *Marketing Scales Handbook* by G. C. Bruner and P. J. Hensel (volume 1 and 2); G. C. Bruner, P. J. Hensel, and K. E. James published by the American Marketing Association (volume 1, 2, and 3) and Thomson (volume 4). The first volume covers scales used in articles published in the 1980s, and volume two covers scales used in articles published from 1990 to 1993. The third volume covers the period from 1994 to 1997. The fourth volume covers marketing scales that were reported in articles published from 1998 to 2001. Also refer to the website: http://www.siu.edu/departments/coba/osr/index.html.

### Index of consumer sentiment toward marketing

1. Listed below are seven statements pertaining to each of the four marketing areas. There is also a fifth section labeled "Marketing in General." It contains four statements.

    For each statement, please "X" the box which best describes how strongly you agree or disagree. For example, if you strongly agree that the quality of most products today is as good as can be expected, then "X" the Strongly Agree box. On the other hand, if you strongly disagree with the statement that the quality of most products today is as good as can be expected, then "X" the Strongly Disagree box. Remember to "X" one box for each statement.

| PRODUCT QUALITY | Strongly Disagree | Somewhat Disagree | Neither Agree nor Disagree | Somewhat Agree | Strongly Agree |
|---|---|---|---|---|---|
| The quality of most products I buy today is as good as can be expected. | ☐ 1 | ☐ 2 | ☐ 3 | ☐ 4 | ☐ 5 |
| I am satisfied with most of the products I buy. | ☐ 1 | ☐ 2 | ☐ 3 | ☐ 4 | ☐ 5 |
| Most products I buy wear out too quickly. | ☐ 1 | ☐ 2 | ☐ 3 | ☐ 4 | ☐ 5 |
| Products are not made as well as they used to be. | ☐ 1 | ☐ 2 | ☐ 3 | ☐ 4 | ☐ 5 |
| Too many of the products I buy are defective in some way. | ☐ 1 | ☐ 2 | ☐ 3 | ☐ 4 | ☐ 5 |
| The companies that make products I buy don't care enough about how well they perform | ☐ 1 | ☐ 2 | ☐ 3 | ☐ 4 | ☐ 5 |
| The quality of products I buy has consistently improved over the years | ☐ 1 | ☐ 2 | ☐ 3 | ☐ 4 | ☐ 5 |

| PRICE OF PRODUCTS | Strongly Disagree | Somewhat Disagree | Neither Agree nor Disagree | Somewhat Agree | Strongly Agree |
|---|---|---|---|---|---|
| Most products I buy are overpriced. | ☐ 1 | ☐ 2 | ☐ 3 | ☐ 4 | ☐ 5 |
| Businesses could charge lower prices and still be profitable. | ☐ 1 | ☐ 2 | ☐ 3 | ☐ 4 | ☐ 5 |
| Most prices are reasonable considering the high cost of doing business. | ☐ 1 | ☐ 2 | ☐ 3 | ☐ 4 | ☐ 5 |

| | | | | | |
|---|---|---|---|---|---|
| Competition between companies keeps prices reasonable. | | | | | |
| Companies are unjustified in charging the prices they charge. | □ 1 | □ 2 | □ 3 | □ 4 | □ 5 |
| Most prices are fair. | □ 1 | □ 2 | □ 3 | □ 4 | □ 5 |
| In general, I am satisfied with the prices I pay. | □ 1 | □ 2 | □ 3 | □ 4 | □ 5 |

| ADVERTISING FOR PRODUCTS | Strongly Disagree | Somewhat Disagree | Neither Agree nor Disagree | Somewhat Agree | Strongly Agree |
|---|---|---|---|---|---|
| Most advertising provides consumers with essential information. | □ 1 | □ 2 | □ 3 | □ 4 | □ 5 |
| Most advertising is very annoying. | □ 1 | □ 2 | □ 3 | □ 4 | □ 5 |
| Most advertising makes false claims. | □ 1 | □ 2 | □ 3 | □ 4 | □ 5 |
| If most advertising was eliminated, consumers could be better off. | □ 1 | □ 2 | □ 3 | □ 4 | □ 5 |
| I enjoy most ads. | □ 1 | □ 2 | □ 3 | □ 4 | □ 5 |
| Advertising should be more closely regulated. | □ 1 | □ 2 | □ 3 | □ 4 | □ 5 |
| Most advertising is intended to deceive rather than to inform consumers. | □ 1 | □ 2 | □ 3 | □ 4 | □ 5 |

| RETAILING OR SELLING | Strongly Disagree | Somewhat Disagree | Neither Agree nor Disagree | Somewhat Agree | Strongly Agree |
|---|---|---|---|---|---|
| Most retail stores serve their customers well. | □ 1 | □ 2 | □ 3 | □ 4 | □ 5 |

| | Strongly Disagree | Somewhat Disagree | Neither Agree nor Disagree | Somewhat Agree | Strongly Agree |
|---|---|---|---|---|---|
| Because of the way retailers treat me, most of my shopping is unpleasant. | ☐ 1 | ☐ 2 | ☐ 3 | ☐ 4 | ☐ 5 |
| I find most retail salespeople to be very helpful. | ☐ 1 | ☐ 2 | ☐ 3 | ☐ 4 | ☐ 5 |
| Most retail stores provide an adequate selection of merchandise. | ☐ 1 | ☐ 2 | ☐ 3 | ☐ 4 | ☐ 5 |
| In general, most middlemen make excessive profits. | ☐ 1 | ☐ 2 | ☐ 3 | ☐ 4 | ☐ 5 |
| When I need assistance in a store, I am usually not able to get it. | ☐ 1 | ☐ 2 | ☐ 3 | ☐ 4 | ☐ 5 |
| Most retailers provide adequate service. | ☐ 1 | ☐ 2 | ☐ 3 | ☐ 4 | ☐ 5 |

| MARKETING IN GENERAL | Strongly Disagree | Somewhat Disagree | Neither Agree nor Disagree | Somewhat Agree | Strongly Agree |
|---|---|---|---|---|---|
| Most businesses operate on the philosophy that the consumer is always right. | ☐ 1 | ☐ 2 | ☐ 3 | ☐ 4 | ☐ 5 |
| Despite what is frequently said, "let the buyer beware" is the guiding philosophy of most businesses. | ☐ 1 | ☐ 2 | ☐ 3 | ☐ 4 | ☐ 5 |
| Most businesses seldom shirk their responsibility to the consumer. | ☐ 1 | ☐ 2 | ☐ 3 | ☐ 4 | ☐ 5 |
| Most businesses are more interested in making profits than in serving consumers. | ☐ 1 | ☐ 2 | ☐ 3 | ☐ 4 | ☐ 5 |

**2.** Now, I'd like to know how satisfied you are, in general, with each of these four marketing areas. Please 'X' the one box which best describes your overall satisfaction with each marketing area.

|  | Very Satisfied | Somewhat Satisfied | Neither Satisfied nor Dissatisfied | Somewhat Dissatisfied | Very Dissatisfied |
|---|---|---|---|---|---|
| The quality of most of the products available to buy. | ☐ 1 | ☐ 2 | ☐ 3 | ☐ 4 | ☐ 5 |
| The prices of most products. | ☐ 1 | ☐ 2 | ☐ 3 | ☐ 4 | ☐ 5 |
| Most of the advertising you read, see, and hear. | ☐ 1 | ☐ 2 | ☐ 3 | ☐ 4 | ☐ 5 |
| The selling conditions at most of the stores at which you buy products. | ☐ 1 | ☐ 2 | ☐ 3 | ☐ 4 | ☐ 5 |

**3.** Listed below are four questions which ask about how often you have had problems with the products you buy, the prices you pay, the advertising you read, see, and hear, and the stores at which you shop.

After each statement, there are five numbers from 1 to 5. Allocating a higher number means you have experienced the problem more often. Allocating a lower number means you have experienced the problem less often.

For each question, please "X" the box which comes closest to how often the problem occurs. Remember to "X" one box for each question.

|  | Very Seldom |  |  |  | Very Often |
|---|---|---|---|---|---|
| How often do you have problems with or complaints about the products you buy? | ☐ 1 | ☐ 2 | ☐ 3 | ☐ 4 | ☐ 5 |
| How often do you have problems with or complaints about the prices you pay? | ☐ 1 | ☐ 2 | ☐ 3 | ☐ 4 | ☐ 5 |
| How often do you have problems with or complaints about advertising? | ☐ 1 | ☐ 2 | ☐ 3 | ☐ 4 | ☐ 5 |

| How often do you have problems with or complaints about the stores at which you buy products? | □ 1 | □ 2 | □ 3 | □ 4 | □ 5 |

*Source*: J. F. Gaski and M. J. Etzel. (Gaski and Etzel, 1986). The index of consumer sentiment toward marketing. *Journal of Marketing*, **50**, 71–81. Reproduced with the permission of the American Marketing Association.

### SERVQUAL-P battery (to assess the quality of service rendered)

*Reliability*
1. Provides the service as promised.
2. Is dependable in handling customers' service problems.
3. Performs the service right the first time.
4. All _____'s employees are well-trained and knowledgeable.

*Responsiveness*
1. Employees of _____ give you prompt service.
2. Employees of _____ are always willing to help you.
3. Employees of _____ are always ready to respond to your requests.
4. _____ gives customers individual attention.

*Responsiveness*
1. Everyone at _____ is polite and courteous.
2. The _____ employees display personal warmth in their behavior.
3. All the persons working at _____ are friendly and pleasant.
4. The _____ employees take the time to know you personally.

*Tangibles*
1. _____ has modern-looking equipment.
2. _____'s physical facilities are visually appealing.
3. _____'s employees have neat and professional appearance.
4. Materials associated with the service (such as pamphlets or statements) are visually appealing at _____.

*Source*: B. Mittal and W. M. Lassar. (Mittal and Lassar, 1996). The role of personalization in service encounters. *Journal of Retailing*, **72**, 95–109. Reproduced with permission of Jai Press, Inc.

## Role ambiguity (salesperson)

| Very False | | | | | | Very True |
|---|---|---|---|---|---|---|
| 1 | 2 | 3 | 4 | 5 | 6 | 7 |

| | |
|---|---|
| 1. I feel certain about how much authority I have in my selling position. | ____ |
| 2. I have clearly planned goals for my selling job. | ____ |
| 3. I am sure I divide my time properly while performing my selling tasks. | ____ |
| 4. I know my responsibilities in my selling position. | ____ |
| 5. I know exactly what is expected of me in my selling position. | ____ |
| 6. I receive lucid explanations of what I have to do in my sales job. | ____ |

Modified from Rizzo, House, and Lirtzman (1970) Role conflict and role ambiguity in complex organizations. *Administrative Science Quarterly*, **15**, p. 156

# CHAPTER 8

## Data collection methods

## Topics discussed

- Sources of data
  - Focus groups
  - Panels
  - Unobtrusive sources
- Data collection methods
  - Interviewing
    - Unstructured and structured interviews
    - Tips for interviewing
    - Face-to-face and telephone interviews
    - Computer-assisted interviews
  - Questionnaires and questionnaire design
    - Personally administered questionnaires and mail questionnaires
    - Principles of wording
    - Principles of measurement
    - General appearance of the questionnaire
    - Electronic questionnaire design
  - Observational studies
    - Participant and nonparticipant observation
    - Structured and unstructured observation
  - Projective tests
- Multimethods and multisources of data collection
- Setting wherefrom data are collected
- International dimensions of surveys
- Managerial implications
- Ethics in data collection

## CHAPTER OBJECTIVES

After completing Chapter 8, you should:

1. Know the difference between primary and secondary data and their sources.
2. Be conversant with the various data collection methods.
3. Know the advantages and disadvantages of each method.
4. Be able to make logical decisions as to the appropriate data collection methods(s) for specific studies.
5. Be able to demonstrate your skills in interviewing others to collect data.
6. Be able to design questionnaires to tap different variables.
7. Be able to evaluate questionnaires, distinguishing the "good" and "bad" questions therein.
8. Be able to identify and minimize the biases in various data collection methods.
9. Be able to discuss the advantages of multisources and multimethods of data collection.
10. Be able to apply what you have learned to class assignments and projects.
11. Understand the issues related to cross-cultural research.

Having examined how variables are measured, we will now discuss the various sources of data and the ways in which data can be gathered for purposes of analysis, testing hypotheses, and answering the research questions. The source of the information and the manner in which data are collected could well make a big difference to the rigor and effectiveness of the research project.

We will first examine the sources of data and then discuss data collection methods.

# Sources of data

Data can be obtained from primary or secondary sources. **Primary data** refer to information obtained first-hand by the researcher on the variables of interest for the specific purpose of the study. **Secondary data** refer to information gathered from sources that already exist, as we saw in Chapter 3 while discussing literature review.

Some examples of sources of primary data are individuals, focus groups, panels of respondents specifically set up by the researcher and from whom opinions may be sought on specific issues from time to time, or some unobtrusive sources such as a trash can. The Internet can also serve as a primary data source when questionnaires are administered over it.

Data can also be obtained from secondary sources, for example, company records or archives, government publications, industry analyses offered by the media, websites, the Internet, and so on. In some cases, the environment or particular settings and events may themselves be sources of data, for example, studying the layout of a plant.

We will first examine the four main primary sources of data – individuals, focus groups, panels, and unobtrusive methods – and then discuss the secondary sources.

## Primary sources of data

Individuals provide information when interviewed, administered questionnaires, or observed. Group depth interviews, or focus groups, are another rich source of primary data.

### Focus groups

**Focus groups** consist typically of eight to ten members with a moderator leading the discussions for about two hours on a particular topic, concept, or product. Members are generally chosen on the basis of their expertise in the topic on which information is sought. For example, computer specialists may be selected to form a focus group to discuss matters related to computers and computing, and women with children may compose a focus group to identify how organizations can help working mothers.

The focus sessions are aimed at obtaining respondents' impressions, interpretations, and opinions, as the members talk about the event, concept, product, or service. The moderator plays a vital role in steering the discussions in a manner that draws out the information sought, and keeps the members on track.

Focus group discussions on a specific topic at a particular location and at a specified time provide the opportunity for a flexible, free-flowing format for the members. The unstructured and spontaneous responses are expected to reflect the genuine opinions, ideas, and feelings of the members about the topic under discussion. Focus groups are relatively inexpensive and can provide fairly dependable data within a short time frame.

#### Role of the moderator

The selection of and role played by the moderator are critical. The moderator introduces the topic, observes, and takes notes and/or tapes the discussions. The moderator never becomes an integral part of the discussions, but merely steers the group persuasively to obtain all the relevant information, and helps the group members to get through any impasse that might occur. The moderator also ensures that all members participate in the discussion and that no member dominates the group. Someone from the research team may also observe the proceedings through a one-way mirror, listening to the verbal statements and noticing the nonverbal cues of the members.

#### The nature of data obtained through focus groups

It should be noted that although data obtained through these homogeneous group members are less expensive than those obtained through the various other data collection methods, and also lend themselves for quick analysis, the content analysis of the data so obtained provides only qualitative and not quantitative information. Also, since the members are not selected scientifically to reflect the opinions of the population at large (see Chapter 10 on Sampling for more details on this), their opinions cannot be considered to be truly representative. However, when exploratory information is collected as a basis for further scientific research, focus groups serve an important function. Consider, for example, the value of focus groups in exploring the concept of "intellectual property." When animated discussions take place, there is a serendipitous flow of new ideas among the group members who discuss the nuances of each thought process. Researchers are thereby helped to obtain valuable insights from the snowballing effects of the discussions.

In sum, focus groups are used for:

1. Exploratory studies
2. Making generalizations based on the information generated by them
3. Conducting sample surveys.

Focus groups have been credited with enlightening investigators as to why certain products are not doing well, why certain advertising strategies are effective, why specific management techniques do not work, and the like.

### Videoconferencing

If regional variations in responses are expected, several focus groups could be formed including trained moderators at different locations. This process is easily facilitated through videoconferencing. By zooming in on a particular member, the nonverbal cues and gestures of that individual can be captured, as and when desired. This also obviates the need for an observer looking through a one-way mirror.

With the great strides made in technological advancement, and with the facility for communication with the moderator by relaying instant messages, videoconferencing as a means of gathering information from different groups in distant locations is indeed a promising prospect for the future.

It should be noted that online focus groups are also common. E-mail, websites, and Internet chat rooms facilitate focus group sessions as well.

### Panels

Panels, like focus groups, are another source of primary information for research purposes. Whereas focus groups meet for a one-time group session, panels (of members) meet more than once. In cases where the effects of certain interventions or changes are to be studied over a period of time, panel studies are very useful. Individuals are randomly chosen to serve as panel members for a research study. For instance, if the effects of a proposed advertisement for a certain brand of coffee are to be assessed quickly, the panel members can be exposed to the advertisement and their intentions of purchasing that brand assessed. This can be taken as the response that could be expected of consumers if, in fact, they had been exposed to the advertisement. A few months later, the product manager might think of introducing a change to the flavor of the same product and might explore its effects on this panel. Thus, a continuing set of "experts" serves as the sample base or the sounding board for assessing the effects of change. Such expert members compose the panel, and research that uses them is called a **panel study**.

The Nielsen television index is based on the television viewing patterns of a panel. The index is designed to provide estimates of the size and nature of the audience for individual television programs. The data are gathered through audimeter instruments hooked to television sets in approximately 1200 cooperating households. The audimeters are connected to a central computer, which records when the set is turned on and spotlights what channel is tuned. From these data, Nielsen develops estimates of the number and percentage of all TV households viewing a given TV show.

Other panels used in marketing research include the National Purchase Diary Panel, the National Family Opinion Panel, and the Consumer Mail Panel.

### Static and dynamic panels

Panels can be either **static** (i.e., the same members serve on the panel over extended periods of time) or **dynamic** (i.e., the panel members change from time to time as various phases of the study are in progress). The main advantage of the static panel is that it offers a good and sensitive measurement of the changes that take place between two points in time – a much better alternative than using two different groups at two different times. The disadvantage, however, is that the panel members could become so sensitized to the changes as a result of the endless continuous interviews that their opinions might no longer be representative of what others in the population might hold. Members could also drop out of the panel from time to time for various reasons, thus raising issues of bias due to mortality. The advantages and disadvantages of the dynamic panel are the reverse of those discussed for the static panel.

In sum, a panel is a source of direct information. Panels may be static or dynamic, and are typically used when several aspects of a product are to be studied from time to time.

### The Delphi Technique

The **Delphi Technique** is a forecasting method that uses a cautiously selected panel of experts in a systematic, interactive manner. These experts answer questionnaires in two or more rounds. In the first round they are asked to answer a series of questions on the likelihood of a future scenario or any other issue about which there is unsure or incomplete knowledge. The contributions from all the experts are then collected, summarized, and fed back in the form of a second-round questionnaire. After reviewing the first-round results, the experts assess the same issue once more, taking the opinions of other experts into account. This process goes on until it is stopped by the researcher. The rationale behind this iterative process is that it eventually may lead to a consensus about the issue that is being investigated.

The identity of participants is usually not revealed, even after the completion of the final report. This should prevent some experts from dominating others, allow experts to unreservedly express their opinions, and encourage experts to admit mistakes, if any, by revising their earlier judgments. The Delphi Technique has been widely used for long-run business forecasting.

## Unobtrusive measures

**Unobtrusive measures**, or trace measures as they are also called, originate from a primary source that does not involve people. One example is the wear and tear of journals in a university library, which offers a good indication of their popularity, frequency of use, or both. The number of different brands of soft drink cans found in trash bags also provides a measure of their consumption levels. Signatures on checks exposed to ultraviolet rays could indicate the extent of forgery and fraud; actuarial records are good sources for collecting data on the births, marriages, and deaths in a community; company records disclose a lot of personal information about employees, the level of company efficiency, and other data as well. Thus, these unobtrusive sources of data and their use are also important in research.

## Secondary sources of data

Secondary data are indispensable for most organizational research. As discussed in Chapter 3, **secondary data** refer to information gathered by someone other than the researcher conducting the current study. Such data can be internal or external to the organization and accessed through the Internet or perusal of recorded or published information.

Secondary data can be used, among other things, for forecasting sales by constructing models based on past sales figures, and through extrapolation.

There are several sources of secondary data, including books and periodicals, government publications of economic indicators, census data, statistical abstracts, databases (as discussed in Chapter 3), the media, annual reports of companies, etc. Case studies and other archival records – sources of secondary data – provide a lot of information for research and problem solving. Such data are, as we have seen, mostly qualitative in nature. Also included in secondary sources are schedules maintained for, or by, key personnel in organizations, the desk calendar of executives, and speeches delivered by them. Much of this internal information, though, may be proprietary and not accessible to all.

Financial databases readily available for research are also secondary data sources. The Compustat database contains information on thousands of companies organized by industry, and information on global companies is also available through Compustat.

The advantage of seeking secondary data sources is savings in time and costs of acquiring information. However, secondary data as the sole source of information has the drawback of becoming obsolete, and not meeting the specific needs of the particular situation or setting. Hence, it is important to refer to sources that offer current and up-to-date information.

Having examined the various sources of data, let us now look at data collection methods.

# Data collection methods

Data collection methods are an integral part of research design, as shown in the shaded portion of Figure 8.1. There are several data collection methods, each with its own advantages and disadvantages. Problems researched with the use of appropriate methods greatly enhance the value of the research.

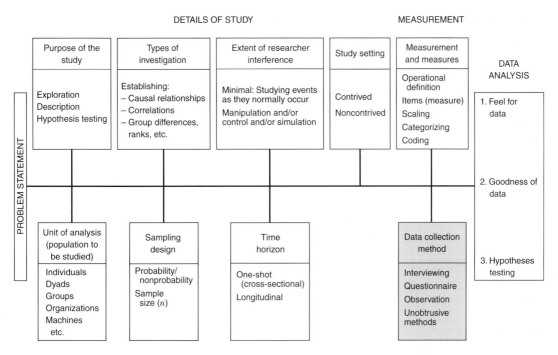

**Figure 8.1:** Research design and how data collection methods fit in.

Data can be collected in a variety of ways, in different settings – field or lab – and from different sources, as we have just discussed. Data collection methods include interviews – face-to-face interviews, telephone interviews, computer-assisted interviews, and interviews through the electronic media – questionnaires that are either personally administered, sent through the mail, or electronically administered; observation of individuals and events with or without videotaping or audio recording; and a variety of other motivational techniques such as projective tests.

Interviewing, administering questionnaires, and observing people and phenomena are the three main data collection methods in survey research. Projective tests and other motivational techniques are also sometimes used to tap variables. In such cases, respondents are usually asked to write a story, complete a sentence, or offer their reactions to ambiguous cues such as inkblots or unlabeled pictures. It is assumed that the respondents project into the responses their own thoughts, feelings, attitudes, and expectations, all of which can be interpreted by trained psychologists.

Although interviewing has the advantage of flexibility in terms of adapting, adopting, and changing the questions as the researcher proceeds with the interviews, questionnaires have the advantage of obtaining data more efficiently in terms of researcher time, energy, and costs. Unobtrusive methods of data collection such as its extraction from company records have the advantage of accuracy. For instance, attendance records will probably give a truer and more reliable picture of the absenteeism of employees than information elicited directly from the respondents. Projective tests are usually administered by researchers who have had training in administering them and interpreting the results. Though some management research has been done using projective techniques, they are more frequently used in marketing research.

Modern technology is increasingly playing a key role in shaping data collection methods. Computer-assisted surveys, which help with both the interviewing process and with preparing and administering questionnaires electronically, are on the increase. Computer-assisted telephone interviewing (CATI), interactive electronic telephonic surveys, as well as administering questionnaires through electronic mail (e-mail), are now being used to facilitate data gathering.

Some of the software available for questionnaire design, response data entry, data analysis, and web and e-mail surveys are SumQuest or SQ Survey Software, Professional Quest, and Perseus.

The choice of data collection method depends on the facilities available, the degree of accuracy required, the expertise of the researcher, the time span of the study, and other costs and resources associated with and available for data gathering.

We will now examine the various data collection methods.

## Interviewing

One method of collecting data is to interview respondents to obtain information on the issues of interest. Interviewing is a useful data collection method, especially during the exploratory stages of research. Where a large number of interviews are conducted with a number of different interviewers, it is important to train the interviewers with care in order to minimize interviewer bias manifested in such ways as voice inflections, differences in wording, and interpretation. Good training decreases interviewer bias.

Interviews may be unstructured or structured, and conducted face to face, by telephone, or online. Unstructured and structured interviews will be discussed first. Some important factors to be borne in mind while interviewing will then be detailed; the advantages and disadvantages of face-to-face interviewing and telephone interviews enumerated thereafter; and finally, computer-assisted interviews described.

### Unstructured and structured interviews

#### Unstructured interviews

**Unstructured interviews** are so labeled because the interviewer does not enter the interview setting with a planned sequence of questions to be asked of the respondent. The objective of the unstructured interview is to bring some preliminary issues to the surface so that the researcher can determine what variables need further in-depth investigation. In Chapter 3, in the discussion of the ''broad problem area,'' we saw several situations where the manager might entertain a vague idea of certain changes taking place in the situation without knowing what exactly they are. Such situations call for unstructured interviews with the people concerned. In order to understand the situation in its totality, the researcher should interview employees at several levels. In the initial stages, only broad, open-ended questions should be asked, and the replies to them should inform the researcher of the perceptions of the individuals. The type and nature of the questions asked of the individuals might vary according to the job level and type of work done by them. For instance, top and middle-level managers might be asked more direct questions about their perceptions of the problem and the situation. Employees at lower levels may have to be approached differently.

Clerical and other employees at lower hierarchical levels may be asked broad, open-ended questions about their jobs and the work environment during unstructured interviews. Supervisors may be asked broad questions relating to their department, the employees under their supervision, and the organization. The following question, for instance, may be put to them during the unstructured interview stage:

*"Tell me something about your unit and department, and perhaps even the organization as a whole, in terms of work, employees, and whatever else you think is important."*

Such a question might elicit an elaborate response from some people; others may just say that everything is fine. Following the leads from the more vocal persons is easy, especially when the interviewer listens carefully to the important messages that they might convey in a very casual manner while responding to a general, global question. As managers and researchers, we should train ourselves to develop these listening skills and identify the critical topics that are touched on. However, when some respondents give a monosyllabic, crisp, short reply that is not informative, the interviewer will have to ask questions that call for details and cannot be answered in one or two words. Such questions might be phrased like the one below:

*"I would like to know something about your job. Please describe to me in detail the things you do in your job on a typical day, from eight in the morning to four in the afternoon."*

Several questions might then be asked as a follow-up to the answer. Some examples of such follow-up questions include:

*"Compared to other units in this organization, what are the strengths and weaknesses of your unit?"*

*"If you could have a problem solved in your unit, or a bottleneck eliminated, or something attended to that blocks your effectiveness, what would that be?"*

If the respondent answers that everything is fine and she has no problems, the interviewer could say: *"That is great! Tell me what contributes to this effectiveness of your unit, because most other organizations usually experience several difficulties."* Such a questioning technique usually brings the respondent's defenses down and makes him or her more amenable to sharing information. Typical of the revised responses to the original question would be something like, "Well, it is not that we never have a problem; sometimes there is delay in getting the jobs done, crash jobs have some defective items, . . . " Encouraging the respondent to talk about both the good things and those not-so-good in the unit can elicit a lot of information. Whereas some respondents do not need much encouragement to speak, others do, and they have to be questioned broadly. Some respondents may show reluctance to be interviewed, and subtly or overtly refuse to cooperate. The wishes of such people must be respected and the interviewer should pleasantly terminate such interviews.

Employees at the shop-floor level, and other nonmanagerial and nonsupervisory employees, might be asked very broad questions relating to their jobs, work environment, satisfactions and dissatisfactions at the workplace, and the like – for example:

*"What do you like about working here?"*

*"If you were to tell me which aspects of your job you like and which you do not, what would they be?"*

*"Tell me something about the reward systems in this place."*

*"If you were offered a similar job elsewhere, how willing would you be to take it and why?"*

*"If I were to seek employment here and request you to describe your unit to me as a newcomer, what would you say?"*

After conducting a sufficient number of such unstructured interviews with employees at several levels and studying the data obtained, the researcher would know the variables that needed greater focus and called for more in-depth information.

This sets the stage for the interviewer to conduct further structured interviews, for which the variables will have been identified.

### Structured interviews

**Structured interviews** are those conducted when it is known at the outset what information is needed. The interviewer has a list of predetermined questions to be asked of the respondents either personally, through the telephone, or through the medium of a PC. The questions are likely to focus on factors that surfaced during the unstructured interviews and are considered relevant to the problem. As the respondents express their views, the researcher notes them down. The same questions will be asked of everybody in the same manner. Sometimes, however, based on the exigencies of the situation, the experienced researcher might take a lead from a respondent's answer and ask other relevant questions not on the interview protocol. Through this process, new factors might be identified, resulting in a deeper understanding. However, to be able to recognize a probable response, the interviewer must comprehend the purpose and goal of each question. This is particularly important when a team of trained interviewers conducts the survey.

Visual aids such as pictures, line drawings, cards, and other materials are also sometimes used in conducting interviews. The appropriate visuals are shown to the interviewees, who then indicate their responses to the questions posed. Marketing research, for example, benefits from such techniques in order to capture the likes and dislikes of customers with regard to different types of packaging, forms of advertising, and so on. Visual aids, including painting and drawing, are particularly useful when children are the focus of marketing research. Visual aids also come in handy while endeavoring to elicit certain thoughts and ideas that are difficult to express or awkward to articulate.

When a sufficient number of structured interviews has been conducted and adequate information obtained to understand and describe the important factors operating in the situation, the researcher stops the interviews. The information is then tabulated and the data analyzed. This helps the researcher to accomplish the task he set out to achieve, such as describing the phenomena, or quantifying them, or identifying the specific problem and evolving a theory of the factors that influence the problem, or finding answers to the research question. Much qualitative research is done in this manner.

### Review of unstructured and structured interviews

The main purpose of the unstructured interview is to explore and probe into the several factors in the situation that might be central to the broad problem area. During this process it might become evident that the problem, as identified by the client, is but a symptom of a more serious and deep-rooted problem. Conducting unstructured interviews with many people in the organization could result in the identification of several critical factors in the situation. These would then be pursued further during structured interviews for eliciting more in-depth information on them. This helps identify the critical problem as well as ways of solving it. In applied research, a tentative theory of the factors contributing to the problem is often conceptualized on the basis of the information obtained from unstructured and structured interviews.

## Training interviewers

When several long interviews are to be conducted, it is often not feasible for one individual to conduct all the interviews. A team of trained interviewers then becomes necessary. Interviewers have to be thoroughly briefed about the research and trained in how to start an interview, how to proceed with the questions, how to motivate respondents to answer, what to look for in the answers, and how to close an interview. They also need to be instructed about taking notes and coding the interview responses. The tips for interviewing, discussed later, should become a part of their repertoire for interviewing.

Good planning, proper training, offering clear guidelines to interviewers, and supervising their work all help in profitably utilizing the interviewing technique as a viable data collection mechanism. Personal interviews provide rich data when respondents spontaneously offer information, in the sense that their answers do not typically fall within a constricted range of responses, as in a questionnaire. However, personal interviews are expensive in terms of time, training costs, and resource consumption.

## Some tips to follow when interviewing

The information obtained during the interviews should be as free as possible of bias. **Bias** refers to errors or inaccuracies in the data collected. Bias could be introduced by the interviewer, the interviewee, or the situation. The interviewer could bias the data if proper trust and rapport are not established with the interviewee, or when the responses are either misinterpreted or distorted, or when the interviewer unintentionally encourages or discourages certain types of response through gestures and facial expressions.

Listening attentively to the interviewee, evincing keen interest in what the respondent has to say, exercising tact in questioning, repeating and/or clarifying the questions posed, and paraphrasing some of the answers to ensure their thorough understanding, go a long way in keeping alive the interest of the respondent throughout the interview. Recording the responses accurately is equally important.

Interviewees can bias the data when they do not come out with their true opinions but provide information that they think is what the interviewer expects of them or would like to hear. Also, if they do not understand the questions, they may feel diffident or hesitant to seek clarification. They may then answer questions without knowing their import, and thus introduce bias.

Some interviewees may be turned off because of personal likes and dislikes, or the dress of the interviewer, or the manner in which the questions are put. They may, therefore, not provide truthful answers, but instead, deliberately offer incorrect responses. Some respondents may also answer questions in a socially acceptable manner rather than indicating their true sentiments.

Biases could be situational as well, in terms of (1) nonparticipants, (2) trust levels and rapport established, and (3) the physical setting of the interview. Nonparticipation, either because of unwillingness or the inability of the interviewee to participate in the study, can bias data inasmuch as the responses of the participants may be different from those of the nonparticipants (which implies that a biased, rather than a representative, set of responses is likely to result). Bias also occurs when different interviewers establish different levels of trust and rapport with their interviewees, thus eliciting answers of varying degrees of openness. The actual setting in which the interview is conducted might sometimes introduce bias. Some individuals, for instance, may not feel quite at ease when interviewed at the workplace and therefore may not respond frankly and honestly.

In door-to-door or telephone interviews, when the respondent cannot be reached due to unavailability at that time, callbacks and further contacts should be attempted so that the sample does not become biased (discussed in Chapter 10 on Sampling). The interviewer can also reduce bias by being consistent with the questioning mode as each person is interviewed, by not distorting or falsifying the information received, and by not influencing the responses of the subjects in any manner.

The above biases can be minimized in several ways. The following strategies will be useful for the purpose.

### Establishing credibility and rapport, and motivating individuals to respond

The projection of professionalism, enthusiasm, and confidence is important for the interviewer. A manager hiring outside researchers would be interested in assessing their abilities and personality predispositions. Researchers must establish rapport with, and gain the confidence and approval of, the hiring client before they can even start their work in the organization. Knowledge, skills, ability, confidence, articulateness, and enthusiasm are therefore qualities a researcher must demonstrate in order to establish credibility with the hiring organization and its members.

To obtain honest information from the respondents, the researcher/interviewer should be able to establish rapport and trust with them. In other words, the researcher should be able to make the respondent sufficiently at ease to give informative and truthful answers without fear of adverse consequences. To this end, the researcher should state the purpose of the interview and assure complete confidentiality about the source of the responses. Establishing rapport with the respondents may not be easy, especially when interviewing employees at lower levels. They are likely to be suspicious of the intentions of the researchers; they may believe that the researchers are on the management's "side," and therefore likely to propose a reduction in the labor force, increase the workload, and so on. Thus, it is important to ensure that everyone concerned is aware of the researchers' purpose as being one of merely understanding the true state of affairs in the organization. The respondents must be tactfully made to understand that the researchers do not intend to take sides; they are not there to harm the staff, and will provide the results of research to the organization only in aggregates, without disclosing the identity of the individuals. This should encourage the respondents to feel secure about responding.

The researcher can establish rapport by being pleasant, sincere, sensitive, and nonevaluative. Evincing a genuine interest in the responses and allaying any anxieties, fears, suspicions, and tensions sensed in the situation will help respondents to feel more comfortable with the researchers. If the respondent is told about the purpose of the study and how he or she was chosen to be one of those interviewed, there should be better communication between the parties. Researchers can motivate respondents to offer honest and truthful answers by explaining to them that their contribution will indeed help, and that they themselves may stand to gain from such a survey, in the sense that the quality of life at work for most of them may improve significantly.

Certain other strategies in how questions are posed also help participants to offer less biased responses. These are discussed below.

### The questioning technique

#### Funneling

At the beginning of an unstructured interview, it is advisable to ask open-ended questions to get a broad idea and form some impressions about the situation. For example a question that could be asked would be:

*"What are some of your feelings about working for this organization?"*

From the responses to this broad question, further questions that are progressively more focused may be asked as the researcher processes the interviewees' responses and notes some possible key issues relevant to the situation. This transition from broad to narrow themes is called the **funneling technique**.

#### Unbiased questions

It is important to ask questions in a way that ensures the least bias in the responses. For example, "Tell me how you experience your job" is a better question than, "Boy, the work you do must be really boring; let me hear how you experience it." The latter question is "loaded" in terms of the interviewer's own perceptions of the job. A loaded question might influence the types of answers received from the respondent. Bias could also be introduced by emphasizing certain words, by tone and voice inflections, and through inappropriate suggestions.

### Clarifying issues

To make sure that the researcher understands issues as the respondent intends to represent them, it is advisable to restate or rephrase important information given by the respondent. For instance, if the interviewee says, "There is an unfair promotion policy in this organization; seniority does not count at all. It is the juniors who always get promoted," the researcher might interject, "So you are saying that juniors always get promoted over the heads of even capable seniors." Rephrasing in this way clarifies the issue of whether or not the respondent considers ability important. If certain things that are being said are not clear, the researcher should seek clarification. For example, if the respondent happens to say, "The facilities here are really poor; we often have to continue working even when we are dying of thirst," the researcher might ask if there is no water fountain or drinking water available in the building. The respondent's reply to this might well indicate that there is a water fountain across the hall, but the respondent would like one on his side of the work area as well.

### Helping the respondent to think through issues

If the respondent is not able to verbalize her perceptions, or replies, "I don't know," the researcher should ask the question in a simpler way or rephrase it. For instance, if a respondent is unable to specify what aspects of the job he dislikes, the researcher might ask the question in a simpler way. For example, the respondent might be asked which task he would prefer to do: serve a customer or do some filing work. If the answer is "serve the customer," the researcher might use another aspect of the respondent's job and ask the paired-choice question again. In this way, the respondent can sort out which aspects of the job he likes better than others.

### Taking notes

When conducting interviews, it is important that the researcher makes written notes as the interviews are taking place, or as soon as the interview is terminated. The interviewer should not rely on memory, because information recalled from memory is imprecise and often likely to be incorrect. Furthermore, if more than one interview is scheduled for the day, the amount of information received increases, as do possible sources of error in recalling from memory as to who said what. Information based solely on recall introduces bias into the research.

The interviews can be recorded on tape if the respondent has no objection. However, taped interviews might bias the respondents' answers because they know that their voices are being recorded, and their anonymity is not preserved in full. Hence, even if the respondents do not object to being taped, there could be some bias in their responses. Before recording or videotaping interviews, one should be reasonably certain that such a method of obtaining data is not likely to bias the information received. Any audio or videotaping should always be done only after obtaining the respondent's permission.

### Review of tips to follow when interviewing

Establishing credibility as able researchers with the client system and the organizational members is important for the success of the research project. Researchers need to establish rapport with the respondents and motivate them to give responses relatively free from bias by allaying whatever suspicions, fears, anxieties, and concerns they may have about the research and its consequences. This can be accomplished by being sincere, pleasant, and nonevaluative. While interviewing, the researcher has to ask broad questions initially and then narrow them down to specific areas, ask questions in an unbiased way, offer clarification when needed, and help respondents to think through difficult issues. The responses should be transcribed immediately and should not be trusted to memory and later recall.

Having looked at unstructured and structured interviews and learned something about how to conduct the interviews, we can now discuss face-to-face and telephone interviews.

## Face-to-face and telephone interviews

Interviews can be conducted either face to face or over the telephone. They may also be computer-assisted. Although most unstructured interviews in organizational research are conducted face to face, structured interviews may be either face to face or through the medium of the telephone, depending on the level of complexity of the issues involved, the likely duration of the interview, the convenience of both parties, and the geographical area covered by the survey. Telephone interviews are best suited when information from a large number of respondents spread over a wide geographic area is to be obtained quickly, and the likely duration of each interview is, say, ten minutes or less. Many market surveys, for instance, are conducted through structured telephone interviews. In addition, **computer-assisted telephone interviews (CATI)** are also possible, and easy to manage.

Face-to-face interviews and telephone interviews have other advantages and disadvantages. These will now be briefly discussed.

### Face-to-face interviews

*Advantages*

The main advantage of face-to-face or direct interviews is that the researcher can adapt the questions as necessary, clarify doubts, and ensure that the responses are properly understood, by repeating or rephrasing the questions. The researcher can also pick up nonverbal cues from the respondent. Any discomfort, stress, or problem that the respondent experiences can be detected through frowns, nervous tapping, and other body language unconsciously exhibited by her. This would be impossible to detect in a telephone interview.

*Disadvantages*

The main disadvantages of face-to-face interviews are the geographical limitations they may impose on the surveys and the vast resources needed if such surveys need to be done nationally or internationally. The costs of training interviewers to minimize interviewer bias (e.g., differences in questioning methods, interpretation of responses) are also high. Another drawback is that respondents might feel uneasy about the anonymity of their responses when they interact face to face with the interviewer.

### Telephone interviews

#### *Advantages*

The main advantage of telephone interviewing, from the researcher's point of view, is that a number of different people can be reached (if need be, across the country or even internationally) in a relatively short period of time. From the respondents' standpoint it eliminates any discomfort that some of them might feel in facing the interviewer. It is also possible that most of them might feel less uncomfortable disclosing personal information over the phone than face to face.

#### *Disadvantages*

A main disadvantage of telephone interviewing is that the respondent could unilaterally terminate the interview without warning or explanation, by hanging up the phone. Caller ID might further aggravate the situation. This is understandable, given the numerous telemarketing calls people are bombarded with on a daily basis. To minimize this type of nonresponse problem, it is advisable to call the interviewee ahead of time to request participation in the survey, giving an approximate idea of how long the interview will last, and setting up a mutually convenient time. Interviewees usually tend to appreciate this courtesy and are more likely to cooperate. It is a good policy not to prolong the interview beyond the time originally stated. As mentioned earlier, another disadvantage of the telephone interview is that the researcher will not be able to see the respondent to read the nonverbal communication.

## Additional sources of bias in interview data

We have already discussed several sources of bias in data collection. Biased data will be obtained when respondents are interviewed while they are extremely busy or are not in good humor. Responses to issues such as strikes, layoffs, or the like could also be biased. The personality of the interviewer, the introductory sentence, inflection of the voice, and such other aspects could introduce additional bias. Awareness of the many sources of bias will enable interviewers to obtain relatively valid information.

Sampling biases, which include inability to contact persons whose telephone numbers have changed, could also affect the quality of the research data. Likewise, people with unlisted numbers who are not contacted could also bias the sample (discussed in Chapter 10), and hence, the data obtained. With the introduction of caller ID, it is possible for telephone interviews to be ridden with complexity.

## Computer-assisted interviewing

With computer-assisted interviews (CAI), thanks to modern technology, questions are flashed onto the computer screen and interviewers can enter the answers of the respondents directly into the computer. The accuracy of data collection is considerably enhanced since the software can be programmed to flag the "offbase" or "out-of-range" responses. CAI software also prevents interviewers from asking the wrong questions or in the wrong sequence since the questions are automatically flashed to the respondent in an ordered sequence. This, to some extent, eliminates interviewer-induced bias.

## CATI and CAPI

There are two types of computer-assisted interview programs: CATI (computer-assisted telephone interviewing) and CAPI (computer-assisted personal interviewing).

CATI, used in research organizations, is useful inasmuch as responses to surveys can be obtained from people all over the world since the PC is networked into the telephone system. The PC monitor prompts the questions with the help of software and the respondent provides the answers. The computer selects the telephone number, dials, and places the responses in a file. The data are analyzed later. Computerized, voice-activated telephone interviews are also possible for short surveys. Data can also be gathered during field surveys through handheld computers that record and analyze responses.

CAPI involves big investments in hardware and software. CAPI has an advantage in that it can be self-administered; that is, respondents can use their own computers to run the program by themselves once they receive the software and enter their responses, thereby reducing errors in recording. However, not everyone is comfortable using a personal computer and some may not have access to one.

The voice recording system assists CATI programs by recording interviewees' responses. Courtesy, ethics, and legal requirements require that the respondents' permission to record be obtained before the voice capture system (VCS) is activated. The VCS allows the computer to capture respondents' answers, which are recorded in a digital mode and stored in a data file. They can be played back later, for example, to listen to customers by region, industry, or any combination of different sets of factors.

In sum, the advantages of computer-assisted interviews can be stated simply as quick and more accurate information gathering, plus faster and easier analysis of data. The field costs are low and automatic tabulation of results is possible. It is more efficient in terms of costs and time, once the initial heavy investment in equipment and software has been made. However, to be really cost-effective, large surveys should be done frequently enough to warrant the heavy front-end investment and programming costs.

### Computer-aided survey services

Several research organizations offer their services to companies who engage in occasional data gathering. For instance, the National Computer Network provides computer survey services for conducting marketing studies. Some of the advantages of using these services are that:

1. The researcher can start analyzing the data even as the field survey is in progress, since results can be transmitted to clients by modem in raw or tabulated form.
2. Data can be automatically "cleaned up" and errors, if any, fixed even as they are being collected.

3. Bias due to ordering questions in a particular way (known as ordering effects) can be eliminated since meaningful random start patterns can be incorporated into the questioning process.
4. Skip patterns (e.g., if the answer to this question is NO, skip to question 19) can be programmed into the process.
5. Questions can be customized to incorporate the respondents' terminology of concepts into subsequent questions.

Computer surveys can be conducted either by mailing the disks to respondents or through online surveys, with the respondents' personal computers being hooked up to computer networks. Survey System, provided by Creative Research Systems, and Interview System, provided by Compaq Co., are two of the several computer survey systems available on the market.

### Advantages of software packages

Field notes taken by interviewers as they collect data generally have to be transcribed, hand-coded, hand-tabulated, and so on – all of which are tedious and time consuming. Computers vastly ease the interviewers' job with regard to these activities. Automatic indexing of the data can be done with special programs. The two modes in operation are:

1. Indexing such that specific responses are coded in a particular way.
2. Retrieval of data with a fast search speed – covering 10 000 pages in less than five seconds.

A text-oriented database management retrieval program allows the user to go through the text, inserting marks that link related units of text. The associative links formed are analytical categories specified by the researcher. Once the links are created, the program allows the user to activate them by opening multiple windows on the screen.

We can thus see that computers make a big impact on data collection. With greater technological advancement and a reduction in hardware and software costs, computer-assisted interviews promise to become a primary method of data collection in the future.

## Review of interviewing

Interviews are one method of obtaining data; they can be either unstructured or structured, and can be conducted face to face, over the telephone, or through the medium of the PC. Unstructured interviews are usually conducted to obtain definite ideas about what is, and is not, important and relevant to particular problem situations. Structured interviews give more in-depth information about specific variables of interest. To minimize bias in responses, the interviewer must establish rapport with the respondents and ask unbiased questions. The face-to-face interview and that conducted over the telephone have their advantages and disadvantages, and both have their uses in different circumstances. Computer-assisted interviewing, which entails heavy initial investment, is an asset for interviewing and for the analysis of qualitative, spontaneous responses. Computer interactive interviews show promise with regard to becoming an increasingly important mode of data collection in the future. Next, we will see how data can be gathered through questionnaires.

# Questionnaires

A **questionnaire** is a preformulated written set of questions to which respondents record their answers, usually within rather closely defined alternatives. Questionnaires are an efficient data collection mechanism when the researcher knows exactly what is required and how to measure the variables of interest. Questionnaires can be administered personally, mailed to the respondents, or electronically distributed.

## Personally administered questionnaires

When the survey is confined to a local area, and the organization is willing and able to assemble groups of employees to respond to questionnaires at the workplace, a good way to collect data is to personally administer the questionnaires. The main advantage of this is that the researcher or a member of the research team can collect all the completed responses within a short period of time. Any doubts that the respondents might have on any question can be clarified on the spot. The researcher is also afforded the opportunity to introduce the research topic and motivate the respondents to offer their frank answers. Administering questionnaires to large numbers of individuals at the same time is less expensive and consumes less time than interviewing; equally, it does not require as much skill to administer a questionnaire as it does to conduct interviews. Wherever possible, questionnaires are best administered personally to groups of people because of these advantages. However, organizations are often unable or disinclined to allow work hours to be spent on data collection, and other ways of getting the questionnaires back after completion may have to be found. In such cases, employees may be given blank questionnaires to be collected from them personally on completion after a few days, or mailed back by a certain date in self-addressed, stamped envelopes provided to them for the purpose. Scanner sheets (the answer sheets that are usually provided for answering multiple-choice questions in exams) are usually sent with the questionnaire, so that respondents can circle their answers to each question on the sheet, which can then be directly entered into the computer as data, without someone having to code and then manually enter them in the computer. Disks containing the questions can also be sent to respondents who have, and can use, personal computers.

## Mail questionnaires

The main advantage of mail questionnaires is that a wide geographical area can be covered in the survey. They are mailed to the respondents, who can complete them at their convenience, in their homes, and at their own pace. However, the return rates of mail questionnaires are typically low. A 30% response rate is considered acceptable. Another disadvantage of the mail questionnaire is that any doubts the respondents might have cannot be clarified. Also, with very low return rates it is difficult to establish the representativeness of the sample because those responding to the survey may not at all represent the population they are supposed to.

However, some effective techniques can be employed for improving the rates of response to mail questionnaires. Sending follow-up letters, enclosing some small monetary amounts as incentives with the questionnaire, providing the respondent with self-addressed, stamped return envelopes, and keeping the questionnaire brief all help.

Mail questionnaires are also expected to meet with a better response rate when respondents are notified in advance about the forthcoming survey, and a reputed research organization administers them with its own introductory cover letter.

The choice of using the questionnaire as a data-gathering method might be restricted if the researcher has to reach subjects with very little education. Adding pictures to the questionnaires, if feasible, might be of help in such cases. For most organizational research, however, after the variables for the research have been identified and the measures therefore found or developed, the questionnaire is a convenient data collection mechanism. Field studies, comparative surveys, and experimental designs often use questionnaires to measure the variables of interest. Because questionnaires are in common use in surveys, it is necessary to know how to design them effectively. A set of guidelines for questionnaire construction follows.

## Guidelines for questionnaire design

Sound questionnaire design principles should focus on three areas. The first relates to the wording of the questions. The second refers to the planning of issues with regard to how the variables will be categorized, scaled, and coded after receipt of the responses. The third pertains to the general appearance of the questionnaire. All three are important issues in questionnaire design because they can minimize bias in research. These issues are discussed below. The important aspects are schematically depicted in Figure 8.2.

### Principles of wording

The principles of wording refer to such factors as:

1. The appropriateness of the content of the questions.
2. How questions are worded and the level of sophistication of the language used.
3. The type and form of questions asked.
4. The sequencing of the questions.
5. The personal data sought from the respondents.

Each of these is explained below.

#### Content and purpose of the questions

The nature of the variable tapped – subjective feelings or objective facts – will determine what kinds of questions are asked. If the variables tapped are of a subjective nature (e.g., satisfaction, involvement), where respondents' beliefs, perceptions, and attitudes are to be measured, the questions should tap the dimensions and elements of the concept. Where objective variables, such as age and educational levels of respondents, are tapped, a single direct question – preferably one that has an ordinal scaled set of categories – is appropriate.

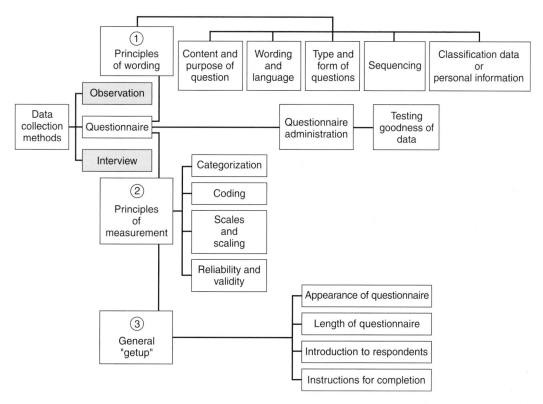

Figure 8.2: Principles of questionnaire design.

Thus, the purpose of each question should be carefully considered so that the variables are adequately measured and yet no superfluous questions are asked.

*Language and wording of the questionnaire*

The language of the questionnaire should approximate the level of understanding of the respondents. The choice of words will depend on their educational level, the usage of terms and idioms in the culture, and the frames of reference of the respondents. For instance, even when English is the spoken or official language in two cultures, certain words may be alien to one culture. Terms such as "working here is a drag," and "she is a compulsive worker," may not be interpreted the same way in different cultures. Some blue-collar workers may not understand terminology such as "organizational structure." Thus, it is essential to word the questions in a way that can be understood by the respondent. If some questions are either not understood or are interpreted differently by the respondent, the researcher will obtain the wrong answers to the questions, and responses will thus be biased. Hence, the questions asked, the language used, and the wording should be appropriate to tap respondents' attitudes, perceptions, and feelings.

*Type and form of questions*

The type of question refers to whether the question is open-ended or closed. The form of the question refers to whether it is positively or negatively worded.

### Open-ended versus closed questions

**Open-ended questions** allow respondents to answer them in any way they choose. An example of an open-ended question is asking the respondent to state five things that are interesting and challenging in the job. Another example is asking what the respondents like about their supervisors or their work environment. A third example is to invite their comments on the investment portfolio of the firm.

A **closed question**, in contrast, asks the respondents to make choices among a set of alternatives given by the researcher. For instance, instead of asking the respondent to state any five aspects of the job that she finds interesting and challenging, the researcher might list 10 or 15 aspects that might seem interesting or challenging in jobs and ask the respondents to rank the first five among these in the order of their preference. All items in a questionnaire using a nominal, ordinal, Likert, or ratio scale are considered closed.

Closed questions help the respondents to make quick decisions to choose among the several alternatives before them. They also help the researcher to code the information easily for subsequent analysis. Care has to be taken to ensure that the alternatives are mutually exclusive and collectively exhaustive. If there are overlapping categories, or if all possible alternatives are not given (i.e., the categories are not exhaustive), the respondents might get confused and the advantage of their being enabled to make a quick decision is thus lost.

Some respondents may find even well-delineated categories in a closed question rather confining and might avail themselves of the opportunity to make additional comments. This is the reason why many questionnaires end with a final open-ended question that invites respondents to comment on topics that might not have been covered fully or adequately. The responses to such open-ended questions have to be edited and categorized for subsequent data analysis.

### Positively and negatively worded questions

Instead of phrasing all questions positively, it is advisable to include some negatively worded questions as well, so the tendency in respondents to mechanically circle the points toward one end of the scale is minimized. For example, let us say that a set of six questions is used to tap the variable "perceived success" on a five-point scale, with 1 being "very low" and 5 being "very high" on the scale. A respondent who is not particularly interested in completing the questionnaire is more likely to stay involved and remain alert while answering the questions when positively and negatively worded questions are interspersed in it. For instance, if the respondent has circled 5 for a positively worded question such as, "I feel I have been able to accomplish a number of different things in my job," he cannot circle number 5 again to the negatively worded question, "I do not feel I am very effective in my job." The respondent is now shaken out of any likely tendency to mechanically respond to one end of the scale. In case this does still happen, the researcher has an opportunity to detect such bias. A good questionnaire should therefore include both positively and negatively worded questions.

The use of double negatives and excessive use of the words "not" and "only" should be avoided in negatively worded questions because they tend to confuse respondents. For instance, it is better to say, "Coming to work is no great fun" than to say "Not coming to work is greater fun than coming to work." Likewise, it is better to say "The rich need no help" than to say "Only the rich do not need help."

## Double-barreled questions

A question that lends itself to different possible responses to its subparts is called a **double-barreled question**. Such questions should be avoided and two or more separate questions asked instead. For example, the question "Do you think there is a good market for the product and that it will sell well?" could bring a "yes" response to the first part (i.e., there is a good market for the product) and a "no" response to the latter part (i.e., it will not sell well for various other reasons). In this case, it would be better to ask two questions: (1) "Do you think there is a good market for the product?" and (2) "Do you think the product will sell well?" The answers might be "yes" to both, "no" to both, "yes" to the first and "no" to the second, or "yes" to the second and "no" to the first. If we combined the two questions and asked a double-barreled question, we would confuse the respondents and obtain ambiguous responses. Hence, double-barreled questions should be eliminated.

## Ambiguous questions

Even questions that are not double-barreled might be ambiguously worded and the respondent may not be sure what exactly they mean. An example of such a question is "To what extent would you say you are happy?" Respondents might find it difficult to decide whether the question refers to their state of feelings in the workplace, or at home, or in general. Because it is an organizational survey, a respondent might presume that the question relates to the workplace. Yet the researcher might have intended to inquire about the general, overall degree of satisfaction that the individual experiences in everyday life – a very global feeling not specific to the workplace alone. Thus, responses to **ambiguous questions** have built-in bias inasmuch as different respondents might interpret such items in the questionnaire differently. The result is a mixed bag of ambiguous responses that do not accurately provide the correct answer to the question.

## Recall-dependent questions

Some questions might require respondents to recall experiences from the past that are hazy in their memory. Answers to such questions might have bias. For instance, if an employee who has had 30 years' service in the organization is asked to state when he first started working in a particular department and for how long, he may not be able to give the correct answers and may be way off in his responses. A better source for obtaining that information would be the personnel records.

## Leading questions

Questions should not be phrased in such a way that they lead the respondents to give the responses that the researcher would like them to give. An example of such a question is: "Don't you think that in these days of escalating costs of living, employees should be given good pay rises?'' By asking a **leading question**, we are signaling and pressuring respondents to say "yes." Tagging the question to rising living costs makes it difficult for most respondents (unless they are the top bosses in charge of budget and finances) to say, "No; not unless their productivity increases too!'' Another way of asking the question about pay rises to elicit less biased responses would be: "To what extent do you agree that employees should be given higher pay rises?'' If respondents think that the employees do not deserve a higher pay rise at all, their response will be "Strongly Disagree"; if they think that respondents should definitely be given a high pay rise, they will respond to the "Strongly Agree" end of the scale, and the in-between points will be chosen depending on the strength of their agreement or disagreement. In this case, the question is not framed in a suggestive manner as in the previous instance.

### Loaded questions

Another type of bias in questions occurs when they are phrased in an emotionally charged manner. An example of such a **loaded question** is asking employees: "To what extent do you think management is likely to be vindictive if the union decides to go on strike?'' The words "strike" and "vindictive" are emotionally charged terms, polarizing management and unions. Hence, asking a question such as the above would elicit strongly emotional and highly biased responses. If the purpose of the question is twofold; that is, to find (1) the extent to which employees are in favor of a strike and (2) the extent to which they fear adverse reactions if they do go on strike, then these are the two specific questions that need to be asked. It may turn out that the employees are not strongly in favor of a strike and they also do not believe that management would retaliate if they did go on strike!

### Social desirability

Questions should not be worded such that they elicit socially desirable responses. For instance, a question such as "Do you think that older people should be laid off?'' would elicit a response of "no," mainly because society would frown on a person who said that elderly people should be fired even if they are capable of performing their jobs satisfactorily. Hence, irrespective of the true feelings of the respondent, a socially desirable answer would be provided. If the purpose of the question is to gauge the extent to which organizations are seen as obligated to retain those above 65 years of age, a differently worded question with less pressure toward social desirability would be: "There are advantages and disadvantages to retaining senior citizens in the workforce. To what extent do you think companies should continue to keep the elderly on their payroll?''

Sometimes certain items that tap social desirability are deliberately introduced at various points in the questionnaire and an index of each individual's social desirability tendency is calculated therefrom. This index is then applied to all other responses given by the individual in order to adjust for social desirability bias (Crowne and Marlowe, 1980; Edwards, 1957).

### Length of questions

Finally, simple, short questions are preferable to long ones. As a rule of thumb, a question or a statement in the questionnaire should not exceed 20 words, or exceed one full line in print (Horst, 1968; Oppenheim, 1986).

*Sequencing of questions*

The sequence of questions in the questionnaire should be such that the respondent is led from questions of a general nature to those that are more specific, and from questions that are relatively easy to answer to those that are progressively more difficult. This funnel approach, as it is called (Festinger and Katz, 1966), facilitates the easy and smooth progress of the respondent through the items in the questionnaire. The progression from general to specific questions might mean that the respondent is first asked questions of a global nature that pertain to the organization, and then is asked more incisive questions regarding the specific job, department, and the like. Easy questions might relate to issues that do not involve much thinking; the more difficult ones might call for more thought, judgment, and decision making in providing the answers.

In determining the sequence of questions, it is advisable not to place contiguously a positively worded and a negatively worded question tapping the same element or dimension of a concept. For instance, placing two questions such as the following, one immediately after the other, is not only awkward but might also seem insulting to the respondent.

*I have opportunities to interact with my colleagues during work hours.*

*I have few opportunities to interact with my colleagues during work hours.*

First, there is no need to ask the very same question in both a positive and a negative way. Second, if for some reason this is deemed necessary (e.g., to check the consistency of the responses), the two questions should be placed in different parts of the questionnaire, as far apart as possible.

The way questions are sequenced can also introduce certain biases, frequently referred to as ordering effects. Though randomly placing the questions in the questionnaire reduces any systematic bias in the responses, it is very rarely done, because of subsequent confusion while categorizing, coding, and analyzing the responses.

In sum, the language and wording of the questionnaire focus on such issues as the type and form of questions asked (i.e., open-ended and closed questions, and positively and negatively worded questions), as well as avoiding double-barreled questions, ambiguous questions, leading questions, loaded questions, questions prone to tap socially desirable answers, and those involving distant recall. Questions should also not be unduly long. Using the funnel approach helps respondents to progress through the questionnaire with ease and comfort.

## Classification data or personal information

Classification data, also known as personal information or demographic questions, elicit such information as age, educational level, marital status, and income. Unless absolutely necessary, it is best not to ask for the name of the respondent. If, however, the questionnaire has to be identified with the respondents for any reason, then the questionnaire can be numbered and connected by the researcher to the respondent's name, in a separately maintained, private document. This procedure should be clearly explained to the respondent. The reason for using the numerical system in questionnaires is to ensure the anonymity of the respondent, should the questionnaires fall into the hands of someone unauthorized in the organization.

Whether questions seeking personal information should appear at the beginning or at the end of the questionnaire is a matter of choice for the researcher. Some researchers ask for personal data at the end rather than the beginning of the questionnaire (Oppenheim, 1986). Their reasoning may be that by the time the respondent reaches the end of the questionnaire he or she has been convinced of the legitimacy and genuineness of the questions framed by the researcher and, hence, is more inclined and amenable to share personal information. Researchers who prefer to elicit most of the personal information at the very beginning may opine that once respondents have shared some of their personal history, they may have psychologically identified themselves with the questionnaire, and may feel a commitment to respond. Thus, whether one asks for this information at the beginning or at the end of the questionnaire is a matter of individual choice. However, questions seeking details of income, or other highly sensitive information – if deemed necessary – are best placed at the very end of the questionnaire. Even so, it is a wise policy to ask for such information by providing a range of response options, rather than seeking exact figures. For example, the variables may be tapped as shown below:

| Age (years) | Annual income |
|---|---|
| Under 20 | Less than $20 000 |
| 20–30 | $20 000–30 000 |
| 31–40 | $30 001–40 000 |
| 41–50 | $40 001–50 000 |
| 51–60 | $50 001–70 000 |
| Over 60 | $70 001–90 000 |
| | Over $90 000 |

In organizational surveys, it is advisable to gather certain demographic data such as age, sex, educational level, job level, department, and number of years in the organization, even if the theoretical framework does not necessitate or include these variables. Such data help to describe the sample characteristics in the report written after data analysis. However, when there are only a few respondents in a department, then questions likely to reveal their identity might render them futile, objectionable, and threatening to employees. For instance, if there is only one female in a department, then she might refrain from responding to the question on gender, because it would establish the source of the data; this apprehension is understandable.

To sum up, certain principles of wording need to be followed while designing a questionnaire. The questions asked must be appropriate for tapping the variable. The language and wording used should be such that it is meaningful to the employees. The form and type of questions should be geared to minimize respondent bias. The sequencing of the questions should facilitate the smooth progress of the responses from start to finish. The personal data should be gathered with due regard to the sensitivity of the respondents' feelings, and with respect for privacy.

## Principles of measurement

Just as there are guidelines to be followed to ensure that the wording of the questionnaire is appropriate to minimize bias, so also are there some principles of measurement to be followed to ensure that the data collected are appropriate to test our hypotheses. These refer to the scales and scaling techniques used in measuring concepts, as well as the assessment of reliability and validity of the measures used, which were all discussed in Chapter 7.

As we have seen, appropriate scales have to be used depending on the type of data that need to be obtained. The different scaling mechanisms that help us to anchor our scales appropriately should be properly used. Wherever possible, the interval and ratio scales should be used in preference to nominal or ordinal scales. Once data are obtained, the "goodness of data" should be assessed through tests of validity and reliability. Validity establishes how well a technique, instrument, or process measures a particular concept, and reliability indicates how stably and consistently the instrument taps the variable. Finally, the data have to be obtained in a manner that makes for easy categorization and coding, both of which are discussed later.

## General appearance or "getup" of the questionnaire

Not only is it important to address issues of wording and measurement in questionnaire design, but it is also necessary to pay attention to how the questionnaire looks. An attractive and neat questionnaire with appropriate introduction, instructions, and well-arrayed set of questions and response alternatives will make it easier for the respondents to answer them. A good introduction, well-organized instructions, and neat alignment of the questions are all important. These elements are briefly discussed with examples.

### A good introduction

A proper introduction that clearly discloses the identity of the researcher and conveys the purpose of the survey is absolutely necessary. It is also essential to establish some rapport with the respondents and motivate them to respond to the questions in the questionnaire wholeheartedly and enthusiastically. Assurance of confidentiality of the information provided by them will allow for less biased answers. The introduction section should end on a courteous note, thanking the respondent for taking the time to respond to the survey. The following is an example of an appropriate introduction.

## EXAMPLE

Dear Participant,                                                                                     Date

This questionnaire is designed to study aspects of life at work. The information you provide will help us better understand the quality of our work life. Because you are the one who can give us a correct picture of how you experience your work life, I request you to respond to the questions frankly and honestly.

Your response will be kept strictly confidential. Only members of the research team will have access to the information you give. In order to ensure the utmost privacy, we have provided an identification number for each participant. This number will be used by us only for follow-up procedures. The numbers, names, and the completed questionnaires will not be made available to anyone other than the research team. A summary of the results will be mailed to you after the data are analyzed.

Thank you very much for your time and cooperation. I greatly appreciate the help of your organization and yourself in furthering this research endeavor.

Cordially,
(Sd)
A. Professor, PhD

### Organizing questions, giving instructions and guidance, and good alignment

Organizing the questions logically and neatly in appropriate sections and providing instructions on how to complete the items in each section will help the respondents to answer them without difficulty. Questions should also be neatly aligned in a way that allows the respondent to complete the task of reading and answering the questionnaire by expending the least time and effort and without straining the eyes.

A specimen of the portion of a questionnaire incorporating the above points follows.

## EXAMPLE

SECTION TWO: ABOUT WORK LIFE

The questions below ask about how you experience your work life. Think in terms of your everyday experiences and accomplishments on the job and put the most appropriate response number for you beside each item, using the scale below.

| Strongly Agree | Agree | Slightly Agree | Neutral | Slightly Disagree | Disagree | Strongly Disagree |
|---|---|---|---|---|---|---|
| 1 | 2 | 3 | 4 | 5 | 6 | 7 |

I do my work best when my job assignments are fairly difficult. ____
When I have a choice, I try to work in a group instead of by myself. ____
In my work assignments, I try to be my own boss. ____
I seek an active role in the leadership of a group. ____
I try very hard to improve on my past performance at work. ____
I pay a good deal of attention to the feelings of others at work. ____
I go my own way at work, regardless of the opinions of others. ____
I avoid trying to influence those around me to see things my way. ____
I take moderate risks, sticking my neck out to get ahead at work. ____
I prefer to do my own work, letting others do theirs. ____
I disregard rules and regulations that hamper my personal freedom. ____

Personal data

Demographic or personal data could be organized as in the example that follows. Note the ordinal scaling of the age variable.

**EXAMPLE**

SECTION ONE: ABOUT YOURSELF

Please circle the numbers representing the most appropriate responses for you in respect of the following items.

**1. Your age (years)**

1 Under 20
2 20–35
3 36–50
4 51–65
5 Over 65

**2. Your highest completed level of education**

1 Elementary school
2 High school
3 College degree
4 Graduate degree
5 Other (specify)

**3. Your gender**

1 Female
2 Male

**4. Your marital status**

1 Married
2 Single
3 Widowed
4 Divorced or separated
5 Other (specify)

**5. Number of preschool children (under 5 years of age)**

1 None
2 One
3 Two
4 Three or more

**6. Age of the eldest child in your care (years)**

1 Under 5
2 5–12
3 13–19
4 Over 19

5 Not applicable

**7. Number of years worked in the organization**

1 Less than 1
2 1–2
3 3–5
4 6–10
5 Over 10

**8. Number of other organizations worked for before joining this organization**

1 None
2 One
3 Two
4 Three
5 Four or more

**9. Present work shift**

1 First
2 Second
3 Third

**10. Job status**

1 Top management
2 Middle management
3 First-level supervisor
4 Nonmanagerial

### Information on income and other sensitive personal data

Although demographic information can be sought either at the beginning or at the end of the questionnaire, information of a very private and personal nature such as income, state of health, and so on, if considered at all necessary for the survey, should be asked at the end of the questionnaire, rather than the beginning. Also, such questions should be justified by explaining how this information might contribute to knowledge and problem solving, so that respondents do not perceive them to be of an intrusive or prying nature (see example below). Postponing such questions to the end will help reduce respondent bias if the individual is vexed by the personal nature of the question.

## EXAMPLE

Because many people believe that income is a significant factor in explaining the type of career decisions individuals make, the following two questions are very important for this research. Like all other items in this questionnaire, the responses to these two questions will be kept confidential. Please circle the most appropriate number that describes your position.

Roughly, *my total yearly* income before taxes and other deductions is:

1  Less than $36 000
2  $36 001–50 000
3  $50 001–70 000
4  $70 001–90 000
5  Over $90 000

Roughly, the *total yearly income* before taxes and other deductions of my *immediate family –* *including* my own job income, income from other sources, and the income of my spouse – is:

1  Less than $36 000
2  $36 001–50 000
3  $50 001–70 000
4  $70 001–90 000
5  $90 001–120 000
6  $120 001–150 000
7  Over $150 000

### Open-ended question at the end

The questionnaire could include an open-ended question at the end, allowing respondents to comment on any aspect they choose. It should end with an expression of sincere thanks to respondents. The last part of the questionnaire could look as follows:

## EXAMPLE

The questions in the survey may not be all-embracing and comprehensive and may not therefore have afforded you an opportunity to report some things you may want to say about your job, the organization, or yourself. Please make any additional comments needed in the space provided.

*How did you feel about completing this questionnaire? Check the face in the following diagram that reflects your feelings.*

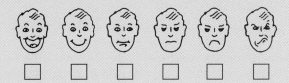

## Concluding the questionnaire

The questionnaire should end on a courteous note, reminding the respondent to check that all the items have been completed, as per the example below.

### EXAMPLE

I sincerely appreciate your time and cooperation. Please check to make sure that you have not skipped any questions inadvertently, and then drop the questionnaire in the locked box, clearly marked for the purpose, at the entrance of your department.

Thank you!

## Review of questionnaire design

We have devoted a lot of attention to questionnaire design because questionnaires are the most common method of collecting data. The principles of questionnaire design relate to how the questions are worded and measured, and how the entire questionnaire is organized. To minimize respondent bias and measurement errors, all the principles discussed have to be followed carefully.

Questionnaires are most useful as a data collection method, especially when large numbers of people are to be reached in different geographical regions. They are a popular method of collecting data because researchers can obtain information fairly easily, and the questionnaire responses are easily coded. When well-validated instruments are used, the findings of the study benefit the scientific community since the results can be replicated and additions to the theory base made.

There are several ways of administering questionnaires. Questionnaires can be personally administered to respondents, inserted in magazines, periodicals, or newspapers, mailed to respondents, or electronically distributed through e-mail – either via the Internet or an intranet. Software is also available to frame subsequent questions based on the subject's response to the preceding question. Companies' websites can also elicit survey responses; for example, reactions to customer service, product utility, and the like. Global research is now vastly facilitated by electronic systems.

## Pretesting of structured questions

Whether it is a structured interview where the questions are posed to the respondent in a predetermined order, or a questionnaire that is used in a survey, it is important to pretest the instrument to ensure that the questions are understood by the respondents (i.e., there is no ambiguity in the questions) and that there are no problems with the wording or measurement. Pretesting involves the use of a small number of respondents to test the appropriateness of the questions and their comprehension. This helps to rectify any inadequacies before administering the instrument orally or through a questionnaire to respondents, and thus reduces bias.

It would be good to debrief the results of the pretest and obtain additional information from the small group of participants (who serve the role of a focus group) on their general reactions to the questionnaire and how they felt about completing the instrument.

## Electronic questionnaire and survey design

Online questionnaire surveys are easily designed and administered when microcomputers are hooked up to computer networks. Data disks can also be mailed to respondents, who may use their own personal computers for responding to the questions. These will, of course, be helpful only when the respondents know how to use the computer and feel comfortable responding in this manner.

CAPPA, which facilitates the preparation and administration of questionnaires, is particularly useful for marketing research. The CAPPA system includes ten programs enabling the user to design a sophisticated computerized questionnaire, computerize the data collection process, and analyze the data collected. More reliable data are likely to result since the respondent can go back and forth and easily change a response, and various on- and off-screen stimuli are provided to sustain respondents' interest.

A program is designed in the CAPPA system, which checks for syntactical or logical errors in the coding. Even as the survey is in progress, descriptive summaries of the cumulative data can be obtained either on the screen or in printed form. After data collection is complete, a data-editing program identifies missing or out-of-range data (e.g., a 6 in response to a question on a five-point scale). The researcher can set the parameters to either delete missing responses if there are too many of them, or compute the mean of other responses and substitute this figure for the missing response. CAPPA also includes data analytic programs such as cross-tabs, ANOVA, multiple regression, and others (discussed later in the book). Randomization of questions and the weighting of respondents to ensure more representative results (in cases where the sample either overrepresents or underrepresents certain population groups – discussed in Chapter 10 on Sampling) are some of the attractive features of CAPPA.

Several programs have been developed to administer questionnaires electronically. As disks are inexpensive, mailing them across the country is no problem either. However, the PC medium nonresponse rates may not be any lower than those for mail questionnaires. With increases in computer literacy, we can expect electronic questionnaire administration to take on an increasing role in the future.

SPSS (Statistical Package for the Social Sciences) has several software programs for research purposes including (1) SPSS Data Entry Builder for creating surveys that can be administered over the web, phone, or mail; (2) SPSS Data Entry Enterprise Server for entering the responses; and (3) SPSS 11.0 for data analysis and charts.

The advantages and disadvantages of personal or face-to-face interviews, telephone interviews, personally administered questionnaires, mail questionnaires, and questionnaires distributed through the electronic system are presented in Table 8.1.

It should be pointed out that information obtained from respondents either through interviews or questionnaires, being self-report data, could be biased. That is the reason why data should be collected from different sources and by different methods, as discussed later.

## Other methods of data collection

### Observational studies

Whereas interviews and questionnaires elicit responses from the subjects, it is possible to gather data without asking questions of respondents. People can be observed in their natural work environment or in a lab setting, and their activities and behaviors or other items of interest can be noted and recorded.

Apart from the activities performed by the individuals under study, their movements, work habits, the statements made and meetings conducted by them, their facial expressions of joy, anger, and other emotions, and body language can be observed. Other environmental factors such as layout, work-flow patterns, the closeness of the seating arrangement, and the like, can also be noted. Children can be observed as to their interests and attention span with various stimuli, such as their involvement with different toys. Such observation would help toy manufacturers, child educators, day-care administrators, and others deeply involved in, or responsible for, children's development, to design and model ideas based on children's interests, which are more easily observed than traced in any other manner.

The researcher can play one of two roles while gathering field observational data – that of a nonparticipant-observer or participant-observer.

#### Nonparticipant-observer

The researcher may act as a **nonparticipant-observer** by collecting the necessary data without becoming an integral part of the organizational system. For example, the researcher might sit in the corner of an office and watch and record how the manager spends her time. Observation of all the activities of managers, over a period of several days, will allow the researcher to make

| TABLE 8.1 | Advantages and disadvantages of interviews and questionnaires. | |
|---|---|---|

| Mode of data collection | Advantages | Disadvantages |
|---|---|---|
| Personal or face-to-face interviews | Can establish rapport and motivate respondents. Can clarify the questions, clear doubts, add new questions. Can read nonverbal cues. Can use visual aids to clarify points. Rich data can be obtained. CAPI can be used and responses entered in a portable computer. | Takes personal time. Costs more when a wide geographic region is covered. Respondents may be concerned about confidentiality of information given. Interviewers need to be trained. Can introduce interviewer bias. Respondents can terminate the interview at any time. |
| Telephone interviews | Less costly and speedier than personal interviews. Can reach a wide geographic area. Greater anonymity than personal interviews. Can be done using CATI. | Nonverbal cues cannot be read. Interviews will have to be kept short. Obsolete telephone numbers could be contacted, and unlisted ones omitted from the sample. |
| Personally administered questionnaires | Can establish rapport and motivate respondent. Doubts can be clarified. Less expensive when administered to groups of respondents. Almost 100% response rate ensured. Anonymity of respondent is high. | Organizations may be reluctant to give up company time for the survey with groups of employees assembled for the purpose. |
| Mail questionnaires | Anonymity is high. Wide geographic regions can be reached. | Response rate is almost always low. A 30% rate is quite acceptable. Cannot clarify questions. |

| | | |
|---|---|---|
| | Token gifts can be enclosed to seek compliance. | Follow-up procedures for nonresponses are necessary. |
| | Respondent can take more time to respond at convenience. Can be administered electronically, if desired. | |
| Electronic questionnaires | Easy to administer. | Computer literacy is a must. |
| | Can reach globally. | Respondents must have access to the facility. |
| | Very inexpensive. | |
| | Fast delivery. | Respondent must be willing to complete the survey. |
| | Respondents can answer at their convenience like the mail questionnaire. | |

some generalizations on how managers typically spend their time. By merely observing the activities, recording them systematically, and tabulating them, the researcher is able to come up with some findings. This, however, renders it necessary that observers are physically present at the workplace for extended periods of time, making observational studies time consuming.

### Participant-observer

The researcher may also play the role of the **participant-observer**. Here, the researcher enters the organization or the research setting and becomes a part of the work team. For instance, if a researcher wants to study group dynamics in work organizations, then she may join the organization as an employee and observe the dynamics in groups while being a part of the work organization and the relevant work groups. Much anthropological research is conducted in this manner, where researchers become a part of an alien culture, which they are interested in studying in depth.

### Structured versus unstructured observational studies

As we have seen, observational studies may be of either the nonparticipant-observer or the participant-observer type. Both of these, again, may be either structured or unstructured.

#### *Structured observational studies*

Where the observer has a predetermined set of categories of activities or phenomena to be studied, it is a **structured observational study**. Formats for recording the observations can be specifically designed and tailored to each study to suit the goal of that research.

Usually, matters that pertain to the feature of interest, such as the duration and frequency of the event, as well as certain activities that precede and follow it, are recorded. Environmental conditions and any changes in setting are also noted, if considered relevant. Task-relevant behaviors of the actors, their perceived emotions, verbal and nonverbal communication, and such, are recorded. Observations that are recorded in worksheets or field notes are then systematically analyzed, with minimal personal inferences made by the investigator. Categories can then be developed for further analysis, as described in later chapters on Data Analysis.

### Unstructured observational studies

At the beginning of a study, it is possible that the observer has no definite ideas regarding the particular aspects that need focus. Observing events as they take place may also be a part of the plan, as in many qualitative studies. In such cases, the observer will record practically everything that is observed. Such a study is an **unstructured observational study**.

Unstructured observational studies are claimed to be the hallmark of qualitative research. The investigator might entertain a set of tentative hypotheses that serve as a guide as to who, when, where, and how they will observe. Once the necessary information has been observed and recorded over a period of time, patterns can be traced, and inductive discovery can then pave the way for subsequent theory building and hypothesis testing.

### Advantages and disadvantages of observational studies

There are some specific advantages and disadvantages to gathering data through observation, as listed in the next two sections.

### Advantages of observational studies

The following are among the advantages of observational studies.

1. The data obtained through observation of events as they normally occur are generally more reliable and free from respondent bias.
2. In observational studies, it is easier to note the effects of environmental influences on specific outcomes. For example, the weather (hot, cold, rainy), the day of the week (midweek as opposed to Monday or Friday), and other such factors that might have a bearing on, for example, the sales of a product, traffic patterns, absenteeism, and the like, can be noted and meaningful patterns might emerge from this type of data.
3. It is easier to observe certain groups of individuals – for example, very young children and extremely busy executives – from whom it may be otherwise difficult to obtain information.

The above three advantages are perhaps unique to observational studies.

### Disadvantages of observational studies

The following drawbacks of observational studies have also to be noted.

1. It is necessary for the observer to be physically present (unless a camera or another mechanical system can capture the events of interest), often for prolonged periods of time.
2. This method of collecting data is not only slow, but also tedious and expensive.

3. Because of the long periods for which subjects are observed, observer fatigue can easily set in, which might bias the recorded data.

4. Though moods, feelings, and attitudes can be guessed by observing facial expressions and other nonverbal behaviors, the cognitive thought processes of individuals cannot be captured.

5. Observers have to be trained in what and how to observe, and ways to avoid observer bias.

### Bias in observational studies

Data observed from the researcher's point of view are likely to be prone to observer bias. There may be recording errors, memory lapses, or errors in interpreting activities, behaviors, events, and nonverbal cues. Moreover, where several observers are involved, interobserver reliability has to be established before the data can be accepted. Observation of the happenings day in and day out, over extended periods of time, could afflict the observers with ennui and introduce bias in the recording of the observations. To minimize observer bias, observers are usually given training on how to observe and what to record. Good observational studies also establish interobserver reliability. This may be established during the training of the observers when videotaped stimuli may be used to determine interobserver reliability. A simple formula can be used for the purpose – dividing the number of agreements among the trainees by the number of agreements and disagreements – thus establishing the reliability coefficient.

Respondent bias could also be a threat to the validity of the results of observational studies, because those who are observed may behave differently during the period of the study, especially if the observations are confined to a short period of time. However, in studies of longer duration, the employees become more relaxed as the study progresses and tend to behave normally. For these reasons, researchers doing observational studies discount the data recorded in the first few days, if they seem to be quite different from what is observed later.

### Summary of observational studies

Observational studies have a formulated research purpose and are systematically planned. Such studies can be structured or unstructured, with the investigator being a participant or nonparticipant in the study setting. All phenomena of interest are systematically recorded and quality control can be exercised by eliminating bias. Observational studies can provide rich data and insights into the nature of the phenomena observed. They have offered much understanding of interpersonal and group dynamics. Interestingly, observational data can also be quantified through tabulation.

## Data collection through mechanical observation

There are situations where machines can provide data by recording the events of interest as they occur, without a researcher being physically present. Nielsen ratings is an oft-cited example in this regard. Other examples include collection of details of products sold by type or brand tracked through optical scanners and bar codes at the checkout stand, and tracking systems keeping a record of how many individuals utilize a facility or visit a website. Films and electronic recording devices such as video cameras can also be used to record data. Such mechanically observed data are error-free.

### Projective methods

Certain ideas and thoughts that cannot be easily verbalized or that remain at the unconscious levels in the respondents' minds can usually be brought to the surface through motivational research. This is typically done by trained professionals who apply different probing techniques in order to bring to the surface deep-rooted ideas and thoughts in the respondents. Familiar techniques for gathering such data are word association, sentence completion, thematic apperception tests (TAT), inkblot tests, and the like.

**Word association** techniques, such as asking the respondent to quickly associate a word – say, work – with the first thing that comes to mind, are often used to get at true attitudes and feelings. The reply gives an indication of what work means to the individual. Similarly, sentence completion asks the respondent to quickly complete a sentence, such as "Work is . . . ." One respondent might say, "Work is a lot of fun," whereas another might say "Work is drudgery." These responses may provide some insights into individuals' feelings and attitudes toward work.

**Thematic apperception tests** (TAT) call for the respondent to weave a story around a picture that is shown. Several need patterns and personality characteristics of employees can be traced through these tests.

**Inkblot tests**, another form of motivational research, use colored inkblots that are interpreted by the respondents, who explain what they see in the various patterns and colors.

Although these types of projective tests are useful for tapping attitudes and feelings that are difficult to obtain otherwise, they cannot be resorted to by researchers who are not trained to conduct motivational research.

Consumer preferences, buying attitudes and behaviors, product development, and other marketing research strategies make substantial use of in-depth probing. TAT and inkblot tests are on their way out in marketing research since advertisers and others now use sentence completion tests and word association tests more frequently. Sketch drawings, collages from magazine pictures, filling in the balloon captions of cartoon characters, and other strategies are also being followed to see how individuals associate different products, brands, advertisements, and so on, in their minds. Agencies frequently ask subjects to sketch "typical" users of various brands and narrate stories about them. The messages conveyed through the unsophisticated drawings are said to be very powerful, helping the development of different marketing strategies.

The idea behind motivational research is that "emotionality" ("I identify with it" feeling) rather than "rationality" ("it is good for me" thought), which is what keeps a product or practice alive, is captured. Emotions are powerful motivators of actions, and knowledge of what motivates individuals to act is very useful. The failure of attempts to trade in the "New Coke" for "Classic Coke" is an oft-cited example of the emotional aspect. Emotionality is clearly at the nonrational, subconscious level, lending itself to capture by projective techniques alone.

## Multimethods of data collection

Because almost all data collection methods have some bias associated with them, collecting data through multimethods and from multiple sources lends rigor to research. For instance, if the responses collected through interviews, questionnaires, and observation are strongly correlated with one another, then we will have more confidence about the goodness of the collected data. If the same question fetches discrepant answers in the questionnaire and during the interview, then an air of uncertainty emerges and we will be inclined to discard both data as being biased.

Likewise, if data obtained from several sources bear a great degree of similarity, we will have stronger conviction in the goodness of the data. For example, if an employee rates his performance as 4 on a five-point scale, and his supervisor gives him a similar rating, we may be inclined to consider him a better than average worker. On the contrary, if he gives himself a 5 on the five-point scale and his supervisor gives him a rating of 2, then we will not know to what extent there is a bias and from which source. Therefore, high correlations among data obtained on the same variable from different sources and through different data collection methods lend more credibility to the research instrument and to the data obtained through these instruments. Good research entails collection of data from multiple sources and through multiple data collection methods. Such research, though, is more costly and time consuming.

## Review of the advantages and disadvantages of different data collection methods and when to use each

Having discussed the various data collection methods, we will now briefly recount the advantages and disadvantages of the three most commonly used methods – interviews, questionnaires, and observation – and examine when each method can be most profitably used.

**Face-to-face interviews** provide rich data, offer the opportunity to establish rapport with the interviewees, and help to explore and understand complex issues. Many ideas ordinarily difficult to articulate can also be brought to the surface and discussed during such interviews. On the negative side, face-to-face interviews have the potential for introducing interviewer bias and can be expensive if a large number of subjects are involved. Where several interviewers become necessary, adequate training becomes a necessary first step. Face-to-face interviews are best suited to the exploratory stages of research when the researcher is trying to get a handle on concepts or the situational factors.

**Telephone interviews** help to contact subjects dispersed over various geographic regions and obtain immediate responses from them. This is an efficient way of collecting data when one has specific questions to ask, needs the responses quickly, and has a sample spread over a wide geographic area. On the negative side, the interviewer cannot observe the nonverbal responses of the respondents, and the interviewee can block a call. Telephone interviews are best suited for asking structured questions where responses need to be obtained quickly from a sample that is geographically spread.

**Personally administering questionnaires** to groups of individuals helps to (1) establish rapport with the respondents while introducing the survey, (2) provide clarification sought by the respondents on the spot, and (3) collect the questionnaires immediately after they are completed. In that sense, there is a 100% response rate. On the negative side, administering questionnaires personally is expensive, especially if the sample is geographically dispersed. Personally administered questionnaires are best suited when data are collected from organizations that are located in close proximity to one another and groups of respondents can be conveniently assembled in the company's conference (or other) rooms.

Mail questionnaires are advantageous when responses to many questions have to be obtained from a sample that is geographically dispersed, or it is difficult or not possible to conduct telephone interviews without much expense. On the negative side, mailed questionnaires usually have a low response rate and one cannot be sure if the data obtained are biased since the nonrespondents may be different from those who did respond. The mailed questionnaire survey is best suited (and perhaps the only alternative open to the researcher) when information is to be obtained on a substantial scale through structured questions, at a reasonable cost, from a sample that is widely dispersed geographically.

Observational studies help to comprehend complex issues through direct observation (either as a participant or a nonparticipant-observer) and then, if possible, asking questions to seek clarification on certain issues. The data obtained are rich and uncontaminated by self-report bias. On the negative side, they are expensive, since long periods of observation (usually encompassing several weeks or even months) are required, and observer bias may well be present in the data. Because of the costs involved, very few observational studies are done in business. Henry Mintzberg's study of managerial work is one of the best-known published works that used an observational data collection method. Observational studies are best suited for research requiring non-self-report descriptive data; that is, when behaviors are to be understood without directly asking the respondents themselves. Observational studies can also capture "in-the-stores buying behaviors."

## Setting from which data are gathered

Data can be collected in any one of the aforementioned ways in the natural environment of the workplace. Data may also be collected in artificial lab settings where variables are controlled and manipulated, or they can be gathered in the homes of the respondents, on the street, in malls, or in a setting where a LAN (local area network) system is available. It is not unusual to find marketers conducting what are known as intercept interviews in malls and fairs, to obtain vast amounts of marketing information.

# International dimensions of surveys

We have so far discussed instrument development for eliciting responses from subjects within a country. With the globalization of business operations, managers often need to compare the business effectiveness of their subsidiaries in different countries. Researchers engaged in cross-cultural research also endeavor to trace the similarities and differences in the behavioral and attitudinal responses of employees at various levels in different cultures. When data are collected through questionnaires and occasionally through interviews, one should pay attention to the measuring instruments and how data are collected, in addition to being sensitive to cultural differences in the use of certain terms. Surveys should also be tailored to the different cultures, as discussed below.

## Special issues in instrumentation for cross-cultural research

Certain special issues need to be addressed while designing instruments for collecting data from different countries. Since different languages are spoken in different countries, it is important to ensure that the translation of the instrument to the local language matches accurately to the original language. For this purpose, the instrument should be first translated by a local expert. Supposing a comparative survey is to be done between Japan and the United States, and the researcher is a US national, then the instrument has first to be translated from English to Japanese. Then, another bilinguist should translate it back to English. This back translation, as it is called, ensures vocabulary equivalence (i.e., that the words used have the same meaning). Idiomatic equivalence could also become an issue, where some idioms unique to one language just do not lend themselves for translation to another language. Conceptual equivalence, where the meanings of certain words could differ in different cultures, is yet another issue to which attention has to be paid. As stated earlier, the meaning of the concept ''love'' may differ in different cultures. All these issues can be taken care of through good back translation by persons who are facile with the relevant languages and are also knowledgeable about the customs and usages in the cultures concerned.

The following examples culled from *Business Week* show the pitfalls in cross-cultural advertising and emphasize the need for back translation of messages for idiomatic and conceptual equivalence. Not only is the meaning lost in some advertisement messages by literally translating the English words into the native languages, but in some cases they actually become offensive. Here are some examples:

### EXAMPLE

1. GM took a step back when it tried to market the NOVA in Central and South America. In Spanish, ''No va'' means ''It doesn't go.''
2. Pepsi's ''Come alive with the Pepsi generation,'' when translated into Chinese, means ''Pepsi brings your ancestors from the grave.''
3. Frank Perdue's chicken slogan, ''It takes a strong man to make a tender chicken'' translates in Spanish to, ''It takes an aroused man to make a chicken affectionate.''
4. When American Airlines wanted to advertise its new leather first-class seats to Mexico, its ''Fly in Leather'' campaign would have literally translated to ''Fly Naked'' in Spanish.
5. The ''Got Milk?'' slogan in Spanish would translate to ''Are you lactating?''

## Issues in data collection

At least three issues are important for cross-cultural data collection – response equivalence, timing of data collection, and the status of the individual collecting the data. Response equivalence is ensured by adopting uniform data collection procedures in the different cultures. Identical methods of introducing the study, the researcher, task instructions, and closing remarks, in personally administered questionnaires, provide equivalence in motivation, goal orientation, and response attitudes. Timing of data collected across cultures is also critical for cross-cultural comparison. Data collection should be completed within acceptable time frames in the different countries – say within three to four months. If too much time elapses in collecting data in the different countries, much might change during the time interval in any one country or all the countries.

As pointed out as early as 1969 by Mitchell, in interview surveys, the egalitarian oriented interviewing style used in the West may not be appropriate in societies that have well-defined status and authority structures. Also, when a foreigner comes to collect data, the responses might be biased for fear of portraying the country to a "foreigner" in an "adverse light" (Sekaran, 1983). The researcher has to be sensitive to these cultural nuances while engaging in cross-cultural research. It is worthwhile collaborating with a local researcher while developing and administering the research instrument, particularly when the language and customs of the respondents are different from those of the researcher.

# Managerial implications

As a manager, you will perhaps engage consultants to do research and may not be collecting data yourself through interviews, questionnaires, or observation. However, during those instances, when you will perforce have to obtain work-related information through interviews with clients, employees, or others, you will know how to phrase unbiased questions to elicit the right types of useful response. Moreover, you, as the sponsor of research, will be able to decide at what level of sophistication you want data to be collected, based on the complexity and gravity of the situation. Moreover, as a constant participant-observer of all that goes on around you at the workplace, you will be able to understand the dynamics operating in the situation. Also, as a manager, you will be able to differentiate between good and bad questions used in surveys, with sensitivity to cultural variations, not only in scaling but also in developing the entire survey instrument, and in collecting data, as discussed in this chapter.

# Ethics in data collection

Several ethical issues should be addressed while collecting data. As previously noted, these pertain to those who sponsor the research, those who collect the data, and those who offer them. The sponsors should ask for the study to be done to better the purpose of the organization, and not for any other self-serving reason. They should respect the confidentiality of the data obtained by the researcher, and not ask for the individual or group responses to be disclosed to them, or ask to see the questionnaires. They should have an open mind in accepting the results and recommendations in the report presented by the researchers.

## Ethics and the researcher

1.  Treating the information given by the respondent as strictly confidential and guarding his or her privacy is one of the primary responsibilities of the researcher. If the vice president or some other top executive wishes to take a look at the completed question-naires, the obligatory need to preserve the confidentiality of the documents should then be pointed out. They should be reminded that prior understanding of this had already been reached with them before starting the survey.

    Also, data for a subgroup of, say, less than ten individuals, should be dealt with tactfully to preserve the confidentiality of the group members. The data can be combined with others, or treated in another unidentifiable manner. It is difficult to sanitize reports to protect sources and still preserve the richness of detail of the study. An acceptable alternative has to be found, since preserving confidentiality is the fundamental goal.

2.  The researcher should not misrepresent the nature of the study to subjects, especially in lab experiments. The purpose of the research must be explained to them.

3.  Personal or seemingly intrusive information should not be solicited, and if it is absolutely necessary for the project, it should be tapped with high sensitivity to the respondent, offering specific reasons.

4.  Whatever the nature of the data collection method, the self-esteem and self-respect of the subjects should never be violated.

5.  No one should be forced to respond to the survey and if someone does not want to avail themselves of the opportunity to participate, the individual's desire should be respected. Informed consent of the subjects should be the goal of the researcher. This holds true even when data are collected through mechanical means, such as recording interviews, video-taping, and the like.

6.  Nonparticipant-observers should be as unintrusive as possible. In qualitative studies, personal values could easily bias the data. It is necessary for the researcher to make explicit his or her assumptions, expectations, and biases, so that informed decisions regarding the quality of the data can be made by the manager.

7.  In lab studies, the subjects should be debriefed with full disclosure of the reason for the experiment after they have participated in the study.

8.  Subjects should never be exposed to situations where they could be subject to physical or mental harm. The researcher should take personal responsibility for their safety.

9.  There should be absolutely no misrepresentation or distortion in reporting the data collected during the study.

## Ethical behavior of respondents

1.  The subject, once having exercised the choice to participate in a study, should cooperate fully in the tasks ahead, such as responding to a survey or taking part in an experiment.

2. The respondent also has an obligation to be truthful and honest in the responses. Misrepresentation or giving information, knowing it to be untrue, should be avoided.

## SUMMARY

In this chapter we examined various sources of data and several data collection methods. We discussed the advantages and disadvantages as well as the bias inherent in each data collection method. We also examined the impact of technology on data collection. Because of the inherent bias in each of the data collection methods, the collection of data from multiple sources and through multiple methods was recommended. The final decision will, of course, be governed by considerations of cost, and the degree of rigor that the given research goal calls for. We also pointed out some issues in cross-cultural research, such as back translation, and alerted the reader to the pitfalls while collecting data in a different culture.

## DISCUSSION QUESTIONS

1. Describe the different data sources, explaining their usefulness and disadvantages.
2. As a manager, you have invited a research team to come in, study, and offer suggestions on how to improve the performance of your staff. What steps will you take to allay staff apprehensions even before the research team sets foot in your department?
3. What is bias, and how can it be reduced during interviews?
4. Explain the principles of wording, stating how these are important in questionnaire design, citing examples not in the book.
5. What are projective techniques and how can they be used profitably?
6. How are multiple methods of data collection and from multiple sources related to the reliability and validity of the measures?
7. "Every data collection method has its own built-in biases. Therefore, resorting to multimethods of data collection is only going to compound the biases." How would you critique this statement?
8. "One way to deal with discrepancies found in the data obtained from multiple sources is to average the figures and take the mean as the value of the variable." What is your reaction to this?
9. How has the advancement in technology helped data gathering?
10. How would you use the data from observational study to reach scientific conclusions?
11. The fewer the biases in measurement and in data collection procedures, the more scientific the research. Comment on this statement.

Now do Exercises 8.1, 8.2, 8.3, 8.4, and 8.5

## EXERCISE 8.1

A production manager wants to assess the reactions of the blue-collar workers in his department (including foremen) to the introduction of computer-integrated manufacturing (CIM) systems. He is particularly interested to know how they perceive the effects of CIM on:

**a.** their future jobs
**b.** additional training that they will have to receive
**c.** future job advancement.

Design a questionnaire for the production manager.

## EXERCISE 8.2

Seek permission from a professor to sit in two sessions of his or her class, and do an unstructured, nonparticipant-observer study. Give your conclusions on the data, and include in the short report your observation sheets and tabulations.

## EXERCISE 8.3

First conduct an unstructured and later a structured interview, to learn about how people use and process information to choose among alternative brands when they are looking for furniture, clothing, household appliances, and the like. Select a specific product and ask people, for instance, about the product attributes they consider, and how important these attributes are. Write up the results, and include the formats you used for both stages of the research.

## EXERCISE 8.4

Design a questionnaire that you could use to assess the quality of your on-campus dining facilities. Make sure you can test the following hypotheses:

$H_1$: *There is a positive relationship between the service quality of the on-campus dining facilities and customer loyalty.*

$H_2$: *The relationship between service quality and customer loyalty is mediated by customer satisfaction.*

## EXERCISE 8.5

Design an interview schedule to assess the "intellectual capital" as perceived by employees in an organization – the dimensions and elements for which you developed earlier.

# CHAPTER 9

## Experimental designs

## Topics discussed

- Lab and field experiments
- Control
- Manipulation
- Controlling the contaminating variables
  - Matching
  - Randomization
- Internal validity
- External validity
- Trade-off between internal and external validity
- Factors affecting validity
  - History effects
  - Maturation effects
  - Testing effects
  - Instrumentation effects
  - Selection effects
  - Statistical regression effects
  - Mortality effects
- Internal validity in case studies
- Types of experimental designs and validity
  - Quasi-experimental designs
  - True experimental designs
  - Ex post facto designs
- Simulation
- Ethical issues in experimental research
- Managerial implications
- Appendix: further experimental designs

## CHAPTER OBJECTIVES

After completing Chapter 9, you should be able to:

1. Distinguish between causal and correlational analysis.
2. Explain the difference between lab and field experiments.
3. Explain the following terms: nuisance variables, manipulation, experimental and control groups, treatment effect, matching, and randomization.
4. Discuss internal and external validity in experimental designs.
5. Discuss the seven possible threats to internal validity in experimental designs.
6. Describe the different types of experimental designs.
7. Discuss the Solomon four-group design and its implications for internal and external validity.
8. Apply what has been learned to class assignments and exams.

In Chapter 5, we examined the basic research designs. We distinguished causal from correlational studies and explained that experimental studies are typically used when the researcher is interested in establishing cause-and-effect relationships.

Consider the following three scenarios.

## EXAMPLE

**Scenario A**     A manufacturer of luxurious cars has decided to launch a global brand communications campaign to reinforce the image of its cars. An 18-month campaign is scheduled that will be rolled out worldwide, with advertising in television, print and electronic media. Under the title "Bravura", a renowned advertising agency developed three different campaign concepts. In order to determine which of these concepts is most effective, the car manufacturer wants to test their effects on the brand's image. But how can the car manufacturer test the effectiveness of these concepts?

**Scenario B**     A study of absenteeism and the steps taken to curb it indicates that companies use the following incentives to reduce it:

> 14% give bonus days
> 39% offer cash
> 39% present recognition awards
> 4% award prizes
> 4% pursue other strategies

Asked about their effectiveness,

22% of the companies said they were very effective
66% said they were somewhat effective
12% said they were not at all effective

What does the above information tell us? How do we know what kinds of incentives cause people not to absent themselves? What particular incentive(s) did the 22% of companies that found their strategies to be "very effective" offer? Is there a direct causal connection between one or two specific incentives and absenteeism?

**Scenario C**

The dagger effect of layoffs is that there is a sharp drop in the commitment of workers who are retained, even though they might well understand the logic of the reduction in the workforce.

Does layoff really cause employee commitment to drop off, or is something else operating in this situation?

The answers to the questions raised in Scenarios A, B, and C might be found by using experimental designs in researching the issues.

In Chapter 5 we touched on experimental designs. In this chapter, we will discuss both lab experiments and field experiments in detail. Experimental designs, as we know, are set up to examine possible cause-and-effect relationships among variables, in contrast to correlational studies, which examine the relationships among variables without necessarily trying to establish if one variable causes another.

In order to establish that a change in the independent variable *causes* a change in the dependent variable, *all four* of the following conditions should be met:

1. The independent and the dependent variable should covary.
2. The independent variable (the presumed causal factor) should precede the dependent variable.
3. No other factor should be a possible cause of the change in the dependent variable.
4. A logical explanation (a theory) is needed about why the independent variable affects the dependent variable.

The third condition implies that to establish causal relationships between two variables in an organizational setting, several variables that might covary with the dependent variable have to be controlled. This then allows us to say that variable X, and variable X alone, causes the dependent variable Y. However, it is not always possible to control all the covariates while manipulating the causal factor (the independent variable that is causing the dependent variable) in organizational settings, where events flow or occur naturally and normally. It is, however, possible to first isolate the effects of a variable in a tightly controlled artificial setting (the lab setting), and after testing and establishing the cause-and-effect relationship under these tightly controlled conditions, see how generalizable such relationships are to the field setting.

Let us illustrate this with an example.

## EXAMPLE

Suppose a manager believes that staffing the accounting department completely with personnel with M.Acc. (Master of Accountancy) degrees will increase its productivity. It is well nigh impossible to transfer all those without the M.Acc. degree currently in the department to other departments and recruit fresh M.Acc. degree holders to take their place. Such a course of action is bound to disrupt the work of the entire organization inasmuch as many new people will have to be trained, work will slow down, employees will get upset, and so on. However, the hypothesis that possession of an M.Acc. degree would cause increases in productivity can be tested in an artificially created setting (i.e., not at the regular workplace) in which an accounting job can be given to three groups of people: those with an M.Acc. degree, those without an M.Acc. degree, and a mixed group of those with and without an M.Acc. degree (as is the case in the present work setting). If the first group performs exceedingly well, the second group poorly, and the third group falls somewhere in the middle, there will be evidence to indicate that the M. Acc. degree qualification might indeed cause productivity to rise. If such evidence is found, then planned and systematic efforts can be initiated to gradually transfer those without the M.Acc. degree in the accounting department to other departments and recruit others with this degree to this department. It is then possible to see to what extent productivity does, in fact, go up in the department because all the staff members are M. Acc. degree holders.

As we saw earlier, experimental designs fall into two categories: experiments done in an artificial or contrived environment, known as **lab experiments**, and those done in the natural environment in which activities regularly take place, known as **field experiments**.

# The lab experiment

As stated earlier, when a cause-and-effect relationship between an independent and a dependent variable of interest is to be clearly established, then all other variables that might contaminate or confound the relationship have to be tightly controlled. In other words, the possible effects of other variables on the dependent variable have to be accounted for in some way, so that the actual causal effects of the investigated independent variable on the dependent variable can be determined. It is also necessary to manipulate the independent variable so that the extent of its causal effects can be established. The control and manipulation are best done in an artificial setting (the laboratory), where the causal effects can be tested. When control and manipulation are introduced to establish cause-and-effect relationships in an artificial setting, we have laboratory experimental designs, also known as lab experiments.

Because we use the terms control and manipulation, let us examine what these concepts mean.

## Control

When we postulate cause-and-effect relationships between two variables X and Y, it is possible that some other factor, say A, might also influence the dependent variable Y. In such a case, it will not be possible to determine the extent to which Y occurred only because of X, since we do not know how much of the total variation in Y was caused by the presence of the other factor A. For instance, a Human Resource Development manager might arrange special training for a set of newly recruited secretaries in creating web pages, to prove to the VP (his boss) that such training causes them to function more effectively. However, some of the new secretaries might function more effectively than others, mainly or partly because they have had previous intermittent experience with the web. In this case, the manager cannot prove that the special training alone caused greater effectiveness, since the previous intermittent experience of some secretaries with the web is a contaminating factor. If the true effect of the training on learning is to be assessed, then the learners' previous experience has to be controlled. This might be done by not including in the experiment those who already have had some experience with the web. This is what we mean when we say we have to control the contaminating factors, and we will later see how this is done.

## Manipulation of the independent variable

In order to examine the causal effects of an independent variable on a dependent variable, certain manipulations need to be tried. Manipulation simply means that we create different levels of the independent variable to assess the impact on the dependent variable. For example, we may want to test the theory that depth of knowledge of various manufacturing technologies is caused by rotating the employees on all the jobs on the production line and in the design department, over a four-week period. Then we can manipulate the independent variable, "rotation of employees," by rotating one group of production workers and exposing them to all the systems during the four-week period, rotating another group of workers only partially during the four weeks (i.e., exposing them to only half of the manufacturing technologies), and leaving the third group to continue to do what they are currently doing, without any special rotation. By measuring the depth of knowledge of these groups both before and after the manipulation (also known as the treatment), it is possible to assess the extent to which the treatment caused the effect, after controlling the contaminating factors. If deep knowledge is indeed caused by rotation and exposure, the results will show that the third group had the lowest increase in depth of knowledge, the second group had some significant increase, and the first group had the greatest gains!

Let us look at another example on how causal relationships are established by manipulating the independent variable.

## EXAMPLE

Let us say we want to test the effects of lighting on worker production levels among sewing machine operators. To establish a cause-and-effect relationship, we must first measure the production levels of all the operators over a 15-day period with the usual amount of light they work with – say 60-watt lamps. We might then want to split the group of 60 operators into three groups of 20 members each, and while allowing one subgroup to continue to work under the same conditions as before (60-watt electric lightbulbs), we might want to manipulate the intensity of the light for the other two subgroups, by making one group work with 75-watt and the other with 100-watt lightbulbs. After the different groups have worked with these varying degrees of light exposure for 15 days, each group's total production for these 15 days may be analyzed to see if the difference between the preexperimental and the postexperimental production among the groups is directly related to the intensity of the light to which they have been exposed. If our hypothesis that better lighting increases the production levels is correct, then the subgroup that did not have any change in the lighting (called the **control group**), should have no increase in production and the other two groups should show increases, with those having the most light (100 watts) showing greater increases than those who had the 75-watt lighting.

In the above case the independent variable, lighting, has been manipulated by exposing different groups to different degrees of changes in it. This manipulation of the independent variable is also known as the **treatment**, and the results of the treatment are called treatment effects.

Let us illustrate how variable X can be both controlled and manipulated in the lab setting through another example.

## EXAMPLE

Let us say an entrepreneur – the owner of a toy factory – is rather disappointed with the number of imitation Batman action figures produced by his workers, who are paid wages at an hourly rate. He might wonder whether paying them piece rates would increase their production levels. However, before implementing the piece-rate system, he wants to make sure that switching over to the new system would indeed achieve the objective.

In a case like this, the researcher might first want to test the causal relationships in a lab setting, and if the results are encouraging, conduct the experiment later in a field setting. In designing the lab experiment, the researcher should first think of possible factors affecting the production level of the workers, and then try to control these. Other than piece rates, previous job experience might also influence the rate of production because familiarity with the job makes it easy for people to increase their productivity levels. In some cases, where the jobs are very strenuous and require muscular strength, gender differences may affect productivity. Let us say that for the type of production job discussed earlier, age, gender, and prior experience of the employees are the factors that influence the production levels of the employees. The researcher needs to control these three variables. Let us see how this can be done.

Suppose the researcher intends to set up four groups of 15 people each for the lab experiment – one to be used as the control group, and the other three subjected to three different pay manipulations. Now, the variables that may impact on the cause-and-effect relationship can be controlled in two different ways: either by matching the groups or through randomization. These concepts are explained before we proceed further.

## Controlling the contaminating exogenous or "nuisance" variables

### Matching groups

One way of controlling the contaminating or "nuisance" variables is to match the various groups by picking the confounding characteristics and deliberately spreading them across groups. For instance, if there are 20 women among the 60 members, then each group will be assigned five women, so that the effects of gender are distributed across the four groups. Likewise, age and experience factors can be matched across the four groups, such that each group has a similar mix of individuals in terms of gender, age, and experience. Because the suspected contaminating factors are matched across the groups, we may take comfort in saying that variable X alone causes variable Y, if such is the result of the study.

### Randomization

Another way of controlling the contaminating variables is to assign the 60 members randomly (i.e., with no predetermination) to the four groups. That is, every member will have a known and equal chance of being assigned to any of these four groups. For instance, we might throw the names of all the 60 members into a hat and draw their names. The first 15 names drawn may be assigned to the first group, the second 15 to the second group, and so on, or the first person drawn might be assigned to the first group, the second person drawn to the second group, and so on. Thus, in randomization, the process by which individuals are drawn (i.e., everybody has a known and equal chance of being drawn) and their assignment to any particular group (each individual could be assigned to any one of the groups set up) are both random. By thus randomly assigning members to the groups we are distributing the confounding variables among the groups equally. That is, the variables of age, sex, and previous experience – the controlled variables – will have an equal probability of being distributed among the groups.

The process of randomization ideally ensures that each group is comparable to the others, and that all variables, including the effects of age, sex, and previous experience, are controlled. In other words, each of the groups will have some members who have more experience mingled with those who have less or no experience. All groups will have members of different age and sex composition. Thus, randomization ensures that if these variables do indeed have a contributory or confounding effect, we have controlled their confounding effects (along with those of other unknown factors) by distributing them across groups. This is achieved because when we manipulate the independent variable of piece rates by having no piece rate system at all for one group (control) and having different piece rates for the other three groups (experimental), we can determine the causal effects of the piece rates on production levels. Any errors or biases caused by age, sex, and previous experience are now distributed equally among all four groups. Any causal effects found will be over and above the effects of the confounding variables.

To make it clear, let us illustrate this with some actual figures as in Table 9.1. Note that because the effects of experience, sex, and age were controlled in all the four groups by randomly assigning the members to them, and the control group had no increase in productivity, it can be reliably concluded from the result that the percentage increases in production are a result of the piece rate (treatment effects). In other words, piece rates are the cause of the increase in the number of toys produced. We cannot now say that the cause-and-effect relationship has been confounded by other "nuisance" variables, because they have been controlled through the process of randomly assigning members to the groups. Here, we have high internal validity or confidence in the cause-and-effect relationship.

**Advantages of randomization**

The difference between matching and randomization is that in the former case individuals are deliberately and consciously matched to control the differences among group members, whereas in the latter case we expect that the process of randomization will distribute the inequalities among the groups, based on the laws of normal distribution. Thus, we need not be particularly concerned about any known or unknown confounding factors.

| TABLE 9.1 | Cause-and-effect relationship after randomization. |  |
|---|---|---|

| Groups | Treatment | Treatment effect (% increase in production over pre-piece rate system) |
|---|---|---|
| Experimental group 1 | $1.00 per piece | 10 |
| Experimental group 2 | $1.50 per piece | 15 |
| Experimental group 3 | $2.00 per piece | 20 |
| Control group (no treatment) | Old hourly rate | 0 |

In sum, compared to randomization, matching might be less effective, since we may not know all the factors that could possibly contaminate the cause-and-effect relationship in any given situation, and hence fail to match some critical factors across all groups while conducting an experiment. Randomization, however, will take care of this, since all the contaminating factors will be spread across all groups. Moreover, even if we know the confounding variables, we may not be able to find a match for all such variables. For instance, if gender is a confounding variable, and if there are only two women in a four-group experimental design, we will not be able to match all the groups with respect to gender. Randomization solves these dilemmas as well. Thus, lab experimental designs involve control of the contaminating variables through the process of either matching or randomization, and the manipulation of the treatment.

## Internal validity of lab experiments

Internal validity refers to the confidence we place in the cause-and-effect relationship. In other words, it addresses the question, "To what extent does the research design permit us to say that the independent variable A causes a change in the dependent variable B?" As Kidder and Judd (1986) note, in research with high internal validity, we are relatively better able to argue that the relationship is causal, whereas in studies with low internal validity, causality cannot be inferred at all. In lab experiments where cause-and-effect relationships are substantiated, internal validity can be said to be high.

So far we have talked about establishing cause-and-effect relationships within the lab setting, which is an artificially created and controlled environment. You might yourself have been a subject taking part in one of the lab experiments conducted by the psychology or other departments on campus at some time. You might not have been specifically told what cause-and-effect relationships the experimenter was looking for, but you would have been told what is called a "cover story." That is, you would have been apprised in general terms of some reason for the study and your role in it, without divulging its true purpose. After the end of the experiment you would also have been debriefed and given a full explanation of the experiment, and any questions you might have had would have been answered. This is how lab experiments are usually conducted: subjects are selected and assigned to different groups through matching or randomization; they are moved to a lab setting; they are given some details of the study and a task to perform; and some kind of questionnaire or other tests are administered both before and after the task is completed. The results of these studies indicate the cause-and-effect relationship between the variables under investigation.

## External validity or generalizability of lab experiments

To what extent are the results found in the lab setting transferable or generalizable to actual organizational or field settings? In other words, if we do find a cause-and-effect relationship after conducting a lab experiment, can we then confidently say that the same cause-and-effect relationship will also hold true in the organizational setting?

Consider the following situation. If, in a lab experimental design, the groups are given the simple production task of screwing bolts and nuts onto a plastic frame, and the results indicate that the groups who were paid piece rates were more productive than those who were paid hourly rates, to what extent can we then say that this would be true of the sophisticated nature of the jobs performed in organizations? The tasks in organizational settings are far more complex, and there might be several confounding variables that cannot be controlled – for example, experience. Under such circumstances, we cannot be sure that the cause-and-effect relationship found in the lab experiment is necessarily likely to hold true in the field setting. To test the causal relationships in the organizational setting, field experiments are carried out. These will now be briefly discussed.

# The field experiment

A **field experiment**, as the name implies, is an experiment done in the natural environment in which work goes on as usual, but treatments are given to one or more groups. Thus, in the field experiment, even though it may not be possible to control all the nuisance variables because members cannot be either randomly assigned to groups, or matched, the treatment can still be manipulated. Control groups can also be set up in field experiments. The experimental and control groups in the field experiment may be made up of the people working at several plants within a certain radius, or from the different shifts in the same plant, or in some other way. If there are three different shifts in a production plant, for instance, and the effects of the piece-rate system are to be studied, one of the shifts can be used as the control group, and the two other shifts given two different treatments or the same treatment – that is, different piece rates or the same piece rate. Any cause-and-effect relationship found under these conditions will have wider generalizability to other similar production settings, even though we may not be sure to what extent the piece rates alone were the cause of the increase in productivity, because some of the other confounding variables could not be controlled.

## External validity

What we just discussed can be referred to as an issue of external validity versus internal validity. **External validity** refers to the extent of generalizability of the results of a causal study to other settings, people, or events, and **internal validity** refers to the degree of our confidence in the causal effects (i.e., that variable X causes variable Y). Field experiments have more external validity (i.e., the results are more generalizable to other similar organizational settings), but less internal validity (i.e., we cannot be certain of the extent to which variable X alone causes variable Y). Note that in the lab experiment, the reverse is true: the internal validity is high but the external validity is rather low. In other words, in lab experiments we can be sure that variable X causes variable Y because we have been able to keep the other confounding exogenous variables under control, but we have so tightly controlled several variables to establish the cause-and-effect relationship that we do not know to what extent the results of our study can be generalized, if at all, to field settings. In other words, since the lab setting does not reflect the "real world" setting, we do not know to what extent the lab findings validly represent the realities in the outside world.

# Trade-off between internal and external validity

There is thus a trade-off between internal validity and external validity. If we want high internal validity, we should be willing to settle for lower external validity and vice versa. To ensure both types of validity, researchers usually try first to test the causal relationships in a tightly controlled artificial or lab setting, and once the relationship has been established, they try to test the causal relationship in a field experiment. Lab experimental designs in the management area have thus far been done to assess, among other things, gender differences in leadership styles and managerial aptitudes. However, gender differences and other factors found in the lab settings are frequently not found in field studies (Osborn and Vicars, 1976). These problems of external validity usually limit the use of lab experiments in the management area. Field experiments are also infrequently undertaken because of the resultant unintended consequences – personnel becoming suspicious, rivalries and jealousies being created among departments, and the like.

# Factors affecting the validity of experiments

Even the best designed lab studies may be influenced by factors that might affect the internal validity of the lab experiment. That is, some confounding factors might still be present that could offer rival explanations as to what is causing the dependent variable. These possible confounding factors pose a threat to internal validity. The seven major threats to internal validity are the effects of history, maturation, (main) testing, selection, mortality, statistical regression, and instrumentation, and these are explained below with examples. Two threats to external validity are (interactive) testing and selection. These threats to the validity of experiments are discussed next.

## History effects

Certain events or factors that have an impact on the independent variable–dependent variable relationship might unexpectedly occur while the experiment is in progress, and this history of events would confound the cause-and-effect relationship between the two variables, thus affecting the internal validity. For example, let us say that the manager of a Dairy Products

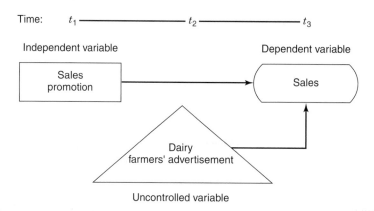

Figure 9.1: Illustration of history effects in experimental design.

Division wants to test the effects of the "buy one, get one free" sales promotion on the sale of the company-owned brand of packaged cheese for a week. She carefully records the sales of the packaged cheese during the previous two weeks to assess the effect of the promotion. However, on the very day that her sales promotion goes into effect, the Dairy Farmers' Association unexpectedly launches a multimedia advertisement on the benefits of consuming dairy products, especially cheese. The sales of all dairy products, including cheese, go up in all the stores, including the one where the experiment had been in progress. Here, because of an unexpected advertisement, one cannot be sure how much of the increase in sales of the packaged cheese in question was due to the sales promotion and how much to the advertisement by the Dairy Farmers' Association! The effects of history have reduced the internal validity or the faith that can be placed on the conclusion that the sales promotion caused the increase in sales. The history effects in this case are illustrated in Figure 9.1.

To give another example, let us say a bakery is studying the effects of adding to its bread a new ingredient that is expected to enrich it and offer more nutritional value to children under 14 years of age within 30 days, subject to a certain daily intake. At the start of the experiment the bakery takes a measure of the health of 30 children through some medical yardsticks. Thereafter, the children are given the prescribed intakes of bread daily. Unfortunately, on day 20 of the experiment, a flu virus hits the city in epidemic proportions affecting most of the children studied. This unforeseen and uncontrollable effect of history, flu, has contaminated the cause-and-effect relationship study for the bakery.

## Maturation effects

Cause-and-effect inferences can also be contaminated by the effects of the passage of time – another uncontrollable variable. Such contamination effects are denoted **maturation effects**. The maturation effects are a function of the processes – both biological and psychological – operating within the respondents as a result of the passage of time. Examples of maturation processes include growing older, getting tired, feeling hungry, and getting bored. In other

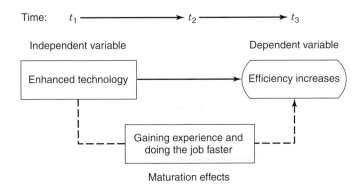

**Figure 9.2:** Illustration of maturation effects on a cause-and-effect relationship.

words, there could be a maturation effect on the dependent variable purely because of the passage of time. For instance, let us say that an R & D director contends that increases in the efficiency of workers will result within three months' time if advanced technology is introduced in the work setting. If, at the end of the three months, increased efficiency is indeed found, it will be difficult to claim that the advanced technology (and it alone) increased the efficiency of workers because, with the passage of time, employees will also have gained experience, resulting in better job performance and therefore in improved efficiency. Thus, the internal validity also gets reduced owing to the effects of maturation inasmuch as it is difficult to pinpoint how much of the increase is attributable to the introduction of the enhanced technology alone. Figure 9.2 illustrates the maturation effects in the above example.

## Testing effects

Frequently, to test the effects of a treatment, subjects are given what is called a pretest. That is, first a measure of the dependent variable is taken (the **pretest**), then the treatment is given, and after that a second measure of the dependent variable is taken (the **posttest**). The difference between the posttest and the pretest scores is then attributed to the treatment. However, the exposure of participants to the pretest may affect both the internal and external validity of the findings. Indeed, the aforementioned process may lead to two types of testing effects.

A *main testing effect* occurs when the prior observation (the pretest) affects *the later observation* (the posttest). Main testing effects typically occur because participants want to be consistent. Let us assume that we have tested the effect of a television commercial (the treatment) on attitudes towards the brand using a pretest and a posttest. Suppose that no significant difference in attitude towards the brand was found. This finding could lead to the conclusion that the commercial was ineffective. However, an alternative explanation is that our participants tried to be consistent and answered the later questions so that their answers were similar to the answers they gave the first time. The pretest may thus have affected the results of the experiment. Along these lines, main testing effects are another threat to internal validity.

*Interactive testing effects* occur when the pretest affects the participant's *reaction to the treatment* (the independent variable). Again, let's assume that we are testing the effect of a television commercial on attitude towards the brand using a pretest and a posttest. It is possible that because of the pretest, the participants watch the television commercial more closely than consumers that do not take part in the experiment. For this reason, any effects that are found may not necessarily be generalizable to the population. Hence, interactive treatment effects are a threat to the external validity of an experiment.

In sum, testing effects may affect both the internal and external validity of our findings. Main testing effects threaten the internal validity, whereas interactive testing effects threaten the external validity.

## Selection bias effects

Another threat to both the internal and external validity of our findings is the selection of participants. First, we will discuss how selection may affect the external validity of our findings. Then, we will discuss how selection may affect the internal validity.

In a lab setting, the types of participants selected for the experiment may be very different from the types of employees recruited by organizations. For example, students in a university might be allotted a task that is manipulated to study the effects on their performance. The findings from this experiment cannot be generalized, however, to the real world of work, where the employees and the nature of the jobs are both quite different. Thus, subject selection poses a threat to external validity.

The threat to internal validity comes from improper or unmatched selection of subjects for the experimental and control groups. For example, if a lab experiment is set up to assess the impact of the working environment on employees' attitudes toward work, and if one of the experimental conditions is to have a group of subjects work for about two hours in a room with some mild stench, an ethical researcher might disclose this condition to prospective subjects, who may decline to participate in the study. However, some volunteers might be lured through incentives (say a payment of $70 for the two hours of participation in the study). The volunteers so selected may be quite different from the others (inasmuch as they may come from an environment of deprivation) and their responses to the treatment might be quite different. Such bias in the selection of the subjects might contaminate the cause-and-effect relationships and pose a threat to internal validity as well. Hence, newcomers, volunteers, and others who cannot be matched with the control groups pose a threat to internal validity in certain types of experiment. For this reason, randomization or matching groups is highly recommended.

## Mortality effects

Another confounding factor on the cause-and-effect relationship is the **mortality** or attrition of the members in the experimental or control group, or both, as the experiment progresses. When the group composition changes over time across the groups, comparison between the groups becomes difficult, because those who dropped out of the experiment may confound the results.

Again, we will not be able to say how much of the effect observed arises from the treatment, and how much is attributable to the members who dropped out, since those who stayed with the experiment may have reacted differently from those who dropped out. Let us see an example.

## EXAMPLE

A sales manager had heard glowing reports about three different training programs that train salespersons in effective sales strategies. All three were of six weeks' duration. The manager was curious to know which one would offer the best results for the company. The first program took the trainees daily on field trips and demonstrated effective and ineffective sales strategies through practical experience. The second program trained groups on the same strategies but indoors in a classroom type of setting, lecturing, role playing, and answering questions from the participants. The third program used mathematical models and simulations to increase sales effectiveness. The manager chose eight trainees each for the three different programs and sent them to training. By the end of the fourth week, three trainees from the first group, one from the second group, and two from the third group had dropped out of the training programs due to a variety of reasons including ill health, family exigencies, transportation problems, and a car accident. This attrition from the various groups made it impossible to compare the effectiveness of the various programs. Thus, mortality can also lower the internal validity of an experiment.

## Statistical regression effects

The effects of **statistical regression** are brought about when the members chosen for the experimental group have extreme scores on the dependent variable to begin with. For instance, if a manager wants to test whether he can increase the "salesmanship" repertoire of the sales personnel through Dale Carnegie-type programs, he should not choose those with extremely low or extremely high abilities for the experiment. This is because we know from the laws of probability that those with very low scores on a variable (in this case, current sales ability) have a greater probability of showing improvement and scoring closer to the mean on the posttest after being exposed to the treatment. This phenomenon of low scorers tending to score closer to the mean is known as "regressing toward the mean" (statistical regression). Likewise, those with very high abilities also have a greater tendency to regress toward the mean – they will score lower on the posttest than on the pretest. Thus, those who are at either end of the continuum with respect to a variable will not "truly" reflect the cause-and-effect relationship. The phenomenon of statistical regression is thus yet another threat to internal validity.

## Instrumentation effects

**Instrumentation effects** are yet another source of threat to internal validity. These might arise because of a change in the measuring instrument between pretest and posttest, and not because of the treatment's differential impact at the end (Cook and Campbell, 1979a). For instance, an observer who is involved in observing a particular pattern of behavior in respondents before a treatment might start concentrating on a different set of behaviors after the treatment. The frame of measurement of behavior (in a sense, the measuring instrument) has now changed and will not reflect the change in behavior that can be attributed to the treatment. This is also true in the case of physical measuring instruments like the spring balance or other finely calibrated instruments that might lose their accuracy due to a loss of tension with constant use, resulting in erroneous final measurement.

In organizations, instrumentation effects in experimental designs are possible when the pretest is done by the experimenter, treatments are given to the experimental groups, and the posttest on measures such as performance is done by different managers. One manager might measure performance by the final units of output, a second manager might take into account the number of rejects as well, and a third manager might also take into consideration the amount of resources expended in getting the job done! Here, there are at least three different measuring instruments, if we treat each manager as a performance measuring instrument.

Thus, instrumentation effects also pose a threat to internal validity in experimental design.

# Identifying threats to validity

Let us examine each of the possible seven threats to validity in the context of the following scenario.

## EXAMPLE

An organizational consultant wanted to demonstrate to the president of a company, through an experimental design, that the democratic style of leadership best enhances the morale of employees. She set up three experimental groups and one control group for the purpose and assigned members to each of the groups randomly. The three experimental groups were headed by an autocratic leader, a democratic leader, and a laissez-faire leader, respectively.

The members in the three experimental groups were administered a pretest. Since the control group was not exposed to any treatment, they were not given a pretest. As the experiment progressed, two members in the democratic treatment group got quite excited and started moving around to the other members saying that the participative atmosphere was "great" and "performance was bound to be high in this group." Two members from each of the autocratic and laissez-faire groups left after the first hour saying they had to go and could no longer participate in the experiment. After two hours of activities, a posttest was administered to all the participants, including the control group members, on the same lines as the pretest.

1. *History effects.* The action of the two members in the participative group by way of unexpectedly moving around in an excited manner and remarking that participative leadership is "great" and the "performance is bound to be high in this group" might have boosted the morale of all the members in the group. It would be difficult to separate out how much of the increase in morale was due to the participative condition alone and how much to the sudden enthusiasm displayed by the two members.

2. *Maturation effects.* It is doubtful that maturation had any effect on morale in this situation, since the passage of time, in itself, may not have anything much to do with increases or decreases in morale.

3. *Testing effects.* The pretests are likely to have sensitized the respondents to both the treatment and the posttest. Thus, main and interactive testing effects exist. However, if all the groups had been given both the pre- and the posttests, the main testing effects (but not the interactive testing effects!) across all groups would have been taken care of (i.e., nullified) and the posttests of each of the experimental groups could have been compared with that of the control group to detect the effects of the treatment. Unfortunately, the control group was not given the pretest, and thus, this group's posttest scores were not biased by the pretest – a phenomenon that could have occurred in the experimental groups. Hence, it is incorrect, on the face of it, to compare the experimental groups' scores with those of the control group. Interactive testing poses a threat to the external validity of the findings.

4. *Selection bias effects.* Since members were randomly assigned to all groups, selection bias should not have affected the internal validity of the findings. The external validity of the findings should also not have been threatened by selection: there is no reason to assume that the participants selected for the experiment are different from the other employees of the organization.

5. *Mortality effects.* Since members dropped out of two experimental groups, the effects of mortality could affect internal validity.

6. *Statistical regression effects.* Though not specifically stated, we can assume that all the members participating in the experiment were selected randomly from a normally distributed population, in which case the issue of statistical regression contaminating the experiment does not arise.

7. *Instrumentation effects.* Since the same questionnaire measured morale both before and after the treatment for all members, there should not have been any instrumentation bias.

In effect, three of the seven threats to internal validity do apply in this case. The history, main testing, and mortality effects are of concern and hence the internal validity will not be high. Interactive testing effects threaten the external validity of the findings.

# Internal validity in case studies

If there are several threats to internal validity even in a tightly controlled lab experiment, it should be quite clear why we cannot draw conclusions about causal relationships from case studies that describe the events that occurred during a particular time. Unless a well-designed experimental study, randomly assigning members to experimental and control groups and successfully manipulating the treatment, indicates possible causal relationships, it is impossible to say which factor causes another. For instance, there are several causes attributed to "Slice," the soft drink introduced by Pepsico Inc., not taking off after its initial success. Among the reasons given are (1) a cutback in advertisements for Slice, (2) operating on the mistaken premise that the juice content in Slice would appeal to health-conscious buyers, (3) Pepsico's attempts to milk the brand too quickly, (4) several strategic errors made by Pepsico, (5) underestimation of the time taken to build a brand, and the like.  While all the above could provide the basis for developing a theoretical framework for explaining the variance in the sales of a product such as Slice, conclusions about cause-and-effect relationships cannot be determined from anecdotal events.

# Review of factors affecting internal and external validity

Whereas internal validity raises questions about whether it is the treatment alone or some additional extraneous factor that causes the effects, external validity raises issues about the generalizability of the findings to other settings.

Interactive testing and selection effects may restrict the external validity of our findings. These threats to external validity can be combated by creating experimental conditions that are as close as possible to the situations to which the results of the experiment are to be generalized.

At least seven contaminating factors exist that might affect the internal validity of experimental designs. These are the effects of history, maturation, (main) testing, instrumentation, selection, statistical regression, and mortality. It is, however, possible to reduce these biases by enhancing the level of sophistication of the experimental design. Whereas some of the more sophisticated designs, discussed next, help to increase the internal validity of the experimental results, they also become expensive and time consuming.

The different types of experimental design and the extent to which internal and external validity are met in each are discussed next.

# Types of experimental design and validity

Let us consider some of the commonly used experimental designs and determine the extent to which they guard against the seven factors that could contaminate the internal validity of experimental results. The shorter the time span of the experiments, the less the chances are of encountering history, maturation, and mortality effects. Experiments lasting an hour or two do not usually meet with many of these problems. It is only when experiments are spread over an extended period of, say, several months, that the possibility of encountering more of the confounding factors increases.

## Quasi-experimental designs

Some studies expose an experimental group to a treatment and measure its effects. Such an experimental design is the weakest of all designs, and it does not measure the true cause-and-effect relationship. This is so because there is no comparison between groups, nor any recording of the status of the dependent variable as it was prior to the experimental treatment and how it changed after the treatment. In the absence of such control, the study is of no scientific value in determining cause-and-effect relationships. Hence, such a design is referred to as a *quasi-experimental design*. The following three designs are quasi-experimental designs.

### Pretest and posttest experimental group design

An experimental group (without a control group) may be given a pretest, exposed to a treatment, and then given a posttest to measure the effects of the treatment. This can be illustrated as in Table 9.2, where $O$ refers to some process of observation or measurement, $X$ represents the exposure of a group to an experimental treatment, and the $X$ and $O$s in the row are applied to the same specific group. Here, the effects of the treatment can be obtained by measuring the difference between the posttest and the pretest $(O_2 - O_1)$. Note, however, that testing effects might contaminate both the internal (main testing effects) and external (interactive testing effects) validity of the findings. If the experiment is extended over a period of time, history, mortality, and maturation effects may also confound the results.

### Posttests only with experimental and control groups

Some experimental designs are set up with an experimental and a control group, the former alone being exposed to a treatment and not the latter. The effects of the treatment are studied by assessing the difference in the outcomes – that is, the posttest scores of the experimental and control groups. This is illustrated in Table 9.3 Here is a case where the testing effects have

| **TABLE 9.2** | **Pretest and posttest experimental group design.** | | |
|---|---|---|---|
| Group | Pretest score | Treatment | Posttest score |
| Experimental group | $O_1$ | $X$ | $O_2$ |
| Treatment effect $= (O_2 - O_1)$ | | | |

| TABLE 9.3    Posttest only with experimental and control groups. | | |
| --- | --- | --- |
| Group | Treatment | Outcome |
| Experimental group | X | $O_1$ |
| Control group | | $O_2$ |
| Treatment effect $= (O_1 - O_2)$ | | |

been avoided because there is no pretest, only a posttest. Care has to be taken, however, to make sure that the two groups are matched for all the possible contaminating "nuisance" variables. Otherwise, the true effects of the treatment cannot be determined by merely looking at the difference in the posttest scores of the two groups. Randomization would take care of this problem.

Mortality (the dropout of individuals from groups) is a problem for all experimental designs, including this one. It can confound the results, and thus pose a threat to internal validity.

### Time series design

A time series design (sometimes called an interrupted time series design) differs from the aforementioned designs in that it collects data on the same variable at regular intervals (for instance weeks, months, or years). A time series design thus allows the researcher to assess the impact of a treatment over time. Figure 9.3 visually describes a time series design. It shows that a series of measurements on the dependent variable is taken before and after the treatment is administered (either by the researcher or naturally).

Figure 9.4 depicts the results of a time series experiment testing the effect of price reduction (in week 4) on sales. The horizontal or x-axis is divided into weeks, and the vertical or y-axis shows the values of sales (the dependent variable) as they fluctuate over a period of nine weeks. Assuming that other factors, such as the other marketing-mix variables and the marketing mix of competitors, stay the same, the impact of the price cut is the difference in sales before and after the change. From Figure 9.4 it is easy to see that there was an increase in sales after the price of the product went down. The question is, however, whether the increase in sales, depicted by the two horizontal lines in Figure 9.4, is significant. Bayesian moving average models (for instance, Box and Jenkins, 1970) are frequently used to test the impact of a treatment on the dependent variable when a time series design is used.

$$O_1 \; O_2 \; O_3 \; O_4 \; O_5 \; X \; O_6 \; O_7 \; O_8 \; O_9 \; O_{10}$$

Figure 9.3: Time series design.

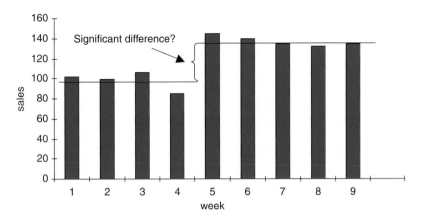

Figure 9.4: Effect of price cut in week 4.

A key problem of time series is history: certain events or factors that have an impact on the independent variable–dependent variable relationship might unexpectedly occur while the experiment is in progress. Other problems are main and interactive testing effects, mortality, and maturation.

## True experimental designs

Experimental designs which include both the treatment and control groups and record information both before and after the experimental group is exposed to the treatment are known as ex post facto experimental designs. These are discussed below.

### Pretest and posttest experimental and control group design

This design can be visually depicted as in Table 9.4. Two groups – one experimental and the other control – are both exposed to the pretest and the posttest. The only difference

| TABLE 9.4 | Pretest and posttest experimental and control groups. | | |
|---|---|---|---|
| Group | Pretest | Treatment | Posttest |
| Experimental group | $O_1$ | X | $O_2$ |
| Control group | $O_3$ | | $O_4$ |
| | Treatment effect $= [(O_2 - O_1) - (O_4 - O_3)]$ | | |

between the two groups is that the former is exposed to a treatment whereas the latter is not. Measuring the difference between the differences in the post- and pretest scores of the two groups gives the net effects of the treatment. Both groups have been exposed to both the pre- and posttests, and both groups have been randomized; thus we can expect the history, maturation, main testing, and instrumentation effects to have been controlled. This is so due to the fact that whatever happened with the experimental group (e.g., maturation, history, main testing, and instrumentation) also happened with the control group, and in measuring the net effects (the difference in the differences between the pre- and posttest scores) we have controlled these contaminating factors. Through the process of randomization, we have also controlled the effects of selection bias and statistical regression.

Mortality could, again, pose a problem in this design. In experiments that take several weeks, as in the case of assessing the impact of training on skill development, or measuring the impact of technology advancement on effectiveness, some of the subjects in the experimental group may drop out before the end of the experiment. It is possible that those who drop out are in some way different from those who stay on until the end and take the posttest. If so, mortality could offer a plausible rival explanation for the difference between $O_2$ and $O_1$. Interactive testing effects could also cause a problem in this design; the fact that the participants in the experimental group are asked to do a pretest could make them more sensitive to the manipulation.

## Solomon four-group design

To gain more confidence in internal validity in experimental designs, it is advisable to set up two experimental groups and two control groups for the experiment. One experimental group and one control group can be given both the pretest and the posttest, as shown in Table 9.5. The other two groups will be given only the posttest. Here, the effects of the treatment can be calculated in several different ways, as indicated in the figure. To the extent that we come up with almost the same results in each of the different calculations, we can attribute the effects to the treatment. This increases the internal validity of the results of the experimental design.

**TABLE 9.5    Solomon four-group design.**

| Group | Pretest | Treatment | Posttest |
|---|---|---|---|
| 1. Experimental | $O_1$ | X | $O_2$ |
| 2. Control | $O_3$ | | $O_4$ |
| 3. Experimental | | X | $O_5$ |
| 4. Control | | | $O_6$ |

This design, known as the **Solomon four-group design**, is perhaps the most comprehensive and the one with the least number of problems with internal validity.

**Solomon four-group design and threats to validity**

The Solomon four-group design, also known as the four-group six-study design, is a highly sophisticated experimental design. This design controls for all the threats to internal validity, except for mortality (which is a problem for all experimental designs) and also for interactive testing effects. For this reason, the Solomon four-group design is very useful when interactive testing effects are expected.

Treatment effect ($E$) could be judged by:

$$E = (O_2 - O_1)$$
$$E = (O_2 - O_4)$$
$$E = (O_5 - O_6)$$
$$E = (O_5 - O_3)$$
$$E = [(O_2 - O_1) - (O_4 - O_3)]$$

If all $E$s are similar, the cause-and-effect relationship is highly valid.

To be able to calculate the effect of the experimental treatment, an estimate of the prior measurements is needed for Groups 3 and 4. The best estimate of this premeasure is the average of the two pretests; that is, $^1/_2(O_1 + O_3)$. Together with the six pre- and posttest observations, the estimates of the premeasures can then be used to generate estimations of the impact of the experimental treatment ($E$), interactive testing effects ($I$), and the effects of uncontrolled variables ($U$). Estimates of these effects are made by comparing the before and after measures of the four groups.

The following equations provide an overview of the potential impact of the experimental treatment ($E$), interactive testing effects ($I$), and uncontrolled variables ($U$) for each group:

*Group 1.* $(O_2 - O_1) = E + I + U$
*Group 2.* $(O_4 - O_3) = U$
*Group 3.* $(O_5 - ^1/_2(O_1 + O_3)) = E + U$
*Group 4.* $(O_6 - ^1/_2(O_1 + O_3)) = U$

We can use these equations to estimate the effects of $E$, $I$, and $U$ by comparing the pre- and posttests of the groups. For instance, to estimate the effect of the experimental stimulus ($E$) the results of Groups 3 and 4 are used:

$$[O_5 - ^1/_2(O_1 + O_3)] - [O_6 - ^1/_2(O_1 + O_3)] = [E + U] - U = E$$

To calculate the effect of $I$ (the interactive testing effect) the results of Groups 1 and 3 are used:

$$(O_2 - O_1) - [O_5 - ^1/_2(O_1 + O_3)] = (E + I + U) - (E + U) = I.$$

Thus we are able to control for interactive testing effects that threaten the external validity of our findings. Let us now examine how the threats to internal validity are taken care of in the Solomon four-group design.

It is important to note that subjects should be randomly selected and randomly assigned to groups. This removes the statistical regression and selection biases. Group 2, the control group that was exposed to both the pre- and posttest, helps us to see whether or not history, maturation, (main) testing, instrumentation, or regression threaten internal validity. Mortality (the loss of participants during the course of the experiment) is a potential problem for all experimental designs, even for this one.

Thus, the Solomon four-group experimental design guarantees the maximum internal and external validity, ruling out many other rival hypotheses. Where establishing a cause-and-effect relationship is critical for the survival of businesses, for example pharmaceutical companies, which often face lawsuits for questionable products, the Solomon four-group design is eminently useful. However, because of the number of subjects that need to be recruited, the care with which the study has to be designed, the time that needs to be devoted to the experiment, and other reasons, the cost of conducting such an experiment is high. For this reason it is rarely used.

Table 9.6 summarizes the threats to validity covered by the different experimental designs. If the subjects have all been randomly assigned to the groups, then selection bias and statistical regression are eliminated in all cases.

### Double-blind studies

When extreme care and rigor are needed in experimental designs, as in the case of discovery of new medicines that could impact on human lives, blind studies are conducted to avoid

| TABLE 9.6 | **Major threats to validity in different experimental designs when members are randomly selected and assigned.** |
|---|---|
| Types of experimental design | Major threats to validity |
| 1. Pretest and posttest with one experimental group only | History, maturation, main testing, interactive testing, mortality |
| 2. Pretest and posttest with one experimental and one control group | Interactive testing, mortality |
| 3. Posttests only with one experimental and one control group | Mortality |
| 4. Solomon four-group design | Mortality |

any bias that might creep in. For example, pharmaceutical companies experimenting with the efficacy of newly developed drugs in the prototype stage ensure that the subjects in the experimental and control groups are kept unaware of who is given the drug, and who the placebo. Such studies are called blind studies.

When Aviron tested and announced the Flu-mist vaccine, neither the subjects nor the researchers who administered the vaccine to them were aware of the "true" versus the "placebo" treatment. The entire process was conducted by an outside testing agency which alone knew who got what treatment. Since, in this case, both the experimenter and the subjects are blinded, such studies are called **double-blind studies**. Since there is no tampering with the treatment in any way, such experimental studies are the least biased.

As mentioned previously, managers rarely undertake the study of cause-and-effect relationships in organizations using experimental designs because of the inconvenience and disruption they cause to the system.

## Ex post facto designs

Cause-and-effect relationships are sometimes established through what is called the ex post facto design. Here, there is no manipulation of the independent variable in the lab or field setting, but subjects who have already been exposed to a stimulus and those not so exposed are studied. For instance, training programs might have been introduced in an organization two years earlier. Some might have already gone through the training while others might not. To study the effects of training on work performance, performance data might now be collected for both groups. Since the study does not immediately follow after the training, but much later, it is an ex post facto design.

More advanced experimental designs such as the completely randomized design, randomized block design, Latin square design, and the factorial design are described in the appendix to this chapter, for the student interested in these.

# Simulation

An alternative to lab and field experimentation currently being used in business research is simulation. Simulation uses a model-building technique to determine the effects of changes, and computer-based simulations are becoming popular in business research. A simulation can be thought of as an experiment conducted in a specially created setting that very closely represents the natural environment in which activities are usually carried out. In that sense, the simulation lies somewhere between a lab and a field experiment, insofar as the environment is artificially created but not too different from "reality." Participants are exposed to real-world experiences over a period of time, lasting anywhere from several hours to several weeks, and they can be randomly assigned to different treatment groups. If managerial behavior as a function of a specific treatment is to be studied, subjects will be asked to operate in an environment very much like an office, with desks, chairs, cabinets, telephones, and the like. Members will be randomly assigned the roles of directors, managers, clerks, and so on, and specific stimuli will be presented to them. Thus, while the researcher retains control over the assignment and manipulation, the subjects are left free to operate as in a real office. In essence, some factors will be built into or incorporated in the simulated system and others left free to vary (participants' behavior, within the rules of the game). Data on the dependent variable can be obtained through observation, videotaping, audio recording, interviews, or questionnaires.

Causal relationships can be tested since both manipulation and control are possible in simulations. Two types of simulation can be made: one in which the nature and timing of simulated events are totally determined by the researcher (called experimental simulation), and the other (called free simulation) where the course of activities is at least partly governed by the reaction of the participants to the various stimuli as they interact among themselves. Looking Glass, the free simulation developed by Lombardo, McCall, and DeVries (1983) to study leadership styles, has been quite popular in the management area.

Cause-and-effect relationships are better established in experimental simulations where the researcher exercises greater control. In simulations involving several weeks, however, there may be a high rate of attrition of members. Experimental and free simulations are both expensive, since creating real-world conditions in an artificial setting and collecting data over extended periods of time involve the deployment of many types of resources. Simulations can be done in specially created settings using subjects, computers, and mathematical models. Steufert, Pogash, and Piasecki (1988), who assessed managerial competence through a six-hour computer-assisted simulation, are of the opinion that simulation technology may be the only viable method to simultaneously study several types of executive style.

Computer-based simulations are frequently used in the accounting and finance areas. For example, the effectiveness of various analytic review procedures in detecting errors in account balances has been tested through simulations (Knechel, 1986). In the finance area, risk management has been studied through simulations. Simulations have also been used to understand the complex relationships in the financing of pension plans and making important investment decisions (Perrier and Kalwarski, 1989). It is possible to vary several variables (workforce demographics, inflation rates, etc.) singly or simultaneously in such models.

Prototypes of machines and instruments are often the result of simulated models. Simulation has also been used by many companies to test the robustness and efficacy of various products. We are also familiar with flight simulators, driving simulators, and even nuclear reactor simulators. Here, the visual patterns presented keep changing in response to the reactions of the individual (the pilot, the driver, or the emergency handler) to the previous stimulus presented, and not in any predetermined order. Entire business operations, from office layout to profitability, can be simulated using different prospective scenarios. With increasing access to sophisticated technology, and the advancement of mathematical models, simulation is becoming an important managerial decision-making tool. It is quite likely that we will see simulation being used as a managerial tool, to enhance motivation, leadership, and the like, in the future. Simulation can also be applied as a problem-solving managerial tool in other behavioral and administrative areas. Programmed, computer-based simulation models in behavioral areas could serve managerial decision making very well indeed.

# Ethical issues in experimental design research

It is appropriate at this juncture to briefly discuss a few of the many ethical issues involved in doing research, some of which are particularly relevant to conducting lab experiments. The following practices are considered unethical:

- Putting pressure on individuals to participate in experiments through coercion, or applying social pressure.
- Giving menial tasks and asking demeaning questions that diminish their self-respect.
- Deceiving subjects by deliberately misleading them as to the true purpose of the research.
- Exposing participants to physical or mental stress.
- Not allowing subjects to withdraw from the research when they want to.
- Using the research results to disadvantage the participants, or for purposes not to their liking.
- Not explaining the procedures to be followed in the experiment.
- Exposing respondents to hazardous and unsafe environments.
- Not debriefing participants fully and accurately after the experiment is over.
- Not preserving the privacy and confidentiality of the information given by the participants.
- Withholding benefits from control groups.

The last item is somewhat controversial as to whether or not it should be an ethical dilemma, especially in organizational research. If three different incentives are offered for three experimental groups and none is offered to the control group, it is a fact that the control group has participated in the experiment with absolutely no benefit. Similarly, if four different experimental groups receive four different levels of training but the control group does not, the other four groups have gained expertise that the control group has been denied. But should this be deemed an ethical dilemma preventing experimental designs with control groups in organizational research? Perhaps not, for at least three reasons. One is that several others in the system who did not participate in the experiment did not benefit either. Second, even in the experimental groups, some would have benefited more than others (depending on the extent to which the causal factor was manipulated). Finally, if a cause-and-effect relationship is found, the system will, in all probability, implement the new-found knowledge sooner or later and everyone will ultimately stand to gain. The assumption that the control group did not benefit from participating in the experiment may not be a sufficient reason not to use lab or field experiments.

Many universities have a "human subjects committee" to protect the right of individuals participating in any type of research activity involving people. The basic function of these committees is to discharge the moral and ethical responsibilities of the university system by studying the procedures outlined in the research proposals and giving their stamp of approval to the study. The human subjects committee might require the investigators to modify their procedures or inform the subjects fully, if occasion demands it.

# Managerial implications

Before using experimental designs in research studies, it is essential to consider whether they are necessary at all, and if so, at what level of sophistication. This is because experimental designs call for special efforts and varying degrees of interference with the natural flow of activities. Some questions that need to be addressed in making these decisions are the following:

1. Is it really necessary to identify causal relationships, or would it suffice if the correlates that account for the variance in the dependent variable were known?
2. If it is important to trace the causal relationships, which of the two, internal validity or external validity, is needed more, or are both needed? If only internal validity is important, a carefully designed lab experiment is the answer; if generalizability is the more important criterion, then a field experiment is called for; if both are equally important, then a lab study should be first undertaken, followed by a field experiment, if the results of the former warrant the latter.
3. Is cost an important factor in the study? If so, would a less rather than a more sophisticated experimental design do?

These decision points are illustrated in the chart in Figure 9.5.

Though managers may not often be interested in cause-and-effect relationships, a good knowledge of experimental designs could foster some pilot studies to be undertaken to examine whether factors such as bonus systems, piece rates, rest pauses, and so on lead to positive outcomes such as better motivation, improved job performance, and other favorable working conditions at the workplace. Marketing managers could use experimental designs to study the effects on sales of advertisements, sales promotions, pricing, and the like. Awareness of the usefulness of simulation as a research tool can also result in creative research endeavors in the management area, as it currently does in the manufacturing side of businesses.

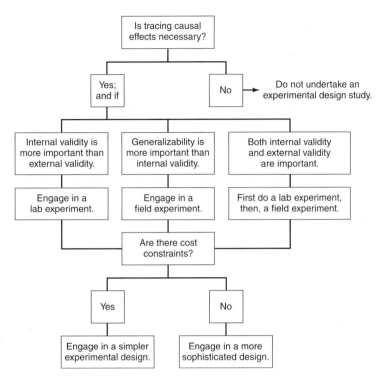

Figure 9.5: Decision points for embarking on an experimental design.

## SUMMARY

This chapter covered experimental designs, with particular reference to lab and field experiments. We examined how the contaminating variables in detecting the cause-and-effect relationship can be controlled through the processes of matching and randomization. Issues of internal and external validity and the seven factors that can affect internal validity were discussed. Also, some types of experimental designs that can be used to test cause-and-effect relationships and their usefulness in the context of validity and practicality were examined. We also described the ethical issues involved in conducting experimental research and the implications for managers in using experimental designs.

## DISCUSSION QUESTIONS

1. What are the differences between causal and correlational studies? pg 110
2. In what ways do lab experiments differ from field experiments?

3. Define the terms control and manipulation. Describe a possible lab experiment where you would need to control a variable. Include also a variable over which you would have no control but which could affect your experiment.
4. Explain the possible ways in which you can control "nuisance" variables.
5. What is internal validity and what are the threats it stands exposed to?
6. Explain the concept of "trade-off between internal validity and external validity."
7. Explain how the selection of participants may affect both the internal and external validity of your experiments.
8. Explain the difference between main and interactive testing effects. Why is this difference important?
9. History is a key problem in a time series design. Other problems are main and interactive testing effects, mortality, and maturation. Explain.
10. Explain why mortality remains a problem even when a Solomon four-group design is used.
11. "If a control group is a part of an experimental design, one need not worry about controlling other exogenous variables." Discuss this statement.
12. "The Solomon four-group design is the answer to all our research questions pertaining to cause-and-effect relationships because it guards against all the threats to internal validity." Comment.
13. Below is an adapted note from *Business Week* published some time ago. After reading it, apply what you have learned in this chapter, and design a study after sketching the theoretical framework.

## EXAMPLE

### The vital role of self-esteem

Why do some people earn more than others? Economists focused on the importance of education, basic skills, and work experience – what they called human capital – on increased productivity, and said these were reflected in greater earning power. Researchers also found that self-esteem was instrumental in acquiring human capital.

14. Design a study to examine the following situation.

## EXAMPLE

An organization would like to introduce one of two types of new manufacturing process to increase the productivity of workers, and both involve heavy investment in expensive technology. The company wants to test the efficacy of each process in one of its small plants.

# Further experimental designs

In this chapter we discussed different types of experimental design where groups were subjected to one or more treatments and the effects of the manipulation measured. However, we may sometimes wish to assess the simultaneous effects of two or more variables on a dependent variable, and this calls for more complex designs. Among the many advanced experimental designs available, we will examine here the completely randomized design, the randomized block design, the Latin square design, and the factorial design.

It would be useful to understand some terms before describing the various designs. The term "factor" is used to denote an independent variable – for example, price. The term "level" is used to denote various gradations of the factor – for example, high price, medium price, low price – while making it clear as to what these gradations signify (e.g., high price is anything over $2 per piece; medium is $1–$2 per piece; low price is anything less than $1 per piece). "Treatment" refers to the various levels of the factors. A "blocking factor" is a preexisting variable in a given situation that might have an effect on the dependent variable in addition to the treatment, the impact of which is important to assess. In effect, a blocking factor is an independent variable that has an effect on the dependent variable, but which preexists in a given situation: for example, the number of women and men in an organization; or teenagers, middle-aged men, and senior citizens as customers of a store, and so on.

## The completely randomized design

Let us say that a bus transportation company manager wants to know the effects of fare reduction by 5, 7, and 10 cents on the average daily increase in the number of passengers using the bus as a means of transportation. He may take 27 routes that the buses usually ply, and randomly assign nine routes for each of the treatments (i.e., reduction of fares by 5, 7, and 10 cents) for a two-week period. His experimental design is shown in Table 9.7, where the Os on the left indicate the number of passengers that used the bus for the two weeks preceding the treatment; $X_1$, $X_2$, and $X_3$ indicate the three different treatments (fare reductions of 5, 7, and 10 cents per mile), and the Os on the right indicate the number of passengers that used the bus as a transportation mode during the two weeks when the fares were reduced. The manager will be able to assess the impact of the three treatments by deducting each of the three Os on the left from its corresponding O on the right. The results of this study will provide the answer to the bus company manager's question.

| TABLE 9.7 | Illustration of a completely randomized design. | | |

| Routes | Number of passengers before | Treatment | Number of passengers after |
|---|---|---|---|
| Group 1 of nine routes | $O_1$ | $X_1$ | $O_2$ |
| Group 2 of nine routes | $O_3$ | $X_2$ | $O_4$ |
| Group 3 of nine routes | $O_5$ | $X_3$ | $O_6$ |

## Randomized block design

In the foregoing case, the bus company manager was interested only in the effects of different levels of price reduction on the increase in the number of passengers in general. He may be more interested, however, in targeting the price reduction on the right routes or sectors. For example, it is likely that the reduction in fares will be more welcome to senior citizens and residents of crowded urban areas where driving is stressful, than to car owners living in the suburbs, who may not be equally appreciative of and sensitive to price reduction. Thus, reductions in fares will probably attract more passengers if targeted at the right groups (i.e., the right blocking factor – the residential areas). In this case, the bus company manager should first identify the routes that fall into the three blocks – those in suburbs, crowded urban areas, or residential areas with retirees. Thus, the 27 routes will get assigned to one or other of three blocks and will then be randomly assigned, within the blocks, to the three treatments. The experimental design is shown in Table 9.8.

Through the above randomized block design, not only can the direct effect of each treatment (i.e., the main effect of the level, which is the effect of each type of fare reduction) be assessed, but also the joint effects of price and the residential area route (the interaction effect). For example, the general effect of a 5 cent reduction for all routes will be known by the increase in passengers across all three residential areas, and the general effect of a 5 cent reduction on those in the suburbs alone will also be known by seeing the effects in the first cell. If the highest average daily number of increased passengers is 75 for a 7 cent decrease for the crowded urban area route, followed by an increase of 30 for the retirees' areas for the 10 cent decrease, and an increase of five passengers for a 5 cent reduction for the suburbs, the bus company manager can work out a cost–benefit analysis and decide on the course of action to be taken. Thus, the randomized block design is a more powerful technique, providing more information for decision making. However, the cost of this experimental design will be higher.

**TABLE 9.8**    Illustration of a randomized block design. Note that the *X*s only indicate various levels of the blocking factor and the *O*s (the number of passengers before and after each treatment at each level) are not shown, though these measures will be taken.

| Fare reduction | Blocking factor: residential areas | | |
| --- | --- | --- | --- |
| | Suburbs | Crowded urban areas | Retirement areas |
| 5c | $X_1$ | $X_1$ | $X_1$ |
| 7c | $X_2$ | $X_2$ | $X_2$ |
| 10c | $X_3$ | $X_3$ | $X_3$ |

## Latin square design

Whereas the randomized block design helps the experimenter to minimize the effects of one nuisance variable (variation among the rows) in evaluating the treatment effects, the Latin square design is very useful when two nuisance blocking factors (i.e., variations across both the rows and the columns) are to be controlled. Each treatment appears an equal number of times in any one ordinal position in each row. For instance, in studying the effects of bus fare reduction on passengers, two nuisance factors could be (1) the day of the week: (a) midweek (Tuesday through Thursday), (b) weekend, (c) Monday and Friday, and (2) the (three) residential localities of the passengers. A three by three Latin square design can be created in this case, to which will be randomly assigned the three treatments (5, 7, and 10 cent fare reductions), such that each treatment occurs only once in each row and column intersection. The Latin square design is shown in Table 9.9. After the experiment is carried out and the net increase in passengers under each treatment calculated, the average treatment effects can be gauged. The price reduction that offers the best advantage can also be assessed.

A problem with the Latin square design is that it presupposes the absence of interaction between the treatments and blocking factors, which may not always be the case. We also need as many cells as there are treatments. Furthermore, it is an uneconomical design compared to some others.

| TABLE 9.9 | Illustration of the Latin square design. |
|---|---|

| Residential area | Day of the week | | |
|---|---|---|---|
| | Midweek | Weekend | Monday/Friday |
| Suburbs | $X_1$ | $X_2$ | $X_3$ |
| Urban | $X_2$ | $X_3$ | $X_1$ |
| Retirement | $X_3$ | $X_1$ | $X_2$ |

## Factorial design

Thus far we have discussed experimental designs in the context of examining a cause-and-effect relationship between one independent variable and the dependent variable. The factorial design enables us to test the effects of two or more manipulations at the same time on the dependent variable. In other words, two treatments can be simultaneously manipulated and their single and joint (known as main and interaction) effects assessed. For example, the manager of the bus company might be interested in knowing passenger increases if he used three different types of buses (Luxury Express, Standard Express, and Regular) and manipulated both the fare reduction and the type of vehicle used, simultaneously. Table 9.10 illustrates the $3 \times 3$ factorial design that would be used for the purpose.

Here, two factors are used with three levels in each. The above is completely randomized, since the fares are randomly assigned to one of nine treatment combinations. A wealth of information can be obtained from this design. For example, the bus company manager will know the increase in passengers for each fare reduction, for each type of vehicle, and for the two in combination. Thus, the main effects of the two independent variables as well as the

| TABLE 9.10 | Illustration of a $3 \times 3$ factorial design. |
|---|---|

| Type of bus | Bus fare reduction rates | | |
|---|---|---|---|
| | 5c | 7c | 10c |
| Luxury Express | $X_1Y_1$ | $X_2Y_1$ | $X_3Y_1$ |
| Standard Express | $X_2Y_2$ | $X_1Y_2$ | $X_3Y_2$ |
| Regular | $X_3Y_3$ | $X_2Y_3$ | $X_1Y_3$ |

interactions among them can be assessed. For this reason, the factorial design is more efficient than several single-factor randomized designs.

It is also statistically possible to control one or more variables through covariance analysis. For example, it may be suspected that even after randomly assigning members to treatments, there is a further "nuisance" factor. It is possible to statistically block such factors while analyzing the data.

Several other complex experimental designs are also available and are treated in books devoted to experimental designs.

# CHAPTER 10

## Sampling

## Topics discussed

- Population, element, population frame, sample, subject, sampling
- Reasons for sampling
- Representativeness of the sample
- Probability sampling
  - Simple random sampling
  - Systematic sampling
  - Stratified random sampling: proportionate and disproportionate
  - Cluster sampling: single-stage and multistage clusters
  - Area sampling
  - Double sampling
- Nonprobability sampling
  - Convenience sampling
  - Judgment sampling
  - Quota sampling
- Sampling in cross-cultural research
- Issues of precision and confidence in determining sample size
- Precision and confidence trade-offs
- Sample data and hypothesis testing
- Sample size
- Efficiency in sampling
- Sampling in qualitative studies
- Managerial implications

## CHAPTER OBJECTIVES

After completing Chapter 10, you should be able to:

1. Define sampling, sample, population, element, sampling unit, and subject.
2. Describe and discuss the sampling process
3. Describe and discuss the different sampling designs.
4. Identify the use of appropriate sampling designs for different research purposes.
5. Explain why sample data are used to test hypotheses.
6. Discuss precision and confidence.
7. Estimate sample size.
8. Discuss the factors to be taken into consideration for determining sample size.
9. Discuss efficiency in sampling.
10. Discuss generalizability in the context of sampling designs.
11. Apply the material learned in this chapter to class assignments and projects.

Surveys are useful and powerful in finding answers to research questions through data collection and subsequent analyses, but they can do more harm than good if the population is not correctly targeted. That is, if data are not collected from the people, events, or objects that can provide the correct answers to solve the problem, the survey will be in vain. The process of selecting the right individuals, objects, or events as representatives for the entire population is known as sampling, which we will examine in some detail in this chapter.

# Population, element, sample, sampling unit, and subject

In learning how representative data (i.e., as reflected in the universe) can be collected, a few terms, as described below, have first to be understood.

## Population

The population refers to the entire group of people, events, or things of interest that the researcher wishes to investigate. It is the group of people, events, or things of interest for which the researcher wants to make inferences (based on sample statistics). For instance, if the CEO of a computer firm wants to know the kinds of advertising strategies adopted by computer firms in the Silicon Valley, then all computer firms situated there will be the population. If an organizational consultant is interested in studying the effects of a four-day work week on the white-collar workers in a telephone company in Ireland, then all white-collar workers in that company will make up the population. If regulators want to know how patients in nursing homes run by a company in France are cared for, then all the patients in all the nursing homes run by them will form the population. If, however, the regulators are interested only in one particular nursing home run by that company, then only the patients in that specific nursing home will form the population.

## Element

An **element** is a single member of the population. If 1000 blue-collar workers in a particular organization happen to be the population of interest to a researcher, each blue-collar worker therein is an element. If 500 pieces of machinery are to be approved after inspecting a few, there will be 500 elements in this population. Incidentally, the census is a count of all elements in the human population.

## Sample

A **sample** is a subset of the population. It comprises some members selected from it. In other words, some, but not all, elements of the population form the sample. If 200 members are drawn from a population of 1000 blue-collar workers, these 200 members form the sample for the study. That is, from a study of these 200 members, the researcher will draw conclusions about the entire population of 1000 blue-collar workers. Likewise, if there are 145 in-patients in a hospital and 40 of them are to be surveyed by the hospital administrator to assess their level of satisfaction with the treatment received, then these 40 members will be the sample.

A sample is thus a subgroup or subset of the population. By studying the sample, the researcher should be able to draw conclusions that are generalizable to the population of interest.

## Sampling unit

The **sampling unit** is the element or set of elements that is available for selection in some stage of the sampling process. Examples of sampling units in a multistage sample are city blocks, households, and individuals within the households.

## Subject

A **subject** is a single member of the sample, just as an element is a single member of the population. If 200 members from the total population of 1000 blue-collar workers form the sample for the study, then each blue-collar worker in the sample is a subject. As another example, if a sample of 50 machines from a total of 500 machines is to be inspected, then every

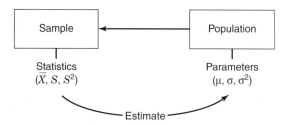

Figure 10.1: The relationship between sample and population.

one of the 50 machines is a subject, just as every single machine in the total population of 500 machines is an element.

# Parameters

The characteristics of the population such as $\mu$ (the population mean), $\sigma$ (the population standard deviation), and $\sigma^2$ (the population variance) are referred to as its *parameters.* The central tendencies, the dispersions, and other statistics in the sample of interest to the research are treated as approximations of the central tendencies, dispersions, and other parameters of the population. As such, all conclusions drawn about the sample under study are generalized to the population. In other words, the sample statistics – $X$ (the sample mean), $S$ (the standard deviation), and $S^2$ (the variation in the sample) – are used as estimates of the population parameters $\mu$, $\sigma$, and $\sigma^2$. Figure 10.1 shows the relationship between the sample and the population.

# Reasons for sampling

The reasons for using a sample, rather than collecting data from the entire population, are self-evident. In research investigations involving several hundreds and even thousands of elements, it would be practically impossible to collect data from, or test, or examine every element. Even if it were possible, it would be prohibitive in terms of time, cost, and other human resources. Study of a sample rather than the entire population is also sometimes likely to produce more reliable results. This is mostly because fatigue is reduced and fewer errors therefore result in collecting data, especially when a large number of elements is involved. In a few cases, it would also be impossible to use the entire population to gain knowledge about, or test, something. Consider, for instance, the case of electric bulbs. In testing the life of bulbs, if we were to burn every single bulb produced, there would be none left to sell! This is known as *destructive sampling.*

# Representativeness of samples

The need to choose the right sample for a research investigation cannot be overemphasized. We know that rarely will the sample be an exact replica of the population from which it is drawn. For instance, very few sample means ($X$) are likely to be exactly equal to the population means ($\mu$). Nor is the standard deviation of the sample ($S$) likely to be the same as the standard deviation of the population ($\sigma$). However, if we choose the sample in a scientific way, we can be reasonably sure that the sample statistic (e.g., $X$, $S$, or $S^2$) is fairly close to the population parameter (i.e., $\mu$, $\sigma$, or $\sigma^2$). To put it differently, it is possible to choose the sample in such a way that it is representative of the population. There is always a slight probability, however, that sample values might fall outside the population parameters.

# Normality of distributions

Attributes or characteristics of the population are generally normally distributed. For instance, when attributes such as height and weight are considered, most people will be clustered around the mean, leaving only a small number at the extremes who are either very tall or very short, very heavy or very light, and so on, as indicated in Figure 10.2. If we are to estimate the population characteristics from those represented in a sample with reasonable accuracy, the sample has to be so chosen that the distribution of the characteristics of interest follows the same pattern of normal distribution in the sample as it does in the population. From the central limit theorem, we know that the sampling distribution of the sample mean is normally distributed. As the sample size $n$ increases, the means of the random samples taken from practically any population approach a normal distribution with mean $\mu$ and standard deviation $\sigma$. In sum, irrespective of whether or not the attributes of the population are normally distributed, if we take a sufficiently *large number of* samples and *choose* them with care, we will have a sampling distribution of the means that has normality. This is the reason why two important issues in sampling are the sample size ($n$) and the sampling design, as discussed later.

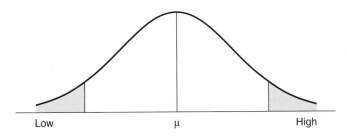

Figure 10.2: Normal distribution in a population.

When the properties of the population are not overrepresented or underrepresented in the sample, we have a representative sample. When a sample consists of elements in the population that have extremely high values on the variable we are studying, the sample mean X will be far higher than the population mean $\mu$. If, in contrast, the sample subjects consist of elements in the population with extremely low values on the variable of interest, the sample mean will be much lower than the true population mean $\mu$. If our sampling design and sample size are right, however, the sample mean X will be within close range of the true population mean $\mu$. Thus, through appropriate sampling design, we can ensure that the sample subjects are not chosen from the extremes, but are truly representative of the properties of the population. The more representative of the population the sample is, the more generalizable are the findings of the research. Recall that generalizability is one of the hallmarks of scientific research, as we saw in Chapter 2.

While, in view of our concern about generalizability, we may be particular about choosing representative samples for most research, some cases may not call for such regard to generalizability. For instance, at the exploratory stages of fact finding, we may be interested only in "getting a handle" on the situation, and therefore limit the interview to only the most conveniently available people. The same is true when time is of the essence, and urgency in getting information overrides a high level of accuracy in terms of priority. For instance, a film agency might want to find out quickly the impact on the viewers of a newly released film shown the previous evening. The interviewer might question the first 20 people leaving the theater after seeing the film and obtain their reactions. On the basis of their replies, she may form an opinion as to the likely success of the film. As another example, a restaurant manager might want to find the reactions of customers to a new item added to the menu to determine whether or not it has been a popular and worthwhile addition. For this purpose, the first 15 people who chose the special item might be interviewed, and their reactions obtained. In such cases, having instant information may be more gainful than obtaining the most representative facts. It should, however, be noted that the results of such convenient samples are not reliable and can never be generalized to the population.

# The sampling process

Sampling is the *process* of selecting a sufficient number of the right elements from the population, so that a study of the sample and an understanding of its properties or characteristics make it possible for us to generalize such properties or characteristics to the population elements. The major steps in sampling include:

1. Define the population.
2. Determine the sample frame.
3. Determine the sampling design.
4. Determine the appropriate sample size.
5. Execute the sampling process.

## Defining the population

Sampling begins with precisely defining the target population. The target population must be defined in terms of elements, geographical boundaries, and time. For instance, for a banker interested in saving habits of blue-collar workers in the mining industry in the United States, the target population might be all blue-collar workers in that industry throughout the country. For an advertising agency interested in reading habits of elderly people, the target population might be the German population aged 50 and over. These examples illustrate that the research objective and the scope of the study play a crucial role in defining the target population.

## Determining the sample frame

The sampling frame is a (physical) representation of all the elements in the population from which the sample is drawn. The payroll of an organization would serve as the sampling frame if its members are to be studied. Likewise, the university registry containing a listing of all students, faculty, administrators, and support staff in the university during a particular academic year or semester could serve as the sampling frame for a study of the university population. A roster of class students could be the sampling frame for the study of students in a class. The telephone directory is also frequently used as a sampling frame for some types of study, even though it has an inherent bias inasmuch as some numbers are unlisted and certain others may have become obsolete.

Although the sampling frame is useful in providing a listing of each element in the population, it may not always be a current, up-to-date document. For instance, the names of members who have recently left the organization or dropped out of the university, as well as members who have only recently joined the organization or the university may not appear in the organization's payroll or the university registers on a given day. The most recently installed or disconnected telephones will not, likewise, be included in the current telephone directory. Hence, though the sampling frame may be available in many cases, it may not always be entirely correct or complete. When the sampling frame does not exactly match the population *coverage error* occurs. In some cases, the researcher might recognize this problem and not be too concerned about it, because the discrepancy between the target population and the sampling frame is small enough to ignore. However, in most cases, the researcher should deal with this error by either redefining the target population in terms of the sampling frame, screening the respondents with respect to important characteristics to ensure that they meet the criteria for the target population, or adjusting the collected data by a weighting scheme to counterbalance the coverage error.

## Determining the sampling design

There are two major types of sampling design: probability and nonprobability sampling. In **probability sampling**, the elements in the population have some known, non-zero chance or probability of being selected as sample subjects. In **nonprobability sampling**, the elements do not have a known or predetermined chance of being selected as subjects. Probability sampling designs are used when the representativeness of the sample is of importance in the interests of wider generalizability. When time or other factors, rather than generalizability, become critical, nonprobability sampling is generally used. Each of these two major designs has different sampling strategies. Depending on the extent of generalizability desired, the demands of time and other resources, and the purpose of the study, different types of probability and nonprobability sampling design are chosen.

The choice of the sampling procedure is a very important one. Therefore, this chapter will elaborately discuss the different types of sampling designs, bearing in mind the following points in the determination of the choice:

- What is the relevant target population of focus to the study?
- What exactly are the parameters we are interested in investigating?
- What kind of a sampling frame is available?
- What costs are attached to the sampling design?
- How much time is available to collect the data from the sample?

## Determining the sample size

Is a sample size of 40 large enough? Or do you need a sample size of 75, 180, 384, or 500? Is a large sample better than a small sample; that is, is it more representative? The decision about how large the sample size should be can be a very difficult one. We can summarize the factors affecting decisions on sample size as:

1. The research objective;
2. The extent of precision desired (the confidence interval);
3. The acceptable risk in predicting that level of precision (confidence level);
4. The amount of variability in the population itself;
5. The cost and time constraints;
6. In some cases, the size of the population itself.

Thus, how large your sample should be is a function of these six factors. We will have more to say about sample size later on in this chapter, after we have discussed sampling designs.

## Executing the sampling process

The following two examples illustrate how, in the final stage of the sampling process, decisions with respect to the target population, the sampling frame, the sample technique, and the sample size have to be implemented.

## EXAMPLE

A satisfaction survey was conducted for a computer retailer in New Zealand. The objective of this survey was to improve internal operations and thus to retain more customers. The survey was transactional in nature; service satisfaction and several related variables were measured following a service encounter (i.e., a visit to the retailer). Hence, customer feedback was obtained while the service experience was still fresh. To obtain a representative sample of customers of the computer retailer (*the target population*), every 10th person, leaving one out of ten randomly selected stores, in randomly selected cities, in randomly selected regions, was approached during a one-week period (*the sampling technique*). Trained interviewers that were sent out with standardized questionnaires approached 732 customers leaving the stores (*the sample size*).

A young researcher was investigating the antecedents of salesperson performance. To examine his hypotheses, data were collected from chief sales executives in the United Kingdom (*the target population*) via mail questionnaires. The sample was initially drawn from a published business register (*the sampling frame*), but supplemented with respondent recommendations and other additions, in a *judgment sampling methodology*. Before distributing the questionnaires, the young researcher called each selected company to obtain the name of the chief sales executive, who was contacted and asked to participate in the study. The questionnaires were subsequently distributed to chief sales executives of 450 companies (*the sample size*). To enhance the response rate, pre-addressed and pre-stamped envelopes were provided, anonymity was assured, and a summary of the research findings as an incentive to the participants was offered. Several follow-up procedures, such as telephone calls and new mailings, were planned in order to receive as many responses as possible.

## Non-response and non-response error

A failure to obtain information from a number of subjects included in the sample (non-response) may lead to non-response error. **Non-response error** exists to the extent that those who did respond to your survey are different from those who did not on (one of the) characteristics of interest in your study. Two important sources of non-response are not-at-homes and refusals. An effective way to reduce the incidence of not-at-homes is to call back at another time, preferably at a different time of day. The rate of refusals depends, among other things, on the length of the survey, the data collection method, and the patronage of the research. Hence, a decrease in survey length, in the data collection method (personal interviews instead of mail questionnaires), and the auspices of the research often improve the overall return rate. Personalized cover letters, a small incentive for participating in the study, and an advance notice that the survey is taking place may also help you to increase the response rate. Nonetheless, it is almost impossible to entirely avoid non-response in surveys. In these cases you may have to turn to methods to deal with non-response error, such as generalizing the results to the respondents only or statistical adjustment (weighting the data by observable variables).

# Probability sampling

When elements in the population have a known chance of being chosen as subjects in the sample, we resort to a probability sampling design. Probability sampling can be either unrestricted (simple random sampling) or restricted (complex probability sampling) in nature.

## Unrestricted or simple random sampling

In the **unrestricted probability sampling** design, more commonly known as **simple random sampling**, every element in the population has a *known and equal* chance of being selected as a subject. Let us say there are 1000 elements in the population, and we need a sample of 100. Suppose we were to drop pieces of paper in a hat, each bearing the name of one of the elements, and draw 100 of those from the hat with our eyes closed. We know that the first piece drawn will have a 1/1000 chance of being drawn, the next one a 1/999 chance of being drawn, and so on. In other words, we know that the probability of any one of them being chosen is 1 in the number of the population, and we also know that each single element in the hat has the same or equal probability of being chosen. We certainly know that computers can generate random numbers and one does not have to go through the tedious process of pulling out names from a hat!

When we thus draw the elements from the population, it is most likely that the distribution patterns of the characteristics we are interested in investigating in the population are also likewise distributed in the subjects we draw for our sample. This sampling design, known as simple random sampling, has the least bias and offers the most generalizability. However, this sampling process could become cumbersome and expensive; in addition an entirely updated listing of the population may not always be available. For these and other reasons, other probability sampling designs are often chosen instead.

## Restricted or complex probability sampling

As an alternative to the simple random sampling design, several complex probability sampling (restricted probability) designs can be used. These probability sampling procedures offer a viable, and sometimes more efficient, alternative to the unrestricted design we just discussed. Efficiency is improved in that more information can be obtained for a given sample size using some of the complex probability sampling procedures than the simple random sampling design. The five most common complex probability sampling designs – systematic sampling, stratified random sampling, cluster sampling, area sampling, and double sampling – will now be discussed.

## Systematic sampling

The **systematic sampling** design involves drawing every $n$th element in the population starting with a randomly chosen element between 1 and $n$. The procedure is exemplified below.

### EXAMPLE

If we wanted a sample of 35 households from a total population of 260 houses in a particular locality, then we could sample every seventh house starting from a random number from 1 to 7. Let us say that the random number was 7, then houses numbered 7, 14, 21, 28, and so on, would be sampled until the 35 houses were selected. The one problem to be borne in mind in the systematic sampling design is the probability of a systematic bias creeping into the sample. In the above example, for instance, let us say that every seventh house happened to be a corner house. If the focus of the research study conducted by the construction industry was to control "noise pollution" experienced by residents through the use of appropriate filtering materials, then the residents of corner houses may not be exposed to as much noise as the houses that are in between. Information on noise levels gathered from corner house dwellers might therefore bias the researcher's data. The likelihood of drawing incorrect conclusions from such data is thus high. In view of the scope for such systematic bias, the researcher must consider the plans carefully and make sure that the systematic sampling design is appropriate for the study, before deciding on it. For market surveys, consumer attitude surveys, and the like, the systematic sampling design is often used, and the telephone directory frequently serves as the sampling frame for this sampling design.

## Stratified random sampling

While sampling helps to estimate population parameters, there may be identifiable subgroups of elements within the population that may be expected to have different parameters on a variable of interest to the researcher. For example, to the Human Resources Management Director interested in assessing the extent of training that the employees in the system feel they need, the entire organization will form the population for study. But the extent, quality, and intensity of training desired by middle-level managers, lower-level managers, first-line supervisors, computer analysts, clerical workers, and so on will be different for each group. Knowledge of the kinds of differences in needs that exist for the different groups will help the director to develop useful and meaningful training programs for each group in the organization. Data will therefore have to be collected in a manner that will help the assessment of needs at each subgroup level in the population. The unit of analysis then will be at the group level and the stratified random sampling process will come in handy.

Stratified random sampling, as its name implies, involves a process of stratification or segregation, followed by random selection of subjects from each stratum. The population is first divided into mutually exclusive groups that are relevant, appropriate, and meaningful in the context of the study. For instance, if the president of a company is concerned about low motivational levels or high absenteeism rates among the employees, it makes sense to stratify the population of organizational members according to their job levels. When the data are collected and the analysis is done, we may find that, contrary to expectations, it is the middle-level managers that are not motivated. This information will help the president to focus on action at the right level and devise better methods to motivate this group. Tracing the differences in the parameters of the subgroups within a population would not be possible without the stratified random sampling procedure. If either the simple random sampling or the systematic sampling procedure were used in a case like this, then the high motivation at some job levels and the low motivation at other levels would cancel each other out, thus masking the real problems that exist at a particular level or levels.

Stratification also helps when research questions such as the following are to be answered:

1. Are the machinists more accident prone than clerical workers?
2. Are Hispanics more loyal to the organization than Native Americans?

Stratifying customers on the basis of life stages, income levels, and the like to study buying patterns and stratifying companies according to size, industry, profits, and so forth to study stock market reactions are common examples of the use of stratification as a sampling design technique.

Stratification is an efficient research sampling design; that is, it provides more information with a given sample size. Stratification should follow the lines appropriate to the research question. If we are studying consumer preferences for a product, stratification of the population could be by geographical area, market segment, consumers' age, consumers' gender, or various combinations of these. If an organization contemplates budget cuts, the effects of these cuts on employee attitudes can be studied with stratification by department, function, or region. Stratification ensures homogeneity within each stratum (i.e., very few differences or dispersions on the variable of interest within each stratum), but heterogeneity (variability) between strata. In other words, there will be more between-group differences than within-group differences.

### Proportionate and disproportionate stratified random sampling

Once the population has been stratified in some meaningful way, a sample of members from each stratum can be drawn using either a simple random sampling or a systematic sampling procedure. The subjects drawn from each stratum can be either proportionate or disproportionate to the number of elements in the stratum. For instance, if an organization employs 10 top managers, 30 middle managers, 50 lower-level managers, 100 supervisors, 500 clerks, and 20 secretaries, and a stratified sample of about 140 people is needed for some

| | | Number of subjects in the sample | |
| | | Proportionate sampling (20% of the elements) | Disproportionate sampling |
| Job level | Number of elements | | |
|---|---|---|---|
| Top management | 10 | 2 | 7 |
| Middle-level management | 30 | 6 | 15 |
| Lower-level management | 50 | 10 | 20 |
| Supervisors | 100 | 20 | 30 |
| Clerks | 500 | 100 | 60 |
| Secretaries | 20 | 4 | 10 |
| Total | 710 | 142 | 142 |

**TABLE 10.1    Proportionate and disproportionate stratified random sampling.**

specific survey, the researcher might decide to include in the sample 20% of members from each stratum. That is, members represented in the sample from each stratum will be *proportionate* to the total number of elements in the respective strata. This would mean that two from the top, six from the middle, and ten from the lower levels of management would be included in the sample. In addition, 20 supervisors, 100 clerks, and four secretaries would be represented in the sample, as shown in the third column of Table 10.1. This type of sampling is called a **proportionate stratified random sampling** design.

In situations like the one above, researchers might sometimes be concerned that information from only two members at the top and six from the middle levels would not truly reflect how all members at those levels would respond. Therefore, a researcher might decide, instead, to use a **disproportionate stratified random sampling** procedure. The number of subjects from each stratum would now be altered, while keeping the sample size unchanged. Such a sampling design is illustrated in the far right-hand column in Table 10.1. The idea here is that the 60 clerks might be considered adequate to represent the population of 500 clerks; seven out of ten managers at the top level might also be considered representative of the top managers, and likewise 15 out of the 30 managers at the middle level. This redistribution of the numbers in the strata might be considered more appropriate and representative for the study than the previous proportionate sampling design.

Disproportionate sampling decisions are made either when some stratum or strata are too small or too large, or when there is more variability suspected within a particular stratum. As an example, the educational levels among supervisors, which may be considered to influence perceptions, may range from elementary school to master's degrees. Here, more people will be sampled at the supervisory level. Disproportionate sampling is also sometimes done when it is easier, simpler, and less expensive to collect data from one or more strata than from others.

In summary, stratified random sampling involves stratifying the elements along meaningful levels and taking proportionate or disproportionate samples from the strata. This sampling design is more efficient than the simple random sampling design because, for the same sample size, each important segment of the population is better represented, and more valuable and differentiated information is obtained with respect to each group.

## Cluster sampling

Cluster samples are samples gathered in groups or chunks of elements that, ideally, are natural aggregates of elements in the population. In cluster sampling, the target population is first divided into clusters. Then, a random sample of clusters is drawn and for each selected cluster either all the elements or a sample of elements are included in the sample. Cluster samples offer more heterogeneity within groups and more homogeneity among groups – the reverse of what we find in stratified random sampling, where there is homogeneity within each group and heterogeneity across groups.

A specific type of cluster sampling is area sampling. In this case, clusters consist of geographic areas such as counties, city blocks, or particular boundaries within a locality. If you wanted to survey the residents of a city, you would get a city map, take a sample of city blocks and select respondents within each city block. Sampling the needs of consumers before opening a 24-hour convenience store in a particular part of town would involve area sampling. Location plans for retail stores, advertisements focused specifically on local populations, and TV and radio programs beamed at specific areas could all use an area sampling design to gather information on the interests, attitudes, predispositions, and behaviors of the local area people.

Area sampling is less expensive than most other probability sampling designs, and it is not dependent on a sampling frame. A city map showing the blocks of the city is adequate information to allow a researcher to take a sample of the blocks and obtain data from the residents therein. Indeed, the key motivation for cluster sampling is cost reduction. The unit costs of cluster sampling are much lower than those of other probability sampling designs of simple or stratified random sampling or systematic sampling. However, cluster sampling exposes itself to greater bias and is the least generalizable of all the probability sampling designs, because most naturally occurring clusters in the organizational context do not contain heterogeneous elements. In other words, the conditions of intracluster heterogeneity and intercluster homogeneity are often not met.

For these reasons, the cluster sampling technique is not very common in organizational research. Moreover, for marketing research activities, naturally occurring clusters, such as clusters of residents, buyers, students, or shops, do not have much heterogeneity among the elements. As stated earlier, there is more intracluster homogeneity than heterogeneity in such clusters. Hence, cluster sampling, though less costly, does not offer much efficiency in terms of precision or confidence in the results. However, cluster sampling offers convenience. For example, it is easier to inspect an assortment of units packed inside, say, four boxes (i.e., all the elements in the four clusters) than to open 30 boxes in a shipment in order to inspect a few units from each at random.

### Single-stage and multistage cluster sampling

We have thus far discussed single-stage cluster sampling, which involves the division of the population into convenient clusters, randomly choosing the required number of clusters as sample subjects, and investigating all the elements in each of the randomly chosen clusters. Cluster sampling can also be done in several stages and is then known as **multistage cluster sampling**. For instance, if we were to do a national survey of the average monthly bank deposits, cluster sampling would first be used to select the urban, semiurban, and rural geographical locations for study. At the next stage, particular areas in each of these locations would be chosen. At the third stage, banks within each area would be chosen. In other words, multistage cluster sampling involves a probability sampling of the primary sampling units; from each of these primary units, a probability sample of the secondary sampling units is then drawn; a third level of probability sampling is done from each of these secondary units, and so on, until we have reached the final stage of breakdown for the sample units, when we sample every member in those units.

## Double sampling

This plan is resorted to when further information is needed from a subset of the group from which some information has already been collected for the same study. A sampling design where initially a sample is used in a study to collect some preliminary information of interest, and later a subsample of this primary sample is used to examine the matter in more detail, is called **double sampling**. For example, a structured interview might indicate that a subgroup of the respondents has more insight into the problems of the organization. These respondents might be interviewed again and asked additional questions. This research adopts a double sampling procedure.

## Review of probability sampling designs

There are two basic probability sampling plans: the unrestricted or simple random sampling, and the restricted or complex probability sampling plans. In the simple random sampling design, every element in the population has a known and equal chance of being selected as a subject. The complex probability plan consists of five different sampling designs. Of these five, the cluster sampling design is probably the least expensive as well as the least dependable, but is used when no list of the population elements is available. The stratified random sampling design is probably the most efficient, in the sense that for the same number of sample subjects, it offers precise and detailed information. The systematic sampling design has the built-in hazard of possible systematic bias. Area sampling is a popular form of cluster sampling, and double sampling is resorted to when information in addition to that already obtained by using a primary sample has to be collected using a subgroup of the sample.

# Nonprobability sampling

In **nonprobability sampling** designs, the elements in the population do not have any probabilities attached to their being chosen as sample subjects. This means that the findings from the study of the sample cannot be confidently generalized to the population. As stated earlier, however, researchers may, at times, be less concerned about generalizability than obtaining some preliminary information in a quick and inexpensive way. They might then resort to nonprobability sampling. Sometimes nonprobability sampling is the only way to obtain data, as discussed later.

Some of the nonprobability sampling plans are more dependable than others and could offer some important leads to potentially useful information with regard to the population. Nonprobability sampling designs, which fit into the broad categories of convenience sampling and purposive sampling, are discussed next.

## Convenience sampling

As its name implies, **convenience sampling** refers to the collection of information from members of the population who are conveniently available to provide it. One would expect the "Pepsi Challenge" contest to have been administered on a convenience sampling basis. Such a contest, with the purpose of determining whether people prefer one product to another, might be held at a shopping mall visited by many shoppers. Those inclined to take the test might form the sample for the study of how many people prefer Pepsi over Coke or product X to product Y. Such a sample is a convenience sample.

Consider another example. A convenience sample of five officers who attended the competitor's showcase demonstration at the county fair the previous evening offered the vice president of the company information on the "new" products of the competitor and their pricing strategies, which helped the VP to formulate some ideas on the next steps to be taken by the company.

Convenience sampling is most often used during the exploratory phase of a research project and is perhaps the best way of getting some basic information quickly and efficiently.

## Purposive sampling

Instead of obtaining information from those who are most readily or conveniently available, it might sometimes become necessary to obtain information from specific target groups. The sampling here is confined to specific types of people who can provide the desired information, either because they are the only ones who have it, or conform to some criteria set by the researcher. This type of sampling design is called **purposive sampling**, and the two major types of purposive sampling – judgment sampling and quota sampling – will now be explained.

## Judgment sampling

Judgment sampling involves the choice of subjects who are most advantageously placed or in the best position to provide the information required. For instance, if a researcher wants to find out what it takes for women managers to make it to the top, the only people who can give first-hand information are the women who have risen to the positions of presidents, vice presidents, and important top-level executives in work organizations. They could reasonably be expected to have expert knowledge by virtue of having gone through the experiences and processes themselves, and might perhaps be able to provide good data or information to the researcher. Thus, the judgment sampling design is used when a limited number or category of people have the information that is sought. In such cases, any type of probability sampling across a cross-section of the entire population is purposeless and not useful.

Judgment sampling may curtail the generalizability of the findings, due to the fact that we are using a sample of experts who are conveniently available to us. However, it is the only viable sampling method for obtaining the type of information that is required from very specific pockets of people who alone possess the needed facts and can give the information sought. In organizational settings, and particularly for market research, opinion leaders who are very knowledgeable are included in the sample. Enlightened opinions, views, and knowledge constitute a rich data source.

Judgment sampling calls for special efforts to locate and gain access to the individuals who do have the requisite information. As already stated, this sampling design may be the only useful one for answering certain types of research question.

## Quota sampling

Quota sampling, a second type of purposive sampling, ensures that certain groups are adequately represented in the study through the assignment of a quota. Generally, the quota fixed for each subgroup is based on the total numbers of each group in the population. However, since this is a nonprobability sampling plan, the results are not generalizable to the population.

Quota sampling can be considered a form of proportionate stratified sampling, in which a predetermined proportion of people are sampled from different groups, but on a convenience basis. For instance, it may be surmised that the work attitude of blue-collar workers in an organization is quite different from that of white-collar workers. If there are 60% blue-collar workers and 40% white-collar workers in this organization, and if a total of 30 people are to be interviewed to find the answer to the research question, then a quota of 18 blue-collar workers and 12 white-collar workers will form the sample, because these numbers represent 60% and 40% of the sample size. The first 18 conveniently available blue-collar workers and 12 white-collar workers will be sampled according to this quota. Needless to say, the sample may not be totally representative of the population; hence the generalizability of the findings will be restricted. However, the convenience it offers in terms of effort, cost, and time makes quota sampling attractive for some research efforts. Quota sampling also becomes a necessity when a subset of the population is underrepresented in the organization – for example, minority groups, foremen, and so on. In other words, quota sampling ensures that all the subgroups in the population are adequately represented in the sample. Quota samples are basically stratified samples from which subjects are selected nonrandomly.

In a workplace (and society) that is becoming increasingly heterogeneous because of the changing demographics, quota sampling can be expected to be used more frequently in the future. For example, quota sampling can be used to gain some idea of the buying predispositions of various ethnic groups, to get a feel of how employees from different nationalities perceive the organizational culture, and so on.

Although quota sampling is not generalizable like stratified random sampling, it does offer some information, based on which further investigation, if necessary, can proceed. That is, it is possible that the first stage of research will use the nonprobability design of quota sampling, and once some useful information has been obtained, a probability design will follow. The converse is also entirely possible. A probability sampling design might indicate new areas for research, and nonprobability sampling designs might be used to explore their feasibility.

### Review of nonprobability sampling designs

There are two main types of nonprobability sampling design: convenience sampling and purposive sampling. Convenience sampling is the least reliable of all sampling designs in terms of generalizability, but sometimes it may be the only viable alternative when quick and timely information is needed, or for exploratory research purposes. Purposive sampling plans fall into two categories: judgment and quota sampling designs. Judgment sampling, though restricted in generalizability, may sometimes be the best sampling design choice, especially when there is a limited population that can supply the information needed. Quota sampling is often used on considerations of cost and time and the need to adequately represent minority elements in the population. Although the generalizability of all nonprobability sampling designs is very restricted, they have certain advantages and are sometimes the only viable alternative for the researcher.

Table 10.2 summarizes the probability and nonprobability sampling designs discussed thus far, and their advantages and disadvantages. Figure 10.3 offers some decision choice points as to which design might be useful for specific research goals.

## Examples of when certain sampling designs would be appropriate

### Simple random sampling

This sampling design is best when the generalizability of the findings to the whole population is the main objective of the study. Consider the following two examples.

| TABLE 10.2 | Probability and nonprobability sampling designs. | | |
|---|---|---|---|
| Sampling design | Description | Advantages | Disadvantages |
| **Probability sampling** | | | |
| 1. Simple random sampling | All elements in the population are considered and each element has an equal chance of being chosen as the subject. | High generalizability of findings. | Not as efficient as stratified sampling. |
| 2. Systematic sampling | Every $n$th element in the population is chosen starting from a random point in the sampling frame. | Easy to use if sampling frame is available. | Systematic biases are possible. |
| 3. Stratified random sampling (Str.R.S.)<br><br>Proportionate Str. R.S.<br><br>Disproportionate Str.R.S. | Population is first divided into meaningful segments; thereafter subjects are drawn in proportion to their original numbers in the population.<br><br>Based on criteria other than their original population numbers. | Most efficient among all probability designs.<br><br>All groups are adequately sampled and comparisons among groups are possible. | Stratification must be meaningful. More time-consuming than simple random sampling or systematic sampling.<br><br>Sampling frame for each stratum is essential. |
| 4. Cluster sampling | Groups that have heterogeneous members are first identified; then some are chosen at random; all the members in each of the randomly chosen groups are studied. | In geographic clusters, costs of data collection are low. | The least reliable and efficient among all probability sampling designs since subsets of clusters are more homogeneous than heterogeneous. |
| 5. Area sampling | Cluster sampling within a particular area or locality. | Cost-effective. Useful for decisions relating to a particular location. | Takes time to collect data from an area. |

(continued)

**TABLE 10.2** (Continued)

| Sampling design | Description | Advantages | Disadvantages |
|---|---|---|---|
| 6. Double sampling | The same sample or a subset of the sample is studied twice. | Offers more detailed information on the topic of study. | Original biases, if any, will be carried over. Individuals may not be happy responding a second time. |
| **Nonprobability sampling** | | | |
| 7. Convenience sampling | The most easily accessible members are chosen as subjects. | Quick, convenient, less expensive. | Not generalizable at all. |
| 8. Judgment sampling | Subjects selected on the basis of their expertise in the subject investigated. | Sometimes, the only meaningful way to investigate. | Generalizability is questionable; not generalizable to entire population. |
| 9. Quota sampling | Subjects are conveniently chosen from targeted groups according to some predetermined number or quota. | Very useful where minority participation in a study is critical. | Not easily generalizable. |

## EXAMPLE

The human resources director of a company with 82 people on its payroll has been asked by the vice president to consider formulating an implementable flextime policy. The director feels that such a policy is not necessary since everyone seems happy with the 9-to-5 hours, and no one has complained. Formulating such a policy now, in the opinion of the director, runs the risk of creating domestic problems for the staff and scheduling problems for the company. She wants, however, to resort to a simple random sampling procedure to do an initial survey, and with the results, convince the V.P. that there is no need for flextime, and urge him to drop the matter. Since simple random sampling offers the greatest generalizability of the results to the entire population, and the V.P. needs to be convinced, it is important to resort to this sampling design.

The regional director of sales operations of a medium-sized company, which has 20 retail stores in each of its four geographical regions of operation, wants to know what types of sales gimmicks worked best for the company overall during the past year. This is to help formulate some general policies for the company *as a whole* and prioritize sales

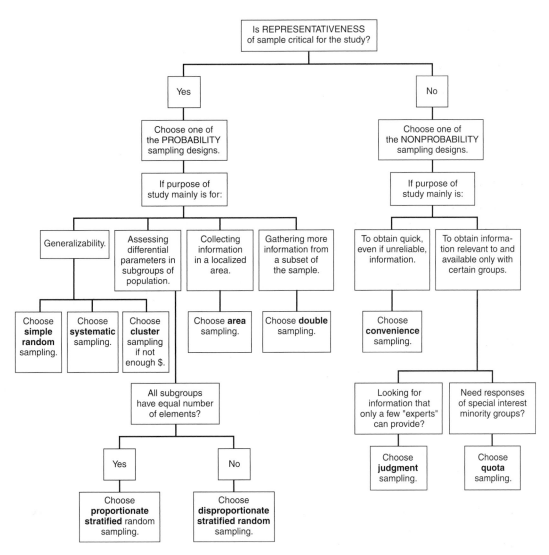

**Figure 10.3:** Choice points in sampling design.

promotion strategies for the coming year. Instead of studying each of the 80 stores, some *dependable* (i.e., *representative* and *generalizable*) information can be had, based on the study of a few stores drawn through a simple random sampling procedure. That is, each one of the 80 stores would have an equal chance of being included in the sample, and the results of the study would be the most generalizable. A simple random sampling procedure is recommended in this case since the policy is to be formulated for the company as a whole. This implies that the most representative information has to be obtained that can be generalized to the entire company. This is best accomplished through this design.

It has to be noted that in some cases, where *cost* is a primary consideration (i.e., resources are limited), and the number of elements in the population is very large and/or geographically dispersed, the simple random sampling design may not be the most desirable, because it could become quite expensive. Thus, both the criticality of generalizability and considerations of cost come into play in the choice of this sampling design.

## Stratified random sampling

This sampling design, which is the most efficient, is a good choice when differentiated information is needed regarding various strata within the population, which are known to differ in their parameters. See the examples below.

## EXAMPLE

The director of human resources of a manufacturing firm wants to offer stress management seminars to the personnel who experience high levels of stress. He conjectures that three groups are most prone to stress: the workmen who constantly handle dangerous chemicals, the foremen who are held responsible for production quotas, and the counselors who, day in and day out, listen to the problems of the employees, internalize them, and offer them counsel, with no idea of how much they have really helped the clients. To get a feel for the experienced level of stress within each of the three groups and the rest of the firm, the director might stratify the sample into four distinct categories: (1) the workmen handling the dangerous chemicals, (2) the foremen, (3) the counselors, and (4) all the rest. He might then choose a *disproportionate random sampling* procedure [since group (3) can be expected to be very small, and groups (2) and (1) are much smaller than group (4)].

This is the only sampling design that would allow the designing of stress management seminars in a meaningful way, targeted at the right groups.

If, in the earlier example, the regional director had wanted to know which sales promotion gimmick offered the best results for *each* of the geographical areas, so that different sales promotion strategies (according to regional preferences) could be developed, then the 80 stores would first be stratified on the basis of the geographical region, and then a representative sample of stores would be drawn from each of the geographical regions (strata) through a simple random sampling procedure. In this case, since each of the regions has 20 stores, a proportionate stratified random sampling process (say, five stores from each region) would be appropriate. If, however, the northern region had only 3 stores, the southern had 15, and the eastern and western regions had 24 and 38 stores, respectively, then a *disproportionate stratified random sampling* procedure would be the right choice, with all three stores in the northern region being studied, because of the small number of elements in that population. If the sample size was retained at 20, then the north, south, east, and west regions would probably have samples respectively of three, four, five and eight. It is interesting to note that sometimes when stratified random sampling might seem logical, it might not really be necessary. For example, when test-marketing results show that Cubans, Puerto Ricans, and Mexicans perceive and consume a particular product the same way, there is no need to segment the market and study each of the three groups using a stratified sampling procedure.

## Systematic sampling

If the sampling frame is large, and a listing of the elements is conveniently available in one place (as in the telephone directory, company payroll, chamber of commerce listings, etc.), then a systematic sampling procedure will offer the advantages of ease and quickness in developing the sample, as illustrated by the following two examples.

### EXAMPLE

An administrator wants to assess the reactions of employees to a new and improved health benefits scheme that requires a modest increase in the premiums to be paid by the employees for their families. The administrator can assess the enthusiasm for the new scheme by using a systematic sampling design. The company's records will provide the sampling frame, and every $n$th employee can be sampled. A stratified plan is not called for here since the policy is for the entire company.

If customers' interest in a highly sophisticated telephone is to be gauged by an entrepreneur, a systematic sampling procedure with the telephone directory as the sampling frame will be the easiest and quickest way to obtain the information, while still ensuring representativeness of the population studied.

📖 Note

Systematic sampling is inadvisable where systematic bias can be anticipated to be present. For example, systematic sampling from the personnel directory of a company (especially when it has an equal number of employees in each department), which lists the names of the individuals department-wise, with the head of the department listed first, and the secretary listed next, has inherent bias. The possibility of systematic bias creeping into the data cannot be ruled out in this case, since the selection process may end up picking each of the heads of the department or the departmental secretaries as the sample subjects. The results from such a sample will clearly be biased and not generalizable, despite the use of a probability sampling procedure. Systematic sampling will have to be scrupulously avoided in cases where known systematic biases are possible.

## Cluster sampling

This sampling design is most useful when a heterogeneous group is to be studied at one time. Two examples are offered below.

**EXAMPLE**

A human resources director is interested in knowing why staff resign. Cluster sampling will be useful in this case for conducting exit interviews of all members completing their final papers in the human resources department on the same day (cluster), before resigning. The clusters chosen for interview will be based on a simple random sampling of the various clusters of personnel resigning on different days. The interviews will help to understand the reasons for turnover of a heterogeneous group of individuals (i.e., from various departments), and the study can be conducted at a low cost.

A financial analyst wishes to study the lending practices of banks in The Netherlands. All the banks in each city will form a cluster. By randomly sampling the clusters, the analyst will be able to draw conclusions on the lending practices.

## Area sampling

Area sampling is best suited when the goal of the research is confined to a particular locality or area, as per the example below.

**EXAMPLE**

A telephone company wants to install a public telephone outlet in a locality where crime is most rampant, so that victims can have access to a telephone. Studying the crime statistics and interviewing the residents in a particular area will help to choose the right location for installation of the phone.

## Double sampling

This design provides added information at minimal additional expenditure. See the example below.

**EXAMPLE**

In the previous exit interview example, some individuals (i.e., a subset of the original cluster sample) might have indicated that they were resigning because of philosophical differences with the company's policies. The researcher might want to do an in-depth interview with these individuals to obtain further information regarding the nature of the policies disliked, the actual philosophical differences, and why these particular issues were central to the individuals' value systems. Such additional detailed information from the target group through the double sampling design could help the company to look for ways of retaining employees in the future.

## Convenience sampling

This nonprobability design, which is not generalizable at all, is used at times to obtain some "quick" information to get a "feel" for the phenomenon or variables of interest. See the example below.

### EXAMPLE

The accounts executive has established a new accounting system that maximally utilizes computer technology. Before making further changes, he would like to get a feel for how the accounting clerks react to the new system without making it seem that he has doubts about their acceptability. He may then "casually" talk to the first five accounting personnel that walk into his office, trying to gauge their reactions.

📖 Note

Convenience sampling should be resorted to in the interests of expediency, with the full knowledge that the results are not generalizable at all.

## Judgment sampling: one type of purposive sampling

A judgment sampling design is used where the collection of "specialized informed inputs" on the topic area researched is vital, and the use of any other sampling design would not offer opportunities to obtain the specialized information, as per the example that follows.

### EXAMPLE

A pharmaceutical company wants to trace the effects of a new drug on patients with specific health problems (muscular dystrophy, sickle cell anemia, rheumatoid arthritis, etc.). It then contacts such individuals and, with a group of voluntarily consenting patients, tests the drug. This is a judgment sample because data are collected from appropriate special groups.

## Quota sampling: a second type of purposive sampling

This sampling design allows for the inclusion of *all* groups in the system researched. Thus, groups who are small in number are not neglected, as per the example below.

### EXAMPLE

A company is considering operating an on-site kindergarten facility. But before taking further steps, it wants to get the reactions of four groups to the idea: (1) Employees who are parents of kindergarten-age children, and where both are working outside of the home, (2) employees who are parents of kindergarten-age children, but where one of them is *not* working outside of the home, (3) single parents with kindergarten-age children, and (4) all those without children of kindergarten age. If the four groups are expected to represent 60%, 7%, 23%, and 10% respectively, in the population of 420 employees in the company, then a quota sampling will be appropriate to represent the four groups.

---

📖 Note

The last group should also be included in the sample since there is a possibility that they may perceive this as a facility that favors only the parents of kindergarten children, and therefore resent the idea. It is easy to see that resorting to quota sampling would be important in a case such as this.

---

In effect, as can be seen from the discussions on sampling designs thus far, *decisions on which design to use* depend on many factors, including the following:

1. Extent of prior knowledge in the area of research undertaken.
2. The main objective of the study – generalizability, efficiency, knowing more about subgroups within a population, obtaining some quick (even if unreliable) information, etc.
3. Cost considerations – is exactitude and generalizability worth the extra investment of time, cost, and other resources in resorting to a more, rather than less, sophisticated sampling design? Even if it is, is suboptimization because of cost or time constraints called for? (See also Figure 10.3.)

The advantages and disadvantages of the different probability and nonprobability sampling designs are listed in Table 10.2.

In sum, choosing the appropriate sampling plan is one of the important research design decisions the researcher has to make. The choice of a specific design will depend broadly on the goal of research, the characteristics of the population, and considerations of cost.

# Sampling in cross-cultural research

Just as in instrument development and data collection, while engaging in cross-cultural research, one has to be sensitive to the issue of selecting matched samples in the different countries. The nature and types of organizations studied, whether subjects are from rural or urban areas, and the types of sampling design used, should all be similar in the different countries to enable true comparisons.

# Issues of precision and confidence in determining sample size

Having discussed the various probability and nonprobability sampling designs, we now need to focus attention on the second aspect of the sampling design issue – the sample size. Suppose we select 30 people from a population of 3000 through a simple random sampling procedure. Will we be able to generalize our findings to the population with confidence, since we have chosen a probability design that has the most generalizability? What is the sample size required to make reasonably precise generalizations with confidence? What do precision and confidence mean? These issues will be considered now.

A reliable and valid sample should enable us to generalize the findings from the sample to the population under investigation. In other words, the sample statistics should be reliable estimates and reflect the population parameters as closely as possible within a narrow margin of error. No sample statistic ($X$, for instance) is going to be *exactly* the same as the population parameter ($\mu$), no matter how sophisticated the probability sampling design is. Remember that the very reason for a probability design is to increase the probability that the sample statistics will be as close as possible to the population parameters! Though the point estimate $X$ may not accurately reflect the population mean, $\mu$, an interval estimate can be made within which $\mu$ will lie, with probabilities attached – that is, at particular confidence levels. The issues of confidence interval and confidence level are addressed in the following discussions on precision and confidence.

## Precision

Precision refers to how close our estimate is to the true population characteristic. Usually, we estimate the population parameter to fall within a range, based on the sample estimate. For example, let us say that from a study of a simple random sample of 50 of the total 300 employees in a workshop, we find that the average daily production rate per person is 50 pieces of a particular product ($\overline{X} = 50$). We might then (by doing certain calculations, as we shall see later) be able to say that the true average daily production of the product ($\mu$) lies anywhere between 40 and 60 for the population of employees in the workshop. In saying this, we offer an interval estimate, within which we expect the true population mean production to be ($\mu = 50 \pm 10$). The narrower this interval, the greater the precision. For instance, if we are able to estimate that the population mean will fall anywhere between 45 and 55 pieces of production ($\mu = 50 \pm 5$) rather than 40 and 60 ($\mu = 50 \pm 10$), then we have more precision. That is, we now estimate the mean to lie within a narrower range, which in turn means that we estimate with greater exactitude or precision.

Precision is a function of the range of variability in the sampling distribution of the sample mean. That is, if we take a number of different samples from a population, and take the mean of each of these, we will usually find that they are all different, are normally distributed, and have a dispersion associated with them. The smaller this dispersion or variability, the greater the probability that the sample mean will be closer to the population mean. We need not necessarily take several different samples to estimate this variability. Even if we take only one sample of 30 subjects from the population, we will still be able to estimate the variability of the sampling distribution of the sample mean. This variability is called the standard error, denoted by $S_{\overline{X}}$. The standard error is calculated by the following formula:

$$S_{\overline{X}} = \frac{S}{\sqrt{n}}$$

where $S$ is the standard deviation of the sample, $n$ is the sample size, and $S_{\overline{X}}$ indicates the standard error or the extent of precision offered by the sample.

Note that the standard error varies inversely with the square root of the sample size. Hence, if we want to reduce the standard error given a particular standard deviation in the sample, we need to increase the sample size. Another noteworthy point is that the smaller the variation in the population, the smaller the standard error, which in turn implies that the sample size need not be large. Thus, low variability in the population requires a smaller sample size.

In sum, the closer we want our sample results to reflect the population characteristics, the greater the precision we should aim at. The greater the precision required, the larger the sample size needed, especially when the variability in the population itself is large.

## Confidence

Whereas precision denotes how close we estimate the population parameter based on the sample statistic, confidence denotes how *certain* we are that our estimates will really hold true for the population. In the previous example of production rate, we know we are more precise when we estimate the true mean production ($\mu$) to fall somewhere between 45 and 55 pieces, than somewhere between 40 and 60. However, we may have more confidence in the latter estimation than in the former. After all, anyone can say with 100% certainty or confidence that the mean production ($\mu$) will fall anywhere between zero and infinity! Other things being equal, the narrower the range, the lower the confidence. In other words, there is a trade-off between precision and confidence for any given sample size, as we shall see later in this chapter.

In essence, confidence reflects the level of certainty with which we can state that our estimates of the population parameters, based on our sample statistics, will hold true. The level of confidence can range from 0 to 100%. 95% confidence is the conventionally accepted level for most business research, most commonly expressed by denoting the significance level as $p \leq 0.05$. In other words, we say that at least 95 times out of 100 our estimate will reflect the true population characteristic.

# Sample data, precision, and confidence in estimation

Precision and confidence are important issues in sampling because when we use sample data to draw inferences about the population, we hope to be fairly "on target," and have some idea of the extent of possible error. Because a point estimate provides no measure of possible error, we do an interval estimation to ensure a *relatively accurate* estimation of the population parameter. Statistics that have the same distribution as the sampling distribution of the mean are used in this procedure, usually a $z$ or a $t$ statistic.

For example, we may want to estimate the mean dollar value of purchases made by customers when they shop at department stores. From a sample of 64 customers sampled through a systematic sampling design procedure, we may find that the sample mean $\overline{X} = 105$, and the sample standard deviation $S = 10$. $\overline{X}$, the sample mean, is a point estimate of $\mu$, the population mean. We could construct a confidence interval around $X$ to estimate the range within which $\mu$ will fall. The standard error $S_{\overline{X}}$ and the percentage or level of confidence we require will determine the width of the interval, which can be represented by the following formula, where $K$ is the $t$ statistic for the level of confidence desired.

$$\mu = X \pm KS$$

We already know that:

$$S_{\overline{X}} = \frac{S}{\sqrt{n}}$$

Here,

$$S_{\overline{X}} = \frac{10}{\sqrt{64}} = 1.25$$

From the table of critical values for $t$ in any statistics book (see Table II, columns 5, 6, and 9, at the end of this book), we know that:

For a 90% confidence level, the K value is 1.645.
For a 95% confidence level, the K value is 1.96.
For a 99% confidence level, the K value is 2.576.

If we desire a 90% confidence level in the above case, then $\mu = 105 \pm 1.645$ (1.25) (i.e., $\mu = 105 \pm 2.056$). $\mu$ thus falls between 102.944 and 107.056. These results indicate that using a sample size of 64, we could state with 90% confidence that the true population mean value of purchases for all customers would fall between $102.94 and $107.06. If we now want to be 99% confident of our results without increasing the sample size, we necessarily have to sacrifice precision, as may be seen from the following calculation: $\mu = 105 \pm 2.576$ (1.25). The value of $\mu$ now falls between 101.78 and 108.22. In other words, the width of the interval has increased and we are now less precise in estimating the population mean, though we are a lot more confident about our estimation. It is not difficult to see that if we want to maintain our original precision while increasing the confidence, or maintain the confidence level while increasing precision, or we want to increase both the confidence and the precision, we need a larger sample size.

In sum, the sample size, $n$, is a function of:

1. the variability in the population
2. precision or accuracy needed
3. confidence level desired
4. type of sampling plan used – for example, simple random sampling versus stratified random sampling.

# Trade-off between confidence and precision

We have noted that if we want more precision, or more confidence, or both, the sample size needs to be increased – unless, of course, there is very little variability in the population itself. However, if the sample size ($n$) cannot be increased, for whatever reason – say, we cannot afford the costs of increased sampling – then, with the same $n$, the only way to maintain the same level of precision is to forsake the confidence with which we can predict our estimates. That is, we reduce the confidence level or the certainty of our estimate. This trade-off between precision and confidence is illustrated in Figures 10.4(a) and (b). Figure 10.4(a) indicates that 50% of the time the true mean will fall within the narrow range indicated in the figure, the 0.25 in each tail representing the 25% nonconfidence, or the probability of making errors, in our estimation on either side. Figure 10.4(b) indicates that 99% of the time we expect the true mean $\mu$ to fall within the much wider range indicated in the figure and there is only a 0.005% chance that we are making an error in this estimation. That is, in Figure 10.4(a), we have more precision but less confidence (our confidence level is only 50%). In Figure 10.4(b), we have high confidence (99%), but then we are far from being precise – that is, our estimate falls within a broad interval range.

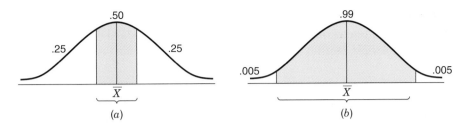

**Figure 10.4:** Illustration of the trade-off between precision and confidence. (a) More precision but less confidence; (b) more confidence but less precision.

It thus becomes necessary for researchers to consider at least four aspects while making decisions on the sample size needed to do the research:

1. How much precision is really needed in estimating the population characteristics of interest – that is, what is the *margin* of allowable error?
2. How much confidence is really needed – that is, how much *chance* can we take of making errors in estimating the population parameters?
3. To what extent is there *variability* in the population on the characteristics investigated?
4. What is the *cost–benefit* analysis of increasing the sample size?

# Sample data and hypothesis testing

So far we have discussed sample data as a means of estimating the population parameters, but sample data can also be used to test hypotheses about population values rather than simply to estimate population values. The procedure for this testing incorporates the same information as in interval estimation, but the goals behind the two methods are somewhat different.

Referring to the earlier example of the average dollar value purchases of customers in a department store, instead of trying to estimate the average purchase value of the store's customers with a certain degree of accuracy, let us say that we now wish to determine whether or not customers expend the same average amount in purchases in Department Store A as in Department Store B. From Chapter 4, we know that we should first set the null hypothesis, which will state that there is no difference in the dollar values expended by customers shopping at the two different stores. This is expressed as:

$$H_0 : \mu A - \mu B = 0$$

The alternate hypothesis of differences will be stated nondirectionally (since we have no idea whether customers buy more at Store A or Store B) as:

$$H_A : \mu A - \mu B \neq 0$$

If we take a sample of 20 customers from each of the two stores and find that the mean dollar value purchases of customers in Store A is 105 with a standard deviation of 10, and the corresponding figures for Store B are 100 and 15, respectively, we see that:

$$X_A - X_B = 105 - 100 = 5$$

whereas our null hypothesis had postulated no difference (difference = 0). Should we then conclude that our alternate hypothesis is to be accepted? We cannot say! To determine this we must first find the probability or likelihood of the two group means having a difference of 5 in the context of the null hypothesis of a difference of 0. This can be done by converting the difference in the sample means to a $t$ statistic and seeing what the probability is of finding a $t$ of that value. The $t$ distribution has known probabilities attached to it [see Table II ($t$ table) in the appendix at the end of the book]. Looking at the $t$ distribution table, we find that, with two samples of 20 each [the degrees of freedom become $(n1 + n2) - 2 = 38$], for the $t$ value to be significant at the 0.05 level, the critical value should be around 2.021 (see $t$ table column 6 against $v40$). We need to use the two-tailed test since we do not know whether the difference between Store A and Store B will be positive or negative. For even a 90% probability, it should be at least 1.684 (see the number to the left of 2.021). The $t$ statistic can be calculated for testing our hypothesis as follows:

$$t = \frac{(\overline{X}_1 - \overline{X}_2) - (\mu_1 - \mu_2)}{S_{\overline{X}_1 - \overline{X}_2}}$$

$$S_{\overline{X}_1 - \overline{X}_2} = \sqrt{\frac{n_1 s_1^2 + n_2 s_2^2}{(n_1 + n_2 - 2)} \left(\frac{1}{n_1} + \frac{1}{n_2}\right)}$$

$$= \sqrt{\frac{(20 \times 10^2) + (20 \times 15^2)}{20 + 20 + -2} \left(\frac{1}{20} + \frac{1}{20}\right)}$$

$$t = \frac{(\overline{X}_A - \overline{X}_B) - (\mu_A - \mu_B)}{4.136}$$

We already know that

$$\overline{X}_A - \overline{X}_B = 5 \text{ (the difference in the means of the two stores)}$$

and

$$\mu_A - \mu_B = 0 \text{ (from our null hypothesis)}$$

Then

$$t = \frac{5 - 0}{4.136} = 1.209$$

This $t$ value of 1.209 is way below the value of 2.021 [for 40 degrees of freedom for a two-population $t$-test, the closest to the actual 38 $df$ {(20 + 20) − 2}] required for the conventional

95% probability, and even for the 90% probability, which requires a value of 1.684. We can thus say that the difference of 5 that we found between the two stores is not significantly different from 0. The conclusion, then, is that there is no significant difference between how much customers buy (dollars expended) at Department Store A and Department Store B. We will thus accept the null hypothesis and reject the alternative.

Sample data can thus be used not only for estimating the population parameters, but also for testing hypotheses about population values, population correlations, and so forth, as we will see more fully in Chapter 13.

# Determining the sample size

Now that we are aware of the fact that the sample size is governed by the extent of precision and confidence desired, how do we determine the sample size required for our research? The procedure can be illustrated through an example.

## EXAMPLE

Suppose a manager wants to be 95% confident that the expected monthly withdrawals in a bank will be within a confidence interval of ± $500. Let us say that a study of a sample of clients indicates that the average withdrawals made by them have a standard deviation of $3500. What would be the sample size needed in this case?

We noted earlier that the population mean can be estimated by using the formula:

$$\mu = \overline{X} \pm K \, S_{\overline{X}}$$

Since the confidence level needed here is 95%, the applicable $K$ value is 1.96 ($t$ table). The interval estimate of ± $500 will have to encompass a dispersion of (1.96 × standard error). That is,

$$500 = 1.96 \times S_{\overline{X}}\overline{X}$$

We already know that

$$S_{\overline{X}} = \frac{S}{\sqrt{n}}$$

$$255.10 = \frac{3500}{\sqrt{n}}$$

$$n = 188$$

The sample size indicated above is 188. However, let us say that this bank has a total clientele of only 185. This means we cannot sample 188 clients. We can, in this case, apply a correction formula and see what sample size would be needed to have the same level of precision and confidence given the fact that we have a total of only 185 clients. The correction formula is as follows:

$$S\overline{X} = \frac{S}{\sqrt{n}} \times \sqrt{\frac{N-n}{N-1}}$$

where $N$ is the total number of elements in the population, $n$ is the sample size to be estimated, $S\overline{X}$ is the standard error of the estimate of the mean, and $S$ is the standard deviation of the sample mean.

Applying the correlation formula, we find that

$$255.10 = \frac{3500}{\sqrt{n}} \times \sqrt{\frac{185-n}{184}}$$
$$n = 94$$

We would now sample 94 of the total 185 clients.

To understand the impact of precision and/or confidence on the sample size, let us try changing the confidence level required in the bank withdrawal example, which needed a sample size of 188 for a confidence level of 95%. Let us say that the bank manager now wants to be 99% sure that the expected monthly withdrawals will be within the interval of ±$500. What will be the sample size now needed?

$S\overline{X}$ *will now be*

$$\frac{500}{2.576} = 194.099$$
$$194.099 = \frac{3500}{\sqrt{n}}$$
$$n = 325$$

The sample has now to be increased 1.73 times (from 188 to 325) to increase the confidence level from 95% to 99%!

Try calculating the sample size if the precision has to be narrowed down from $500 to $300 for a 95% and a 99% confidence level! Your answers should show the sample sizes needed as 523 and 902, respectively. These results dramatically highlight the costs of increased precision, confidence, or both. It is hence a good idea to think through how much precision and confidence one really needs, before determining the sample size for the research project.

So far we have discussed sample size in the context of precision and confidence with respect to one variable only. However, in research, the theoretical framework has several variables of interest, and the question arises as to how one should come up with a sample size when all the factors are taken into account. Krejcie and Morgan (1970) greatly simplified the size decision by providing a table that ensures a good decision model. Table 10.3 provides that

| TABLE 10.3 | Sample size for a given population size. | | | | |
|---|---|---|---|---|---|
| N | S | N | S | N | S |
| 10 | 10 | 220 | 140 | 1200 | 291 |
| 15 | 14 | 230 | 144 | 1300 | 297 |
| 20 | 19 | 240 | 148 | 1400 | 302 |
| 25 | 24 | 250 | 152 | 1500 | 306 |
| 30 | 28 | 260 | 155 | 1600 | 310 |
| 35 | 32 | 270 | 159 | 1700 | 313 |
| 40 | 36 | 280 | 162 | 1800 | 317 |
| 45 | 40 | 290 | 165 | 1900 | 320 |
| 50 | 44 | 300 | 175 | 2000 | 322 |
| 55 | 48 | 320 | 181 | 2200 | 327 |
| 60 | 52 | 340 | 191 | 2400 | 331 |
| 65 | 56 | 360 | 196 | 2600 | 335 |
| 70 | 59 | 380 | 205 | 2800 | 338 |
| 75 | 63 | 400 | 210 | 3000 | 341 |
| 80 | 66 | 420 | 217 | 3500 | 346 |
| 85 | 70 | 440 | 226 | 4000 | 351 |
| 90 | 73 | 460 | 242 | 4500 | 354 |
| 95 | 76 | 480 | 248 | 5000 | 357 |
| 100 | 80 | 500 | 260 | 6000 | 361 |
| 110 | 86 | 550 | 265 | 7000 | 364 |
| 120 | 92 | 600 | 274 | 8000 | 367 |
| 130 | 97 | 650 | 278 | 9000 | 368 |
| 140 | 103 | 700 | 169 | 10 000 | 370 |
| 150 | 108 | 750 | 186 | 15 000 | 375 |

(*continued*)

| TABLE 10.3 | (Continued) | | | | |
|---|---|---|---|---|---|
| N | S | N | S | N | S |
| 160 | 113 | 800 | 201 | 20 000 | 377 |
| 170 | 118 | 850 | 214 | 30 000 | 379 |
| 180 | 123 | 900 | 234 | 40 000 | 380 |
| 190 | 127 | 950 | 254 | 50 000 | 381 |
| 200 | 132 | 1000 | 269 | 75 000 | 283 |
| 210 | 136 | 1100 | 285 | 1 000 000 | 384 |

generalized scientific guideline for sample size decisions. The interested student is advised to read Krejcie and Morgan (1970) as well as Cohen (1969) for decisions on sample size.

# Importance of sampling design and sample size

It is now possible to see how both sampling design and the sample size are important to establish the representativeness of the sample for generalizability. If the appropriate sampling design is not used, a large sample size will not, in itself, allow the findings to be generalized to the population. Likewise, unless the sample size is adequate for the desired level of precision and confidence, no sampling design, however sophisticated, will be useful to the researcher in meeting the objectives of the study. Hence, sampling decisions should consider both the sampling design and the sample size. Too large a sample size, however (say, over 500) could also become a problem inasmuch as we would then be prone to committing Type II errors. That is, we would accept the findings of our research, when in fact we should reject them. In other words, with too large a sample size, even weak relationships (say a correlation of 0.10 between two variables) might reach significance levels, and we would be inclined to believe that these significant relationships found in the sample were indeed true of the population, when in reality they may not be. Thus, neither too large nor too small sample sizes help research projects.

Another point to consider, even with the appropriate sample size, is whether statistical significance is more relevant than practical significance. For instance, a correlation of 0.25 may be statistically significant, but since this explains only about 6% of the variance ($0.25^2$), how meaningful is it in terms of practical utility?

Roscoe (1975) proposes the following rules of thumb for determining sample size:

1. Sample sizes larger than 30 and less than 500 are appropriate for most research.
2. Where samples are to be broken into subsamples; (males/females, juniors/seniors, etc.), a minimum sample size of 30 for each category is necessary.

3. In multivariate research (including multiple regression analyses), the sample size should be several times (preferably ten times or more) as large as the number of variables in the study.
4. For simple experimental research with tight experimental controls (matched pairs, etc.), successful research is possible with samples as small as 10 to 20 in size.

# Efficiency in sampling

**Efficiency in sampling** is attained when, for a given level of precision (standard error), the sample size could be reduced, or for a given sample size ($n$), the level of precision could be increased. Some probability sampling designs are more efficient than others. The simple random sampling procedure is not always the most efficient plan to adopt; some other probability sampling designs are often more efficient. A stratified random sampling plan is often the most efficient, and a disproportionate stratified random sampling design has been shown to be more efficient than a proportionate sampling design in many cases. Cluster sampling is less efficient than simple random sampling because there is generally more homogeneity among the subjects in the clusters than is found in the elements in the population. Multistage cluster sampling is more efficient than single-stage cluster sampling when there is more heterogeneity found in the earlier stages. There is often a trade-off between time and cost efficiencies (as achieved in nonprobability sampling designs) and precision efficiencies (as achieved in many probability sampling plans). The choice of a sampling plan thus depends on the objectives of the research, as well as on the extent and nature of efficiency desired.

# Sampling as related to qualitative studies

Sampling for qualitative research is as important as sampling for quantitative research. Qualitative sampling begins with precisely defining the *target population*. As a sampling technique, qualitative research generally uses *nonprobability sampling* as it does not aim to draw statistical inference. *Purposive sampling* is one technique that is often employed in qualitative investigation: subjects are selected on the basis of expertise in the subject that is being investigated. It is important that the subjects are chosen in such a way that they reflect the diversity of the population.

One form of purposive sampling is *theoretical sampling*, introduced by Glaser and Strauss (1967) in their work on grounded theory. The term **grounded theory** expresses the idea that theory will emerge from data through an iterative process that involves repeated sampling, collection of data, and analysis of data until 'theoretical saturation' is reached. *Theoretical saturation* is reached when no new information about the subject emerges in repeated cases.

Theoretical sampling may or may not begin with purposive sampling, but the sampling of additional subjects is directed by the emerging theoretical framework. According to Glaser (1978) theoretical sampling takes place when "the analyst jointly collects, codes, and analyzes his data and decides what data to collect next and where to find them, in order to develop his theory as it emerges" (p. 36).

Because it is impossible to predict when theoretical saturation is reached, you cannot determine how many subjects will need to be sampled at the beginning of your study. Instead, the general rule in qualitative research is that you continue to sample until you are not getting any new information or are no longer gaining new insights. Note that the sample size will, therefore, at least partly, depend on the heterogeneity of the population.

# Managerial implications

Awareness of sampling designs and sample size helps managers to understand why a particular method of sampling is used by researchers. It also facilitates understanding of the cost implications of different designs, and the trade-off between precision and confidence vis-à-vis the costs. This enables managers to understand the risk they take in implementing changes based on the results of the research study. While reading journal articles, this knowledge also helps managers to assess the generalizability of the findings and analyze the implications of trying out the recommendations made therein in their own system.

## SUMMARY

Sampling design decisions are important aspects of research design and include both the sampling plan to be used and the sample size that will be needed. Probability sampling plans lend themselves to generalizability and nonprobability sampling designs, though not generalizable, offer convenience and timely information. Some probability plans are more efficient than others. Though nonprobability sampling plans have limitations in terms of generalizability, they are often the only designs available for certain types of investigation, as in the case of exploratory research, or where information is needed quickly, or is available with only certain special groups.

The sample size is determined by the level of precision and confidence desired in estimating the population parameters, as well as the variability in the population itself. Cost considerations could also play a part. The generalizability of the findings from a study of the sample to the population is dependent on its representativeness – that is, the sophistication of the sampling design used, and the sample size. Sample data are used for both estimating population parameters and hypothesis testing.

Care should be taken not to overgeneralize the results of any study to populations that are *not* represented by the sample. This is a problem common in some research studies.

In the next two chapters, we will see how the data gathered from a sample of respondents in the population are analyzed to test the hypotheses generated and find answers to the research questions.

## DISCUSSION QUESTIONS

1. Identify the relevant population for the following research foci, and suggest the appropriate sampling design to investigate the issues, explaining *why* they are appropriate. Wherever necessary, identify the sampling frame as well.
   a. A company wants to investigate the initial reactions of heavy soft-drink users to a new "all natural" soft drink.
   b. A hospital administrator wants to find out if the single parents working in the hospital have a higher rate of absenteeism than parents who are not single.
   c. A researcher would like to assess the extent of pilferage in the materials storage warehouses of manufacturing firms.
   d. The director of human resources wants to investigate the relationship between drug abuse and dysfunctional behavior of blue-collar workers in a particular plant.
   e. A marketer wants to generate some ideas on how women differ from men in acquiring product knowledge about cars.

2. a. Explain why cluster sampling is a probability sampling design.
   b. What are the advantages and disadvantages of cluster sampling?
   c. Describe a situation where you would consider the use of cluster sampling.

3. a. Explain what precision and confidence are and how they influence sample size.
   b. Discuss what is meant by the statement: "There is a trade-off between precision and confidence under certain conditions."

4. The use of a convenience sample used in organizational research is correct because all members share the same organizational stimuli and go through almost the same kinds of experience in their organizational life. Comment.

5. "Use of a sample of 5000 is not necessarily better than one of 500." How would you react to this statement?

6. Nonprobability sampling designs ought to be preferred to probability sampling designs in some cases. Explain with an example.

7. Because there seems to be a trade-off between accuracy and confidence for any given sample size, accuracy should always be considered more important than precision. Explain with reasons why you do or do not agree.

8. Overgeneralizations give rise to much confusion and other problems for researchers who try to replicate the findings. Explain what is meant by this.

9. Double sampling is probably the least used of all sampling designs in organizational research. Do you agree? Provide reasons for your answer.

> **10.** Why do you think the sampling design should feature in a research proposal?

Now do Exercises 10.1, 10.2, 10.3, 10.4, 10.5, and 10.6

For the situations presented in Exercises 10.1 to 10.6 below, indicate what would be the relevant population and the most appropriate sampling design. Make sure you discuss the reasons for your answers.

## EXERCISE 10.1

A medical inspector wants to estimate the overall average monthly occupancy rates of the cancer wards in 80 different hospitals that are evenly located in the northwestern, southeastern, central, and southern suburbs of New York City.

## EXERCISE 10.2

A magazine article suggested that "Consumers aged 35 to 44 will soon be the nation's biggest spenders, so advertisers must learn how to appeal to this over-the-thrill crowd." If this suggestion appeals to an apparel manufacturer, what should the sampling design be to assess the tastes of this group?

## EXERCISE 10.3

The McArthur Co. produces special vacuum cleaners for conveniently cleaning the inside of cars. About a thousand of these, with stamped serial numbers, are produced every month and stored serially in a stockroom. Once a month an inspector does a quality control check on 50 of these. When he certifies them as to quality, the units are released from the stockroom for sale. The production and sales managers, however, are not satisfied with the quality control check since, quite often, many of the units sold are returned by customers because of various types of defect. What would be the most useful sampling plan to test the 50 units?

## EXERCISE 10.4

A consultant had administered a questionnaire to some 285 employees using a simple random sampling procedure. As she looked at the responses, she suspected that two questions might not have been clear to the respondents. She would like to know if her suspicion is well-founded.

## EXERCISE 10.5

The executive board of a relatively small university located in Europe wants to determine the attitude of their students toward various aspects of the university. The university, founded in 1928, is a fully accredited government-financed university with 11 000 students. The university specializes in the social sciences and humanities and has five faculties, six service departments, eight research centers, and two graduate schools. The executive board has asked you to come up with a sampling plan. Develop a sampling plan and pay attention to the following aspects: target population, the sampling frame, the sample technique and the sample size

## EXERCISE 10.6

T-Mobile is a mobile network operator headquartered in Bonn, Germany. The company has enlisted your help as a consultant to develop and test a model on the determinants of subscriber churn in the German mobile telephone market. Develop a sampling plan and pay specific attention to the following aspects.

Define the target population. Discuss in as much detail as possible the sampling frame and the sampling design that you would use. Give reasons for your choice.

# CHAPTER 11

## Quantitative data analysis

## Topics discussed

- Getting the data ready for analysis
  - Coding and data entry
  - Editing data
  - Omissions
  - Data transformation
- Getting a feel for the data
  - Frequencies
  - Bar charts and pie charts
  - Measures of central tendency and dispersion
  - Relationships between variables
    - Relationship between two nominal variables: $\chi^2$ test
    - Correlations
- Excelsior Enterprises – descriptive statistics part 1
- Testing goodness of data
  - Reliability
  - Validity
- Excelsior Enterprises – checking the reliability of the multi-item measures.
- Excelsior Enterprises – descriptive statistics part 2
- Summary

## CHAPTER OBJECTIVES

After completing Chapter 11 you should be able to:

1. Code and enter interview responses
2. Edit interview responses

3. Handle omissions
4. Transform data
5. Create a data file
6. Get a feel for the data
7. Test the goodness of data

After data have been collected from a representative sample of the population, the next step is to analyze them to test the research hypotheses. However, before we can start analyzing the data to test hypotheses, some preliminary steps need to be completed. These help to ensure that the data are accurate, complete, and suitable for further analysis. This chapter addresses these preliminary steps in detail.

The easiest way to illustrate data analysis is through a case. We will therefore introduce the Excelsior Enterprises case first.

## EXAMPLE

Excelsior Enterprises is a medium-sized company, manufacturing and selling instruments and supplies needed by the health care industry, including blood pressure instruments, surgical instruments, dental accessories, and so on. The company, with a total of 360 employees working three shifts, is doing reasonably well but could do far better if it did not experience employee turnover at almost all levels and in all departments. The president of the company called in a research team to study the situation and to make recommendations on the turnover problem.

Since access to those who had left the company would be difficult, the research team suggested to the president that they talk to the current employees and, based on their input and a literature survey, try to get at the factors influencing employees' intentions to stay with, or leave, the company. Since past research has shown that intention to leave (ITL) is an excellent predictor of actual turnover, the president concurred.

The team first conducted an unstructured interview with about 50 employees at various levels and from different departments. Their broad statement was: "We are here to find out how you experience your work life. Tell us whatever you consider is important for you in your job, as issues relate to your work, the environment, the organization, supervision, and whatever else you think is relevant. If we get a good handle on the issues involved, we may be able to make appropriate recommendations to management to enhance the quality of your work life. We would just like to talk to you now, and administer a questionnaire later."

Each interview typically lasted about 45 minutes, and notes on the responses were written down by the team members. When the responses were tabulated, it became clear that the issues most frequently brought up by the respondents, in one form or another, related to three main areas: the job (employees said the jobs were dull or too complex; there was lack of freedom to do the job as one wanted to, etc.), perceived inequities (remarks such as "I put much more in my work than I get out of it."); and burnout (comments such as "there is so much work to be done that by the end of the day we are physically and emotionally exhausted"; "we feel the frequent need to take time off because of exhaustion"; etc.).

A literature survey confirmed that these variables were good predictors of intention to leave and subsequent turnover. In addition, job satisfaction was also found to be an important predictor of intention to leave. A theoretical framework was developed based on the interviews and the literature survey, and four hypotheses (stated later) were developed.

Next, a questionnaire was designed incorporating well-validated and reliable measures for job enrichment, perceived equity, burnout, job satisfaction, and intention to leave. Perceived equity was measured by five survey items: (1) "I invest more in my work than I get out of it"; (2) "I exert myself too much considering what I get back in return"; (3) 'For the efforts I put into the organization, I get much in return" (reversed); (4) "If I take into account my dedication, the company ought to give me better training"; and (5) "In general, the benefits I receive from the organization outweigh the effort I put in it" (reversed). Job enrichment was measured on a four-item Likert scale: (1) "The job is quite simple and repetitive" (reversed); (2) "The job requires me to use a number of complex or higher-level skills"; (3) "The job requires a lot of cooperative work with other people"; and (4) "The job itself is not very significant or important in the broader scheme of things" (reversed). Participants responded to these items on a five-point scale, ranging from "I disagree completely" (1) to "I agree completely" (5). Burnout was measured with *The Burnout Measure Short Version* (*BMS*). The BMS includes ten items that measure levels of physical, emotional, and mental exhaustion of the individual. Respondents are asked to rate the frequency with which they experience each of the items appearing in the questionnaire (e.g., being tired or helpless) on a scale ranging from 1 (*never*) to 5 (*always*). Job satisfaction was measured by a single-item rating of "satisfaction with your current job", using a five-point "not at all–very much" scale. Intention to leave was measured using two survey items: "With what level of certainty do you intend to leave this organization within the next year for another type of job" (item 1) "for a similar type of job" (item 2)? Participants indicated on a four-point rating scale their level of certainty. Demographic variables such as age, education, gender, tenure, department, and work shift were also included in the questionnaire.

The questionnaire was administered personally to 174 employees who were chosen on a disproportionate stratified random sampling basis. The responses were entered into the computer. Thereafter, the data were submitted for analysis to test the following hypotheses, which were formulated by the researchers:

$H_1$: *Job enrichment has a negative effect on intention to leave.*
$H_2$: *Perceived equity has a negative effect on intention to leave.*
$H_3$: *Burnout has a positive effect on intention to leave.*
$H_4$: *Job satisfaction mediates the relationship between job enrichment, perceived equity, and burnout on intention to leave.*

It may be pertinent to point out here that the four hypotheses derived from the theoretical framework are particularly relevant for finding answers to the turnover issue. The results of testing the hypotheses will certainly offer insights into how much of the variance in intention to leave can be explained by the independent variables, and what corrective action, if any, needs to be taken.

# Getting the data ready for analysis

After data are obtained through questionnaires, they need to be coded, keyed in, and edited. That is, a categorization scheme has to be set up before the data can be typed in. Then, outliers, inconsistencies, and blank responses, if any, have to be handled in some way. Each of these stages of data preparation is discussed below.

## Coding and data entry

The first step in data preparation is data coding. **Data coding** involves assigning a number to the participants' responses so they can be entered into a database. In Chapter 8, we discussed the convenience of using scanner sheets for collecting questionnaire data; such sheets facilitate the entry of the responses directly into the computer without manual keying in of the data. However, if, for whatever reason, this cannot be done, then it is perhaps a good idea to use a coding sheet first to transcribe the data from the questionnaire and then key in the data. This method, in contrast to flipping through each questionnaire for each item, avoids confusion, especially when there are many questions and a large number of questionnaires as well.

### Coding the responses

In the Excelsior Enterprises questionnaire, we have 22 items measuring perceived justice, job enrichment, burnout, job satisfaction, and intention to leave, and six demographic variables, as shown in Figure 11.1, a sample questionnaire.

The responses of this particular employee (participant # 1 in the data file) to the first 22 questions can be coded by using the actual number circled by the respondent (1, 2, 3, 1, 4, 5, 1, 3, 3, etc.). Coding the demographic variables is somewhat less obvious. For instance, tenure is a special case, because it is a two-category variable. It is possible to use a coding approach that assigns a 1 = part-time and a 2 = full-time. However, using 0 = part-time and 1 = full-time (this is called *dummy coding*) is by far the most popular and recommended approach because it makes our lives easier in the data analysis stage. Hence, we code tenure (full-time) with 1 for participant #1. Work shift (third shift) can be coded 3, department (production) 2, and age 54. Gender can be coded 0 (male), and finally education (less than high school) can be coded 1.

*Circle the number that represents your feelings at this particular moment best. There are no right or wrong answers. Please answer every question.*

|  | I disagree completely |  |  |  | I agree completely |
|---|---|---|---|---|---|
| 1. I invest more in my work than I get out of it | ①  | 2 | 3 | 4 | 5 |
| 2. I exert myself too much considering what I get back in return | 1 | ② | 3 | 4 | 5 |
| 3. For the efforts I put into the organization, I get much in return | 1 | 2 | ③ | 4 | 5 |
| 4. If I take into account my dedication, the company ought to give me better training | ① | 2 | 3 | 4 | 5 |
| 5. In general, the benefits I receive from the organization outweigh the effort I put in it | 1 | 2 | 3 | ④ | 5 |

|  | I disagree completely |  |  |  | I agree completely |
|---|---|---|---|---|---|
| 6. My job is quite simple and repetitive | 1 | 2 | 3 | 4 | ⑤ |
| 7. My job requires me to use a number of complex or higher-level skills | ① | 2 | 3 | 4 | 5 |
| 8. My job requires a lot of cooperative work with other people | 1 | 2 | ③ | 4 | 5 |
| 9. My job itself is not very significant or important in the broader scheme of things | 1 | 2 | ③ | 4 | 5 |

*When you think about your work, how often do you feel the following:*

|  | Never |  |  |  | Always |
|---|---|---|---|---|---|
| 10. Tired | 1 | 2 | ③ | 4 | 5 |
| 11. Disappointed with people | 1 | ② | 3 | 4 | 5 |
| 12. Hopeless | ① | 2 | 3 | 4 | 5 |
| 13. Trapped | 1 | ② | 3 | 4 | 5 |
| 14. Helpless | ① | 2 | 3 | 4 | 5 |
| 15. Depressed | 1 | ② | 3 | 4 | 5 |
| 16. Weak/Sickly | 1 | ② | 3 | 4 | 5 |
| 17. Insecure/A failure | 1 | ② | 3 | 4 | 5 |
| 18. Sleep difficulties | ① | 2 | 3 | 4 | 5 |
| 19. "I have had it" | 1 | 2 | ③ | 4 | 5 |

|  | Not at all |  |  |  | Very much |
|---|---|---|---|---|---|
| 20. To what extent are you satisfied with your current job? | 1 | 2 | 3 | 4 | ⑤ |

With what level of certainty do you intend to leave this organization within the next year:

|  | Very uncertain |  |  | Very certain |
|---|---|---|---|---|
| 21. ...for another type of job? | ① | 2 | 3 | 4 |
| 22. ...for a similar type of job? | 1 | ② | 3 | 4 |

**Finally we would like you to provide some background information.**

23. Do you have a part-time or a full-time job at Excelsior Enterprises?
O      Part-time
⊗     Full-time

24. What shift do you currently work?
O      First shift (1)
O      Second shift (2)
⊗     Third shift (3)

25. What is your department?

| | | | |
|---|---|---|---|
| O Marketing (1) | O Maintenance (4) | O Finance (7) |
| ⊗ Production (2) | O Servicing (5) | O Personnel (8) |
| O Sales (3) | O Public Relations (6) | O Accounting (9) |

26. What is your age?
<u>  54  </u>

Figure 11.1: Sample questionnaire.

---

27. What is your gender
⊗          Male
O          Female

28. What is the highest level of education you have completed?
⊗          Less than High School (1)
O          High School/GED Equivalent (2)
O          College Degree (3)
O          Masters Degree (4)
O          Doctoral Degree (5)

THIS WAS THE FINAL QUESTION OF THIS QUESTIONNAIRE.
THANK YOU VERY MUCH FOR YOUR COOPERATION!

---

**Figure 11.1:** *Continued*

At this stage you should also think about how you want to code non-responses. Some researchers leave non-responses blank, others assign a '9', a '99' or a '.' All the approaches are fine, as long as you code all the non-responses in the same way.

Human errors can occur while coding. At least 10% of the coded questionnaires should therefore be checked for coding accuracy. Their selection may follow a systematic sampling procedure. That is, every *n*th form coded could be verified for accuracy. If many errors are found in the sample, all items may have to be checked.

## Data entry

After responses have been coded, they can be entered into a database. Raw data can be entered through any software program. For instance, the SPSS Data Editor, which looks like a spreadsheet and is shown in Figure 11.2, can enter, edit, and view the contents of the data file.

Each row of the editor represents a case or observation (in this case a participant of our study – 174 in the Excelsior Enterprises study), and each column represents a *variable* (here variables are defined as the different items of information that you collect for your cases; there are thus 28 variables in the Excelsior Enterprises questionnaire).

It is important to always use the first column for identification purposes; assign a number to every questionnaire, write this number on the first page of the questionnaire, and enter this number in the first column of your data file. This allows you to compare the data in the data file with the answers of the participants, even after you have rearranged your data file.

Then, start entering the participants' responses into the data file.

## Editing data

After the data are keyed in, they need to be edited. For instance, the blank responses, if any, have to be handled in some way, and inconsistent data have to be checked and followed up. Data editing deals with detecting and correcting illogical, inconsistent, or illegal data and omissions in the information returned by the participants of the study.

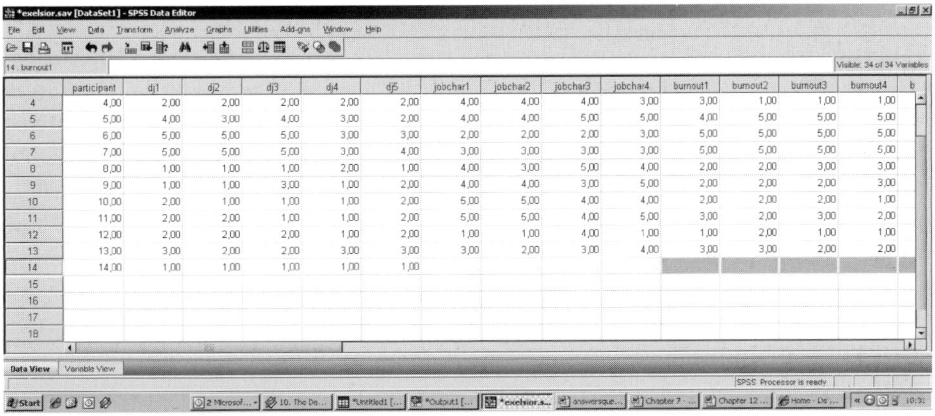
*exelsior.sav [DataSet1] - SPSS Data Editor
File Edit View Data Transform Analyze Graphs Utilities Add-ons Window Help
14 : burnout1
Visible: 34 of 34 Variables
participant dj1 dj2 dj3 dj4 dj5 jobchar1 jobchar2 jobchar3 jobchar4 burnout1 burnout2 burnout3 burnout4 b
4 4,00 2,00 2,00 2,00 2,00 2,00 4,00 4,00 4,00 3,00 3,00 1,00 1,00 1,00
5 5,00 4,00 3,00 4,00 3,00 2,00 4,00 4,00 5,00 5,00 4,00 5,00 5,00 5,00
6 6,00 5,00 5,00 5,00 3,00 3,00 2,00 2,00 2,00 3,00 5,00 5,00 5,00 5,00
7 7,00 5,00 5,00 5,00 3,00 4,00 3,00 3,00 3,00 3,00 5,00 5,00 5,00 5,00
8 8,00 1,00 1,00 1,00 2,00 1,00 4,00 3,00 5,00 4,00 2,00 2,00 3,00 3,00
9 9,00 1,00 1,00 3,00 1,00 2,00 4,00 4,00 3,00 5,00 2,00 2,00 2,00 3,00
10 10,00 2,00 1,00 1,00 1,00 2,00 5,00 5,00 4,00 4,00 2,00 2,00 2,00 1,00
11 11,00 2,00 2,00 1,00 1,00 2,00 5,00 5,00 4,00 5,00 3,00 2,00 3,00 2,00
12 12,00 2,00 2,00 2,00 1,00 2,00 1,00 1,00 4,00 1,00 1,00 2,00 1,00 1,00
13 13,00 3,00 2,00 2,00 3,00 3,00 3,00 2,00 3,00 4,00 3,00 3,00 2,00 2,00
14 14,00 1,00 1,00 1,00 1,00 1,00
15
16
17
18
Data View Variable View
SPSS Processor is ready
Start

Figure 11.2: The SPSS Data Editor.

An example of an *illogical response* is an outlier response. An outlier is an observation that is substantially different from the other observations. An outlier is not always an error even though data errors (entry errors) are a likely source of outliers. Because outliers have a large impact on the research results they should be investigated carefully to make sure that they are correct. You can check the dispersion of nominal and/or ordinal variables by obtaining minimum and maximum values and frequency tables. This will quickly reveal the most obvious outliers. For interval and ratio data, visual aids (such as a scatterplot or a boxplot) are good methods to check for outliers.

*Inconsistent responses* are responses that are not in harmony with other information. For instance, a participant in our study might have answered the perceived equity statements as in Figure 11.3. Note that all the answers of this employee indicate that the participant finds that the benefits she receives from the organization balance the efforts she puts into her job, except for the answer to the third statement. From the other four responses we might infer that the participant in all probability feels that, for the efforts she puts into the organization, she *does* get much in return and has made a mistake in responding to this particular statement. The response to this statement could then be edited by the researcher.

| | *I disagree completely* | | | | *I agree completely* |
|---|---|---|---|---|---|
| 1. I invest more in my work than I get out of it | (1) | 2 | 3 | 4 | 5 |
| 2. I exert myself too much considering what I get back in return | 1 | (2) | 3 | 4 | 5 |
| 3. For the efforts I put into the organization, I get much in return | (1) | 2 | 3 | 4 | 5 |
| 4. If I take into account my dedication, the company ought to give me better training | (1) | 2 | 3 | 4 | 5 |
| 5. In general, the benefits I receive from the organization outweigh the effort I put in it | 1 | 2 | 3 | 4 | (5) |

Figure 11.3: Example of a possible inconsistent answer.

It is, however, possible that the respondent deliberately indicated that she does not get much in return for the efforts she puts into the organization. If such were to be the case, we would be introducing a bias by editing the data. Hence, great care has to be taken in dealing with inconsistent responses such as these. Whenever possible, it is desirable to follow up with the respondent to get the correct data, even though this is an expensive solution.

*Illegal codes* are values that are not specified in the coding instructions. For example, a code of "6" in question 1 (I invest more in my work than I get out of it) would be an illegal code. The best way to check for illegal codes is to have the computer produce a frequency distribution and check it for illegal codes.

Not all respondents answer every item in the questionnaire. *Omissions* may occur because respondents did not understand the question, did not know the answer, or were not willing to answer the question.

If a substantial number of questions – say, 25% of the items in the questionnaire – have been left unanswered, it may be a good idea to throw out the questionnaire and not include it in the data set for analysis. In this event, it is important to mention the number of returned but unused responses due to excessive missing data in the final report submitted to the sponsor of the study. If, however, only two or three items are left blank in a questionnaire with, say, 30 or more items, we need to decide how these blank responses are to be handled.

One way to handle a blank response is to ignore it when the analyses are done. This approach is possible in all statistical programs and is the default option in most of them. A disadvantage of this approach is that, of course, it will reduce the sample size, sometimes even to an inappropriate size, whenever that particular variable is involved in the analyses. Moreover, if the missing data are not missing completely at random, this method may bias the results of your study. For this reason, ignoring the blank responses is best suited to instances in which we have gathered a large amount of data, the number of missing data is relatively small, and relationships are so strong that they are not affected by the missing data (Hair *et al.*, 1995).

An alternative solution would be to look at the participant's pattern of responses to other questions and, from these answers, deduce a logical answer to the question for the missing response. A second alternative solution would be to assign to the item the mean value of the responses of all those who have responded to that particular item. In fact, there are many ways of handling blank responses (see Hair *et al.*, 1995), each of them having its own particular advantages and disadvantages.

Note that if many of the respondents have answered "don't know" to a particular item or items, further investigation may well be worthwhile. The question might not have been clear or, for some reason, participants could have been reluctant or unable to answer the question.

## Data transformation

Data transformation, a variation of data coding, is the process of changing the original numerical representation of a quantitative value to another value. Data are typically changed to avoid problems in the next stage of the data analysis process. For example, economists often use a logarithmic transformation so that the data are more evenly distributed. If, for instance, income data, which are often unevenly distributed, are reduced to their logarithmic value, the high incomes are brought closer to the lower end of the scale and provide a distribution closer to a normal curve.

Another type of data transformation is reverse scoring. Take, for instance, the perceived inequity measure of the Excelsior Enterprises case. Perceived inequity is measured by five survey items: (1) "I invest more in my work than I get out of it"; (2) "I exert myself too much considering what I get back in return"; (3) "For the efforts I put into the organization, I get much in return" (reversed); (4) "If I take into account my dedication, the organization ought to give me a better practical training"; and (5) "In general, the benefits I receive from the organization outweigh the effort I put in" (reversed). For the first, second, and fourth items, a score indicating high agreement would be negative, but for the third and fifth questions, a score indicating high agreement would be positive. To maintain consistency in the meaning of a response, the first, second, and fourth items have to be reverse scored (note that we are measuring equity and not inequity). In this case, a 5 (I completely agree) would be transformed to a 1 (I completely disagree), a 4 to a 2, and so forth.

Data transformation is also necessary when several questions have been used to measure a single concept. In such cases, scores on the original questions have to be combined into a single score (but only *after* we have established that the interitem consistency is satisfactory! (see Testing Goodness of Data discussed later on in this chapter). For instance, because five items have been used to measure the concept "perceived equity", a new "perceived equity" score has to be calculated from the scores on the five individual items (but only after items 1, 2, and 4 have been reverse coded). This involves calculating the summed score (per case/participant) and then dividing it by the number of items (five in this case). For example, our employee # 1 has circled, respectively, 1, 2, 3, 1, and 4 on the five participation in decision-making questions; his or her scores on the items once items 1, 2, and 4 have been reverse coded are 5, 4, 3, 5, and 4. The combined score on perceived justice would be ($5 + 4 + 3 + 5 + 4 = 21/5 = 4, 2$). This combined score is included in a new column in SPSS. It is easy to compute the new variables, using the *Compute* dialog box, which opens when the *Transform* icon is chosen (Figure 11.4).

Note that it is useful to set up a scheme for categorizing the responses such that the several items measuring a concept are all grouped together. If the questions measuring a concept are not contiguous but scattered over various parts of the questionnaire, care has to be taken to include all the items without any omission or wrong inclusion.

# Getting a feel for the data

We can acquire a feel for the data by obtaining a visual summary or by checking the central tendency and the dispersion of a variable. We can also get to know our data by examining the relation between two variables. In Chapter 6, we explained that different statistical operations on variables are possible, depending on the level at which a variable is measured. Table 11.1

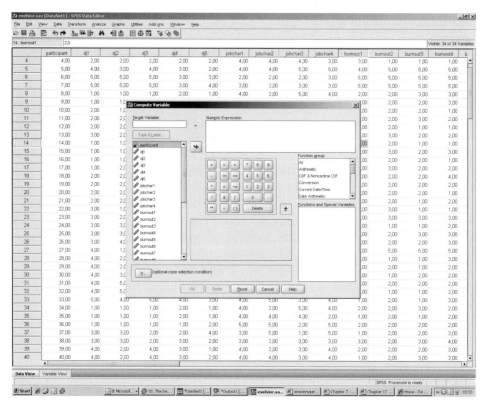

**Figure 11.4:** Transforming data with SPSS.

summarizes the relationship between scale type, data analysis, and methods of obtaining a visual summary for variables.

Table 11.1 shows that, depending on the scale of our measures, the mode, median, or mean, and the semi-interquartile range, standard deviation, or variance will give us a good idea of how the participants in our study have reacted to the items in the questionnaire. These statistics can be easily obtained, and will indicate whether the responses range satisfactorily over the scale. If the response to each individual item in a scale does not have a good spread (range) and shows very little variability, then the researcher may suspect that the particular question was probably not properly worded. Biases, if any, may also be detected if the respondents have tended to respond similarly to all items – that is, they have stuck to only certain points on the scale. Remember that if there is no variability in the data, then no variance can be explained! Getting a feel for the data is thus the necessary first step in all data analysis. Based on this initial feel, further detailed analyses may be undertaken to test the goodness of the data.

Researchers go to great lengths to obtain the central tendency, the range, the dispersion, and other statistics for every single item measuring the dependent and independent variables, especially when the measures for a concept are newly developed.

Descriptive statistics for a single variable are provided by frequencies, measures of central tendency, and dispersion. These are now described.

| TABLE 11.1 | Scale type, data analysis, and methods of obtaining a visual summary for variables. |
|---|---|

| Scale | Measures of central tendency . . . for a single variable | Measures of dispersion . . . for a single variable | Visual summary . . . for a single variable | Measure of relation . . . between variables | Visual summary of relation . . . between variables |
|---|---|---|---|---|---|
| *Nominal* | Mode | — | Bar chart, pie chart | Contingency table (Cross-tab) | Stacked bars, Clustered bars |
| *Ordinal* | Median | Semi-interquartile range | Bar chart, pie chart | Contingency table (Cross-tab) | Stacked bars, Clustered bars |
| *Interval* | Arithmetic mean | Minimum, maximum, standard deviation, variance, coefficient of variation | Histogram, scatterplot, box-and-whisker plot | Correlations | Scatterplots |
| *Ratio* | Arithmetic or geometric mean | Minimum, maximum, standard deviation, variance, coefficient of variation | Histogram, scatterplot, box-and-whisker plot | Correlations | Scatterplots |

## Frequencies

**Frequencies** simply refer to the number of times various subcategories of a certain phenomenon occur, from which the percentage and the cumulative percentage of their occurrence can be easily calculated.

**Excelsior Enterprises – frequencies**

The frequencies for the number of individuals in the various departments for the Excelsior Enterprises sample are shown in Output 11.1. It may be seen therefrom that the greatest

## Output 11.1 Frequencies

From the menus, choose:

Analyze
*Descriptive Statistics*
*Frequencies*
(Select the relevant variables)
Choose needed:
Statistics . . .
Charts . . .
Format (for the order in which the results are to be displayed)

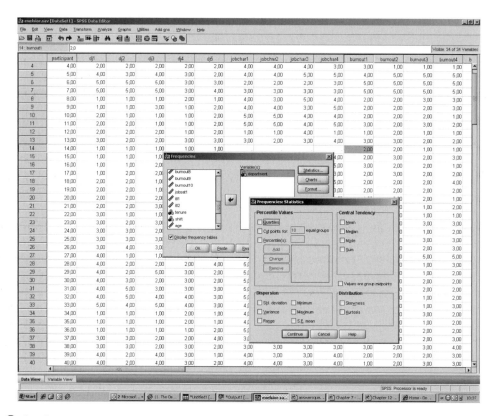

**Output**

Respondent's department

| | Frequency | Percent | Valid percent | Cumulative percent |
|---|---|---|---|---|
| Marketing | 13 | 7.5 | 7.5 | 7.5 |
| Production | 49 | 28.1 | 28.1 | 35.6 |

| | | | | |
|---|---|---|---|---|
| Sales | 44 | 25.3 | 25.3 | 60.9 |
| Finance | 5 | 2.9 | 2.9 | 63.8 |
| Servicing | 34 | 19.5 | 19.5 | 83.3 |
| Maintenance | 5 | 2.9 | 2.9 | 86.2 |
| Personnel | 16 | 9.2 | 9.2 | 95.4 |
| Public Relations | 3 | 1.7 | 1.7 | 97.1 |
| Accounting | 5 | 2.9 | 2.9 | 100.0 |
| Total | 174 | 100.0 | 100.0 | 100.0 |

number of individuals in the sample came from the Production Department (28.1%), followed by the Sales Department (25.3%). Only three individuals (1.7%) came from Public Relations, and five individuals each from the Finance, Maintenance, and Accounting Departments (2.9% from each). The low numbers in the sample in some of the departments are a function of the total population (very few members) in those departments.

From the frequencies obtained for the other variables (results not shown here) it was found that 79.9% of the respondents were men and 20,1% women; about 62% worked the first shift, 20% the second shift, and 18% the third shift. About 16% of the respondents worked part time and 84% full time. About 8% had less than a high school degree, 39% a high school diploma, 32% a college degree, 20% a master's degree, and 1% had doctoral degrees.

We thus have a profile of the employees in this organization, which is useful for describing the sample in the Methods Section of the Written Report (see Chapter 14). Other instances where frequency distributions would be useful are when (1) a marketing manager wants to know how many units (and what proportions or percentages) of each brand of coffee are sold in a particular region during a given period, (2) a tax consultant wishes to keep count of the number of times different sizes of firms (small, medium, large) are audited by the IRS, and (3) the financial analyst wants to keep track of the number of times the shares of manufacturing, industrial, and utility companies lose or gain more than ten points on the New York Stock Exchange over a six-month period.

## Bar charts and pie charts

Frequencies can also be visually displayed as bar charts, histograms, or pie charts. Bar charts, histograms, and pie charts help us to understand our data.

### Excelsior Enterprises – bar chart

Figure 11.5 provides a graphic representation of the results listed in the table in Output 11.1.

Frequency distributions, bar charts, histograms, and pie charts provide a great deal of basic information about the data. Measures of central tendency and dispersion will help us to further understand our data. These are discussed next.

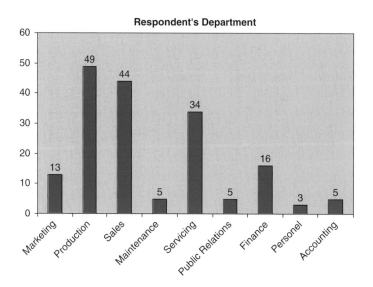

Figure 11.5: Bar chart of categories of employees.

## Measures of central tendency and dispersion

There are three measures of central tendency: the mean, the median, and the mode. Measures of dispersion include the range, the standard deviation, and the variance (where the measure of central tendency is the mean), and the interquartile range (where the measure of central tendency is the median).

### Measures of central tendency

#### The mean

The **mean**, or the *average*, is a measure of central tendency that offers a general picture of the data without unnecessarily inundating one with each of the observations in a data set. For example, the production department might keep detailed records on how many units of a product are being produced each day. However, to estimate the raw materials inventory, all that the manager might want to know is how many units per month, *on average*, the department has been producing over the past six months. This measure of central tendency – that is, the *mean* – might offer the manager a good idea of the quantity of materials that need to be stocked.

The mean or average of a set of, say, ten observations, is the sum of the ten individual observations divided by ten (the total number of observations).

#### The median

The **median** is the *central item* in a group of observations when they are arrayed in either an ascending or a descending order. Let us take an example to examine how the median is determined as a measure of central tendency.

## EXAMPLE

Let's say the annual salaries of nine employees in a department are as follows: $65 000, $30 000, $25 000, $64 000, $35 000, $63 000, $32 000, $60 000, and $61 000. The mean salary here works out to be about $48 333, but the median is $60 000. That is, when arrayed in ascending order, the figures will be as follows: $25 000, $30 000, $32 000, $35 000, $60 000, $61 000, $63 000, $64 000, $65 000, and the figure in the middle is $60 000. If there is an even number of employees, then the median will be the average of the middle two salaries.

## The mode

In some cases, a set of observations does not lend itself to a meaningful representation through either the mean or the median, but can be signified by the *most frequently occurring phenomenon*. For instance, in a department where there are 10 white women, 24 white men, 3 African American women, and 2 Asian women, the most frequently occurring group – the **mode** – is the white men. Neither a mean nor a median is calculable or applicable in this case. There is also no way of indicating any measure of dispersion.

We have illustrated how the mean, median, and the mode can be useful measures of central tendency, based on the type of data we have. We will now examine dispersion.

## Measures of dispersion

Apart from knowing that the measure of central tendency is the mean, median, or mode (depending on the type of available data), one would also like to know about the variability that exists in a set of observations. Like the measure of central tendency, the measure of dispersion is also unique to nominal and interval data.

Two sets of data might have the same mean, but the dispersions could be different. For example, if Company A sold 30, 40, and 50 units of a product during the months of April, May, and June, respectively, and Company B sold 10, 40, and 70 units during the same period, the average units sold per month by both companies is the same – 40 units – but the variability or the *dispersion* in the latter company is larger.

The three measurements of dispersion connected with the mean are the range, the variance, and the standard deviation, which are explained below.

### Range

**Range** refers to the extreme values in a set of observations. The range is between 30 and 50 for Company A (a dispersion of 20 units), while the range is between 10 and 70 units (a dispersion of 60 units) for Company B. Another more useful measure of dispersion is the variance.

### Variance

The **variance** is calculated by subtracting the mean from each of the observations in the data set, taking the square of this difference, and dividing the total of these by the number of observations. In the above example, the variance for each of the two companies is:

$$\text{Variance for Company A} = \frac{(30-40)^2 + (40-40)^2 + (50-40)^2}{3} = 66.7$$

$$\text{Variance for Company B} = \frac{(10-40)^2 + (40-40)^2 + (70-40)^2}{3} = 600$$

As we can see, the variance is much larger in Company B than Company A. This makes it more difficult for the manager of Company B to estimate how many goods to stock than it is for the manager of Company A. Thus, variance gives an indication of how dispersed the data in a data set are.

Standard deviation

The **standard deviation**, which is another measure of dispersion for interval and ratio scaled data, offers an index of the spread of a distribution or the variability in the data. It is a very commonly used measure of dispersion, and is simply the square root of the variance. In the case of the above two companies, the standard deviation for Companies A and B would be $\sqrt{66.7}$ and $\sqrt{600}$ or 8.167 and 24.495, respectively.

The mean and standard deviation are the most common descriptive statistics for interval and ratio scaled data. The standard deviation, in conjunction with the mean, is a very useful tool because of the following statistical rules, in a normal distribution:

1. Practically all observations fall within three standard deviations of the average or the mean.
2. More than 90% of the observations are within two standard deviations of the mean.
3. More than half of the observations are within one standard deviation of the mean.

Other measures of dispersion

When the *median* is the measure of central tendency, percentiles, deciles, and quartiles become meaningful. Just as the median divides the total realm of observations into two equal halves, the *quartile* divides it into four equal parts, the *decile* into ten, and the *percentile* into 100 equal parts. The percentile is useful when huge masses of data, such as the GRE or GMAT scores, are handled. When the area of observations is divided into 100 equal parts, there are 99 percentile points. Any given score has a probability of 0.01 that it will fall in any one of those points. If John's score is in the 16th percentile, it indicates that 84% of those who took the exam scored better than he did, while 15% did worse.

Oftentimes we are interested in knowing where we stand in comparison to others – are we in the middle, in the upper 10 or 25%, or in the lower 20 or 25%, or where? For instance, if in a company-administered test, Mr Chou scores 78 out of a total of 100 points, he may be unhappy if he is in the bottom 10% among his colleagues (the test-takers), but may be reasonably pleased if he is in the top 10%, despite the fact that his score remains the same. His standing in relation to the others can be determined by the central tendency median and the percentile he falls in.

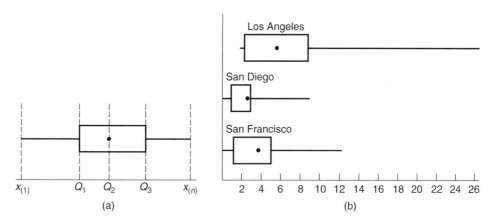

Figure 11.6: (a) Box-and-whisker plot; (b) comparison of telephone bills in three cities.

The measure of dispersion for the median, the **interquartile range**, consists of the middle 50% of the observations (i.e., observations excluding the bottom and top 25% quartiles). The interquartile range is very useful when comparisons are to be made among several groups. For instance, telephone companies can compare long-distance charges of customers in several areas by taking samples of customer bills from each of the cities to be compared. By plotting the first and third quartiles and comparing the median and the spread, they can get a good idea of where billings tend to be highest, to what extent customers vary in the frequency of use of long-distance calls, and so on. This is done by creating a box-and-whisker plot for each area. The box-and-whisker plot is a graphic device that portrays central tendency, percentiles, and variability. A box is drawn, extending from the first to the third quartile, and lines are drawn from either side of the box to the extreme scores, as shown in Figure 11.6(a). Figure 11.6(b) has the median represented by a dot within each box. Side-by-side comparisons of the various plots clearly indicate the highest value, the range, and the spread for each area or city. For a fuller discussion on this, refer to Salvia (1990).

In sum, we have illustrated how the mean, median, and the mode can be useful measures of central tendency, depending on the type of available data. Likewise, we have shown how the standard deviation (and variance, which is the square of standard deviation), and the interquartile range are useful measures of dispersion. Obviously, there is no measure of dispersion associated with the mode.

## Relationships between variables

In a research project that includes several variables, beyond knowing the descriptive statistics of the variables, we would often like to know how one variable is related to another. That is, we would like to see the nature, direction, and significance of the *bivariate* relationships of the variables used in the study (that is, the relationship between any two variables among the variables tapped in the study).

Nonparametric tests are available to assess the relationship between variables measured on a nominal or an ordinal scale. Spearman's rank correlation and Kendall's rank correlation are used to examine relationships between two ordinal variables. A correlation matrix is used to examine relationships between interval and/or ratio variables.

### Relationship between two nominal variables: $\chi^2$ test

We might sometimes want to know if there is a relationship between two nominal variables or whether they are independent of each other. As examples: (1) Is viewing a television advertisement of a product (yes/no) related to buying that product by individuals (buy/don't buy)? (2) Is the type of job done by individuals (white-collar job/blue-collar job) a function of the color of their skin (white/nonwhite)? Such comparisons are possible by organizing data by groups or categories and seeing if there are any statistically significant relationships. For example, we might collect data from a sample of 55 individuals whose color of skin and nature of jobs, culled from a frequency count, might be illustrated as in Table 11.2 in a two-by-two contingency table. Just by looking at Table 11.2, a clear pattern seems to emerge that those who are white hold white-collar jobs. Only a few of the nonwhites hold white-collar jobs. Thus, there does seem to be a relationship between the color of the skin and the type of job handled; the two do not seem to be independent. This can be statistically confirmed by the **chi-square** ($\chi^2$) **test** – a nonparametric test – which indicates whether or not the observed pattern is due to chance. As we know, nonparametric tests are used when normality of distributions cannot be assumed as in nominal or ordinal data. The $\chi^2$ test compares the expected frequency (based on probability) and the observed frequency, and the $\chi^2$ statistic is obtained by the formula:

$$\chi^2 = \sum \frac{(Oi - Ei)^2}{Ei}$$

where $\chi^2$ is the chi-square statistic; $Oi$ is the observed frequency of the $i$th cell; and $Ei$ is the expected frequency. The $\chi^2$ statistic with its level of significance can be obtained for any set of nominal data through computer analysis.

**TABLE 11.2    Contingency table of skin color and job type.**

| Skin color | White collar | Blue collar | Total |
|---|---|---|---|
| White | 30 | 5 | 35 |
| Nonwhite | 2 | 18 | 20 |
| Total | 32 | 23 | 55 |

Thus, in testing for differences in relationships among nominally scaled variables, the $\chi^2$ (chi-square) statistic comes in handy. The null hypothesis would be set to state that there is no significant relationship between two variables (color of skin and nature of the job, in the above example), and the alternative hypothesis would state that there is a significant relationship.

The chi-square statistic is associated with the degrees of freedom ($df$), which denote whether or not a significant relationship exists between two nominal variables. The number of degrees of freedom is one less than the number of cells in the columns and rows. If there are four cells (two in a column and two in a row), then the number of degrees of freedom would be 1, i.e. [(2–1) × (2–1)]. The chi-square statistic for various $df$ is provided in Table III at the end of the book.

The $\chi^2$ statistic can also be used for multiple levels of two nominal variables. For instance, one might be interested to know if four groups of employees – production, sales, marketing, and R & D personnel – react to a policy in four different ways (i.e., with no interest at all, with mild interest, moderate interest, and intense interest). Here, the $\chi^2$ value for the test of independence is generated by cross-tabulating the data in 16 cells – that is, classifying the data in terms of the four groups of employees and the four categories of interest. The degrees of freedom here will be 9, i.e. [(4–1) × (4–1)].

The $\chi^2$ test of significance thus helps us to see whether or not two nominal variables are related. Besides the $\chi^2$ test, other tests, such as the *Fisher exact probability test* and the *Cochran Q test* are used to determine the relationship between two nominally scaled variables.

## Correlations

A Pearson correlation matrix will indicate the direction, strength, and significance of the bivariate relationships among all the variables that were measured at an interval or ratio level. The correlation is derived by assessing the variations in one variable as another variable also varies. For the sake of simplicity, let us say we have collected data on two variables – price and sales – for two different products. The volume of sales at every price level can be plotted for each product, as shown in the scatter diagrams in Figure 11.7(a) and 11.7(b).

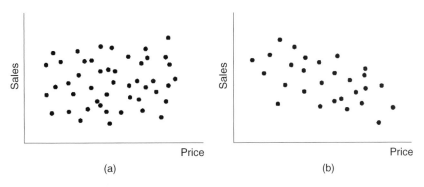

**Figure 11.7:** (a) Scatter diagram with no discernible pattern; (b) scatter diagram indicating a downward or negative slope.

Figure 11.7(b) indicates a discernible pattern of how the two factors vary simultaneously (the trend of the scatter is that of a downward straight line), whereas Figure 11.7(a) does not. Looking at the scatter diagram in Figure 11.7(b), it would seem there is a direct negative correlation between price and sales for this product. That is, as the price increases, sales of the product drop consistently. Figure 11.7(a) suggests no interpretable pattern for the other product.

A correlation coefficient that indicates the strength and direction of the relationship can be computed by applying a formula that takes into consideration the two sets of figures – in this case, different sales volumes at different prices.

Theoretically, there could be a perfect positive correlation between two variables, which is represented by 1.0 (plus 1), or a perfect negative correlation which would be –1.0 (minus 1). However, neither of these will be found in reality when assessing correlations between any two variables expected to be different from each other.

While the correlation could range between $-1.0$ and $+1.0$, we need to know if any correlation found between two variables is significant or not (i.e., if it has occurred solely by chance or if there is a high probability of its actual existence). As we know, a significance of $p = 0.05$ is the generally accepted conventional level in social science research. This indicates that 95 times out of 100, we can be sure that there is a true or significant correlation between the two variables, and there is only a 5% chance that the relationship does not truly exist. If there is a correlation of 0.56 (denoted as $r = 0.56$) between two variables A and B, with $p < 0.01$, then we know that there is a positive relationship between the two variables and the probability of this not being true is 1% or less. That is, over 99% of the time we would expect this correlation to exist. The correlation of 0.56 also indicates that the variables explain the variance in one another to the extent of 31.4% $(0.56^2)$.

We do not know which variable *causes* which, but we do know that the two variables are associated with each other. Thus, a hypothesis that postulates a significant positive (or negative) relationship between two variables can be tested by examining the correlation between the two.

The Pearson correlation coefficient is appropriate for interval- and ratio-scaled variables, and the Spearman Rank or the Kendall's Tau coefficients are appropriate when variables are measured on an ordinal scale. Any bivariate correlation can be obtained by clicking the relevant menu, identifying the variables, and seeking the appropriate parametric or nonparametric statistics.

# Excelsior Enterprises – descriptive statistics part 1

Descriptive statistics such as maximum, minimum, means, standard deviations, and variance were obtained for the interval-scaled items of the Excelsior Enterprises study. The procedure is shown in Output 11.2.

The results presented in the table in Output 11.2 indicate that:

- there are missing observations for every item except for the items burnout10, itl1 and itl2;
- there are illegal codes for items jobchar1 (a 6 has been entered in at least one cell), burnout3 (again, a 6 has been entered in at least one cell), and itl2 (a 5 has been entered in at least one cell);
- the responses to each individual item have a good spread.

## Output 11.2 Descriptive statistics: central tendencies and dispersions

From the menus, choose:

Analyze
*Descriptive Statistics*
    *Descriptives*
    (Select the variables)
    *Options . . .*
    (Choose the relevant statistics needed)

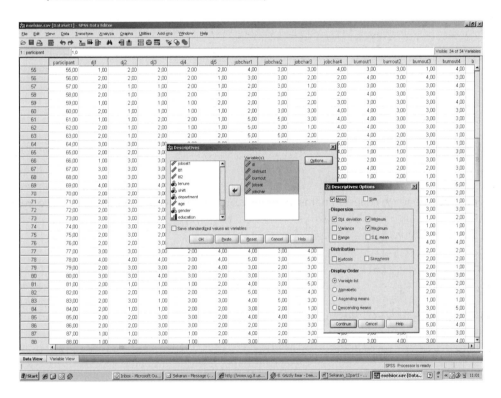

### Output

|  | dj1 | dj2 | dj3 | dj4 | dj5 | jobchar1 | jobchar2 | jobchar3 | jobchar4 | burnout1 | burnout2 |
|---|---|---|---|---|---|---|---|---|---|---|---|
| *N* valid | 171 | 171 | 171 | 171 | 171 | 170 | 170 | 170 | 170 | 171 | 171 |
| *N* missing | 3 | 3 | 3 | 3 | 3 | 4 | 4 | 4 | 4 | 3 | 3 |
| Mean | 2.351 | 2.240 | 2.509 | 2.304 | 2.211 | 3.517 | 3.435 | 3.165 | 3.471 | 2.474 | 2.433 |
| Std deviation | 1.014 | 0.968 | 1.129 | 0.895 | 0.965 | 1.132 | 1.082 | 1.253 | 1.116 | 2.474 | 2.433 |
| Variance | 1.029 | 0.936 | 1.275 | 0.801 | 0.932 | 1.281 | 1.170 | 1.570 | 1.245 | 1.557 | 1.047 |
| Minimum | 1 | 1 | 1 | 1 | 1 | 1 | 1 | 1 | 1 | 1 | 1 |
| Maximum | 5 | 5 | 5 | 5 | 5 | 6 | 5 | 5 | 5 | 5 | 5 |

(Cont'd)

| | burnout3 | burnout4 | burnout5 | burnout6 | burnout7 | burnout8 | burnout9 | burnout10 | jobsat | itl1 | itl2 |
|---|---|---|---|---|---|---|---|---|---|---|---|
| *N* valid | 171 | 171 | 173 | 173 | 173 | 173 | 173 | 174 | 173 | 174 | 174 |
| *N* missing | 3 | 3 | 1 | 1 | 1 | 1 | 1 | 0 | 1 | 0 | 0 |
| Mean | 2.462 | 2.526 | 2.653 | 2.567 | 2.761 | 2.792 | 2.792 | 2.264 | 3.243 | 2.224 | 2.161 |
| Std deviation | 1.014 | 0.968 | 1.129 | 0.895 | 0.965 | 1.132 | 1.082 | 1.253 | 1.116 | 2.474 | 2.433 |
| Variance | 1.029 | 0.936 | 1.275 | 0.801 | 0.932 | 1.281 | 1.170 | 1.570 | 1.245 | 1.557 | 1.047 |
| Minimum | 1 | 1 | 1 | 1 | 1 | 1 | 1 | 1 | 1 | 1 | 1 |
| Maximum | 6 | 5 | 5 | 5 | 5 | 5 | 5 | 4 | 5 | 4 | 5 |

Appropriate actions were taken to correct the illegal entries. A further inspection of the missing data revealed that every participant answered either all or the vast majority of the questions. Therefore, no questionnaires were thrown out. Missing data will be ignored during subsequent analyses.

From here, we can proceed with further detailed analyses to test the goodness of our data.

# Testing goodness of data

The reliability and validity of the measures can now be tested.

## Reliability

As discussed in Chapter 7, the reliability of a measure is established by testing for both consistency and stability. Consistency indicates how well the items measuring a concept hang together as a set. Cronbach's alpha is a reliability coefficient that indicates how well the items in a set are positively correlated to one another. Cronbach's alpha is computed in terms of the average intercorrelations among the items measuring the concept. The closer Cronbach's alpha is to 1, the higher the internal consistency reliability.

Another measure of consistency reliability used in specific situations is the split-half reliability coefficient. Since this reflects the correlations between two halves of a set of items, the coefficients obtained will vary depending on how the scale is split. Sometimes split-half reliability is obtained to test for consistency when more than one scale, dimension, or factor, is assessed. The items across each of the dimensions or factors are split, based on some predetermined logic (Campbell, 1976). In almost every case, Cronbach's alpha is an adequate test of internal consistency reliability. You will see later in this chapter how Cronbach's alpha is obtained through computer analysis.

As discussed in Chapter 7, the stability of a measure can be assessed through parallel form reliability and test–retest reliability. When a high correlation between two similar forms of a measure (see Chapter 7) is obtained, parallel form reliability is established. Test–retest reliability can be established by computing the correlation between the same tests administered at two different time periods.

**Excelsior Enterprises – checking the reliability of the multi-item measures**

Because distributive justice, burnout, job enrichment, and intention to leave were measured with multi-item scales, the consistency of the respondents' answers to the scale items has to be tested for each measure. In Chapter 7, we explained that Cronbach's alpha is a popular test of interitem consistency. Table 11.3 provides an overview of Cronbach's alpha for the four variables. This table shows that the alphas were all well above 0.60.

In general, reliabilities less than 0.60 are considered to be poor, those in the 0.70 range, acceptable, and those over 0.80 good. Thus, the internal consistency reliability of the measures used in this study can be considered to be acceptable for the job enrichment measure and good for the other measures.

It is important to note that all the negatively worded items in the questionnaire should first be reversed before the items are submitted for reliability tests. Unless all the items measuring a variable are in the same direction, the reliabilities obtained will be incorrect.

A sample of the result obtained for the Cronbach's alpha test for job enrichment, together with instructions on how it is obtained, is shown in Output 11.3.

The reliability of the job enrichment measure is presented in the first table in Output 11.3. The second table provides an overview of the alphas if we take one of the items out of the measure. For instance, it is shown that if the first item (Jobchar1) is taken out, Cronbach's alpha of the new three-item measure will be 0.577. This means that the alpha will go down if we take item 1 out of our measure. On the other hand, if we take out item 3, our alpha will go up and become 0.851. Note that, in this case, we would not take out item 3 for two reasons. First, our alpha is above 0.7 so we do not have to take any remedial actions. Second, if we took item 3 out, the validity of our measure would probably decrease. We did not include item 3 for nothing in the original measure!

If, however, our Cronbach's alpha was too low (under 0.60) then we could use this table to find out which of the items would have to be removed from our measure to increase the interitem consistency. Note that, usually, taking out an item, although improving the reliability of our measure, affects the validity of our measure in a negative way.

Now that we have established that the interitem consistency is satisfactory for perceived equity, job enrichment, burnout, and intention to leave, the scores on the original questions can be combined into a single score. For instance, a new "perceived equity" score can be calculated from

**TABLE 11.3    Reliability of the Excelsior Enterprises measures.**

| Variable | Number of items | Cronbach's alpha |
|---|---|---|
| Distributive justice | 5 | 0.862 |
| Job enrichment | 4 | 0.715 |
| Burnout | 10 | 0.806 |
| Intention to leave | 2 | 0.866 |

## Output 11.3    Reliability analysis

From the menus, choose:

Analyze
> Scale
>> *Reliability Analysis* . . .
>> Select the variables constituting the scale.
>> Choose *Model Alpha* (this is the default option).
>> Click on *Statistics*.
>> Select *Scale* if item deleted under *Descriptives*

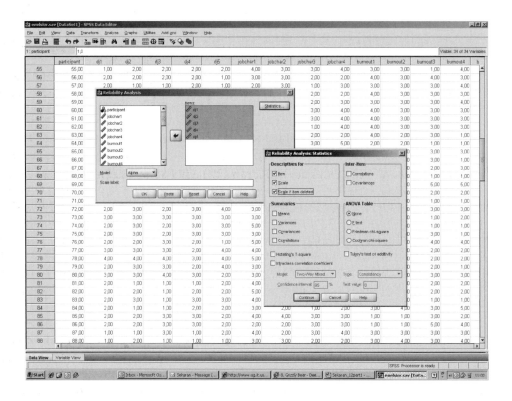

Output

| Reliability statistics | |
|---|---|
| Cronbach's alpha | Number of items |
| 0.715 | 4 |

| Item-total statistics | | | | |
|---|---|---|---|---|
| | Scale mean if item deleted | Scale variance if item deleted | Corrected item-total variation | Cronbach's alpha if item deleted |
| Jobchar1 | 10.0706 | 6.480 | 0.624 | 0.577 |
| Jobchar2 | 10.1471 | 6.552 | 0.646 | 0.568 |
| Jobchar3 | 10.4176 | 8.481 | 0.171 | 0.851 |
| Jobchar4 | 10.1118 | 6.325 | 0.664 | 0.552 |

the scores on the five individual "perceived equity" items (but only after items 1, 2, and 4 have been reverse coded). Likewise, a new "job enrichment" score can be calculated from the scores on the four individual "job enrichment" items, and so on. We have already explained that this involves calculating the summed score (per case/participant) and then dividing it by the number of items.

## Validity

**Factorial validity** can be established by submitting the data for factor analysis. The results of factor analysis (a multivariate technique) will confirm whether or not the theorized dimensions emerge. Recall from Chapter 6 that measures are developed by first delineating the dimensions so as to operationalize the concept. Factor analysis reveals whether the dimensions are indeed tapped by the items in the measure, as theorized. **Criterion-related validity** can be established by testing for the power of the measure to differentiate individuals who are known to be different (refer to discussions regarding concurrent and predictive validity in Chapter 7). **Convergent validity** can be established when there is a high degree of correlation between two different sources responding to the same measure (e.g., both supervisors and subordinates respond similarly to a perceived reward system measure administered to them). **Discriminant validity** can be established when two distinctly different concepts are not correlated to each other (for example, courage and honesty; leadership and motivation; attitudes and behavior). Convergent and discriminant validity can be established through the multitrait multimethod matrix, a full discussion of which is beyond the scope of this book. The student interested in knowing more about factor analysis and the multitrait multimethod matrix can refer to books on those subjects. When well-validated measures are used, there is no need, of course, to establish their validity again for each study. The reliability of the items can, however, be tested.

# Excelsior Enterprises – descriptive statistics part 2

Once the new scores for perceived equity, job enrichment, burnout, and intention to leave have been calculated, we are ready to further analyze the data. Descriptive statistics such as maximum, minimum, means, standard deviations, and variance can now be obtained for the multi-item, interval-scaled independent and dependent variables. What's more, a correlation matrix can also be obtained to examine how the variables in our model are related to each other.

This will help us to answer questions like:

- What are the employees' perceptions on job enrichment?
- How many employees have which degrees of burnout?
- Are the employees satisfied with their jobs?
- Is there much variance in the extent to which employees perceive the relationship with the company as equitable?
- What percentage of employees is inclined to leave the organization?
- What are the relationships between perceived equity, burnout, job enrichment, job satisfaction, and intention to leave?

Descriptive statistics such as maximum, minimum, means, standard deviations, and variance were obtained for the interval-scaled independent and dependent variables in the Excelsior Enterprises study. The results are shown in Table 11.4. It may be mentioned that all variables except ITL were tapped on a five-point scale. ITL was measured on a four-point scale.

From the results, it may be seen that the mean on perceived equity is rather low (2.32 on a five-point scale), as is the mean on experienced burnout (2.55). Job satisfaction is about average (3.22 on a five-point scale), and the job is perceived as somewhat enriched (3.40). The mean of 2.21 on a four-point scale for ITL indicates that most of the respondents are neither bent on leaving nor staying. The minimum of 1 indicates that there are some who do not intend to leave at all, and the maximum of 4 indicates that some are seriously considering leaving. Table 11.5 provides a more detailed account of employees' intentions to leave. This table shows that a large group of

| TABLE 11.4 | Descriptive statistics for independent and dependent variables. | | | | | |
|---|---|---|---|---|---|---|
| | $N$ | Minimum | Maximum | Mean | Std deviation | Variance |
| ITL | 174 | 1.00 | 4.00 | 2.19 | 0.97 | 0.94 |
| Job satisfaction | 173 | 1.00 | 5.00 | 3.24 | 1.32 | 1.74 |
| Perceived equity | 171 | 1.00 | 5.00 | 2.32 | 0.97 | 0.94 |
| Burnout | 171 | 1.00 | 5.00 | 2.55 | 0.66 | 0.43 |
| Jobchar | 170 | 1.50 | 5.00 | 3.40 | 0.84 | 0.706 |

| TABLE 11.5 | Frequency table intention to leave. | | | |
|---|---|---|---|---|
| | Frequency | Percentage | Valid percentage | Cumulative percentage |
| 1.00 | 39 | 22.4 | 22.4 | 22.4 |
| 1.50 | 23 | 13.2 | 13.2 | 35.6 |
| 2.00 | 49 | 28.2 | 28.2 | 63.8 |
| 2.50 | 7 | 4.0 | 4.0 | 67.8 |
| 3.00 | 21 | 12.1 | 12.1 | 79.9 |
| 3.50 | 22 | 12.6 | 12.6 | 92.5 |
| 4.00 | 13 | 7.5 | 7.5 | 100.0 |
| Total | 174 | 100.0 | 100.0 | |

employees seriously considers leaving Excelsior Enterprises! Testing our hypotheses will improve our understanding of why employees consider leaving Excelsior Enterprises and will provide us with useful tools to reduce employees' intentions to leave the company.

In sum, the perceived equity is rather low, not much burnout is experienced, the job is perceived to be fairly enriched, there is average job satisfaction, and there is neither a strong intention to stay with the organization nor to leave it. The variance for all the variables is rather high, indicating that participants' answers are not always very close to the mean on all the variables.

The Pearson correlation matrix obtained for the five interval-scaled variables is shown in Table 11.6.

From the results, we see that the intention to leave is, as would be expected, significantly negatively correlated to job satisfaction, perceived equity, and job enrichment. That is, the intention to leave is low if job satisfaction and equitable treatment are experienced, and the job is enriched. However, when individuals experience burnout (physical and emotional exhaustion), their intention to leave also increases (positive correlation of 0.531). Job satisfaction is also positively correlated to perceived equity, and an enriched job. It is negatively correlated to burnout and ITL. The correlations are all in the expected direction.

It is important to note that no correlation exceeded 0.55 for this sample. If correlations between the *dependent variables* were higher (say, 0.75 and above), we might have had a collinearity problem in our regression analysis.

After we have obtained descriptive statistics for the independent and dependent variables in our study, we can test our hypotheses. Hypothesis testing is discussed in the next chapter.

**TABLE 11.6    Correlations between independent and dependent variables**

|  | Intention to leave | Job satisfaction | Perceived equity | Burnout | Job enrichment |
|---|---|---|---|---|---|
| Intention to leave | 1.000 | −0.489 | −0.366 | 0.531 | −0.387 |
| Sig. (two-tailed) |  | 0.000 | 0.000 | 0.000 | 0.000 |
| N | 174 | 173 | 171 | 170 | 170 |
| Job satisfaction | −0.489 | 1.000 | 0.270 | −0.349 | 0.212 |
| Sig. (two-tailed) | 0.000 |  | 0.000 | 0.000 | 0.006 |
| N | 173 | 173 | 170 | 169 | 169 |
| Perceived equity | −0.366 | 0.270 | 1.000 | −0.208 | 0.364 |
| Sig. (two-tailed) | 0.000 | 0.000 |  | 0.007 | 0.000 |
| N | 171 | 170 | 171 | 167 | 167 |
| Burnout | 0.531 | −0.349 | −0.208 | 1.000 | −0.320 |
| Sig. (two-tailed) | 0.000 | 0.000 | 0.007 |  | 0.000 |
| N | 170 | 170 | 167 | 166 | 166 |
| Job enrichment | −0.387 | 0.212 | 0.364 | −0.320 | 1.000 |
| Sig. (two-tailed) | 0.000 | 0.006 | 0.000 | 0.000 |  |
| N | 170 | 169 | 167 | 166 | 170 |

## SUMMARY

In this chapter we covered the initial steps of the procedure for analyzing data once they are collected. Through the example of the research on Excelsior Enterprises, we saw the steps necessary to get the data ready for analysis – editing, coding, and categorizing. We also obtained descriptive statistics for the variables in the Excelsior Enterprises case. Finally we tested the goodness of data using Cronbach's alpha.

## DISCUSSION QUESTIONS

1. What activities are involved in getting the data ready for analysis?
2. What does coding the data involve?
3. Data editing deals with detecting and correcting illogical, inconsistent, or illegal data in the information returned by the participants of the study. Explain the difference between illogical, inconsistent, and illegal data.
4. How would you deal with missing data?
5. What is reverse scoring and when is reverse scoring necessary?
6. There are three measures of central tendency: the mean, the median, and the mode. Measures of dispersion include the range, the standard deviation, and the variance (where the measure of central tendency is the mean), and the interquartile range (where the measure of central tendency is the median). Describe these measures and explain which of these measures you would use to provide an overview of (a) nominal, (b) ordinal and (c) interval data?
7. A researcher wants to provide an overview of the gender of the respondents in his sample. The gender is measured like this: What is your gender? ☐ Male ☐ Female. What is the best way to provide an overview of the gender of the respondents?
8. Consider the following reliability analysis for the variable customer differentiation. What could you conclude from it?

RELIABILITY ANALYSIS - SCALE (ALPHA)

Item-total statistics

|  | Scale Mean if item deleted | Scale Variance if item deleted | Corrected Item-Total correlation | Alpha if item deleted |
|---|---|---|---|---|
| CUSDIF1 | 10.0405 | 5.4733 | 0.2437 | 0.7454 |
| CUSDIF2 | 9.7432 | 5.0176 | 0.5047 | 0.3293 |
| CUSDIF3 | 9.6486 | 5.3754 | 0.4849 | 0.3722 |

Reliability Coefficients
N of Cases = 111.0     N of Items = 3
Alpha = 0.5878

## EXERCISE 11.1

The following data are available:

| Respondent | Age | Exam mark | Paper mark | Sex | Year in college | IQ |
|---|---|---|---|---|---|---|
| 1 | 21 | 87 | 83 | M | 2 | 80 |
| 2 | 19 | 83 | 80 | M | 1 | 100 |
| 3 | 23 | 85 | 86 | M | 4 | 98 |
| 4 | 21 | 81 | 75 | F | 1 | 76 |
| 5 | 21 | 81 | 75 | F | 3 | 82 |
| 6 | 20 | 67 | 68 | F | 3 | 99 |
| 7 | 26 | 75 | 88 | F | 2 | 120 |
| 8 | 24 | 92 | 78 | F | 4 | 115 |
| 9 | 26 | 78 | 92 | M | 4 | 126 |
| 10 | 30 | 89 | 95 | F | 3 | 129 |
| 11 | 21 | 72 | 80 | F | 1 | 86 |
| 12 | 19 | 81 | 65 | M | 2 | 80 |
| 13 | 17 | 75 | 77 | M | 1 | 70 |
| 14 | 19 | 76 | 85 | F | 1 | 99 |
| 15 | 35 | 80 | 83 | F | 3 | 99 |
| 16 | 27 | 75 | 60 | F | 2 | 60 |
| 17 | 21 | 85 | 80 | M | 3 | 89 |
| 18 | 27 | 79 | 75 | M | 4 | 70 |
| 19 | 21 | 90 | 93 | F | 3 | 140 |
| 20 | 22 | 97 | 95 | M | 3 | 165 |
| 21 | 21 | 90 | 82 | M | 2 | 115 |
| 22 | 19 | 87 | 86 | F | 3 | 119 |
| 23 | 32 | 95 | 90 | M | 2 | 120 |
| 24 | 19 | 68 | 57 | F | 3 | 89 |

*Note:* Maximum exam mark = 100, Maximum paper mark = 100, Sex: M = male, F = female, Year in college: 1 = Freshman; 2 = Sophomore; 3 = Junior; 4 = Senior.

1. Data handling
   a. Enter the data in SPSS. Save the file to your USB flashdrive. Name the file "resmethassignment1".
   b. Provide appropriate variable labels, value labels, and scaling indications to the variables.
2. Descriptives
   a. Use Analyze, Descriptive statistics, Descriptives to summarize metric variables.
   b. Use Analyze, Descriptive statistics, Frequencies to summarize nonmetric variables.

c. Create a pie-chart for Year in college.

d. Create a histogram for IQ and include the normal distribution.

e. Make a scatter plot with IQ on the *x*-axis and exam grade on the *y*-axis. What do you conclude?

f. Recode the sex variable such that it is 1 for females and 0 for males.

g. Make a scatter plot with sex on the *x*-axis and IQ on the *y*-axis. What do you conclude?

h. Compute the mean IQ for males and for females. Conclusion?

i. Create a new dummy variable, IQdum, which is 1 if the IQ is larger than or equal to 100, and 0 otherwise.

# CHAPTER 12

## Quantitative data analysis: hypothesis testing

## Topics discussed

- Type I errors, type II errors and statistical power
- Choosing the appropriate statistical technique
- Testing a hypothesis about a single mean
- Testing hypotheses about two related means
- Testing hypotheses about two unrelated means
- Testing hypotheses about several means
- Regression analysis
  - Standardized regression coefficients
  - Regression with dummy variables
  - Multicollinearity
  - Testing moderation using regression analysis: interaction effects
- Other multivariate tests and analyses
- Excelsior Enterprises – hypothesis testing
- Data warehousing, data mining, and operations research
- Some software packages useful for data analysis

## CHAPTER OBJECTIVES

After completing Chapter 12, you should be able to:

1. Describe the process followed in hypothesis testing.
2. Describe the concepts type I error, type II error, and statistical power.

3. Describe how to choose the appropriate statistical technique to test hypotheses.
4. Explain when and how to use the most important statistical techniques to examine hypotheses.
5. Explain how to use regression analysis to test moderation and mediation.

# Introduction

In Chapter 4 we discussed the steps to be followed in hypothesis development and testing. These steps are:

1. State the null and the alternate hypotheses.
2. Determine the level of significance desired ($p = 0.05$, or more, or less).
3. Choose the appropriate statistical test depending on the type of scales that have been used (nominal, ordinal, interval, or ratio).
4. See if the output results from computer analysis indicate that the significance level is met. When the resultant value is larger than the critical value, the null hypothesis is rejected, and the alternate accepted. If the calculated value is less than the critical value, the null hypothesis is accepted and the alternate hypothesis rejected.

In this chapter we will discuss hypothesis testing. First, we will pay attention to *type I errors*, *type II errors*, and *statistical power*. Then, we will discuss various univariate and bivariate statistical tests that can be used to test hypotheses. Finally, we will come back to the Excelsior Enterprises case and test the hypotheses that were developed in the previous chapter.

# Type I errors, type II errors, and statistical power

In Chapter 4 we explained that the hypothetico-deductive method requires hypotheses to be falsifiable. For this reason, null hypotheses are developed. These null hypotheses ($H_0$) are thus set up to be rejected in order to support the alternate hypothesis, termed $H_A$.

The null hypothesis is presumed true until statistical evidence, in the form of a hypothesis test, indicates otherwise. The required statistical evidence is provided by inferential statistics, such as regression analysis or MANOVA. Inferential statistics help us to draw conclusions (or to make inferences) *about the population* from a sample.

The purpose of hypothesis testing is to determine *accurately* if the null hypothesis can be rejected in favor of the alternate hypothesis. Based on the sample data the researcher can reject the null hypothesis (and therefore accept the alternate hypothesis) *with a certain degree of confidence*: there is always a risk that the inference that is drawn about the population is incorrect.

There are two kinds of errors (or two ways in which a conclusion can be incorrect), classified as *type I errors* and *type II errors*. A **type I error**, also referred to as alpha ($\alpha$), is the probability of rejecting the null hypothesis when it is actually true. In the Excelsior Enterprises example introduced in Chapter 11, a type I error would occur if we concluded, based on the data, that burnout affects intention to leave when, in fact, it does not. The probability of type I error, also known as the *significance level*, is determined by the researcher. Typical significance levels in business research are 5% (<0.05) and 1% (<0.01).

A **type II error**, also referred to as beta ($\beta$), is the probability of failing to reject the null hypothesis given that the alternate hypothesis is actually true; e.g., concluding, based on the data, that burnout does not affect intention to leave when, in fact, it does. The probability of type II error is inversely related to the probability of type I error: the smaller the risk of one of these types of error, the higher the risk of the other type of error.

A third important concept in hypothesis testing is *statistical power* $(1 - \beta)$. **Statistical power**, or just power, is the probability of correctly rejecting the null hypothesis. In other words, power is the probability that statistical significance will be indicated if it is present. Statistical power depends on:

1. Alpha ($\alpha$): the statistical significance criterion used in the test. If alpha moves closer to zero (for instance, if alpha moves from 5% to 1%), then the probability of finding an effect when there is an effect decreases. This implies that the lower the $\alpha$ (that is, the closer $\alpha$ moves to zero) the lower the power; the higher the alpha, the higher the power.
2. Effect size: the effect size is the size of a difference or the strength of a relationship *in the population*: a large difference (or a strong relationship) in the population is more likely to be found than a small difference (similarity, relationship).
3. The size of the sample: at a given level of alpha, increased sample sizes produce more power, because increased sample sizes lead to more accurate parameter estimates. Thus, increased sample sizes lead to a higher probability of finding what we were looking for. However, increasing the sample size can also lead to too much power, because even very small effects will be found to be statistically significant.

Along these lines, there are four interrelated components that affect the inferences you might draw from a statistical test in a research project: the power of the test, the alpha, the effect size, and the sample size. Given the values for any three of these components, it is thus possible to calculate the value of the fourth. Generally, it is recommended to establish the power, the alpha, and the required precision (effect size) of a test first, and then, based on the values of these components, determine an appropriate sample size.

> The focus of business research is usually on type I error. However, power (e.g., to determine an appropriate sample size) and in some situations, type II error (e.g., if you are testing the effect of a new drug) must also be given serious consideration.

# Choosing the appropriate statistical technique

After you have selected an acceptable level of statistical significance to test your hypotheses, the next step is to decide on the appropriate method to test the hypotheses. The choice of the

## Univariate techniques:

Testing a hypothesis on a single mean:

|  |  |
|---|---|
| *Metric data:* | One sample *t*-test |
| *Nonmetric data:* | Chi-square |

Testing hypotheses about two related means

*Independent samples*

|  |  |
|---|---|
| *Metic data:* | Independent samples *t*-test |
| *Nonmetric data:* | Chi-square |
|  | Mann–Whitney *U*-test |

*Related samples*

|  |  |
|---|---|
| *Metic data* | Paired samples *t*-test |
| *Nonmetric data:* | Chi-square |
|  | Wilcoxon |
|  | McNemar |

Testing hypotheses about several means

|  |  |
|---|---|
| Metric data: | One-way analysis of variance |
| Nonmetric data: | Chi-square |

## Multivariate techniques:

*One metric dependent variable*

Analysis of variance and covariance
Multiple regression analysis
Conjoint analysis

*One nonmetric dependent variable*

Discriminant analysis
Logistic regression

*More than one metric dependent variable*

Multivariate analysis of variance
Canonical correlation

Figure 12.1: Overview of univariate and multivariate statistical techniques.

appropriate statistical technique largely depends on the number of (independent and dependent) variables you are examining and the scale of measurement (metric or nonmetric) of your variable(s). Other aspects that play a role are whether the assumptions of parametric tests are met and the size of your sample.

*Univariate statistical techniques* are used when you want to examine two-variable relationships. For instance, if you want to examine the effect of gender on the number of candy bars that students eat per week, univariate statistics are appropriate. If you, on the other hand, are interested in the relationships between many variables, such as in the Excelsior Enterprises case, *multivariate statistical techniques* are required. The appropriate univariate or multivariate test largely depends on the measurement scale you have used, as Figure 12.1 illustrates.

Chi-square analysis was discussed in the previous chapter. This chapter will discuss the other techniques listed in Figure 12.1. Note that some techniques are discussed more elaborately than others. A detailed discussion of all these techniques is beyond the scope of this book.

# Testing a hypothesis about a single mean

The **one sample $t$-test** is used to test the hypothesis that the mean of the *population* from which a sample is drawn is equal to a comparison standard. Assume that you have read that the average student studies 32 hours a week. From what you have observed so far, you think that students from your university (the population from which your sample will be drawn) study more. Therefore, you ask twenty class mates how long they study in an average week. The average study time per week turns out to be 36.2 hours, 4 hours and 12 minutes more than the study time of students in general. The question is: is this a coincidence?

In the above example, the *sample* of students from your university differs from the typical student. What you want to know, however, is whether your fellow students come from a different population than the rest of the students. In other words, did you select a group of motivated students by chance? Or is there a "true" difference between students from your university and students in general?

In this example the null hypothesis is:

$H_0$: *The number of study hours of students from our university is equal to the number of study hours of students in general.*

The alternate hypothesis is:

$H_1$: *The number of study hours of students from our university differs from the number of study hours of students in general.*

The way to decide whether there is a significant difference between students from your university and students in general depends on three aspects: the value of the sample mean (36.2 hours); the value of the comparison standard (32 hours); and the degree of uncertainty concerning how well the sample mean represents the population mean (the standard error of the sample mean).

Along these lines, the following formula is used to compute the $t$-value:

$$t_{n-1} = \frac{X - \mu}{s/\sqrt{n}}$$

Assume that the observed standard deviation is 8. Hence, the $t$-statistic becomes:

$$t = \frac{36.2 - 32}{8/\sqrt{20}} = 2.438$$

Having calculated the $t$-statistic, we can now compare the $t$-value with a standard table of $t$-values with $n - 1$ degrees of freedom to determine whether the $t$-statistic reaches the threshold of statistical significance. When the *t*-statistic is larger than the appropriate table value, the null hypothesis (no significant difference) is rejected.

Our *t*-statistic (2.438) is larger than the appropriate table value (1.729). This means that the difference between 36.2 and 32 is statistically significant. The null hypothesis must thus be rejected: there is a significant difference in study time between students from our university and students in general.

How does this work in SPSS?

Under the Analyze menu, choose Compare Means, then One-Sample T Test. Move the dependent variable into the "Test Variable(s)" box. Type in the value you wish to compare your sample to in the box called "Test Value."

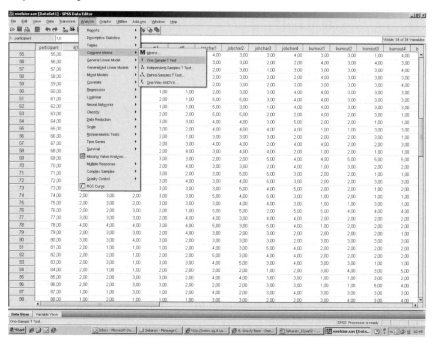

# Testing hypotheses about two related means

We can also do a (paired samples) *t*-test to examine the differences in the same group before and after a treatment. For example, would a group of employees perform better *after* undergoing training than they did *before?* In this case, there would be two observations for each employee, one before the training and one after the training. We would use a paired samples *t*-test to test the null hypothesis that the average of the differences between the before and after measure is zero.

How does this work in SPSS?

Under the Analyze menu, choose Compare Means, then Paired-Samples T Test. Move each of the two variables whose means you want to compare to the "Paired Variables" list.

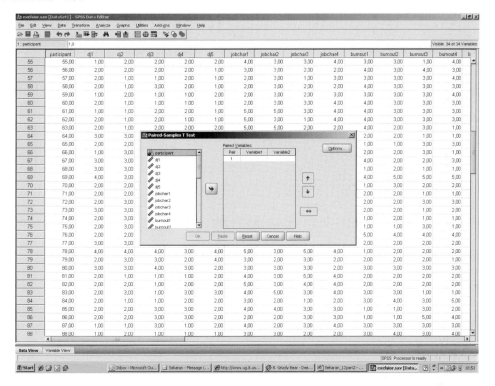

## EXAMPLE

A university professor was interested in the effect of her teaching program on the performance of her students. For this reason, ten students were given a math test in the first week of the semester and their scores were recorded. Subsequently, the students were given an equivalent test during the last week of the semester. The professor now wants to know whether the students' math scores have increased.

Table 12.1 depicts the scores of students on the math test in the first and in the last week of the semester.

TABLE 12.1    **Math scores of ten students in the first and last week of the semester.**

| Student | Math scores | | |
| | Score first week | Score last week | Difference |
|---|---|---|---|
| 1 | 55 | 75 | + 20 |
| 2 | 65 | 80 | + 15 |
| 3 | 70 | 75 | + 5 |
| 4 | 55 | 60 | + 5 |
| 5 | 40 | 45 | + 5 |
| 6 | 60 | 55 | − 5 |
| 7 | 80 | 75 | − 5 |
| 8 | 35 | 70 | + 35 |
| 9 | 55 | 75 | + 20 |
| 10 | 60 | 90 | + 30 |
| Average score | 57.5 | 70 | 22.5 |

To find out if there is a significant difference in math scores we need a test statistic. The test statistic is the average difference$/s_{\text{difference}}/\sqrt{n}$.

In this example we get: $22.5/13.79412/\sqrt{10} = 5.158$.

Having calculated the $t$-statistic, we can now compare the $t$-value with a standard table of $t$-values with $n - 1$ degrees of freedom to determine whether the $t$-statistic reaches the threshold of statistical significance. Again, when the $t$-statistic is larger than the appropriate table value, the null hypothesis (no significant difference) is rejected.

Our $t$-statistic is larger than the appropriate table value (1.83). This means that the difference between 70 and 57.5 is statistically significant. The null hypothesis must thus be rejected: there is a significant increase in math score.

The **Wilcoxon signed-rank test** is a nonparametric test for examining significant differences between two related samples or repeated measurements on a single sample. It is used as an alternative to a paired samples $t$-test when the population cannot be assumed to be normally distributed.

How does this work in SPSS?

Under the Analyze menu, choose Nonparametric Tests, then Two Related Samples. Move the variables you want to compare into the "Test Pairs" box. Select Wilcoxon from the Test Type group and click OK.

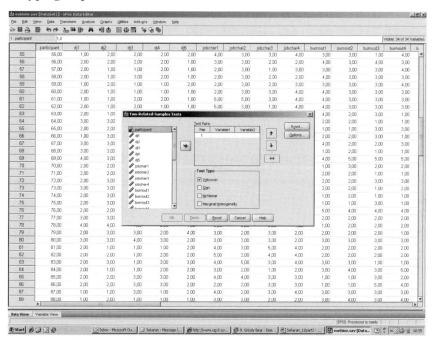

**McNemar's test** is a nonparametric method used on nominal data. It assesses the significance of the difference between two dependent samples when the variable of interest is dichotomous. It is used primarily in before–after studies to test for an experimental effect.

In the following example, a researcher wants to determine whether the use of a new training method (called CARE) has an effect on the performance of athletes. Counts of individual athletes are given in Table 12.2. The performance (average/good) before the treatment (the new training method) is given in the columns (244 athletes delivered an average performance before they trained with the CARE method, whereas 134 athletes delivered a good performance before they adopted this method). You can find the performance after the treatment (average/good) in the rows (190 athletes delivered an average performance after using the new training method; the number of athletes that delivered a good performance increased to 188).

The cells of Table 12.2 can be represented by the letters $a$, $b$, $c$, and $d$. The totals across rows and columns are marginal totals ($a + b$, $c + d$, $a + c$, and $b + d$). The grand total is represented by $n$, as shown in Table 12.3.

McNemar's test is a rather straightforward technique to test marginal homogeneity. *Marginal homogeneity* refers to equality (or the lack of a significant difference) between one or more of the

| TABLE 12.2 | Performance of athletes before and after new training method. | | |
|---|---|---|---|

| | | **Before** | | |
|---|---|---|---|---|
| | | average | good | totals |
| **After** | average | 112 | 78 | 190 |
| | good | 132 | 56 | 188 |
| | totals | 244 | 134 | 378 |

| TABLE 12.3 | A more abstract representation of Table 12.2. | | |
|---|---|---|---|

| | | **Before** | | |
|---|---|---|---|---|
| | | average | good | totals |
| **After** | average | $a$ | $b$ | $a+b$ |
| | good | $c$ | $d$ | $c+d$ |
| | totals | $a+c$ | $b+d$ | $n$ |

marginal row totals and the corresponding marginal column totals. In this example, marginal homogeneity implies that the row totals are equal to the corresponding column totals, or

$$a + b = a + c$$

$$c + d = b + d.$$

Marginal homogeneity would mean there was no effect of the treatment. In this case it would mean that the new training method would not affect the performance of athletes.

The McNemar test uses the $\chi^2$ distribution, based on the formula: $(|b - c| - 1)^2) / (b + c) \cdot$ $\chi^2$ is a statistic with 1 degree of freedom (# rows − 1 x # columns −1). The marginal frequencies are *not* homogeneous if the $\chi^2$ result is significant at $p < 0.05$.

The $\chi^2$ value in this example is: $(|78 - 132| - 1)^2)/(78 + 132) = 53^2/210 = 13.376$.

The table of the distribution of chi-square, with 1 degree of freedom, reveals that the difference between samples is significant: at the 0.05 level: the critical value of chi-square is 3.841. Since 13.376 computed for the example above exceeds this value, the difference between samples is significant. Hence, we can conclude that the new training method has a positive effect on the performance of athletes.

Note that if $b$ and/or $c$ are small ($b + c < 20$) then $\chi^2$ is not approximated by the Chi-square distribution. Instead a *sign test* should be used.

How does this work in SPSS?

Under the Analyze menu, choose Nonparametric Tests, then Two Related Samples. Move the variables you want to compare into the "Test Pairs" box. Select McNemar from the "Test Type" group and click OK.

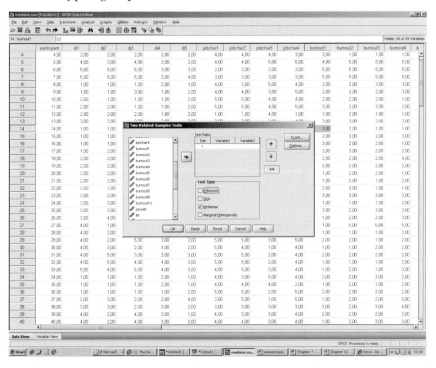

# Testing hypotheses about two unrelated means

There are many instances when we are interested to know whether two groups are different from each other on a particular interval-scaled or ratio-scaled variable of interest. For example, would men and women press their case for the introduction of flextime at the workplace to the same extent, or would their needs be different? Do MBAs perform better in organizational settings than business students with only a bachelor's degree? Do individuals in urban areas have a different investment pattern for their savings than those in semi-urban areas? Do CPAs perform better than non-CPAs in accounting tasks? To find answers to such questions, an **independent samples *t*-test** is carried out to see if there are any significant differences in the means for two groups in the variable of interest. That is, a **nominal** variable that is split into two subgroups (for example, smokers and nonsmokers; employees in the marketing department and those in the accounting department; younger and older employees) is tested to see if there is a significant mean difference between the two split groups on a dependent variable, which is measured on an **interval** or **ratio** scale (for instance, extent of well-being; pay; or comprehension level).

How does this work in SPSS?

Under the Analyze menu, choose Compare Means, then Independent Samples T Test. Move the dependent variable into the "Test Variable(s)" box. Move the independent variable (that is, the variable whose values define the two groups) into the "Grouping Variable" box. Click "Define Groups" and specify how the groups are defined (for instance 0 and 1 or 1 and 2).

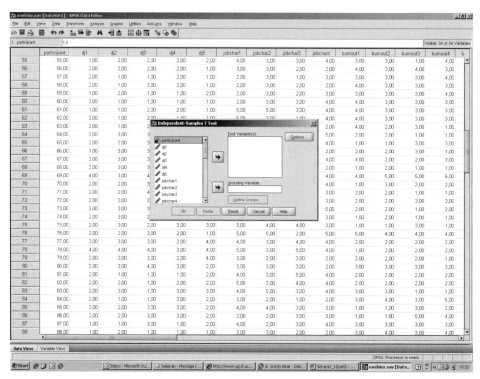

# Testing hypotheses about several means

Whereas the (independent samples) *t*-test indicates whether or not there is a significant mean difference in a dependent variable between two groups, an **analysis of variance (ANOVA)** helps to examine the significant mean differences among more than two groups on an interval or ratio-scaled dependent variable. For example, is there a significant difference in the amount of sales by the following four groups of salespersons: those who are sent to training schools; those who are given on-the-job training during field trips; those who have been tutored by the sales manager; and those who have had none of the above? Or is the rate of promotion significantly different for those who have assigned mentors, choose their own mentors, and have no mentors in the organizational system?

The results of ANOVA show whether or not the means of the various groups are significantly different from one another, as indicated by the $F$ statistic. The $F$ statistic shows whether two sample variances differ from each other or are from the same population. The $F$ distribution is a probability distribution of sample variances and the family of distributions changes with changes in the sample size. Details of the $F$ statistic may be seen in Table IV at the end of the book.

How does this work in SPSS?

Under the Analyze menu, choose Compare Means, then One-Way ANOVA. Move the dependent variable into the "Dependent List". Move the Independent variable (that is, the variable whose values define the groups) into the "Factor" box. Click OK.

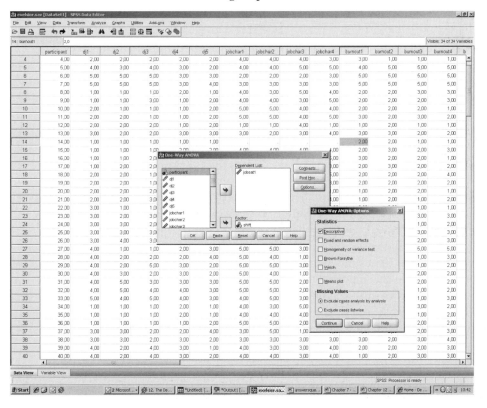

When significant mean differences among the groups are indicated by the $F$ statistic, there is no way of knowing from the ANOVA results alone where they lie; that is, whether the significant difference is between Groups A and B, or between B and C, or A and C, and so on. It is therefore unwise to use multiple $t$-tests, taking two groups at a time, because the greater the number of $t$-tests done, the lower the confidence we can place on results. For example, three $t$-tests done simultaneously decrease the confidence level from 95% to 86% $(0.95)^3$. However, several tests, such as Scheffe's test, Duncan Multiple Range test, Tukey's test, and Student–Newman–Keul's test are available and can be used, as appropriate, to detect where exactly the mean differences lie.

# Regression analysis

Simple **regression analysis** is used in a situation where one independent variable is hypothesized to affect one dependent variable. For instance, assume that we propose that the propensity to buy a product depends only on the perceived quality of that product.[1] In this case we would have to gather information on perceived quality and propensity to buy a product. We could then plot the data to obtain some first ideas on the relationship between these variables.

From Figure 12.2 we can see that there is a linear relationship between perceived quality and propensity to buy the product. We can model this linear relationship by a *least squares function*.

A simple linear regression equation represents a straight line. Indeed, to summarize the relationship between perceived quality and propensity to buy, we can draw a straight line through the data points, as in Figure 12.3

We can also express this relationship in an equation:

$$Y_i = \beta_0 + \beta_1 X_{1i} + \varepsilon_i$$

The parameters $\beta_0$ and $\beta_1$ are called regression coefficients. They are the intercept $(\beta_0)$ and the slope $(\beta_1)$ of the straight line relating propensity to buy $(Y)$ to perceived quality $(X_1)$. The slope can be interpreted as the number of units by which propensity to buy would increase if perceived quality increased by a unit. The error term denotes the error in prediction or the difference between the estimated propensity to buy and the actual propensity to buy.

In this example the intercept $(\beta_0)$ was not significant whereas the slope $(\beta_1)$ was. The unstandardized regression coefficient $\beta_1$ was 0.832. This means that if perceived quality is rated 2 (on a five-point scale), the *estimated* propensity to buy is 1.664. On the other hand, if perceived quality is rated 4 (on a five-point scale), the *estimated* propensity to buy is 3.328.

---

[1] In reality, any effort to model the effect of perceived quality on propensity to buy a product without careful attention to other factors that affect propensity to buy would cause a serious statistical problem ("omitted variables bias").

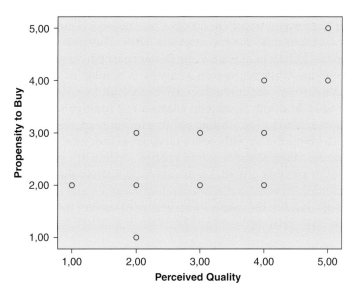

Figure 12.2:  Scatter plot of perceived quality versus propensity to buy.

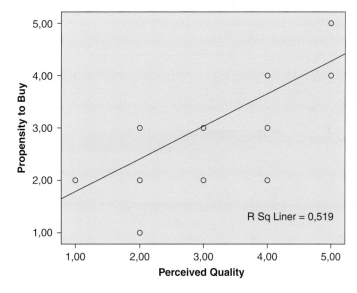

Figure 12.3:  Regression of propensity to buy on perceived quality.

The coefficient of determination, $R^2$, provides information about the goodness of fit of the regression model: it is a statistical measure of how well the regression line approximates the real data points. $R^2$ is the percentage of variance in the dependent variable that is explained by the variation in the independent variable. If $R^2$ is near to 1, most of the variation in the dependent variable can be explained by the regression model. In other words, the regression model fits the data well. On the other hand, if $R^2$ is near to 0, most of the data variation cannot be explained by the regression model. In this case, the regression model fits the data poorly. In the aforementioned example, $R^2$ for the model is 0.519. This means that almost 52% of the variance in propensity to buy is explained by variance in perceived quality.

The basic idea of **multiple regression analysis** is similar to that of simple regression analysis. Only in this case, we use more than one independent variable to explain variance in the dependent variable. Multiple regression analysis is a multivariate technique that is used very often in business research. The starting point of multiple regression analysis is, of course, the conceptual model (and the hypotheses derived from that model) that the researcher has developed in an earlier stage of the research process.

Multiple regression analysis provides a means of objectively assessing the degree and the character of the relationship between the independent variables and the dependent variable: the regression coefficients indicate the relative importance of each of the independent variables in

How does this work in SPSS?

Under the Analyze menu, choose Regression, then Linear. Move the dependent variable into the "Dependent" box. Move the independent variables into the "Independent(s)" list and click OK.

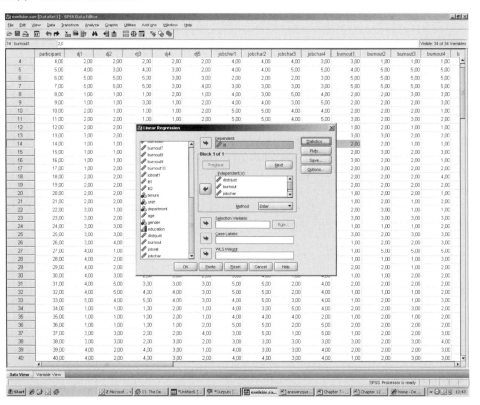

the prediction of the dependent variable. For example, suppose that a researcher believes that the variance in performance can be explained by four independent variables, A, B, C, and D (say, pay, task difficulty, supervisory support, and organizational culture). When these variables are jointly regressed against the dependent variable in an effort to explain the variance in it, the sizes of the individual regression coefficients indicate how much an increase of one unit in the independent variable would affect the dependent variable, assuming that all the other independent variables remain unchanged. What's more, the individual correlations between the independent variables and the dependent variable collapse into what is called a *multiple r* or multiple correlation coefficient. The square of multiple *r*, R-square, or $R^2$ as it is commonly known, is the amount of variance explained in the dependent variable by the predictors.

## Standardized regression coefficients

**Standardized regression coefficients or beta coefficients** are the estimates resulting from a multiple regression analysis performed on variables that have been standardized (a process whereby the variables are transformed into variables with a mean of 0 and a standard deviation of 1). This is usually done to allow the researcher to compare the relative effects of independent variables on the dependent variable, when the independent variables are measured in different units of measurement (for example, income measured in dollars and household size measured in number of individuals).

## Regression with dummy variables

A **dummy variable** is a variable that has two or more distinct levels, which are coded 0 or 1. Dummy variables allow us to use nominal or ordinal variables as independent variables to explain, understand, or predict the dependent variable.

Suppose that we are interested in the relationship between work shift and job satisfaction. In this case, the variable "work shift", which has three categories (see the Excelsior Enterprises case), would have to be coded in terms of two dummy variables, since one of the three categories should serve as the reference category. This might be done as shown in Table 12.4. Note that the third shift serves as the reference category.

### TABLE 12.4  Recoding work shift into dummy codes.

| Work shift | Original code | Dummy $D_1$ | Dummy $D_2$ |
|---|---|---|---|
| First shift | 1 | 1 | 0 |
| Second shift | 2 | 0 | 1 |
| Third shift | 3 | 0 | 0 |

Next, the dummy variables $D_1$ and $D_2$ have to be included in a regression model. This would look like this:

$$Y_i = \beta_0 + \beta_1 D_{1i} + \beta_{2i} D_{2i} + \varepsilon_i$$

In this example workers from the third shift have been selected as the reference category. For this reason, this category has not been included in the regression equation. For workers in the third shift, $D_1$ and $D_2$ assume a value of 0, and the regression equation thus becomes:

$$Y_i = \beta_0 + \varepsilon_i$$

For workers in the first shift the equation becomes:

$$Y_i = \beta_0 + \beta_1 D_{1i} + \varepsilon_i$$

The coefficient $\beta_1$ is the difference in predicted job satisfaction for workers in the first shift, as compared to workers in the third shift. The coefficient $\beta_2$ has the same interpretation. Note that any of the three shifts could have been used as a reference category.

Now do Exercises 12.1 and 12.2

## EXERCISE 12.1

Provide the equation for workers in the second shift.

## EXERCISE 12.2

Use the data of the Excelsior Enterprises case to estimate the effect of work shift on job satisfaction.

## Multicollinearity

**Multicollinearity** is an often encountered statistical phenomenon in which two or more independent variables in a multiple regression model are highly correlated. In its most severe case (if the correlation between two independent variables is equal to 1 or −1) multicollinearity makes the estimation of the regression coefficients impossible. In all other cases it makes the estimates of the regression coefficients unreliable.

The simplest and most obvious way to detect multicollinearity is to check the correlation matrix for the independent variables. The presence of high correlations (most people consider correlations of 0.70 and above high) is a first sign of sizeable multicollinearity. However, when multicollinearity is the result of complex relationships among several independent variables, it may not be revealed by this approach. More common measures for identifying multicollinearity are therefore the *tolerance value* and the *variance inflation factor* (*VIF* – the inverse of the tolerance value). These measures indicate the degree to which one independent variable is explained by the other independent variables. A common cutoff value is a tolerance value of 0.10, which corresponds to a VIF of 10.

How does this work in SPSS?

Under the Analyze menu, choose Regression, then Linear. Move the dependent variable into the "Dependent" box. Move the independent variables into the "Independent(s)" list. Select "Statistics" by clicking the button on the right-hand side. Select "Collinearity diagnostics" and click continue. Then click OK.

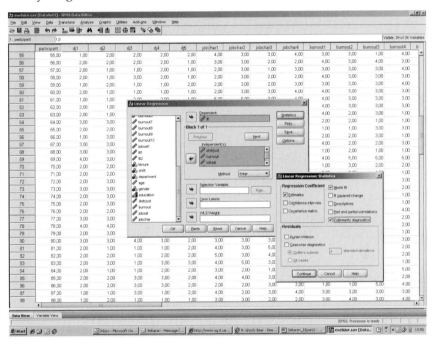

Note that multicollinearity is *not* a serious problem if the purpose of the study is to predict or forecast future values of the dependent variable, because even though the estimations of the regression coefficients may be unstable, multicollinearity does not affect the reliability of the forecast. However, if the objective of the study is to reliably estimate the individual regression coefficients, multicollinearity is a problem. In this case, we may use one or more of the following methods to reduce it:

- Reduce the set of independent variables to a set that are not collinear (note that this may lead to omitted variable bias, which is also a serious problem).
- Use more sophisticated ways to analyze the data, such as ridge regression.
- Create a new variable that is a composite of the highly correlated variables.

## Testing moderation using regression analysis: interaction effects

Earlier in this book we described a moderating variable as a variable that modifies the original relationship between an independent variable and the dependent variable. This means that the effect of one variable ($X_1$) on $Y$ depends on the value of another variable; the moderating variable ($X_2$). Such *interactions* are included as *the product* of two variables in a regression model.

Suppose that we have developed the following hypothesis:

$H_1$: *The students' judgment of the university's library is affected by the students' judgment of the computers in the library.*

Now suppose that we also believe that, even though this relationship will hold for all students, it will be nonetheless contingent on computer ownership. That is, we believe that the relationship between the judgment of computers in the library and the judgment of the library is affected by computer ownership (indeed computer ownership is a *dummy variable*). Therefore, we hypothesize that:

$H_2$: *The relationship between the judgment of the library and judgment of computers in the library is moderated by computer ownership.*

The relationship between the judgment of the library and judgment of computers in the library can be modelled as follows:

$$Y_i = \beta_0 + \beta_1 X_{1i} + \varepsilon_i \tag{1}$$

We have also hypothesized that the effect of $X_1$ on $Y$ depends on $X_2$. This can be modelled as follows:

$$\beta_1 = \gamma_0 + \gamma_1 X_{2i} \tag{2}$$

Adding the second equation into the first one leads to the following model:

$$Y_i = \beta_0 + \gamma_0 X_{1i} + \gamma_1 (X_{1i} \times X_{2i}) + \varepsilon_i \tag{3}$$

Model (3) states that the slope of model (1) is a function of variable $X_2$. Although this model allows us to test moderation, the following model is better:

$$Y_i = \beta_0 + \gamma_0 X_{1i} + \gamma_1 (X_{1i} \times X_{2i}) + \gamma_2 X_{2i} + \varepsilon_i \tag{4}$$

You may have noticed that model (4) includes a direct effect of $X_2$ on $Y$. This allows us to differentiate between *pure moderation* and *quasi moderation*, (compare Sharma, Durand and Gur-Arie, 1981) explained next.

If $\gamma_1 = 0$, and $\gamma_2 \neq 0$, $X_2$ is not a moderator but simply an independent predictor variable. If $\gamma_1 \neq 0$, $X_2$ is a moderator. Model (4) allows us to differentiate between pure moderators and quasi moderators as follows: if $\gamma_1 \neq 0$, and $\gamma_2 = 0$, $X_2$ is a pure moderator; that is, $X_2$ moderates the relationship between $X_1$ and $Y$, but it has no direct effect on $Y$. If $\gamma_1 \neq 0$, and $\gamma_2 \neq 0$, $X_2$ is a quasi moderator; that is, $X_2$ moderates the relationship between $X_1$ and $Y$, but it also has a direct effect on $Y$.

Suppose that data analysis leads to the following model:

$$\hat{Y}_i = 4.3 + 0.4X_{1i} - 0.01X_{2i} - 0.2(X_{1i} \times X_{2i}) \tag{5}$$

where $\beta_0 \neq 0$, $\gamma_0 \neq 0$, $\gamma_1 \neq 0$, and $\gamma_2 = 0$.

Based on the results we can conclude that (1) the judgment of computers in the library has a positive effect on the judgment of the library and (2) that this effect is moderated by computer possession: If a student has no computer ($X_{2i} = 0$) the *marginal* effect is 0.4; if the student has a computer ($X_{2i} = 1$) the *marginal* effect is 0.2. Thus, computer possession has a negative moderating effect.

Now do Exercises 12.3, 12.4, and 12.5

## EXERCISE 12.3

Why could it be important to differentiate between quasi moderators and pure moderators?

## EXERCISE 12.4

Is computer possession a pure moderator or a quasi moderator? Explain.

## EXERCISE 12.5

Provide a logical explanation for the negative moderating effect of computer possession.

The previous example shows that dummy variables can be used to allow the effect of one independent variable on the dependent variable to change depending on the value of the dummy variable. It is, of course, also possible to include metric variables as moderators in a model. In such cases, the procedure to test moderation is exactly the same as in the previous example.

In this section, we have explained how moderation can be tested with regression analysis. Note that it is also possible to test mediation with regression analysis. We will explain this later on in this chapter using the Excelsior Enterprises data.

# Other multivariate tests and analyses

We will now briefly describe five other multivariate techniques: discriminant analysis, logistic regression, conjoint analysis, multivariate analysis of variance (MANOVA), and canonical correlations.

How does this work in SPSS?
    Under the Analyze menu, choose Classify, then Discriminant. Move the dependent variable into the "Grouping" box. Move the independent variables into the "Independent(s)" list and click OK.

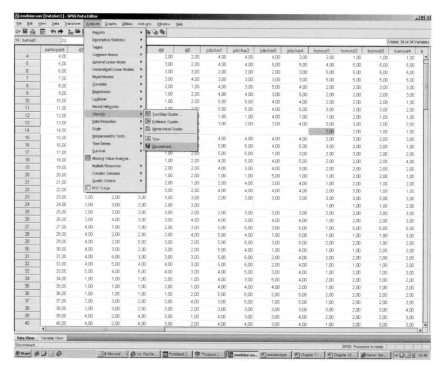

## Discriminant analysis

**Discriminant analysis** helps to identify the independent variables that discriminate a nominally scaled dependent variable of interest – say those who are high on a variable from those who are low on it. The linear combination of independent variables indicates the discriminating function showing the large difference that exists in the two group means. In other words, the independent variables measured on an interval or ratio scale discriminate the groups of interest to the study.

## Logistic regression

**Logistic regression** is also used when the dependent variable is nonmetric. However, when the dependent variable has only two groups, logistic regression is often preferred, because it does not face the strict assumptions that discriminant analysis faces and because it is very similar to regression analysis. Although regression analysis and logistic regression analysis are very different from a statistical point of view, they are very much alike from a practical viewpoint. Both methods produce prediction equations and in both cases the regression coefficients measure the predictive capability of the independent variables. Thus, logistic regression allows the researcher to predict a discrete outcome, such as "will purchase the product/will not purchase the product", from a set of variables that may be continuous, discrete, or dichotomous.

How does this work in SPSS?

Under the Analyze menu, choose Regression, then Binary Logistic. Move the dependent variable into the "Dependent" box. Move the independent variables into the "Covariate(s)" list and click OK.

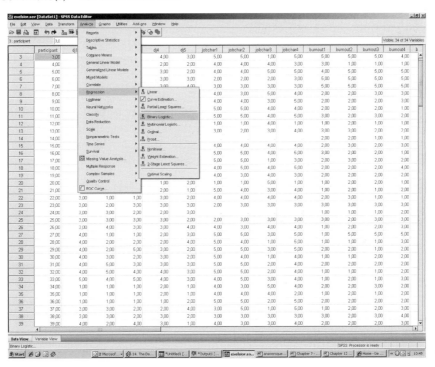

## Conjoint analysis

Conjoint analysis is a statistical technique that is used in many fields including marketing, product management, and operations research. Conjoint analysis requires participants to make a series of trade-offs. In marketing, conjoint analysis is used to understand how consumers develop preferences for products or services. Conjoint analysis is built on the idea that consumers evaluate the value of a product or service by combining the value that is provided by each attribute. An attribute is a general feature of a product or service, such as price, product quality, or delivery speed. Each attribute has specific levels. For instance, for the attribute "price", levels might be €249, €279, and €319. Along these lines, we might describe a mobile telephone using the attributes "memory", "battery life", "camera" and "price". A specific mobile phone would be described as follows: memory, 12 Mbytes; battery life, 24 hours; camera 5 megapixels; and price €249.

Conjoint analysis takes these attribute and level descriptions of products and services and uses them by asking participants to make a series of choices between different products. For instance:

*Would you choose phone X or phone Y?*

|  | **Phone X** | **Phone Y** |
|---|---|---|
| Memory | 12 Mbytes | 16 Mbytes |
| Battery life | 24 hours | 12 hours |
| Camera | 5 megapixels | 8 megapixels |
| Price | €249 | €319 |

By asking for enough choices, it is possible to establish how important each of the levels is relative to the others; this is known as the utility of the level. Conjoint analysis is traditionally carried out with some form of multiple regression analysis. More recently, the use of hierarchical Bayesian analysis has become widespread to develop models of individual consumer decision-making behavior.

## Two-way ANOVA

**Two-way ANOVA** can be used to examine the effect of two nonmetric independent variables on a single metric dependent variable. Note that, in this context, an independent variable is often referred to as a factor and this is why a design that aims to examine the effect of two nonmetric independent variables on a single metric dependent variable is often called a *factorial design*. The factorial design is very popular in the social sciences. Two-way ANOVA enables us to examine main effects (the effects of the independent variables on the dependent variable) but also interaction effects that exist between the independent variables (or factors). An interaction effect exists when the effect of one independent variable (or one factor) on the dependent variable depends on the level of the other independent variable (factor).

## MANOVA

**MANOVA** is similar to ANOVA, with the difference that ANOVA tests the mean differences of more than two groups on *one* dependent variable, whereas MANOVA tests mean differences among groups across *several* dependent variables simultaneously, by using sums of squares and cross-product matrices. Just as multiple *t*-tests would bias the results (as explained earlier), multiple ANOVA tests, using one dependent variable at a time, would also bias the results, since the dependent variables are likely to be interrelated. MANOVA circumvents this bias by simultaneously testing all the dependent variables, cancelling out the effects of any intercorrelations among them.

In MANOVA tests, the independent variable is measured on a nominal scale and the dependent variables on an interval or ratio scale.

The null hypothesis tested by MANOVA is:

$$H_0 : \mu1 = \mu2 = \mu3 \dots \mu n.$$

The alternate hypothesis is:

$$H_A : \mu1 \neq \mu2 \neq \mu3 \neq \dots \mu n.$$

## Canonical correlation

**Canonical correlation** examines the relationship between two or more dependent variables and several independent variables; for example, the correlation between a set of job behaviors (such as engrossment in work, timely completion of work, and number of absences) and their influence on a set of performance factors (such as quality of work, the output, and rate of rejects). The focus here is on delineating the job behavior profiles associated with performance that result in high-quality production.

In sum, several univariate, bivariate, and multivariate techniques are available to analyze sample data. Using these techniques allows us to generalize the results obtained from the sample to the population at large. It is, of course, very important to use the correct statistical technique to test the hypotheses of your study. We have explained earlier in this chapter that the choice of the appropriate statistical technique depends on the number of variables you are examining, on the scale of measurement of your variable(s), on whether the assumptions of parametric tests are met, and on the size of your sample.

# Excelsior Enterprises – hypothesis testing

The following hypotheses were generated for this study, as stated earlier:

$H_1$: *Job enrichment has a negative effect on intention to leave.*
$H_2$: *Perceived equity has a negative effect on intention to leave.*
$H_3$: *Burnout has a positive effect on intention to leave.*
$H_4$: *Job satisfaction mediates the relationship between job enrichment, perceived equity, and burnout on intention to leave.*

How does this work in SPSS?

Under the Analyze menu, choose General Linear Model, then Multivariate. Move the dependent variables into the "Dependent" box. Move the independent variables into the "Fixed Factor(s)" list. Select any of the dialog boxes by clicking the buttons on the right-hand side.

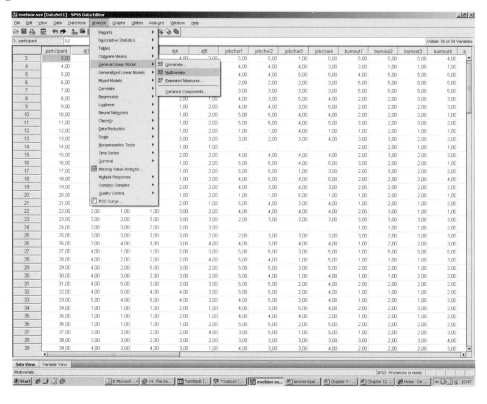

These hypotheses call for the use of mediated regression analysis (all the variables are measured at an interval level). The results of these tests and their interpretation are discussed below.

To test the hypothesis that job satisfaction mediates the effect of perceived justice, burnout, and job enrichment on employees' intentions to leave three regression models were estimated, following Baron and Kenny (1986): model 1, regressing job satisfaction on perceived justice, burnout, and job enrichment; model 2, regressing intention to leave on perceived justice, burnout, and job enrichment; and model 3, regressing employees' intentions to leave on perceived justice, burnout, job enrichment, and job satisfaction. Separate coefficients for each equation were estimated and tested. To establish mediation the following conditions must hold: perceived justice, burnout, and job enrichment must affect job satisfaction in model 1; perceived justice, burnout, and job enrichment must be shown to impact employees' intention to leave in model 2; and job satisfaction must affect employees' intention to leave in model 3 (while controlling for perceived justice, burnout, and job enrichment). If these conditions all hold in the predicted direction, then the effect of perceived justice, burnout, and job enrichment must be less in model 3 than in model 2. Perfect mediation holds if perceived justice, burnout, and job enrichment have no effect on intention to leave (in other words, the effect of these variables on intention to leave is no longer significant) when the effect of job satisfaction is controlled for (model 3); partial mediation is established if perceived justice, burnout, and job enrichment still affect intention leave in model 3. The R square of the first regression model (model 1) was ,165 and the model was statistically significant. In this model perceived justice and burnout were significant predictors of job satisfaction, whereas job enrichment was not. The R square of the second regression model (model 2) was ,393 and this model was also statistically significant. Model 2, as depicted in Table 12.5 indicated that perceived justice, burnout, and job enrichment affected employees' intention to leave. The R square of the last model (model 3) was ,487 and again the model was statistically significant. In this model, job satisfaction was a significant predictor of intention to leave. Perceived justice and burnout were significant predictors of intention to leave when job satisfaction was controlled for. The effect of perceived justice and burnout on intention to leave was less in the third model than in the second 1 model. Thus, all conditions for partial mediation were met for perceived justice and burnout. Job enrichment was related to neither job satisfaction nor to intention to leave (when job satisfaction was controlled for).

We performed follow-up analyses to test for the indirect effect of perceived justice and burnout on intention to leave via job satisfaction. Baron and Kenny (1986) provide an approximate significance test for the *indirect* effect of perceived justices and burnout on employees' intentions. The path from, respectively, perceived justice and burnout to job satisfaction is denoted $a$ and its standard error $s_a$; the path from job satisfaction to intention to leave is denoted $b$ and its standard error $s_b$. The product $ab$ is the estimate of the indirect effect of perceived justice and burnout on employees' intentions to leave. The standard error of $ab$ is:

$$SE_{ab} = \sqrt{b^2 s_a^2 + a^2 s_b^2 + s_a^2 s_b^2}$$

The ratio $ab/SE_{ab}$ can be interpreted as a $z$ statistic. Indirect effects of perceived justice (2.175, $p < 0.05$) and burnout (2.985, $p < 0.01$) were both significant.

## Overall interpretation and recommendations to the president

From the results of the hypothesis tests, it is clear that perceived justice and burnout affect employees' intentions to leave through job satisfaction. From the descriptive results, we have already seen that the mean on perceived equity is rather low (2.32 on a five-point scale), as is the mean on experienced burnout (2.55). Hence, if retention of employees is a top priority for the president, it is important to formulate policies and practices that help to enhance justice perceptions and to further reduce or prevent burnout. Whatever is done to improve employees' perceptions of justice and to either prevent or to reduce burnout will improve job satisfaction and thus help employees to think less about leaving and induce them to stay.

The president would therefore be well advised to rectify inequities in the system if they really exist, or to clear misperceptions of inequities if this is actually the case. Preventing or

**TABLE 12.5    Mediation analysis.**

*Step 1 model, with job satisfaction as the dependent variable*

|  | Coefficient | p-value |
|---|---|---|
| Constant | 3.575 | 0.000 |
| Perceived justice | 0.302 | 0.018 |
| Burnout | −0.538 | 0.000 |
| Job enrichment | 0.120 | 0.332 |

Model fit = 0.165

*Step 2 model, with intention to leave (ITL) as the dependent variable*

|  | Coefficient | p-value |
|---|---|---|
| Constant | 1.840 | 0.000 |
| Perceived justice | −0.307 | 0.000 |
| Burnout | 0.643 | 0.000 |
| Job enrichment | −0.165 | 0.039 |

Model fit = 0.393

*Step 3 model, including job satisfaction as an independent variable and with ITL as the dependent variable*

|  | Coefficient | p-value |
|---|---|---|
| Constant | 2.744 | 0.000 |
| Perceived justice | −0.231 | 0.003 |
| Burnout | 0.507 | 0.000 |
| Job enrichment | −0.134 | 0.068 |
| Job satisfaction | −0.253 | 0.000 |

Model fit = 0.487

*Note.* Parameters are unstandardized regression weights, with significance levels of *t*-values. Two-sided tests. $N = 174$.

remedying burnout may require both individual and organizational change. To solve the problem of burnout, the president may need to change the work environment and educate workers on how to adapt and cope better to the stresses of the workplace.

The fact that only 50% of the variance in "intention to leave" was explained by the four independent variables considered in this study still leaves 50% unexplained. In other words, there are other additional variables that are important in explaining ITL that have not been considered in this study. Further research might be necessary to explain more of the variance in ITL, if the president wishes to pursue the matter further.

Now do Exercises 12.6, 12.7, and 12.8

## EXERCISE 12.6

Discuss: what do the unstandardized coefficients and their *p*-values in the first model imply? In other words, what happens to job satisfaction if perceived justice, burnout, and job enrichment change by one unit?

## EXERCISE 12.7

Provide the tolerance values and the variance inflation factors for all the independent variables in model 1. Discuss: do we have a multicollinearity problem?

## EXERCISE 12.8

Does work shift moderate the relationship between job satisfaction and intention to leave for Excelsior Enterprises employees?

We have now seen how different hypotheses can be tested by applying the appropriate statistical tests in data analysis. Based on the interpretation of the results, the research report is then written, making necessary recommendations and discussing the pros and cons of each, together with cost–benefit analysis.

# Data warehousing, data mining, and operations research

Data warehousing and data mining are aspects of information systems. Most companies are now aware of the benefits of creating a **data warehouse** that serves as the central repository of all data collected from disparate sources including those pertaining to the company's finance, manufacturing, sales, and the like. The data warehouse is usually built from data collected through the different departments of the enterprise and can be accessed through various online analytical processing (OLAP) tools to support decision making. Data warehousing can be described as the process of extracting, transferring, and integrating data spread across multiple external databases and even operating systems, with a view to facilitating analysis and decision making.

Complementary to the functions of data warehousing, many companies resort to data mining as a strategic tool for reaching new levels of business intelligence. Using algorithms to analyze data in a meaningful way, **data mining** more effectively leverages the data warehouse by identifying hidden relations and patterns in the data stored in it. For instance, data mining makes it possible to trace retail sales patterns by ZIP code and the time of day of the purchases, so that optimal stocking of items becomes possible. Such "mined" data pertaining to the vital areas of the organization can be easily accessed and used for different purposes. For example, staffing for different times of the day can be planned, as can the number of check-out counters that need to be kept open in retail stores, to ensure efficiency as well as effectiveness. We can see that data mining helps to clarify the underlying patterns in different business activities, which in turn facilitates decision making.

**Operations research** (OR) or *management science* (MS) is another sophisticated tool used to simplify and thus clarify certain types of complex problem that lend themselves to quantification. OR uses higher mathematics and statistics to identify, analyze, and ultimately solve intricate problems of great complexity faced by the manager. It provides an additional tool to the manager by using quantification to supplement personal judgment. Areas of problem solving that easily lend themselves to OR include those relating to inventory, queuing, sequencing, routing, and search and replacement. OR helps to minimize costs and increase efficiency by resorting to *decision trees, linear programming, network analysis,* and *mathematical models.*

Other information systems such as *management information systems (MIS), the decision support system, the executive information system,* and *the expert system* are good decision-making aids, but not necessarily involved with data collection and analyses in the strict sense.

In sum, a good information system collects, mines, and provides a wide range of pertinent information relating to aspects of both the external and internal environments of the organization. By using the wide variety of tools and techniques available for solving problems of differing magnitude, executives, managers, and others entrusted with responsibility for results at various levels of the organization can find solutions to various concerns merely by securing access to these data available in the system and analyzing them.

It should be ensured that the data in the information system are error-free and are frequently updated. After all, decision making can only be as good as the data made available to managers.

# Some software packages useful for data analysis

There is a wide variety of analytical software that may help you to analyze your data. Based on your specific needs, your research problem, and/or conceptual model you might consider the following software packages:

- **LISREL**: from Scientific Software International;
- **MATLAB**®: from the MathWorks, Inc.;
- **SAS/STAT**: from SAS Institute;
- **SPSS**: Complex Samples. from SPSS Inc.;
- **Stata**: from Stata Corporation.

LISREL is designed to estimate and test structural equation models. Structural equation models are complex, statistical models of linear relationships among latent (unobserved) variables and manifest (observed) variables. You can also use LISREL to carry out exploratory factor analysis and confirmatory factor analysis.

MATLAB is a computer program that was originally designed to simplify the implementation of numerical linear algebra routines. It is used to implement numerical algorithms for a wide range of applications.

SAS is an integrated system of software products, capable of performing a broad range of statistical analyses such as descriptive statistics, multivariate techniques, and time series analyses. Because of its capabilities, it is used in many disciplines, including medical sciences, biological sciences, social sciences, and education.

SPSS (Statistical Package for the Social Sciences) is a data management and analysis program designed to do statistical data analysis, including descriptive statistics such as plots, frequencies, charts, and lists, as well as sophisticated inferential and multivariate statistical procedures like analysis of variance (ANOVA), factor analysis, cluster analysis, and categorical data analysis.

Stata is a general purpose statistical software package that supports various statistical and econometric methods, graphics, and enhanced features for data manipulation, programming, and matrix manipulation.

## SUMMARY

In this chapter we covered the procedure for hypothesis testing. We have discussed type I errors, type II errors, and statistical power. We have observed various statistical analyses and tests used to examine different hypotheses to answer research questions. We discussed the use of dummy variables, multicollinearity, and moderated regression analysis. Through the example of the research on Excelsior Enterprises, we observed hypothesis testing using mediated regression analysis and learned how the computer results are interpreted.

## DISCUSSION QUESTIONS

1. What kinds of biases do you think could be minimized or avoided during the data analysis stage of research?
2. When we collect data on the effects of treatment in experimental designs, which statistical test is most appropriate to test the treatment effects?
3. A tax consultant wonders whether he should be more selective about the class of clients he serves so as to maximize his income. He usually deals with four categories of clients: the very rich, rich, upper middle class, and middle class. He has records of each and every client served, the taxes paid by them, and how much he has charged them. Since many particulars in respect of the clients vary (number of dependants, business deductibles, etc.), irrespective of the category they belong to, he would like an appropriate analysis to be done to see which among the four categories of clientele he should choose to continue to serve in the future. *What kind of analysis should be done in this case and why?*

Now do Exercises 12.9 and 12.10

## EXERCISE 12.9

Open the file "resmethassignment1" (you created this file doing the exercise from the previous chapter). Answer the following questions.

a. Is the exam grade significantly larger than 75?
b. Are there significant differences in the exam grade for men and women?
c. Is there a significant difference between the exam grade and the paper grade?
d. Are there significant differences in the paper grade for the four year groups?
e. Is the sample representative for the IQ level, for which it is known that 50% of the population has an IQ below 100, and 50% has an IQ of 100 or higher?
f. Obtain a correlation matrix for all relevant variables and discuss the results.
g. Do a multiple regression analysis to explain the variance in paper grades using the independent variables of age, sex (dummy coded), and IQ, and interpret the results.

## EXERCISE 12.10

Below are Tables 12A to 12D, summarizing the results of data analyses of research conducted in a sales organization that operates in 50 different cities of the country, and employs a total sales force of about 500. The number of salespersons sampled for the study was 150.

a. Interpret the information contained in each of the tables in as much detail as possible.
b. Summarize the results for the CEO of the company.
c. Make recommendations based on your interpretation of the results.

TABLE 12 A    **Means, standard deviations, minimum, and maximum.**

| Variable | Mean | Std. deviation | Minimum | Maximum |
|---|---|---|---|---|
| Sales (in 1000s of $) | 75.1 | 8.6 | 45.2 | 97.3 |
| No. of salespersons | 25 | 6 | 5 | 50 |
| Population (in 100s) | 5.1 | 0.8 | 2.78 | 7.12 |
| Per capita income (in 1000s of $) | 20.3 | 20.1 | 10.1 | 75.9 |
| Advertisement (in 1000s of $) | 10.3 | 5.2 | 6.1 | 15.7 |

## TABLE 12 B    Correlations among the variables.

|  | Sales | Salespersons | Population | Income | Advertisement |
|---|---|---|---|---|---|
| Sales | 1.0 | | | | |
| No. of salespersons | 0.76 | 1.0 | | | |
| Population | 0.62 | 0.06 | 1.0 | | |
| Income | 0.56 | 0.21 | 0.11 | 1.0 | |
| Ad. expenditure | 0.68 | 0.16 | 0.36 | 0.23 | 1.0 |

All figures above 0.15 are significant at $p = 0.05$.
All figures above 0.35 are significant at $p \leq 0.001$.

## TABLE 12 C    Results of one-way ANOVA: sales by level of education.

| Source of variation | Sums of squares | df | Mean squares | F | Significance of F |
|---|---|---|---|---|---|
| Between groups | 50.7 | 4 | 12.7 | 3.6 | 0.01 |
| Within groups | 501.8 | 145 | 3.5 | | |
| Total | 552.5 | 150 | | | |

## TABLE 12 D    Results of regression analysis.

| | |
|---|---|
| Multiple $R$ | 0.65924 |
| $R$ square | 0.43459 |
| Adjusted $R$ square | 0.35225 |
| Standard error | 0.41173 |
| df | (5.144) |
| F | 5.278 |
| Sig | 0.000 |

*(continued)*

**TABLE 12 D    (Continued)**

| Multiple $R$ | 0.65924 | | |
|---|---|---|---|
| $R$ square | 0.43459 | | |
| Adjusted $R$ square | 0.35225 | | |
| Standard error | 0.41173 | | |
| df | (5.144) | | |
| $F$ | 5.278 | | |
| Sig | 0.000 | | |
| Variable | Beta | $t$ | Sig. $t$ |
| Training of salespersons | 0.28 | 2.768 | 0.0092 |
| No. of salespersons | 0.34 | 3.55 | 0.00001 |
| Population | 0.09 | 0.97 | 0.467 |
| Per capita income | 0.12 | 1.200 | 0.089 |
| Advertisement | 0.47 | 4.54 | 0.00001 |

# CHAPTER 13

## Qualitative data analysis

## Topics discussed

- Data reduction
- Data display
- Drawing conclusions
- Content analysis
- Reliability and validity in qualitative research

### CHAPTER OBJECTIVES

After completing Chapter 13 you should be able to:

1. Understand the general approach to qualitative data analysis.
2. Describe three important steps in qualitative data analysis: data reduction, data display, and drawing conclusions.
3. Describe how reliability and validity have a different meaning in qualitative research in comparison to quantitative research.
4. Explain how reliability and validity are achieved in qualitative research.

## Introduction

Qualitative data are data in the form of words. Examples of qualitative data are interview notes, transcripts of focus groups, answers to open-ended questions, transcriptions of video recordings, accounts of experiences with a product on the Internet, news articles, and the like.

Qualitative data can come from a wide variety of primary sources and/or secondary sources, such as individuals, focus groups, company records, government publications, and the Internet. The analysis of qualitative data is aimed at making valid inferences from the often overwhelming amount of collected data.

Earlier in this book we explained that you can search the Internet for books, journals articles, conference proceedings, company publications, and the like. However, the Internet is more than a mere source of documents; it is also a rich source of textual information for qualitative research. For instance, there are many *social networks* on the Internet structured around products and services such as computer games, mobile telephones, movies, books, and music. Through an analysis of these social networks researchers may learn a lot about the needs of consumers, about the amount of time consumers spend in group communication, or about the social network that underlies the virtual community. In this way, social networks on the Internet may provide researchers and marketing and business strategists with valuable, strategic information.

The possibilities for qualitative research on the Internet are unlimited, as the following example illustrates. In an effort to find out what motivates consumers to construct *protest websites*, Ward and Ostrom (2006) examined and analyzed protest websites. A content analysis revealed that consumers construct complaint websites to demonstrate their power, to influence others, and to gain revenge on the organization that betrayed them. This example illustrates how the Internet can be a valuable source of rich, authentic qualitative information. With increasing usage of the Internet, it will undoubtedly become even more important as a source of qualitative and quantitative information.

Qualitative research may involve repeated sampling, collection of data, and analysis of data. As a result, qualitative data analysis may start after only some of the data have been collected. The analysis of qualitative data is not easy. The problem is that, in comparison with quantitative data analysis, there are relatively few well-established and commonly accepted rules and guidelines for analyzing qualitative data. Over the years, however, some general approaches for the analysis of qualitative data have been developed. The approach discussed in this chapter is largely based on work of Miles and Huberman (1994). According to Miles and Huberman, there are generally three steps in qualitative data analysis: data reduction, data display, and the drawing of conclusions.

The first step in qualitative data analysis is concerned with data reduction. **Data reduction** refers to the process of selecting, coding, and categorizing the data. **Data display** refers to ways of presenting the data. A selection of quotes, a matrix, a graph, or a chart illustrating patterns in the data may help the researcher (and eventually the reader) to understand the data. In this way, data displays may help you to draw conclusions based on patterns in the reduced set of data.

Note that qualitative data analysis is not a step-by-step, linear process. Instead, **data coding** may help you simultaneously to develop ideas on how the data may be displayed, as well as to draw some preliminary conclusions. In turn, preliminary conclusions may feed back into the way the raw data are coded, categorized, and displayed.

This chapter will discuss data reduction, data display, and drawing and verifying conclusions in some detail. To illustrate these steps in qualitative data analysis, we will introduce a case. We will use the case, by means of boxes throughout the chapter, to illustrate key parts of the qualitative research process.

# Case: Instigations of customer anger

## Introduction
Suppose that you are in a fashion shop and that you have just found a clothing item that you like. You go to the counter to pay for the item. At the counter you find a shop assistant who is talking to a friend on the telephone. You have to wait. You wait for a couple of minutes, but the shop assistant is in no hurry to finish the phone call.

This event may make you angry. Waiting for service is a common cause of anger: the longer the delay, the angrier customers tend to be (Taylor, 1994).

## Research objective
Prior research in marketing has applied appraisal theory to understand why anger is experienced in such situations (e.g., Folkes *et al.*, 1987; Nyer, 1997; Taylor, 1994). Appraisal refers to the process of judging the significance of an event for personal well-being. The basic premise of appraisal theory is that emotions are related to the interpretations that people have about events: people may differ in the specific appraisals that are elicited by a particular event (for instance waiting for service), but the same patterns of appraisal give rise to the same emotions. Most appraisal theories see appraisals as being a cause of emotions (Parrott, 2001). Along these lines, appraisal theory has been used to understand why anger is experienced in service settings.

Although appraisal theory provides useful insights into the role of cognition in emotional service encounters, recent research suggests that, although they are clearly associated with anger, none of the aforementioned appraisals is a necessary or sufficient condition for anger to arise (Kuppens *et al.*, 2003; Smith and Ellsworth, 1987). What's more, for the specific purpose of avoiding customer anger, appraisal theory is too abstract to be diagnostic for services management. That is, service firm management may benefit more from a classification of incidents that are considered to be unfair (for instance, waiting for service and core service failures), than from the finding that unfair events are generally associated with customer anger.

In other words, in order to be able to avoid customer anger, it is crucial that service firm management knows what specific precipitating events typically elicit this emotion in customers. After all, it is easier to manage such events than the appraisals that may or may not be associated with these particular events.

Therefore, this study investigates events that typically instigate customer anger in services. This study builds on a rich tradition of research in psychology that has specified typical instigations of anger in everyday life. In addition, it builds on research in marketing that has identified and classified service failures, retail failures, and behaviors of service firms that cause customers to switch services (Bitner, Booms and Tetreault, 1990; Keaveney, 1995; Kelley, Hoffman and Davis, 1993).

## Method
*Procedure.* Following related research in marketing, the critical incident technique (CIT) was used to identify critical behaviors of service providers that instigate customer anger (e.g., Bitner, Booms and Tetreault, 1990; Keaveney, 1995; Kelley, Hoffman and Davis,

1993; Mangold, Miller and Brockway, 1999). Critical incidents were collected by 30 trained research assistants, who were instructed to collect 30 critical incidents each. In order to obtain a sample representative of customers of service organizations, they were instructed to collect data from a wide variety of people. Participants were asked to record their critical incidents on a standardized form in the presence of the interviewer. This has several advantages such as availability of the interviewer to answer questions and to provide explanations.

*Questionnaire.* Participants were asked to record their answers on a standardized questionnaire, which was modeled after previous applications of CIT in services (e.g., Keaveney, 1995; Kelley, Hoffman and Davis, 1993). The questionnaire began by asking participants to indicate which of 30 different services they had purchased during the previous six-month period. Next, participants were asked to recall the last negative incident with a service provider that made them feel angry. They were asked to describe the incident in detail by means of open-ended questions. The open-ended questions were "What service are you thinking about?", "Please tell us, in your own words, what happened. Why did you get angry?" and "Try to tell us exactly what happened: where you were, what happened, what the service provider did, how you felt, what you said, and so forth."

*Sample.* Critical incidents were defined as events, combinations of events, or series of events between a customer and a service provider that caused customer anger. The interviewers collected 859 incidents. The participants (452 males, 407 females) represented a cross-section of the population. Their ages ranged between 16 and 87 with a mean age of 37.4. Approximately 2% of the participants had less than a completed high school education, whereas 45.1% had at least a bachelor's degree. The reported incidents covered more than 40 different service businesses, including banking and insurance, personal transportation (by airplane, bus, ferry, taxi, or train), hospitals, physicians, and dentists, repair and utility services, (local) government and the police, (virtual) stores, education and child care, entertainment, hospitality, restaurants, telecommunication companies, health clubs, contracting firms, hairdressers, real-estate agents, driving schools, rental companies, and travel agencies. On average, the negative events that participants reported had happened 18 weeks earlier.

# Data reduction

Qualitative data collection produces large amounts of data. The first step in data analysis is therefore the reduction of data through coding and categorization. **Coding** is the analytic process through which the qualitative data that you have gathered are reduced, rearranged, and integrated to form theory. The purpose of coding is to help you to draw meaningful conclusions about the data. *Codes* are labels given to units of text which are later grouped and turned into categories. Coding is often an iterative process; you may have to return to your data repeatedly to increase your understanding of the data (that is, to be able to recognize patterns in the data, to discover connections between the data, and to organize the data into coherent categories).

Coding begins with selecting the coding unit. Indeed, qualitative data can be analyzed at many levels. Examples of coding units include words, sentences, paragraphs, and themes. The smallest unit that is generally used is the word. A larger, and often more useful, unit of content analysis is the theme: "a single assertion about a subject" (Kassarjian, 1977, p. 12). When you are using the theme as a coding unit, you are primarily looking for the expression of an idea (Minichiello *et al.*, 1990). Thus, you might assign a code to a text unit of any size, as long as that unit of text represents a single theme or issue. Consider, for instance, the following critical incident:

"After the meal I asked for the check. The waitress nodded and I expected to get the check. After three cigarettes there was still no check. I looked around and saw that the waitress was having a lively conversation with the bartender."

This critical incident contains two themes:

1. The waitress does not provide service at the time she promises to: "The waitress nodded and I expected to get the check. After three cigarettes there was still no check."
2. The waitress pays little attention to the customer: She is not late because she is very busy; instead of bringing the check, she is engaged in a lively conversation with the bartender.

Accordingly, the aforementioned critical incident was coded as: "delivery promises" (that were broken) and "personal attention" (that was not provided).

This example illustrates how the codes "delivery promises" and "personal attention" help to reduce the data to a more manageable amount. Note that proper coding not only involves reducing the data but also making sure that no relevant data are eliminated. Hence, it is important that the codes "delivery promises" and "personal attention" capture the meaning of the coded unit of text.

## Data analysis

**Unit of analysis.** Since the term "critical incident" can refer to either the overall story of a participant or to discrete behaviors contained within this story, the first step in data analysis is to determine the appropriate unit of analysis (Kassarjian, 1977). In this study, *critical behavior* was chosen as the unit of analysis. For this reason, 600 critical incidents were coded into 886 critical behaviors. For instance, a critical incident in which a service provider does not provide prompt service and treats a customer in a rude manner was coded as containing two critical behaviors ("unresponsiveness" and "insulting behavior").

**Categorization** is the process of organizing, arranging, and classifying coding units. Codes and categories can be developed both inductively and deductively. In situations where there is no theory available, you must generate codes and categories inductively from the data. In its extreme form, this is what has been called **grounded theory**.

Grounded theory is a systematic set of procedures to develop an inductively derived theory from the data (Strauss and Corbin, 1990). Important tools in grounded theory are theoretical sampling, coding, and constant comparison. Theoretical sampling is "the process of data collection for generating theory whereby the analyst jointly collects, codes, and analyzes the data and decides what data to collect next and where to find them, in order to develop his theory as it emerges" (Glaser and Strauss, 1967, p. 45). In constant comparison you compare data (for instance an interview) to other data (for instance another interview). After a theory has emerged from this process you compare new data to your theory. If there is a bad fit between data (interviews), or between the data and your theory, then the categories and theories have to be modified until your categories and your theory fit the data. In constant comparison, discrepant and disconfirming cases play an important role in rendering categories and (grounded) theory.

In many situations, however, you will have a preliminary theory on which you can base your codes and categories. In these situations you can construct an initial list of codes and categories from the theory, and, if necessary, change or refine these during the research process as new codes and categories emerge inductively (Miles and Huberman, 1994). The benefit of the adoption of existing codes and categories is that you are able to build on and/or expand prevailing knowledge.

## Data analysis

**Categorization**. Qualitative data analysis was used to examine the data (Kassarjian, 1977). As a first step, two judges coded critical incidents into critical behaviors. Next, (sub)categories were developed based upon these critical behaviors. Two judges (A and B) independently developed mutually exclusive and exhaustive categories and subcategories for responses 1 to 400 (587 critical behaviors). Two other trained judges (C and D), independently sorted the critical behaviors into the categories provided by judges A and B. Finally, a fifth, independent judge (E) carried out a final sort.

As you begin to organize your data into categories and subcategories you will begin to notice patterns and relationships between the data. Note that your list of categories and subcategories may change during the process of analyzing the data. For instance, new categories may have to be identified, definitions of categories may have to be changed, and categories may have to be broken into subcategories. This is all part of the iterative process of qualitative data analysis.

## Results

*Categories.* Participants reported a wide range of critical behaviors that made them angry. Some of these behaviors were closely related to the *outcome* of the service process (e.g., "My suitcase was heavily damaged"). Other behaviors were related to *service delivery* (e.g., "For three days in a row I tried to make an appointment ( . . . ) via the telephone. The line was always busy.") or *interpersonal relationships* (e.g., "She did not stir a finger. She was definitely not intending to help me."). Finally, customers got angry because of *inadequate responses to service failures* (e.g., "He did not even apologize." or "He refused to give me back my money."). These four specific behavior types represent the four overarching categories of events that instigate customer anger.

Two of these categories were further separated into, respectively, three categories representing service delivery or procedural failures ("unreliability", "inaccessibility", and "company policies") and two categories representing interpersonal relationships or interactional failures ("insensitive behavior" and "impolite behavior"). The main reason for this was that the categories "procedural failures" and "interactional failures" would otherwise be too heterogeneous with respect to their composition and, more importantly, with respect to ways of avoiding or dealing with these failures. For instance, avoiding anger in response to unreliability (not performing in accordance with agreements) will most likely call for a different – and maybe even opposite – approach than avoiding anger in response to company policies (performing in accordance with company rules and procedures), even though these failures are both procedural; that is, related to service delivery.

Sometimes you may want to capture the number of times a particular theme or event occurs, or how many respondents bring up certain themes or events. Quantification of your qualitative data may provide you with a rough idea about the (relative) importance of the categories and subcategories.

Table 13.1 indicates that "price agreements that were broken" (category "unreliability", subcategory "pricing") was mentioned 12 times as a cause of anger. Hence, broken price agreements represent 1.35% of the total number of critical behaviors (886) and 2% of the total number of the reported critical incidents (600). The sixth column indicates that nine participants mentioned broken price agreements as the sole cause of their anger, whereas three participants mentioned at least one additional critical behavior (column 7).

**TABLE 13.1  Instigations of anger in service consumption settings.**

| (Sub)category | (Sub)category definition | No. of behaviors | No. of behaviors in % of behaviors | No. of behaviors in % of incidents | No. of behaviors in single-factor incidents | No. of behaviors in multi-factor Incidents | Example(s) |
|---|---|---|---|---|---|---|---|
| **Procedural failures** | | | | | | | |
| *Unreliability* | *Service firm does not perform the service dependably.* | 156 | 17.61 | 26.00 | 73 | 83 | |
| Delivery promises | Service provider does not provide services at the time it promises to do so. | 104 | 11.74 | 17.33 | 42 | 62 | Wait for appointment with dentist, physician, or hairdresser, or on a plane, train, or taxi |
| Service provision | Service provider does not provide the service that was agreed upon. | 40 | 4.52 | 6.67 | 22 | 18 | Client receives different car than agreed upon with car rental company or different apartment than agreed upon with travel agent. Bicycle repairers, car mechanics, or building contractors carry out different work than agreed upon or work that was not agreed upon with their clients. |
| Pricing | Price agreements are broken. | 12 | 1.35 | 2.00 | 9 | 3 | "After a party we called a cab. We were with a party of five. A van would take us home for a fixed, low price. However, upon arrival, the driver asked the regular clock price." |
| *Inaccessibility* | *Customers experience difficulties with engaging in the service process.* | 47 | 5.30 | 7.83 | 17 | 30 | |
| Communicative inaccessibility | Inaccessibility via telephone, fax, e-mail and/or the Internet. | 26 | 2.93 | 4.33 | 9 | 17 | "For three days in a row I tried to make an appointment with my physician via the telephone. The line was always busy." |

| | | | | | | | |
|---|---|---|---|---|---|---|---|
| Physical inaccessibility of service elements | Customers experience difficulties with accessing a certain element or part of the service. | 12 | 1.35 | 2.00 | 4 | 8 | "Check-in counter of an airline company, cash-point of a supermarket, service desk of a holiday resort, or baggage claim at an airport." |
| Physical inaccessibility of service provider | Difficult physical accessibility of service provider because of inconvenient locations or opening hours. | 9 | 1.02 | 1.50 | 4 | 5 | "It was three o'clock on a Saturday afternoon and the dry cleaner was already closed" |
| *Company policies* | *Service provider's rules and procedures or the execution of rules and procedures by service staff is perceived to be unfair.* | 76 | 8.57 | 12.67 | 45 | 31 | |
| Rules and procedures | Inefficient, ill-timed, and unclear rules and procedures | 66 | 7.45 | 11.00 | 38 | 28 | "It turned out that the [Cystic Fibrosis] foundation used unfair procedures for assigning families with cystic fibrosis to vacations. For example, some families were invited for years in a row even though this is not allowed." "Only two days before our wedding my wife was ordered to leave the country by the immigration office" "I went to the local administration to report a change of address. At the same time I wanted to apply for a parking license. In that case you must draw a number for the change of address first and later on you must draw a second number for the parking license. I got angry and asked why on earth that was necessary." |
| Inflexible service staff | Service staff does not adapt rules and procedures to reflect individual circumstances of customer | 10 | 1.12 | 1.67 | 7 | 3 | "It was an exceptionally hot day. The second-class compartments of the train were overcrowded. To avoid the bad atmosphere I went to a first-class compartment. When the guard came he sent us away. At that moment I flew into a rage." |

*(continued)*

**TABLE 13.1    (Continued)**

| (Sub)category | (Sub)category definition | No. of behaviors | No. of behaviors in % of behaviors | No. of behaviors in % of incidents | No. of behaviors in single-factor incidents | No. of behaviors in multi-factor Incidents | Example(s) |
|---|---|---|---|---|---|---|---|
| Interactional failures | | | | | | | |
| *Impolite behavior* | *Service provider behaves rudely.* | 84 | 9.48 | 14.00 | 46 | 38 | |
| Insulting behavior | Service provider is behaving offensively. | 32 | 3.61 | 5.33 | 15 | 17 | "The physician was getting fluid out of my knee. This was rather painful, so I told him that it hurt. He directly stopped even though there was some fluid left. When I asked him why he had stopped he said 'because you are such a moaner'. That's no way to treat people." |
| Not taking client seriously | Service provider does not take client seriously. | 28 | 3.16 | 4.67 | 15 | 13 | "For some time I was hearing strange noises when I was driving my car. Again and again they [garage] fobbed me off with 'Yes, dear . . .' and 'Yes, love . . .' Eventually they had to replace the engine." |
| Dishonesty | Service provider tries to earn money in an improper manner. | 16 | 1.81 | 2.67 | 10 | 6 | "After we went to the theater, we took a cab. The driver made a huge detour. I was mad because this was a plain rip-off." |
| Discrimination | Person or group is treated unfairly, usually because of prejudice about race, ethnic group, age group, or gender. | 8 | 0.90 | 1.33 | 6 | 2 | "I was refused access to the bar because of my race, even though I was immaculately dressed. They literally told me that they did not care for my kind of people." |
| *Insensitive behavior* | *Service provider does not make an effort to appreciate the customer's needs and/or pays little attention to customers or their belongings.* | 195 | 22.01 | 32.50 | 76 | 119 | |

| | | | | | | | |
|---|---|---|---|---|---|---|---|
| Unresponsiveness | Unresponsive staff does not provide prompt service to customers or does not respond to customers' requests at all | 80 | 9.03 | 33 | 13.33 | 47 | "I went to a cash desk [of a drugstore] but the salesperson walked away. At another cash desk two persons were helping one client. One of them looked at me but did not show any intention to help me. It took forever before I was finally served." "I asked a girl to help me find the right size [clothes] for my grandson. She did not stir a finger. She was definitely not intending to help me." |
| Incomplete/ incorrect information | Service provider withholds information from client or provides incomplete, imprecise, or incorrect information | 61 | 6.88 | 21 | 10.17 | 40 | "Our plane was not there. I got mad because they did not tell us why not or what to do." |
| Inaccuracy with personal data | Service provider handles personal information of client rather carelessly. | 16 | 1.81 | 5 | 2.67 | 11 | "I was looking for a summer job and signed up at an employment agency. When I asked them about the state of affairs a couple of weeks later, I found out that I had not been signed up yet. They told me that they had lost my application form." |
| Personal attention | Service provider pays little attention to the customer. | 15 | 1.69 | 8 | 2.50 | 7 | "After the meal I asked for the check. The waitress nodded and I expected to get the check. After three cigarettes there was still no check. I looked around and saw that the waitress was having a lively conversation with the bartender." |
| Impersonal treatment | Service provider does not provide tailor-made solutions. | 9 | 1.02 | 3 | 1.50 | 6 | "I got angry because she [hairdresser] did not cut my hair the way I had asked her to . . ." "The mortgage counsellor was very dominant during the conversation. My own point of view was not sufficiently addressed." |

(continued)

**TABLE 13.1  (Continued)**

| (Sub)category | (Sub)category definition | No. of behaviors | No. of behaviors in % of behaviors | No. of behaviors in % of incidents | No. of behaviors in single-factor incidents | No. of behaviors in multi-factor Incidents | Example(s) |
|---|---|---|---|---|---|---|---|
| Inconvenience | Customer ends up in inconvenient or uncomfortable situation, often leading to physical distress. | 8 | 0.90 | 1.33 | 2 | 6 | "After landing [airplane], we had to stay in our seats for 1.5 hours. It was very uncomfortable". |
| Privacy matters | Service provider invades or disregards a person's privacy | 3 | 0.34 | 0.50 | 2 | 1 | "The welfare worker left the door open during our private conversation." |
| Irresponsible behavior | Service staff behaves irresponsibly | 3 | 0.34 | 0.50 | 2 | 1 | "The schoolteacher let my very young children walk to their homes on their own when I was a little late to pick them up." |
| *Outcome failures* | *Quality of core service itself* | *191* | *21.56* | *31.84* | *76* | *115* | |
| Service mistakes | Small or big mistakes, which may cause damage to the customer or belongings of the customer. | 115 | 12.98 | 18.50 | 47 | 68 | "The waitress brought the wrong meal." "The physician prescribed the wrong medicine." "As a consequence of the operation I will not be able to ever walk again." "My suitcase was heavily damaged." |
| Defective tangibles | Inoperative, broken, badly prepared, or unsatisfactory tangibles. | 35 | 3.95 | 5.83 | 6 | 29 | "My cash card was not working." "After three weeks the coffee machine [bought in shop] broke down." "The food was cold." "We booked a very expensive holiday. However, the hotel was an old, dirty, run-down slum, with holes |

| Category | Description | | | | | | Example quote |
|---|---|---|---|---|---|---|---|
| Billing errors | Customers are mischarged for services. | 25 | 2.82 | 4.17 | 10 | 15 | "in the carpeting. The swimming pool was unpainted and 95 centimeters deep. The dining-room looked like a stable." |
| High prices | Service provider's prices are considered to be too high relative to an internal reference price or relative to prices of competitors | 16 | 1.81 | 2.67 | 13 | 3 | "I ordered two drinks at the bar. I had to pay 12. That is really an absurd price!"<br><br>"The price of the DVD-player was 1250. At another store it was only 900." |
| *Inadequate responses to service failures* | | 137 | 15.46 | 22.83 | 10 | 127 | |
| Interactional unfairness | Service employees' interpersonal behavior during the service recovery. | 80 | 9.03 | 13.33 | 4 | 76 | "He [waiter] did not even apologize" |
| Outcome unfairness | The outcome of the service recovery. | 37 | 4.17 | 6.17 | 5 | 32 | "I did not receive the newspaper. I called them on the phone and they promised that I would receive the newspaper that same day. Nothing happened."<br><br>"He [hairdresser] refused to give me back my money." |
| Procedural unfairness | The perceived fairness of the service recovery process. | 20 | 2.26 | 3.33 | 1 | 19 | "Recently I bought a house. After moving in I noticed that the bathroom tap was defective. The contractor admitted that it was the firm's responsibility. However, it took forever before they took action. Only after the chief executive of the company intervened did they cover the expenses." |

# Data display

According to Miles and Huberman (1994) data display is the second major activity which you should go through when analyzing your qualitative data. **Data display** involves taking your reduced data and displaying them in an organized, condensed manner. Along these lines, charts, matrices, diagrams, graphs, frequently mentioned phrases, and/or drawings may help you to organize the data and to discover patterns and relationships in the data so that the drawing of conclusions is eventually facilitated.

In our example, a matrix was considered to be the appropriate display to bring together the qualitative data. The selected data display technique may depend on researcher preference, the type of data set, and the purpose of the display. A matrix is, by and large, descriptive in nature, as the aforementioned example illustrates. Other displays, such as networks or diagrams, allow you to present causal relationships between concepts in your data.

In our study into events that typically elicit customer anger in service consumption settings, we developed a matrix to organize and arrange the qualitative data. This allowed us to extract higher order themes from the data: we were able to combine the 28 subcategories into seven categories and four "super-categories". The seven categories were "unreliability", "inaccessibility", and "company policies" (procedural failures), "insensitive behaviour" and "impolite behaviour" (interactional failures), "outcome failures", and "inadequate responses to service failures". These categories and subcategories are defined in the second column of Table 13.1. The eighth column provides typical examples of critical behavior per subcategory.

Table 13.1 illustrates how data display organizes qualitative information in a way that helps you to draw conclusions. Categories and corresponding subcategories of events that typically instigate anger are presented in column 1 and defined in column 2. Column 3 provides information on how many times specific themes were mentioned by the participants. Column 4 provides information about how many times a specific theme was mentioned as a percentage of the total number of themes (885). Column 5 contains the percentage of participants that mentioned a specific category or subcategory. Columns 6 and 7 provide an overview of the distribution of incidents over one- or multi-factor incidents. Column 8 provides (verbatim) examples of critical behaviors, attitudes, and manners of service providers.

# Drawing conclusions

Conclusion drawing is the "final" analytical activity in the process of qualitative data analysis. It is the essence of data analysis; it is at this point where you answer your research questions by determining what identified themes stand for, by thinking about explanations for observed patterns and relationships, or by making contrasts and comparisons.

## Discussion

The identification of precipitating events of anger is critical to understanding this emotion. What's more, for service firm management, it is important to understand what critical behaviors from their side typically elicit anger in customers. For this reason, this exploratory study investigated precipitating events of customer anger in services.

The results of this study provide an adequate, unambiguous representation of precipitating events of customer anger and expand existing (appraisal) theories of antecedents of customer anger. Specifically, seven event categories were found to instigate anger, including unreliability, inaccessibility, and company policies (the procedural failures), insensitive behavior and impolite behavior (the interactional failures), outcome failures, and inadequate responses to service failures. Each of these events was found to be a sufficient cause of customer anger. However, the compound incidents that were reported by the participants in this study suggest that critical behaviors of service providers may also interact in their effects on customer anger.

The foregoing findings imply certain extensions to service marketing research. Researchers have previously examined the effects of core service failures and waiting for service on anger. However, this study shows that the antecedents of anger are not limited to these two factors. For service firm management, the seven categories suggest areas in which managers might take action to prevent customer anger. For example, the finding that inaccessibility of services causes customers to get angry suggests that service providers may benefit from being easily accessible for consumers. The finding that customer anger may be caused by insensitivity and impoliteness of service staff implies that hiring the right people, adequate training of service employees, and finding ways to motivate service staff to adequately perform services also reduces customer anger.

The present results partly converge with prior studies that have categorized dis-satisfying experiences with service firm employees (Bitner, Booms and Tetreault, 1990) and retail failures (Kelley, Hoffman and Davis, 1993). Besides these similarities, there are important differences with the aforementioned studies as well. For instance, incidents reported by the participants of this study include difficulties with engaging in the service process and unfair rules and procedures (company policies). These behaviors, which account for more than 20% of the reported anger-provoking incidents, did not come forward as unfavorable behaviors of service providers in earlier research. This shows how the classification scheme developed here builds on and extends earlier models of service and retail failures.

# Reliability and validity in qualitative research

It is important that the conclusions that you have drawn are verified in one way or another. That is, you must make sure that the conclusions that you derive from your qualitative data are plausible, reliable, and valid.

Reliability and validity have a slightly different meaning in qualitative research in comparison to quantitative research. Reliability in qualitative data analysis includes category and interjudge reliability. **Category reliability** "depends on the analyst's ability to formulate categories and present to competent judges definitions of the categories so they will agree on which items of a certain population belong in a category and which do not" (Kassarjian, 1977, p. 14). Thus, category reliability relates to the extent to which judges are able to use category definitions to classify the qualitative data. Well-defined categories will lead to higher category reliability and eventually to higher interjudge reliability (Kassarjian, 1977), discussed next. However, categories that are defined in a very broad manner will also lead to higher category reliability. This can lead to the oversimplification of categories, which reduces the relevance of the research findings. For instance, McKellar (1949) in an attempt to classify instigations of anger distinguished between *need situations* and *personality instigations*. Need situations were defined as "any interference with the pursuit of a personal goal", such as missing a bus. Personality situations included the imposition of physical or mental pain or the violation of personal values, status, and possession. This classification, which focuses on whether an anger-provoking event can be classified as a personality situation or a need situation, will undoubtedly lead to high category and interjudge reliability, but it seems to be too broad to be relevant to service firm management trying to avoid customer anger. Therefore, Kassarjian (1977) suggests that the researcher must find a balance between category reliability and the relevance of categories. **Interjudge reliability** can be defined as a degree of consistency between coders processing the same data (Kassarjian, 1977). A commonly used measure of interjudge reliability is the percentage of coding agreements out of the total number of coding decisions. As a general guideline, agreement rates at or above 80% are considered to be satisfactory.

Earlier in this book, **validity** was defined as the extent to which an instrument measures what it purports to measure. In this context, however, validity has a different meaning. It refers to the extent to which the research results (1) accurately represent the collected data (internal validity) and (2) can be generalized or transferred to other contexts or settings (external validity). Two methods that have been developed to achieve validity in qualitative research are:

- Supporting generalizations by counts of events. This can address common concerns about the reporting of qualitative data: that anecdotes supporting the researcher's theory have been selected, or that too much attention has been paid to a small number of events, at the expense of more common ones.
- Ensuring representativeness of cases and the inclusion of deviant cases (cases that may contradict your theory). The selection of deviant cases provides a strong test of your theory.

Triangulation is a technique that is also often associated with reliability and validity in qualitative research. The idea behind triangulation is that one can be more confident in a result if the use of different methods or sources leads to the same results. Triangulation requires that research is addressed from multiple perspectives. Several kinds of triangulation are possible:

- Method triangulation: using multiple methods of data collection and analysis.
- Data triangulation: collecting data from several sources and/or at different time periods.
- Researcher triangulation: multiple researchers collect and/or analyze the data.
- Theory triangulation: multiple theories and/or perspectives are used to interpret and explain the data.

You can also enhance the validity of your research by providing an in-depth description of the research project. Anyone who wishes to transfer the results to another context is then responsible for judging how valid such a transfer is.

## Reliability and validity

A rigorous classification system should be "intersubjectively unambiguous" (Hunt, 1983), as measured by interjudge reliability. The interjudge reliability averaged 0.84, and no individual coefficients were lower than 0.80. The content validity of a critical incident classification scheme is regarded as satisfactory if themes in the confirmation sample are fully represented by the categories and subcategories developed in the classification sample. In order to determine whether the sample size was appropriate, two confirmation samples (hold-out samples from the original 859 samples) of 100 new incidents (299 critical behaviors) were sorted into the classification scheme with an eye to developing new categories. No new categories emerged, indicating that the set of analyzed critical incidents forms an adequate representation of the precipitating events of anger in services.

# Some other methods of gathering and analyzing qualitative data

## Content analysis

**Content analysis** is an observational research method that is used to systematically evaluate the symbolic contents of all forms of recorded communications (Kolbe and Burnett, 1991).

Content analysis can be used to analyze newspapers, websites, advertisements, recordings of interviews, and the like. The method of content analysis enables the researcher to analyze (large amounts of) textual information and systematically identify its properties, such as the presence of certain words, concepts, characters, themes, or sentences. To conduct a content analysis on a text, the text is coded into categories and then analyzed using conceptual analysis or relational analysis.

**Conceptual analysis** establishes the existence and frequency of concepts (such as words, themes, or characters) in a text. Conceptual analysis analyzes and interprets text by coding the text into manageable content categories. **Relational analysis** builds on conceptual analysis by examining the relationships among concepts in a text.

The results of conceptual or relational analysis are used to make inferences about the messages within the text, the effects of environmental variables on message content, the effects of messages on the receiver, and so on. Along these lines, content analysis has been used to analyze press coverage of election campaigns, to assess the effects of the content of advertisements on consumer behavior, and to provide a systematic overview of tools that online media use to encourage interactive communication processes.

## Narrative analysis

A narrative is a story or ''an account involving the narration of a series of events in a plotted sequence which unfolds in time'' (Denzin, 2000). **Narrative analysis** is an approach that aims to elicit and scrutinize the stories we tell about ourselves and their implications for our lives. Narrative data are often collected via interviews. These interviews are designed to encourage the participant to describe a certain incident in the context of his or her life history. In this way, narrative analysis differs from other qualitative research methods; it is focused on a process or temporal order, for instance by eliciting information about the antecedents and consequences of a certain incident in order to relate this incident to other incidents. Narrative analysis has thus been used to study impulsive buying (Rook, 1987), customers' responses to advertisements (Mick and Buhl, 1992), and relationships between service providers and consumers (Stern, Thomson and Arnould, 1998).

## SUMMARY

The analysis of qualitative data is aimed at making valid inferences from data in the form of words. There are relatively few well-established and commonly accepted rules and guidelines for analyzing qualitative data. Over the years, however, some general approaches for the analysis of qualitative data have been developed. In this chapter we have briefly discussed the approach of Miles and Huberman (1999). We have explained that during the first step in qualitative data analysis data are reduced, rearranged, and integrated to form theory through coding and categorization. The second major activity, data display, helps you to present the data and eventually to draw conclusions from the data (step three). These conclusions should be verified; that is, you must assess the reliability and validity of your findings.

## DISCUSSION QUESTIONS

1. What is qualitative data? How do qualitative data differ from quantitative data?
2. Describe the main steps in qualitative data analysis.
3. Define reliability and validity in the context of qualitative research.
4. How can you assess the reliability and validity of qualitative research?
5. What is grounded theory?
6. How does narrative analysis differ from content analysis?

# CHAPTER 14

## The research report

## Topics discussed

- The written report
  - Purpose
  - Different types of reports
  - Audience
  - Characteristics of a good report
- Contents of the research report
  - Title of the report
  - Table of contents
  - Copy of authorization letter
  - Executive summary or synopsis
  - The introductory section
  - Method section
  - Results section
  - Discussion section
  - Recommendations and implementation
  - Summary
  - Acknowledgments
  - References
  - Appendix
- Oral presentation
  - Content
  - Visual aids
  - Presentation
  - Handling questions

## CHAPTER OBJECTIVES

After completing Chapter 14 you should:

1. Know what the contents of a research report are.
2. Be able to tailor the report format to meet the needs of different types of research (basic and applied), different research goals that need reports of varying lengths, and different audiences.
3. Be able to write a good:
   *Executive summary or synopsis*
   *Introductory section*
   *Methods section*
   *Data analysis section*
   *Interpretation of the results* (using tables and pictorial representations, wherever appropriate.)
4. Give your recommendations and suggestions for implementation, as necessary.
5. Write the summary and acknowledgment.
6. Provide the appropriate references.
7. Include appropriate materials in the appendix
8. Critique research reports and published studies.
9. Know the components of, and be able to make, a good oral presentation.

# The report

It is important that the results of the study and the recommendations for solving the problem are effectively communicated to the sponsor, so that the suggestions made are accepted and implemented. Otherwise, all the effort hitherto expended on the investigation would have been in vain. Writing the report concisely, convincingly, and with clarity is perhaps as important, if not more so, than conducting a perfect research study. Hence, a well-thought-out written report and oral presentation are critical.

The contents and organization of both modes of communication – the written report and the oral presentation – depend on the purpose of the research study, and the audience to which it is targeted. The relevant aspects of the written report and oral presentation are discussed in this chapter.

# The written report

The written report enables the manager to weigh the facts and arguments presented therein, and implement the acceptable recommendations, with a view to closing the gap between the existing state of affairs and the desired state. To achieve its goal, the written report has to focus on the issues discussed below.

## The purpose of the written report

Reports can have different purposes and hence the form of the written report will vary according to the situation. It is important to identify the purpose of the report, so that it can be tailored accordingly. If the purpose is simply to offer details on some specific areas of interest requested by a manager, the report can be very narrowly focused and provide the desired information to the manager in a brief format, as in the example below. If, on the other hand, the report is intended to "sell an idea" to management, then it has to be more detailed and convincing as to how the proposed idea is an improvement and why it should be adopted. Here the emphasis would be directed on presenting all the relevant information backed by the necessary data, to persuade the reader to "buy into the idea." An example of the purpose of such a report and its contents can be seen in the second example. A different form of report will be prescribed in some cases, where a manager asks for several alternative solutions or recommendations to rectify a problem in a given situation. Here the researcher provides the requested information and the manager chooses from among the alternatives and makes the final decision. In this case, a more detailed report surveying past studies, the methodology used for the present study, different perspectives generated from interviews and current data analyses, and alternative solutions based on the conclusions drawn therefrom will have to be provided. How each alternative helps to improve the problem situation will also have to be discussed. The advantage and disadvantages of each of the proposed solutions, together with a cost–benefit analysis in terms of dollars and/or other resources, will also have to be presented to help the manager make the decision. A situation like that in the third example would warrant this kind of a report. Such a report can also be found in Report 3 of the appendix to this chapter.

Yet another type of report might require the researcher to identify the problem and provide the final solution as well. That is, the researcher might be called in to study a situation, determine the nature of the problem, and offer a report of the findings and recommendations. Such a report has to be very comprehensive, following the format of a full-fledged study, as detailed later in this chapter. A fifth kind of research report is the very scholarly publication presenting the findings of a basic study that one usually finds published in academic journals.

## EXAMPLE

### A simple descriptive report

If a study is undertaken to understand, in detail, certain factors of interest in a given situation (variations in production levels, composition of employees, and the like), then a report describing the phenomena of interest, in the manner desired, is all that is called for.

For instance, let us say a human resources manager wants to know how many employees have been recruited during the past 18 months in the organization, their gender composition, educational level, and the average proportion of days that these individuals have absented themselves since recruitment. A simple report giving the desired information would suffice.

In this report, a statement of the purpose of the study will be first given (e.g., it was desired that a profile of the employees recruited during the past 18 months in the company, and an idea of their rate of absenteeism be provided. This report offers those details). The methods or procedures adopted to collect the data will then be given (e.g., the payroll of the company and the personal files of the employees were examined). Finally, a narration of the actual results, reinforced by visual tabular and graphical forms of representation of the data, will be provided. Frequency distributions, cross-tabulations, and other data will be presented in a tabular form, and illustrations will include bar charts (for gender), pie charts (to indicate the proportions of individuals at various educational levels), and so on. This section will summarize the data and may look as follows:

A total of 27 employees were recruited during the past 18 months, of whom 45% are women and 55% are men. Twenty percent have a masters degree, 68% a bachelor's degree, and 12% a high school diploma. The average proportion of days that these employees remained absent during the past 18 months is six.

These details provide the information required by the manager. It may, however, be a good idea to provide a further gender-wise breakdown of the mean proportion of days of absence of the employees in an appendix, even though this information might not have been specifically requested. If considered relevant, a similar breakdown can also be furnished for people at different job levels.

A short simple report of the type discussed above is provided in Report 1 in the appendix to this chapter.

## EXAMPLE

### Details of a report to "sell" an idea

The objective of a report may be to sell an idea to top management. For example, the information systems (IS) manager might want to suggest to the top executives that an executive information system (EIS) would greatly enhance the effectiveness of top executives by virtue of the speed and timeliness of the electronic information delivery system. With up-to-the-minute information available at the fingertips of executives – something that the current paper reporting system lacks – informed decisions could be made with much confidence. When the executives realize that they can perform their information-intensive activities with ease and speed, and at the same time enhance the quality of their decisions, they should readily buy into the idea. But then the research report for this purpose will have a different thrust and will focus in greater detail on the following:

1. An explanation, in clear and simple terms, of what an EIS is, and how it will be a powerful executive tool for effective decision making.
2. How it will save time (e.g., by giving immediate access to the specific information the executive needs, without the frustrating experience of shuffling papers and ending up with not finding what is needed).
3. How it will have an advantage over, and be better than, the current system (e.g., since all information is updated two times daily, the EIS will provide executives all the current data needed – marvelously enhancing the quality of the decisions made).
4. How it will boost savings in resources in the long run (backed by a detailed cost–benefit analysis). For instance, compare the costs of training executives in using the system and updating information on a daily basis, versus the benefits of savings accrued through more informed and timely decisions, as in the case of the establishment of a viable "just-in-time" inventory system, with resultant substantial savings to the organization.
5. An illustration of examples from past company history (within the past two months, if possible) of how an EIS system would have helped the executives to make more informed decisions in those instances, and how it could have saved the system money/resources.
6. A final forceful and convincing recommendation to adopt EIS as a way of organizational decision making.

A specimen of the type of report discussed above relating to recommending sabbaticals for managers is provided in Report 2 in the appendix to this chapter.

## EXAMPLE

### A situation where a comprehensive report, offering alternative solutions, is needed

The president of a tire company wants several recommendations to be made on planning for the future growth of the company, taking into consideration the manufacturing, marketing, accounting, and financial perspectives. In this case, only a broad objective is stated: corporate growth. There may currently be several impediments that retard growth. One has to carefully examine the situation to determine the obstacles to expansion and how these may be overcome through strategic planning from production, marketing, management, financial, and accounting perspectives. Identification of the problems or impediments in the situation would call for intensive interviews, literature review, industry analysis, formulation of a theoretical perspective, generation of several hypotheses to come up with different alternative solutions, data gathering, data analysis, and then exploration of alternative ways of attaining corporate growth through different strategies. To enable the president to evaluate the alternatives proposed, the pros and cons of implementing each of the alternative solutions, and a statement of the costs and benefits attached to each, would follow.

This report will be more elaborate than the previous two, detailing each of the steps in the study, emphasizing the results of data analysis, and furnishing a strong basis for the various recommendations. The alternatives generated and the pros and cons of each in a report such as this are likely to follow the format of Report 3 in the appendix. Report 4 in the appendix relates to basic research on an issue that was examined by a researcher.

As we can see, the contents and format of a report will depend on the purpose of the study and the needs of the sponsors to whom it is submitted.

## The audience for the written report

The organization of a report, its length, focus on details, data presentation, and illustrations will, in part, be a function of the audience for whom it is intended. The letter of transmittal of the report will clearly indicate to whom the report is being sent. An executive summary placed at the beginning will offer busy executives just the right amount of vital details – in less than three pages. This will help the busy managers to quickly grasp the essentials of the study and its findings, and turn to the pages that offer more detailed information on aspects that are of special interest to them.

Some managers are distracted by data presented in the form of tables and feel more comfortable with graphs and charts, while others want to see "facts and figures". Both tables and figures are visual forms of representation and need to be presented in reports. Which of these are to be prominently highlighted in the report and which relegated to an appendix is a function of the awareness of the idiosyncracies of the ultimate user of the report. If a report is to be handled by different executives, with different orientations, it should be packaged such that they know where to find the information that meets their preferred mode of information processing. For example, in addition to mentioning market share in the text, it can be illustrated through a pie chart, and the raw data also presented in a tabular form.

The length, organization, and presentation modes of the report will, among other things, depend at least in part on the target audience. Some businesses might also prescribe their own format for report writing. In all cases, a good report is a function of the audience for whom it is intended and its exact purpose. As we have seen, some reports may have to be long and detailed, and others brief and specific.

Sometimes, the findings of a study may be unpalatable to the executive (e.g., the organizational policies are outdated and the system is very bureaucratic), or may reflect poorly on management, tending to make them react defensively (e.g., the system has an ineffective top-down approach). In such cases, tact should be exercised in presenting the conclusions without compromising on the actual findings. That is, while there is no need to suppress the unpalatable findings, they can be presented in a nonjudgmental, non-fault-finding or finger-pointing manner, using objective data and facts that forcefully lead to, and convince the managers of the correctness of, the conclusions drawn. If this is not done, the report will be read defensively, the recommendations will not be accepted, and the problem will remain unsolved.

Tact and diplomacy combined with honesty and objectivity are essential in report writing and presentation. While this is true for both internal and external research teams, the task of the internal team in writing the research report in such cases becomes even more difficult. Being a part of the very system on which such findings are reported, the internal team might be perceived as challenging the authority of the hierarchy. Although, as a result, chances exist of being intimidated by power and authority, the internal research team, while being polite, should package its findings in a professional, unbiased, and tactful manner, thereby preserving the integrity of the findings and the process.

As an example of such a presentation, if the system has outmoded policies (or is highly bureaucratic), the report can be formatted thus: after presenting the data to support the facts, it might say that these policies (and the system) were perhaps appropriate at the time they were formulated, but the current goals of the present management, coupled with the passage of time, call for a change. It can also highlight the fact that the present system is receptive to changes and changing the policies (or the structure of the organization) will not, therefore, pose difficult problems. A similar appropriate strategy can be followed to change the top-down approach to a bottom-up management style.

## Characteristics of a well-written report

Despite the fact that report writing is a function of the purpose of the study and the type of audience to which it is presented, and accordingly has to be tailored to meet both, certain basic features are integral to all written reports. Clarity, conciseness, coherence, the right emphasis on important aspects, meaningful organization of paragraphs, smooth transition from one topic to the next, apt choice of words, and specificity are all important features of a good report. The report should, to the extent possible, be free of technical or statistical jargon unless it happens to be of a technical or statistical nature. Care should also be taken to eliminate grammatical and spelling errors.

Any assumptions made by the researcher should be clearly stated in the report, and facts, rather than opinions, provided. The report should be organized in a manner that enhances the meaningful and smooth flow of materials, as the reader progresses through it. The importance of the appearance of the report and its readability cannot be overemphasized.

Appropriate headings and subheadings help organize the report in a logical manner and allow the reader to follow the transitions easily. A double-spaced, typed report with wide margins on all sides enables the reader to make notes/comments while perusing the contents.

## Contents of the research report

It is obvious that the research report should bear a title that indicates, in a succinct manner, what the study is about. It should have at the beginning a table of contents, the research proposal, a copy of the authorization to conduct the study, and an executive summary (in the case of applied research) or a synopsis (in the case of basic research).

All reports should have an introductory section detailing the purpose of the study, giving some background of what it relates to, and stating the problem studied, setting the stage for what the reader should expect in the rest of the report. The body of the report should contain details regarding the framework of the study, hypotheses, if any, sampling design, data collection methods, analysis of data, and the results obtained. The final part of the report should present the findings and draw conclusions. If recommendations have been called for, they will be included, with a cost–benefit analysis provided with respect to each. Such information clarifies the net advantages of implementing each of the recommendations. The details provided in the report should be such as to convince the reader of the thoroughness of the study, and induce confidence in accepting the results and the recommendations made. Every professional report should also point out the limitations of the study (for example, in sampling, data collection, and the like).

Good descriptions and lucid explanations, smooth and easy flow of materials, recommendations that flow logically from the results of data analysis, and an explicit statement of any limitations to the study, provide scientific authenticity to the report. The transmittal letter is best written with a personal touch, wherever appropriate.

In sum, a rigorous, well-conducted study loses all its value when it is not properly presented in writing. To be considered useful, a report should provide a good rationale for the study, clearly present the problem studied, present the results of data analysis fully and adequately, and interpret the data in a manner that is easily understood by the reader. The conclusion drawn from the findings should indicate a clear solution to the problem.

The report can be organized in parts, sections, or chapters and should be tailored to meet the needs of the situation. Good, crisp, and clear writing, figures, charts, and tables that succinctly support or highlight the salient issues, and attractive packaging are some of the essential characteristics of a good report. The writing style should be simple, interesting, precise, and comprehensible. Unbiased and objective presentation of the findings and specific reference to the limitations of the study lend credibility to the research work. Tact and diplomacy are required in presenting unpalatable findings without distortion, and in an objective, nonthreatening, and useful manner that does not offend the sponsor. The format and style of reporting should be tailored to the audience and meet the purpose of the study. The report should end with a summary and acknowledgment of the help received from various individuals and sources. A list of references cited in the report should then follow.

Appendices, if any, should be attached to the report. A report on the factors influencing the upward mobility of women in accounting firms can be found in Report 4 of the appendix to this chapter. We will now discuss the different parts of the report.

## Integral parts of the report

### The title page

The title of the report should succinctly indicate what the study is all about. Examples of some good report titles are:

1. A Study of Customer Satisfaction with the Pizza Hut at Sunshine City, Illinois
2. Factors Influencing the Burnout of Nurses in Monroe Hospital
3. Antecedents and Consequences of White-Collar Employees' Resistance to Mechanization in Service Industries
4. Factors Affecting the Upward Mobility of Women in Accounting Firms
5. A Study of Portfolio Balancing and Risk Management in Investment Firms

The first two projects will relate to applied research, whereas the last three will be in the realm of basic research.

In addition to the title of the project, the title page will indicate the name of the sponsor of the study, the names of the researchers and their affiliations, and the date of the final report.

### Table of contents

The table of contents usually lists the important headings and subheadings in the report with page references. A separate list of tables and figures should also be listed in the table of contents.

### The research proposal and the authorization letter

A copy of the letter of authorization from the sponsor of the study approving the investigation and detailing its scope will be attached at the beginning of the report along with the research proposal. The authorization letter makes clear to the reader that the goals of the study have the full blessing of the organization.

### The executive summary or synopsis

The executive summary (or synopsis) is a brief account of the research study that provides an overview, and highlights the following important information related to it: the problem statement, sampling design, data collection methods used, results of data analysis, findings, and recommendations, with suggestions for their implementation. The executive summary (or synopsis) will be brief – usually three pages or less in length.

An example of a synopsis of the study of customer satisfaction with the Pizza Hut in Sunshine City follows.

## EXAMPLE

## Synopsis of Pizza Hut study

### Introduction and relevant details

At the request of the manager of Pizza Hut in Sunshine City, a survey was conducted to assess customer satisfaction. The sample comprised 240 customers who were administered a short questionnaire during a period of two months from July 15 to September 14. Each day, four customers who walked into the Pizza Hut at 12:00 noon, 3:00 p.m., 6:00 p.m., and 9:00 p.m.. were requested to respond to a short questionnaire on site, after they had eaten the pizza. The questionnaire, requiring less than three minutes for completion, asked respondents to give information on their gender and age, and to indicate on a five-point scale the extent of their satisfaction with (1) the flavor and texture of the pizza, (2) its taste, (3) nutritional value, (4) price, (5) the quality of service, and (6) the ambiance of the eating place. An open-ended question also asked them to offer additional comments they might wish to make. Customers dropped off their responses in a locked box with a slit at the top, kept near the exit.

### Results of data analysis

Analysis of the data indicated that of the 240 respondents, about 60% were men and 40% women. Most of them were over 25 years of age. Customers expressed greatest satisfaction with the taste of the pizza (a mean of 4.5 on a five-point scale), followed by its flavor and texture (mean of 4). They were neither pleased nor displeased with the price or the quality of service (3 on a five-point scale). They were not particularly happy, however, with the ambiance or the nutritional value (mean of 2.5 for each). The comments offered in the open-ended question indicated that some 25 individuals felt that the amount of cheese in the pizza might increase their cholesterol level to the detriment of their health.

### Conclusions and recommendations

These results indicate that customers do like the pizza and have no specific complaints about the price or the service. Should the manager be concerned about the displeasure of the customers with the ambiance or the nutritional value, he could handle it fairly easily. It is possible, for instance, to improve the ambiance with flowers and hanging baskets of plants. Candlelight on the tables in the evenings would also contribute to an improvement.

As for dissatisfaction with the nutritional value, information about the use of only low-fat cheese in the pizza as a health safeguard could be disseminated through the menu card and advertisements. The option of pizza with nonfat cheese may also be offered to the customers.

If enhancement of the level of customer satisfaction is desired, a short training program could be introduced for the waiters for this purpose, and their service thereafter supervised until the "service with a smile" motto was internalized by them.

## The introductory section

The introductory section starts with a statement of the problem under investigation. The research objective, together with background information on why and how the study was initiated, is also stated. In the case of basic research, the introductory section will offer an idea of the topic that is researched, and why it is important to study it. The arguments will focus on the relevancy, timeliness, and appropriateness of the research, in the context of current factors and trends in society and/or organizations.

The research objective and the problem statement to be studied are clearly set forth in this section.

## The body of the report

In this part, the details of the interviews conducted, the literature survey, the theoretical framework, and the hypotheses are furnished. The design details, such as sampling and data collection methods, as well as the nature and type of study, the time horizon, the field setting, and the unit of analysis, are described.

The details of the types of data analysis done to test the hypotheses, and the findings therefrom, will be provided next. Tabular and pictorial depictions of the results of data analysis will find a place here. A few of the various ways in which data can be pictorially presented in written reports and oral presentations are illustrated in Figure 14.1.

## The final part of the report

The final part of the report will contain the conclusions drawn from the findings. In most cases (depending on the scope of the project), a list of recommendations for implementation will follow. Frequently, a cost–benefit analysis will also be provided. Any limitations to the study, for example, flaws in sampling due to circumstances beyond one's control, will find a place herein. A brief summation paragraph will also be provided at the end.

## Acknowledgments

Help received from others is next acknowledged. Usually, the people who assisted in the study by collecting the questionnaires, acting as liaison persons, helping in data analysis, and so on, are recognized and thanked. The organization is thanked for the facilities provided, and its members for responding to the survey.

It should now be easy to see, given the variety of information covered in the report, why it is important to have appropriate headings and subheadings throughout. This assists the reader to progress through the report smoothly, easily, and quickly, while wide margins on all sides help the reader to jot down points or make notes, wherever considered necessary, as one goes through the report.

## References

Immediately after the acknowledgments, starting on a fresh page, a list of the references cited in the literature review and in other places in the report will be given. The format of the

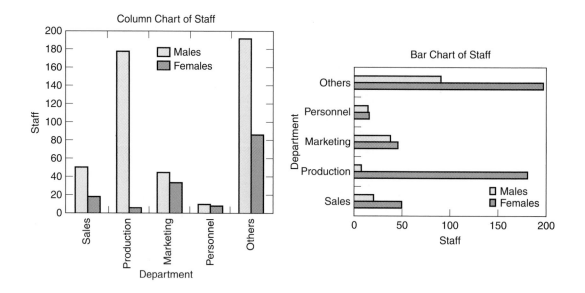

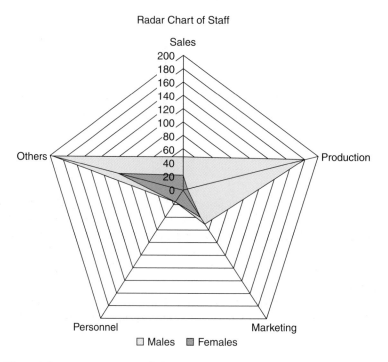

Figure 14.1: Pictorial representation of data.

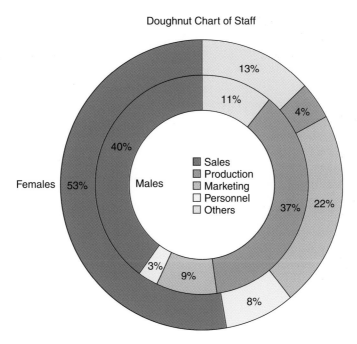

Figure 14.1: (Continued).

references has been discussed and illustrated in the appendix to Chapter 3. Footnotes, if any in the text, are referenced either separately at the end of the report, or at the bottom of the page where the footnote occurs.

## Appendix

The appendix, which comes last, is the appropriate place for the organization chart, newspaper clippings or other materials that substantiate the text of the report, detailed verbatim narration of interviews with members, and whatever else might help the reader follow the text. It should also contain a copy of the questionnaire administered to the respondents. If there are several appendices, they should be referenced as Appendix A, Appendix B, and so on, and appropriately labeled.

The above will make clear that the Table of Contents (mentioned earlier) following the title page and the letter of transmittal, will look somewhat as indicated below, with some possible variations.

### Table of Contents
- Research proposal
- Letter of authorization

- Introduction
  - Problem studied
  - Background information
  - Research goals
- Preliminary details
  - Unstructured and structured interviews
  - Literature survey
  - Theoretical framework
  - Hypotheses formulated
- Research design
  - Type and nature of the study
  - Sampling design
  - Data collection methods
  - Data analytic techniques used
- Results of data analysis
  - Hypotheses substantiated/unsubstantiated
- Conclusions
- Recommendations
- Limitations of study
- Acknowledgments
- References
- Tables
- Graphs
- Appendices

# Oral presentation

Usually organizations (and instructors in classes) require about a 20-minute oral presentation of the research project, followed by a question and answer session. The oral presentation calls for considerable planning. Imagine a study that spanned several months having to be presented in 20 minutes to a live audience! Those who have not read the report at all, or at best only superficially, have to be convinced that the recommendations made therein will indeed prove to be beneficial to the organization. All this will have to be effectively accomplished in the matter of a few minutes.

The challenge is to present the important aspects of the study so as to hold the interest of the audience, while still providing statistical and quantitative information, which may drive many to ennui. Different stimuli (overheads, slides, charts, pictorial and tabular depiction, etc.) have to be creatively provided to the audience to consistently sustain their interest throughout the presentation. To make all this possible, time and effort have to be expended in planning, organizing, and rehearsing the presentation.

Slides, overheads, charts, graphs, handouts – all in large, bold print, and preferably in multiple colors – help the presenter to sustain the interest of the audience. They also help the presenter discuss and explain the research project coherently, without reading from prepared notes.

Factors irrelevant to the written report, such as dress, mannerisms, gestures, voice modulation, and the like, take on added importance in oral presentations. Speaking audibly, clearly, without distracting mannerisms, and at the right speed for the audience to comprehend is vital for holding their attention. Varying the length of the sentences, establishing eye contact, tone variations, voice modulation, and the rate of flow of information make all the difference to audience receptivity. Use of 3 × 5 cards for orderly presentation helps smooth transitions during the presentation. Thus, the contents of the presentation and the style of delivery should both be planned in detail.

## Deciding on the content

Because a lot of material has to be covered in perhaps a 20-minute presentation, it becomes necessary to decide on the points to focus on and the importance to be given to each. Remembering that the listener absorbs only a small proportion of all that he or she has heard, it is important to determine what the presenter would like the listener to walk away with, and then organize the presentation accordingly.

Obviously, the problem investigated, the results found, the conclusions drawn, the recommendations made, and the ways in which they can be implemented are of vital interest to organizational members, and need to be emphasized during the presentation. The design aspects of the study, details of the sample, data collection methods, details of data analysis, and the like, can be mentioned in passing to be picked up at the question and answer session by interested members.

However, depending on the type of audience, it may become necessary to put more stress on the data analytic aspects. For example, if the presentation is being made to a group of statisticians in the company, or in a research methods class, the data analyses and results will receive more time than if the project is being presented to a group of managers whose main interest lies in the solution to the problem and implementation of the recommendations. Thus, the time and attention devoted to the various components of the study will require adjustment, depending on the audience.

## Visual aids

Graphs, charts, and tables help to drive home the points one wishes to make much faster and more effectively, true to the adage that a picture is worth a thousand words. Visual aids provide a captivating sensory stimulus that sustains the attention of the audience. Modern PowerPoint technology makes it possible for color graphics to be produced on personal computers and projected onto a screen. Slides, transparencies, flip charts, the chalkboard, and handout materials also help the audience to easily follow the points of the speaker's focus. The selection of specific visual modes of presentation will depend, among other things, on the size of the room, the availability of a good screen for projection, and the cost constraints of developing sophisticated visuals. All visuals should be produced with an eye on easy visibility from the far end of the presentation hall. Large, easily readable visuals that are properly labeled in big size bold letters help the audience to focus on the presentation. Visuals that present side-by-side comparisons of the existing and would-be state of affairs via graphs or pie charts drive home the points made much more forcefully than elaborate and laborious verbal explanations.

Integrated multimedia presentations using PowerPoint, CD-ROMs, and other visuals are quite common in this technological age. Digital whiteboards facilitate digital storage of intricate diagrams that can be used in conjunction with electronic projective systems to serve as electronic flipcharts. When planning a presentation using PowerPoint or integrated multimedia, it is important to ensure before the presentation starts that the related equipment is properly hooked up and tested so that the presentation can go smoothly without interruptions.

## The presenter

An effective presentation is also a function of how "unstressed" the presenter is. The speaker should establish eye contact with the audience, speak audibly and understandably, and be sensitive to the nonverbal reactions of the audience. Strict adherence to the time frame and concentration on the points of interest to the audience are critical aspects of presentation. A display of extreme nervousness throughout the presentation, stumbling for words, fumbling with the notes or audiovisuals, speaking inaudibly and/or with distracting mannerisms, straying away from the main focus of the study, and exceeding the time limit all detract from effectiveness. One should also not minimize the importance of the impression created on the audience by dress, posture, bearing, and the confidence with which one carries oneself. Such simple things as covering the materials on the visuals until they need to be exhibited, and voice modulation, help to focus the attention of the audience on the discussion.

## The presentation

The opening remarks set the stage for riveting the attention of the audience. Certain aspects such as the problem investigated, the findings, the conclusions drawn, the recommendations made and their implementation are, as previously mentioned, important aspects of the presentation. The speaker should drive home these points at least three times – once in the beginning, again when each of these areas is covered, and finally, while summarizing and bringing the presentation to a conclusion.

## Handling questions

Concentrated and continuous research on the research topic over a considerable period of time indisputably makes the presenter more knowledgeable about the project than anyone else in the audience. Hence, it is not difficult to handle questions from the members with confidence and poise. It is important to be nondefensive when questions are posed that seemingly find fault with some aspect of the research. Openness to suggestions also helps, as the audience might, at times, come up with some excellent ideas or recommendations that the researcher might not have thought of. Such ideas must always be acknowledged graciously. If a question or a suggestion from a member in the audience happens to be flawed, it is best addressed in a nonjudgmental fashion.

The question and answer session, when handled well, leaves the audience with a sense of involvement and satisfaction. Questioning should be encouraged and responded to with care. This interactive question and answer session offers an exciting experience both to the audience and to the presenter.

As may be readily seen, a 20-minute presentation and a short question and answer session thereafter do call for substantial planning, anticipation of audience concerns, psychological preparedness, and good impression management skills.

Reporting has to be done in an honest and straightforward manner. It is unethical to fail to report findings that are unpalatable to the sponsors or that reflect poorly on management. As suggested earlier, it is possible to be tactful in presenting such findings without withholding or distorting information to please the sponsors. Internal researchers, in particular, will have to find ways of presenting unpopular information in a tactful manner. It is also important to state the limitations of the study – and practically every study has some limitation – so that the audience is not misled.

## SUMMARY

The components of various types of written research report were discussed in this chapter. It was emphasized that the purpose of the report and the composition of the intended audience are critical factors in deciding what aspects of the study will be stressed the most. Examples of different kinds of reports were offered and additional examples can be found in the appendix to this chapter. Ways of making effective oral presentations were also discussed, stressing both the contents of the presentation and the style of delivery.

## DISCUSSION QUESTIONS

1. Discuss the purpose and contents of the executive summary.
2. What are the similarities and differences between basic and applied research reports?
3. How have technological advancements helped in writing and presenting research reports?
4. Why is it necessary to specify the limitations of the study in the research report?

5. What aspects of a class research project would be stressed by you in the written report and in the oral presentation?

Now do Exercises 14.1 and 14.2

## EXERCISE 14.1

Critique Report 4 in the appendix. Discuss it in terms of good and bad research, suggesting how the study could have been improved, what aspects of it are good, and how scientific it is.

## EXERCISE 14.2

Give a title to and write the introductory section of any study you might like to conduct.

# Report 1: Sample of a report involving a descriptive study

SEKRAS COMPANY

> **TO:** Mr L. Raiburn, Chairman
>    Strategic Planning Committee
> **FR:** Joanne Williams
>    Public Relations Officer
> **RE:** Report requested by Mr Raiburn

Attached is the report requested by Mr Raiburn. If any further information or clarification is needed, please let me know.

Encl: Report

## Report for the strategic planning committee

### Introduction

Vice President Raiburn, Chairman of the Strategic Planning Committee, requested two pieces of information:

1. The sales figures of the top five retailers in the country.
2. Customers' ideas of what improvements can be made to Sekras to enhance their satisfaction. For this purpose, he desired that a quick survey of the company's customers be done to elicit their opinions.

### Method used for obtaining the requisite information

Figures of sales of the top five retailers in the country were obtained from *Business Week*, which periodically publishes many kinds of industry statistics.

To obtain customers' inputs on improvements that could be made by the company, a short questionnaire (specimen in Appendix A) was mailed to 300 of our credit card customers – 100 who had most frequently used the card in the last 18 months, 100 who most infrequently used it during the same period, and 100 average users. Questionnaires in three different colors were sent to the three groups. Respondents were offered a complimentary magnet for responses received within a week. The questionnaire asked for responses to three questions:

1. What are some of the things you like best about shopping at Sekras?
2. What are some of the things that you dislike and would like to see improved at Sekras? Please explain in as much detail as possible.
3. What are your specific suggestions for making improvements to enhance the quality of our service to customers like you?

## Findings

*Sales figures of the top five retailers*

Information regarding sales of the top five retailers in 2000 and 2003 is provided in Table 14.1.

As can be seen, Wal-Mart and Home Depot retained their top positions in 2003. Kroger (a supermarket chain with 2532 grocery stores in 32 states) which was not among the top five in 2000, occupied the third place in 2003, whereas Costco (an international chain of membership warehouses, primarily under the "Costco Wholesale" name) occupied the fourth place. Target

**TABLE 14.1   Comparative sales figures of the five top retail companies during 2000 and 2003.**

| | Top retailers in 2000 | | | Top retailers in 2003 | |
| Company | Sales in billions of $ | Share among top five | Company | Sales in billions of $ | Share among top five |
|---|---|---|---|---|---|
| Wal-Mart Stores | 191.33 | 54.7% | Wal-Mart Stores | 256.0 | 53.4% |
| Home Depot | 45.74 | 13.1% | Home Depot | 73.10 | 15.2% |
| Sears, Roebuck | 40.94 | 11.7% | Kroger | 56.40 | 11.8% |
| Kmart | 36.50 | 10.3% | Costco | 47.15 | 9.8% |
| Target | 35.51 | 10.2% | Target | 46.80 | 9.8% |

*Source: Business Week*

(the company's stores offer men's and women's clothing, home furnishings, electronic products, sports products, toys, and entertainment products) retained the fifth position in 2003. Sears, Roebuck and Kmart did not find a place among the top five retailers during 2003. It may be observed that even though Wal-Mart increased its sales by about 1.33 times during the three-year period, its share among the top five did not increase.

*Customer suggestions for improvements*

Of the 300 surveys sent out, 225 were received, a 75% response rate. Of the 100 most frequent users of our credit card to whom questionnaires were sent, 80 responded; among the most infrequent users, 60 responded; and among the average users, 85 responded.

About 75% of the respondents were women. The majority of the customers were between the ages of 35 and 55 (62%).

The responses to the three open-ended questions were analyzed. The information needed by the Committee on the suggested improvements is tabulated (see Table 14.2). Responses to the other two questions on features liked by the customers, and their specific suggestions for improvement, are provided in the two tables in the appendix. The following are suggestions received from one or two respondents only:

1. Have more water fountains on each floor.
2. The pushcarts could be lighter, so they will be less difficult to push.
3. More seats for resting after long hours of shopping would help.
4. Prices of luxury items are too high.

From looking at Table 14.2, it can be seen that the most dissatisfaction stems from (1) out of stock small appliances, and (2) inability to locate store assistants who could guide customers in locating what they need (44% each). The need for child care services is expressed by 38% of the customers. Twenty percent also indicate that the cafeteria should cater to the international spicy type of foods. The next two important items pertain to the temperature (18%) and billing mistakes (16%). Some customers (16%) also wish the store was open 24 hours.

The rest of the suggestions were offered by less than 10% of the customers and, hence, can perhaps be attended to later.

A note of caution is in order at this juncture. We are not sure how representative our sample is. We thought that a mix of high, average, and infrequent users of our credit card would provide us with some useful insights. If a more detailed study obtaining information from a sample of all the customers who come to the store is considered necessary, we will initiate it quickly. In the meantime, we are also interviewing a few of the customers who shop here daily. If we find anything of significance from these interviews, we will inform you.

## Improvements indicated by these suggestions

Based on the current sample of customers who have responded to our survey, the following improvements and actions seem called for:

TABLE 14.2    Suggested areas for improvement.

| Features | Frequent users no. | Medium users no. | Infrequent users no. | Total no. | % |
|---|---|---|---|---|---|
| 1. Small appliances such as mixers, blenders are often not in stock. This is irritating. | 30 | 48 | 22 | 100 | 44 |
| 2. The cafeteria serves only bland, uninteresting food. How about some spicy international food? | 26 | 14 | 5 | 45 | 20 |
| 3. Often, we are unable to locate where the items we want are! | 3 | 6 | 14 | 23 | 10 |
| 4. It would be nice if you could have a child care service so we can shop without distractions. | 28 | 32 | 25 | 85 | 38 |
| 5. It is often difficult to locate an assistant who can help us with answers to our questions. | 29 | 49 | 22 | 100 | 44 |
| 6. I wish it were a 24-hour store. | 17 | 13 | 7 | 37 | 16 |
| 7. Sometimes, there is a mistake in billing. We have to make some telephone calls before charges are corrected. This is a waste of our time. | 4 | 12 | 14 | 20 | 16 |
| 8. Allocate some floor space for kids to play video games. | 2 | — | 4 | 6 | 2 |
| 9. Import more Eastern apparel like the kimono, sarees, sarongs. | — | 8 | 4 | 12 | 5 |
| 10. Regulate the temperature better; often, it is too cold or too hot. | 15 | 12 | 17 | 44 | 18 |

1. Small appliances need to be adequately stocked (44% complained about this). An effective reorder inventory system has to be developed for this department to minimize customer dissatisfaction and avoid loss of sales for lack of sufficient stock. The research team can help in this, if requested.

2. Customers seem to need help to locate store items and would appreciate help from store assistants (44% expressed this need). If providing assistance is a primary concern, it would be a good idea to have liveried store personnel with badges to indicate they are there to

assist customers. During idle hours, if any (when there are no customers seeking help), these individuals can be deployed as shelf organizers.

3. Need for child care has been expressed by more than a third of our customers (38%). It would be a good idea to earmark a portion of the front of the building for parents to drop off their children while shopping. The children will have to be supervised by a trained child care professional recruited by the organization. An assistant could be recruited later if needed. From the cost–benefit analysis in Exhibit 7, it may be seen that this additional expenditure will pay off multifold in sales revenue, and at the same time, create a fund of goodwill for the company.

4. Adding to the variety of foods served in the cafeteria (a need expressed by 20%) is at once a simple and a complex matter. We need further ideas and details as to what types of food need to be added. This information can be obtained through a short survey, if Mr Raiburn so desires.

5. Billing errors should not occur (16% indicated this). The billing department should be warned that such mistakes should be avoided and should not recur. Performance assessment should be tied to such mistakes.

6. Regulation of temperature (16% identified this) is easy. This, in fact, could be immediately attended to by the engineering department personnel.

I hope this report contains all the information sought by Mr Raiburn. As stated earlier, if the non-credit card customers also have to be sampled, this can be easily arranged.

# Report 2: Sample of a report where an idea has to be "sold"

Mueller Pharmaceuticals

June 15
  **TO:** The Board of Directors
  **FR:** Harry Wood, VP.
      (Through: President Michael Osborn)
  **RE:** Sabbatical for Managers

Enclosed is a brief report on the need for a sabbatical policy for our managers and R & D personnel, for discussion at our next board meeting. We will also plan on a more detailed presentation at that time.

## Why sabbaticals for managers are necessary

### Introduction

At the company's board meeting last month, the members were concerned that no new products have been developed during the past four years and that the profits of the company are considerably down. One of the board members suggested that a sabbatical given to the managers and key staff of our company might rejuvenate them, and help creativity flow again. At that time, the matter was treated casually and not given any further consideration. Sensing the need to consider this option seriously, I have since talked to a few companies who do offer this benefit to their managers. I have further obtained some data from them, which demonstrate the efficacy of sabbaticals.

Based on the available information, there is a strong case for introducing a sabbatical policy in our company. Details of my discussions with other companies and their data are presented below.

## Gist of telephone conversations with vice presidents and presidents of companies

I talked to the presidents, vice presidents, and directors of IBM, Tandem, Apple Computers, Eli Lilly, and Time Warner Inc. All these companies have had sabbatical policies for at least the past nine years. Some presidents to whom I spoke said they initiated the policy because they found that their own productivity went up after they had had some time away from their jobs doing different kinds of things. Some said that they introduced the sabbatical because they felt that their managerial staff experienced burnout after long years of nonstop work at a hectic pace and became ineffective.

Without exception, everyone said that it makes good business sense to offer managers a chance to refurbish their lives and recharge their batteries every six years or so, so that they come back to work with renewed vigor. Among the many advantages recounted by those to whom I spoke are:

1. More enthusiasm and zest for work.
2. Better working relationships with staff.
3. A fresh approach to problem solving with less competitiveness among the different departments.
4. More creative flow of ideas, new marketing strategies, and product development ideas.
5. A more dynamic workplace in terms of interpersonal interactions, interdepartmental collegiality, and joint problem solving.

## Some hard data

The appendix, which contains the information provided by two companies, shows that the number of new products developed quadrupled in one company and increased fivefold in the other during the years following the introduction of the sabbatical. As they themselves acknowledge, the increase cannot be attributed to the sabbatical alone, but they have also documented that most of the new products developed were under the leadership of the managers after their return from a three-month sabbatical. You will note that new product development statistics for these managers, before and after their sabbaticals, are indeed compelling! Reinforcing our theory is also the decline in the figures after the fourth or fifth year of their return from sabbatical and the pickup again after the next sabbatical. Noteworthy too is that the "pickup" years were no different from the others in terms of the economic environment, technology advancement, or other factors that might have a direct impact on innovation!

I have also placed in the appendix a copy of the article on executive life, which appeared in a top journal on July 3, 2007, and which you have probably already read. Is it not astonishing and amusing that many of the executives who try something new during the sabbatical, ultimately want to get back to their old jobs? The case cited of the law firm partner, Axinn, who missed the rigors of his old job and could just not shake off the lawyer in him when he tried to be a rabbi-in-training during his sabbatical, is particularly interesting.

### Benefits of sabbatical

The benefits of sabbatical to the managers are obvious; they refresh themselves trying their hands at new things or doing the things they have dreamed of (such as learning to play the flute or paint or write). These activities seem to offer them a new lease on their professional lives, but the benefits to the corporation seem to be even greater, as experienced by the companies that already have this scheme in place. Apple Computer's revenues are stated to have quadrupled under the leadership of Mr John Sculley, who took nine-week sabbaticals. Again no one is attributing a cause-and-effect relationship, but there might be a strong correlation possible there! Mr Lerman, partner of Wilmer, Cutler & Pickering, strongly affirms that when managers come back from sabbatical, they are more effective and invigorated.

### Recommendation

Given the qualitative and quantitative evidence generated from a number of organizations that have implemented the sabbatical policy, I strongly recommend that we also establish a sabbatical policy in our company. The suggestion is to offer a paid, three-month sabbatical for all our R & D scientists, and managerial and executive staff, after every six years of service. The costs of implementing this with respect to our senior scientists, managers, and executives are worked out and shown in Exhibit 4. The likely benefits within ten years of our initiating such a policy in terms of new product development, increased sales, and joint problem-solving endeavors due to higher energy levels of department heads, are also shown in the same exhibit.

I will ask the HRM Director to collect information from more companies having sabbatical policies and ask him to make a presentation to the Board at our next meeting. In the meantime, if you need more information or clarification, feel free to give me a call.

In conclusion, our company is at a crossroads and our scientists and managers need to be energized to enhance their performance and productivity. Constant pressure and ceaseless toil are wearing them out. Many are frustrated by the demands imposed by the jobs. "All work and no play" has banished their zest for working and drained them of their creative ideas. It is high time we inject some vitality into our system through sabbaticals.

# Report 3: Sample of a report offering alternative solutions and explaining the pros and cons of each alternative

**TO:** Mr Charles Orient, CEO

    Lunard Manufacturing Company
**FR:** Alex Ventura, Senior Researcher
    Beam Research Team
**RE:** Suggestions on alternative ways of cutting costs in anticipation of recession.

Enclosed is the report requested by Mr Orient. If any additional information or clarification is needed, please let me know.
Encl: Report

## Report on alternative ways of handling recessionary times without massive layoffs

### Introduction

The Beam Research Team was asked to suggest alternative ways of tiding over the anticipated recession over the next several months, when a slowdown of the economy is expected. A recent article in *Business Week* entitled "Hunkering Down in a Hurry" indicated that executives in a large number of companies are slashing costs mostly through layoffs and restructuring. Mr Orient wanted the Beam Research Team to suggest other alternatives besides layoffs.

This report provides five alternatives citing the advantages and disadvantages of each.

### Method used for developing the alternatives

The team studied the economic indicators and the published industry analyses, read the Federal Reserve Board Chairman's speeches, examined the many ways in which companies cut costs during nonrecessionary periods as well as recessions, and, based on these, suggests the following five alternatives.

Alternatives suggested

1. A moratorium on all capital expenditure.
2. Hiring freeze.
3. Recovery of bad debts through sustained efforts.
4. Trimming of operating expenditure with substantial reduction in travel and entertainment expenditure.
5. Discontinuance of the manufacture of low-profit-margin products.

## Advantages and disadvantages of each of the above

Itemized details of the cost–benefit analysis for each of the above suggestions are furnished in the appendix. We give only the net benefits for each alternative here.

### Moratorium on all capital expenditure

It makes good sense to desist from all capital expenditure since manufacture of most of the items will slow down during recession. Except for parts for existing machines, there is no need to buy capital equipment, and all proposals in this regard should be shelved.

This strategy will cut down expenditure to the extent of 7 to 10% of revenue. See appendix for full details. A reserve fund can be created to catch up with future orders when the economy returns to normal.

### Hiring freeze

The annual increase in the strength of staff during the past four years has been about 15%. With a slowdown of the economy, a hiring freeze in all branch offices will save over $10 million annually.

This might initially result in some extra workload for the staff and cause some job dissatisfaction, but once they get used to it, and the impact of the actual recession hits them, employees will be thankful for the job they have. It will be a good idea to explain in advance the reasons for the hiring freeze to the employees so that they understand the motive behind the company's policy, and appreciate having been informed.

### Recovery of bad debts through aggressive efforts

Bad debts of the company have been on the increase over the past three years, and no intensive efforts to recover them seem to have been made hitherto.

We suggest that collection agents who have successfully recovered bad debts for other companies be hired immediately. Such agents may have to be paid more than other collection agents, but the extra cost will be well worth it. About a billion dollars can be collected within a few weeks of their being on the job, and this will help the financial cash flow of the company.

### Trimming of operating expenditure

Several operating expenses can be cut down – the travel expenses of managers in particular – as shown in Exhibit 4 of the appendix. Videoconferencing costs much less and is quicker, and should be encouraged for most of the meetings and negotiations. This alone will result in savings of more than $175 000 per month.

Another way of considerably curtailing expenditure is to restrict entertainment expenses only for such purposes and to such managers as actively promote the business of the company or are essential for public relations.

These changes will have a negative impact on morale, but managers understand the economic situation, and will adjust to the new system once the initial mental resistance wears off.

### Eliminating the manufacture of low-margin products

The team found from a detailed study of the company records of manufacturing, sales, and profits figures for the various products that all the items listed in Exhibit 5 of the appendix have very low profit margins. It is evident from the data provided that considerable time and effort are expended in manufacturing and selling these items.

It will be useful to phase out the manufacture of these items and divert the resources to the high-profit items suggested in Exhibit 6. From the cost–benefit analysis in Exhibit 7, it may be seen that several billions can be saved through this strategy.

It is possible to put into effect all of the five alternatives above and handle the onslaught of the recession with confidence.

# Report 4: Example of an abridged basic research report

## Factors affecting the upward mobility of women in public accounting

### Introduction

A substantial number of women have entered the public accounting profession in the past 15 years or so. However, less than 4% of the partners in the big eight accounting firms are women, indicating a lack of upward mobility for women in the accounting profession. Against the backdrop of the fact that the women students perform significantly better during their academic training than their male counterparts, it is unfortunate that their intellectual ability and knowledge remain underutilized during their professional careers. The recent costly litigation and discrimination suits filed make it imperative for us to study the factors that affect the upward mobility of women and examine how the situation can be rectified.

### A brief literature review

Studies of male and female accounting majors indicate that the percentage of women accounting students has increased severalfold since 1977 (Kurian, 1998). Based on the analysis of longitudinal data collected over a 15-year period, Mulcher, Turner and Williams (2000) found that female students' grades in senior accounting courses were significantly higher than those of the male students. This higher level of academic performance has been theorized as being due to the higher need and desire that women have to achieve and overcome stereotypes (Messing, 2000), having higher career aspirations (Tinsley *et al.*, 1999), or having a higher aptitude for accounting (Jones and Alexander, 2001; Riley, 2001). Empirical studies by Fraser, Lytle and Stolle (1998), and Johnson and Meyer (1999), however, found no significant differences in personality predispositions or behavioral traits among male and female accounting majors.

Several surveys of women accountants in the country pinpoint three major factors that hinder women's career progress in the public accounting field (see, for instance, Kaufman, 1986; Larson, 1999; Walkup and Fenman, 2001). They are (1) the long hours of work demanded by the profession (a factor that conflicts with family demands), (2) failure to be entrusted with responsible assignments, and (3) discrimination. In sum, the lack of upward mobility seems to be due to factors over which the organization has some control.

### Research question

Do long work hours, failure to be handed greater responsibilities, and discrimination account for the lack of upward mobility of women in public accounting?

## Theoretical framework

The variance in the dependent variable, upward mobility, can be explained by the three independent variables: long hours of work, not handling greater responsibilities, and discrimination. As women are expected to, and do indeed, take on responsibility for household work and childrearing, they are not able to work beyond regular work hours at the workplace. This creates the wrong impression among higher-ups in the organization that women are less committed to their work. Because of this perception, they are not entrusted with significant responsibilities. This further hinders their progress as they are not afforded exposure to the intricacies of accounting practices as much as men. Hence, women are overlooked at the time of promotion.

Deliberate discriminatory practices due to sex-role stereotypes, as evidenced in the well-known case of Hopkins vs. Price Waterhouse & Co., also arrest women's progress. If women are not valued for their potential and are expected to conform to sex-typed behavior (which confines them to inconspicuous roles), their chances of moving up the career ladder are significantly reduced.

Thus, the three independent variables considered here would significantly explain the variance in the upward mobility of women in public accounting. The impracticability of putting in long hours of work, lack of opportunities to handle greater responsibilities, and sex-role stereotyping all negatively impact upward mobility.

## Hypotheses

If women spend more hours on the job after regular work hours, they will be given greater responsibilities.

If women are entrusted with higher levels of responsibility, they will have more opportunities to move up in the organization.

If women are not expected to conform to stereotypical behavior, their chances for upward mobility will increase.

All three independent variables will significantly explain the variance in women CPAs' upward mobility.

## Method section

### Study design

In this cross-sectional correlational field study, data on the three independent variables and the dependent variable were collected from women CPAs in several public accounting organizations in the country through mail questionnaires.

### Population and sample

The population for the study comprised all women CPAs in the country. A systematic sampling procedure was first used to select 30 cities from the various regions of the country, from which a sample of accounting firms would be drawn. Then, through a simple random sampling procedure, five CPA firms from each of the cities were chosen for the study. Data were collected from all the women in each of the firms so chosen. The total sample size was 300 and responses were received from 264 women CPAs, for an 88% response rate for the mail questionnaires, which is pretty good. The unit of analysis was the individuals who responded to the survey.

All respondents had, as expected, the CPA degree. Their ages ranged from 28 to 66. About 60% of the women were over 45 years of age. The average number of children in the house below the age of 13 was two. The average number of years of work in the organization was 15, and the average number of organizations worked for was two. The average number of hours spent daily at home on office-related matters was 1.4.

### Variables and measures

All demographic variables such as age, number of years in the organization, number of other organizations in which the individual had worked, number of hours spent at home on office-related matters, and number of children in the house and their ages, were tapped by direct single questions.

*Upward mobility.* This dependent variable indicates the extent to which individuals are expected to progress in their career during the succeeding three to ten years. Hall (1986) developed four items to measure this variable, a sample item being: I see myself being promoted to the next level quite easily. The measure is reported to have convergent and discriminant validity, and Cronbach's alpha for the four items for this sample was 0.86.

*Sex-role stereotyping.* This independent variable was measured using Hall and Humphreys' (1972) eight-item measure. An example item is: Men in this organization do not consider women's place to be primarily in the home. Cronbach's alpha for the measure for this sample was 0.82.

*Responsibilities assigned.* This was tapped by three items from Sonnenfield and McGrath (1983), which asked respondents to indicate their levels of assigned responsibility to (a) make important decisions, (b) handle large accounts, and (c) account for the annual profits of the firm. Cronbach's alpha for the three items was 0.71 for this sample.

### Data collection method

Questionnaires were mailed to 300 women CPAs in the United States. After two reminders, 264 completed questionnaires were received within a period of six weeks. The high return rate of 88% can be attributed to the shortness of the questionnaire and perhaps the motivation of the women CPAs to respond to a topic close to their heart.

Questionnaires were not electronically administered for various reasons, including the advantage it afforded to the busy respondents to reply without switching on the computer.

*Data analysis and results*

After determining the reliabilities (Cronbach's alpha) for the measures for this sample, frequency distributions for the demographic variables were obtained. These may be seen in Exhibit 1. Then a Pearson correlation matrix was obtained for the four independent and dependent variables. This may be seen in Exhibit 2. It is to be noted that no correlation exceeded 0.6.

Each hypothesis was then tested. The correlation matrix provided the answer to the first three hypotheses. The first hypothesis stated that the number of hours put in beyond work hours on office-related matters would be positively correlated to the responsibilities assigned. The correlation of 0.56 ($p < 0.001$) between the number of hours spent on office work beyond regular work hours and the entrusted responsibilities substantiates this hypothesis.

The second hypothesis stated that if women were given higher responsibilities, their upward mobility would improve. The positive correlation of 0.59 ($p < 0.001$) between the two variables substantiates this hypothesis. That is, the greater the entrusted responsibilities, the higher are the perceived chances of being promoted.

The third hypothesis indicated that sex-role stereotyping would be negatively correlated to upward mobility. The correlation of –0.54 ($p < 0.001$) substantiates this hypothesis as well. That is, the greater the expected conformity to stereotyped behavior, the less the chances of upward mobility.

To test the fourth hypothesis that the number of hours spent beyond regular work hours on job-related matters, assignment of higher responsibilities, and expectations of conformity with stereotyped behavior will significantly explain the variance in perceived upward mobility, the three independent variables were regressed against the dependent variable. The results, which are shown in Exhibit 3, indicate that this hypothesis is also substantiated. That is, the $R^2$ value of 0.43 at a significance level of $p < 0.001$, with df (3.238), confirms that 43% of the variance in upward mobility is significantly explained by the three independent variables.

*Discussion of results*

The results of this study confirm that the variables considered in the theoretical framework are important. By focusing solely on the number of hours worked, ignoring the quality of work done, the organization is perhaps not harnessing the full potential and encouraging the development of the talents of the women CPAs adequately. It seems worthwhile to remedy this situation.

It would be useful if the top executive were to assign progressively higher levels of responsibility to women. This would utilize their abilities fully and, in turn, enhance the effectiveness of the firm. If executives are helped to modify their mental attitudes and sex-role expectations, they should tend to expect less stereotypical behavior and encourage the upward mobility of women CPAs. Knowing women bring a different kind of perspective to organizational matters (Smith, 1999; Vernon, 2001), it is quite possible that having them as partners of the firm will enhance the organizational effectiveness as well.

### Recommendations

It is recommended that a system be set up to assess the value of the contributions of each individual in discharging his or her duties, and use that, rather than the number of hours of work put in, as a yardstick for promotion.

Second, women CPAs should be given progressively more responsibility after they have served three to five years in the system. Assigning a mentor to train them will facilitate smooth functioning of the firm.

Third, a short seminar should be organized for executives to sensitize them to the adverse effects of sex-role stereotyping at the workplace. This will help them to beneficially utilize the talents of women CPAs. If viewed as professionals with career goals and aspirations, rather than in stereotyped ways, women CPAs will be enabled to handle more responsibilities and advance in the system. The organization also stands to benefit from their contributions.

In conclusion, it would be worthwhile for public accounting firms to modify their mental orientations toward, and expectations of, women CPAs. It is a national waste if their potential is not fully tapped and utilized.

# A FINAL NOTE TO STUDENTS

If you have enjoyed learning about research and built up a repertoire of research skills, you are prepared and ready for your professional life. As you must have realized from the discussions in this book, research is an integral part of organizational reality that helps businesses to continuously improve and grow progressively. Though you may not have become an *expert* researcher after one semester of coursework, and perhaps a research project, I am sure you would have gained an intelligent appreciation of, and an adequate depth of knowledge for business research– great assets in dealing effectively with consultants. The ability to discriminate between the good and the not so good research will also be invaluable to you in sifting through the materials you will undoubtedly read in the practitioner and academic journals in your professional life as managers. And, more important, as you get deluged by all the information from various sources, including the Internet, newspapers, talk shows, and the like, you will be better able to evaluate the validity of the messages and judge them for what they truly represent. You are thus armed to handle the information overload that one faces in today's Information Age.

If you have satisfactorily met the following objectives, you can be confident that you have taken a giant step toward becoming even more effective as a manager:

- Developing a sensitivity to, and being able to identify, important variables operating in a particular situation.
- Being able to sense problems that may be surfacing from time to time in your environment.
- Being able to gather information quickly by asking appropriate questions of the right sources in an unbiased manner.
- Locating and being able to extract relevant information from published sources.
- Being able to clearly conceptualize the logical relationships among variables in any given situation.
- Becoming sensitive to sources of biases in both published articles and project reports given to you by consultants and researchers, and thus becoming a more discriminating and sophisticated consumer of research.
- Knowing which aspects of a study could be advantageously applied to a problem encountered in your own work situation.
- Recognizing the limitations of a research study, even though they may not have been enumerated in the report.
- Being able to carry out a small research project in an organization.

Research is the excitement of exploring avenues for problem solving, and as a manager you will find the research knowledge and skills you have now acquired to be extremely useful. Scientific research, when applied with good common sense, yields the desired results.

*I wish you success in your personal, academic, and professional careers!*
**Uma Sekaran**

# STATISTICAL TABLES

**Table I**

Cumulative Normal Probabilities

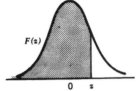

$F(z)$

| $z$ | $F(z)$ | $z$ | $F(z)$ | $z$ | $F(z)$ |
|---|---|---|---|---|---|
| 0.00 | 0.5000000 | 0.30 | 0.6179114 | 0.60 | 0.7257469 |
| 0.01 | 0.5039894 | 0.31 | 0.6217195 | 0.61 | 0.7290691 |
| 0.02 | 0.5079783 | 0.32 | 0.6255158 | 0.62 | 0.7323711 |
| 0.03 | 0.5119665 | 0.33 | 0.6293000 | 0.63 | 0.7356527 |
| 0.04 | 0.5159534 | 0.34 | 0.6330717 | 0.64 | 0.7389137 |
| 0.05 | 0.5199388 | 0.35 | 0.6368307 | 0.65 | 0.7421539 |
| 0.06 | 0.5239222 | 0.36 | 0.6405764 | 0.66 | 0.7453731 |
| 0.07 | 0.5279032 | 0.37 | 0.6443088 | 0.67 | 0.7485711 |
| 0.08 | 0.5318814 | 0.38 | 0.6480273 | 0.68 | 0.7517478 |
| 0.09 | 0.5358564 | 0.39 | 0.6517317 | 0.69 | 0.7549029 |
| 0.10 | 0.5398278 | 0.40 | 0.6554217 | 0.70 | 0.7580363 |
| 0.11 | 0.5437953 | 0.41 | 0.6590970 | 0.71 | 0.7611479 |
| 0.12 | 0.5477584 | 0.42 | 0.6627573 | 0.72 | 0.7642375 |
| 0.13 | 0.5517168 | 0.43 | 0.6664022 | 0.73 | 0.7673049 |
| 0.14 | 0.5556700 | 0.44 | 0.6700314 | 0.74 | 0.7703500 |
| 0.15 | 0.5596177 | 0.45 | 0.6736448 | 0.75 | 0.7733726 |
| 0.16 | 0.5635595 | 0.46 | 0.6772419 | 0.76 | 0.7763727 |
| 0.17 | 0.5674949 | 0.47 | 0.6808225 | 0.77 | 0.7793501 |
| 0.18 | 0.5714237 | 0.48 | 0.6843863 | 0.78 | 0.7823046 |
| 0.19 | 0.5753454 | 0.49 | 0.6879331 | 0.79 | 0.7852361 |
| 0.20 | 0.5792597 | 0.50 | 0.6914625 | 0.80 | 0.7881446 |
| 0.21 | 0.5831662 | 0.51 | 0.6949743 | 0.81 | 0.7910299 |
| 0.22 | 0.5870604 | 0.52 | 0.6984682 | 0.82 | 0.7938919 |
| 0.23 | 0.5909541 | 0.53 | 0.7019440 | 0.83 | 0.7967306 |
| 0.24 | 0.5948349 | 0.54 | 0.7054015 | 0.84 | 0.7995458 |
| 0.25 | 0.5987063 | 0.55 | 0.7088403 | 0.85 | 0.8023375 |
| 0.26 | 0.6025681 | 0.56 | 0.7122603 | 0.86 | 0.8051055 |
| 0.27 | 0.6064199 | 0.57 | 0.7156612 | 0.87 | 0.8078498 |
| 0.28 | 0.6102612 | 0.58 | 0.7190427 | 0.88 | 0.8105703 |
| 0.29 | 0.6140919 | 0.59 | 0.7224047 | 0.89 | 0.8132671 |

(*continued*)

**Table I**    (*Continued*)

| z | F(z) | z | F(z) | z | F(z) |
|------|-----------|------|-----------|------|-----------|
| 0.90 | 0.8159399 | 1.37 | 0.9146565 | 1.84 | 0.9671159 |
| 0.91 | 0.8185887 | 1.38 | 0.9162067 | 1.85 | 0.9678432 |
| 0.92 | 0.8212136 | 1.39 | 0.9177356 | 1.86 | 0.9685572 |
| 0.93 | 0.8238145 | 1.40 | 0.9192433 | 1.87 | 0.9692581 |
| 0.94 | 0.8263912 | 1.41 | 0.9207302 | 1.88 | 0.9699460 |
| 0.95 | 0.8289439 | 1.42 | 0.9221962 | 1.89 | 0.9706210 |
| 0.96 | 0.8314724 | 1.43 | 0.9236415 | 1.90 | 0.9712834 |
| 0.97 | 0.8339768 | 1.44 | 0.9250663 | 1.91 | 0.9719334 |
| 0.98 | 0.8364569 | 1.45 | 0.9264707 | 1.92 | 0.9725711 |
| 0.99 | 0.8389129 | 1.46 | 0.9278550 | 1.93 | 0.9731966 |
| 1.00 | 0.8413447 | 1.47 | 0.9292191 | 1.94 | 0.9738102 |
| 1.01 | 0.8437524 | 1.48 | 0.9305634 | 1.95 | 0.9744119 |
| 1.02 | 0.8461358 | 1.49 | 0.9318879 | 1.96 | 0.9750021 |
| 1.03 | 0.8484950 | 1.50 | 0.9331928 | 1.97 | 0.9755808 |
| 1.04 | 0.8508300 | 1.51 | 0.9344783 | 1.98 | 0.9761482 |
| 1.05 | 0.8531409 | 1.52 | 0.9357445 | 1.99 | 0.9767045 |
| 1.06 | 0.8554277 | 1.53 | 0.9369916 | 2.00 | 0.9772499 |
| 1.07 | 0.8576903 | 1.54 | 0.9382198 | 2.01 | 0.9777844 |
| 1.08 | 0.8599289 | 1.55 | 0.9394292 | 2.02 | 0.9783083 |
| 1.09 | 0.8621434 | 1.56 | 0.9406201 | 2.03 | 0.9788217 |
| 1.10 | 0.8643339 | 1.57 | 0.9417924 | 2.04 | 0.9793248 |
| 1.11 | 0.8665005 | 1.58 | 0.9429466 | 2.05 | 0.9798178 |
| 1.12 | 0.8686431 | 1.59 | 0.9440826 | 2.06 | 0.9803007 |
| 1.13 | 0.8707619 | 1.60 | 0.9452007 | 2.07 | 0.9807738 |
| 1.14 | 0.8728568 | 1.61 | 0.9463011 | 2.08 | 0.9812372 |
| 1.15 | 0.8749281 | 1.62 | 0.9473839 | 2.09 | 0.9816911 |
| 1.16 | 0.8769756 | 1.63 | 0.9484493 | 2.10 | 0.9821356 |
| 1.17 | 0.8789995 | 1.64 | 0.9494974 | 2.11 | 0.9825708 |
| 1.18 | 0.8809999 | 1.65 | 0.9505285 | 2.12 | 0.9829970 |
| 1.19 | 0.8829768 | 1.66 | 0.9515428 | 2.13 | 0.9834142 |
| 1.20 | 0.8849303 | 1.67 | 0.9525403 | 2.14 | 0.9838226 |
| 1.21 | 0.8868606 | 1.68 | 0.9535213 | 2.15 | 0.9842224 |
| 1.22 | 0.8887676 | 1.69 | 0.9544860 | 2.16 | 0.9846137 |
| 1.23 | 0.8906514 | 1.70 | 0.9554345 | 2.17 | 0.9849966 |
| 1.24 | 0.8925123 | 1.71 | 0.9563671 | 2.18 | 0.9853713 |
| 1.25 | 0.8943502 | 1.72 | 0.9572838 | 2.19 | 0.9857379 |
| 1.26 | 0.8961653 | 1.73 | 0.9581849 | 2.20 | 0.9860966 |
| 1.27 | 0.8979577 | 1.74 | 0.9590705 | 2.21 | 0.9864474 |
| 1.28 | 0.8997274 | 1.75 | 0.9599408 | 2.22 | 0.9867906 |
| 1.29 | 0.9014747 | 1.76 | 0.9607961 | 2.23 | 0.9871263 |
| 1.30 | 0.9031995 | 1.77 | 0.9616364 | 2.24 | 0.9874545 |
| 1.31 | 0.9049021 | 1.78 | 0.9624620 | 2.25 | 0.9877755 |
| 1.32 | 0.9065825 | 1.79 | 0.9632730 | 2.26 | 0.9880894 |
| 1.33 | 0.9082409 | 1.80 | 0.9640697 | 2.27 | 0.9883962 |
| 1.34 | 0.9098773 | 1.81 | 0.9648521 | 2.28 | 0.9886962 |
| 1.35 | 0.9114920 | 1.82 | 0.9656205 | 2.29 | 0.9889893 |
| 1.36 | 0.9130850 | 1.83 | 0.9663750 | 2.30 | 0.9892759 |

**Table I**   (*Continued*)

| z | F(z) | z | F(z) | z | F(z) |
|------|------------|------|------------|------|------------|
| 2.31 | 0.9895559 | 2.45 | 0.9928572 | 2.59 | 0.9952012 |
| 2.32 | 0.9898296 | 2.46 | 0.9930531 | 2.60 | 0.9953388 |
| 2.33 | 0.9900969 | 2.47 | 0.9932443 | 2.70 | 0.9965330 |
| 2.34 | 0.9903581 | 2.48 | 0.9934309 | 2.80 | 0.9974449 |
| 2.35 | 0.9906133 | 2.49 | 0.9936128 | 2.90 | 0.9981342 |
| 2.36 | 0.9908625 | 2.50 | 0.9937903 | 3.00 | 0.9986501 |
| 2.37 | 0.9911060 | 2.51 | 0.9939634 | 3.20 | 0.9993129 |
| 2.38 | 0.9913437 | 2.52 | 0.9941323 | 3.40 | 0.9996631 |
| 2.39 | 0.9915758 | 2.53 | 0.9942969 | 3.60 | 0.9998409 |
| 2.40 | 0.9918025 | 2.54 | 0.9944574 | 3.80 | 0.9999277 |
| 2.41 | 0.9920237 | 2.55 | 0.9946139 | 4.00 | 0.9999683 |
| 2.42 | 0.9922397 | 2.56 | 0.9947664 | 4.50 | 0.9999966 |
| 2.43 | 0.9924506 | 2.57 | 0.9949151 | 5.00 | 0.9999997 |
| 2.44 | 0.9926564 | 2.58 | 0.9950600 | 5.50 | 0.9999999 |

This table is condensed from Table 1 of the *Biometrika Tables for Statisticians,* Vol. 1 (1st ed.), edited by E. S. Pearson and H. O. Hartley. Reproduced with the kind permission of E. S. Pearson and the trustees of *Biometrika.*

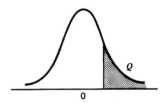

### Table II
Upper Percentage Points of the *t* Distribution

| $v$ | $Q = 0.4$<br>$2Q = 0.8$ | 0.25<br>0.5 | 0.1<br>0.2 | 0.05<br>0.1 | 0.025<br>0.05 | 0.01<br>0.02 | 0.005<br>0.01 | 0.001<br>0.002 |
|---|---|---|---|---|---|---|---|---|
| 1 | 0.325 | 1.000 | 3.078 | 6.314 | 12.706 | 31.821 | 63.657 | 318.31 |
| 2 | 0.289 | 0.816 | 1.886 | 2.920 | 4.303 | 6.965 | 9.925 | 22.326 |
| 3 | 0.277 | 0.765 | 1.638 | 2.353 | 3.182 | 4.541 | 5.841 | 10.213 |
| 4 | 0.271 | 0.741 | 1.533 | 2.132 | 2.776 | 3.747 | 4.604 | 7.173 |
| 5 | 0.267 | 0.727 | 1.476 | 2.015 | 2.571 | 3.365 | 4.032 | 5.893 |
| 6 | 0.265 | 0.718 | 1.440 | 1.943 | 2.447 | 3.143 | 3.707 | 5.208 |
| 7 | 0.263 | 0.711 | 1.415 | 1.895 | 2.365 | 2.998 | 3.499 | 4.785 |
| 8 | 0.262 | 0.706 | 1.397 | 1.860 | 2.306 | 2.896 | 3.355 | 4.501 |
| 9 | 0.261 | 0.703 | 1.383 | 1.833 | 2.262 | 2.821 | 3.250 | 4.297 |
| 10 | 0.260 | 0.700 | 1.372 | 1.812 | 2.228 | 2.764 | 3.169 | 4.144 |
| 11 | 0.260 | 0.697 | 1.363 | 1.796 | 2.201 | 2.718 | 3.106 | 4.025 |
| 12 | 0.259 | 0.695 | 1.356 | 1.782 | 2.179 | 2.681 | 3.055 | 3.930 |
| 13 | 0.259 | 0.694 | 1.350 | 1.771 | 2.160 | 2.650 | 3.012 | 3.852 |
| 14 | 0.258 | 0.692 | 1.345 | 1.761 | 2.145 | 2.624 | 2.977 | 3.787 |
| 15 | 0.258 | 0.691 | 1.341 | 1.753 | 2.131 | 2.602 | 2.947 | 3.733 |
| 16 | 0.258 | 0.690 | 1.337 | 1.746 | 2.120 | 2.583 | 2.921 | 3.686 |
| 17 | 0.257 | 0.689 | 1.333 | 1.740 | 2.110 | 2.567 | 2.898 | 3.646 |
| 18 | 0.257 | 0.688 | 1.330 | 1.734 | 2.101 | 2.552 | 2.878 | 3.610 |
| 19 | 0.257 | 0.688 | 1.328 | 1.729 | 2.093 | 2.539 | 2.861 | 3.579 |
| 20 | 0.257 | 0.687 | 1.325 | 1.725 | 2.086 | 2.528 | 2.845 | 3.552 |
| 21 | 0.257 | 0.686 | 1.323 | 1.721 | 2.080 | 2.518 | 2.831 | 3.527 |
| 22 | 0.256 | 0.686 | 1.321 | 1.717 | 2.074 | 2.508 | 2.819 | 3.505 |
| 23 | 0.256 | 0.685 | 1.319 | 1.714 | 2.069 | 2.500 | 2.807 | 3.485 |
| 24 | 0.256 | 0.685 | 1.318 | 1.711 | 2.064 | 2.492 | 2.797 | 3.467 |
| 25 | 0.256 | 0.684 | 1.316 | 1.708 | 2.060 | 2.485 | 2.787 | 3.450 |
| 26 | 0.256 | 0.684 | 1.315 | 1.706 | 2.056 | 2.479 | 2.779 | 3.435 |
| 27 | 0.256 | 0.684 | 1.314 | 1.703 | 2.052 | 2.473 | 2.771 | 3.421 |
| 28 | 0.256 | 0.683 | 1.313 | 1.701 | 2.048 | 2.467 | 2.763 | 3.408 |
| 29 | 0.256 | 0.683 | 1.311 | 1.699 | 2.045 | 2.462 | 2.756 | 3.396 |
| 30 | 0.256 | 0.683 | 1.310 | 1.697 | 2.042 | 2.457 | 2.750 | 3.385 |
| 40 | 0.255 | 0.681 | 1.303 | 1.684 | 2.021 | 2.423 | 2.704 | 3.307 |
| 60 | 0.254 | 0.679 | 1.296 | 1.671 | 2.000 | 2.390 | 2.660 | 3.232 |
| 120 | 0.254 | 0.677 | 1.289 | 1.658 | 1.980 | 2.358 | 2.617 | 3.160 |
| ∞ | 0.253 | 0.674 | 1.282 | 1.645 | 1.960 | 2.326 | 2.576 | 3.090 |

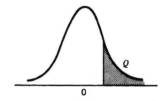

**Table III**
Upper Percentage Points of the $\chi^2$ Distribution

| $Q$ $v$ | 0.995 | 0.990 | 0.975 | 0.950 | 0.900 | 0.750 | 0.500 |
|---|---|---|---|---|---|---|---|
| 1 | $392704 \cdot 10^{-10}$ | $157088 \cdot 10^{-9}$ | $982069 \cdot 10^{-9}$ | $393214 \cdot 10^{-8}$ | 0.0157908 | 0.1015308 | 0.454937 |
| 2 | 0.0100251 | 0.0201007 | 0.0506356 | 0.102587 | 0.210720 | 0.575364 | 1.38629 |
| 3 | 0.0717212 | 0.114832 | 0.215795 | 0.351846 | 0.584375 | 1.212534 | 2.36597 |
| 4 | 0.206990 | 0.297110 | 0.484419 | 0.710721 | 1.063623 | 1.92255 | 3.35670 |
| 5 | 0.411740 | 0.554300 | 0.831211 | 1.145476 | 1.61031 | 2.67460 | 4.35146 |
| 6 | 0.675727 | 0.872085 | 1.237347 | 1.63539 | 2.20413 | 3.45460 | 5.34812 |
| 7 | 0.989265 | 1.239043 | 1.68987 | 2.16735 | 2.83311 | 4.25485 | 6.34581 |
| 8 | 1.344419 | 1.646482 | 2.17973 | 2.73264 | 3.48954 | 5.07064 | 7.34412 |
| 9 | 1.734926 | 2.087912 | 2.70039 | 3.32511 | 4.16816 | 5.89883 | 8.34283 |
| 10 | 2.15585 | 2.55821 | 3.24697 | 3.94030 | 4.86518 | 6.73720 | 9.34182 |
| 11 | 2.60321 | 3.05347 | 3.81575 | 4.57481 | 5.57779 | 7.58412 | 10.3410 |
| 12 | 3.07382 | 3.57056 | 4.40379 | 5.22603 | 6.30380 | 8.43842 | 11.3403 |
| 13 | 3.56503 | 4.10691 | 5.00874 | 5.89186 | 7.04150 | 9.29906 | 12.3398 |
| 14 | 4.07468 | 4.66043 | 5.62872 | 6.57063 | 7.78953 | 10.1653 | 13.3393 |
| 15 | 4.60094 | 5.22935 | 6.26214 | 7.26094 | 8.54675 | 11.0365 | 14.3389 |
| 16 | 5.14224 | 5.81221 | 6.90766 | 7.96164 | 9.31223 | 11.9122 | 15.3385 |
| 17 | 5.69724 | 6.40776 | 7.56418 | 8.67176 | 10.0852 | 12.7919 | 16.3381 |
| 18 | 6.26481 | 7.01491 | 8.23075 | 9.39046 | 10.8649 | 13.6753 | 17.3379 |
| 19 | 6.84398 | 7.63273 | 8.90655 | 10.1170 | 11.6509 | 14.5620 | 18.3376 |
| 20 | 7.43386 | 8.26040 | 9.59083 | 10.8508 | 12.4426 | 15.4518 | 19.3374 |
| 21 | 8.03366 | 8.89720 | 10.28293 | 11.5913 | 13.2396 | 16.3444 | 20.3372 |
| 22 | 8.64272 | 9.54249 | 10.9823 | 12.3380 | 14.0415 | 17.2396 | 21.3370 |
| 23 | 9.26042 | 10.19567 | 11.6885 | 13.0905 | 14.8479 | 18.1373 | 22.3369 |
| 24 | 9.88623 | 10.8564 | 12.4011 | 13.8484 | 15.6587 | 19.0372 | 23.3367 |
| 25 | 10.5197 | 11.5240 | 13.1197 | 14.6114 | 16.4734 | 19.9393 | 24.3366 |
| 26 | 11.1603 | 12.1981 | 13.8439 | 15.3791 | 17.2919 | 20.8434 | 25.3364 |
| 27 | 11.8076 | 12.8786 | 14.5733 | 16.1513 | 18.1138 | 21.7494 | 26.3363 |
| 28 | 12.4613 | 13.5648 | 15.3079 | 16.9279 | 18.9392 | 22.6572 | 27.3363 |
| 29 | 13.1211 | 14.2565 | 16.0471 | 17.7083 | 19.7677 | 23.5666 | 28.3362 |
| 30 | 13.7867 | 14.9535 | 16.7908 | 18.4926 | 20.5992 | 24.4776 | 29.3360 |
| 40 | 20.7065 | 22.1643 | 24.4331 | 26.5093 | 29.0505 | 33.6603 | 39.3354 |
| 50 | 27.9907 | 29.7067 | 32.3574 | 34.7642 | 37.6886 | 42.9421 | 49.3349 |
| 60 | 35.5346 | 37.4848 | 40.4817 | 43.1879 | 46.4589 | 52.2938 | 59.3347 |
| 70 | 43.2752 | 45.4418 | 48.7576 | 51.7393 | 55.3290 | 61.6983 | 69.3344 |
| 80 | 51.1720 | 53.5400 | 57.1532 | 60.3915 | 64.2778 | 71.1445 | 79.3343 |
| 90 | 59.1963 | 61.7541 | 65.6466 | 69.1260 | 73.2912 | 80.6247 | 89.3342 |
| 100 | 67.3276 | 70.0648 | 74.2219 | 77.9295 | 82.3581 | 90.1332 | 99.3341 |
| $z_Q$ | $-2.5758$ | $-2.3263$ | $-1.9600$ | $-1.6449$ | $-1.2816$ | $-0.6745$ | 0.0000 |

*(continued)*

**Table III**   continued

| $\nu$ | 0.250 | 0.100 | 0.050 | 0.025 | 0.010 | 0.005 | 0.001 |
|---|---|---|---|---|---|---|---|
| 1 | 1.32330 | 2.70554 | 3.84146 | 5.02389 | 6.63490 | 7.87944 | 10.828 |
| 2 | 2.77259 | 4.60517 | 5.99147 | 7.37776 | 9.21034 | 10.5966 | 13.816 |
| 3 | 4.10835 | 6.25139 | 7.81473 | 9.34840 | 11.3449 | 12.8381 | 16.266 |
| 4 | 5.38527 | 7.77944 | 9.48773 | 11.1433 | 13.2767 | 14.8602 | 18.467 |
| 5 | 6.62568 | 9.23635 | 11.0705 | 12.8325 | 15.0863 | 16.7496 | 20.515 |
| 6 | 7.84080 | 10.6446 | 12.5916 | 14.4494 | 16.8119 | 18.5476 | 22.458 |
| 7 | 9.03715 | 12.0170 | 14.0671 | 16.0128 | 18.4753 | 20.2777 | 24.322 |
| 8 | 10.2188 | 13.3616 | 15.5073 | 17.5346 | 20.0902 | 21.9550 | 26.125 |
| 9 | 11.3887 | 14.6837 | 16.9190 | 19.0228 | 21.6660 | 23.5893 | 27.877 |
| 10 | 12.5489 | 15.9871 | 18.3070 | 20.4831 | 23.2093 | 25.1882 | 29.588 |
| 11 | 13.7007 | 17.2750 | 19.6751 | 21.9200 | 24.7250 | 26.7569 | 31.264 |
| 12 | 14.8454 | 18.5494 | 21.0261 | 23.3367 | 26.2170 | 28.2995 | 32.909 |
| 13 | 15.9839 | 19.8119 | 22.3621 | 24.7356 | 27.6883 | 29.8194 | 34.528 |
| 14 | 17.1170 | 21.0642 | 23.6848 | 26.1190 | 29.1413 | 31.3193 | 36.123 |
| 15 | 18.2451 | 22.3072 | 24.9958 | 27.4884 | 30.5779 | 32.8013 | 37.697 |
| 16 | 19.3688 | 23.5418 | 26.2962 | 28.8454 | 31.9999 | 34.2672 | 39.252 |
| 17 | 20.4887 | 24.7690 | 27.5871 | 30.1910 | 33.4087 | 35.7185 | 40.790 |
| 18 | 21.6049 | 25.9894 | 28.8693 | 31.5264 | 34.8053 | 37.1564 | 42.312 |
| 19 | 22.71578 | 27.2036 | 30.1435 | 32.8523 | 36.1908 | 38.5822 | 43.820 |
| 20 | 23.8277 | 28.4120 | 31.4104 | 34.1696 | 37.5662 | 39.9968 | 45.315 |
| 21 | 24.9348 | 29.6151 | 32.6705 | 35.4789 | 38.9321 | 41.4010 | 46.797 |
| 22 | 26.0393 | 30.8133 | 33.9244 | 36.7807 | 40.2894 | 42.7956 | 48.268 |
| 23 | 27.1413 | 32.0069 | 35.1725 | 38.0757 | 41.6384 | 44.1813 | 49.728 |
| 24 | 28.2412 | 33.1963 | 36.4151 | 39.3641 | 42.9798 | 45.5585 | 51.179 |
| 25 | 29.3389 | 34.3816 | 37.6525 | 40.6465 | 44.3141 | 46.9278 | 52.620 |
| 26 | 30.4345 | 35.5631 | 38.8852 | 41.9232 | 45.6417 | 48.2899 | 54.052 |
| 27 | 31.5284 | 36.7412 | 40.1133 | 43.1944 | 46.9630 | 49.6449 | 55.476 |
| 28 | 32.6205 | 37.9159 | 41.3372 | 44.4607 | 48.2782 | 50.9933 | 56.892 |
| 29 | 33.7109 | 39.0875 | 42.5569 | 45.7222 | 49.5879 | 52.3356 | 58.302 |
| 30 | 34.7998 | 40.2560 | 43.7729 | 46.9792 | 50.8922 | 53.6720 | 59.703 |
| 40 | 45.6160 | 51.8050 | 55.7585 | 59.3417 | 63.6907 | 66.7659 | 73.402 |
| 50 | 56.3336 | 63.1671 | 67.5048 | 71.4202 | 76.1539 | 79.4900 | 86.661 |
| 60 | 66.9814 | 74.3970 | 79.0819 | 83.2976 | 88.3794 | 91.9517 | 99.607 |
| 70 | 77.5766 | 85.5271 | 90.5312 | 95.0231 | 100.425 | 104.215 | 112.317 |
| 80 | 88.1303 | 96.5782 | 101.879 | 106.629 | 112.329 | 116.321 | 124.839 |
| 90 | 98.6499 | 107.565 | 113.145 | 118.136 | 124.116 | 128.299 | 137.208 |
| 100 | 109.141 | 118.498 | 124.342 | 129.561 | 135.807 | 140.169 | 149.449 |
| $z_Q$ | +0.6745 | +1.2816 | +1.6449 | +1.9600 | +2.3263 | +2.5758 | +3.0902 |

**Table IV**

Percentage Points of the $F$ Distribution: Upper 5% Points

| $v_2$ \ $v_1$ | 1 | 2 | 3 | 4 | 5 | 6 | 7 | 8 | 9 | 10 | 12 | 15 | 20 | 24 | 30 | 40 | 60 | 120 | ∞ |
|---|---|---|---|---|---|---|---|---|---|---|---|---|---|---|---|---|---|---|---|
| 1 | 161.4 | 199.5 | 215.7 | 224.6 | 230.2 | 234.0 | 236.8 | 238.9 | 240.5 | 241.9 | 243.9 | 245.9 | 248.0 | 249.1 | 250.1 | 251.1 | 252.2 | 253.3 | 254.3 |
| 2 | 18.51 | 19.00 | 19.16 | 19.25 | 19.30 | 19.33 | 19.35 | 19.37 | 19.38 | 19.40 | 19.41 | 19.43 | 19.45 | 19.45 | 19.46 | 19.47 | 19.48 | 19.49 | 19.50 |
| 3 | 10.13 | 9.55 | 9.28 | 9.12 | 9.01 | 8.94 | 8.89 | 8.85 | 8.81 | 8.79 | 8.74 | 8.70 | 8.66 | 8.64 | 8.62 | 8.59 | 8.57 | 8.55 | 8.53 |
| 4 | 7.71 | 6.94 | 6.59 | 6.39 | 6.26 | 6.16 | 6.09 | 6.04 | 6.00 | 5.96 | 5.91 | 5.86 | 5.80 | 5.77 | 5.75 | 5.72 | 5.69 | 5.66 | 5.63 |
| 5 | 6.61 | 5.79 | 5.41 | 5.19 | 5.05 | 4.95 | 4.88 | 4.82 | 4.77 | 4.74 | 4.68 | 4.62 | 4.56 | 4.53 | 4.50 | 4.46 | 4.43 | 4.40 | 4.36 |
| 6 | 5.99 | 5.14 | 4.76 | 4.53 | 4.39 | 4.28 | 4.21 | 4.15 | 4.10 | 4.06 | 4.00 | 3.94 | 3.87 | 3.84 | 3.81 | 3.77 | 3.74 | 3.70 | 3.67 |
| 7 | 5.59 | 4.74 | 4.35 | 4.12 | 3.97 | 3.87 | 3.79 | 3.73 | 3.68 | 3.64 | 3.57 | 3.51 | 3.44 | 3.41 | 3.38 | 3.34 | 3.30 | 3.27 | 3.23 |
| 8 | 5.32 | 4.46 | 4.07 | 3.84 | 3.69 | 3.58 | 3.50 | 3.44 | 3.39 | 3.35 | 3.28 | 3.22 | 3.15 | 3.12 | 3.08 | 3.04 | 3.01 | 2.97 | 2.93 |
| 9 | 5.12 | 4.26 | 3.86 | 3.63 | 3.48 | 3.37 | 3.29 | 3.23 | 3.18 | 3.14 | 3.07 | 3.01 | 2.94 | 2.90 | 2.86 | 2.83 | 2.79 | 2.75 | 2.71 |
| 10 | 4.96 | 4.10 | 3.71 | 3.48 | 3.33 | 3.22 | 3.14 | 3.07 | 3.02 | 2.98 | 2.91 | 2.85 | 2.77 | 2.74 | 2.70 | 2.66 | 2.62 | 2.58 | 2.54 |
| 11 | 4.84 | 3.98 | 3.59 | 3.36 | 3.20 | 3.09 | 3.01 | 2.95 | 2.90 | 2.85 | 2.79 | 2.72 | 2.65 | 2.61 | 2.57 | 2.53 | 2.49 | 2.45 | 2.40 |
| 12 | 4.75 | 3.89 | 3.49 | 3.26 | 3.11 | 3.00 | 2.91 | 2.85 | 2.80 | 2.75 | 2.69 | 2.62 | 2.54 | 2.51 | 2.47 | 2.43 | 2.38 | 2.34 | 2.30 |
| 13 | 4.67 | 3.81 | 3.41 | 3.18 | 3.03 | 2.92 | 2.83 | 2.77 | 2.71 | 2.67 | 2.60 | 2.53 | 2.46 | 2.42 | 2.38 | 2.34 | 2.30 | 2.25 | 2.21 |
| 14 | 4.60 | 3.74 | 3.34 | 3.11 | 2.96 | 2.85 | 2.76 | 2.70 | 2.65 | 2.60 | 2.53 | 2.46 | 2.39 | 2.35 | 2.31 | 2.27 | 2.22 | 2.18 | 2.13 |
| 15 | 4.54 | 3.68 | 3.29 | 3.06 | 2.90 | 2.79 | 2.71 | 2.64 | 2.59 | 2.54 | 2.48 | 2.40 | 2.33 | 2.29 | 2.25 | 2.20 | 2.16 | 2.11 | 2.07 |
| 16 | 4.49 | 3.63 | 3.24 | 3.01 | 2.85 | 2.74 | 2.66 | 2.59 | 2.54 | 2.49 | 2.42 | 2.35 | 2.28 | 2.24 | 2.19 | 2.15 | 2.11 | 2.06 | 2.01 |
| 17 | 4.45 | 3.59 | 3.20 | 2.96 | 2.81 | 2.70 | 2.61 | 2.55 | 2.49 | 2.45 | 2.38 | 2.31 | 2.23 | 2.19 | 2.15 | 2.10 | 2.06 | 2.01 | 1.96 |
| 18 | 4.41 | 3.55 | 3.16 | 2.93 | 2.77 | 2.66 | 2.58 | 2.51 | 2.46 | 2.41 | 2.34 | 2.27 | 2.19 | 2.15 | 2.11 | 2.06 | 2.02 | 1.97 | 1.92 |
| 19 | 4.38 | 3.52 | 3.13 | 2.90 | 2.74 | 2.63 | 2.54 | 2.48 | 2.42 | 2.38 | 2.31 | 2.23 | 2.16 | 2.11 | 2.07 | 2.03 | 1.98 | 1.93 | 1.88 |
| 20 | 4.35 | 3.49 | 3.10 | 2.87 | 2.71 | 2.60 | 2.51 | 2.45 | 2.39 | 2.35 | 2.28 | 2.20 | 2.12 | 2.08 | 2.04 | 1.99 | 1.95 | 1.90 | 1.84 |
| 21 | 4.32 | 3.47 | 3.07 | 2.84 | 2.68 | 2.57 | 2.49 | 2.42 | 2.37 | 2.32 | 2.25 | 2.18 | 2.10 | 2.05 | 2.01 | 1.96 | 1.92 | 1.87 | 1.81 |
| 22 | 4.30 | 3.44 | 3.05 | 2.82 | 2.66 | 2.55 | 2.46 | 2.40 | 2.34 | 2.30 | 2.23 | 2.15 | 2.07 | 2.03 | 1.98 | 1.94 | 1.89 | 1.84 | 1.78 |
| 23 | 4.28 | 3.42 | 3.03 | 2.80 | 2.64 | 2.53 | 2.44 | 2.37 | 2.32 | 2.27 | 2.20 | 2.13 | 2.05 | 2.01 | 1.96 | 1.91 | 1.86 | 1.81 | 1.76 |
| 24 | 4.26 | 3.40 | 3.01 | 2.78 | 2.62 | 2.51 | 2.42 | 2.36 | 2.30 | 2.25 | 2.18 | 2.11 | 2.03 | 1.98 | 1.94 | 1.89 | 1.84 | 1.79 | 1.73 |
| 25 | 4.24 | 3.39 | 2.99 | 2.76 | 2.60 | 2.49 | 2.40 | 2.34 | 2.28 | 2.24 | 2.16 | 2.09 | 2.01 | 1.96 | 1.92 | 1.87 | 1.82 | 1.77 | 1.71 |
| 26 | 4.23 | 3.37 | 2.98 | 2.74 | 2.59 | 2.47 | 2.39 | 2.32 | 2.27 | 2.22 | 2.15 | 2.07 | 1.99 | 1.95 | 1.90 | 1.85 | 1.80 | 1.75 | 1.69 |
| 27 | 4.21 | 3.35 | 2.96 | 2.73 | 2.57 | 2.46 | 2.37 | 2.31 | 2.25 | 2.20 | 2.13 | 2.06 | 1.97 | 1.93 | 1.88 | 1.84 | 1.79 | 1.73 | 1.67 |
| 28 | 4.20 | 3.34 | 2.95 | 2.71 | 2.56 | 2.45 | 2.36 | 2.29 | 2.24 | 2.19 | 2.12 | 2.04 | 1.96 | 1.91 | 1.87 | 1.82 | 1.77 | 1.71 | 1.65 |
| 29 | 4.18 | 3.33 | 2.93 | 2.70 | 2.55 | 2.43 | 2.35 | 2.28 | 2.22 | 2.18 | 2.10 | 2.03 | 1.94 | 1.90 | 1.85 | 1.81 | 1.75 | 1.70 | 1.64 |
| 30 | 4.17 | 3.32 | 2.92 | 2.69 | 2.53 | 2.42 | 2.33 | 2.27 | 2.21 | 2.16 | 2.09 | 2.01 | 1.93 | 1.89 | 1.84 | 1.79 | 1.74 | 1.68 | 1.62 |
| 40 | 4.08 | 3.23 | 2.84 | 2.61 | 2.45 | 2.34 | 2.25 | 2.18 | 2.12 | 2.08 | 2.00 | 1.92 | 1.84 | 1.79 | 1.74 | 1.69 | 1.64 | 1.58 | 1.51 |
| 60 | 4.00 | 3.15 | 2.76 | 2.53 | 2.37 | 2.25 | 2.17 | 2.10 | 2.03 | 1.99 | 1.92 | 1.84 | 1.75 | 1.70 | 1.65 | 1.59 | 1.53 | 1.47 | 1.39 |
| 120 | 3.92 | 3.07 | 2.68 | 2.45 | 2.29 | 2.17 | 2.09 | 2.02 | 1.96 | 1.91 | 1.83 | 1.75 | 1.66 | 1.61 | 1.55 | 1.50 | 1.43 | 1.35 | 1.25 |
| ∞ | 3.84 | 3.00 | 2.60 | 2.37 | 2.21 | 2.10 | 2.01 | 1.94 | 1.88 | 1.83 | 1.75 | 1.67 | 1.57 | 1.52 | 1.46 | 1.39 | 1.32 | 1.22 | 1.00 |

*(continued)*

**Table IV** (*continued*)
Upper 2.5% Points

| $v_2$ \ $v_1$ | 1 | 2 | 3 | 4 | 5 | 6 | 7 | 8 | 9 | 10 | 12 | 15 | 20 | 24 | 30 | 40 | 60 | 120 | ∞ |
|---|---|---|---|---|---|---|---|---|---|---|---|---|---|---|---|---|---|---|---|
| 1 | 647.8 | 799.5 | 864.2 | 899.6 | 921.8 | 937.1 | 948.2 | 956.7 | 963.3 | 968.6 | 976.7 | 984.9 | 993.1 | 997.2 | 1001 | 1006 | 1010 | 1014 | 1018 |
| 2 | 38.51 | 39.00 | 39.17 | 39.25 | 39.30 | 39.33 | 39.36 | 39.37 | 39.39 | 39.40 | 39.41 | 39.43 | 39.45 | 39.46 | 39.46 | 39.47 | 39.48 | 39.49 | 39.50 |
| 3 | 17.44 | 16.04 | 15.44 | 15.10 | 14.88 | 14.73 | 14.62 | 14.54 | 14.47 | 14.42 | 14.34 | 14.25 | 14.17 | 14.12 | 14.08 | 14.04 | 13.99 | 13.95 | 13.90 |
| 4 | 12.22 | 10.65 | 9.98 | 9.60 | 9.36 | 9.20 | 9.07 | 8.98 | 8.90 | 8.84 | 8.75 | 8.66 | 8.56 | 8.51 | 8.46 | 8.41 | 8.36 | 8.31 | 8.26 |
| 5 | 10.01 | 8.43 | 7.76 | 7.39 | 7.15 | 6.98 | 6.85 | 6.76 | 6.68 | 6.62 | 6.52 | 6.43 | 6.33 | 6.28 | 6.23 | 6.18 | 6.12 | 6.07 | 6.02 |
| 6 | 8.81 | 7.26 | 6.60 | 6.23 | 5.99 | 5.82 | 5.70 | 5.60 | 5.52 | 5.46 | 5.37 | 5.27 | 5.17 | 5.12 | 5.07 | 5.01 | 4.96 | 4.90 | 4.85 |
| 7 | 8.07 | 6.54 | 5.89 | 5.52 | 5.29 | 5.21 | 4.99 | 4.90 | 4.82 | 4.76 | 4.67 | 4.57 | 4.47 | 4.42 | 4.36 | 4.31 | 4.25 | 4.20 | 4.14 |
| 8 | 7.57 | 6.06 | 5.42 | 5.05 | 4.82 | 4.65 | 4.53 | 4.43 | 4.36 | 4.30 | 4.20 | 4.10 | 4.00 | 3.95 | 3.89 | 3.84 | 3.78 | 3.73 | 3.67 |
| 9 | 7.21 | 5.71 | 5.08 | 4.72 | 4.48 | 4.32 | 4.20 | 4.10 | 4.03 | 3.96 | 3.87 | 3.77 | 3.67 | 3.61 | 3.56 | 3.51 | 3.45 | 3.39 | 3.33 |
| 10 | 6.94 | 5.46 | 4.83 | 4.47 | 4.24 | 4.07 | 3.95 | 3.85 | 3.78 | 3.72 | 3.62 | 3.52 | 3.42 | 3.37 | 3.31 | 3.26 | 3.20 | 3.14 | 3.08 |
| 11 | 6.72 | 5.26 | 4.63 | 4.28 | 4.04 | 3.88 | 3.76 | 3.66 | 3.59 | 3.53 | 3.43 | 3.33 | 3.23 | 3.17 | 3.12 | 3.06 | 3.00 | 2.94 | 2.88 |
| 12 | 6.55 | 5.10 | 4.47 | 4.12 | 3.89 | 3.73 | 3.61 | 3.51 | 3.44 | 3.37 | 3.28 | 3.18 | 3.07 | 3.02 | 2.96 | 2.91 | 2.85 | 2.79 | 2.72 |
| 13 | 6.41 | 4.97 | 4.35 | 4.00 | 3.77 | 3.60 | 3.48 | 3.39 | 3.31 | 3.25 | 3.15 | 3.05 | 2.95 | 2.89 | 2.84 | 2.78 | 2.72 | 2.66 | 2.60 |
| 14 | 6.30 | 4.86 | 4.24 | 3.89 | 3.66 | 3.50 | 3.38 | 3.29 | 3.21 | 3.15 | 3.05 | 2.95 | 2.84 | 2.79 | 2.73 | 2.67 | 2.61 | 2.55 | 2.49 |
| 15 | 6.20 | 4.77 | 4.15 | 3.80 | 3.58 | 3.41 | 3.29 | 3.20 | 3.12 | 3.06 | 2.96 | 2.86 | 2.76 | 2.70 | 2.64 | 2.59 | 2.52 | 2.46 | 2.40 |
| 16 | 6.12 | 4.69 | 4.08 | 3.73 | 3.50 | 3.34 | 3.22 | 3.12 | 3.05 | 2.99 | 2.89 | 2.79 | 2.68 | 2.63 | 2.57 | 2.51 | 2.45 | 2.38 | 2.32 |
| 17 | 6.04 | 4.62 | 4.01 | 3.66 | 3.44 | 3.28 | 3.16 | 3.06 | 2.98 | 2.92 | 2.82 | 2.72 | 2.62 | 2.56 | 2.50 | 2.44 | 2.38 | 2.32 | 2.25 |
| 18 | 5.98 | 4.56 | 3.95 | 3.61 | 3.38 | 3.22 | 3.10 | 3.01 | 2.93 | 2.87 | 2.77 | 2.67 | 2.56 | 2.50 | 2.44 | 2.38 | 2.32 | 2.26 | 2.19 |
| 19 | 5.92 | 4.51 | 3.90 | 3.56 | 3.33 | 3.17 | 3.05 | 2.96 | 2.88 | 2.82 | 2.72 | 2.62 | 2.51 | 2.45 | 2.39 | 2.33 | 2.27 | 2.20 | 2.13 |
| 20 | 5.87 | 4.46 | 3.86 | 3.51 | 3.29 | 3.13 | 3.01 | 2.91 | 2.84 | 2.77 | 2.68 | 2.57 | 2.46 | 2.41 | 2.35 | 2.29 | 2.22 | 2.16 | 2.09 |
| 21 | 5.83 | 4.42 | 3.82 | 3.48 | 3.25 | 3.09 | 2.97 | 2.87 | 2.80 | 2.73 | 2.64 | 2.53 | 2.42 | 2.37 | 2.31 | 2.25 | 2.18 | 2.11 | 2.04 |
| 22 | 5.79 | 4.38 | 3.78 | 3.44 | 3.22 | 3.05 | 2.93 | 2.84 | 2.76 | 2.70 | 2.60 | 2.50 | 2.39 | 2.33 | 2.27 | 2.21 | 2.14 | 2.08 | 2.00 |
| 23 | 5.75 | 4.35 | 3.75 | 3.41 | 3.18 | 3.02 | 2.90 | 2.81 | 2.73 | 2.67 | 2.57 | 2.47 | 2.36 | 2.30 | 2.24 | 2.18 | 2.11 | 2.04 | 1.97 |
| 24 | 5.72 | 4.32 | 3.72 | 3.38 | 3.15 | 2.99 | 2.87 | 2.78 | 2.70 | 2.64 | 2.54 | 2.44 | 2.33 | 2.27 | 2.21 | 2.15 | 2.08 | 2.01 | 1.94 |
| 25 | 5.69 | 4.29 | 3.69 | 3.35 | 3.13 | 2.97 | 2.85 | 2.75 | 2.68 | 2.61 | 2.51 | 2.41 | 2.30 | 2.24 | 2.18 | 2.12 | 2.05 | 1.98 | 1.91 |
| 26 | 5.66 | 4.27 | 3.67 | 3.33 | 3.10 | 2.94 | 2.82 | 2.73 | 2.65 | 2.59 | 2.49 | 2.39 | 2.28 | 2.22 | 2.16 | 2.09 | 2.03 | 1.95 | 1.88 |
| 27 | 5.63 | 4.24 | 3.65 | 3.31 | 3.08 | 2.92 | 2.80 | 2.71 | 2.63 | 2.57 | 2.47 | 2.36 | 2.25 | 2.19 | 2.13 | 2.07 | 2.00 | 1.93 | 1.85 |
| 28 | 5.61 | 4.22 | 3.63 | 3.29 | 3.06 | 2.90 | 2.78 | 2.69 | 2.61 | 2.55 | 2.45 | 2.34 | 2.23 | 2.17 | 2.11 | 2.05 | 1.98 | 1.91 | 1.83 |
| 29 | 5.59 | 4.20 | 3.61 | 3.27 | 3.04 | 2.88 | 2.76 | 2.67 | 2.59 | 2.53 | 2.43 | 2.32 | 2.21 | 2.15 | 2.09 | 2.03 | 1.96 | 1.89 | 1.81 |
| 30 | 5.57 | 4.18 | 3.59 | 3.25 | 3.03 | 2.87 | 2.75 | 2.65 | 2.57 | 2.51 | 2.41 | 2.31 | 2.20 | 2.14 | 2.07 | 2.01 | 1.94 | 1.87 | 1.79 |
| 40 | 5.42 | 4.05 | 3.46 | 3.13 | 2.90 | 2.74 | 2.62 | 2.53 | 2.45 | 2.39 | 2.29 | 2.18 | 2.07 | 2.01 | 1.94 | 1.88 | 1.80 | 1.72 | 1.64 |
| 60 | 5.29 | 3.93 | 3.34 | 3.01 | 2.79 | 2.63 | 2.51 | 2.41 | 2.33 | 2.27 | 2.17 | 2.06 | 1.94 | 1.88 | 1.82 | 1.74 | 1.67 | 1.58 | 1.48 |
| 120 | 5.15 | 3.80 | 3.23 | 2.89 | 2.67 | 2.52 | 2.39 | 2.30 | 2.22 | 2.16 | 2.05 | 1.94 | 1.82 | 1.76 | 1.69 | 1.61 | 1.53 | 1.43 | 1.31 |
| ∞ | 5.02 | 3.69 | 3.12 | 2.79 | 2.57 | 2.41 | 2.29 | 2.19 | 2.11 | 2.05 | 1.94 | 1.83 | 1.71 | 1.64 | 1.57 | 1.48 | 1.39 | 1.27 | 1.00 |

## Upper 1% Points

| $\nu_2$ \ $\nu_1$ | 1 | 2 | 3 | 4 | 5 | 6 | 7 | 8 | 9 | 10 | 12 | 15 | 20 | 24 | 30 | 40 | 60 | 120 | ∞ |
|---|---|---|---|---|---|---|---|---|---|---|---|---|---|---|---|---|---|---|---|
| 1 | 4052 | 4999.5 | 5403 | 5625 | 5764 | 5859 | 5928 | 5982 | 6022 | 6056 | 6106 | 6157 | 6209 | 6235 | 6261 | 6287 | 6313 | 6339 | 6366 |
| 2 | 98.50 | 99.00 | 99.17 | 99.25 | 99.30 | 99.33 | 99.36 | 99.37 | 99.39 | 99.40 | 99.42 | 99.43 | 99.45 | 99.46 | 99.47 | 99.47 | 99.48 | 99.49 | 99.50 |
| 3 | 34.12 | 30.82 | 29.46 | 28.71 | 28.24 | 27.91 | 27.67 | 27.49 | 27.35 | 27.23 | 27.05 | 26.87 | 26.69 | 26.60 | 26.50 | 26.41 | 26.32 | 26.22 | 26.13 |
| 4 | 21.20 | 18.00 | 16.69 | 15.98 | 15.52 | 15.21 | 14.98 | 14.80 | 14.66 | 14.55 | 14.37 | 14.20 | 14.02 | 13.93 | 13.84 | 13.75 | 13.65 | 13.56 | 13.46 |
| 5 | 16.26 | 13.27 | 12.06 | 11.39 | 10.97 | 10.67 | 10.46 | 10.29 | 10.16 | 10.05 | 9.89 | 9.72 | 9.55 | 9.47 | 9.38 | 9.29 | 9.20 | 9.11 | 9.02 |
| 6 | 13.75 | 10.92 | 9.78 | 9.15 | 8.75 | 8.47 | 8.26 | 8.10 | 7.98 | 7.87 | 7.72 | 7.56 | 7.40 | 7.31 | 7.23 | 7.14 | 7.06 | 6.97 | 6.88 |
| 7 | 12.25 | 9.55 | 8.45 | 7.85 | 7.46 | 7.19 | 6.99 | 6.84 | 6.72 | 6.62 | 6.47 | 6.31 | 6.16 | 6.07 | 5.99 | 5.91 | 5.82 | 5.74 | 5.65 |
| 8 | 11.26 | 8.65 | 7.59 | 7.01 | 6.63 | 6.37 | 6.18 | 6.03 | 5.91 | 5.81 | 5.67 | 5.52 | 5.36 | 5.28 | 5.20 | 5.12 | 5.03 | 4.95 | 4.86 |
| 9 | 10.56 | 8.02 | 6.99 | 6.42 | 6.06 | 5.80 | 5.61 | 5.47 | 5.35 | 5.26 | 5.11 | 4.96 | 4.81 | 4.73 | 4.65 | 4.57 | 4.48 | 4.40 | 4.31 |
| 10 | 10.04 | 7.56 | 6.55 | 5.99 | 5.64 | 5.39 | 5.20 | 5.06 | 4.94 | 4.85 | 4.71 | 4.56 | 4.41 | 4.33 | 4.25 | 4.17 | 4.08 | 4.00 | 3.91 |
| 11 | 9.65 | 7.21 | 6.22 | 5.67 | 5.32 | 5.07 | 4.89 | 4.74 | 4.63 | 4.54 | 4.40 | 4.25 | 4.10 | 4.02 | 3.94 | 3.86 | 3.78 | 3.69 | 3.60 |
| 12 | 9.33 | 6.93 | 5.95 | 5.41 | 5.06 | 4.82 | 4.64 | 4.50 | 4.39 | 4.30 | 4.16 | 4.01 | 3.86 | 3.78 | 3.70 | 3.62 | 3.54 | 3.45 | 3.36 |
| 13 | 9.07 | 6.70 | 5.74 | 5.21 | 4.86 | 4.62 | 4.44 | 4.30 | 4.19 | 4.10 | 3.96 | 3.82 | 3.66 | 3.59 | 3.51 | 3.43 | 3.34 | 3.25 | 3.17 |
| 14 | 8.86 | 6.51 | 5.56 | 5.04 | 4.69 | 4.46 | 4.28 | 4.14 | 4.03 | 3.94 | 3.80 | 3.66 | 3.51 | 3.43 | 3.35 | 3.27 | 3.18 | 3.09 | 3.00 |
| 15 | 8.68 | 6.36 | 5.42 | 4.89 | 4.56 | 4.32 | 4.14 | 4.00 | 3.89 | 3.80 | 3.67 | 3.52 | 3.37 | 3.29 | 3.21 | 3.13 | 3.05 | 2.96 | 2.87 |
| 16 | 8.53 | 6.23 | 5.29 | 4.77 | 4.44 | 4.20 | 4.03 | 3.89 | 3.78 | 3.69 | 3.55 | 3.41 | 3.26 | 3.18 | 3.10 | 3.02 | 2.93 | 2.84 | 2.75 |
| 17 | 8.40 | 6.11 | 5.18 | 4.67 | 4.34 | 4.10 | 3.93 | 3.79 | 3.68 | 3.59 | 3.46 | 3.31 | 3.16 | 3.08 | 3.00 | 2.92 | 2.83 | 2.75 | 2.65 |
| 18 | 8.29 | 6.01 | 5.09 | 4.58 | 4.25 | 4.01 | 3.84 | 3.71 | 3.60 | 3.51 | 3.37 | 3.23 | 3.08 | 3.00 | 2.92 | 2.84 | 2.75 | 2.66 | 2.57 |
| 19 | 8.18 | 5.93 | 5.01 | 4.50 | 4.17 | 3.94 | 3.77 | 3.63 | 3.52 | 3.43 | 3.30 | 3.15 | 3.00 | 2.92 | 2.84 | 2.76 | 2.67 | 2.58 | 2.49 |
| 20 | 8.10 | 5.85 | 4.94 | 4.43 | 4.10 | 3.87 | 3.70 | 3.56 | 3.46 | 3.37 | 3.23 | 3.09 | 2.94 | 2.86 | 2.78 | 2.69 | 2.61 | 2.52 | 2.42 |
| 21 | 8.02 | 5.78 | 4.87 | 4.37 | 4.04 | 3.81 | 3.64 | 3.51 | 3.40 | 3.31 | 3.17 | 3.03 | 2.88 | 2.80 | 2.72 | 2.64 | 2.55 | 2.46 | 2.36 |
| 22 | 7.95 | 5.72 | 4.82 | 4.31 | 3.99 | 3.76 | 3.59 | 3.45 | 3.35 | 3.26 | 3.12 | 2.98 | 2.83 | 2.75 | 2.67 | 2.58 | 2.50 | 2.40 | 2.31 |
| 23 | 7.88 | 5.66 | 4.76 | 4.26 | 3.94 | 3.71 | 3.54 | 3.41 | 3.30 | 3.21 | 3.07 | 2.93 | 2.78 | 2.70 | 2.62 | 2.54 | 2.45 | 2.35 | 2.26 |
| 24 | 7.82 | 5.61 | 4.72 | 4.22 | 3.90 | 3.67 | 3.50 | 3.36 | 3.26 | 3.17 | 3.03 | 2.89 | 2.74 | 2.66 | 2.58 | 2.49 | 2.40 | 2.31 | 2.21 |
| 25 | 7.77 | 5.57 | 4.68 | 4.18 | 3.85 | 3.63 | 3.46 | 3.32 | 3.22 | 3.13 | 2.99 | 2.85 | 2.70 | 2.62 | 2.54 | 2.45 | 2.36 | 2.27 | 2.17 |
| 26 | 7.72 | 5.53 | 4.64 | 4.14 | 3.82 | 3.59 | 3.42 | 3.29 | 3.18 | 3.09 | 2.96 | 2.81 | 2.66 | 2.58 | 2.50 | 2.42 | 2.33 | 2.23 | 2.13 |
| 27 | 7.68 | 5.49 | 4.60 | 4.11 | 3.78 | 3.56 | 3.39 | 3.26 | 3.15 | 3.06 | 2.93 | 2.78 | 2.63 | 2.55 | 2.47 | 2.38 | 2.29 | 2.20 | 2.10 |
| 28 | 7.64 | 5.45 | 4.57 | 4.07 | 3.75 | 3.53 | 3.36 | 3.23 | 3.12 | 3.03 | 2.90 | 2.75 | 2.60 | 2.52 | 2.44 | 2.35 | 2.26 | 2.17 | 2.06 |
| 29 | 7.60 | 5.42 | 4.54 | 4.04 | 3.73 | 3.50 | 3.33 | 3.20 | 3.09 | 3.00 | 2.87 | 2.73 | 2.57 | 2.49 | 2.41 | 2.33 | 2.23 | 2.14 | 2.03 |
| 30 | 7.56 | 5.39 | 4.51 | 4.02 | 3.70 | 3.47 | 3.30 | 3.17 | 3.07 | 2.98 | 2.84 | 2.70 | 2.55 | 2.47 | 2.39 | 2.30 | 2.21 | 2.11 | 2.01 |
| 40 | 7.31 | 5.18 | 4.31 | 3.83 | 3.51 | 3.29 | 3.12 | 2.99 | 2.89 | 2.80 | 2.66 | 2.52 | 2.37 | 2.29 | 2.20 | 2.11 | 2.02 | 1.92 | 1.80 |
| 60 | 7.08 | 4.98 | 4.13 | 3.65 | 3.34 | 3.12 | 2.95 | 2.82 | 2.72 | 2.63 | 2.50 | 2.35 | 2.20 | 2.12 | 2.03 | 1.94 | 1.84 | 1.73 | 1.60 |
| 120 | 6.85 | 4.79 | 3.95 | 3.48 | 3.17 | 2.96 | 2.79 | 2.66 | 2.56 | 2.47 | 2.34 | 2.19 | 2.03 | 1.95 | 1.86 | 1.76 | 1.66 | 1.53 | 1.38 |
| ∞ | 6.63 | 4.61 | 3.78 | 3.32 | 3.02 | 2.80 | 2.64 | 2.51 | 2.41 | 2.32 | 2.18 | 2.04 | 1.88 | 1.79 | 1.70 | 1.59 | 1.47 | 1.32 | 1.00 |

# GLOSSARY

**Action research:** A method of initiating change processes, with an incremental focus, for narrowing the gap between the desired and actual states.

**Alternate hypothesis:** An educated conjecture that sets the parameters one expects to find. The alternate hypothesis is tested to see whether or not the null is to be rejected.

**Ambiguous questions:** Questions that are not clearly worded and are likely to be interpreted by respondents in different ways.

**Analytical study:** A study that tries to explain why or how certain variables influence the dependent variable of interest to the researcher.

**ANOVA:** Stands for Analysis of Variance, which tests for significant mean differences in variables among multiple groups.

**Applied research:** Research conducted in a particular setting with the specific objective of solving an existing problem in the situation.

**Area sampling:** Cluster sampling within a specified area or region; a probability sampling design.

**Attitudinal factors:** People's feelings, dispositions, and reactions toward the organization and factors in the work environment such as the work itself, co-workers, or supervision.

**Basic research:** Research conducted to generate knowledge and understanding of phenomena (in the work setting) that adds to the existing body of knowledge (about organizations and management theory).

**Behavioral factors:** Actual behavior of employees on the job, such as being late, working hard, remaining absent, or quitting work.

**Bias:** Any error that creeps into the data. Biases can be introduced by the researcher, the respondent, the measuring instrument, the sample, and so on.

**Bibliography:** A listing of books, articles, and other relevant materials, alphabetized according to the last name of the authors, referencing the titles of their works, and indicating where they can be located.

**Broad problem area:** A situation where one senses a possible need for research and problem solving, even though the specific problem is not clear.

**Canonical correlation:** A statistical technique that examines the relationship between two or more dependent variables and several independent variables.

**Case study:** The documented history of noteworthy events that have taken place in a given institution.

**Categorization:** The process of organizing, arranging, and classifying coding units (in qualitative data analysis).

**Category reliability:** The extent to which judges are able to use category definitions to classify qualitative data.

**Category scale:** A scale that uses multiple items to seek a single response.

**Causal analysis:** Analysis done to detect cause-and-effect relationships between two or among more variables.

**Causal study:**  A research study conducted to establish cause-and-effect relationships among variables.

**Chi-square test:**  A nonparametric test that establishes the independence or otherwise between two nominal variables.

**Classification data:**  Personal information or demographic details of the respondents such as age, marital status, and educational level.

**Closed questions:**  Questions with a clearly delineated set of alternatives that confine the respondents' choice to one of them.

**Cluster sampling:**  A probability sampling design in which the sample comprises groups or chunks of elements with intragroup heterogeneity and intergroup homogeneity.

**Coding:**  The analytic process through which the qualitative data that you have gathered are reduced, rearranged, and integrated to form theory (compare Data coding).

**Comparative scale:**  A scale that provides a benchmark or point of reference to assess attitudes, opinions, and the like.

**Comparative study:**  A study conducted by collecting data from several settings or organizations.

**Complex probability sampling:**  Several probability sampling designs (such as systematic and stratified random), which offer an alternative to the cumbersome, simple random sampling design.

**Computer-assisted telephone interviews (CATI):**  Interviews in which questions are prompted onto a PC monitor that is networked into the telephone system, to which respondents provide their answers.

**Conceptual analysis:**  Establishes the existence and frequency of concepts (such as words, themes, or characters) in a text.

**Concurrent validity:**  Relates to criterion-related validity, which is established at the same time the test is administered.

**Confidence:**  The probability estimate of how much reliance can be placed on the findings; the usual accepted level of confidence in social science research is 95%.

**Conjoint analysis:**  A multivariate statistical technique used to determine the relative importance respondents attach to attributes and the utilities they attach to specific levels of attributes.

**Consensus scale:**  A scale developed through consensus or the unanimous agreement of a panel of judges as to the items that measure a concept.

**Constant sum rating scale:**  A scale where the respondents distribute a fixed number of points across several items.

**Construct validity:**  Testifies to how well the results obtained from the use of the measure fit the theories around which the test was designed.

**Content analysis:**  An observational research method that is used to systematically evaluate the symbolic contents of all forms of recorded communication.

**Content validity:**  Establishes the representative sampling of a whole set of items that measures a concept, and reflects how well the dimensions and elements thereof are delineated.

**Contextual factors:**  Factors relating to the organization under study such as the background and environment of the organization, including its origin and purpose, size, resources, financial standing, and the like.

**Contrived setting:** An artificially created or "lab" environment in which research is conducted.

**Control group:** The group that is not exposed to any treatment in an experiment.

**Controlled variable:** Any exogenous or extraneous variable that could contaminate the cause-and-effect relationship, but the effects of which can be controlled through a process of either matching or randomization.

**Convenience sampling:** A nonprobability sampling design in which information or data for the research are gathered from members of the population conveniently accessible to the researcher.

**Convergent validity:** That which is established when the scores obtained by two different instruments measuring the same concept, or by measuring the concept by two different methods, are highly correlated.

**Correlational analysis:** Analysis done to trace the mutual influence of variables on one another.

**Correlational study:** A research study conducted to identify the important factors associated with the variables of interest.

**Criterion-related validity:** That which is established when the measure differentiates individuals on a criterion that it is expected to predict.

**Criterion variable:** The variable of primary interest to the study, also known as the dependent variable.

**Cross-cultural research:** Studies done across two or more cultures to understand, describe, analyze, or predict phenomena.

**Cross-sectional study:** A research study for which data are gathered just once (stretched though it may be over a period of days, weeks, or months) to answer the research question.

**Data coding:** In quantitative research data coding involves assigning a number to the participants' responses so they can be entered into a database.

**Data display:** Taking the reduced qualitative data and displaying them in an organized, condensed manner.

**Data mining:** Helps to trace patterns and relationships in the data stored in the data warehouse.

**Data reduction:** Breaking down data into manageable pieces.

**Data transformation:** The process of changing the original numerical representation of a quantitative value to another value.

**Data warehouse:** A central repository of all information gathered by the company.

**Deductive reasoning:** The application of a general theory to a specific case.

**Delphi technique:** A forecasting method that uses a cautiously selected panel of experts in a systematic, interactive manner.

**Dependent variable:** *See* Criterion variable.

**Descriptive statistics:** Statistics such as frequencies, the mean, and the standard deviation, which provide descriptive information about a set of data.

**Descriptive study:** A research study that describes the variables in a situation of interest to the researcher.

**Dichotomous scale:** Scale used to elicit a Yes/No response, or an answer to two different aspects of a concept.

**Directional hypothesis:** An educated conjecture as to the direction of the relationship, or differences among variables, which could be positive or negative, or more or less, respectively.

**Discriminant analysis:** A statistical technique that helps to identify the independent variables that discriminate a nominally scaled dependent variable of interest.

**Discriminant validity:** That which is established when two variables are theorized to be uncorrelated, and the scores obtained by measuring them are indeed empirically found to be so.

**Disproportionate stratified random sampling:** A probability sampling design that involves a procedure in which the number of sample subjects chosen from various strata is not directly proportionate to the total number of elements in the respective strata.

**Double-barreled question:** Refers to the improper framing of a question that should be posed as two or more separate questions, so that the respondent can give clear and unambiguous answers.

**Double-blind study:** A study where neither the experimenter nor the subjects are aware as to who is given the real treatment and who the placebo.

**Double sampling:** A probability sampling design that involves the process of collecting information from a set of subjects twice – such as using a sample to collect preliminary information, and later using a subsample of the primary sample for more information.

**Dummy variable:** A variable that has two or more distinct levels, which are coded 0 or 1.

**Dynamic panel:** Consists of a changing composition of members in a group who serve as the sample subjects for a research study conducted over an extended period of time.

**Editing data:** The process of going over the data and ensuring that they are complete and acceptable for data analysis.

**Efficiency in sampling:** Attained when the sampling design chosen either results in a cost reduction to the researcher or offers a greater degree of accuracy in terms of the sample size.

**Electronic questionnaire:** Online questionnaire administered when a microcomputer is hooked up to computer networks.

**Element:** A single member of the population.

**Ethics:** Code of conduct or expected societal norms of behavior.

**Exogenous variable:** A variable that exerts an influence on the cause-and-effect relationship between two variables in some way, and needs to be controlled.

**Experimental design:** A study design in which the researcher might create an artificial setting, control some variables, and manipulate the independent variable to establish cause-and-effect relationships.

**Experimental group:** The group exposed to a treatment in an experimental design.

**Exploratory study:** A research study where very little knowledge or information is available on the subject under investigation.

**Ex post facto design:** Studying subjects who have already been exposed to a stimulus and comparing them to those not so exposed, so as to establish cause-and-effect relationships (in contrast to establishing cause-and-effect relationships by manipulating an independent variable in a lab or a field setting).

**External consultants:** Research experts outside the organization who are hired to study specific problems to find solutions.

**External validity:** The extent of generalizability of the results of a causal study to other field settings.

**Faces scale:** A particular representation of the graphic scale, depicting faces with expressions that range from smiling to sad.

**Face-to-face interview:** Information gathering when both the interviewer and interviewee meet in person.

**Face validity:** An aspect of validity examining whether the item on the scale, on the face of it, reads as if it indeed measures what it is supposed to measure.

**Factorial validity:** That which indicates, through the use of factor analytic techniques, whether a test is a pure measure of some specific factor or dimension.

**Field experiment:** An experiment done to detect cause-and-effect relationships in the natural environment in which events normally occur.

**Field study:** A study conducted in the natural setting with a minimal amount of researcher interference in the flow of events in the situation.

**Fixed rating scale:** *See* Constant sum rating scale.

**Focus group:** A group consisting of eight to ten members randomly chosen, who discuss a product or any given topic for about two hours with a moderator present, so that their opinions can serve as the basis for further research.

**Forced choice:** Elicits the ranking of objects relative to one another.

**Formative scale:** Used when a construct is viewed as an explanatory combination of its indicators.

**Frequencies:** The number of times various subcategories of a phenomenon occur, from which the percentage and cumulative percentage of any occurrence can be calculated.

**Fundamental research:** *See* Basic research.

**Funneling technique:** The questioning technique that consists of initially asking general and broad questions, and gradually narrowing the focus thereafter to more specific themes.

**Generalizability:** The applicability of research findings in one setting to others.

**Goodness of measures:** Attests to the reliability and validity of measures.

**Graphic rating scale:** A scale that graphically illustrates the responses that can be provided, rather than specifying any discrete response categories.

**Grounded theory:** A systematic set of procedures to develop an inductively derived theory from the data.

**Group videoconferencing:** Video transmittal technology that enables remote groups of people to participate in a conference using video cameras and monitors.

**History effects:** A threat to the internal validity of the experimental results, when events unexpectedly occur while the experiment is in progress and contaminate the cause-and-effect relationship.

**Hypothesis:** A tentative, yet testable, statement that predicts what you expect to find in your empirical data.

**Hypothesis testing:** A means of testing if the if–then statements generated from the theoretical framework hold true when subjected to rigorous examination.

**Hypothetico-deductive method of research:** A seven-step process of identifying a broad problem area, defining the problem statement, developing hypotheses, determining measures, data collection, data analysis, and the interpretation of data.

**Independent samples *t*-test:** Test that is done to see if there are significant differences in the means for two groups in the variable of interest.

**Independent variable:**   A variable that influences the dependent or criterion variable and accounts for (or explains) its variance.

**Inductive reasoning:**   A process where we observe specific phenomena and on this basis arrive at general conclusions.

**Inferential statistics:**   Statistics that help to establish relationships among variables and draw conclusions therefrom.

**Inkblot tests:**   A motivational research technique that uses colored patterns of inkblots to be interpreted by the subjects.

**Instrumentation effects:**   The threat to internal validity in experimental designs caused by changes in the measuring instrument between the pretest and the posttest.

**Interitem consistency reliability:**   A test of the consistency of responses to all the items in a measure to establish that they hang together as a set.

**Interjudge reliability:**   The degree of consistency between coders processing the same (qualitative) data.

**Internal consistency:**   Homogeneity of the items in the measure that tap a construct.

**Internal consultants:**   Research experts within the organization who investigate and find solutions to problems.

**Internal validity of experiments:**   Attests to the confidence that can be placed in the cause-and-effect relationship found in experimental designs.

**Interrater reliability:**   The consistency of the judgment of several raters on how they see a phenomenon or interpret the activities in a situation.

**Interval scale:**   A multipoint scale that taps the differences, the order, and the equality of the magnitude of the differences in the responses.

**Intervening variable:**   A variable that surfaces as a function of the independent variable, and helps in conceptualizing and explaining the influence of the independent variable on the dependent variable.

**Interviewing:**   A data collection method in which the researcher asks for information verbally from the respondents.

**Intranet:**   A network that connects people and resources within the organization.

**Itemized rating scale:**   A scale that offers several categories of response, out of which the respondent picks the one most relevant for answering the question.

**Judgment sampling:**   A purposive, nonprobability sampling design in which the sample subject is chosen on the basis of the individual's ability to provide the type of special information needed by the researcher.

**Lab experiment:**   An experimental design set up in an artificially contrived setting where controls and manipulations are introduced to establish cause-and-effect relationships among variables of interest to the researcher.

**Leading questions:**   Questions phrased in such a manner as to lead the respondent to give the answers that the researcher would like to obtain.

**Likert scale:**   An interval scale that specifically uses the five anchors of *Strongly Disagree, Disagree, Neither Disagree nor Agree, Agree,* and *Strongly Agree.*

**Literature review:**   The documentation of a comprehensive review of the published work from secondary sources of data in the areas of specific interest to the researcher.

**Literature survey:**   *See* Literature review.

**Loaded questions:** Questions that elicit highly biased emotional responses from subjects.

**Logistic regression:** A specific form of regression analysis in which the dependent variable is a nonmetric, dichotomous variable.

**Longitudinal study:** A research study for which data are gathered at several points in time to answer a research question.

**Manipulation:** How the researcher exposes the subjects to the independent variable to determine cause-and-effect relationships in experimental designs.

**MANOVA:** A statistical technique that is similar to ANOVA, with the difference that ANOVA tests the mean differences of more than two groups on *one* dependent variable, whereas MANOVA tests mean differences among groups across *several* dependent variables simultaneously, by using sums of squares and cross-product matrices.

**Matching:** A method of controlling known contaminating factors in experimental studies, by deliberately spreading them equally across the experimental and control groups, so as not to confound the cause-and-effect relationship.

**Maturation effects:** A threat to internal validity that is a function of the biological, psychological, and other processes taking place in the respondents as a result of the passage of time.

**McNemar's test:** A nonparametric method used on nominal data. It assesses the significance of the difference between two dependent samples when the variable of interest is dichotomous.

**Mean:** The average of a set of figures.

**Measure of central tendency:** Descriptive statistics of a *data set* such as the mean, median, or mode.

**Measure of dispersion:** The variability in a set of observations, represented by the range, variance, standard deviation, and the interquartile range.

**Median:** The central item in a group of observations arranged in an ascending or descending order.

**Mediating variable:** A variable that surfaces as a function of the independent variable, and helps in conceptualizing and explaining the influence of the independent variable on the dependent variable.

**Mode:** The most frequently occurring number in a data set.

**Moderating variable:** A variable on which the relationship between two other variables is contingent. That is, if the moderating variable is present, the theorized relationship between the two variables will hold good, but not otherwise.

**Mortality:** The loss of research subjects during the course of the experiment, which confounds the cause-and-effect relationship.

**Motivational research:** A particular data-gathering technique directed toward surfacing information, ideas, and thoughts that are not either easily verbalized, or remain at the unconscious level in the respondents.

**Multicollinearity:** A statistical phenomenon in which two or more independent variables in a multiple regression model are highly correlated.

**Multiple regression analysis:** A statistical technique to predict the variance in the dependent variable by regressing the independent variables against it.

**Multistage cluster sampling:** A probability sampling design that is a stratified sampling of clusters.

**Narrative analysis:**   A qualitative approach that aims to elicit and scrutinize the stories we tell about ourselves and their implications for our lives.

**Nominal scale:**   A scale that categorizes individuals or objects into mutually exclusive and collectively exhaustive groups, and offers basic, categorical information on the variable of interest.

**Noncontrived setting:**   Research conducted in the natural environment where activities take place in the normal manner (i.e., the field setting).

**Nondirectional hypothesis:**   An educated conjecture of a relationship between two variables, the directionality of which cannot be guessed.

**Nonparametric statistics:**   Statistics used to test hypotheses, when the population from which the sample is drawn cannot be assumed to be normally distributed.

**Nonparticipant-observer:**   A researcher who collects observational data without becoming an integral part of the system.

**Nonprobability sampling:**   A sampling design in which the elements in the population do not have a known or predetermined chance of being selected as sample subjects.

**Non-response error:**   Exists to the extent that those who did respond to your survey are different from those who did not on (one of the) characteristics of interest in your study. Two important sources of non-response are not-at-homes and refusals.

**Nuisance variable:**   A variable that contaminates the cause-and-effect relationship.

**Null hypothesis:**   The conjecture that postulates no differences or no relationship between or among variables.

**Numerical scale:**   A scale with bipolar attributes with five points or seven points indicated on the scale.

**Objectivity:**   Interpretation of the results on the basis of the results of data analysis, as opposed to subjective or emotional interpretations.

**Observational survey:**   Collection of data by observing people or events in the work environment and recording the information.

**One sample *t*-test:**   A test that is used to test the hypothesis that the mean of the population from which a sample is drawn is equal to a comparison standard.

**One-shot study:**   *See* Cross-sectional study.

**Open-ended questions:**   Questions that the respondent can answer in a free-flowing format without restricting the range of choices to a set of specific alternatives suggested by the researcher.

**Operational definition:**   Definition of a construct in measurable terms by reducing it from its level of abstraction through the delineation of its dimensions and elements.

**Operations research:**   A quantitative approach taken to analyze and solve problems of complexity.

**Ordinal scale:**   A scale that not only categorizes the qualitative differences in the variable of interest, but also allows for the rank-ordering of these categories in a meaningful way.

**Paired comparisons:**   Respondents choose between two objects at a time, with the process repeated with a small number of objects.

**Paired samples *t*-test:**   Test that examines the differences in the same group before and after a treatment.

**Panel studies:**   Studies conducted over a period of time to determine the effects of certain changes made in a situation, using a panel or group of subjects as the sample base.

**Parallel-form reliability:**   That form of reliability which is established when responses to two comparable sets of measures tapping the same construct are highly correlated.

**Parametric statistics:**   Statistics used to test hypotheses when the population from which the sample is drawn is assumed to be normally distributed.

**Parsimony:**   Efficient explanation of the variance in the dependent variable of interest through the use of a smaller, rather than a larger number of independent variables.

**Participant-observer:**   A researcher who collects observational data by becoming a member of the system from which data are collected.

**Population:**   The entire group of people, events, or things that the researcher desires to investigate.

**Population frame:**   A listing of all the elements in the population from which the sample is drawn.

**Posttest:**   A test given to the subjects to measure the dependent variable after exposing them to a treatment.

**Precision:**   The degree of closeness of the estimated sample characteristics to the population parameters, determined by the extent of the variability of the sampling distribution of the sample mean.

**Predictive study:**   A study that enables the prediction of the relationships among the variables in a particular situation.

**Predictive validity:**   The ability of the measure to differentiate among individuals as to a criterion predicted for the future.

**Predictor variable:**   *See* Independent variable.

**Pretest:**   A test given to subjects to measure the dependent variable before exposing them to a treatment.

**Pretesting survey questions:**   Test of the understandability and appropriateness of the questions planned to be included in a regular survey, using a small number of respondents.

**Primary data:**   Data collected first-hand for subsequent analysis to find solutions to the problem researched.

**Probability sampling:**   The sampling design in which the elements of the population have some known chance or probability of being selected as sample subjects.

**Problem definition:**   A precise, succinct statement of the question or issue that is to be investigated.

**Problem statement:**   *See* Problem definition.

**Projective methods:**   Ways of eliciting responses difficult to obtain, otherwise than through such means as word association, sentence completion, and thematic apperception tests.

**Proportionate stratified random sampling:**   A probability sampling design in which the number of sample subjects drawn from each stratum is proportionate to the total number of elements in the respective strata.

**Pure research:**   *See* Basic research.

**Purposiveness in research:**   The situation in which research is focused on solving a well-identified and defined problem, rather than aimlessly looking for answers to vague questions.

**Purposive sampling:**   A nonprobability sampling design in which the required information is gathered from special or specific targets or groups of people on some rational basis.

**Qualitative data:**   Data that are not immediately quantifiable unless they are coded and categorized in some way.

**Qualitative study:**   Research involving analysis of data/information that are descriptive in nature and not readily quantifiable.

**Questionnaire:**   A preformulated written set of questions to which the respondent records the answers, usually within rather closely delineated alternatives.

**Quota sampling:**   A form of purposive sampling in which a predetermined proportion of people from different subgroups is sampled.

**Randomization:**   The process of controlling the nuisance variables by randomly assigning members among the various experimental and control groups, so that the confounding variables are randomly distributed across all groups.

**Range:**   The spread in a set of numbers indicated by the difference in the two extreme values in the observations.

**Ranking scale:**   Scale used to tap preferences between two or among more objects or items.

**Rating scale:**   Scale with several response categories that evaluate an object on a scale.

**Ratio scale:**   A scale that has an absolute zero origin, and hence indicates not only the magnitude, but also the proportion, of the differences.

**Recall-dependent question:**   Question that elicits from the respondents information that involves recall of experiences from the past that may be hazy in their memory.

**Reflective scale:**   Each item in a reflective scale is assumed to share a common basis (the underlying construct of interest).

**Regression analysis:**   Used in a situation where one or more metric independent variable(s) is (are) hypothesized to affect a metric dependent variable.

**Relational analysis:**   Builds on conceptual analysis by examining the relationships among concepts in a text.

**Reliability:**   Attests to the consistency and stability of the measuring instrument.

**Replicability:**   The repeatability of similar results when identical research is conducted at different times or in different organizational settings.

**Representativeness of the sample:**   The extent to which the sample that is selected possesses the same characteristics as the population from which it is drawn.

**Research:**   An organized, systematic, critical, scientific inquiry or investigation into a specific problem, undertaken with the objective of finding answers or solutions thereto.

**Research proposal:**   A document that sets out the purpose of the study and the research design details of the investigation to be carried out by the researcher.

**Researcher interference:**   The extent to which the person conducting the research interferes with the normal course of work at the study site.

**Restricted probability designs:**   *See* Complex probability sampling.

**Rigor:**   The theoretical and methodological precision adhered to in conducting research.

**Sample:**   A subset or subgroup of the population.

**Sample size:**   The actual number of subjects chosen as a sample to represent the population characteristics.

**Sampling:**   The process of selecting items from the population so that the sample characteristics can be generalized to the population. Sampling involves both design choice and sample size decisions.

**Sampling unit:**   The element or set of elements that is available for selection in some stage of the sampling process.

**Scale:**   A tool or mechanism by which individuals, events, or objects are distinguished on the variables of interest in some meaningful way.

**Scientific investigation:**   A step-by-step, logical, organized, and rigorous effort to solve problems.

**Secondary data:**   Data that have already been gathered by researchers, data published in statistical and other journals, and information available from any published or unpublished source available either within or outside the organization, all of which might be useful to the researcher.

**Selection effects:**   The threat to internal validity that is a function of improper or unmatched selection of subjects for the experimental and control groups.

**Semantic differential scale:**   Usually a seven-point scale with bipolar attributes indicated at its extremes.

**Simple random sampling:**   A probability sampling design in which every single element in the population has a known and equal chance of being selected as a subject.

**Simulation:**   A model-building technique for assessing the possible effects of changes that might be introduced in a system.

**Social desirability:**   The respondents' need to give socially or culturally acceptable responses to the questions posed by the researcher even if they are not true.

**Solomon four-group design:**   The experimental design that sets up two experimental groups and two control groups, subjecting one experimental group and one control group to *both* the pretest and the posttest, and the other experimental group and control group to *only* the posttest.

**Split-half reliability:**   The correlation coefficient between one half of the items measuring a concept and the other half.

**Stability of a measure:**   The ability of the measure to repeat the same results over time with low vulnerability to changes in the situation.

**Standard deviation:**   A measure of dispersion for parametric data; the square root of the variance.

**Standardized regression coefficients (or beta coefficients):**   The estimates resulting from a multiple regression analysis performed on variables that have been standardized (a process whereby the variables are transformed into variables with a mean of 0 and a standard deviation of 1).

**Stapel scale:**   A scale that measures both the direction and intensity of the attributes of a concept.

**Static panel:**   A panel that consists of the same group of people serving as subjects over an extended period of time for a research study.

**Statistical power $(1 - \beta)$:**   The probability of correctly rejecting the null hypothesis.

**Statistical regression:**   The threat to internal validity that results when various groups in the study have been selected on the basis of their extreme (very high or very low) scores on some important variables.

**Stratified random sampling:**   A probability sampling design that first divides the population into meaningful, nonoverlapping subsets, and then randomly chooses the subjects from each subset.

**Structural variables:**   Factors related to the form and design of the organization such as roles and positions, communication channels, control systems, reward systems, and span of control.

**Structured interviews:**   Interviews conducted by the researcher with a predetermined list of questions to be asked of the interviewee.

**Structured observational studies:**   Studies in which the researcher observes and notes specific activities and behavior that have been clearly delineated as important factors for observation, before the commencement of the study.

**Subject:**   A single member of the sample.

**Synopsis:**   A brief summary of the research study.

**Systematic sampling:**   A probability sampling design that involves choosing every $n$th element in the population for the sample.

**$t$-test:**   A statistical test that establishes a significant mean difference in a variable between two groups.

**Telephone interview:**   The information-gathering method by which the interviewer asks the interviewee *over the telephone,* rather than face to face, for information needed for the research.

**Test–retest reliability:**   A way of establishing the stability of the measuring instrument by correlating the scores obtained through its administration to the same set of respondents at two different points in time.

**Testability:**   The ability to subject the data collected to appropriate statistical tests, in order to substantiate or reject the hypotheses developed for the research study.

**Testing effects:**   The distorting effects on the experimental results (the posttest scores) caused by the prior sensitization of the respondents to the instrument through the pretest.

**Thematic apperception test (TAT):**   A projective test that requires the respondent to develop a story around a picture.

**Theoretical framework:**   A logically developed, described, and explained network of associations among variables of interest to the research study.

**Treatment:**   The manipulation of the independent variable in experimental designs so as to determine its effects on a dependent variable of interest to the researcher.

**Two-way ANOVA:**   A statistical technique that can be used to examine the effect of two nonmetric independent variables on a single metric dependent variable.

**Type I error ($\alpha$):**   The probability of rejecting the null hypothesis when it is actually true.

**Type II error ($\beta$):**   The probability of failing to reject the null hypothesis given that the alternative hypothesis is actually true.

**Unbalanced rating scale:**   An even-numbered scale that has no neutral point.

**Unbiased questions:**   Questions posed in accordance with the principles of wording and measurement, and the right questioning technique, so as to elicit the least biased responses.

**Unit of analysis:**   The level of aggregation of the data collected during data analysis.

**Unobtrusive measures:**   Measurement of variables through data gathered from sources other than people, such as examination of birth and death records or count of the number of cigarette butts in the ashtray.

Unrestricted probability sampling:   *See* Simple random sampling.

Unstructured interviews:   Interviews conducted with the primary purpose of identifying some important issues relevant to the problem situation, without prior preparation of a planned or predetermined sequence of questions.

Unstructured observational studies:   Studies in which the researcher observes and makes notes of almost all activities and behavior that occur in the situation without predetermining what particular variables will be of specific interest to the study.

Validity:   Evidence that the instrument, technique, or process used to measure a concept does indeed measure the intended concept.

Variable:   Anything that can take on differing or varying values.

Variance:   Indicates the dispersion of a variable in the data set, and is obtained by subtracting the mean from each of the observations, squaring the results, summing them, and dividing the total by the number of observations.

Wilcoxon signed-rank test:   A nonparametric test used to examine differences between two related samples or repeated measurements on a single sample. It is used as an alternative to a paired samples *t*-test when the population cannot be assumed to be normally distributed.

Word association:   A projective method of identifying respondents' attitudes and feelings by asking them to associate a specified word with the first thing that comes to their mind.

# BIBLIOGRAPHY

Abbott, C. C. (1966) *Basic Research in Finance: Needs and Prospects*. Charlottesville, VA: University Press.

Abdel-khalik, A. R. and Ajinkya, B. B. (1979) *Empirical Research in Accounting: A Methodological Viewpoint*. Sarasota, FL: American Accounting Association.

Amabile, T. M., Hill, K. G., Hennessey, B. A. and Tighe, E. M. (1994) The work preference inventory: Assessing intrinsic and extrinsic motivational orientations. *Journal of Personality and Social Psychology*, **66**, 950–967.

American Psychological Association. (2001) *Publication Manual of the American Psychological Association* (4th ed.) Washington, DC.

Angell, R. C. and Freedman, R. (1966) The use of documents, records, census materials, and indices. In L. Festinger and D. Katz (Eds.), *Research Methods in the Behavioral Sciences*. New York: Holt, Rinehart and Winston.

Baker, R. L. and Schutz, R. E. (Eds.), (1972) *Instructional Product Research*. New York: Van Nostrand.

Balsley, H. L. and Clover, V. T. (1988) *Research for Business Decisions. Business research methods* (4th ed.). Columbus, OH: Publishing Horizons.

Baron, R. M. and Kenny, D. A. (1986) The moderator-mediator variable distinction in social psychological research: conceptual, strategic, and statistical considerations. *Journal of Personality and Social Psychology*, **51**, 1173–1182.

Barry, H. (1969) Cross-cultural research with matched pairs of societies. *Journal of Social Psychology*, **79**, 25–33.

Bending, A. W. (1954) Transmitted information and the length of rating scales. *Journal of Experimental Psychology*, **47**, 303–308.

Bentley, T. J. and Forkner, I. H. (1983) *Making Information Systems Work for You: How to Make Better Decisions using Computer-generated Information*. Englewood Cliffs, NJ: Prentice Hall.

Billings, R. S. and Wroten, S. P. (1978) Use of path analysis in industrial/organizational psychology: Criticisms and suggestions. *Journal of Applied Psychology*, **63**(6), 677–688.

Bitner, M. J., Booms, B. H. and Tetreault, M. S. (1990), The Service Encounter – Diagnosing Favorable and Unfavorable Incidents. *Journal of Marketing*, **54**, 71–84.

Blank, G. (1989). Finding the right statistic with statistical navigator. *PC Magazine*, March 14, p. 97.

Boot, J. C. G. and Cox, E. B. (1970) *Statistical Analysis for Managerial Decisions*. New York: McGraw-Hill.

Bordens, K. S. and Abbott, B. B. (1988) *Research Design and Methods: A Process Approach*. Mountain View, CA: Mayfield Publishing.

Box, G. and Jenkins, G. (1970) *Time Series Analysis: Forecasting and Control*. San Francisco: Holden-Day.

Brown, L. D. and Vasarhelyi, M. A. (1985) *Accounting Research Directory: The Database of Accounting Literature*. New York: Markus Wiener Publishing.

Bruner II G. C., Hensel P. J. and James K. E. (2005) *Marketing Scales Handbook*. Chicago: Thomson South-Western Co.

Burton, S. and Lichtenstein, D.R. (1988) The Effect of Ad Claims and Ad Context on Attitude toward the Advertisement. *Journal of Advertising*, **17**, 3–11.

Cacioppo, J. T. and Petty, R. E. (1982) The need for cognition. *Journal of Personality and Social Psychology*, **42**, 116–131.

Campbell, A. A. and Katona, G. (1966) The sample survey: A technique for social science research. In L. Festinger and D. Katz (Eds.) *Research Methods in the Behavioral Sciences*. New York: Holt, Rinehart and Winston.

Campbell, D. T. (1976) Psychometric theory. In M. D. Dunnette (Ed.) *Handbook of Industrial and Organizational Psychology*. Chicago: Rand McNally.

Campbell, D. T. and Fiske, D. W. (1959) Convergent and discriminant validation by the multitrait-multimethod matrix. *Psychological Bulletin*, **56**, 81–105.

Campbell, D. T. and Stanley, J. C. (1966) *Experimental and Quasi-experimental Designs for Research*. Chicago: Rand-McNally.

Cannell, C. F. and Kahn, R. L. (1966) The collection of data by interviewing. In L. Festinger and D. Katz (Eds.) *Research Methods in the Behavioral Sciences*. New York: Holt, Rinehart and Winston.

Carlsmith, M., Ellsworth, P. C. and Aronson, E. (1976) *Methods of Research in Social Psychology*. Reading, MA: Addison-Wesley.

Cattell, R. B. (1966) The scree test for the number of factors. *Multivariate Behavioral Research*, **1**, 245–276.

Chein, L. (1959) An introduction to sampling. In C. Selltiz, M. Jahoda, M. Deutsch, and S. W. Cook (Eds.) *Research Methods in Social Relations*. New York: Holt, Rinehart and Winston.

*Chicago Manual of Style*, 15th ed.(2003) Chicago: University of Chicago Press.

Churchill, G. A. (1987) *Marketing Research: Methodological Foundations*. Chicago: Dryden Press.

Clark, D. and Bank, D. (1998) Microsoft, Sony agree to work together to link consumer-electronic devices. *Wall Street Journal*, April 8, p. B6.

Cohen, J. (1969) *Statistical Power Analysis for the Behavioral Sciences*. New York: Academic Press.

Cohen, J. (1990) Things I have learned (so far). *American Psychologist*, 1304–1312.

Cook, T. D. and Campbell, D. T. (1979a) *Quasi-experimentation: Design and Analysis Issues for Field Settings*. Boston: Houghton-Mifflin.

Cook, T. D. and Campbell, D. T. (1979b) Four kinds of validity. In R. T. Mowday and R. M. Steers (Eds.) *Research in Organizations: Issues and Controversies*. Santa Monica, CA: Goodyear Publishing.

Cooke, A. (2001) *A Guide to Finding Quality Information on the Internet: Selection and Evaluation Strategies* (2nd ed.), London: Library Association.

Coombs, C. H. (1966) Theory and methods of social measurement. In L. Festinger and D. Katz (Eds.) *Research Methods in the Behavioral Sciences*. New York: Holt, Rinehart and Winston.

Cortada, J. W. (1996) *Information Technology as Business History: Issues in the History and Management of Computers*. Westport, CT: Greenwood Press.

Coulter, M. K. (2002) *Strategic Management in Action*. Englewood Cliffs, NJ: Prentice Hall.

Cronbach, L. J. (1946) Response sets and test validating. *Educational and Psychological Measurement*, **6**, 475–494.

Cronbach, L. J. (1990) *Essentials of Psychological Testing* (5th ed.). New York: Harper & Row.

Cronin, M. J. (1998a) Business secrets of the billion-dollar website. *Fortune*, February 2, p. 142.

Cronin, M. J. (1998b) Ford's Intranet success. *Fortune*, March 30, p. 158.

Crosby, L. A. and Stephens N. (1987) Effects of Relationship Marketing on Satisfaction, Retention, and Prices in the Life Insurance Industry. *Journal of Marketing Research*, **24**, 404–411.

Crowne, D. P. and Marlowe, D. (1980) *The Approval Motive: Studies in Evaluative Dependence*. Westport, CT: Greenwood Press.

Cummings, L. L. (1977) Emergence of the instrumental organization. In P. S. Goodman and J. M. Pennings (Eds) *New Perspectives on Organizational Effectiveness*, San Francisco, CA: Jossey-Bass, pp. 56-62.

Davies, G. R. and Yoder, D. (1937) *Business Statistics*. New York: John Wiley.

Davis, D. and Cosenza, R. M. (1988) *Business Research for Decision Making* (2nd ed.). Boston: PWS-Kent Publishing.

DeArmond, S, Tye M., Chen P. Y., Krauss A., Rogers D. A. and Sintek E. (2006) Age and gender stereotypes: new challenges in a changing workplace and workforce. *Journal of Applied Social Psychology*, **36**, 2184–2214.

De Jong, M. (2006) *Response Bias in International Marketing Research*, Doctoral Dissertation, Tilburg University.

Denzin, N. K. (2000) The Practices and Politics of Interpretation. In N. K. Denzin and Y. S. Lincoln (Eds.) *Handbook of Qualitative Research*, 2nd ed. Thousand Oaks, CA: Sage.

Drenkow, G. (1987) Data acquisition software that adapts to your needs. *Research and Development*, April, 84–87.

Edwards, A. L. (1957) *Manual for the Edwards Personal Preference Schedule*. New York: Psychological Corporation.

Elmore, P. E. and Beggs, D. L. (1975) Salience of concepts and commitment to extreme judgements in response pattern of teachers. *Education*, **95**(4), 325–334.

Emory, C. W. (1985) *Business Research Methods* (3rd ed.). Homewood, IL: Richard D. Irwin.

Etzioni, A. (1960) Interpersonal and structural factors in the study of mental hospitals. *Psychiatry*, **23**, 13–22.

*Express Computer* (1998) Data mining captures the imagination, March 2, p. 19.

*Express Computer* (1998) Beyond microprocessors, May 11, p. 22.

Ferris, K. R. (1988) *Behavioral Accounting Research: A Critical Analysis*. Columbus, OH: Century VII Publishing.

Festinger, L. (1966) Laboratory experiments. In L. Festinger and D. Katz (Eds.) *Research Methods in the Behavioral Sciences*. New York: Holt, Rinehart and Winston.

Festinger, L. and Katz, D. (1966) *Research Methods in the Behavioral Sciences*. New York: Holt, Rinehart and Winston.

Fiedler, F. (1967) *A Theory of Leadership Effectiveness*. New York: McGraw-Hill.

Fishbein, M. (1967) *Readings in Attitude Theory and Measurement*. New York: John Wiley.

Folkes, V. S., Koletsky, S. and Graham, J. L. (1987) A Field Study of Causal Inferences and Consumer Reaction: The View from the Airport. *Journal of Consumer Research*, **13**, 534–539.

Fornell, C. (1987) A Second Generation of Multivariate Analysis: Classification of Methods and Implications for Marketing Research. In M. Houston (Ed.), *Review of Marketing*, Chicago, IL: American Marketing Association.

Fornell, C. and Bookstein, F. L. (1982) Two structural equation models: LISREL and PLS applied to consumer exit-voice theory. *Journal of Marketing Research*, **19**, 440–452.

French, J. R. P. (1966) Experiments in field settings. In L. Festinger and D. Katz (Eds.) *Research Methods in the Behavioral Sciences*. New York: Holt, Rinehart and Winston.

Garten, J. E. (1998) Why the global economy is here to stay. *Business Week*, March 23, p. 21.

Gaski, J. F. and Etzel, M. J. (1986) The index of consumer sentiment toward marketing. *Journal of Marketing*, **50**, 71–81.

Georgopolous, B. S. and Tannenbaum, A. S. (1957) The study of organizational effectiveness. *American Sociological Review*, **22**, 534–540.

Glaser, B. (1978) *Theoretical Sensitivity*. Mill Valley, CA: Sociology Press.

Glaser, B. G. and Strauss, A. L. (1967) *The Discovery of Grounded Theory*. Chicago: Aldine.

Gordon, R. A. (1973) An explicit estimation of the prevalence of commitment to a training school, to age 18, by race and by sex. *Journal of the American Statistical Association*, **68**, 547–553.

Gorsuch, R. L. (1974) *Factor Analysis*. Philadelphia: Saunders.

Gorsuch, R. L. (1983) *Factor Analysis* (2nd ed.). Philadelphia: Saunders.

Green, P. E., Kedia, P. K. and Nikhil, R. S. (1985) *Electronic Questionnaire Design and Analysis with CAPPA*. Palo Alto, CA: The Scientific Press.

Hair, J. F., Jr., Anderson, R. E., Tatham, R. L. and Black, W. C. (1995) *Multi-variate Data Analysis*. Englewood Cliffs, NJ: Prentice Hall.

Harnett, D. L. and Horrell, J. F. (1998) *Data, Statistics, and Decision Models with Excel*. New York: John Wiley.

Heggestad, E. D. and Kanfer, R. (1999) *Individual differences in trait motivation. Development of the Motivational Trait Questionnaire*. Poster presented at the Annual Meetings of the Society of Industrial and Organizational Psychology, Atlanta, Georgia, April.

Hoel, P. G. and Jessen, R. J. (1971) *Basic Statistics for Business and Economics*. New York: John Wiley.

Horst, P. (1968) *Personality: Measurement of Dimensions*. San Francisco: Jossey-Bass.

Hunt, S.D. (1983) *Marketing Theory: The Philosophy of Marketing Science*. Homewood, IL: Richard D. Irwin.

Izard, C. E. (1977) *Human Emotions*. New York: Plenum.

Jarvis, C. B., MacKenzie, S. B. and Podsakoff, P. M. (2003) A Critical Review of Construct Indicators and Measurement Model Misspecification in Marketing and Consumer Research. *Journal of Consumer Research*, **30**(2), 199–218.

Kanuk, L. and Berenson, C. (1975) Mail surveys and response rates: A literature review. *Journal of Marketing Research*, **12**, 440–453.

Kaplan, A. (1979) *The Conduct of Inquiry: Methodology for Behavioral Science*. New York: Harper & Row.

Kassarjian, H. H. (1977) Content-analysis in consumer research. *Journal of Consumer Research*, **4**, 8–18.

Katz, D. (1966) *Research Methods in the Behavioral Sciences*. New York: Holt, Rinehart and Winston.

Katz, D. and Kahn, R. L. (1966) *Organizations and the System Concept: The Social Psychology of Organizations*. John Wiley & Sons, Inc. Reprinted in Shafritz, J. and Ott, J. S. (2001) *Classics of Organization Theory*. Fort Worth: Harcourt College Publishers.

Keaveney, S. M. (1995) Customer Switching Behavior in Service Industries – an Exploratory Study. *Journal of Marketing*, **59**, 71–82.

Kelley, S. W., Hoffman, K. D. and Davis, M. A. (1993) A Typology of Retail Failures and Recoveries, *Journal of Retailing*, **69**, 429–452.

Kelly, F. J., Beggs, D. L., McNeil, K. A., Eichelberger, T. and Lyon, J. (1969) *Research Design in the Behavioral Sciences: Multiple Regression Approach*. Carbondale, IL: Southern Illinois University Press.

Kerlinger, R. N. (1986) *Foundations of Behavioral Research* (3rd ed.) New York: Holt, Rinehart and Winston.

Kidder, L. H. and Judd, C. H. (1986) *Research Methods in Social Relations*. New York: Holt, Rinehart and Winston.

Kilmer, B. and Harnett, D. L. (1998) *KADDSTAT: Statistical Analysis Plug-in to Microsoft Excel*. New York: John Wiley.

Kirby, C. (2001) Snail mail's loss could be e-mail's gain. *San Francisco Chronicle*, October 23, p. B1.

Kirk, R. E. (1982) *Experimental Design: Procedures for the Behavioral Sciences*. Belmont, CA: Brooks/Cole.

Kish, L. (1965) *Survey Sampling*. New York: John Wiley.

Kish, L. (1966) Selection of the sample. In L. Festinger and D. Katz (Eds.) *Research Methods in the Behavioral Sciences*. New York: Holt, Rinehart and Winston.

Knechel, W. R. (1986) A simulation study of the relative effectiveness of alternative analytical review procedures. *Decision Sciences*, **17**(3), 376–394.

Kolbe, R. H. and Burnett, M. S. (1991) Content analysis research: an examination of applications with directives for improving research reliability and objectivity. *Journal of Consumer Research*, **18**, 243–250.

Kornhauser, A. and Sheatsley, P. B. (1959) Questionnaire construction and interview procedure. In C. Sellitz, M. Jahoda, M. Deutsch and S. W. Cook (Eds.) *Research Methods in Social Relations*. New York: Holt, Rinehart and Winston.

Krejcie, R. and Morgan, D. (1970) Determining sample size for research activities. *Educational and Psychological Measurement*, **30**, 607–610.

Kuder, G. F. and Richardson, M. W. (1937) The theory of the estimation of test reliability. *Psychometrika*, **2**, 151–160.

Kuppens, P., Van Mechelen I., Smits D. J. M. and De Boeck, P. (2003) The Appraisal Basis of Anger: Specificity, Necessity, and Sufficiency of Components. *Emotion*, **3**(3), 254–269.

Labaw, P. (1980) *Advanced Questionnaire Design*. Cambridge, MA: Abt Books.

Lazarsfeld, P. F. (1935) The art of asking why. *National Marketing Research*, **1**, 26–38.

Leedy, P. D. (1985) *Practical Research: Planning and Design* (3rd ed.). New York: Macmillan Publishing.

Leshin, C. B. (1997) *Management on the World Wide Web*. Englewood Cliffs, NJ: Prentice Hall.

Likert, R. (1932) A technique for the measurement of attitudes. *Archives of Psychology*, No. 140.

Lombardo, M. L., McCall, M. and DeVries, D. L. (1983) *Looking Glass*. Glenview, IL: Scott Foresman, Co.

Luconi, F. L., Malone, T. W. and Scott Morton, M. S. (1986) Expert systems: The next challenge for managers. *Sloan Management Review*, **27**(4), 3–14.

Luftman, J. N. (1996) *Competing in the Information Age: Strategic Alignment in Practice*. New York: Oxford University Press.

Mangold, W. G., Miller, F. and Brockway, G. R. (1999) Word-of-Mouth Communication in the Service Marketplace. *Journal of Services Marketing*, **13**, 73–89.

Marascuilo, L. A. and McSweeney, M. (1977) *Nonparametric and Distribution-free Methods for the Social Sciences*. Monterey, CA: Brooks/Cole.

Martin, M. H. (1998) Smart managing: Best practices, careers, and ideas. *Fortune*, February 2, p. 149.

McClave, J. T. and Benson, P. G. (1988) *Statistics for Business and Economics* (4th ed.). San Francisco: Dellen Publishing Co.

McKellar, P. (1949) The Emotion of Anger in the Expression of Human Aggressiveness. *British Journal of Psychology*, **39**, 148–155.

McNeil, K. A., Kelly, F. J. and McNeil, J. T. (1975) *Testing Research Hypotheses using Multiple Linear Regression*. Carbondale, IL: Southern Illinois University Press.

Meltzer, M. E. (1981) *Information: The Ultimate Management Resource*. New York: Amacom.

Merton, R. K. and Kendall, P. L. (1955) The focused interview. In P. F. Lazarsfeld and M. Rosenberg (Eds.) *The Language of Social Research*. New York: The Free Press.

Mick, D. and Buhl C. (1992) A Meaning-Based Model of Advertising Experiences. *Journal of Consumer Research*, **19**, 317–338.

Miles, M. B. and Huberman, A. M. (1994) *Qualitative Data Analysis* (2nd ed.). Thousand Oaks, CA: SAGE.

Minichiello, V., Aroni, R., Timewell, E. and Alexander, L. (1990) *In-depth Interviewing: Researching People*. Melbourne: Longman Cheshire.

Mitchell, R. E. (1969) Survey materials collected in developing countries: Sampling, measurement, and interviewing obstacles to intra- and international comparisons. In J. Boddewyn (Ed.) *Comparative Management and Marketing* (pp. 232–252). Glenview, IL: Scott, Foresman & Co.

Mittal, B. and Lassar, W. M. (1996) The role of personalization in service encounters. *Journal of Retailing*, **72**, 95–109.

Muehling, D. D. (1987) An investigation of factors underlying attitude toward advertising in general. *Journal of Advertising*, **16**(1), 32–40.

Murdick, P. G. and Cooper, D. R. (1982) *Business Research: Concepts and Guides*. Columbus, OH: Grid Publishing.

Namboodiri, N. K., Carter, L. F. and Blalock, H. M. (1975) *Applied Multivariate Analysis and Experimental Designs*. New York: McGraw-Hill.

Nasr-Bechwati, N. and Morrin M. (2003) Outraged Consumers: Getting Even at the Expense of Getting a Good Deal. *Journal of Consumer Psychology*, **13**, 440–453.

Norusis, M. J. (1998) *SPSS 8.0 Guide to Data Analysis*. Englewood Cliffs, NJ: Prentice Hall.

Nyer, P. U. (1997) A Study of the Relationships Between Cognitive Appraisals and Consumption Emotions. *Journal of the Academy of Marketing Science*, **25**, 296–304.

Oliver, R. L. (1996) *Satisfaction: A Behavioral Perspective on the Consumer*. New York: McGraw-Hill.

O'Neil, D., Hopkins, M. M. and Bilimoria, D. (2008) Women's careers at the start of the 21st century: patterns and paradoxes. *Journal of Business Ethics*, **80**, 727–743.

Oppenheim, A. N. (1986) *Questionnaire Design and Attitude Measurement*. Great Britain: Gower Publishing.

Osborn, R. N. and Vicars, W. M. (1976) Sex stereotypes: An artifact in leader behavior and subordinate satisfaction analysis? *Academy of Management Journal*, **19**, 439–449.

Parrott, W. G. (2001) *Emotions in Social Psychology: Essential Readings*. Philadelphia: Psychology Press.

Payne, S. L. (1951) *The Art of Asking Questions*. Princeton, NJ: Princeton University Press.

Peak, H. (1966) Problems of objective observation. In L. Festinger and D. Katz (Eds.), *Research Methods in the Behavioral Sciences*. New York: Holt, Rinehart and Winston.

Pedhazur, E. J. (1982) *Multiple Regression in Behavioral Research: Explanation and Prediction* (2nd ed.). New York: CBS College Publishing.

Pelosi, M. K., Sandifer, T. M. and Letkowski, J. J. (1998) *Doing Statistics with Excel™ 97: Software Instruction and Exercise Activity Supplement*. New York: John Wiley & Sons, Inc.

Perrier, C. and Kalwarski, G. (1989) Stimulating Simulations: Technique shows relationship between risk, funding. *Pensions and Investment Age*, October 30, 41–43.

Pfeffer, J. (1977) The ambigiuty of leadership. *The Academy of Management Review*, **2**.

Popper, K. R. (2002a) *The Logic of Scientific Discovery*, London: Routledge.

Popper, K. R. (2002b) *Conjectures and Refutations*, London: Routledge.

Price, J. (1997) Handbook of Organizational Measurement. *International Journal of Manpower*, **18** (4/5/6), 301–558.

Price J. L. and Mueller C. W. (1986) *Handbook of Organizational Measurement*. Marshfield, Mass.: Pitman.

Rao, C. R. (1973) *Linear Statistical Inference and its Applications* (2nd ed). New York: John Wiley.

Resta, P. A. (1972) *The Research Report*. New York: American Book Co.

Riley, M. W. and Nelson, E. E. (1974) *Sociological observation: A strategy for new social knowledge*. New York: Basic Books.

Rizzo, J. R., House, R. J. and Lirtzman, S. L. (1970) Role conflict and role ambiguity in complex organizations. *Administrative Science Quarterly*, **15**, 150–163.

Rook, D. W. (1987) The buying impulse. *Journal of Consumer Research*, **14**(2), 189–199.

Roscoe, J. T. (1975) *Fundamental Research Statistics for the Behavioral Sciences* (2nd ed.). New York: Holt, Rinehart and Winston.

Runkel, P. J. and McGrath, J. E. (1972) *Research on Human Behavior: A Systematic Guide to Method*. New York: Holt, Rinehart and Winston.

Salvia, A. A. (1990) *Introduction to Statistics*. Philadelphia: Saunders.

Schein, V. E. (2007) Women in management: reflections and projections. *Women in Management Review*, **22** (1), 6–18.

Schlesinger, L. and Heskett, J. (1991) The Service-Driven Service Company. *Harvard Business Review*, **69**, 71–81.

Schmitt, N. W. and Klimoski, R. J. (1991) *Research Methods in Human Resources Management*. Cincinnati, OH: South-Western Publishing.

Sekaran, U. (1983) Methodological and theoretical issues and advancements in cross-cultural research. *Journal of International Business*, Fall, 61–73.

Sekaran, U. (1986) *Dual-career Families: Contemporary Organizational and Counseling Issues*. San Francisco: Jossey-Bass.

Sekaran, U. and Martin, H. J. (1982) An examination of the psychometric properties of some commonly researched individual differences, job, and organizational variables in two cultures. *Journal of International Business Studies*, Spring/Summer, 51–66.

Sekaran, U. and Trafton, R. S. (1978) The dimensionality of jobs: Back to square one. *Twenty-fourth Midwest Academy of Management Proceedings*, 249–262.

Selltiz, C., Jahoda, M., Deutsch, M. and Cook, S. W. (1959) *Research Methods in Social Relations* (rev. ed.). New York: Holt, Rinehart, and Winston.

Selltiz, C., Wrightsman, L. S. and Cook, S. W. (1981) *Research Methods in Social Relations* (4th ed.). New York: Holt, Rinehart and Winston.

Shapira, Z. (1995) *Risk Taking: A Managerial Perspective*. New York: Russell Sage Foundation.

Sharma, S., Durand, R. M. and Gur-Arie, O. (1981) Identification and analysis of moderator variables. *Journal of Marketing Research*, **18**, 291–300.

Shurter, R. L., Williamson, J. P. and Broehl, W. G., Jr. (1965) *Business Research and Report Writing*. New York: McGraw-Hill.

Smith, C. A. and Ellsworth P. C. (1987) Patterns of Appraisals and Emotions related to Taking an Exam. *Journal of Personality and Social Psychology*, **52**, 475–488.

Smith, C. B. (1981) *A Guide to Business Research: Developing, Conducting, and Writing Research Projects*. Chicago, IL: Nelson-Hall.

Smith, P. C., Kendall, L. and Hulin, C. (1969) *The Measurement of Satisfaction in Work and Retirement*. Chicago: Rand McNally, pp. 79–84.

Stern, B. B., Thompson, C. J. and Arnould, E. J. (1998) Narrative analysis of a marketing relationship: the consumer's perspective. *Psychology and Marketing*, **15**(3), 195–214.

Stern, N. B. and Stern, R. A. (1996) *Computing in the Information Age* (2nd ed.). New York: John Wiley & Sons, Inc.

Steufert, S., Pogash, R. and Piasecki, M. (1988) Simulation-based assessment of managerial competence: Reliability and validity. *Personnel Psychology*, **41**(3), 537–557.

Stone, E. (1978) *Research Methods in Organizational Behavior*. Santa Monica, CA: Goodyear Publishing.

Strauss, A. and Corbin, J. (1990) *Basics of Qualitative Research: Grounded Theory Procedures and Techniques*. Sage Publications.

Super, D. E. (1970) *Work Values Inventory Manual*. Boston, MA: Houghton Mifflin Co.

Taylor, S. (1994) Waiting for Service – the Relationship between Delays and Evaluations of Service, *Journal of Marketing*, **58**, 56–69.

Tomaski, E. A. (1970) *The Computer Revolution: The Executive and the New Information Technology*. New York: Macmillan.

Turabian, K. L. (2007) *A Manual for Writers of Term Papers, Theses, and Dissertations* (7th ed.). Chicago: University of Chicago Press.

Turban, E., McLean, E. and Wetherbe, J. (1998) *Informational Technology for Management: Making Connections for Strategic Advantage*. New York: John Wiley & Sons, Inc.

Ward, J. C. and Ostrom, A. L. (2006) Complaining to the Masses: The Role of Protest Framing in Customer-Created Complaint Web Sites, *Journal of Consumer Research*, **33**, 220–230.

Webb, E. J., Campbell, D. T., Schwartz, P. D. and Sechrest, L. (1966) *Unobtrusive Measures: Non-reactive Research in the Social Sciences*. Chicago, IL: Rand-McNally.

Wetherbe, J. C. (1983) *Computer-based Information Systems*. Englewood Cliffs, NJ: Prentice Hall.

White, J. K. and Ruh, R. A. (1973) Effects of personal values on the relationship between participation and job attitudes. *Administrative Science Quarterly*, **18**(4), 506–514.

Wildstrom, S. H. (1998) Web sites made simpler. *Business Week*, January 26.

Williams, C. T. and Wolfe, G. K. (1979) *Elements of Research: A Guide for Writers*. Sherman Oaks, CA: Alfred Publishing.

Yuchtman, E. and Seashore, S. E. (1967) A system resource approach to organizational effectiveness. *American Sociological Review*, **32**, 891–903.

Zeithaml, V. A., Berry, L. L. and Parasuraman, A. (1996) The Behavioral Consequences of Service Quality. *Journal of Retailing*, **60**, 31–46.

Zetterberg, H. (1955) On axiomatic theories in sociology. In P. F. Lazarsfeld and M. Rosenberg (Eds.) *The Language of Social Research*. New York: The Free Press.

# INDEX

Abstract concepts, operationalization   127, 129, 136
Abstract databases   42
Accounting research   4
Accuracy *see* Goodness of measures; Precision
Achievement motivation, operationalization   129–135
Acknowledgments   399
Action research   31
Alternate hypotheses   89–90, 291, 336
Ambiguous questions   201
Analysis of variance (ANOVA)   346–8
  two-way   358
Anonymity   203–4
ANOVA *see* Analysis of variance
Appendix of report   401
Applied research   5, 6–7, 8–9
  basic research distinguished   8
  generalizability   18
Area sampling   274, 275, 279, 284
Attitude Toward the Offer   163
Attributes of objects, measurement
  126–7
Authorization, letters of   47, 396,
  397

Background information   37–38
Bar charts   315–16, 400
Basic research   6, 7–9
  applied research distinguished   8
  example report   418–422
Behavioural area research   23–24
Beta coefficients   351
Bias   21
  editing data   310
  interviews   189–90, 194, 196, 211
  minimizing   190–3, 198
  observational studies   215
  questionnaires   198, 203, 211
  sampling bias   194
  selection bias effects   238, 241, 242
  systematic   271, 275, 283
  unbiased questions   191–2
Bibliographic databases   41–2, 60
Bibliographies   61
Bivariate relationships   319–320
Box-and-whisker plots   319
Broad problem area *see* Problem area identification

*Business Ethics Quarterly*   15
Business research   2–3
  applied research   5, 6–7, 8–9, 18
  basic research   6, 7–9
  common research areas   4–5
  definition   3
  ethical issues   15
  managers and   3–4, 9–10, 14–15
  types   5–9

Canonical correlation   359
CAPI *see* Computer-assisted personal interviewing
CAPPA   210–11
Case studies   30–1, 103, 109
  internal validity   241–2
  proving causal relationships   241–2
Categorization   374
Category reliability   384
Category scale   149–50
CATI *see* Computer-assisted telephone interviewing
Causal relationships   72, 110
  case studies and   241–2
  establishing   227–8
  identification   120
  simulations and   250
  *see also* Causal studies
Causal studies   110–11
  deductive processes   29
  longitudinal nature   120
  managerial understanding   123
  researcher interference   111–13
  settings   114, 116
Cause-and effect-relationships *see* Causal relationships
Central tendency, measures of   311, 313, 316–17
Chi-squared test   320–1, 344
*Chicago Manual of Style*   44, 61
Citations *see* References
Classification data   203–4, 207–8
Closed questions   200
Cluster sampling   274–5, 279, 284, 297
Cochran Q test   321
Coding of data   306–8, 310
  qualitative data   370, 372–3
Coefficient of determination   349–50
Column charts   400
Comparative scales   156

Completely randomized design   255–6
Complex probability sampling   270–1, 275
Computer-aided surveys   186, 195–6
Computer-assisted interviews   193, 194–5, 196–7
Computer-assisted personal interviewing (CAPI)   195
Computer-assisted telephone interviewing (CATI)   186, 193, 195
Computer-based simulations   250
Conceptual analysis   386
Conceptual models   81
Conclusions   264, 382–383, 399
Concurrent validity   159, 160
Conference proceedings   40
Confidence   21
    estimation and   289–90
    sample size and   288–9, 294
    trade-off with precision   290–1
Confidence intervals   21
Confidence levels   21
Conjoint analysis   357–8
Consensus scale   154
Consistency   324
    measures   162–3
Constant sum scale   152–3
Construct validity   160–1
Consultants see Researchers
Consumer Mail Panel   183
Contaminating variables   229, 231–3
Content analysis   385–6
Content validity   158–9, 160
Continuous variables   70
Contrived settings   114, 116
Control groups   230
    ethical issues   251–2
    posttest only with experimental and control
        groups   243–4, 248
    pretest and posttest experimental and control group
        design   245–6, 248
Convenience sampling   276, 278, 280, 285
Convergent validity   160, 327
Correlation matrix   320
Correlational analysis   160
Correlational studies   110–11, 227
    managerial understanding   123
    researcher interference   111, 112
    settings   114
Correlations   321–2
Cost-benefit analysis   399
Costs   110
    research design and   121
    sampling design and   282
    see also Resources
Countries, as units of analysis   118–19
"Cover stories"   233

Coverage error   267
Criterion variables see Dependent variables
Criterion-related validity   159, 160, 327
Cronbach's alpha   162, 163, 324
    example   325–7
Cross-cultural research
    instrumentation issues   219
    operationalization of variables   137
    sampling   287
    see also International issues
Cross-sectional studies   119

Data analysis   26, 28
    editing data   308–10
    example case   304–5
    goodness of data   324–7
    initial impressions   311–13
    objectivity   22
    preparation of data   306–11
    software packages   364–5
Data coding   306–8
    illegal codes   310
    qualitative data   370, 372–3
Data collection   26, 27
    cross-cultural issues   219–20
    ethical issues   220–2
    interviews see Interviews
    managerial implications   220
    mechanical observation   215
    methods   184–218
    multimethods   216–217
    observational studies see Observational studies
    projective methods   185–186, 216
    questionnaires see Questionnaires
    settings   218
    timing   220
    unobtrusive methods   185
Data display   370, 382
Data entry   308
Data interpretation   26, 28
Data mining   363–4
Data reduction   370, 372–5
Data sources see Sources of data
Data transformation   310–11
Data triangulation   385
Data warehouses   363
Databases   41–2, 60
    online   55–6
Decile   318
Deductive reasoning   28–9, 92
Degrees of freedom   321
Delphi Technique   183
Demographic questions   203–4, 207–8
Dependent variables   70–1, 79, 81

Descriptive statistics 312–19
  example study 322–4, 327–30
Descriptive studies 105–8, 109
  sample reports 391–2, 407–11
Destructive sampling 264
Dichotomous scale 149
Directional hypotheses 88
Discrete variables 70
Discriminant analysis 356
Discriminant validity 160, 327
Dispersion, measures of 311, 313,
  317–19
Disproportionate stratified random sampling 273–4,
  279, 297
Distributions, normal 265–6
Diversity research 105
Divisions, as units of analysis 118
Door-to-door interviews 190
Double sampling 275, 280, 284–5
Double-barreled questions 201
Double-blind studies 248–9
Doughnut chart 401
Dummy coding 306
Dummy variables 351–2
Dyads, as units of analysis 116, 117
Dynamic panels 183

Efficiency in sampling 297
Electronic journals 41
Electronic questionnaires 210–11, 213
Elements 263
Employees, interviewing 187, 188,
  191
Errors
  coverage 267
  measurement 21
  non response 269–70
  standard 288, 289
  Type I 336–7
  Type II 296, 337
Estimation, sample data and 289–90
Ethics
  business research and 15
  data collection 220–2
  experimental design research 251–2
  participants and 221–2
  preliminary stages 50–1
  reporting research 395, 405
  researchers and 221
  telephone interviews 195
Ex post facto experimental designs 245, 249
Executive summary 394, 396, 397–8
Experimental designs 72, 227
  completely randomized 255–6

decision points 252, 253
ethical issues 251–2
factorial design 258–9, 358
field experiments see Field experiments
lab experiments see Lab experiments
Latin square design 257–8
longitudinal nature 120
managerial implications 252–3
quasi-experimental 243–5, 248
randomized block design 256–7
study nature and 115–16
true experimental 245–9
validity 242–51
Experimental simulation 250
Exploratory studies 103–5, 109
  inductive processes 29
External researchers 13–14
External validity
  factors affecting 238, 241, 242
  field experiments 234–5
  interactive testing effects 238, 241, 242
  lab experiments 233–4
  selection bias effects 238, 241, 242
  trade-off with internal validity 235

F distribution 347
F statistics 347
Face validity 159, 160
Face-to-face interviews 193–4, 196, 212,
  217
Factor analysis 161, 327
Factorial design 258–9, 358
Factorial validity 327
Falsifiability 25
Field experiments 114, 116, 228, 234–5
  example 114–15
  validity 234–5
Field studies 114, 116
  example 114
  longitudinal nature 120
Figures, in report 394, 399
Finance research 4
Fisher exact probability test 321
Fixed scale 152–3
Focus groups 105, 181–2
  moderator's role 181
  nature of data obtained 181–2
  online 182
  videoconferencing 182
Footnotes 401
Forced choice scale 155–6
Formative scales 163–4
  quality 164–5
Free simulation 250

Frequencies   313–15, 328–9
Full-text databases   41
Fundamental research *see* Basic research
Funneling technique   191, 203

Generalizability   22–3
  lab experiments   233–4
Goodness of fit   349–50
Goodness of measures   157–63
  item analysis   157
Google Scholar   41
Graphic rating scale   153–4
Grounded theory   297–8, 374
Groups
  matching   231, 232–3, 238
  as units of analysis   116–17, 118

Hawthorne effect   29, 92
History effects   235–6, 241, 243, 245
Hunches   19
Hypotheses
  alternate   89–90, 291, 336
  definition   87
  development of   25, 27, 69, 86–92, 95
  directional   88
  falsifiability   25
  format of statement   87–91
  if-then statements   87
  managerial understanding   96
  nondirectional   88, 90
  null   88–90, 291, 336
  statements of   87–91
  testability   20, 25
  testing *see* Hypothesis testing
  unsupported   26
Hypothesis testing   109
  canonical correlation   359
  case studies and   30
  conjoint analysis   357–8
  deductive/inductive nature   28, 92
  discriminant analysis   356
  example case   359–62
  logistic regression   356–7
  MANOVA   358–9
  negative case analysis   92–3
  purpose   336
  qualitative data and   92–3
  regression analysis   348–55
  sample data and   291–3
  several means   338, 346–8
  single mean   338, 339–40
  steps   91
  studies   108–9
  techniques   337–9

two related means   338, 340–5
two unrelated means   345–6
two-way ANOVA   358
Hypothetico-deductive method
  data analysis   26, 28
  data collection   26, 27
  data interpretation   26, 28
  examples   27–8, 29–30
  hypotheses development   25, 27
  measurement of variables   25, 27
  problem area identification   24, 27
  problem statement definition   25, 27, 45–7
  seven-step process   24–6
  summary   28–9

If-then statements   87
Illogical responses   309
Income data   208
Inconsistent responses   309–10
Independent samples t-test   345–6
Independent variables   72–3, 79, 81
  manipulation   229–31
  moderating variables distinguished   75–6
Individuals, as units of analysis   116, 117
Inductive reasoning   28–9, 92
Industries, as units of analysis   118
Information systems   363–4
Inkblot tests   216
Instrumentation effects   239–40, 241
Interactive testing effects   238, 241, 242
  designs affected   245, 246, 247
Interference with study   111–13
  excessive   113
  minimal   112
  moderate   112–13
Interitem consistency reliability   162, 325
  formative scales   164
Interjudge reliability   384
Internal researchers   12–13, 395
Internal validity
  case studies   241–2
  factors affecting   235–41, 242
  field experiments   234–5
  history effects   235–6, 241, 243, 254
  instrumentation effects   239–40, 241
  lab experiments   233
  maturation effects   236–7, 241, 243, 245
  mortality effects *see* Mortality effects
  selection bias effects   238, 241
  statistical regression effects   239, 241
  testing effects   237–8, 241
  trade-off with external validity   235
International issues
  operationalization of variables   137

scaling 156–7
surveys 218–20
*see also* Cross-cultural research
Internet 41, 370
online resources 56–9
Interquartile range 319
Interrupted time series design 244
Interval scales 143–5, 146, 147–8, 149
data analysis 313
questionnaires 205
Intervening variables *see* Mediating variables
Interview System 196
Interviews 185, 186–97
advantages and disadvantages 212–13
bias 189–90, 194, 196, 211
clarification of issues 192
credibility 190, 193
door-to-door 190
face-to-face 193–4, 196, 212, 217
individuals 105
minimizing bias 190–3
note-taking 192, 193
questioning technique 191–2, 193
rapport 190–1, 193, 196
recording 190, 192
simplification 192
software packages 196
structured 37, 188–9, 196, 210
telephone 190, 193, 194, 196, 212, 217
training interviewers 189
unstructured 37, 186–8, 189, 196
Item analysis 157
Itemized rating scale 151–2

Job Descriptive Index 161, 163–4
*Journal of Business Ethics* 15
Journals 15, 40
electronic 41
quality 43
as source of measures 130
Judgment sampling 269, 277, 278, 280, 285–6

Kendall's Tau rank correlation 320, 322
Kuder–Richardson formulas 162

Lab experiments 114, 116, 228–34
control 229, 231–3
example 115
generalizability 233–4
manipulation 229–31, 233
matching groups 231, 232–3
randomization 231–3
treatment 230, 233
validity 233–4

Latin square design 257–8
Leading questions 201–2
Least squares function 348
Letters of authorization 47, 396, 397
Likert scale 152, 155
Limitations 399
Linear regression equation 348
LISREL 364–5
Literature reviews 37, 38–45
data sources 39–41
documentation 43–4
evaluation 42–3
example 44, 93–4
quality 39
quotations 65–6
references 42, 43–4, 64–5
searching 41–2
theoretical framework and 80
Loaded questions 202
Logistic regression 356–7
Longitudinal studies 119–20
Looking Glass 250

McNemar's test 343–5
Mail questionnaires 197–8, 212–13, 218
Main testing effects 237, 241, 245
Management research 4
example scales 167–71
scientific research and 23–4
Management science 364
Managerial involvement
causal/correlational studies 123
data collection 220
decision points 252, 253
decision-making 2
effectiveness 14–15
experimental designs 252–3
hypotheses 96
problem area identification 50
relationship with researcher 10–11, 14
research 3–4, 9–10, 14–15
research design 122–3
rigor 123
sampling 298
theoretical frameworks 96
variables 96
MANOVA 358–9
*Manual for Writers* (Turabian) 44, 61
Marginal homogeneity 343–4
Marketing research 4
example scales 171–7
visual aids to interviews 188–9
Matching groups 231, 232–3, 238
MATLAB 365

Maturation effects   236–7, 241, 243, 245
Mean   316, 328
Measurement errors   21
Measurement scales *see* Scales
Measurement of variables   25, 27, 126–7
    existing measures   130, 136
    goodness of measures   157–63
    internal consistency   162–3
    stability of measures   162
    *see also* Scales
Mechanical observation methods   215
Median   316–17, 318
Mediating variables   77–9, 81, 84, 85
Method triangulation   385
Mode   317
Moderating variables   73–7, 79, 81, 84, 85
    independent variables distinguished
        75–6
    testing moderation   354–5
Mortality effects   238–9, 241
    designs affected   243, 244, 245, 246, 247, 248
Motivational research   216
Multicollinearity   352–3
Multidimensional scaling   154
Multiple correlation coefficient   351
Multiple regression analysis   350–1
Multistage cluster sampling   275
Multitrait, multimethod matrix of correlations   161
Multivariate statistical techniques   71, 338

Narrative analysis   386
National Computer Network   195
National Family Opinion Panel   183
National Purchase Diary Panel   183
Negative case method   92–3
Negatively worded questions   200–1
Newspapers   40
Nielsen television index   183, 215
Nominal scales   141–2, 146–7, 148–9
    data analysis   313
    example   146–7
    independent samples t-test   345–6
Non responses
    coding   308
    non response error   269–70
Noncontrived settings   114, 116
Nondirectional hypotheses   88, 90
Nonparticipant observers   211, 213, 221
Nonprint media, referencing   63
Nonprobability sampling   268, 276–8, 280, 297
Normality of distributions   265–6
Not-at-homes   269
Null hypotheses   88–90, 291, 336
Numerical scale   150, 156

Objectivity   22
Objects, measurement of attributes   126–7
Observational studies   185, 211–15, 218
    advantages and disadvantages   214–15
    bias   215
    structured   213–14
    unstructured   214
One sample t-test   339–40
One-shot studies   119
Online focus groups   182
Online resources   41–2, 55–9
Online surveys, design   210–11
Open-ended questions   200, 208–9
Operationalization of variables   127–8
    achievement motivation example   129–35
    cognition example   128
    dimensions and elements   129, 131–5
    international aspects   137
Operations research (OR)   364
Oral presentations   402–5
    content   403
    presenter skills   404
    question and answer sessions   402, 404–405
    visual aids   403–404
Ordinal scales   142–3, 146, 147, 149
    data analysis   313
    example   147
Outliers   309

Paired comparison   155
Paired samples t-test   340–1
Panel studies   182
Panels   182–3
    Delphi Technique   183
    dynamic   183
    static   183
Parallel-form reliability   162, 324
Parameters   264
Parsimony   23
Participant observers   213
Pearson correlation matrix   321–2, 329, 330
Percentile   318
Personal information   203–4, 207–8, 221
Personally administered questionnaires   197, 212, 217
Pie charts   315
Pilot studies   109
Population   262–3
    definition   267
    parameters   264
Positively worded questions   200–1
Posttests   237
    posttest only with experimental and control groups   243–4, 248

pretest and posttest experimental and control group
design 245–6, 248
pretest and posttest experimental group design 243,
248
Power 337
Precision 21
estimation and 289–90
sample size and 287–8, 294
trade-off with confidence 290–1
Predictive validity 159, 160
Predictor variables *see* Independent variables
Preliminary information gathering 25, 37–8
background information 37–8
ethical issues 50–1
prevailing knowledge 37, 38
*see also* Literature reviews
Pretests 237
pretest and posttest experimental and control group
design 245–6, 248
pretest and posttest experimental group design 243,
248
Prevailing knowledge 37, 38
Primary data 37, 180, 181–4
Probability sampling 267–8, 270–5,
279–80
Problem area identification 24, 27, 36
managers' inputs 50
Problem statement
definition 25, 27, 45–7
feasibility 46
interest 47
meaning 45
Projective methods 185–6, 216
Proportionate stratified random sampling 272–3, 279
Protest websites 370
Prototypes 250
*Publication Manual of the American Psychological
Association* 43–4, 61
Pure moderation 354–5
Pure research *see* Basic research
Purposive sampling 276, 278, 297
Purposiveness 19

Qualitative data 3, 26, 369–70
Qualitative data analysis
conceptual analysis 386
conclusions 382–3
content analysis 385–6
customer anger study 371–2, 373, 374, 375–81, 382,
383
data coding 370, 372–3
data display 370, 382
data reduction 370, 372–81
hypothesis testing and 92–3

narrative analysis 386
relational analysis 386
reliability 384, 385
sources of data 370
validity 384–5
Qualitative studies
exploratory nature 104
inductive processes 29
sampling and 297–8
Quality of life research 105
Quantitative data 3
analysis *see* Data analysis
descriptive studies and 107
Quantitative studies, deductive processes 29
Quartile 318
Quasi moderation 354–5
Quasi-experimental designs 243–5
posttests only with experimental and control
groups 243–4, 248
pretest and posttest experimental group design 243,
248
time series design 244–5
Question and answer sessions 402, 404–405
Questioning techniques 191–192, 193
Questionnaires 185, 197–211
administering 209–10
advantages and disadvantages 212–13
ambiguous questions 201
appearance 205–9
bias 198, 203, 211
classification data 203–4, 207–8
closed questions 200
coding responses 306–8
concluding 209
content 198–9
data transformation 310–11
design guidelines 198–204
double-barreled questions 201
editing data 308–10
electronic 210–11, 213
illegal codes 310
illogical responses 309
income data 208
inconsistent responses 309–10
international issues 218–20
introduction 205–6
language 199
leading questions 201–2
length of questions 202
loaded questions 202
mail 197–8, 212–13, 218
measurement principles 205
negatively worded questions 200–1
non response 269–70

Questionnaires (*Continued*)
  omissions   310
  open-ended questions   200, 208–9
  ordering effects   203
  personal information   203–4, 207–8
  personally administered   197, 212, 217
  positively worded questions   200–1
  pretesting   210
  purpose of questions   198–9
  question organization   206
  recall-dependent questions   201
  sample   307–8
  scales   205
  sequencing of questions   203
  socially desirable responses   202
  software resources   186
  type of questions   200–2
  wording   199
Questions
  ambiguous   201
  closed   200
  demographic   203–4, 207–8
  double-barreled   201
  leading   201–2
  loaded   202
  negatively worded   200–1
  open-ended   200, 208–9
  positively worded   200–1
  recall-dependent   201
  unbiased   191–2
Quota sampling   277–8, 280, 286
Quotations in text   65–6

Radar charts   400
Randomization   231–3, 238, 246
Randomized block design   256–7
Range   317
Ranking scales   140, 155–6
  comparative scales   156
  forced choice   155–6
  paired comparison   155
  use   156
Rating scales   140, 149–55
  category scale   149–50
  consensus scale   154
  constant sum scale   152–3
  dichotomous scale   149
  fixed scale   152–3
  graphic rating scale   153–4
  itemized rating scale   151–2
  Likert scale   152, 155
  multidimensional scaling   154
  numerical scale   150, 156
  semantic differential scale   150, 156

Stapel scale   153
  use   156
Ratio scales   145, 146, 148, 149
  data analysis   313
  questionnaires   205
Recall-dependent questions   201
Recommendations   399
Reference lists   61
References
  citation   61–3
  literature reviews   42, 43–4, 64–5
  nonprint media   63
  research reports   399, 401
Reflective scales   163
Refusals   269
Regression analysis   348–55
  dummy variables   351–2
  moderation testing   354–5
  multicollinearity   352–3
  multiple   350–1
Regression coefficients   348
Relational analysis   386
Relevance of research   45, 46
Reliability   161–3
  category   384
  checking   324–7
  forms   158
  interitem consistency   162, 164, 325
  interjudge   384
  meaning   157, 161
  parallel-form   162, 324
  qualitative research   384, 385
  questionnaires   205
  split-half   163, 324
  test-retest   162, 324
Replicability   20–1
Reports   40
Representativeness of samples   265, 266
Research   2
  assessing quality   42–3
  relevance   45, 46
  *see also* Business research
Research articles   40
Research design   102–3
  managerial implications   122–3
  purpose of study   103–10
  researcher interference   111–13
  setting   114–16
  summary   120–1
  time horizon   119–20
  type of investigation   110–11
  units of analysis   116–19, 373
Research process model   68
Research proposals   47–50

content   48
example   48–9
managers and   50
in research report   396, 397
Research reports
  acknowledgments   399
  with alternative solutions   393–4,
    415–17
  appendix   401
  audience   394–5
  basic report example   418–22
  body of report   396, 399
  conclusions   399
  contents   396–402
  cost-benefit analysis   399
  descriptive reports   391–2, 407–11
  ethical issues   395, 405
  examples   391–4, 407–22
  executive summary   394, 396, 397–8
  footnotes   401
  ideal characteristics   395
  introductory section   396, 399
  letter of authorization   396, 397
  limitations   399
  pictorial data representation   394, 399, 400–1
  purpose   391
  recommendations   399
  references   399, 401
  research proposal   396, 397
  to "sell" an idea   392–3, 412–14
  synopsis   396, 397–8
  table of contents   396, 397, 401–2
  title   396, 397
  see also Oral presentations
Researcher triangulation   385
Researchers
  ethical issues   221
  external   13–14
  interference see Interference with study
  internal   12–13, 395
  as nonparticipant observers   211, 213, 221
  as participant-observers   213
  personal qualities   191, 193
  relationship with manager   10–11, 14
  status   220
Resources
  research design and   103
  trade-off with rigor   121
  see also Costs
Response equivalence   219–20
Restricted probability sampling   270–1, 275
Reverse scoring   311
Review articles   40
Rigor   19–20

managerial decision   123
multimethods and   216–17
research design and   102, 110
trade-off with resources   121

Sample size   265
  confidence and   288–9, 294
  determination of   268, 290, 293–7
  importance of   296–7
  precision and   287–8, 294
Sampling
  area sampling   274, 275, 279, 284
  bias   194
  cluster sampling   274–5, 279, 284, 297
  complex probability sampling   270–1,
    275
  convenience sampling   276, 278, 280, 285
  cross-cultural research   287
  design see Sampling design
  destructive   264
  disproportionate stratified random sampling
    273–4, 279, 297
  double sampling   275, 280, 284–5
  efficiency in   297
  estimation and   289–90
  execution   268–70
  generalized conclusions   264
  hypothesis testing and   291–3
  judgment sampling   269, 277, 278, 280, 285–6
  managerial implications   298
  meaning   262
  nonprobability sampling   268, 276–8, 280, 297
  probability sampling   267–8, 270–5, 279–80
  process   266–70
  proportionate stratified random sampling   272–3,
    279
  purposive   276, 278, 297
  qualitative studies and   297–8
  quota sampling   277–8, 280, 286
  reasons   264
  representativeness   265, 266
  restricted probability sampling   270–271, 275
  sample frame   267
  sample meaning   263
  sampling unit   263
  simple random sampling   270, 275, 278–82, 297
  size of sample see Sample size
  stratified random sampling   271–2, 275, 279, 282–3,
    297
  systematic sampling   271, 275, 279,
    283
  theoretical   297–8, 374
  unrestricted probability sampling   270,
    275

Sampling design   265, 267–8
    choice points   281
    design selection   278–87
    generalizability and   22
    importance of   296–7
SAS   365
Scale handbooks   130
Scales
    existing   130, 136
    formative   163–4
    international issues   156–7
    interval see Interval scales
    management research examples   167–71
    marketing research examples   171–7
    meaning   141
    nominal see Nominal scales
    ordinal see Ordinal scales
    properties   145–6
    questionnaires   205
    ranking   140, 155–6
    rating   140, 149–55
    ratio see Ratio scales
    reflective   163
Scanner sheets   197
Scatter diagrams   321
Schematic diagrams   81, 83, 85
Scientific investigation   18
Scientific research   18–19
    behavioural areas   23–4
    characteristics   19–23
    confidence   21
    generalizability   22–3
    management areas   23–4
    objectivity   22
    obstacles to   23–4
    parsimony   23
    precision   21
    purposiveness   19
    replicability   20–1
    rigor   19–20
    testability   20
Secondary data   37, 180, 184
Selection bias effects   238, 241, 242
Semantic differential scale   150, 156
Sensitive data   208, 221
Settings of studies   114–16
    contrived   114, 116
    noncontrived   114, 116
Sign test   344
Significance levels   336–337
Simple random sampling   270, 275, 278–282, 297
Simplicity   23
Simulation   249–51
Single-stage cluster sampling   275

Social desirability, question design   202
Social networks   370
Software resources
    data analysis   364–5
    interviews   196
    questionnaires   186
Solomon four-group design   246–7
    threats to validity   247–8
Sources of data   180–4
    focus groups   105, 181–2
    literature reviews   39–41
    panels   182–3
    primary data   37, 180, 181–4
    qualitative data   370
    quality   42–3
    secondary data   37, 180, 184
    unobtrusive measures   183–4
Spearman's rank correlation   320, 322
Split-half reliability   163, 324
SPSS   211, 365
    analysis of variance   347
    Data Editor   308, 309
    data transformation   311, 312
    descriptive statistics   323–4
    discriminant analysis   356
    frequencies   314–15
    independent samples t-test   346
    linear regression   350
    logistic regression   357
    McNemar's test   345
    multicollinearity   353
    one sample t-test   340
    paired samples t-test   341
    reliability analysis   326–7
    Wilcoxon signed-rank test   343
Stability of measures   162
Standard deviation   318, 328
Standard error   288, 289
Standardized regression coefficients   351
Stapel scale   153
Stata   365
Static panels   183
Statistical Package for the Social Sciences (SPSS) see SPSS
Statistical power   337
Statistical regression effects   239, 241
Stratified random sampling   271–2, 275, 279, 282–3, 297
Structured interviews   37, 188–9, 196
    pretesting   210
Structured observational studies   213–14
Studies
    case studies   30–1, 103, 109, 241–2
    causal see Causal studies

correlational *see* Correlational studies
cross-sectional 119
descriptive 105–8, 109, 391–2, 407–11
exploratory 103–5, 109
field experiments *see* Field experiments
field studies *see* Field studies
hypothesis testing 108–9
lab experiments *see* Lab experiments
longitudinal 119–20
panel studies 182
pilot studies 109
purpose 103–10
researcher interference 111–13
setting 114–16
time horizon 119–20
Subject 263–4
Subjective areas 23–4
Survey System 196
Synopsis 396, 397–8
Systematic bias 271, 275, 283
Systematic sampling 271, 275, 279, 283

T-statistic, hypothesis testing 292–3
Table of contents 396, 397, 401–2
Tables, in report 394, 399
TAT *see* Thematic apperception tests
Telephone interviews 190, 193, 194, 196, 212, 217
Test-retest reliability 162, 324
Testability 20, 25
Testing effects 237–8, 241
Textbooks 39–40
Thematic apperception tests (TAT) 216
Theoretical frameworks
    air safety violation example 82–85
    building process 69
    components 80–82
    example 94–95
    literature review and 80
    managerial knowledge 96
    need for 69
Theoretical sampling 297–298, 374
Theoretical saturation 297–8
Theory 81–2
Theory triangulation 385
Theses 40
Thurstone Equal Appearing Interval Scale 154
Time horizon of study 119–20
Time series design 244–5
Title 396, 397
Tolerance value 353
Trace measures *see* Unobtrusive measures
Training

interviewers 189
projective tests 185–6
Treatment 230
Triangulation 385
True experimental designs 245–9
    double-blind studies 248–9
    ex post facto designs 245, 249
    pretest and posttest experimental and control group design 245–6, 248
    Solomon four-group design 246–8
Two-way ANOVA 358
Type I errors 336–7
Type II errors 296, 337

Unbiased questions 191–2
Units of analysis 116–19, 373
    countries 118–19
    divisions 118
    dyads 116, 117
    groups 116–17, 118
    individuals 116, 117
    industries 118
Univariate statistical techniques 338
Unobtrusive measures 183–4
Unpublished manuscripts 40
Unrestricted probability sampling 270, 275
Unstructured interviews 37, 186–8, 189, 196
Unstructured observational studies 214

Validity 158–61
    checking 327
    concurrent validity 159, 160
    construct validity 160–1
    content validity 158–9, 160
    convergent validity 160, 327
    criterion-related validity 159, 160, 327
    discriminant validity 160, 327
    establishing 160–1
    experimental design and 242–51
    external *see* External validity
    face validity 159, 160
    factorial 327
    factors affecting 235–41, 242
    field experiments 234–5
    forms 158
    internal *see* Internal validity
    lab experiments 233–4
    meaning 157
    predictive validity 159, 160
    qualitative research 384–5
    questionnaires 205
    Solomon four-group design and 247–8
    trade-off 235

Variables
    contaminating   229, 231–3
    continuous   70
    definition   80, 81
    dependent   70–1, 79, 81
    descriptive studies   105–6
    discrete   70
    dummy   351–2
    frequencies   313–15, 328–9
    independent *see* Independent variables
    managerial knowledge   96
    meaning   69–70
    measurement of *see* Measurement of variables
    mediating   77–9, 81, 84, 85
    moderating *see* Moderating variables
    operationalization *see* Operationalization of variables
    relationships between   81, 319–22
    types   70–80
    visual summaries   311, 313
Variance   317–18, 328
Variance inflation factor (VIF)   353
VCS *see* Voice capture system
Videoconferencing   182
VIF *see* Variance inflation factor
Visual aids
    interviews   188–9
    presentations   403–4
Visual summaries, variables   311, 313
Voice capture system (VCS)   195

Wilcoxon signed-rank test   342–3
Word association   216
Written reports *see* Research reports